Communications
in Computer and Information Science   1768

Rationale

The CCIS series is devoted to the publication of proceedings of computer science conferences. Its aim is to efficiently disseminate original research results in informatics in printed and electronic form. While the focus is on publication of peer-reviewed full papers presenting mature work, inclusion of reviewed short papers reporting on work in progress is welcome, too. Besides globally relevant meetings with internationally representative program committees guaranteeing a strict peer-reviewing and paper selection process, conferences run by societies or of high regional or national relevance are also considered for publication.

Topics

The topical scope of CCIS spans the entire spectrum of informatics ranging from foundational topics in the theory of computing to information and communications science and technology and a broad variety of interdisciplinary application fields.

Information for Volume Editors and Authors

Publication in CCIS is free of charge. No royalties are paid, however, we offer registered conference participants temporary free access to the online version of the conference proceedings on SpringerLink (http://link.springer.com) by means of an http referrer from the conference website and/or a number of complimentary printed copies, as specified in the official acceptance email of the event.

CCIS proceedings can be published in time for distribution at conferences or as post-proceedings, and delivered in the form of printed books and/or electronically as USBs and/or e-content content licenses for accessing proceedings at SpringerLink. Furthermore, CCIS proceedings are included in the CCIS electronic book series hosted in the SpringerLink digital library at http://link.springer.com/bookseries/7899. Conferences publishing in CCIS are allowed to use Online Conference Service (OCS) for managing the whole proceedings lifecycle (from submission and reviewing to preparing for publication) free of charge.

Publication process

The language of publication is exclusively English. Authors publishing in CCIS have to sign the Springer CCIS copyright transfer form, however, they are free to use their material published in CCIS for substantially changed, more elaborate subsequent publications elsewhere. For the preparation of the camera-ready papers/files, authors have to strictly adhere to the Springer CCIS Authors' Instructions and are strongly encouraged to use the CCIS LaTeX style files or templates.

Abstracting/Indexing

CCIS is abstracted/indexed in DBLP, Google Scholar, EI-Compendex, Mathematical Reviews, SCImago, Scopus. CCIS volumes are also submitted for the inclusion in ISI Proceedings.

How to start

To start the evaluation of your proposal for inclusion in the CCIS series, please send an e-mail to ccis@springer.com.

Guojun Wang · Kim-Kwang Raymond Choo ·
Jie Wu · Ernesto Damiani
Editors

Ubiquitous Security

Second International Conference, UbiSec 2022
Zhangjiajie, China, December 28–31, 2022
Revised Selected Papers

 Springer

Editors
Guojun Wang 🅾
Guangzhou University
Guangzhou, China

Kim-Kwang Raymond Choo 🅾
University of Texas at San Antonio
San Antonio, TX, USA

Jie Wu 🅾
Temple University
Philadelphia, PA, USA

Ernesto Damiani 🅾
Khalifa University of Science and Technology
Abu Dhabi, United Arab Emirates

ISSN 1865-0929   ISSN 1865-0937 (electronic)
Communications in Computer and Information Science
ISBN 978-981-99-0271-2   ISBN 978-981-99-0272-9 (eBook)
https://doi.org/10.1007/978-981-99-0272-9

This Springer imprint is published by the registered company Springer Nature Singapore Pte Ltd.
The registered company address is: 152 Beach Road, #21-01/04 Gateway East, Singapore 189721, Singapore

Preface

The Second International Conference on Ubiquitous Security (UbiSec 2022), held in Zhangjiajie, China on December 28–31, 2022, was jointly organized by Jishou University and Guangzhou University.

UbiSec 2022 built upon the success of the UbiSec 2021 conference in Guangzhou and the previous SpaCCS/UbiSafe/IWCSS conference/symposium/workshop series. Specifically, UbiSec focuses on the security, privacy, and anonymity aspects of cyberspace, the physical world, and social networks (collectively referred to as the metaverse).

UbiSec 2022 received a total of 98 submissions from authors in 14 different countries, and each submission was reviewed by at least three experts with relevant subject matter expertise. Based on the recommendations of the reviewers and subsequent discussions of the Program Committee members, 34 regular papers were selected for oral presentation at the conference and inclusion in this Springer CCIS volume (i.e., an acceptance rate of 34.7%). In addition to the technical presentations, the program included a number of keynote speeches by world-renowned researchers. We thank our distinguished keynote speakers, Richard Hill, Omer Rana, Kouichi Sakurai, Deqing Zou, and Tien N. Nguyen, and our invited speakers, Arcangelo Castiglione, Scott Fowler, Wenjun Jiang, Ryan Ko, Qin Liu, Tian Wang, Carlos Becker Westphall, Yulei Wu, and Yang Xu, for their time and willingness to share their knowledge with the conference attendees.

UbiSec 2022 was only possible because of the support and dedication of a large number of individuals and organizations worldwide. There is a long list of people who volunteered their time and energy to put together the conference and they deserve special thanks. First and foremost, we would like to offer our gratitude to the Steering Committee Chairs, Guojun Wang from Guangzhou University, China, and Kim-Kwang Raymond Choo from the University of Texas at San Antonio, USA, for guiding the entire process of the conference. We are also deeply grateful to all the Program Committee members and reviewers for their time and efforts in reading, commenting on, debating on, and finally selecting the papers.

We would like to offer our gratitude to the General Chairs, Hanpin Wang, Richard Hill, and Aniello Castiglione, for their tremendous support and advice in ensuring the success of the conference. Thanks also go to the Local Organizing Committee Chair, Jianfeng Li; the Publicity Chairs, Carlos Becker Westphall, Scott Fowler, Peter Mueller, Haroon Elahi, Yulei Wu, and Xiangyong Liu; and the Conference Secretary, Wenyin Yang.

Finally, we thank the authors and all participants for their support and contribution. We hope they found the conference a stimulating and exciting forum, and we hope they also enjoyed the beautiful city of Zhangjiajie, China!

January 2023

Guojun Wang
Kim-Kwang Raymond Choo
Jie Wu
Ernesto Damiani

Organization

Executive General Chair

Guojun Wang   Guangzhou University, China

Local Organizing Chair

Jianfeng Li   Jishou University, China

General Chairs

Hanpin Wang   Guangzhou University, China
Richard Hill   University of Huddersfield, UK
Aniello Castiglione   University of Naples Parthenope, Italy

Program Chairs

Guojun Wang   Guangzhou University, China
Kim-Kwang Raymond Choo   University of Texas at San Antonio, USA
Jie Wu   Temple University, USA
Ernesto Damiani   Khalifa University, UAE and Università degli Studi di Milano, Italy

Program Vice Chairs

(1) Cyberspace Security Track

Qin Liu   Hunan University, China
Wenjia Li   New York Institute of Technology, USA
Jie Hu   University of Electronic Science and Technology of China, China
Saed Alrabaee   United Arab Emirates University, UAE
Charalambos (Harrys) Konstantinou   King Abdullah University of Science and Technology, Saudi Arabia

(2) Cyberspace Privacy Track

Yulei Wu	University of Exeter, UK
Wenjun Jiang	Hunan University, China
Saqib Ali	University of Agriculture, Faisalabad, Pakistan
Md Tariqul Islam	Syracuse University, USA
Saad Khan	University of Huddersfield, UK

(3) Cyberspace Anonymity Track

Tian Wang	Beijing Normal University, China
A. S. M. Kayes	La Trobe University, Australia
Oana Geman	University of Suceava, Romania
Mamoun Alazab	Charles Darwin University, Australia
Hudan Studiawan	Institut Teknologi Sepuluh Nopember, Indonesia

Publicity Chairs

Carlos Becker Westphall	Federal University of Santa Catarina, Brazil
Scott Fowler	Linköping University, Sweden
Peter Mueller	IBM Zurich Research Laboratory, Switzerland
Haroon Elahi	Umeå University, Sweden
Yulei Wu	University of Exeter, UK
Xiangyong Liu	Guangzhou University, China

Workshop Chairs

Sabu M. Thampi	Kerala University of Digital Sciences, Innovation and Technology (KUDSIT), India
Arcangelo Castiglione	University of Salerno, Italy
Shuhong Chen	Guangzhou University, China

Publication Chairs

Tao Peng	Guangzhou University, China
Fang Qi	Central South University, China

Registration Chairs

Xiaofei Xing	Guangzhou University, China
Pin Liu	Central South University, China
Pengfei Yin	Jishou University, China

Conference Secretary

Wenyin Yang	Foshan University, China

Web Chairs

Ziwei Xiao	Foshan University, China
Jianguo Jiang	Foshan University, China
Peiqiang Li	Guangzhou University, China

Steering Committee

Guojun Wang (Chair)	Guangzhou University, China
Kim-Kwang Raymond Choo (Chair)	University of Texas at San Antonio, USA
Saqib Ali	University of Agriculture, Faisalabad, Pakistan
Valentina E. Balas	Aurel Vlaicu University of Arad, Romania
Md Zakirul Alam Bhuiyan	Fordham University, USA
Jiannong Cao	Hong Kong Polytechnic University, Hong Kong, China
Aniello Castiglione	University of Naples Parthenope, Italy
Scott Fowler	Linkoping University, Sweden
Oana Geman	University of Suceava, Romania
Richard Hill	University of Huddersfield, UK
Ryan Ko	University of Queensland, Australia
Kuan-Ching Li	Providence University, Taiwan
Jianhua Ma	Hosei University, Japan
Gregorio Martinez	University of Murcia, Spain
Peter Mueller	IBM Zurich Research Laboratory, Switzerland
Kouichi Sakurai	Kyushu University, Japan

Sabu M. Thampi	Indian Institute of Information Technology and Management, Kerala and Kerala University of Digital Sciences, Innovation and Technology (KUDSIT), India
Carlos Becker Westphall	Federal University of Santa Catarina, Brazil
Jie Wu	Temple University, USA
Yang Xu	Hunan University, China
Zheng Yan	Xidian University, China and Aalto University, Finland
Wenyin Yang	Foshan University, China
Haojin Zhu	Shanghai Jiao Tong University, China

Program Committee

Track1: Cyberspace Security

Track Chairs

Qin Liu	Hunan University, China
Wenjia Li	New York Institute of Technology, USA
Jie Hu	University of Electronic Science and Technology of China, China
Saed Alrabaee	United Arab Emirates University, UAE
Charalambos (Harrys) Konstantinou	King Abdullah University of Science and Technology, Saudi Arabia

Program Committee Members

Mohiuddin Ahmed	Edith Cowan University, Australia
Hussain Al-Aqrabi	University of Huddersfield, UK
Dima Alhadidi	University of Windsor, Canada
Man Ho Allen Au	University of Hong Kong, Hong Kong, China
Ali Awad	United Arab Emirates University, UAE
Eduard Babulak	National Science Foundation, USA
Sudip Chakraborty	Valdosta State University, USA
Omar Darwish	Eastern Michigan University, USA
Edwin Dauber	Widener University, USA
Luca Davoli	University of Parma, Italy
Md. Sadek Ferdous	Shahjalal University of Science and Technology, Bangladesh

Elke Franz	Technische Universitat Dresden, Germany
Jeff Garae	CERT Vanuatu, Vanuatu
Gerhard Hancke	City University of Hong Kong, Hong Kong, China
Michael Heinzl	Independent Security Researcher, Austria
Heemeng Ho	Singapore Institute of Technology, Singapore
Mike Johnstone	Edith Cowan University, Australia
Sokratis Katsikas	Norwegian University of Science and Technology, Norway
Mahmoud Khasawneh	Al Ain University, UAE
Abigail Koay	University of Queensland, Australia
Vimal Kumar	University of Waikato, New Zealand
Nuno Laranjeiro	University of Coimbra, Portugal
Jiguo Li	Fujian Normal University, China
Linsen Li	Shanghai Jiao Tong University, China
Kaitai Liang	Delft University of Technology, The Netherlands
Xin Liao	Hunan University, China
Yuhong Liu	Santa Clara University, USA
García Villalba Luis Javier	Universidad Complutense Madrid, Spain
Wissam Mallouli	Montimage EURL, France
Spiros Mancoridis	Drexel University, USA
Hafizah Mansor	International Islamic University Malaysia, Malaysia
Chengying Mao	Jiangxi University of Finance and Economics, China
Iberia Medeiros	University of Lisbon, Portugal
Weizhi Meng	Technical University of Denmark, Denmark
Aleksandra Mileva	University Goce Delcev, Macedonia
David Naccache	ENS, France
Francesco Piccialli	University of Naples Federico II, Italy
Josef Pieprzyk	CSIRO/Data61, Australia
Nikolaos Pitropakis	Edinburgh Napier University, UK
Vincenzo Piuri	University of Milan, Italy
Emil Pricop	Petroleum-Gas University of Ploiesti, Romania
Quan Qian	Shanghai University, China
Vinayakumar Ravi	Prince Mohammad Bin Fahd University, Saudi Arabia
Hassan Raza	National Institute of Standards and Technology (NIST), USA
Joshua Scarsbrook	University of Queensland, Australia
Amartya Sen	Oakland University, USA
Kewei Sha	University of Houston, Clear Lake (UHCL), USA
Paria Shirani	Ryerson University, Canada

Dario Stabili	University of Modena, Italy
Hung-Min Sun	National Tsing Hua University, Taiwan
Omair Uthmani	Glasgow Caledonian University, UK
Konstantinos Votis	Information Technologies Institute, Centre for Research and Technology Hellas, Greece
Lei Wang	Nanjing Forestry University, China
Wei Wang	Nanjing University of Aeronautics and Astronautics, China
Yi Wang	Manhattan College, USA
Yehua Wei	Hunan Normal University, China
Longfei Wu	Fayetteville State University, USA
Liang Xiao	Xiamen University, China
Anjia Yang	Jinan University, China
Baoliu Ye	Nanjing University, China
Chong Yu	University of Nebraska-Lincoln, USA
Nicola Zannone	Eindhoven University of Technology, The Netherlands
Mengyuan Zhang	Hong Kong Polytechnic University, China
Yi Zhang	Sichuan University, China
Yuan Zhang	University of Electronic Science and Technology, China
Yongjun Zhao	Nanyang Technological University, Singapore
Xinliang Zheng	Frostburg State University, USA
Yongbin Zhou	Nanjing University of Science and Technology, China
Congxu Zhu	Central South University, China

Track2: Cyberspace Privacy

Track Chairs

Yulei Wu	University of Exeter, UK
Wenjun Jiang	Hunan University, China
Saqib Ali	University of Agriculture Faisalabad, Pakistan
Md Tariqul Islam	Syracuse University, USA
Saad Khan	University of Huddersfield, UK

Program Committee Members

Tariq Alsboui	University of Huddersfield, UK
Bakhtiar Amen	University of Huddersfield, UK
Faisal Bappy	Syracuse University, Bangladesh

Kamrul Hasan	Tennessee State University, USA
Salima Benbernou	LIPADE, Université de Paris, France
Jorge Bernal Bernabe	University of Murcia, Spain
Ebrima N. Ceesay	Johns Hopkins University, USA
Tianhua Chen	University of Huddersfield, UK
Minh-Son Dao	National Institute of Information and Communications Technology, Japan
Ralph Deters	University of Saskatchewan, Canada
Giovanni Di Stasi	University "Federico II" of Naples, Italy
Yucong Duan	Hainan University, China
James Dyer	University of Huddersfield, UK
Ramadan Elaiess	University of Benghazi, Libya
Philippe Fournier-Viger	Shenzhen University, China
Kambiz Ghazinour	SUNY Canton, USA
Hai Jiang	Arkansas State University, USA
Ashad Kabir	Charles Sturt University, Australia
Vana Kalogeraki	Athens University of Economics and Business, Greece
Konstantinos Kolias	University of Idaho, USA
Ruixuan Li	Huazhong University of Science and Technology, China
Xin Li	Nanjing University of Aeronautics and Astronautics, China
Joan Lu	University of Huddersfield, UK
Changqing Luo	Virginia Commonwealth University, USA
Yuxiang Ma	Henan University, China
Anand Nayyar	Duy Tan University, Viet Nam
Simon Parkinson	University of Huddersfield, UK
Zhan Qin	Zhejiang University, China
Manuel Roveri	Politecnico di Milano, Italy
Sangeet Saha	University of Huddersfield, UK
Ricardo Seguel	Universidad Adolfo Ibañez, Chile
Jaydip Sen	Praxis Business School, Kolkata, India
Junggab Son	Kennesaw State University, USA
Zhiyuan Tan	Napier University, UK
Muhhamad Imran Tariq	Superior University Lahore, Pakistan
Xiuhua Wang	Huazhong University of Science and Technology, China
Yunsheng Wang	Kettering University, USA
Lei Xu	Kent State University, USA
Guisong Yang	University of Shanghai for Science and Technology, China

Shuhui Yang	Purdue University Northwest, USA
Xuanxia Yao	University of Science and Technology Beijing, China
Ji Zhang	University of Southern Queensland, Australia
Youwen Zhu	Nanjing University of Aeronautics and Astronautics, China

Track3: Cyberspace Anonymity

Track Chairs

Tian Wang	Beijing Normal University & UIC, China
A. S. M. Kayes	La Trobe University, Australia
Oana Geman	University of Suceava, Romania
Mamoun Alazab	Charles Darwin University, Australia
Hudan Studiawan	Institut Teknologi Sepuluh Nopember, Indonesia

Program Committee Members

Hamid Ali Abed Al-Asadi	Iraq University College, Iraq
Selcuk Baktir	American University of the Middle East, Kuwait
Fu Chen	Central University of Finance and Economics, China
Honglong Chen	China University of Petroleum, China
Ivan Cvitic	University of Zagreb, Croatia
Ke Gu	Changsha University of Science and Technology, China
Hasan Jamil	University of Idaho, USA
Aleksandar Jevremovic	Singidunum University, Serbia
Frank Jiang	Deakin University, Australia
Marko Krstic	Regulatory Agency for Electronic Communication and Postal Services, Serbia
Massimo Mecella	Sapienza University of Rome, Italy
Jose Andre Morales	Carnegie Mellon University, USA
Klimis Ntalianis	University of West Attica, Greece
Hao Peng	Zhejiang Normal University, China
Dapeng Qu	Liaoning University, China
Imed Romdhani	Edinburgh Napier University, UK
Zeyu Sun	Luoyang Institute of Science and Technology, China
Henry Tufo	University of Colorado Boulder, USA
Ioan Ungurean	"Stefan cel Mare" University, Suceava, Romania
Hongzhi Wang	Harbin Institute of Technology, China

Xiaoliang Wang	Hunan University of Science and Technology, China
Sherali Zeadally	University of Kentucky, USA
Chunsheng Zhu	Southern University of Science and Technology, China

Contents

Cyberspace Privacy

Cyberspace Anonymity

Short Papers

Cyberspace Security

Support Tool Selection in Digital Forensics Training

Sabrina Friedl$^{(\boxtimes)}$ ⓘ, Ludwig Englbrecht ⓘ, Fabian Böhm ⓘ,
and Günther Pernul ⓘ

Regensburg University, Universitätsstraße 31, Regensburg 93053, Germany
{sabrina.friedl,ludwig.englbrecht,fabian.boehm,guenther.pernul}@ur.de
https://go.ur.de/ifs

Abstract. One of the most common challenges for digital forensic investigations is the selection of suitable analysis tools in an ever-changing environment. In recent years, live digital forensic investigations are emerging throughout organizations due to Advanced Persistent Threats (APT). At the same time, the variety and availability of digital forensic tools expand rapidly. As there is no objective guideline to enable decision-support for tool selection, forensic analysts mostly rely on their experience. They apply tools they are familiar with, although, these tools might not be the most suitable ones for the analysis task at hand. We propose a concept that enables a well-considered tool selection for experts based on desired tool characteristics. The concept supports training the right tool selection to be forensically ready for future investigations and to structure cybersecurity knowledge within an organization. To evaluate our approach, we apply the concept to a use case and demonstrate its application and performance.

Keywords: Digital Forensics (DF) · DF training · Forensic readiness · Tool selection · Incident response · Decision-making process · AHP

1 Introduction

Digital Forensics (DF) is an emerging field since the 1990s [5]. It is a process to determine step-by-step those events that led to a specific incident. To get there, scientific processes and principles are employed to analyze electronically stored data [24]. It comprises the five steps (1) Identification, (2) Data backup, (3) Analysis, (4) Documentation, and (5) Preparation of digital evidence [4]. These steps should lead forensic examiners in companies to connecting a crime, like blackmail or data theft, to court-proof evidence.

During such a DF process, the help of multiple tools is required. Hence, experts face a wide range of available forensic tools when a security vulnerability occurs in an organization. Despite their expertise and knowledge of these tools, it is hard to know all functionalities of the vast amount of tools accessible on the market [32]. Thereby, it can be challenging to make a good tool selection

© The Author(s), under exclusive license to Springer Nature Singapore Pte Ltd. 2023
G. Wang et al. (Eds.): UbiSec 2022, CCIS 1768, pp. 3–21, 2023.
https://doi.org/10.1007/978-981-99-0272-9_1

without deep knowledge on available tools, including their functions. Thus, to be prepared for future incidents and train forensic analysts, the proposed concept can be used for training and to create awareness about various tool options. Moreover, organizations can execute and coordinate an incident response as well as a DF investigation more efficiently if they are forensically ready.

In this work, we tackle this research challenge by proposing a combined concept for an appropriate tool selection as a training setup for forensic investigations. Our main contribution is a concept based on the theory of abstraction layers used in live DF analysis to compare and categorize forensic tools. It is divided into three parts. First, the input data with a rule set, second the abstraction layer, and third the output data with a margin of error [3]. To help categorize the tools in the concept, we adapt a typology for characterizing DF tools [15]. This typology does not consider the five steps of DF analysis. For that reason, these are added to link the tool applied to a specific phase of the investigation. A vital step in our concept is the application of an Analytical Hierarchy Process (AHP) to enable decision-support in tool selection as well as to support the decision-making process for experts in tool selection during DF investigations. Security and forensic experts can use our concept as a source of knowledge. By using it, they choose the aspects they consider as relevant for a possible future DF investigation in their organization. That could be Indicators of Compromise (IoC) and other Environmental Influences (EI) like accessible lab equipment. Furthermore, our approach can help to improve an organization's DF Readiness (DFR). The overview and knowledge about relevant DF tools can help reach and hold an appropriate level of DFR [9].

The remainder of the paper is structured as follows. Section 2 provides definitions for several highly relevant terms. Subsequently, in Sect. 3 a compact literature review on DF supported by decision-making processes, is conducted. In Sect. 4 our concept for supporting the tool selection process during live DF is introduced and described, based on the concept of layers of abstraction, the typology for the classification of DF tools, and the AHP. After that, the concept is applied to a use case in Sect. 5, starting with a use case description, followed by the instantiation of the proposed concept and the AHP calculation and results. This procedure is performed to demonstrate a possible tool selection for a live DF analysis training. Subsequently, in Sect. 6 the strengths and weaknesses of the proposed concept are discussed. Finally, Sect. 7 concludes our work and provides future research directions.

2   Background

In order to build a uniform knowledge base, terms that are necessary for understanding our proposed concept are explained below.

Digital Forensics (DF) is a subarea of classical forensics. Classical forensics refers to the observation and interpretation of physical evidence [8]. In DF, processes and events on IT systems are investigated concerning criminal acts to obtain evidence that can be used in court or to detect and correct malfunctions in a system or network. Generally, according to R. McKemmish in the year 1999, DF is defined by the four stages: identification, retention, analysis, and presentation [18]. Followed by the DF Investigation Model, that was first introduced in 2001. This is a linear procedure model that is used for DF investigation. In 2002, Eoghan Casey [4] extended the procedure model to the five steps (1) Identification, (2) Data backup, (3) Analysis, (4) Documentation, and (5) Preparation. While in general for an investigation a distinction is made between a static and dynamic analysis, we focus on dynamic analysis.

Live Forensics (LF), or dynamic analysis, describes a Real-Time System (RTS) in DF. That is a system with a short reaction time to respond to external input (e. g., an incident) and at the same time evaluate it. This type of reaction is referred to as incident response in DF. Incident response serves to minimize possible damage from an occurring incident and to prevent future incidents of the same type. In LF, data is collected while the system is still running. This practice provides additional contextual information that is otherwise lost when collecting data after a system shut down [1,11,23]. LF is a fast-developing field due to the emerging number of newly developed threats that do not reside within static but dynamic memory of a system, like fileless malware [17].

Digital Forensic Readiness (DFR) is defined as the degree to which digital evidence data (e. g., system activities) are sufficient enough available if an incident or attack happens. This is crucial for forensic experts during future investigations to be able to use the gathered evidence with a certainty of authenticity [20]. One of the basic underlying principles in DFR is the ability of an entity managing a system to minimize the cost and ensure the maximum possible extent of digital evidence for forensic investigations [29]. Through applying DFR an organization can be prepared and ease the process of forensic investigations for forensic experts significantly [20,22].

Fileless Malware is a type of malicious software that resides in the volatile memory of a system. In general, a fileless attack is defined as an attack on a system or network through a dynamic link library (DLL) injection. This approach uses the same malicious code-basis as traditional file-based malware. However, the fileless malware attack method is not based on infected files that must be loaded onto the system to gain access. Instead, it uses pre-existing legitimate applications (e. g., browsers) that allow malicious code to enter a system through a vulnerability. Thus, the malicious code is loaded into Random Access Memory (RAM) or injects itself, which means that the fileless malware exists only in a system's RAM and is executed from there. In the RAM of a computer, data is stored only temporarily, during runtime, and is no longer available after a reboot. Therefore, it is almost impossible to find permanent traces of fileless malware [2,17]. These types of malware increase the relevance of a reasonable tool selection to secure possible evidence and IoCs properly.

Multi-Criteria Decision-Making (MCDM) techniques are widely used in different areas of application [30]. This also enables the selection of the right and appropriate tool during a LF investigation. The actions for tool selection relate to the decision-making process and are produced by *1) determining relevant criteria and alternatives, 2) attaching relevance measurements* and *3) processing a ranking of alternatives* [30].

Analytic Hierarchy Process (AHP) is a prioritization technique entirely based on objectivity, if the correct set of data is used, e. g., historical data entries. It applies mathematics to the decision-making process to enable a comparison of different goals. Since people make their decisions in specific situations according to subjective criteria, it is important in critical situations to find a decision that is as objective as possible. AHP was founded by Saaty [25] and is a decomposition of a complex real-world problem in objectives, criteria, and alternatives to obtain a relative preference and to guarantee a high degree of transparency and traceability. The objective is reached via a pairwise comparison of alternatives along with pre-defined criteria and their sub-criteria. The AHP is one of the most used MCDM methods. It transforms a decision problem into hierarchical order. This means an overarching goal is set at the top level. The decision criteria are subsequently related to the top goal and linked to a wide variety of available alternatives at the bottom level. The AHP, in general, has four main steps: *1) determining the sought knowledge, 2) structuring the decision architecture, 3) constructing a set of pairwise comparison matrices, and 4) using the obtained priorities to weigh the elements* [25]. Weights are scaled from zero to nine, implicating that a score of nine is most relevant. This scale is applied in our work within the ranking process for the tool suggestions.

3   Related Work

Saleem et al. [26] build a decision tree to prioritize artifacts along with seven crime cases while using a specific mobile phone. The authors address the problem of selecting the best tool for mobile forensics out of a wide variety of tools for acquiring and analyzing digital evidence. They transform this challenge into a multi-criteria decision and propose a method for selecting the right tool to extract evidence that has the most relevant impact on the digital investigation. Since this approach provides a base for comparing two alternatives, it is useful for a post-mortem analysis. An ever-changing environment by considering the investigator's task during a LF analysis cannot be addressed. Our approach builds upon this idea but provides a new concept. Therefore, the taxonomy is adapted specifically for the field of decision-support during a LF investigation.

Karabiyik and Karabiyik [13] introduce a game-theoretic approach to the tool selection problem. Most of the time, DF investigators deploy tools due to their familiarity, previous experiences, or available organizational resources and funding. This approach aims to support and ease the decision for investigators on which DF tool to apply. When analyzing their model, the authors focus on the use of file carving tools. Their results indicate that the efficiency of an ongoing investigation could increase if the dynamic of strategic tool changes is considered. This approach is realized by using game-theoretic modeling.

Related work addresses the tool selection problem using a decision tree to prioritize DF artifacts and a game-theoretic approach. A disadvantage of decision trees is overfitting (where a model interprets meaning from irrelevant data), it can become a problem if the design of a decision tree is too complex. In addition, they do not work well for continuous variables (e.g., variables that can have more than one value or a spectrum of values) [19]. With an AHP this problem is still present, but not as distinct. Within the game-theoretic approach applied mathematics provides tools for analyzing situations in which parties make interdependent decisions. This method can lead to complex implementations and a restricted applicability [27]. In contrast to existing work, we address the selection problem using an AHP. We chose the AHP to balance the complexity of integration and reduce partially problems of decision trees. To the best of our knowledge, no approaches exist to solve or facilitate the tool selection problem using an AHP to properly train for DF investigations. The AHP methodology is nevertheless a suitable approach. It allows the target and the associated characteristics to be presented in a structured manner on several levels and the results to be determined based on relevance. Adding computational support, a forensic expert can properly train the tool selection process with a picked use case to prepare for future incidents that need to be investigated.

Keeping up-to-date as a cybersecurity professional in organizations is getting more attention as the availability of tools is steadily increasing and new paradigms, like the Internet of Things (IoT) are becoming more integrated [14]. Especially in organizational environments, rapid knowledge processing, promotion, dissemination, and procedures for dealing with incidents are valuable [7]. To address this issue, we propose a concept that helps forensic examiners and investigators in their decision-making and training process when choosing a tool to extract anticipated digital evidence from a system.

4   Support Tool Selection in Digital Forensics Training

In the following, we propose a concept based on the theory of abstraction layers for supporting the training of forensics analysts for tool selection in DF investigation. This theory is enhanced with our extended typology and an AHP for decision-support.

4.1   Layers of Abstraction

DF investigations in organizations require a prepared selection of appropriate, reasonable tools. The theory of abstraction layers was first utilized by Carrier [3] to describe the purpose, meaning, and goal of forensic analysis tools. This enables the categorization of tools and is therefore applicable as an underlying concept to support decision-making for experts to prepare for digital investigation in an organizational environment. Hence, we classify the respective structure as applicable for our goal.

Fig. 1. Abstract concept for DF tool selection training, according to [3].

Generally, the theory of abstraction layers is divided into three areas: *Input*, *Abstraction Layer*, and *Output* as depicted in Fig. 1. The input consists of input data and a rule set that is then applied to the data. The resulting data is processed in the abstraction layer, and then the output data is generated, including an error margin. The concept is not restricted to only one abstraction layer but can contain several abstraction layers on top of each other [3]. As input data, we define possible available IoCs and EI. In order to classify tools according to their characteristics, a typology is required as described in Sect. 4.2 as part one of the rule set. As a second part of the rule set, we apply the AHP. This is done by conducting a questionnaire that determines the relevance of one characteristic versus another, an expert's preferences can be measured. In the abstraction layer itself, the AHP calculation is performed. This results in an output with tool suggestions leading to possible new IoCs.

4.2 Typology

There are no consistently applied software products, procedures, methods, or concepts in IT forensic analysis. This is primarily due to the different capabilities of the programs. The typology for DF tools by Kiper [15] enables a precise classification of tools according to different characteristics and makes them comparable [21]. Further, tools can be assigned to one or more of the five steps of the DF analysis process, as outlined in Sect. 2. Adding those steps as ancillary characteristics provides a further linkage to a specific situation during a DF investigation. Therefore, we extend Kiper's typology [15] to include the five DF process steps as additional characteristics, (1) Identification, (2) Data backup, (3) Analysis, (4) Documentation and (5) Preparation [4].

This typology is used as one part of the layers of abstraction rule set. It is structured into key-value pairs, containing the *Tool Characteristics* and the associated *Values*. This results in the typology consisting of the six categories, into which tool characteristics can be classified, namely *1. Parsing Capabilities, 2. Subject Data, 3. Subject Device, 4. General Tool Characteristics, 5. Pre-Analysis Features*, and *6. DF Process Step*. For each process step in the sixth category, a yes/no criterion is added as an associated value. Meaning, if a tool can be applied during a process step, the value would be yes.

4.3 Decision-Making with AHP

The typology defined in Sect. 4.2 provides categories for the tool classification. These categories build the basis to apply the AHP to our proposed concept.

The AHP functions as the second part of the rule set by providing a question-naire, which is filled out from a forensic expert view and that compares the characteristics. From now on, the six categories into which the characteristics can be sorted according to the typology will be referred to as criteria in the AHP. While training for DF investigations, decisions are based on and influenced by uncertainty to select a relevant tool-set. Uncertainty is always present in investigations due to subjective decisions. These differ from investigator to investigator and result in a different prioritization of digital evidence. The AHP converts a subjective decision into an objective one while processing quantitative and qualitative data. Therefore, applying the AHP in our proposed concept is appropriate and can support the decision-making process. To instantiate our concept, we need to determine the overarching goal of the DF investigation. In our concept, we define this goal as "selecting the most appropriate tool for one specific training situation to be forensically ready for future investigations". The four steps of an AHP (Sect. 2) can be adapted to our model as follows:

First, available forensic tools with their characteristics need to be prepared as the set of alternatives. This is continued by linking the characteristics from the tools with specified criteria from the expert questionnaire. Additionally, it is necessary to build suitable groups of criteria since not every characteristic can be part of the decision-making process. This step includes a well-known understanding of the DF tool and the effect of each functionality. These groups are defined as the six categories from the typology.

Subsequently, all criteria are evaluated against concurrent criteria in an Eigenvector matrix. This matrix is reciprocal; therefore, inverse relationships are mutually represented as fractions. The Eigenvector matrix is a squared matrix with recommendations. Then, all rows of this matrix are summed up. This process is iterative. In addition, all alternatives are rated according to all criteria and this results in the total amounts of matrices $n+2$ (one for every criterion plus two Eigenvectors). Afterwards, the importance of each alternative is weighted in a criterion matrix concerning the remaining alternatives.

Adopting the AHP requires first to define the weight to pursued goals. The goals must be compared holistically with each other and a normalization value is calculated. After creating the goal matrix, each alternative needs to be compared according to each goal. Using the AHP in the context of a DF investigation, the user needs a profound understanding of the available tools' criteria and belonging sub-criteria. These are concurrent to the extended typologies categories and associated characteristics.

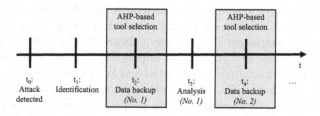

Fig. 2. Illustration of using an AHP during a LF forensic analysis training.

During an IT forensic analysis, several decisions are made. Due to new findings or circumstances during a use case training, a tool selection must be made at several points. Therefore, at different times, the criteria are re-weighted because specific criteria are considered more important than others. For this reason, the concept can be applied at several points in time to find the best suitable tool for the next step of the investigation. The application of the AHP during a LF analysis is illustrated in Fig. 2. In summary, the concept's underlying framework is based on the theory of abstraction layers, and the main components applied to it are the extended typology and the AHP.

5   Applying the Concept to a Use-Case

With a use case as a basis, we apply the proposed concept. Starting with a use case description and a specification of the input for the abstraction layer. Subsequently, the AHP calculation is applied within the abstraction layer itself and afterwards interpreted. Finally, the abstraction layer's output is reached, resulting in a ranking list of the tools to provide decision-support for the expert during a LF investigation training.

5.1   Use Case Description

The presented concept provides an approach for forensic investigators to make the decision to use appropriate tools easier. To illustrate the functionality for organizations in more detail, the concept will now be applied to an example incident from recent years, the "Jeff Bezos Hack". This world-famous attack describes an incident where perpetrators infiltrated the target's smartphone with camouflaged malware to obtain personal and business data. After a meeting of Bezos and the crown prince of Saudi-Arabia in 2017, they exchanged phone numbers and wrote ordinary messages to each other on WhatsApp. After Bezos watched a random and out-of-context video sent by the prince in 2018, his phone started sending out large amounts of data via its web browser and the mail program. Following an investigation and forensic analysis of the phone, the video contained presumably a 14-byte small malicious code. Ancillary, the spyware Pegasus and Galileo are reported as most likely applied tools in this case [12].

In general, this type of camouflaged malware aims to access a person's personal and business data in a senior management position by deploying social engineering. Hence, malware is infiltrated by commonly available and installed programs to the target system. These programs include everyday applications such as WhatsApp, Facebook, e-mail, and others. Important here is that only the social engineering component shapes these malware attacks to be successful. The infected file is disguised as a photo or an apparently harmless e-mail attachment and is additionally transmitted by a trusted and known person. When the target person opens the infected file, the malware is installed in the background and covertly collects data, forwarding it to the perpetrators. This enables espionage in companies and government organizations.

FTI Consulting[1], which conducted the investigation to determine if and what type of malware was planted on Bezos' phone, used various LF tools. A cursory study of the subject determined these tools. As a result, FTI Consulting applied a toolbox including UFED 4PC Ulitmate, Phone Detective, Physical Analyzer, Telerik Fiddler, WireShark, and PowerGREP [12].

5.2 Input for Abstraction Layer Concept

In order to convey the proposed concept in an approachable manner, the interrelationships are explained thoroughly below. Furthermore, Fig. 3 depicts the theory of abstraction layers in detail with the extensions considered necessary. The input data contains two sources. The rule set consists of a typology and a method that are applied. The second step maps the abstraction layer itself, in which the input data is processed and output data is generated. The concept ends with the output, including two possible forms of output data and a margin of error.

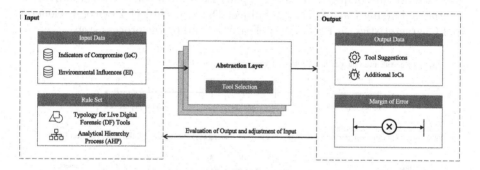

Fig. 3. The proposed concept for training LF tool selection.

Input - Data. The input data is provided and defined by the forensic examiner or investigator. This may involve data in the form of previously encountered or known IoCs or EI. EIs can be limitations in processing power or equipment for investigations. These data inputs build the basis on which the rule set is applied. **Input - Rule Set.** The utilized rule set consists of two methodological components. One is the extended typology for LF tools from Sect. 4.2. The other method is the AHP expert questionnaire (Sect. 4.3). Combining these two approaches enables a tool selection based on desired criteria for the LF expert. **Abstraction Layer - Tool Selection.** This layer acts as a black box to represent the process of tool selection by the expert. Here, forensics experts use their desired criteria as input through the AHP expert questionnaire according to the extended LF tool typology. In this layer, the actual calculation of the AHP is performed that produces tool suggestions. **Output - Data.** In the final step of the abstraction layer model, the calculated tool suggestions are output. These suggestions are proposed in the form of a ranked list to support the

---

[1] https://www.fticonsulting-emea.com/?rl=emea.

forensic examiner during the decision-making process. However, the final tool selection is left to the expert. **Output - Margin of Error.** The margin of error is a statistical expression that reflects the extent of random sampling error in the results of a questionnaire. **Evaluation of Output and Adjustment of Input.** After the expert has deduced the final tool list, there is a possibility to make adjustments to get more suitable or further tool suggestions.

5.3   AHP Calculation

After the design of the AHP including the objective (level 1), the criteria (level 2), the sub-criteria (level 3) as well as the alternatives (level 4), the data is collected from an expert's perspective trying to select a tool for a specific use case. In the current situation, that's the Jeff Bezos Hack use case described before (Sect. 5.1). The conducted questionnaire (Sect. 4.3) consists of 15 questions. The number of questions is calculated on basis of the number of compared criteria $n = 6$ in Eq. 1 [25]. That amount of questions allows a pairwise comparison of the six individual criteria, 1. Parsing Capabilities, 2. Subject Data, 3. Subject Device, 4. General Tool Characteristics, 5. Pre-analysis Features, and 6. DF process step.

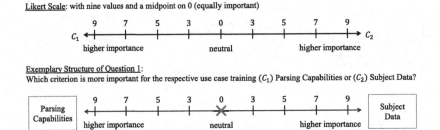

Fig. 4. Likert scale [6] and exemplary structure of question 1 (answer marked with a X at 0).

With the aim of obtaining qualitative data based on subjective opinions, a relative Likert scale [16] with a midpoint is used [6]. The scale with nine value points has a midpoint of 0. While 0 stands for neutral, both sides represent a scale with growing importance from 3 to 9 for a criterion as seen in Fig. 4. The importance of the individual criteria is determined by the expert on the basis of this nine-point scale. With this approach, two criteria C_1 and C_2 are compared with each other until all 15 possible comparisons have been covered. If the expert chooses 0, the two criteria are equally important, if e.g. 9 for C_1 is selected it has a nine times higher importance than C_2 [25].

In order to evaluate the collected data, a squared comparison matrix with rows i and columns j is applied. When filling the matrix, the diagonals are filled with a 1 since these represent the cell value with itself. All other cells in a comparison matrix are filled by the reciprocal values a_{ji} of a matrix element $a_{ij} > 0$ with Eq. 2 [25].

Table 1. Squared comparison matrix for criteria 1–6.

Criteria	1	2	3	4	5	6	$\sum$	w_c
1	1	0.12	0.11	0.14	1.00	1.00	3.37	0.04
2	8.00	1	1.00	4.00	6.00	3.00	23.00	0.27
3	9.00	1.00	1	9.00	9.00	9.00	38.00	0.44
4	7.00	0.25	0.11	1	5.00	3.00	16.36	0.19
5	1.00	0.17	0.11	0.20	1	0.33	2.81	0.03
6	1.00	0.33	0.11	0.33	3.00	1	2.77	0.03
						$\sum$	86.31	

After the matrix is filled, the relative importance of the individual criteria is represented by the calculation of the Eigenvectors. These describe the criteria weight scores w that are based on the principal Eigenvector of the decision matrix. They are obtained with a normalization of the square matrix by calculating the total column sum as in Eq. 3 and dividing each matrix element by it [25]. In Table 1 the resulting weights w_c of the comparison matrix are depicted. Following the principal eigenvalue λ needs to be calculated to check the consistency of the comparison matrix. The eigenvalue λ is calculated with Eq. 4 [25]. For a pairwise comparison the matrix needs to be consistent. A matrix is called consistent or transitive if $a_{ii} = 1$ for all i in $1, ..., n$ and $a_{ij}a_{ji} = 1$ for all i, j in $1, ..., n$ [10]. The consistency is measured with the consistency ratio CR, which is calculated as stated in Eq. 5 [25]. In our example the eigenvalue is $\lambda = 6.562$. The application of this eigenvalue results in a $CR = 9\%$. Utilizing that procedure ensures data quality when $CR < 0.1$ applies [25].

$$c = \frac{n(n-1)}{2} \tag{1}$$

$$a_{ji} = \frac{1}{a_{ij}} \tag{2}$$

$$for \quad column \quad j = \sum_{i=1}^{n} a_{ij} \tag{3}$$

$$\lambda = \frac{1}{n} \sum_{i}^{n} x_i \quad with \quad x_i = \frac{\sum_{j-1}^{n} a_{ji}EV_j}{EV_i} \tag{4}$$

$$CR = \frac{C_i}{R_n} \quad with \quad CI = \frac{\lambda - n}{n - 1} \tag{5}$$

Table 2. Priority ranks of the criteria based on the pairwise comparison.

Criteria	Abbreviation	Priority	Ranking
1. Parsing Capability	PC	3.5%	5
2. Subject Data	SDa	29.0%	2
3. Subject Device	SDe	45.9%	1
4. General Tool Characteristics	GTC	12.6%	3
5. Pre-Analysis Features	P-AF	3.2%	6
6. DF Process Step	DFPS	5.8%	4

In Table 2 the six criteria are listed with their calculated priority and according to their rank. This ranking results from the pairwise comparison of the individual criteria, with the criterion "3. Subject Device" in the first place, "2. Subject Data" in second place and "4. Tool Characteristics" in third place. This ranking shows that the forensic analyst or expert wants to find these first three criteria prioritized in his tool selection.

Table 3. Priority ranks of the tools based on the pairwise comparison.

Alternatives	Priority	Ranking
UFED Ultimate	25.2%	1
MOBILedit Forensic	21.2%	2
Oxygen Forensic	15.5%	3
iXAM	10.4%	4
Pilotlink	7.3%	5
MSAB XRY	4.6%	6
Volatility Framework	4.2%	7
EnCase	2.9%	8
Device Seizure	2.8%	9
WireShark	2.7%	10
Fiddler	1.3%	11
Elcomsoft iOS Forensic Toolkit	1.1%	12
PhoneRescue	1.0%	13

The second pairwise comparison is performed using the same procedure for the available alternatives. While for the criteria $n = 6$ is applied, this procedure is performed with $n = 13$ alternatives, whereas the alternatives are represented by available tools. As a result, a second squared comparison matrix is built for the 13 alternatives. The comparison is carried out by comparing the characteristics of the tools. The resulting priority ranks that emerged from the second pairwise comparison show the order of the tools according to the prioritized criteria in Table 3.

5.4   Results Interpretation of the AHP

The final results of the AHP are presented in Table 4. Here the individual weights w_c of the criteria can be found. The weights of the alternatives are multiplied with the associated criteria weight w_c. Based on this procedure, the global weights w_g can be calculated, which represent the connection between the two comparison matrices (criteria, alternatives). Through the global weights w_g, the most relevant tool can be ascertained; the higher the value, the higher the tool will appear in the ranking. The results in Table 1 illustrate that the criterion found most relevant are *3. Subject Device* with a value of 0.44, followed by *2. Subject Data* (0.27), *4. General Tool Characteristics* (0.19), *1. Parsing Capabilities* (0.04) and ending with *5. Pre-Analysis Features* (0.03) and *6. DF Process Step* (0.03) as least relevant criterion.

Table 4. Final AHP results including a ranking [Note: all values are in 10^{-2} format to increase the visibility].

Alternatives	Criteria						w_g	Ranking
	1. PC	2. SDa	3. SDe	4. GTC	5. P-AF	6. DFPS		
w_c	4.0	27.0	44.0	19.0	3.0	3.0		
1. UFED Ultimate	0.8	5.1	8.3	3.6	0.6	0.6	19.0	1
2. MOBILedit Forensic	0.7	4.6	7.6	3.3	0.5	0.5	17.2	2
3. Oxygen Forensic	0.5	3.7	6.0	2.6	0.5	0.5	13.8	3
4. iXAM	0.5	3.1	5.0	2.2	0.4	0.4	11.6	4
5. Pilotlink	0.4	2.5	4.1	1.8	0.3	0.3	9.4	5
6. Volatility Framework	0.3	1.9	3.0	1.3	0.2	0.2	6.9	6
7. MSAB XRY	0.2	1.6	2.6	1.1	0.3	0.3	6.1	7
8. Device Seizure	0.2	1.3	2.1	1.0	0.1	0.1	4.8	8
9. EnCase	0.2	1.2	2.0	0.9	0.2	0.2	4.7	9
10. WireShark	0.2	1.2	1.9	0.8	0.0	0.0	4.1	10
11. Fiddler	0.1	0.3	0.6	0.2	0.0	0.0	1.2	11
12. Elcomsoft iOS	0.0	0.3	0.4	0.2	0.0	0.0	0.9	12
13. PhoneRescue	0.0	0.2	0.4	0.2	0.0	0.0	0.8	13

A detailed look at Table 4 additionally reveals which tool represents a criterion the most. For example, for criterion *3. Subject Device* the alternative *UFED Ultimate* (8.3) would be most suitable. That means *UFED Ultimate* would be, according to the tool properties, well suited for the device type from the expert's corresponding use case for an iOS-based device (iPhone). For the criterion *2. Subject Data* the AHP results show that *UFED Ultimate* (5.1) would be the most appropriate to analyze or extract data from an iPhone, for instance. Additionally, for the third-most relevant criterion *4. General Tool Characteristics* the alternative *UFED Ultimate* would be the most suitable again, which supports the final ranking with the tool *UFED Ultimate* (3.6) in the first place.

Through an interpretation of the results, we could state that the forensic analyst clearly defined the relevance of the different criteria during the decision-making process. Additionally, the application of the AHP results in a ranking of the most suitable tool for a specific situation. The process described above can be applied several times during an LF investigation. During this process, the weights of the criteria can change, and a different tool recommendation is generated. However, this process can reveal an incorrect assessment of the given situation and lead to a positive effect during the tool selection. In the following, an example of a specific output of the AHP (within the abstraction layer) for the selected use-case is demonstrated.

5.5 Output of Abstraction Layer Concept

The output of our concept is calculated as described in Sect. 5.3 and depicted in Fig. 5 in the form of an AHP. On level 1, the overall goal is to select the most appropriate LF tool for the present use case or investigation. Level 2 describes super-categories as criteria. These are directly followed by characteristics assigned to the individual criteria and are listed as sub-criteria on level 3. All sub-criteria have been chosen based on the information supplied from the FTI consulting report [12]. For that reason, we used the report as a baseline for our use case evaluation and have made useful additions. Finally, on level 4, the alternatives are presented as tool suggestions to the organizational forensic expert. The results are highly dependent on the previously entered characteristics, and the final decision is likewise to be made by the expert.

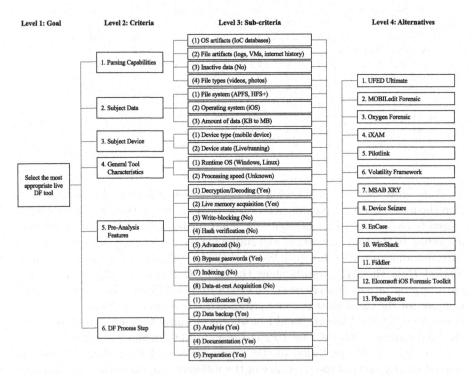

Fig. 5. AHP tool selection process based on the proposed concept.

While the final goal is to enable an effective LF analysis, the additional steps aim to support companies by utilizing the available resources without incurring further costs. This is supported by the focus of the concept of tool suggestions intended to support decision-making but does not make the decision for an expert. Next, the list of tools obtained by applying the AHP through weighting the criteria is examined in more detail. The ranking of the final list of tools is dependent on the previous rating by the importance of the individual criteria. When calculating the AHP priority of the criteria, a ranking emerges, marking the essential criteria. These most important features are then compared with the individual tool features leading to the tool suggestions. The tool suggestions are sorted according to the equality of available features. If that amount is higher, the tool is put higher up; if it is lower, the tool is put further down in the ranking. Consecutively, the extracted tool suggestions are in the follwoing ranking, 1. UFED Ultimate, 2. MOBILedit Forensic, 3. Oxygen Forensic, 4. iXAM, 5. Pilotlink, 6. Volatility Framework, 7. MSAB XRY, 8. EnCase, 9. Device Seizure, 10. WireShark, 11. Fiddler, 12. Elcomsoft iOS Digital Forensic Toolkit and 13. PhoneRescue.

The concept characteristics were filled in based on the input of the "Jeff Bezos Hack" use case. A tool selection is created independently, which is not intended to result in the same tools as those from FTI Consulting. Nevertheless, our concept suggests tools that were applied similarly during the analysis in the use case, such as UFED Ultimate and WireShark. The application of the concept based on AHP has significantly contributed to the decision-support in selecting the best possible tools and resulted in a list of 13 tool proposals. To achieve a fast response time during a LF investigation in organizations, it is advisable to start with tools that do not require installation on the mobile device. In addition, repeated application of the concept over time by adjusting the relevance of characteristics can provide new or more precise tool suggestions.

6 Discussion

The proposed concept provides a methodology to support tool selection during LF training. Especially the combination of the abstraction layers of the forensic analysis with an iterative applied decision-support process enables to react to new information and changing environments in the dynamic area of a LF investigation training setup. The possibility of training with our concept can increase the level of preparation for forensic investigations, thus improving processes and operations in the event of an incident and enabling faster and better prepared DF investigations.

Although the concept provides a well-considered and comprehensible approach to select the most suitable tool, the model suggests the decision only based on the available input data. It must be emphasized that the used data, including the classification for tools with the extended typology, must be continuously updated and that the data must be obtained from trustworthy sources. In addition to the list of tools, features, and characteristics, the tools' successful applications must be documented. This is necessary, because the output of the tool is strongly dependent on the input questions as well as the experts answers.

In our concept, an AHP-based decision-making process is proposed and applied at different tasks during a DF analysis training. Especially during a live analysis, additional tools may have to be applied or removed at reasonable intervals. This makes sense for the investigation, but if there is no history of the tools already used, it can lead to an undesirable endless loop regarding the application or discarding of two tools. Therefore, it is essential to include information from a previous decision in our decision process. Due to the modular concept's great flexibility, this information can also be formulated as a hint, and forensic experts can consider this note and select the next most appropriate tool. We suggest this approach since the exclusion of an already used tool at the end of the decision-making would change the underlying total set of alternatives and result in a substantial deviation after the pairwise comparison (rank reversal problem). Finally, the DF expert has to decide whether a tool is selected more than once, and this option must be considered in the decision-making process.

The proposed approach supports the application of different decision-making tools. Compared to the proposed AHP method, an Analytic Network Process (ANP) would also be applicable. It is a more general form of the AHP that includes the core concepts of a pairwise comparison to assess the weight of the criteria and build a rank of alternatives. Further, an ANP incorporates dependencies between the criteria (and among the alternatives) using this relationship as a network. We used an AHP and assumed independence between the criteria and alternatives since the concept is iteratively applied during a LF investigation, and at every point of the decision, different environments and influences are present. An ANP would need to have the interdependence between criteria and alternatives in specific situations acquired before, which is neither practicable nor realistic.

Nevertheless, the actual application of a specific tool is still the forensic expert's decision since he must have the expertise. Our concept is mainly meant as preparation for the selection of a suitable tool in a very nerve-racking situation. With the AHP method, the amount of relevant criteria and their weighting is consciously considered at the beginning of each decision-making process, making it easier to follow the investigation afterwards. Furthermore, a structured method for collecting expert knowledge is created and forms an approach to describe subjective decisions objectively.

7   Conclusion and Future Work

IT forensics experts are constantly challenged with the latest developments in DF tools and methods for analyzing and investigating new types of attacks. Especially in a LF investigation, the most suitable tool selection at the correct time is a critical success factor. Our paper provides an approach to support DFR with a tool selection in a LF investigation training environment.

The concept builds on recently developed approaches and characterizations of DF tools and combines them with well-known decision-support approaches.

More precisely, we developed a concept for training the tool selection process during LF by extending a topology for DF tools according to their application phases. The concept is instantiated and complemented by a selection process based on the AHP to support and rationalize complex decision-making. The usability of the tool has been applied to a well-known use case and demonstrates the support during a LF investigation training. The strengths and weaknesses have also been discussed in detail.

To support the pairwise comparison and the decision-making process accordingly, we plan to include Visual Security Analytics (VSA) to provide additional support through improved visual cognition of the current situation by enhancing the situational awareness during a LF investigation training to improve DFR.

Further, a direct comparison of the proposed method with existing approaches based on the same underlying use case or decision situation in which a forensic analyst finds himself would be valuable. This would go beyond the scope of this paper, but it is planned in future work to compare existing methods based on variables like, calculation time and differences in tool suggestions.

Additionally, the presented concept for training to select the right or appropriate tools for a LF investigation could also find application in novel forensic areas such as IoT forensics [28]. Here, forensic experts are faced with complex environments and contexts as well as new types of attacks [31]. Targeted training and decision-support in the selection of appropriate tools could enable or accelerate the investigation of IoT incidents.

Moreover, it is planned not only to limit the knowledge to a company but also to share it within the DF community. The tool characteristics, the phase of the LF investigation, and the decisions made are intended to be provided as scenario-based knowledge units, whereby the criteria are defined and weighted in advance. In this way, the concept aims to address a wide range of recipients and promote the comprehensibility of the decision about the selected tool.

References

1. Adelstein, F.: Live forensics: diagnosing your system without killing it first. Commun. ACM **49**, 63–66 (2006)
2. Alzuri, A., Andrade, D., Escobar, Y.N., Zambora, B.M.: The growth of fileless malware. IEEE REM Group, pp. 1–5 (2019)
3. Carrier, B.D.: Defining digital forensic examination and analysis tool using abstraction layers. Int. J. Digit. EVid. **1**, 1–12 (2003)
4. Casey, E.: Handbook of Digital Forensics and Investigation. Elsevier Science, Amsterdam (2009)
5. Casino, F., et al.: Research trends, challenges, and emerging topics in digital forensics: a review of reviews. IEEE Access **10**, 25464–25493 (2022)
6. Chyung, S.Y., Roberts, K., Swanson, I., Hankinson, A.: Evidence-based survey design: the use of a midpoint on the likert scale. Perform. Improv. **56**(10), 15–23 (2017)
7. Corallo, A., Lazoi, M., Lezzi, M., Luperto, A.: Cybersecurity awareness in the context of the industrial internet of things: a systematic literature review. Comput. Ind. **137**, 103614 (2022)

8. Eckert, W.G.: Introduction to Forensic Sciences, 2nd edn. Elsevier Science Publishing Co., New York (1992)
9. Englbrecht, L., Meier, S., Pernul, G.: Towards a capability maturity model for digital forensic readiness. Wirel. Networks **26**(7), 4895–4907 (2020)
10. Farkas, A., Rózsa, P., Stubnya, E.: Transitive matrices and their applications. Linear Algebra Appl. **302**, 423–433 (1999)
11. Farmer, D., Venema, W.: Forensic Discovery, vol. 1. Addison-Wesley Professional, Boston (2004)
12. Ferrante, A.J.: Project cato. https://assets.documentcloud.org/documents/66683 13/FTI-Report-into-Jeff-Bezos-Phone-Hack.pdf (2019). Accessed 07 Dec 2022
13. Karabiyik, U., Karabiyik, T.: A game theoretic approach for digital forensic tool selection. MDPI Math. **8**(5), 1–13 (2020)
14. Keipour, H., Hazra, S., Finne, N., Voigt, T.: Generalizing supervised learning for intrusion detection in IoT mesh networks. In: Wang, G., Choo, K.K.R., Ko, R.K.L., Xu, Y., Crispo, B. (eds.) Ubiquitous Security. UbiSec 2021, pp. 214–228. Springer, Singapore (2022). https://doi.org/10.1007/978-981-19-0468-4_16
15. Kiper, J.R.: Pick a tool, the right tool: developing a practical typology for selecting digital forensics tools. SANS Institute - Information Security Reading Room, pp. 1–24 (2018)
16. Likert, R.: A technique for the measurement of attitudes. Archiv. Psychol. **22**(140), 5–55 (1932)
17. Mansfield-Devine, S.: Fileless attacks: compromising targets without malware. Netw. Secur. **2017**(4), 7–11 (2017)
18. McKemmish, R.: What is forensic computing? Trends Issues Crime Criminal Just. **118**, 1–6 (1999)
19. Mehedi Shamrat, F.J., Chakraborty, S., Billah, M.M., Das, P., Muna, J.N., Ranjan, R.: A comprehensive study on pre-pruning and post-pruning methods of decision tree classification algorithm. In: 2021 5th International Conference on Trends in Electronics and Informatics (ICOEI), pp. 1339–1345 (2021)
20. Menza Karie, N., Karume, S.M., et al.: Digital forensic readiness in organizations: issues and challenges. J. Digital Forens. Secur. Law **12**(4), 5 (2017)
21. NIST: Computer forensics tool catalog (2021). https://toolcatalog.nist.gov/index. php. Accessed 07 Dec 2022
22. Park, S., Kim, Y., Park, G., Na, O., Chang, H.: Research on digital forensic readiness design in a cloud computing-based smart work environment. Sustainability **10**(4), 1203 (2018)
23. Patrascu, A., Patriciu, V.V.: Beyond digital forensics. A cloud computing perspective over incident response and reporting. In: IEEE 8th International Symposium on Applied Computational Intelligence and Informatics, SACI 2013, Timisoara, Romania, 23–25 May 2013, pp. 455–460. IEEE (2013)
24. Raghavan, S.: Digital forensic research: current state of the art. CSI Trans. ICT **1**(1), 91–114 (2013)
25. Saaty, T.L.: How to make a decision: the analytic hierarchy process. Eur. J. Oper. Res. **48**(1), 9–26 (1990)
26. Saleem, S., Popov, O., Baggili, I.: A method and a case study for the selection of the best available tool for mobile device forensics using decision analysis. Digit. Investig. **16**, 55–64 (2016)
27. Shafiee Hasanabadi, S., Habibi Lashkari, A., Ghorbani, A.A.: A survey and research challenges of anti-forensics: evaluation of game-theoretic models in simulation of forensic agents' behaviour. Forensic Sci. Int. Dig. Invest. **35**, 301024 (2020)

28. Stoyanova, M., Nikoloudakis, Y., Panagiotakis, S., Pallis, E., Markakis, E.K.: A survey on the internet of things (IoT) forensics: challenges, approaches, and open issues. IEEE Commun. Surv. Tutor. **22**(2), 1191–1221 (2020)
29. Tan, J.: Forensic readiness. Cambridge, MA:@ Stake 1 (2001)
30. Vaidya, O.S., Kumar, S.: Analytic hierarchy process: an overview of applications. Eur. J. Oper. Res. **169**(1), 1–29 (2006)
31. Woodiss-Field, A., Johnstone, M.N., Haskell-Dowland, P.: Towards evaluating the effectiveness of botnet detection techniques. In: Wang, G., Choo, K.K.R., Ko, R.K.L., Xu, Y., Crispo, B. (eds.) Ubiquitous Security. UbiSec 2021, pp. 292–308. Springer, Singapore (2022). https://doi.org/10.1007/978-981-19-0468-4_22
32. Wu, T., Breitinger, F., O'Shaughnessy, S.: Digital forensic tools: Recent advances and enhancing the status quo. Forensic Sci. Int. Dig. Invest. **34**, 300999 (2020)

Listen to the Music: Evaluating the Use of Music in Audio Based Authentication

Michael Tsai and Vimal Kumar[✉]

School of Computing and Mathematical Sciences, University of Waikato,
Hamilton 3200, New Zealand
mt296@students.waikato.ac.nz, vkumar@waikato.ac.nz

Abstract. Audio based authentication has been proposed to be used as a second or third factor of authentication in Multi-Factor Authentication (MFA). Previous audio fingerprinting work has mostly used tonal frequencies which are not ideal in authentication as humans do not like sharp tonal frequencies as audio. This work investigates the usage of music as the audio for authentication instead of tonal frequencies. We also compare music with Dual Tone Multi Frequency (DTMF) audio. We present the results of our experimentation over source audio, feature extraction and performance under noise in this paper. The results of our experiments show that music in fact offers advantages such as better accuracy and better performance under noise in addition to sounding pleasant.

Keywords: Authentication · Fingerprinting · Audio · Music · Mobile devices

1 Introduction

Mobile device fingerprinting, which is the idea of gathering characteristics that could reliably identify each individual mobile phone is useful in a variety of scenarios. For instance, a vendor may wish to determine their target customers and advertise accordingly, in which case mobile device fingerprinting can be used to perform user tracking. Furthermore, this technique can also be used in criminal investigations [4] in which investigators may need to identify if a particular mobile phone was used in criminal activity. Finally, another major application is authentication, which is also the focus of this paper. Due to the ubiquity of mobile devices, it is convenient as well as cost-efficient to adopt them in multi-factor authentication schemes. Traditional mobile device fingerprinting techniques include the usage of IP addresses, cookies and other identifiers such as IMEI (International Mobile Equipment Identity) or UDID (Unique Device Identifier) for iOS devices. However, these methods are often subjected to user modification, which would be unsuitable in a high-security context such as an access control system. Another idea which has been proposed in previous work is sensor fingerprinting. Mobile devices often contain a large number of sensors.

G. Wang et al. (Eds.): UbiSec 2022, CCIS 1768, pp. 22–37, 2023.
https://doi.org/10.1007/978-981-99-0272-9_2

For example, the audio sensors, which consist of the microphone and the speaker provide the basic functionality of recording and playing sounds. Other sensors such as gyroscope, accelerometer, magnetometer, ambient light sensors and others have also contributed to the abundant features in mobile devices. During the manufacturing process of the sensors however, there are often variations which result in inevitable hardware variances. These variances cause the sensors to produce different output when presented with the same inputs, even within the same make and model of the phones. These different outputs can provide enough entropy to construct reliable fingerprints and be used to perform hardware-level device identification [5, 12].

Previous work in the area of audio based fingerprinting [5, 8] has focused on the usage of single or stepped frequencies with some success. We will use the term tonal frequency for these as the sound produced by them is a pure tone. If such fingerprinting techniques are to be used for authenticating humans that carry these mobile phones, some consideration also has to be given to how user friendly the techniques are. Tonal frequencies as it turns out, especially at the higher end of the audio spectrum are not user friendly at all. This in turn means that while audio based fingerprinting may have high accuracy, the technique may not be usable with tonal frequencies and there is a need to look at other types of source audio for it. In this paper we present our results of experimentation with music as the source audio for audio based authentication. In addition to music, we also experimented with Dual Tone Multi Frequencies (DTMF) commonly used in telephony.

2   Background and Literature Review

The technique of physical device fingerprinting has been proposed in previous research. For example, device-specific *clock skew* can be used to fingerprint a physical device [10]. However, it was not until *AccelPrint* [9] that fingerprinting through hardware sensors for the purpose of mobile device identification was utilised. The core concept of sensor fingerprinting is that natural variations in the sensor manufacturing process produce variances that can cause distorted output. This distortion is consistent and can be measured to form a fingerprint of a device.

Further work in sensor fingerprinting was carried out in [2, 3, 5], while [7, 8, 20], have specifically examined many different aspects of audio based fingerprinting. For audio sensors, such as the speaker and the microphone, the variances are exhibited in the frequency response. Bojinov et al. proposed a technique in [5] that fingerprints both the speaker and the microphone simultaneously by playing a sound and recording it on the mobile phones. Dekker and Kumar in [8] use the same approach. In [8], which our work is based on, the authors experimented with several ideas to improve the existing audio-based sensor fingerprinting technique. These include an increased range of frequencies tested, different length of playback time and other features. The frequencies tested covered the entire audible range (200 Hz to 20000 Hz) with varying frequency steps and length of audio.

The types of source audio that can be used in audio based authentication can be divided into two categories - tonal frequencies and non-tonal frequencies. Tonal frequencies are the most common ones used in previous research [2,5,8,20]. The other type includes audio such as music, DTMF, ringtones and human speech as described in [7]. This type of source audio has received less attention in literature. In this paper we use music and DTMF as source audio and evaluate their usefulness in audio based authentication systems.

3   Source Audio Selection

The source audio is an essential part of the audio sensor authentication process. The choice of which may affect the classification accuracy, noise resistance, user experience, authentication time and more. Dekker and Kumar [8], tested different variations of stepped-frequency. In this work, we focus our attention primarily on music as our source audio and investigate, classification accuracy, noise resistance, and other aspects of audio based authentication. For the purpose of comparison, we also investigate sequential and superimposed DTMFs. Below we describe our source audio in detail.

- Music—The use of music in the authentication process provides a pleasing user experience and therefore is preferable to tonal frequency based approaches. As opposed to the stepped frequencies used in [8], which consist of a single frequency at a time, music contains multiple mixed frequencies. The fingerprints extracted will therefore consist of features from the combination of many frequencies simultaneously, which may result in varying classification performance. In this work, we have selected several music samples from the GTZAN dataset [15,18], a dataset commonly used for music genre classification. The dataset consists of ten music genres, which includes 100 music samples per genre. For our experiments, we have randomly selected one sample per genre, forming a total of ten samples for the music source audio. The selected music samples are listed in Table 1. Furthermore, we have reduced the length of the original music audio from 30 s to 3 s in order to reduce the total authentication time.
- Sequential and Superimposed DTMF Frequencies – For comparison we have also selected source audio that consists of the frequencies adopted in DTMF (Dual Tone Multi-frequency) tones. The DTMF tones are commonly used in telecommunication systems. More specifically, certain pairs of frequencies are used to represent each key press on a DTMF keypad. For example, when the key 1 is pressed, 697 Hz and 1209 Hz are played. These frequencies are mainly selected to reduce harmonic interference as well as the possibility of the tones simulated by the human voice [14]. The main reason for adopting these frequencies are that they are not harmonic with each other, therefore they could be played together simultaneously to achieve shorter playback time. In this type of source audio, we play them both sequentially and simultaneously. We have generated eight tones with the respective frequency of 697, 770, 852, 941,

1209, 1336, 1477 and 1633 Hz. For sequential DTMF audio, each frequency was played for 0.1 and 0.3 s. Meanwhile, for superimposed DTMF audio, each frequency was played for 0.1, 0.3 and 0.5 s. The 0.5-s sequential DTMF audio was not considered due to the resulting lengthy register and authentication time. Moreover, the selection of these durations was based off the frequency play time determined in [8], in which desirable results were obtained for the stepped frequency source audio. The frequency play time longer than one second was not considered in order to shorten the authentication time required.

4   Feature Extraction

The most common feature extraction methods used in the literature are based on extracting the frequency response at each of the played frequency to form the feature vector. However, this method cannot be directly applied to our source audio since music contains a mixture of different frequencies. Furthermore, there are additional features that can be extracted from a piece of audio [6] that may improve the overall classification performance. Below we discuss the Raw FFT feature used in the literature primarily and other spectral features from [6].

- Raw FFT and its variation – The most basic feature extraction method is to generate the feature vectors directly from the raw FFT output values. This method is easy to implement and can be applied to many source audios, however, this method would result in too many irrelevant features for music, which would drastically increase the resource consumption of the system while also negatively impacting the classification performance. Previous research has adopted some filtering techniques to only extract the frequency responses at the played frequency of the source audio. This method reduces the amount of features, while also having the ability to reject unwanted frequency responses from other sources such as noises.
- Spectral Features – In addition to the FFT values, there are other features that can be used to describe a piece of audio. These include features such as spectral centroid which represents the centre of mass of the spectrum, spectral bandwidth which calculates the average distance to each spectral centroid at each frequency bin and other various spectral features. To observe the effect of each spectral feature, we experimented with them individually. In addition, we also compared all the spectral features combined and evaluated it against directly using the FFT output values. The implementation of these features made heavy use of the Librosa Python package [11]. Furthermore, the number of features were reduced by taking the statistical summary of the features, such that the mean, standard deviation, maximum, minimum and median values were calculated to form the final feature vector [19]. The following describes the list of features implemented.

1. MFCC
   The MFCC feature describes the spectrum of an audio by taking into account how the human perceives sound by using a Mel scale. Based on [7], we have extracted 13 MFCC coefficients. We then take the statistical summary as stated previously to form the final feature vectors.

2. Poly Features
   Another useful spectral feature to extract is the poly features. This feature fits an n-th degree polynomial function to each frame of the spectrogram. To construct this feature, we have fitted a linear polynomial to each frame and have extracted the first and second array of coefficients.

3. Spectral Centroid
   The spectral centroid feature calculates the mean value per frame. The resulting feature vector consists of the centroids extracted for every frame. It was observed that the difference between the features were more significant than the previous implemented features and may be beneficial in producing a more accurate model.

4. Spectral Contrast
   The spectral contrast feature calculates the difference between the spectral peak and spectral valley at each sub-band. For the implementation of Librosa, the spectral peak is calculated by taking the mean energy in the top quantile and spectral valley the bottom quantile. It was observed that the spectral contrast values did not vary as much as the spectral centroid value, however, it is still superior to the poly features.

5. Spectral Bandwidth
   The spectral bandwidth feature computes the weighted average distance between each frequency and the spectral centroid in each frequency bin. This feature shows the distribution of frequencies relative to the spectral centroid.

6. Spectral Flatness
   The spectral flatness describes how tone-like or noise-like a sound is. It is computed by measuring the frequency distribution at each frequency sub-band. The resulting feature vector contains the spectral flatness for each frame.

7. Spectral Roll-off
   Finally, spectral roll-off computes a roll-off frequency for each frame, such that under which 85% of the spectral energy is contained. The spectral roll-off feature was also found to be quite distinct comparatively, which may be a suitable candidate for feature extraction as well.

Additionally, the spectral features can be concatenate to form a combined feature vector that describes all the above characteristics of a piece of audio.

5 Implementation

Firstly, the audio sensor fingerprints were collected off a number of devices by playing a pre-loaded source audio through their speakers and recording with their microphones respectively. The collected fingerprints were pre-processed for feature extraction, after which they were utilised for training a machine learning classifier. Finally, the performance of the classifier was evaluated.

5.1 Source Audio Generation

The list of the selected source audio considered in the paper is shown in Table 1, along with the corresponding category, duration and the sampling rate.

Table 1. Complete list of source audio selected

	Category	Duration (s)	Sample Rate
dtmf-01	dtmf-seq	01.80	44100
dtmf-03	dtmf-seq	03.40	44100
music-blues-00079	music	03.07	22050
music-classical-00012	music	03.07	22050
music-country-00040	music	03.07	22050
music-disco-00022	music	03.07	22050
music-hiphop-00035	music	03.07	22050
music-jazz-00075	music	03.07	22050
music-metal-00009	music	03.07	22050
music-pop-00044	music	03.07	22050
music-reggae-00016	music	03.07	22050
music-rock-00006	music	03.07	22050
superimposed-dtmf-01	dtmf-sup	01.10	44100
superimposed-dtmf-03	dtmf-sup	01.30	44100
superimposed-dtmf-05	dtmf-sup	01.50	44100

5.2 Devices Under Test

The devices used in the experimentation are listed in Table 2. A total of 16 devices were used in this research.

Table 2. Device List

Name	Type	Quantity
ASUS Nexus 7	Tablet	2
ASUS ZenFone 3	Phone	2
LG Nexus 4	Phone	3
LG Nexus 5	Phone	3
Motorola Nexus 6	Phone	2
Samsung Galaxy Nexus	Phone	4

5.3 Experiment Architecture

The experiment flow consisted of loading the selected source audio in Table 1 onto each device. Each source audio was played through its speaker and recorded with its microphone. For every device, 20 audio samples were collected and sent to a remote server for further processing.

5.4 Environment

The environment for the experiment comprised of a student lab in a basement of a building. The room was situated at the end of a hallway, thus limiting the amount of outside noise caused by people passing and talking. However, there existed small amount of ambient noise caused by air conditioning and desktop PCs. The audio samples were collected under similar conditions, such that nobody was present in the room during the time of recording. The devices were also placed on the same desk to reduce the number of variables. The process of data collection lasted several weeks, during which no significant changes towards the environment were observed.

6 Classification and Evaluation

With the obtained feature vector derived from using the proposed feature extraction techniques, a machine learning model was trained. Given a set of audio sensor fingerprint features, the model needs to accurately identify the associated device for that fingerprint. To train such a model the audio dataset collected off the devices was split into training and testing sets. The dataset was split into training and testing set based on, the number of phones registered and the size of the training set. The training set was constructed such that num_phones amount of phones were first randomly selected from the pool of 16 devices, where num_phones indicates the number of registered phones. Afterwards, another num_train amount of phones were randomly selected from the 20 audio samples collected off the device, where num_train specifies the size of the training set. Similarly, the testing set was constructed first by including the devices used in the training set, while only including those audio samples that were not used in the training set. The resulting training and testing sets were then used in the classification process.

The classification algorithm adopted was selected based on the previous work [8]. In particular, the Random Forest algorithm was selected due to its superiority in performance. We used scikit-learn [13] for implementing Random Forest. Similar to [8], the default parameters were used and no hyperparameter tuning was performed.

7 Evaluating the Effect of Noise

A major challenge of audio fingerprinting is that noises are an inevitable source of disruption to the fingerprint collection process. One way of evaluating the impact of noise is to collect the fingerprints in various environments and record the associated SNR. Although this should produce the most accurate result, it would require a significant amount of time and resources. Another way to evaluate the impact of noise is to add previously collected noise samples to audio samples. Although simulated, this approach allowed us to compare the effects of different types of noises at different SNR levels. In our approach, it was ensured that the length of noise sample was greater than that of the recorded audio. Therefore, for the processing of noise audio, we first selected a random consecutive portion from the noise audio with the same length as the recorded audio. Afterwards, the noise audio signal was scaled down to the desired SNR by the following formula.

$$SNR_{dB} = 20 log_{10}(\frac{A_{signal}}{A_{noise}}) \tag{1}$$

where A_{signal} denotes the RMS value of the original signal and A_{noise} denotes the RMS value of the noise signal. Finally, the noise signal was added onto the recorded audio signal. The resulting signal was then clipped between 0 and 2^{16} (int max) to avoid the issue of cracked sounds.

All the recorded samples were mixed with three types of noises recorded under different scenarios - busy university restaurant, small office noise and data centre noise. The first two noise samples were obtained from the DEMAND dataset [16] while the last noise sample was downloaded from the Freesound website [1].

Table 3. Selected Noise Samples

Name	Type	Sampling Rate
PRESTO_ch01	University Restaurant	16K
OOFFICE_ch07	Small Office	16K
data_centre	Data Centre	44.1K

8   Results

In this section we present the classification accuracy when different source audio are used along with the usage of various feature extraction techniques. There are two main variables in all of the experiments - number of phones registered and number of audio samples available. In the context of the model training stage, this represents the number of classes and the training samples, respectively. We aim to show the performance of the classification model under various conditions when adopted in an authentication system. For example, the number of phones registered may provide an overview of the effectiveness of the system from the beginning of user enrollment to a state where a number of phones have already been enrolled. Meanwhile, the number of training samples indicates the amount of audio samples to collect for the registration process. This amount directly impacts the time required for users to be enrolled into the system and thus data aggregated by such variable is beneficial to determine the balance between system efficiency and effectiveness. Overall, the results showed a trend in which the accuracy of the classifier slightly decreases as more phones are enrolled into the system. On the other hand, the classifier performance improved as more training samples were available.

8.1   Source Audio Comparison

We first take a look at the accuracy obtained when using various source audio. We used various genres of music as well as sequential and superimposed DTMF tones. We used the combined spectral features for this experiment. We can see in Fig. 1 that over 99% of accuracy was achieved across all source audio, suggesting that the use of source audio does not impact classification performance greatly. Nevertheless, slight difference in the performance was observed from these results. For example, over half of the music category source audio achieved an accuracy of over 99.9% while blues, classical, country and disco music are on the slightly lower side. This suggests that it is possible to adopt certain types of music in audio sensor fingerprinting in order to improve the user experience while achieving robust fingerprint identification capability. Furthermore, all results from superimposed DTMF also achieved over 99.9% accuracy, which suggests the possibility of using shorter source audio (1 s) for extracting the audio sensor fingerprints. Since more than one sample is required for registering a particular device, this result suggests that the time required for registering and authenticating a particular device can be significantly reduced.

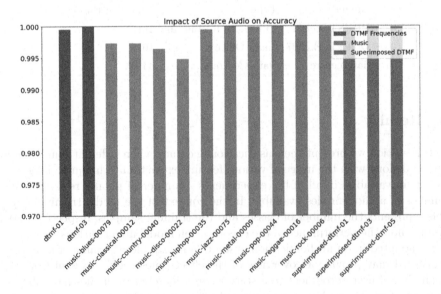

Fig. 1. Source audio accuracy result

8.2   Feature Comparison

We then compared the various features that could be extracted and used for audio based authentication. Dekker and Kumar [8] only targeted stepped frequency source audio but to generalise the audio based authentication idea to a wider range of source audio such as music we need more nuanced features. Additionally, different features produce different length of feature vectors. This could impact the training and testing time of the ML model, thus in turn affect the registration and authentication time. Last but not least, different source audio may require different feature extraction methods in order to reach the peak performance, thus a comparison of such techniques could provide insight into the best combination of source audio and the corresponding features to extract.

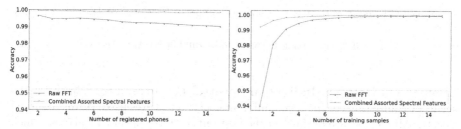

(a) Varying number of registered phones   (b) Varying the number of training samples

Fig. 2. Raw FFT versus combined assorted spectral features

Raw FFT Versus Combined Assorted Spectral Features. Figure 2a shows the accuracy comparison of the two different features used at various number of phones registered. The first conclusion that could be drawn from this result is that the accuracy decreases as more phones were registered. In fact, we also experimented with filtered FFT as a feature but it degrades severely with the number of phones and therefore we have excluded it from the discussion in this paper. It can be easily observed that the use of combined spectral features produced the highest accuracy of nearly 100% while raw FFT achieved slightly worse result albeit maintaining its accuracy around 99%. Similar pattern could also be observed from the aspect of training samples. Figure 2b shows that the combined spectral features achieved over 98% accuracy with only one training sample, whereas the raw FFT approach started at approximately 93%. Despite the fact that the accuracy of raw FFT features converged with that of the combined spectral features at around 9 training samples, it should be noted that this number of training samples indicates a significantly longer registration time. For example, the *dtmf-01* source audio would take around 16 s of play time (exclusive of pause time) while the music source audio would take around 27 s. On the other hand, the *dtmf-01* source audio would only take around 5 s of play time and the music source audio would take around 9 s with combined spectral features. Furthermore, the number of raw FFT features are significantly more than that of the combined spectral features resulting in more intensive computation. Therefore the combined spectral features outperform the raw FFT features.

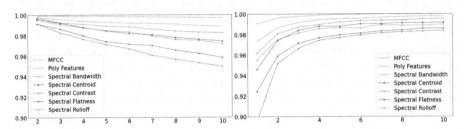

(a) Impact of Number of Registered Phones(b) Impact of Number of Training Samples

Fig. 3. Comparison between individual spectral features

Comparison Between Individual Spectral Features. Figure 3a shows the accuracy comparison of the seven different spectral features used. It was observed that the MFCC feature performed the best out of all the spectral features, which is consistent with the findings in [7]. The next high-performing features were the poly features and the spectral bandwidth, followed by the spectral centroid and spectral roll-off. Two of the worst performing features were the spectral contrast and spectral flatness, which dropped from approximately 99% accuracy to around 95%–96% accuracy with 10 registered phones. The issue may have lied in the fact that these extracted features did not have as much variation as the other features, thus increasing the difficulty for the Random Forest classifier. From the aspect of training samples as shown in Fig. 3b, we can also observe the same pattern. The MFCC feature achieved approximately 99% with one training sample, which increased to near 100% around five training samples. On the other hand, the spectral contrast performed the worst by achieving less than 90% using one training sample. Nevertheless, it still achieved over 95% with three training samples.

8.3   Impact of Phones Registered

It was observed during all the experiments that the performance of the classifiers decreased as more phones were registered. Figure 4a shows the accuracy obtained at different number of registered phones for different types of source audio. The features used were the combined spectral features, and the results were averaged over all the audio within each type. The graph showed several fluctuations but an overall trend of decrease in accuracy. Despite the accuracy being maintained above 99.7% for the maximum number of registered phones available in this experiment, the scalability of this phenomenon for a larger number of phones was unclear due to lack of phones and time available for testing. A definite answer to this would require further experiments with a significantly larger pool of devices.

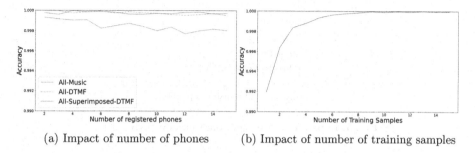

(a) Impact of number of phones   (b) Impact of number of training samples

Fig. 4. Impact of phones and training samples when considered with various audio types and combined spectral features

8.4 Impact of Training Samples

The number of training samples also has a noticeable impact on the performance of the classifier. Figure 4b shows that the average accuracy across all source audio under the adoption of combined spectral features increased with the number of training samples. It could be observed thatb with one training sample, an average of 98.8% accuracy was achieved. However, with nine training samples, the accuracy increased to near 100%. As mentioned previously, the number of training samples affect the time required for registering a device.

8.5 Impact of Noise

In order to evaluate the suitability of audio sensor fingerprinting in real-world scenario, we conducted experiments to simulate noise in the classification process. This was performed by adding the noises outlined in Table 3 at SNR levels of 5, 10 and 15 to the training set as well as the testing set. The processed audio then had the combined spectral features extracted for training and classification. Figure 5 shows the impact of noises on accuracy for an SNR of 10.

The result shows that with a fixed SNR of 10, the university restaurant noise had a greater impact on the accuracy compared to the small office and the data centre noise. It also indicated that under certain scenario, the accuracy of the classifier could decrease to around 90% or even lower. This showed that the proposed technique may not maintain its high performance in noisy environments such as a university cafeteria, however, it could still be applicable in places with less amount and variation of noise such as a small office or a server room.

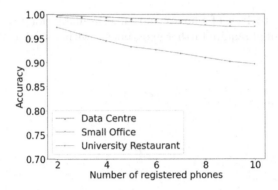

Fig. 5. Impact of noise types on accuracy, SNR = 10

Different Source Audio. The result from the noise simulation was aggregated based upon different types of source audio in order to discover potential noise-resistant source audio. It was found that stepped frequency as used in the earlier work of Dekker and Kumar [8] perform poorly with noise. As our focus in the paper is on music we will skip the details of stepped frequencies but more information can be found in [17]. However, as Fig. 6 shows, the noise simulation hardly impacted the classification performance when music was used. Despite some noticeable difference in performance under the impact of university restaurant noise, the overall accuracy was above 98%. This result indicates that the music source audio may be more suitable for collecting audio sensor fingerprints in a noisy environment.

Different SNR. Finally, the three types of noise were simulated under different SNR to provide insight into the effectiveness of audio sensor fingerprinting under various amount of background noise. The results for the university restaurant noise in Fig. 7a showed that in an environment that is heavily polluted with noise (under SNR of 1), the accuracy could drop to an average of 65% across all source audio with a single training sample. The situation could be improved to achieve over 80% accuracy with at least three training samples. However, the performance gain from increasing the number of training samples would eventually become marginally small. The results for the small office and data centre are presented in Fig. 7b and Fig. 7c respectively. Similar patterns could be observed in the graphs, however, the impact of these two source audio is much less than the university restaurant noise. In the case of data centre noise, the accuracy could still be maintained well above 90% under an SNR of one. Meanwhile for the small office environment, the accuracy could be maintained above 90% if SNR is larger than 5. It should also be noted that the accuracy obtained was trained on the combined spectral features and averaged over all the selected source audio. This could potentially be improved by pairing each source audio sample with their best-performing features, creating an even more robust audio sensor fingerprinting system.

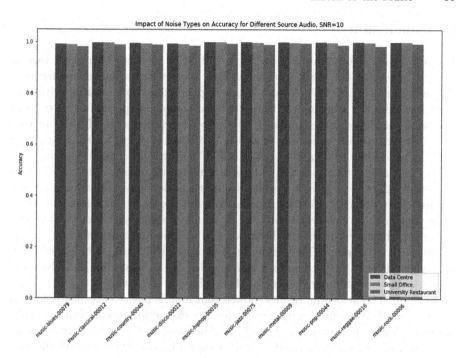

Fig. 6. Impact of noise types on accuracy for different Source Audio, SNR = 10

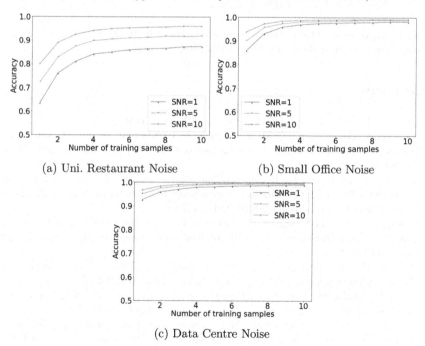

Fig. 7. Impact of noise at different SNR

9   Conclusion

The source audio and feature extraction evaluation in this paper show various interesting results. Our evaluation shows that audio with various mixed frequencies such as music and DTMF can provide high classification accuracy with very short samples. We provided evidence that the combined spectral features work best with the music source audio. It was also observed that the MFCC feature was the most important feature from the combined spectral features, and that it might be feasible to extract only the MFCC features for classification in order to achieve faster training and classification time while maintaining certain level of identification accuracy. Our evaluation with noise show that different types of noises have different effect on the classification accuracy. Therefore, this technique may require more refinement in environments such as a noisy university restaurant, however, it may still work in other environments such as a data centre and a small office. The results have also provided a measurement of accuracy with different levels of noise, which should help to determine the maximum tolerable noise in an environment for this technique to be viable.

In summary, the overall results showed that mobile device classification could achieve over 99% accuracy with various feature extraction mechanisms on multi frequency audio such as music and DTMF. Such audio are also more resistant to noise than tonal frequencies and provide a more pleasant experience to the user during authentication. Taken together this presents a very good case for music to be used in audio based authentication.

Acknowledgments. This work was supported in part by Sir William Gallagher Cyber Security Scholarship at the University of Waikato.

References

1. Freesound. https://freesound.org. Accessed 26 Dec 2020
2. Amerini, I., Becarelli, R., Caldelli, R., Melani, A., Niccolai, M.: Smartphone fingerprinting combining features of on-board sensors. IEEE Trans. Inf. Forensics Secur. **12**(10), 2457–2466 (2017)
3. Amerini, I., Bestagini, P., Bondi, L., Caldelli, R., Casini, M., Tubaro, S.: Robust smartphone fingerprint by mixing device sensors features for mobile strong authentication. Electronic Imaging **2016**(8), 1–8 (2016)
4. Baldini, G., Steri, G.: A survey of techniques for the identification of mobile phones using the physical fingerprints of the built-in components. IEEE Commun. Surv. Tutor. **19**(3), 1761–1789 (2017)
5. Bojinov, H., Michalevsky, Y., Nakibly, G., Boneh, D.: Mobile device identification via sensor fingerprinting. arXiv preprint arXiv:1408.1416 (2014)
6. Cano, P., Batlle, E., Kalker, T., Haitsma, J.: A review of audio fingerprinting. J. VLSI Signal Process. Syst. Signal Image Video Technol. **41**(3), 271–284 (2005)
7. Das, A., Borisov, N., Caesar, M.: Do you hear what i hear? Fingerprinting smart devices through embedded acoustic components. In: Proceedings of the 2014 ACM SIGSAC Conference on Computer and Communications Security, pp. 441–452 (2014)

8. Dekker, M., Kumar, V.: Using audio characteristics for mobile device authentication, pp. 98–113 (2019). https://doi.org/10.1007/978-3-030-36938-56
9. Dey, S., Roy, N., Xu, W., Choudhury, R.R., Nelakuditi, S.: Accelprint: imperfections of accelerometers make smartphones trackable. In: NDSS. Citeseer (2014)
10. Kohno, T., Broido, A., Claffy, K.C.: Remote physical device fingerprinting. IEEE Trans. Dependable Secure Comput. **2**(2), 93–108 (2005)
11. McFee, B., et al.: librosa/librosa: 0.8.0 (2020). https://doi.org/10.5281/zenodo.3955228
12. Nair, A.S., Thampi, S.M.: PUFloc: PUF and location based hierarchical mutual authentication protocol for surveillance drone networks. In: Wang, G., Choo, K.K.R., Ko, R.K.L., Xu, Y., Crispo, B. (eds.) UbiSec 2021, CCIS, vol. 1557, pp. 66–89. Springer, Singapore (2022). https://doi.org/10.1007/978-981-19-0468-4_6
13. Pedregosa, F., et al.: Scikit-learn: machine learning in Python. J. Mach. Learn. Res. **12**, 2825–2830 (2011)
14. Rey, R.: Engineering and operations in the Bell system. AT&T Bell Laboratories (1983)
15. Sturm, B.L.: An analysis of the gtzan music genre dataset. In: Proceedings of the Second International ACM Workshop on Music Information Retrieval with User-Centered and Multimodal Strategies, pp. 7–12 (2012)
16. Thiemann, J., Ito, N., Vincent, E.: Demand: a collection of multi-channel recordings of acoustic noise in diverse environments. In: Proc. Meetings Acoust (2013)
17. Tsai, M.: Optimisation of audio-based sensor fingerprinting system for mobile device authentication. Master's thesis, The University of Waikato (2021)
18. Tzanetakis, G., Essl, G., Cook, P.: Automatic musical genre classification of audio signals (2001). http://ismir2001.ismir.net/pdf/tzanetakis.pdf
19. VanderPlas, J.: Python Data Science Handbook: Essential Tools for Working With Data. O'Reilly Media, Inc. (2016)
20. Zhou, Z., Diao, W., Liu, X., Zhang, K.: Acoustic fingerprinting revisited: Generate stable device id stealthily with inaudible sound. In: Proceedings of the 2014 ACM SIGSAC Conference on Computer and Communications Security, pp. 429–440 (2014)

A Hybrid Secure Two-Party Protocol for Vertical Federated Learning

Wenti Yang[1,2] , Zhaoyang He[2], Yalei Li[1], Haiyan Zhang[1], and Zhitao Guan[2(✉)]

[1] Beijing Key Laboratory of Research and System Evaluation of Power Dispatching
Automation Technology (China Electric Power Research Institute), Beijing 100192, China
[2] School of Control and Computer Engineering, North China Electric Power University,
Beijing 102206, China
guan@ncepu.edu.cn

Abstract. Federated learning (FL) is a promising distributed machine learning technique for solving the privacy leakage problem in machine learning training process. Multiple parties collaborate to train a machine learning model, while the data is kept locally, so as to achieve privacy-preservation of users. However, some studies have shown that an attacker can infer some sensitive information from the interacted data, even if the raw data is not available. It is necessary to adopt some privacy-preserving techniques such as secure multi-party computation and homomorphic encryption to prevent the above problem. Most existing solutions have focused on FL over horizontally partitioned data but ignore the research on FL over vertically partitioned data. In this paper, we present a vertical federated learning scheme with enhanced privacy preservation. Split learning is used to enable cooperative neural network training between multiple parties with vertically partitioned datasets, and a hybrid secure two-party computation protocol is adopted for protecting users' privacy. The experimental results demonstrate the feasibility of our scheme.

Keywords: Vertical federated learning · Split learning · Secure two-party computation · Privacy-preservation

1 Introduction

Since federated learning (FL) was proposed in 2016 [1], it has shown tremendous interest in it from cutting-edge research to industrial applications, which demonstrates the importance people place on privacy preservation. FL enables multiple parties to cooperatively train machine learning models using their local data while ensuring that the privacy of each party's data is not compromised. FL has been applied in many fields such as medical, financial, Internet of Things, etc. [2]. In different application scenarios, FL mainly includes horizontal federated learning (HFL) and vertical federated learning (VFL). HFL supports cooperative training between multiple parties with horizontally partitioned data (e.g., banks in different regions), and most of the existing works are focused on HFL. VFL supports cooperative training between multiple parties with vertically partitioned data (e.g., a bank and a hospital in the same region). Most of the existing works about VFL are only for traditional machine learning training, with less research on vertical neural network FL.

The distributed machine learning training paradigm of FL, however, still poses the threat of privacy leakage. Some studies have shown that attackers can infer sensitive information from training data through only partial gradients or weights [3, 4]. So, some privacy-preserving techniques such as secure multi-party computation, homomorphic encryption, and differential privacy, are adopted to solve the above problems. Those techniques have received extensive attention in the application of HFL.

In practical applications, there are many requirements of VFL between parties with vertically partitioned data [5, 6]. For example, a hospital has the health data of a certain group, a bank has the deposit data of a certain group, and a company has information related to the occupation (label) of the group. Now we want to train a neural network model to predict occupation based on health status and property status. Currently, most of the existing works about VFL are only for traditional machine learning models. Some researchers have proposed split learning to implement vertical federated neural networks [7]. Split learning enables parties to collaboratively train a neural network model, in which the global model is split into several bottom models and a top model. Each client holds a bottom model and a server holds the top model. The clients and server interact to train the model. However, several studies have confirmed that some private information can be inferred from the data of interactions [8–10]. The privacy leakage in split learning needs to be solved urgently.

Potential solutions to address the privacy leakage of split learning include: 1) Differential privacy (DP). The computation and communication overhead of DP are small, but a trade-off between privacy and utility is required. In scenarios with high privacy requirements, the utility of the model will be greatly reduced. 2) Homomorphic encryption (HE). HE has a high computation overhead and can only be evaluated for a limited number of levels, which is not suitable for training deep neural network models. 3) Secure Multi-party Computation (MPC). MPC does not reduce the utility of the model and supports the training of large neural networks, but the communication overhead is relatively high. In this paper, we adopt MPC to achieve privacy preservation in split learning. The motivations and contributions are as follows.

Our Motivations. Our main goal is to protect the privacy of data parties in split learning and prevent attackers from extracting the private information of data parties using property inference attacks and membership inference attacks. We use secure multi-party computation as a privacy preservation technique, which not only ensures the utility of the trained model but also applies to various neural networks.

Our Contributions. 1) We propose a privacy-preserving vertical federated neural networks scheme, in which split learning is used to ensure efficient cooperative training among multiple parties with vertically partitioned data. 2) We adopt a hybrid secure two-party protocol to implement the privacy preservation of the split learning, specifically, arithmetic sharing is adopted to support linear operations in neural networks, Yao's garbled circuit is adopted to support non-linear operations in neural networks.

2   Related Work

Since Google put forward the concept of federated learning in 2016 [1], it has received more and more attention. To deal with the privacy leakage problems in FL, many researchers focused on enhanced privacy preservation techniques including secure multi-party computation, homomorphic encryption, differential privacy, and so on [11–15]. In the following, we elaborate on the existing works from two aspects: horizontal federated learning and vertical federated learning.

Horizontal Federated Learning (HFL): Some studies have shown that adversaries can use gradients or weights to infer the private information about participants in FL [16]. Fereidooni et al. [17] proposed SAFELearn, a general-purpose proprietary federated learning scheme that can effectively perform inference attacks to access the model updates of the client. Xu et al. [18] presented VerifyNet, a privacy-preserving, and verifiable federated learning framework. They proposed a double mask protocol to ensure the confidentiality of the user's local gradients. The scheme in [19] protects data privacy by utilizing a ring signature scheme and anonymous communication techniques. Zhou et al. [20] proposed FED-FI, a detection method to detect malicious models based on feature importance. However, the above schemes are all for the federated learning scenarios of users with horizontally partitioned data and a lack of the vertical FL solution.

Vertical Federated Learning (VFL): With increasing demand, VFL has also gained attention in recent years. Xu et al. [21] proposed FedV, a VFL framework which not only supports rejoining and dynamic deletion during the model training phase, but also greatly reduces the training time. Wu et al. [22] proposed a novel VFL framework, which overcomes the shortcomings of traditional VFL methods and improves resistance performance. Wei et al. [23] designed a VFL system using homomorphic encryption. The row data is exchanged in an encrypted manner to protect data privacy. However, the above work only implements federated learning of machine learning algorithms. Thapa et al. [24] combined split learning and federated learning to eliminate the inherent shortcomings and enhance data privacy and model robustness. Singh et al. [25] studied the communication efficiency of split learning and federated learning and point out that the larger the number of clients, the higher the split learning efficiency. Otoum et al. [26] constructed a secure IDS model by applying split learning, which has higher accuracy and performance.

3   Preliminaries

3.1   Split Learning

Split learning (SL) is a distributed neural network training method. It splits the model into several parts, each of which is trained by a different party. We consider the scenario of multiple data parties and a label party. Each data party holds a bottom model, and the label party holds a top model. Data parties train their models locally in parallel, and sends the output of the bottom models (embeddings) to the label party. The label party aggregates these embeddings to obtain a new matrix or vector as the input of the top model, performs forward propagation through the top model and calculates the loss function, and finally updates the top model parameters. Then, the label party sends the gradients of the first layer (cut layer) to the data parties. Each data party performs the back propagation algorithm to update the bottom model parameters. The above process is executed iteratively until the end of training.

3.2 Arithmetic Sharing

Suppose there is a secret s, arithmetic sharing (or additive secret sharing) ensures that the secret s is not compromised by dividing it into n ($n > 1$) additive shares $s_1, s_2, ..., s_n$ (where $s = s_1 + s_2 + ... + s_n$), which are held by n different parties. The n parties can cooperate to achieve the evaluation of multiple secrets and cannot infer any sensitive information. Here, we give the evaluation (addition and multiplication) method for $n = 2$.

Addition: It's easy to achieve the addition between two secrets. For example, we have two secrets x and y, party A holds $[x]_1$, $[y]_1$, and party B holds $[x]_2$, $[y]_2$,, they only need to compute $[z]_1 = [x]_1 + [y]_1$ and $[z]_2 = [x]_2 + [y]_2$, then $z = [z]_1 + [z]_2 = x + y$.

Multiplication: We need to use the Beaver's triplet to achieve multiplication in arithmetic sharing. Assume that we have two secrets x and y, party A holds $[x]_1$, $[y]_1$ and party B holds $[x]_2$, $[y]_2$, now we want to compute $z = [z]_1 + [z]_2 = x \times y$. The steps are as follows (see Fig. 1):

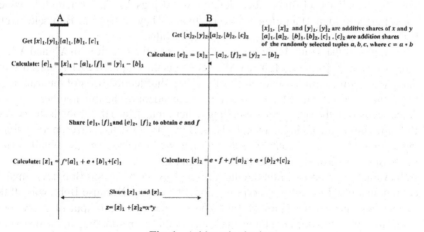

Fig. 1. Arithmetic sharing

1) Randomly generate: a, b, and $c = a * b$.
2) Party A holds $[x]_1, [y]_1, [a]_1, [b]_1, [c]_1$, Party B holds $[x]_2, [y]_2, [a]_2, [b]_2, [c]_2$.
3) Party A computes $[e]_1 = [x]_1 - [a]_1$, $[f]_1 = [y]_1 - [b]_1$, and sends $[e]_1[f]_1$ to B, Party B computes $[e]_2 = [x]_2 - [a]_2$, $[f]_2 = [y]_2 - [b]_2$, and sends $[e]_2[f]_2$ to A.

4) They both compute $e = [e]_1 + [e]_2$ and $f = [f]_1 + [f]_2$.
5) Party A computes $[z]_1 = f \times [a]_1 + e \times [b]_1 + [c]_1$, Party B computes $[z]_2 = e \times f + f \times [a]_2 + e \times [b]_2 + [c]_2$. So we have $z = [z]_1 + [z]_z = x \times y$.

3.3 Garbled Circuit

The garbled circuit (GC) compiles the secure computation function of the participant into the form of the Boolean circuit. We take the Yao - millionaire problem as an example, assume that there are two rich people Alice and Bob, they want to compare who is richer without revealing privacy. The details are as follows:

1) First, we define $A_n A_{n-1}, ..., A_1$, and $B_n, B_{n-1}, ..., B_1$ ($A_i, B_i \in \{0, 1\}$) as the private information of Alice and Bob, now they want to compare $A_n A_{n-1}, ..., A_1$, and $B_n, B_{n-1}, ..., B_1$.
2) Define variables:

$$C_i = \begin{cases} 1, & A_i A_{i-1,...,} A_1 > B_i B_{i-1}, ..., B_1 \\ 0, & A_i A_{i-1,...,} A_1 < B_i B_{i-1}, ..., B_1 \end{cases}$$

where the initial value of C_i is 0.
3) $C_{i+1} = 1 \Leftrightarrow (A_i > B_i) \cup (A_i = B_i \cap C_i = 0)$ can be converted to a logic circuit. But every line in the circuit is in plaintext. It needs to be encrypted with the help of oblivious transfer (OT).
4) Alice generates GC: Alice marks the lines in the circuit diagram, which are the input and output of the module respectively $W_{A_0}, W_{B_0}, W_{C_0}, W_{C_1}$, intermediate results W_D, W_E, W_F. For each line, Alice defines two strings X_i^0, X_i^1 of length k, which corresponds to logic 0 and logic 1, respectively. They are sent to Bob selectively, but he does not know the corresponding logical value.
5) Alice replaces the Truth Table of each logic gate in the circuit with X_i^0 and X_i^1, X_i^0 replaces 0 and X_i^1 replaces 1. Then Alice encrypts the output of each replaced Truth Table twice with symmetric keys. Finally, Alice shuffled the rows of the truth table to get the garbled table. Make the content independent of the line number.
6) Alice sends Bob the string corresponding to her input. Since the string is encrypted, Bob does not know its logical value. Then Bob gets the string corresponding to his input from Alice via OT, but Alice doesn't know which one Bob got. Finally, Alice sends Bob the garbled table of all the logic gates.
7) Bob evaluates the obfuscation circuit generated: After Alice and Bob have finished communicating, Bob starts decrypting along the circuit. Because Bob owns all the input labels and all the Garbled Table, he can decrypt the output of every logic gate. However, Bob does not know the logical value corresponding to the decrypted results to ensure privacy and security.

8) Alice shares the result with Bob, so they both know the result.

4 Overview

4.1 System Model

We consider n ($n \geq 1$) data parties, a label party, and an assistant server in our system. First, the parties initialize the parameters of the neural networks model to be trained. Then, split the model into n bottom models and a top model. Each data party has a bottom model that may be different from other data parties, the label party has the top model. The label party sends the arithmetic sharing shares of parameters (e.g., weights) of the top model to the assistant server. The data parties hold datasets with different features, the label party holds the labels, and the assistant server only assists in performing part of the computation. They collaborate to perform the following steps (see Fig. 2):

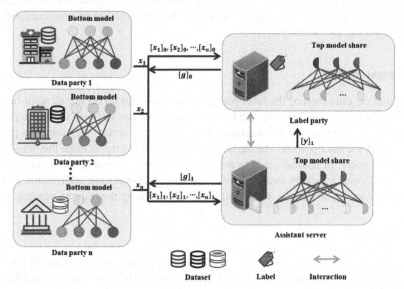

Fig. 2. System model, where x_i represents the output of the cut layer of party i, and $[x_i]_0$, $[x_i]_1$ represent the arithmetic sharing shares of x_i sent to the label party and assistant server respectively.

1) Forward propagation of data parties: Each data party i uses the local dataset to train the corresponding bottom model, and get the output x_i of the last layer (cut layer) of the bottom model. Then the data party i sends the arithmetic sharing shares of x_i (i.e., $[x_i]_0$, $[x_i]_1$), to the label party and the assistant server respectively.

2) Forward propagation of the label party and assistant server: The label party and the assistant server take $[x_i]_0$ and $[x_i]_1$ as input to train the corresponding top model share (require interaction) and get the output $[y']_0$ and $[y']_1$. Then the assistant server sends $[y']_1$ to the label party.

3) The label party recovers the output of the top model $y' = [y']_0 + [y']_1$, and computes δ which is the error of y' and the label y. Then it sends the share $[\delta]_1$ to the assistant server.

4) Back propagation of the label party and assistant server: The label party and the assistant server perform the back propagation algorithm to update the weights of the top model shares and get the gradient shares $[g]_0$ and $[g]_1$ of the first layer (cut layer) of the top model shares. Then they send $[g]_0$ and $[g]_1$ to the data parties.

5) Back propagation of the data parties: Each data party recovers the gradient of the cut layer, that is $g = [g]_0 + [g]_1$, and performs the back propagation algorithm to update the weights of the corresponding bottom model.

6) The above steps are performed iteratively until the model converges. At the end of the training process, the bottom models and the top model shares are consolidated to obtain the global model.

4.2 Threat Model

We set that the data parties, the label party, and the assistant server are all semi-honest. They follow the protocol during the training phase, but are curious about the private information of other parties. For example, all participating parties may mine the private local data of the data parties. The assistant server may also try to mine the data labels of the label party. In addition, due to the potential value of models and datasets, there may be malicious attackers stealing model parameters and private information such as members, features, and labels in the training datasets during the training process.

4.3 Objective

Our main objective is to enable cooperative training of neural networks model between parties with vertically partitioned data (i.e., datasets with different features, and labels), while preventing the data parties, the label party, and the assistant server from extracting the private information of other data parties using property inference attack and membership inference attack.

1. Each data party only sends shares of the output of the cut layer to the label party and the assistant server. Neither the label party nor the assistant server can recover the output data of the cut layer from the secret shares, so it is impossible to infer private information about the training data of the data parties.

2. The label party sends the share of the top model, the share of the label, and the share of the error in the top model output. From the above data share, the assistant server cannot infer any private information about the label and the top model.

5   The Proposed Scheme

The training of data parties is parallel, and the process is similar to traditional neural network training. The forward propagation processes of the label party and assistant server are achieved by the secure two-party computation protocol, which is divided into the linear protocol and non-linear protocol. The secure two-party protocol for back propagation is implemented in a similar way to forward propagation, so we omit it. In this section, we focus on the forward propagation processes of the label party and assistant server.

Notations: We denote matrices in uppercase bold (e.g., W), and vectors in lowercase bold (e.g., x). The superscript letter indicates the dimension of the vector or matrix (e.g., $W^{m \times n}$, x^n), $W_{i,j}$ represents the element of the i-th row and j-th column of the matrix W and x_i represent the i-th element of the vector x. $[y]_0$, $[y]_1$ represent the arithmetic sharing shares of y, which has $[y]_0 + [y]_1 = y$. (a, b, c) is a beaver triple used to assist in secret multiplication, $(a, b, c)^{m \times n}$ means that there are $m \times n$ different beaver tuples.

5.1   Linear Protocol

Fully Connected Layer: The secret sharing algorithm of the fully connected layer is shown in Algorithm 1. The input of the fully connected layer is a vector x, the dot product of the weight matrix W and the vector x needs to be calculated in this layer. In our scheme, the weight matrix W and the vector x are held by the label party and the assistant server in the form of secret shares (i.e., $[W]_0$ and $[W]_1$). With Algorithm 1, the label party and the assistant server get the corresponding secret shares of the dot product of W and x (i.e., $< W^{m \times n} \cdot x^n >$).

Convolution Layer: The secret sharing algorithm of the convolution layer is shown in Algorithm 2. Here we consider a simple example with two-dimensional convolution, 1 feather map, and 1 kernel, stride $= 1$. It can be easily extended to a complex case (e.g., 3 feather maps, multiple kernels). The input of convolution layer is a matrix X, and the kernel is a matrix W. In our scheme, the input feather map $X^{n \times n}$ and the kernel $W^{m \times m}$ are held by the label party and the assistant server in the form of secret shares. We assume that the output feather map is $Y^{l \times l}$, where $l = n - m + 1$. With Algorithm 2, the label party and the assistant server get the corresponding secret shares of the convolution of X and W, that is, the shares output feather map $[Y^{l \times l}]_0$ and $[Y^{l \times l}]_1$.

Algorithm 1

Input:

Label party: $[x^n]_0$, $[W^{m \times n}]_0$, $([a]_0, [b]_0, [c]_0)^{m \times n}$

Assistant server: $[x^n]_1$, $[W^{m \times n}]_1$, $([a]_1, [b]_1, [c]_1)^{m \times n}$

Output:

Label party: $[y^m]_0$

Assistant server: $[y^m]_1$, where $y^m = <W^{m \times n} \cdot x^n>$

Interaction:

/* Runs on label party */

   for $i = 1 \to m$

     for $j = 1 \to n$

       $[e_{i,j}]_0 = [W_{i,j}]_0 - [a_{i,j}]_0$, $[f_{i,j}]_0 = [x_j]_0 - [b_{i,j}]_0$

     end for

   end for

   send $[e_{i,j}]_0$ and $[f_{i,j}]_0$ to the assistant server

/* Runs on assistant server */

   for $i = 1 \to m$

     for $j = 1 \to n$

       $[e_{i,j}]_1 = [W_{i,j}]_1 - [a_{i,j}]_1$, $[f_{i,j}]_1 = [x_j]_1 - [b_{i,j}]_1$

     end for

   end for

   send $[e_{i,j}]_1$ and $[f_{i,j}]_1$ to the label party

Computation:

/* Runs on label party */

   for $i = 1 \to m$

     for $j = 1 \to n$

       $e_{i,j} = [e_{i,j}]_0 + [e_{i,j}]_1$, $f_{i,j} = [f_{i,j}]_0 + [f_{i,j}]_1$

       $[W_{i,j} \cdot x_j]_0 = f_{i,j} \cdot [a_{i,j}]_0 + e_{i,j} \cdot [b_{i,j}]_0 + [c_{i,j}]_0$

     end for

     $[y_i]_0 = \sum_{j=1 \to n} [W_{i,j} \cdot x_j]_0$

   end for

   $[y^m]_0 = ([y_1]_0, [y_2]_0, ..., [y_m]_0)$

/* Runs on assistant server */

   for $i = 1 \to m$

     for $j = 1 \to n$

       $e_{i,j} = [e_{i,j}]_0 + [e_{i,j}]_1$, $f_{i,j} = [f_{i,j}]_0 + [f_{i,j}]_1$

       $[W_{i,j} \cdot x_j]_1 = e_{i,j} \cdot f_{i,j} + f_{i,j} \cdot [a_{i,j}]_1 + e_{i,j} \cdot [b_{i,j}]_1 + [c_{i,j}]_1$

     end for

     $[y_i]_1 = \sum_{j=1 \to n} [W_{i,j} \cdot x_j]_1$

   end for

   $[y^m]_1 = ([y_1]_1, [y_2]_1, ..., [y_m]_1)$

Algorithm 2

Input:

Label party: $[X^{n \times n}]_0$, $[W^{m \times m}]_0$, $([a]_0, [b]_0, [c]_0)^{l \times l \times 4}$

Assistant server: $[X^{n \times n}]_1$, $[W^{m \times m}]_1$, $([a]_1, [b]_1, [c]_1)^{l \times l \times 4}$

Output:

Label party: $[Y^{l \times l}]_0$

Assistant server: $[Y^{l \times l}]_1$

Interaction:

/* Runs on label party */

  for $i = 1 \rightarrow l$

    for $j = 1 \rightarrow l$

      for $k = 1 \rightarrow 4$

        $[e_{i,j,k}]_0 = [W_{i,j,k}]_0 - [a_{i,j,k}]_0$, $[f_{i,j,k}]_0 = [X_{i,j,k}]_0 - [b_{i,j,k}]_0$

      end for

    end for

  end for

  send $[e_{i,j,k}]_0$ and $[f_{i,j,k}]_0$ to the assistant server

/* Runs on assistant server */

  for $i = 1 \rightarrow l$

    for $j = 1 \rightarrow l$

      for $k = 1 \rightarrow 4$

        $[e_{i,j,k}]_1 = [W_{i,j,k}]_1 - [a_{i,j,k}]_1$, $[f_{i,j,k}]_1 = [X_{i,j,k}]_1 - [b_{i,j,k}]_1$

      end for

    end for

  end for

  send $[e_{i,j,k}]_1$ and $[f_{i,j,k}]_1$ to the label party

Computation:

/* Runs on label party */

  for $i = 1 \rightarrow l$

    for $j = 1 \rightarrow l$

      for $k = 1 \rightarrow 4$

        $e_{i,j,k} = [e_{i,j,k}]_0 + [e_{i,j,k}]_1$, $f_{i,j,k} = [f_{i,j,k}]_0 + [f_{i,j,k}]_1$

        $[W_{i,j,k} \cdot X_{i,j,k}]_0 = f_{i,j,k} \cdot [a_{i,j,k}]_0 + e_{i,j,k} \cdot [b_{i,j,k}]_0 + [c_{i,j,k}]_0$

      end for

      $[Y_{i,j}]_0 = \sum_{k=1 \rightarrow 4} [W_{i,j,k} \cdot X_{i,j,k}]_0$

    end for

  end for

/* Runs on assistant server */

  for $i = 1 \rightarrow l$

    for $j = 1 \rightarrow l$

      for $k = 1 \rightarrow 4$

        $e_{i,j,k} = [e_{i,j,k}]_0 + [e_{i,j,k}]_1$, $f_{i,j,k} = [f_{i,j,k}]_0 + [f_{i,j,k}]_1$

        $[W_{i,j,k} \cdot X_{i,j,k}]_1 = f_{i,j,k} \cdot [a_{i,j,k}]_1 + e_{i,j,k} \cdot [b_{i,j,k}]_1 + [c_{i,j,k}]_1$

      end for

      $[Y_{i,j}]_1 = \sum_{k=1 \rightarrow 4} [W_{i,j,k} \cdot X_{i,j,k}]_1$

    end for

  end for

5.2 Non-linear Protocol

Since arithmetic sharing only supports addition and multiplication operations, the non-linear activation functions (e.g., Rectified Linear Activation Function (ReLU)) cannot be implemented. We adopt the ABY framework to achieve the conversion of the arithmetic sharing to the Yao's garbled circuit, so as to complete the calculation of the non-linear activation function. Here, we set $[y]_i^A$ as the arithmetic sharing share, and $[y]_i^Y$ as the Yao sharing share. We give the example of the implementation of Yao's garbled circuit in the fully connection layer (see Algorithm 3). The label party finally gets the outputs of the activation function, and converts them into arithmetic sharing shares for the next layer of the neural networks.

Algorithm 3

Input:

Label party: $[y^m]_0^A$

Assistant server: $[y^m]_1^A$

Output:

Label party: $[y]_0^Y$

Assistant server: $[y]_1^Y$

Circuit construction:

/* Runs on label party */

    for $i = 1 \rightarrow m$

        $[y_i]_0^B \leftarrow [y_i]_0^A$ (y_i is converted from arithmetic sharing to Boolean sharing)

        for each bit of $[y_i]_0^B$

          Generate the garbled circuit

        Execute oblivious transfer (OT) protocol

        The assistant server sends masked $[y_i]_1^B$ to the label party

        Send the garbled circuit and the corresponding key to the assistant server

Circuit computation:

/* Runs on assistant server */

    Decrypt and get the output of the circuit and send it to the label party

/* Runs on label party */

    Get the output the garbled circuit

---

6 Evaluation

Experimental Configuration: Our experimental configuration is shown in Table 1.

Datasets: We use two datasets: MNIST and Bank Marketing Data Set. The MNIST dataset is processed with reference to PyVertical [27], where each image is split into two parts, held by two data parties, and the labels are held by the label party and the assistant server respectively in a secret shared manner. The data in the Bank Marketing Data Set is a vector of 20 features, we set each data party to have 10 features.

Table 1. Experimental configuration.

Item	Version
Operating system	Ubuntu 18.04 on a virtual machine
Intel(R) Core (TM)	i7-12700F
RAM	16GB
GPU	NVIDIA RTX 3060
Python	3.7
Pytorch	1.4.0
Pysyft	0.2.4
CrypTen	\

Neural Networks Architecture: Each bottom model consists of two fully connected layers, the number of neurons is 32 and 64 respectively, the activation function is ReLU. The top model consists of two fully connected layers either, the number of neurons is 64 and 128 respectively.

Experimental Results: We give a comparison of our scheme with PyVertical on two datasets MNIST and Bank Marketing Data Set. As shown in Table 2, the accuracy of our scheme is close to that of PyVertical. The training time of our scheme is about 2 orders of magnitude slower than PyVertical, since the secure multi-party computation requires the label party to interact with the assistant server. Even so, our scheme is still feasible in scenarios with privacy preservation requirement.

Table 2. Experimental results.

	Dataset	Accuracy	Training time (s)
PyVertical	MNIST	91.3%	1350
	Bank Marketing Data Set	93.5%	340
Our scheme	MNIST	91.5%	114761
	Bank Marketing Data Set	92.8%	25650

7 Conclusion

In this paper, we proposed a vertical federated neural networks scheme with enhanced privacy preservation. We adopted split learning to achieve federated learning between multiple parties with vertically partitioned data. A hybrid secure two-party protocol is used to protect the privacy of data parties. We introduced an assistant server to assist the label party to achieve secure multi-party computation. The arithmetic sharing is used to support linear operations in neural networks, and the Yao's garbled circuit is used to support non-linear operations in neural networks. Finally, we gave experiments to verify the feasibility of our scheme.

Acknowledgments. This work is supported by Open Fund of Beijing Key Laboratory of Research and System Evaluation of Power Dispatching Automation Technology (China Electric Power Research Institute) (No.DZB51202101270).

References

1. Konečný, J., McMahan, H.B., Yu, F.X., Richtárik, P., Suresh, A. T., Bacon, D.: Federated learning: strategies for improving communication efficiency. arXiv preprint arXiv:1610.05492 (2016)
2. Liu, W., Feng, W., Yu, B., Peng, T: Security and privacy for sharing electronic medical records based on blockchain and federated learning. In: Wang, G., Choo, KK.R., Ko, R.K.L., Xu, Y., Crispo, B. (eds.) Ubiquitous Security. UbiSec 2021. CCIS, vol. 1557, pp 13–24. Springer, Singapore (2022). https://doi.org/10.1007/978-981-19-0468-4_2
3. Hu, H., Salcic, Z., Sun, L., Dobbie, G., Zhang, X.: Source inference attacks in federated learning. In: 2021 IEEE International Conference on Data Mining (ICDM), pp. 1102–1107. IEEE, Auckland, New Zealand (2021)
4. Luo, X., Wu, Y., Xiao, X., Ooi, B.C.: Feature inference attack on model predictions in vertical federated learning. In: 2021 IEEE 37th International Conference on Data Engineering (ICDE), pp. 181–192. IEEE, Chania, Greece (2021)
5. Liao, S., Wu, J., Mumtaz, S., Li, J., Morello, R., Guizani, M.: Cognitive balance for fog computing resource in internet of things: an edge learning approach. IEEE Trans. Mob. Comput. **21**(5), 1596–1608 (2022)
6. Lin, X., Wu, J., Bashir, A.K., Li, J., Yang, W., Piran, M.J.: Blockchain-based incentive energy-knowledge trading in IoT: joint power transfer and AI design. IEEE Internet Things J. **9**(16), 14685–14698 (2022)
7. Vepakomma, P., Gupta, O., Swedish, T., Raskar, R.: Split learning for health: distributed deep learning without sharing raw patient data. arXiv preprint arXiv:1812.00564 (2018)
8. Pasquini, D., Ateniese, G., Bernaschi, M.: Unleashing the tiger: Inference attacks on split learning. In: Proceedings of the 2021 ACM SIGSAC Conference on Computer and Communications Security. pp. 2113–2129. ACM, Virtual Event Republic of Korea (2021)
9. Li, O., et al.: Label leakage and protection in two-party split learning. arXiv preprint arXiv: 2102.08504 (2021)
10. Zheng, Z., Li, Z., Jiang, H., Zhang, L., Tu, D.: Semantic-aware privacy-preserving online location trajectory data sharing. IEEE Trans. Inf. Forensics Secur. **17**, 2256–2271 (2022)
11. Wang, N., Yang, W., Wang, X., et al.: A blockchain based privacy-preserving federated learning scheme for Internet of Vehicles. Digital Commun. Networks (2022). https://doi.org/10.1016/j.dcan.2022.05.020
12. Liu, Q. Yang, J., Jiang, H., et al.: When deep learning meets steganography: protecting inference privacy in the dark. In: IEEE INFOCOM 2022 - IEEE Conference on Computer Communications, pp. 590–599. IEEE, London, United Kingdom (2022)
13. Kanagavelu, R., Li, Z., Samsudin, J., et al.: Two-phase multi-party computation enabled privacy-preserving federated learning. In: 2020 20th IEEE/ACM International Symposium on Cluster, Cloud and Internet Computing (CCGRID), pp.410–419. IEEE, Melbourne, VIC, Australia (2020)

14. Wei, K., Li, J., Ding, M., et al.: Federated learning with differential privacy: algorithms and performance analysis. IEEE Trans. Inf. Forensics Secur. **15**, 3454–3469 (2020)
15. Zhao, Y., Zhao, J., Yang, M., et al.: Local differential privacy-based federated learning for internet of things. IEEE Internet Things J. **8**(11), 8836–8853 (2020)
16. Nasr, M., Reza, S., Amir, H.: Comprehensive privacy analysis of deep learning: passive and active white-box inference attacks against centralized and federated learning. In: 2019 IEEE symposium on security and privacy (SP), pp.739–753. IEEE, San Francisco, CA, USA (2019)
17. Fereidooni, H., Marchal, S., Miettinen, M., et al.: SAFELearn: secure aggregation for private federated learning. In: 2021 IEEE Security and Privacy Workshops (SPW), pp. 56–62. IEEE, San Francisco, CA, USA (2021)
18. Xu, G., Li, H., Liu, S., et al.: Verifynet: secure and verifiable federated learning. IEEE Trans. Inf. Forensics Secur. **15**, 911–926 (2019)
19. Yang, W., Wang, N., Guan, Z., Wu, L., Du, X., Guizani, M.: A practical cross-device federated learning framework over 5G networks. IEEE Wirel. Commun. (2022). https://doi.org/10.1109/MWC.005.2100435
20. Zhou, C., Sun, Y., Wang, D., et al.: Fed-Fi: federated learning malicious model detection method based on feature importance. Security Commun. Networks **2022**, 1–11 (2022)
21. Xu, R., Baracaldo, N., Zhou, Y., et al.: Fedv: privacy-preserving federated learning over vertically partitioned data. In: Proceedings of the 14th ACM Workshop on Artificial Intelligence and Security, pp. 181–192. ACM, Virtual Event, Republic of Korea (2021)
22. Wu, Z., Li. Q., He. B.: Exploiting Record Similarity for Practical Vertical Federated Learning. arXiv preprint arXiv:2106.06312 (2021)
23. Wei, O., Zeng, J., Yan, W., et al.: A homomorphic-encryption-based vertical federated learning scheme for rick management. Comput. Sci. Inf. Syst. **17**(3), 819–834 (2020)
24. Thapa, C., Arachchige, P.C.M., Camtepe, S., et al.: Splitfed: when federated learning meets split learning. In: Proceedings of the AAAI Conference on Artificial Intelligence, vol. 36, issue 8, pp. 8485–8493 (2022)
25. Singh, A., Vepakomma, P., Gupta, O., et al.: Detailed comparison of communication efficiency of split learning and federated learning. arXiv preprint arXiv:1909.09145 (2019)
26. Otoum, S., Nadra G., Hussein M.: On the feasibility of split learning, transfer learning and federated learning for preserving security in ITS systems. IEEE Trans. Intell. Transp. Syst. (2022). https://doi.org/10.1109/TITS.2022.3159092
27. Romanini, D., et al.: Pyvertical: a vertical federated learning framework for multi-headed splitnn. arXiv preprint arXiv:2104.00489 (2021)

Detecting Unknown Vulnerabilities in Smart Contracts with Multi-Label Classification Model Using CNN-BiLSTM

Wanyi Gu, Guojun Wang$^{(\boxtimes)}$ (iD), Peiqiang Li, Xubin Li, Guangxin Zhai, Xiangbin Li, and Mingfei Chen

School of Computer Science and Cyber Engineering, Guangzhou University, Guangzhou 510006, China
csgjwang@gzhu.edu.cn

Abstract. Smart contracts are frequently targeted by hackers because they hold large amounts of money and cannot be modified once they are published. Existing detection methods mainly focus on known vulnerabilities with clear features and cannot deal with unknown vulnerabilities. As a consequence, proposing a method for detecting unknown vulnerabilities in smart contracts represents a significant advancement in the field of smart contract security. Aiming at this problem, based on the idea that the opcode sequences of transactions containing unknown vulnerabilities have similarities to the opcode sequences of transactions containing known vulnerabilities, we propose a novel approach for unknown vulnerability detection in smart contracts using a CNN-BiLSTM model. Our model determines whether a vulnerability is unknown by detecting the opcode sequence representing the entire execution process of a transaction. Experimental results with the opcode sequences of transactions show that the model can achieve 82.86% accuracy and 83.63% F1-score.

Keywords: Smart contracts · Unknown vulnerabilities · Vulnerability detection · CNN-BiLSTM · Opcode sequences

1 Introduction

Ethereum [25] has emerged as one of the representative platforms for blockchain technology due to its capability for smart contracts in contrast to Bitcoin. One of the most important features of Ethereum is its capacity to execute complicated smart contracts [31]. Smart contracts are developed in high-level languages (e.g., Solidity), allowing trusted transactions to be made without a third party, and these transactions are traceable and irrevocable. Smart contracts cannot be modified once they are published, so vulnerabilities in smart contracts cannot be easily fixed. Furthermore, smart contracts hold large amounts of money, as a result of which, are frequently targeted by hackers. A prominent example is the DAO attack, the hacker utilized the re-entrancy vulnerability in the DAO contract and stole more than $50 million [11]. The frequent smart contract security

G. Wang et al. (Eds.): UbiSec 2022, CCIS 1768, pp. 52–63, 2023.
https://doi.org/10.1007/978-981-99-0272-9_4

issues have not only resulted in significant cash losses but have also damaged the blockchain's credit system. Therefore, more and more people are becoming interested in the study on smart contract vulnerability detection.

The vulnerabilities of smart contracts raise several challenges. Re-entrancy vulnerability, integer overflow vulnerability [4], timestamp dependency vulnerability, etc, exist with Ethereum, for instance. However, existing detectors for smart contracts available focus only on known vulnerabilities, for example, two well-known symbolic execution tools Manticore [17] and Maian [18], as well as two popular fuzzy testing tools Regurad [13] and ContractFuzzer [12]. Liu et al. [14,15] design SlimBox, which rapidly screens out potentially malicious packets in constant time while incurring only moderate communication overhead.

To the best of our knowledge, numerous academics have studied unknown vulnerabilities in software applications. There is relatively little research on unknown vulnerabilities in smart contracts, while the majority of existing research in smart contract vulnerability detection is focused on detecting known vulnerabilities with clear features in smart contracts. As a result, proposing a method for detecting unknown vulnerabilities in smart contracts represents a significant advancement in the field of smart contract security.

TXSPECTOR [28] can detect vulnerabilities in smart contracts from transactions, which coincides with our previous work to transparently check the integrity of the system using the Intel Management Engine (IME) [29]. Arif et al. [3] propose a two-tiered architecture intended to serve as a baseline for safeguarding users' privacy and integrity when conducting online purchases and other associated activities. Furthermore, the opcode sequence of a transaction essentially represents the entire execution process of a transaction. As a consequence, we directly detect opcode sequences of transactions obtained by Geth instrumentation [23] to find unknown vulnerabilities in smart contracts. Based on the idea that the opcode sequences of transactions containing unknown vulnerabilities have similarities to the opcode sequences of transactions containing known vulnerabilities, we propose a novel approach for unknown vulnerability detection in smart contracts using a CNN-BiLSTM neural network. The set of opcode sequences of transactions is used to train the CNN-BiLSTM model. Furthermore, the CNN-BiLSTM model is applied to determine the probability for each label, and the two thresholds are applied to determine whether an unknown vulnerability exists. In this way, we successfully detect unknown vulnerabilities in smart contracts. Experimental results with the opcode sequences of transactions obtained by Geth instrumentation show that the model was able to achieve 82.86% accuracy and 83.63% F1-score.

In summary, we make the following main contributions:

(1) We propose a model to detect unknown vulnerabilities in smart contracts, which is the first to detect unknown vulnerabilities in smart contracts.
(2) Our model can dynamically detect unknown vulnerabilities after a smart contract has been published, minimizing user losses.
(3) We make an extensive evaluation over >1500 real-world opcode sequences of transactions, demonstrating that the model is effective and can detect

significantly unknown vulnerabilities and achieve 82.86% accuracy and 83.63% F1-score.

2   Related Work

We now discuss the work that is most closely related to ours.

SODA [5] as a general online detection framework, with good scalability to detect 8 types of vulnerabilities and the transactions trigger the execution of vulnerable codes in smart contracts. TXSPECTOR [28] as a generic, logic-driven framework can detect transactions that trigger the execution of vulnerable code in smart contracts, which can discover three kinds of vulnerabilities. The two tools mentioned above can gain dynamic information, unlike static analysis tools. Oyente [16] is the first symbolic tool to detect vulnerabilities in smart contracts, which applies symbolic execution to interpret the bytecode of smart contracts. Although symbolic execution is a great tool for finding vulnerabilities, it suffers from the problem of path explosion. ILF [7] is an imitation learning-based fuzzer that attempts to learn fuzzing policies from training sequences generated from symbolic execution, providing accurate and high-coverage detection.

In the field of machine learning, TMP [30] is a smart contract vulnerability detection tool based on graph neural networks that leverage a novel temporal message propagation network (TMP) to learn vulnerabilities from normalized graphs. ContractWard [24] is a machine learning-based smart contract vulnerability detection tool, which was built by extracting bigram features from simplified opcodes of smart contracts, one smart contract corresponds to one opcode sequence. The opcode sequence used here has different meanings than ours. SCS-Guard [10] is a novel deep learning detection framework using Gated Recurrent Unit (GRU) with attention mechanism learning from the N-gram bytecode patterns to determine whether a smart contract is malicious or not. SaferSC [22] is a sequential learning model using LSTM network to detect known vulnerabilities in smart contracts.

In the field of unknown vulnerability, singh et al. [21] propose a framework that acts as an integrated method for unknown vulnerability detection. Albashir [2] proposes a novel method called HVD to detect unknown vulnerabilities in a software system, which results in providing opportunities for software developers to fix unknown vulnerabilities. Periyasamy et al. [19] propose a vulnerability prediction scheme named Prediction of Future Vulnerability Discovery in Software Applications using Vulnerability Syntax Tree (PFVD-VST) which comprises five phases to solve the unknown vulnerability detection problem. Abri et al. [1] demonstrate the effectiveness of machine and deep learning classifiers in detecting unknown malware.

Although the tools mentioned above are effective at detecting known vulnerabilities with clear features in smart contracts, none of them can detect unknown vulnerabilities in smart contracts. In contrast, our model is capable of detecting unknown vulnerabilities in smart contracts.

3 Implementation

Opcode Sequences. The following concept needs to be explained before our model is described:

Opcodes are low-level machine instructions, which will be fetched, decoded, and executed by EVM [26]. There are two different definitions of opcode sequences. The first is the opcode sequences of transactions that Geth instrumentation collects, each sequence consists of multiple opcodes, such as CALLDATALOAD, MSTORE, STOP, PUSH1, PUSH2, ADD, SUB, STOP. The length of the series is variable. Essentially, each sequence represents the entire execution process of a transaction. And the other is the opcode sequences created by decompiling smart contracts, one smart contract corresponds to one opcode sequence. The opcode sequences of safe transactions discussed are those generated by transactions that trigger the normal execution of smart contracts, and the opcode sequences of dangerous transactions are those generated by transactions that trigger the execution of vulnerable codes in smart contracts.

Detection Model Description. As shown in Fig. 1, we first gather a big number of the opcode sequences of transactions by Geth instrumentation. Opcodes are then transformed into One-hot vectors by One-hot encoding. Furthermore, we build the CNN-BiLSTM model to get the probability for each label. Finally, based on the probability for each label, the two thresholds are used to determine whether an unknown vulnerability exists.

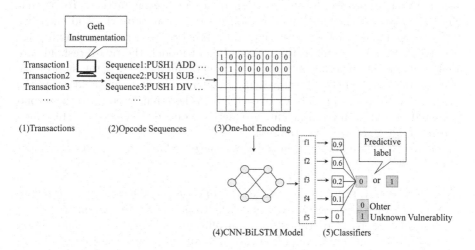

Fig. 1. The process of detecting unknown vulnerability.

Classification Model. A convolutional neural network (CNN) is a feedforward neural network with a deep structure, which consists of an input layer, a convolutional layer, a ReLU layer, a pooling layer, and a fully connected layer.

This model has addressed several problems in image processing and automatic natural language processing such as opinion analysis, text summary, etc. [20].

Long Short-Term Memory Neural Networks (LSTM), an extension of recurrent neural network (RNN), were proposed by Hochreiter and Schmidhuber in 1997 [9]. They mainly solve the regular RNN memory problem, in which text information at a distance cannot be utilized, and text information at a closer distance but not semantically relevant produces excessive interference. Bidirectional Long ShortTerm Memory (BiLSTM) combines the information of the input sequence in both forward and backward directions based on LSTM. BiLSTM has proven good results in natural language processing [27].

Our model combines two neural networks, namely CNN and BiLSTM, which allow extracting the maximum amount of information from the opcode sequences of transactions using CNN. This output becomes the BiLSTM input, allowing keeping the chronological order between the data in both directions. Meanwhile, since the length of the series is variable, CNN can play the role of dimensionality reduction.

Combining the advantages of both models, the vectors created by the preprocessing part are used as the input to CNN to extract high-level features. The Rectified Linear Unit (ReLU) function [6] for each convolutional layer reduces the non-linearity of the network. Then, three filters of 3, 4, and 5, respectively are applied 128 times each. After each filter, a layer of max pooling is applied to update and reduce the size of the data.

The max pooling layer outputs are then utilized as prior knowledge input to the BiLSTM. The outputs of this stage are sent into the concat layer for feature fusion, which improves the propagation of features even further. To prevent overfitting, we use dropout [8] to optimize the neural network. And then, we apply the sigmoid function as an activation function to get the probability for each label. Finally, based on the CNN-BiLSTM model, the two thresholds are used to determine whether an unknown vulnerability exists. If the sum of the probabilities of all labels is greater than or equal to the first threshold α and the maximum value of the probability of each label is less than or equal to the second threshold β, and both requirements are met, the opcode sequence is determined to contain an unknown vulnerability.

Therefore, our model consists of three parts, which are described in more detail below (Fig. 2):

(1) Preprocessing part: In this stage, the opcode sequences are converted to One-hot vectors using One-hot encoding to prepare data for convolution.
(2) Convolution part: In this stage, convolution and max pooling layers are applied for extracting high-level features and can play the role of dimensionality reduction. The output of this stage is subsequently applied to the BiLSTM layer.
(3) BiLSTM part: In this stage, BiLSTM layer is used to determine whether an unknown vulnerability exists.

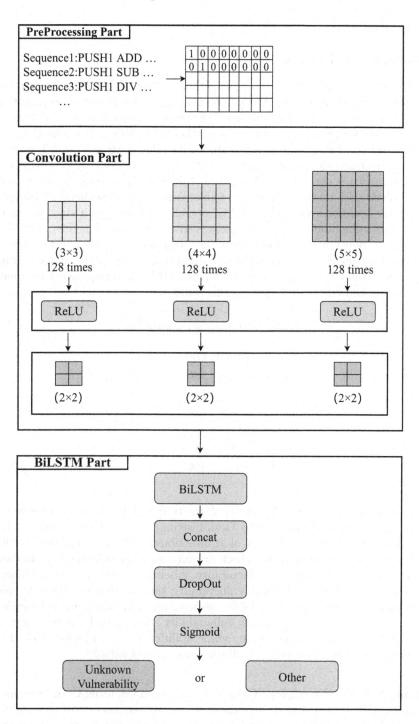

Fig. 2. CNN-BiLSTM model architecture.

4   Evaluation

Training Set and Labels

(1) Training Set: We replay the transactions on the Ethereum platform and employ SODA to extract the safe transactions and dangerous transactions with five types of vulnerabilities. The opcode sequences of safe transactions and dangerous transactions are gathered by Geth instrumentation. The description of the training set is shown in Table 1, S0, S1, S2, S3, S4, and S5 correspond to opcode sequences with no vulnerability, opcode sequences with incorrect check for authorization vulnerability, opcode sequences with no check after contract invocation vulnerability, opcode sequences with missing the transfer event vulnerability, opcode sequences with strict check for balance vulnerability, opcode sequences with timestamp dependency & block number dependency vulnerability. The training set with a total of 1733 opcode sequences of transactions is divided into two parts, namely training and validation, distributed as follows: 70% (1213 sequences) for model training and 30% (520 sequences) for validation.

Table 1. Training set description

Total	1733
S0	*788*
S1	*155*
S2	*156*
S3	*79*
S4	*55*
S5	*500*

(2) Labels: We employ SODA to label all the transactions, the opcode sequences of transactions are gathered by Geth instrumentation. Thus we finish labeling all the opcode sequences of transactions, and each sequence has five labels representing incorrect check for authorization vulnerability, no check after contract invocation vulnerability, missing the transfer event vulnerability, strict check for balance vulnerability, timestamp dependency & block number dependency vulnerability, respectively. The labels are independent of each other in each type of vulnerability. For example, a transaction's opcode sequence can have many vulnerabilities at once, in which case there would be multiple labels of 1, all 0 means no vulnerability.

Testing Set. We also employ SODA to get transactions, using Geth instrumentation to gather their opcode sequences. 6 opcode sequences with re-entrancy vulnerability, and 788 opcode sequences with unexpected function invocation vulnerability as opcode sequences with unknown vulnerabilities, a total of 735

S0-S5 as other sequences. The description of the testing set is shown in Table 2, the testing set consists of 794 opcode sequences with unknown vulnerabilities and 735 other sequences.

Table 2. Testing set description

Total	1529
Sequences with unknown vulnerabilities	*794*
Other sequences	*735*

Performance Measures. We use the accuracy metric to evaluate the performance of the CNN-BiLSTM model.

$$Accuracy = \frac{true\ positive + true\ negative}{total\ tested} \tag{1}$$

However, the accuracy metric is no longer useful in the imbalanced distribution problem. Consequently, three additional metrics, respectively, precision, recall, and F1-score are used to evaluate the performance of the CNN-BiLSTM model. We denote an opcode sequence with unknown vulnerability correctly detected as true positive, an opcode sequence with unknown vulnerability wrongly detected as false negative, one other sequence correctly detected as a true negative and one other sequence detected wrongly as a false positive.

$$Precision = \frac{true\ positive}{true\ positive + false\ positive} \tag{2}$$

$$Recall = \frac{true\ positive}{true\ positive + false\ negative} \tag{3}$$

$$F1 - score = 2 \times \frac{Precision \times Recall}{Precision + Recall} \tag{4}$$

Experimental Results. Our experiment environment is shown in Table 3.

Table 3. The experiment environment

Software and Hardware	Configurations
Server Model	*Lenovo Legion Y7000*
Operating System	*Windows 11*
CPU	*Intel i5-10200H*
RAM	*16.0 GB*

As shown in Fig. 3, from approximately 1000000 opcode sequences of transactions obtained by Geth instrumentation, nearly 80% of the sequences are less than 3000 in length. Therefore, in order to sufficiently cover the majority of opcode sequences of transactions, we choose to set the maximum CNN-BiLSTM sequence input length at 3000.

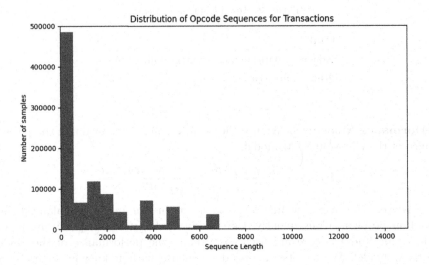

Fig. 3. Histogram of the length of opcode sequences for transactions.

Our experiment is implemented in Python and Keras, an open-source learning library based on TensorFlow. Regarding our Experimental parameters, the value of batch_size is 64, 100 iterations are performed, the optimizer Adam is used, and the learning rate is 0.001. We change α and β separately and conduct 45 control experiments. A part of the experimental results is attached as shown in Fig. 4, α is finally set to 0.2 and β is set to 0.999.

As shown in Table 4, the CNN-BiLSTM model can achieve 82.86% accuracy and 83.63% F1-score, demonstrating that the model is effective and can detect unknown vulnerabilities.

Table 4. Detection measures

Performance measure	Model(%)
Accuracy	82.86
Precision	83.00
Recall	84.26
F1-Score	83.63

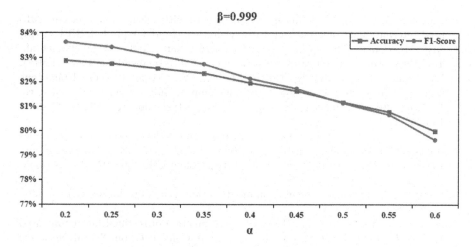

Fig. 4. Line graph of detection measures at different thresholds.

5 Conclusion

Smart contracts are frequently targeted by hackers because they hold large amounts of money and cannot be modified once they are published. However, there is relatively little research on unknown vulnerabilities in smart contracts. Therefore, based on the idea that the opcode sequences of transactions containing unknown vulnerabilities have similarities to the opcode sequences of transactions containing known vulnerabilities, we propose a novel approach to detecting unknown vulnerabilities in smart contracts. The key idea is an end-to-end classification model that determines whether a vulnerability is unknown by detecting the opcode sequence representing the entire execution process of a transaction. We make an extensive evaluation demonstrating that the model is effective and can detect unknown vulnerabilities.

In future work, we will add the attention mechanism to our model. Furthermore, our data set will be made available as open source so that anybody can utilize it.

Acknowledgements. This work was supported in part by the National Key Research and Development Program of China (2020YFB1005804), and in part by the National Natural Science Foundation of China under Grants 61632009, 61872097, and 61802076.

References

1. Abri, F., Siami-Namini, S., Khanghah, M.A., Soltani, F.M., Namin, A.S.: Can machine/deep learning classifiers detect zero-day malware with high accuracy? In: 2019 IEEE International Conference on Big Data (Big Data), pp. 3252–3259. IEEE (2019)

2. Albashir, A.A.A.N.: Detecting unknown vulnerabilities using honeynet. In: 2015 First International Conference on Anti-Cybercrime (ICACC), pp. 1–4. IEEE (2015)
3. Arif, M., Sohail, S.S., Alam, M.T., Ubaid, S., Nafis, M.T., Wang, G., et al.: Towards a two-tier architecture for privacy-enabled recommender systems (PeRS). In: Wang, G., Choo, KK.R., Ko, R.K.L., Xu, Y., Crispo, B. (eds) Ubiquitous Security. UbiSec 2021. Communications in Computer and Information Science, vol 1557. pp. 268–278. Springer, Singapore (2022). https://doi.org/10.1007/978-981-19-0468-4_20
4. Atzei, N., Bartoletti, M., Cimoli, T.: A survey of attacks on ethereum smart contracts (SoK). In: Maffei, M., Ryan, M. (eds.) POST 2017. LNCS, vol. 10204, pp. 164–186. Springer, Heidelberg (2017). https://doi.org/10.1007/978-3-662-54455-6_8
5. Chen, T., et al.: Soda: A generic online detection framework for smart contracts. In: NDSS (2020)
6. Hara, K., Saito, D., Shouno, H.: Analysis of function of rectified linear unit used in deep learning. In: 2015 International Joint Conference on Neural Networks (IJCNN), pp. 1–8. IEEE (2015)
7. He, J., Balunović, M., Ambroladze, N., Tsankov, P., Vechev, M.: Learning to fuzz from symbolic execution with application to smart contracts. In: Proceedings of the 2019 ACM SIGSAC Conference on Computer and Communications Security, pp. 531–548 (2019)
8. Hinton, G.E., Srivastava, N., Krizhevsky, A., Sutskever, I., Salakhutdinov, R.R.: Improving neural networks by preventing co-adaptation of feature detectors. arXiv preprint arXiv:1207.0580 (2012)
9. Hochreiter, S., Schmidhuber, J.: Long short-term memory. Neural Comput. 9(8), 1735–1780 (1997)
10. Hu, H., Bai, Q., Xu, Y.: Scsguard: deep scam detection for ethereum smart contracts. In: IEEE INFOCOM 2022-IEEE Conference on Computer Communications Workshops (INFOCOM WKSHPS), pp. 1–6. IEEE (2022)
11. Insider, B.: Digital currency ethereum is cratering because of a $50 million hack. https://www.businessinsider.com/dao-hacked-ethereum-crashing-in-value-tens-of-millions-allegedly-stolen-2016-6?r=UK
12. Jiang, B., Liu, Y., Chan, W.K.: ContractFuzzer: fuzzing smart contracts for vulnerability detection. In: 2018 33rd IEEE/ACM International Conference on Automated Software Engineering (ASE), pp. 259–269. IEEE (2018)
13. Liu, C., Liu, H., Cao, Z., Chen, Z., Chen, B., Roscoe, B.: Reguard: finding reentrancy bugs in smart contracts. In: 2018 IEEE/ACM 40th International Conference on Software Engineering: Companion (ICSE-Companion), pp. 65–68. IEEE (2018)
14. Liu, Q., Peng, Y., Jiang, H., Wu, J., Wang, T., Peng, T., Wang, G.: Slimbox: lightweight packet inspection over encrypted traffic. IEEE Trans. Depend. Secure Comput. Early Access (2022)
15. Liu, Q., Peng, Y., Wu, J., Wang, T., Wang, G.: Secure multi-keyword fuzzy searches with enhanced service quality in cloud computing. IEEE Trans. Netw. Serv. Manage. 18(2), 2046–2062 (2020)
16. Luu, L., Chu, D.H., Olickel, H., Saxena, P., Hobor, A.: Making smart contracts smarter. In: Proceedings of the 2016 ACM SIGSAC Conference on Computer and Communications Security, pp. 254–269 (2016)
17. Mossberg, M., et al.: Manticore: a user-friendly symbolic execution framework for binaries and smart contracts. In: 2019 34th IEEE/ACM International Conference on Automated Software Engineering (ASE), pp. 1186–1189. IEEE (2019)

18. Nikolić, I., Kolluri, A., Sergey, I., Saxena, P., Hobor, A.: Finding the greedy, prodigal, and suicidal contracts at scale. In: Proceedings of the 34th Annual Computer Security Applications Conference, pp. 653–663 (2018)
19. Periyasamy, K., Arirangan, S.: Prediction of future vulnerability discovery in software applications using vulnerability syntax tree (PFVD-VST). Int. Arab J. Inf. Technol. **16**(2), 288–294 (2019)
20. Rhanoui, M., Mikram, M., Yousfi, S., Barzali, S.: A CNN-BILSTM model for document-level sentiment analysis. Mach. Learn. Knowl. Extract. **1**(3), 832–847 (2019)
21. Singh, U.K., Joshi, C., Kanellopoulos, D.: A framework for zero-day vulnerabilities detection and prioritization. J. Inf. Secur. Appl. **46**, 164–172 (2019)
22. Tann, W.J.W., Han, X.J., Gupta, S.S., Ong, Y.S.: Towards safer smart contracts: a sequence learning approach to detecting security threats. arXiv preprint arXiv:1811.06632 (2018)
23. Wang, G., et al.: Generating opcode sequences by replaying ethereum transaction data. Application Number: 202211531992.1 (2022–12–01)
24. Wang, W., Song, J., Xu, G., Li, Y., Wang, H., Su, C.: Contractward: Automated vulnerability detection models for ethereum smart contracts. IEEE Trans. Netw. Sci. Eng. **8**(2), 1133–1144 (2020)
25. Wood, G., et al.: Ethereum: a secure decentralised generalised transaction ledger. Ethereum Project Yellow Paper **151**(2014), 1–32 (2014)
26. Wu, S., et al.: Time-travel investigation: toward building a scalable attack detection framework on ethereum. ACM Trans. Softw. Eng. Methodol. **31**(3), 1–33 (2022)
27. Yin, W., Kann, K., Yu, M., Schütze, H.: Comparative study of CNN and RNN for natural language processing. arXiv preprint arXiv:1702.01923 (2017)
28. Zhang, M., Zhang, X., Zhang, Y., Lin, Z.: TXSPECTOR: uncovering attacks in ethereum from transactions. In: 29th USENIX Security Symposium (USENIX Security 2020), pp. 2775–2792 (2020)
29. Zhou, I., et al.: A coprocessor-based introspection framework via intel management engine. IEEE Trans. Depend. Secure Comput. **18**(4), 1920–1932 (2021)
30. Zhuang, Y., Liu, Z., Qian, P., Liu, Q., Wang, X., He, Q.: Smart contract vulnerability detection using graph neural network. In: IJCAI, pp. 3283–3290 (2020)
31. Zou, Y., Peng, T., Zhong, W., Guan, K., Wang, G.: Reliable and controllable data sharing based on blockchain. In: Wang, G., Choo, KK.R., Ko, R.K.L., Xu, Y., Crispo, B. (eds) Ubiquitous Security. UbiSec 2021. Communications in Computer and Information Science, vol. 1557. pp. 229–240. Springer, Singapore (2022).https://doi.org/10.1007/978-981-19-0468-4_17

CATS: A Serious Game in Industry Towards Stronger Cloud Security

Tiange Zhao[1,2]($\boxtimes$) , Ulrike Lechner[3] , Maria Pinto-Albuquerque[4] ,
Ece Ata[3] , and Tiago Gasiba[1]

[1] Siemens AG, 81739 Munich, Germany
{tiange.zhao,tiago.gasiba}@siemens.com
[2] Universität der Bundeswehr München, 85579 Munich, Germany
[3] Technische Universität München, 80333 Munich, Germany
[4] (ISCTE-IUL), ISTAR, University Institute of Lisbon, 1649-026 Lisbon, Portugal

Abstract. Cloud computing has become a widely applied technology in the industry. Broad network access as a characteristic of cloud computing brings business value. It poses threats to cloud assets due to a greater attack surface than on-premises and other service models. Industry standards aim to regulate cloud security by enforcing best practices. To comply with the standards, practitioners in the industry are mandated to be trained to understand basic concepts of attack and defense mechanisms in cloud security to protect assets in the cloud. This work presents a serious game: Cloud of Assets and Threats (CATS), as an enrichment to the traditional training material to raise awareness about the cloud security challenges. In this paper, we introduce the design elements and implementation details of CATS. We organized eight game events with 94 industrial practitioners to validate our design. We applied a questionnaire and conducted semi-structured interviews with the game participants to evaluate the impact of the game and collect feedback. The evaluation indicates that CATS is a promising innovative method for promoting awareness of cloud security issues among practitioners in the industry, regardless of their technical background. Our main contributions are the design of such a game and the understanding of the impact of playing the CATS game in the industry.

Keywords: Serious game · Cloud security · Awareness · Industry

1 Introduction

The size and number of cloud-based applications have risen significantly in the industry. The National Institute for Standards and Technology (NIST [32]) summarizes five characteristics of cloud computing [33]: On-demand Self Service; Broad network access; Resource Pooling; Rapid Elasticity, and Measured Service. The great flexibility and convenience contribute to development efficiency and business success. However, cloud assets are prone to various cyber-security threats [1]. Due to the broad network exposure and architecture that involves

G. Wang et al. (Eds.): UbiSec 2022, CCIS 1768, pp. 64–82, 2023.
https://doi.org/10.1007/978-981-99-0272-9_5

cloud service providers and customers, the attack surface increases compared to on-premise and other service provisioning models. Also, there are security challenges that are specific to the cloud. The Cloud Security Alliance (CSA[1]) provides a ranking table of the top 11 threats in cloud computing [7]. One possible way to counter the increase of threats in cloud systems is to raise awareness of industry practitioners about cloud security. Due to the complexity of cloud deployments, a better understanding on the individual responsibilities of each stakeholder on how to secure the company assets is desired.

Numerous industry security standards propose requirements and best practices in cloud security. The Cloud Control Matrix [2] from CSA maps and compares the different existing standards. The study of Gleeson [18] has shown the complexity of those standards. Shared-responsibility model describes the responsibility of cloud service providers and cloud service customers for a cloud service based on different service models: Infrastructure as a Service (IaaS), Platform as a Service (PaaS), and Software as a Service (SaaS). In all three service models, it is the cloud service customers' responsibility to configure the cloud service securely. Cloud service customers are the users of a cloud service, and among them, there are different roles and responsibilities too.

Cloud security is a complex yet important topic that industry practitioners need to understand. In the work of Andrei-Cristian et al. [24], they examined the quality of infrastructure as code (IaC) in open code repositories in terms of security and found almost 300,000 security violations from over 8000 code repositories. Their study concludes that the developers miss basic concepts of cloud security and that we need to improve awareness about certain issues on cloud deployment in an industrial environment. Those fundamental concepts are generally conveyed to the developers through training. Traditional training is typically lecture-based in a face-to-face or virtual format. In recent years, there are various cyber-security serious games designed to enrich or provide an alternative to the traditional training method. Yet, none of the existing games targets the challenges in cloud security. Therefore, we designed a serious game, Cloud of Assets and Threats (CATS) to help raise awareness of cloud security in the industry. In this work, we present the design of the game and evaluate the impact of the game on industrial practitioners by means of open discussion, semi-structured interviews, and surveys.

Our work contributes to the existing body of knowledge by proposing the design of the CATS game following the design science research paradigm [22,23]. The evaluation process of CATS gives insight into the impact of such a game on the cloud security awareness of industrial practitioners and validates the usefulness of CATS. Industrial practitioners benefit from the game as their awareness on cloud security improves by participating in the game events. Researchers could utilize the design and evaluation details of CATS as a blueprint for the further serious game and understand the possible impact of serious games on raising IT security awareness.

---

[1] https://cloudsecurityalliance.org/.

This paper is organized as follows. After the introduction, in Sect. 2 we analyze some work related to the application of the serious game in the context of the cyber-security field. Then, we describe the method we propose to guide our research activity in Sect. 3. In Sect. 4, we share details of the CATS game design and implementation. Section 5 presents the result of eight game events that took place in the industry. Section 6 shares our thought and discussion on the collected results. Section 7 concludes our work and briefly presents an outlook on the future study.

2   Related Work

In the industry, standards define necessary protections for cloud assets. The best known among them is the ISO 27017 [26] and ISO 27001 [25], which require the practitioners to participate in training to learn about security technologies and raise awareness on cyber-security issues. The CSA CCM (Cloud Security Alliance Cloud Controls Matrix) [2] compares 44 cloud security standards and shows an overview of the coverage of cloud security controls. MITRE ATT&CK cloud matrix [4] categorizes cloud attack actions and defense mechanisms based on real-world observations. It provides us with an adequate framework to derive the important game elements in CATS.

In the field of serious game design, Dörner et al. established a baseline for developing serious games [8]. In their seminal work, serious games are a type of game with more than just entertainment purposes. These types of games contrast with gamification. However, Landers [30] shows that both methods contain parallels and similarities. Our game, CATS, is a serious game with the purpose of assisting the players in learning important concepts in cloud security and raising awareness on cloud security problems. Raising awareness of cyber-security topics is important in practice, and various serious games have been designed in recent years for the cyber-security domain, hinting that serious games are a possible solution to cyber-security issues. Nevertheless, these games need to be well designed to achieve their goal, as shown by Landers [31]. A well-established register of games designed for cyber-security is maintained by Shostack [35].

One example is the game Riskio from Hart et al. [21], which successfully increases cyber-security awareness for people without technical backgrounds working in organizations. Riskio is a tabletop game that focuses on both defensive and offensive skills in IT security in general, however, the complicated topic of cloud security involving different stakeholders and cloud specific security challenges and mitigation are not included in depth in Riskio.

Another example is Another Week at the Office (AWATO) [12] by Ferro et al. They designed the game based on a systematic literature review and focus on the human factor that provides possibilities for phishing attacks. The primary use case is phishing attack instead of cloud security. The evaluation of AWATO shows that it is an effective tool for improving users' awareness of cyber-security best practices. Their work hints that serious game is a useful approach to solving awareness issues.

The work of Valdemar et al. [36] shows that creating serious games contributes to fostering adversary thinking. In their study over three semesters, undergraduate students learn methods of network attack and defense by creating educational games in a cyber range. The students report they had a unique opportunity to deeply understand the topic. The game is played by their collegemate, who rated the quality and educational value of the games overwhelmingly positively. Their work shows exciting results in the academic environment. Our work focuses on the specific topic of cloud security with a setting in the industry.

One work that emphasizes security mitigation in cloud deployment is the CyberSecurity Challenges from Gasiba et al. [10]. They extend their secure coding teaching platform SiFu [13,14] with challenges addressing Terraform-aided[2] cloud deployment on Amazon Web Services [11]. The player gets flags by fixing vulnerabilities in Terraform code. It requires more technical know-how on secure coding for the players to participate and benefit the most from the game. However, their work does not cover different roles and their responsibilities in cloud security.

In [28], Jakóbik et al. present a theoretical framework to model security attack scenarios for cloud environments. Their model enables to automatically find strategies and decisions that minimize the impact that attackers can cause while maximizing the impact of the defense strategy. These derived decisions can be used by cloud administrators and also by service providers. Jakóbik refines his game and model in [27] to address a defensive strategy for threats on information confidentiality and integrity in terms of leakage and corruption. However, both these previous works do not cover industry standards, such as the Cloud Control Matrix.

The present work also builds on the work on IT security awareness by Hänsch et al. [20], and on its extension by Gasiba [16]. In their work, Hänsch et al. define three dimensions of IT security awareness: perception, protection, and behavior. These three dimensions are used to evaluate our artifact in the industry, and also to understand how the game affects the cyber security awareness of the players on cloud security.

3   Method

Gleasure [17] describes that when the prescriptive aspect of a research problem is less mature than its descriptive or normative dimensions, the information system (IS) research problem is 'wicked'. Such problems are not suitable for traditional science approaches and instead require the situated theorizing afforded in the context of active design. Our work is guided by the design science research paradigm [22,23] proposed by Hevner et al., since design science research can handle the changing and unstable requirements we encounter in practice and in the industry. In the work of Hevner et al., they describe the core of design science research as the cycle of Design & Implement and Justify & Evaluate. We applied the method in our research. We designed and implemented the serious game artifact and organized game events for justification and evaluation.

---

[2] https://www.terraform.io/.

We organize our study in a two-phase approach: in phase 1, we organize game events. Directly after each game event, we use survey and round-table open discussion to collect feedback. In phase 2, we randomly choose players who have participated in the game event two weeks to one month after the game events take place to understand the impact of the game on the players.

In phase 1, eight game events were organized in the first half of 2022. During these events, a total of 94 industry practitioners took part in our study. Some of the game events were integrated into a CyberSecurity Challenge (CSC) [14,15] event. CSC is a type of event similar to Capture-the-flag (CTF), where CATS is a category of challenges to be solved. Players work in teams and get points by solving attack scenarios in CATS. Other game events are integrated into training. Players first attend a full-day cyber-security awareness training, in which cloud security is included as a topic. Then, the players are invited as single players instead of in teams to join the CATS game. In all the eight game events, we collected 2077 submissions, as shown in Table 1.

Table 1. Overview of game events organized in the first half of 2022 - phase 1

Game event	Date	Player	Team	CSC or Training	Valid submissions
1	2022-01-21	17	4	CSC	177
2	2022-03-15	14	–	Training	477
3	2022-03-22	14	–	Training	493
4	2022-03-29	13	–	Training	312
5	2022-04-14	13	4	CSC	178
6	2022-04-26	11	–	Training	100
7	2022-05-03	8	–	Training	171
8	2022-06-02	4	2	CSC	169
Total number of players	94				
Total number of submissions	2077				

In the survey we distributed in phase 1, we collected 24 answers. The focus of the questionnaire is on the impact of awareness, game experience, and security knowledge, as shown in Table 2. Awareness of IT security is not standardized. In this work, we extended the classification proposed by Hänsch et al. [20] from IT security to cloud security. In their work, they suggest a classification of the different meanings of IT security awareness into three groups: Perception, Protection, and Behavior. In the questionnaire, we included questions to measure Perception and Protection. Behavior is evaluated in the game's dynamic activities.

In phase 2, we randomly selected 22 of the 94 players that participated in phase 1 and invited them into a semi-structured interview (SSI) in online meetings, 15 of them showed up in the meeting, and 7 of them turned down the invitation due to time conflict, as shown in Table 3. The focus of a SSI is on the

Table 2. Overview of questions and theoretical construct - phase 1

Theoretical construct	ID	Questions
Perception	Ph1Q1	Playing this cloud security game helps me to understand roles and responsibilities
Perception	Ph1Q2	Playing this cloud security game helps me to understand cloud attacks and defenses
Game Experience	Ph1Q3	I benefit from the collaboration with teammates in this cloud security game
Game Experience	Ph1Q4	I benefit from the discussion with teammates in the cloud security game
Protection	Ph1Q5	I feel my cloud security know-how has improved by playing this cloud security game
Game Background	Ph1Q6	I would recommend this cloud security game to other colleagues
Protection	Ph1Q7	Our strategy for cloud security will improve by repeatedly playing this cloud security game
Security Knowledge	Ph1Q8	I think it is hard to calculate the actual probability of a successful defense
Security Knowledge	Ph1Q9	I think it is hard to consider all relevant factors for a successful defense

impact of awareness. Table 4 shows the questions for SSI. In questions 2 to question 8 (Ph2Q2 to Ph2Q8), we ask the respondent to assign a certain defense card to either business responsibility or technical responsibility. The asked defense cards are; Logging & Monitoring, Network Segmentation, Audit, Password Policy, Account Use Policy, Account Management, and Intrusion Detection System (IDS).

Table 3. Overview of semi-structured interview - phase 2

Number of game event participants	94
Number of invited interviewees	22
Number of show-up interviewees	15
Date of SSI	2022-04-29–2022-05-25
Average duration of interview	11 min 13 s
Number of questions	15

4 Design and Implementation

In this section, the game design and the implementation are introduced. We detail the CATS game and the game process with the important elements in game design and implementation.

Table 4. Overview of questions in SSI - phase 2

Theoretical construct	ID	Questions
Perception	Ph2Q1	Please rate how much do you still remember from the cloud security game
Protection	Ph2Q2~8	Does the defense XXX belong to Business Responsibility or Technical Responsibility?
Protection	Ph2Q9	Please identify the cards that was helpful in your defense strategy
Perception	Ph2Q10	What is the most important thing you learn from the Cloud Security Game?
Behavior	Ph2Q11	What have you changed in your daily work after the game?
General	Ph2Q12	Do you want to add any feedback or suggestion about the Cloud Security Game?
Perception	Ph2Q13	The game helped me in understanding the weakness in cloud security
Behavior	Ph2Q14	I think my cloud asset is secure
Behavior	Ph2Q15	I think I still need more training in cloud security

4.1 Overview of CATS

We first proposed our serious game Cloud of Assets and Threats (CATS) in our previous work [40]. To the best of our knowledge, CATS is currently the only serious game that focuses solely on raising awareness about different roles and responsibilities in secure cloud deployments. In the beginning, it was designed to be a board game with cards for two to six players. The players are divided into defense and attack teams and play cards to build attack and defense plans. More details about the game prototype and organized trial runs can be found in [39]. We initiated and refined the game design in two design iterations [41]. In the current pandemic, many face-to-face events are adapted to a virtual format. To cope with this situation, we designed and built a digital platform for CATS, where players can join as a single player or play in a team online. The players can drag and drop cards to defend themselves against cloud security attacks. In the next sections, we give a brief overview of the important game elements in CATS. We refer to CATS as the virtual board game on the digital platform.

Game Process. The flowchart in Fig. 1 shows the game process. As the game starts, the players first follow a tutorial to learn about the rules and game elements. The players are free to choose from the available attack scenarios. Details about the attack scenario are provided in the next section. During the game event, we offer the players two attack scenarios for the tutorials and four attack scenarios to be solved. We will introduce the details of attack scenarios in the

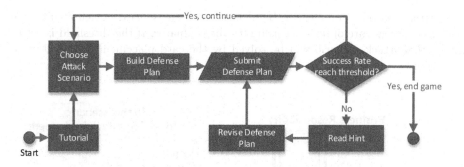

Fig. 1. The game process from player perspective

next sections. The goal of the game is for players to build a defense plan by assigning defense cards to the correct responsibility. When the defense plan is ready, players submit their defense plan to the back end by clicking a "submit" button. The back end then performs an evaluation of the chances of the cloud deployment being attacked based on the scenario and the players' selected cards and their positions. The evaluator calculates a success rate, which is the probability that the submitted defense plan withstands the given attack scenario. The game is pre-configured with a threshold, which is visible to the player in the game interface. If the calculated success rate is bigger or equal to the given threshold, the player has successfully solved the scenario and can move on to the next one. If the success rate does not reach the threshold, hints are automatically generated and sent back to the player. These hints provide a justification to the player why the card selection did or did not work. At this stage, the player is given a further chance to adjust the defense plan based on the received hints. The player can change the defense plan and submit the new plan to the back end until the game scenario is solved.

Game Interface. In Fig. 2 we show an example of the game interface. Depicted on the left side are the six chosen cards that are assigned either to "Business Responsibility" or "Technical Responsibility" area. "Business Responsibility" refers to the high-level defense actions in which important business-related decisions should be made, typically by the asset owners. "Technical Responsibilities" refers to the concrete technical defense actions, typically implemented by the asset manager. On the right side, the attack scenario is listed with three steps: step 1, initial access; step 2, launch attack; and step 3, make impact. In the first step, attack "Abuse Credential" can be mitigated by defense card "Audit"; attack "Cloud Infrastructure Discovery" can be defended by "Account Management." In the second step, attack "Abuse Trusted Relationship" and "Account Manipulation" can also be secured with the defense "Account Management." The defense card "Logging & Monitoring" can detect "Impair Defense." In the last step, the defense card "Backup Concept" can alleviate the attack "Defacement." There are in total 24 defense cards for the players to choose from. In this example, all the attack actions are defended by at least one defense card, which results in a defense success rate of 98% according to the evaluator. If the threshold is set to 95%, this attack scenario will be solved by the card placement as depicted on the right.

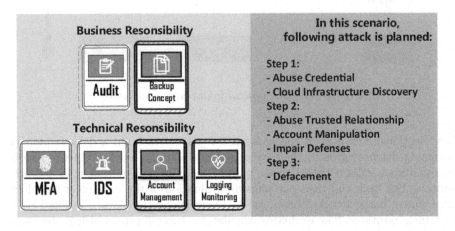

Fig. 2. Illustrative example of the game design elements

4.2   Design of CATS

In this section, we explain the design details of the important elements in CATS: Attack scenario, Submission, and Success rate.

Attack Scenario and Defense Action. To reflect facts in cloud security, the attack scenarios are derived based on real-world cyber-security attacks that have occurred and were reported in practice. In 2022 Koay et al. proposed SDGen as an approach to generate real-world cyber-security datasets [29], which is a promising proof-of-concept. In our research, we use MITRE ATT&CK cloud matrix as the source for acquiring such information [4]. We simplified the attack kill-chain into a three-step pattern: initial access, launch attack, and make impact. The effective defense actions are based on the mitigation listed for each technique [3] in the cloud matrix. In Table 5, we summarize the difficulty level and goal of each attack scenario. We derived 6 attack scenarios in total. AS1 and AS2 are the tutorial attack scenarios, where we show the impact of effective cards and correct roles. AS3 is the first attack scenario where the players are required to build a full defense plan without pre-selected cards. In AS4 and AS5, the difficulty is increased by raising the threshold. In AS6, a seldom-used attack "Exploit Unused Region" is used to increase the coverage of different attack actions and reduce repetitions from previous scenarios.

Table 5. The difficulty level and goal of each attack scenario

Attack scenario	Difficulty level	Goal
AS1	Tutorial	Show the player the impact of choosing effective defense cards
AS2	Tutorial	Show the player the impact of assigning effective cards to the correct roles
AS3	Elementary	Let the player build the first full defense plan without pre-selected cards
AS4	Advanced	Increase the difficulty by raising threshold
AS5	Advanced	Increase the difficulty by raising threshold
AS6	Expert	Increase defense coverage by using seldom used card

Submission. By hitting the "Submit" button on the game interface, the player triggers the back end to calculate the defense success rate. The submission that is sent to the back end is encoded in a JSON format [9]. It sent data includes the chosen defense cards and their corresponding assignment to the responsibilities and roles. Each submission is captured in the back end as dynamic game data for analysis. We present a brief statistic on the captured submission data in Sect. 5.

Success Rate. The success rate describes the quality of the submitted defense plan against the given attack scenario. The result is a percentage value that is limited between 0% to 99%. The success rate never reaches 100%, reflecting that in reality, a perfectly secure system does not exits. An evaluator calculates the success rate; the algorithm that is used for the computation is described in [39]. There are two reasons for a low success rate: 1) the defense card chosen does not mitigate the attack actions used in the attack scenario, and 2) the defense card is assigned to an incorrect responsibility, and thus, the defense cannot be performed.

4.3 Implementation of CATS

The game platform is implemented as a single-page web application. In the front end, we use Konva [19], a Javascript library providing the gadget necessary for the game interface, for instance, a canvass, floating images of defense cards, and a magnetic effect when the player is dragging and dropping the cards in the supposed area. In the back end, we implemented the evaluator with Python3 [34]. It calculates the success rate based on the presented attack scenario and the submission, then sends results and hints to the front-end. The application is packed into a docker image and deployed in AWS EC2 virtual machine [5]. Previous to each game event, we prepare a new virtual machine in AWS with automated scripts, and after the game event, we collect the data and dispose of the used AWS resources.

5   Design Evaluation

This section presents the design evaluation obtained during the eight game events that took place in the industry in phase 1 and the result obtained from the SSI in phase 2. In the first part, we show the result from game dynamic data on the correlation of the player behavior in relation to our expectancy. In the second part, we present the result collected from the questionnaire and SSI. In the third part, we share the feedback in open discussion.

5.1   Game Dynamic Evaluation

The players can choose from the 24 defense cards provided during the game. Each card can be helpful or useless in defending different attack actions in the given scenario, depending on if it is assigned to the correct role and if it defends any of the attack actions as provided in the attack scenario. We count the number of attack actions in our attack scenarios, to which the defense card is a proper mitigation. In that way, we can get a ranking of theoretically most helpful cards, as Table 6 shows in the third column. The card "Account Management" is in the first place, which indicates it is helpful mitigation in most of the attack actions in our scenarios.

In the game dynamic data, we counted the number of each card that appeared in all the valid submissions and got another "Ranking in Game" list in the fourth column of Table 6. In the most optimal condition, assuming the players know completely which defense cards are helpful against which attack action in all scenarios, we should get the same ranking list in the third and fourth column in Table 6. Measuring the similarity and correlation helps to gain an insight of how well the players performed over all. There are various ways to compare the similarity and correlation of the two ranking lists. In this work, we use Spearman's ρ [38] as a way to measure the correlation of two ranking lists.

5.2   Questionnaire and SSI Evaluation

Directly after each game event, we distributed a questionnaire to the participants in phase 1. Based on the eight game events we organized, we have obtained 24 valid answers from 94 participants. Table 7 gives an overview of the questions asked and the distribution of the answers. We listed nine statements in the questionnaire in Table 7. The respondents were asked to answer whether they "Strongly Disagree $(--)$", "Disagree $(-)$", "Neutral (N)", "Agree $(+)$", or "Strongly Agree $(++)$" to the statement.

Two weeks to one month after each game event, we randomly selected game participants and invited them to join an SSI in phase 2. We list the questions in Table 4. The Table 8 depicts the result of question Ph2Q1, Ph2Q13 to Ph2Q15.

We present the results of questions Ph2Q2 to Ph2Q8 in Fig. 3. The blue bar shows the players' performance in-game and the red bar shows the percentage of the correct answer in the survey in terms of assigning the defense actions to a correct role. We see that the players perform nicely in the game and survey for

Table 6. The defense cards ranking in theory, in game and in survey

No.	Defense card	Ranking in theory	Ranking in game	Ranking in SSI
1	Account Management	1	7	2
2	Network Segmentation	2	3	1
3	Restrict Permission	3	11	2
4	Logging & Monitoring	4	1	6
5	Asset Management	5	12	2
6	Filter Network Traffic	5	8	6
7	Password Policy	7	2	6
8	Audit	7	6	11
9	MFA	7	13	2
10	Critical Data Protection	10	10	11
11	Update Software	10	18	17
12	Information Encryption	10	16	20
13	Backup Concept	13	14	6
14	Application Isolation and Sandboxing	13	9	6
15	Vulnerability Scan	13	15	11
16	OS Hardening	13	16	17
17	IDS	13	5	11
18	Remove Unnecessary Feature	13	21	22
19	Application Developer Guidance	19	19	22
20	User Training	19	20	11
21	Account Use Policy	19	4	11
22	Software Configuration	22	22	20
23	Code Signing	23	24	17
24	ACP Process	24	23	22
Spearman's ρ			0.66	0.75

some defenses such as Intrusion Detection System (IDS) and Network Segmentation. However, in some other defenses, the players made more mistakes in the survey at least two weeks after the game event.

In Ph2Q9, we asked them to identify the helpful cards. We ranked their answer and summarized the result into the last column in Table 6. As shown in the Table 6, the correlation to the ranking in theory is reflected by Spearman's ρ and the SSI value is higher than the game value. The rest of the questions are open-ended questions and the result will be summarized and presented in the next part.

5.3 Evaluation from Open Discussion and Open-Ended Questions in SSI

We asked the players for their opinion in the open discussion after each game event. In Table 9, we present a selection of the feedback and answers to the

Table 7. Questionnaire after each game event - phase 1

No.	Questions	$--$	$-$	N	$+$	$++$
Ph1Q1	Playing this cloud security game helps me to understand roles and responsibilities	0%	0%	16%	63%	21%
Ph1Q2	Playing this cloud security game helps me to understand cloud attacks and defenses	0%	0%	4%	79%	17%
Ph1Q3	I benefit from the collaboration with teammates in this cloud security game	0%	8%	38%	29%	25%
Ph1Q4	I benefit from the discussion with teammates in the cloud security game	0%	8%	29%	42%	21%
Ph1Q5	I feel my cloud security know-how has improved by playing this cloud security game	0%	13%	8%	75%	4%
Ph1Q6	I would recommend this cloud security game to other colleagues	0%	8%	4%	58%	30%
Ph1Q7	Our strategy for cloud security will improve by repeatedly playing this cloud security game	0%	12%	29%	42%	17%
Ph1Q8	I think it is hard to calculate the actual probability of a successful defense	0%	0%	25%	42%	23%
Ph1Q9	I think it is hard to consider all relevant factors for a successful defense	0%	0%	21%	42%	27%

Table 8. Questions in SSI - phase 2

No.	Question	$--$	$-$	N	$+$	$++$	N.A
Ph2Q1	Please rate how much do you still remember from the cloud security game	0%	0%	20%	67%	13%	–
Ph2Q13	The game helped me in understanding the weakness in cloud security	13%	0%	13%	67%	7%	–
Ph2Q14	I think my cloud asset is secure	0%	6%	7%	27%	20%	40%
Ph2Q15	I think I still need more training in cloud security	13%	7%	27%	20%	33%	–

open-ended questions. The second column represents whether the feedback is collected in the discussion of phase 1 (Ph1D) or the answers to open-ended questions in phase 2 (Ph2Q10, Ph2Q11 and Ph2Q12). In general, the comments we received were quite positive. We will discuss the feedback in more depth in the next section.

6   Discussion

In this section, we discuss the results and share our thoughts upon them.

In Table 6, we see that in theory, the card "Account Management" helps defend against most of the attack actions. The importance of account management is sufficiently discussed in the work of Tang et al. in [37] regarding active

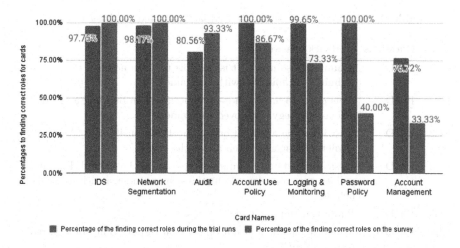

Fig. 3. The percentage of finding correct roles for cards on the survey

malicious accounts detection. However, in the game it is not the most selected card, being at the seventh position in the ranking list in the game. In the game, the most selected card is "Logging & Monitoring". This indicates that participants believe relying on logging and monitoring will improve cloud security, whereas account management contributes more in defending cloud assets. We use Spearman's ρ as a way to measure the correlation between two ranking lists. We refer to the Table 10 to interpret the calculated value as proposed in [6]. Spearman's ρ has a range between "-1" and "1". The value "-1" suggests that the two compared ranking lists are negatively correlated. That is the case when one list is the reserve of the other. "0" suggests there is no correlation between the two lists. "1" suggests that the two compared ranking lists are perfectly correlated. That is the case when two lists are identical. In our case, Spearman's ρ of our expectancy and the players' behavior in the game reached 0.66, which suggests a moderate correlation as shown in Table 10. This is a positive indicator that players' performance in the game seconds our expectancy. The players understand the game logic and grasp the fundamental concept of cloud security. In the last column of Table 6, we calculated the correlation of the expectation and the SSI, the value reached 0.75, which shows a strong correlation according to Table 10. We take it as a positive sign that the players' understanding of cloud security defense actions has improved. One possible explanation could be, during the game, the player is learning about the defenses and attacks, thus players might make mistakes. By correcting the mistakes, players deepen their knowledge about defenses and attacks and remember them. In the survey, when they are asked again, their answer shows more similarity to the optimal case. Since the SSI was conducted two weeks to one month after the game event, we can interpret the results as a possible indicator on the retention of knowledge and also on the impact of the game on the players.

Table 7 summarizes the answers to the questionnaire in phase 1. Most respondents agree that CATS helps them understand roles and responsibilities in cloud

Table 9. Selection of representative feedback collected in phase 1 and 2

No.	Questions	Feedback/Answer
FB1	Ph1D	"Thank you so much! It is possible to learn new technical vocabulary (with the game)"
FB2	Ph1D	"It is great to have hands-on experiences in building a cloud defense strategy! I enjoyed the game"
FB3	Ph1D	"Provide some explanations for both responsibilities (Asset Owner/Manager) as well as for the cards"
FB4	Ph1D	"Less abstraction and more context would be helpful. E.g. an architecture overview about the system under attack would be helpful"
FB5	Ph1D	"More time for the game"
FB6	Ph2Q10	"Cloud deployment is not one person responsibility but shared responsiblity"
FB7	Ph2Q10	"I improve my awareness"
FB8	Ph2Q10	"The game is too abstract to learn anything"
FB9	Ph2Q11	"I did't change anything"
FB10	Ph2Q12	"Add animations to the hints"

Table 10. Degree of correlation according to Spearman's Rho

Range	Degree of correlation
$0 < |\rho| < 0.3$	Weak
$0.3 < |\rho| < 0.7$	Moderate
$|\rho| > 0.7$	Strong

security, and know-how is improved by playing CATS. We imply that the player's perception of cloud security is improved by the game and the player is more aware of how to protect cloud assets. Most of them would recommend CATS to other colleagues. We interpret those answers as a positive sign that the players enjoyed CATS and could benefit from it. In question Ph1Q6, 30% of the respondents strongly agree and 58% of them agree that they would recommend the game to other colleagues, which hints at a good design of the game. In the questionnaire, we did not get any "strongly disagree" answers to all the questions, which shows the game was well received by the participants.

Table 9 shows some of the feedback and answers collected in open discussion in phase 1 and open-ended questions in phase 2. Most of them are excited about using the game as a method to learn (FB1). They are embracing the interactive exercises (FB2) and want to spend more time with the game (FB5). For some of them, the game is too abstract (FB8) and more concrete examples (FB4) and explanations (FB3) are wished. The players learned that cloud security is a shared responsibility (FB6) and they feel their awareness of cloud security is improved by playing the game (FB7). Some give constructive feedback on how to improve the game interface (FB10). We will take it into consideration in the next design iteration. In question Ph2Q11, we received lots of answers that the game did not trigger any change in their daily work (FB9) despite the increase in awareness. We would like to conduct future research on the reason behind that and to improve the game further. According to the feedback and answer we collected, it is safe to conclude that the game is suitable to raise awareness of cloud security, especially the defenses versus the attacks and the roles and responsibilities.

In our observation of eight game events, the participants mostly identify the card "Account Management" to be helpful in lots of attack scenarios. They learn about the impact of this card in the game and in the SSI in phase 2, they rank "Account Management" as the second most helpful card as shown in Table 6. This indicates that they use the game to correct their wrong understanding. Additionally, the participants seem to enjoy the game.

In phase 2, we asked the respondents to assign certain defense cards to the correct role. The results are illustrated in Fig. 3, which reflects what the players still remember after the game. For some cards such as "IDS" (Intrusion Detection Systems), "Network Segmentation", and "Audit", the correct rate increases in SSI of phase 2. For cards such as "Account Use Policy", "Logging & Monitoring", "Password Policy" and "Account Management", the correct rate decreases. Surprisingly, although the participants understand the importance of "Account Management", only 33% of the participants assigned it to the correct role in the SSI of phase 2. The card "Password Policy" has a 100% of correct rate on the role assignment during the game, however, the correct rate drops to only 40% in the SSI. There might be multiple factors that could lead to such results, e.g. daily work and chores. We need to conduct further research to understand the cause of decreasing in correct rate. It might be an indicator that the game should be played more often to solidify the lessons learned, which seconds with the results of Ph1Q7 in Table 7, almost 60% of the participants agree or strongly agree that their defense strategy for cloud security will be improved by repeatedly playing CATS.

7   Conclusion

In this work, we present CATS, a serious game dedicated to raising awareness about cloud security issues in the industry. We introduced the design elements and implementation details of CATS, and we invited 94 industrial practitioners to join the game and collect feedback from them. There are positive indicators that the participants enjoyed the interactive game, and their understanding of basic concepts in cloud security was improved. We validated our design and ideas with eight game events. We provided a preliminary analysis of collected game dynamic data and proposed a measurable way to evaluate the level of understanding of cloud security basic concepts of our game participants. We used questionnaires and semi-structured interviews to collect feedback, and the result is presented and discussed. Our work shows CATS has the potential to be applied as a useful artifact to raise awareness of cloud security in the industry. The contribution of this work is: 1) to propose an innovative serious game as an enrichment of traditional lecture-based virtual and physical training; 2) to extend the understanding of the usage of CATS in an industrial environment.

In the future, we would like to refine the evaluator algorithm and collect further feedback for improvement in additional CATS game events.

Acknowledgements. This work is partially financed by Portuguese national funds through FCT - Fundação para a Ciência e Tecnologia, I.P., under the projects FCT UIDB/04466/2020 and FCT UIDP/04466/2020. Furthermore, the third author thanks the Instituto Universitário de Lisboa and ISTAR, for their support. We acknowledge funding for project LIONS by dtec.bw.

References

1. Al Nafea, R., Almaiah, M.A.: Cyber security threats in cloud: literature review. In: 2021 International Conference on Information Technology (ICIT), pp. 779–786. IEEE (2021)
2. Cloud Security Alliance: Cloud controls matrix v4 (2021). https://cloudsecurity alliance.org/artifacts/cloud-controls-matrix-v4/
3. ATT&CK, M.: Techniques, May 2017. https://attack.mitre.org/techniques/
4. ATT&CK, M.: MITRE ATT&CK Cloud Matrix (2020). https://attack.mitre.org/versions/v8/matrices/enterprise/cloud/
5. AWS: Amazon EC2 secure and resizable compute capacity for virtually any workload, May 2022. https://aws.amazon.com/ec2
6. Casinillo, L., Tavera, G.: On the dark side of learning calculus: evidence from agribusiness students. IJIET (Int. J. Indonesian Educ. Teach.) **5**, 52–60 (2021). https://doi.org/10.24071/ijiet.v5i1.2825
7. CSA: Top threats to cloud computing: The egregious 11. BLACKHAT2019 (2019)
8. Dörner, R., Göbel, S., Effelsberg, W., Wiemeyer, J. (eds.): Serious Games. Foundations, Concepts and Practice, Springer, Cham (2016). https://doi.org/10.1007/978-3-319-40612-1
9. ECMA-404: Json format, May 2022. https://www.json.org/json-en.html
10. Espinha Gasiba, T., Andrei-Cristian, I., Lechner, U., Pinto-Albuquerque, M.: Raising security awareness of cloud deployments using infrastructure as code through cybersecurity challenges. In: The 16th International Conference on Availability, Reliability and Security. ARES 2021, Association for Computing Machinery, New York, NY, USA (2021). https://doi.org/10.1145/3465481.3470030
11. Espinha Gasiba, T., Andrei-Cristian, I., Lechner, U., Pinto-Albuquerque, M.: Raising security awareness of cloud deployments using infrastructure as code through cybersecurity challenges. In: The 16th International Conference on Availability, Reliability and Security, pp. 1–8 (2021)
12. Ferro, L.S., Marrella, A., Catarci, T., Sapio, F., Parenti, A., De Santis, M.: AWATO: a serious game to improve cybersecurity awareness. In: Fang, X. (ed.) HCI in Games, vol. 13334, pp. 508–529. Springer, Cham (2022). https://doi.org/10.1007/978-3-031-05637-6_33

13. Gasiba, T., Lechner, U., Pinto-Albuquerque, M.: Sifu-a cybersecurity awareness platform with challenge assessment and intelligent coach. Cybersecurity **3**(1), 1–23 (2020)

14. Gasiba, T., Lechner, U., Pinto-Albuquerque, M.: CyberSecurity challenges for software developer awareness training in industrial environments. In: Ahlemann, F., Schütte, R., Stieglitz, S. (eds.) WI 2021. LNISO, vol. 47, pp. 370–387. Springer, Cham (2021). https://doi.org/10.1007/978-3-030-86797-3_25

15. Gasiba, T., Lechner, U., Pinto-Albuquerque, M.: Cybersecurity challenges: serious games for awareness training in industrial environments. Federal Office for Information Security (ed.) Germany Digital Secure. 30 Years BSI - Proceedings of the 17th German IT Security Congress 2021, February 2021

16. Gasiba, T., Hodzic, S., Lechner, U., Albuquerque, M.P.: Raising awareness on secure coding in the industry through CyberSecurity challenges. Ph.D. thesis, Universität der Bundeswehr München (2021)

17. Gleasure, R.: What is a 'wicked problem' for is research? In: SIG Prag Workshop on IT Artefact Design & Workpractice Improvement, 5 June 2013, Tilburg, The Netherlands (2013)

18. Gleeson, N., Walden, I.: 'It's a jungle out there'?: Cloud Computing, Standards and the Law. SSRN Electron. J. (2014). https://doi.org/10.2139/ssrn.2441182

19. Group, K.: Konva.js - html5 2D canvas js library for desktop and mobile applications, May 2022. https://konvajs.org/

20. Hänsch, N., Benenson, Z.: Specifying IT security awareness. In: 2014 25th International Workshop on Database and Expert Systems Applications, pp. 326–330. IEEE (2014)

21. Hart, S., Margheri, A., Paci, F., Sassone, V.: Riskio: a serious game for cyber security awareness and education. Comput. Secur. **95**, 101827 (2020). https://doi.org/10.1016/j.cose.2020.101827

22. Hevner, A.: A three cycle view of design science research. Scand. J. Inf. Syst. **19**, 4 (2007)

23. Hevner, A., March, S., Park, J.: Design science in information systems research. Manage. Inf. Syst. Q. **28**, 75–105 (2004)

24. Iosif, A.C., Gasiba, T.E., Zhao, T., Lechner, U., Pinto-Albuquerque, M.: A large-scale study on the security vulnerabilities of cloud deployments. In: Wang, G., Choo, K.K.R., Ko, R.K.L., Xu, Y., Crispo, B. (eds.) Ubiquitous Security (UbiSec 2021), pp. 171–188. Springer, Singapore (2022). https://doi.org/10.1007/978-981-19-0468-4_13

25. ISO27002: ISO/IEC 27002:2013 information technology - security techniques - code of practice for information security controls (2013). https://www.iso.org/standard/54533.html

26. ISO27017: ISO/IEC 27017:2015 information technology - security techniques - code of practice for information security controls based on ISO/IEC 27002 for cloud services (2015). https://www.iso.org/standard/43757.html

27. Jakóbik, A.: Stackelberg game modeling of cloud security defending strategy in the case of information leaks and corruption. Simul. Model. Pract. Theory **103**, 102071 (2020)

28. Jakóbik, A., Palmieri, F., Kołodziej, J.: Stackelberg games for modeling defense scenarios against cloud security threats. J. Netw. Comput. Appl. **110**, 99–107 (2018)

29. Koay, A.M.Y., Xie, M., Ko, R.K.L., Sterner, C., Choi, T., Dong, N.: SDGen: a scalable, reproducible and flexible approach to generate real world cyber security

datasets. In: Wang, G., Choo, K.K.R., Ko, R.K.L., Xu, Y., Crispo, B. (eds.) Ubiquitous Security (UbiSec 2021), pp. 102–115. Springer, Singapore (2022). https://doi.org/10.1007/978-981-19-0468-4_8

30. Landers, R.N.: Developing a theory of gamified learning: linking serious games and gamification of learning. Simul. Gaming **45**(6), 752–768 (2014)

31. Landers, R.N.: Gamification misunderstood: how badly executed and rhetorical gamification obscures its transformative potential. J. Manag. Inq. **28**(2), 137–140 (2019)

32. NIST: National institute of standards and technology (2022). https://www.nist.gov/

33. Peter Mell (NIST), T.G.N.: SP 800–145 the NIST definition of cloud computing, September 2011. https://csrc.nist.gov/publications/detail/sp/800-145/final

34. Python3: Python is a programming language that lets you work quickly and integrate systems more effectively, May 2022. https://www.python.org/

35. Shostack, A.: Tabletop security games & cards (2021). https://shostack.org/games.html

36. Švábenský, V., Vykopal, J., Cermak, M., Laštovička, M.: Enhancing cybersecurity skills by creating serious games. In: Proceedings of the 23rd Annual ACM Conference on Innovation and Technology in Computer Science Education, pp. 194–199 (2018)

37. Tang, Y., Zhang, D., Liang, W., Li, K.C., Sukhija, N.: Active malicious accounts detection with multimodal fusion machine learning algorithm. In: Wang, G., Choo, K.K.R., Ko, R.K.L., Xu, Y., Crispo, B. (eds.) Ubiquitous Security (UbiSec 2021), vol. 1557, pp. 38–52. Springer, Singapore (2022). https://doi.org/10.1007/978-981-19-0468-4_4

38. Wiki, E.: Spearman's rank correlation coefficient (1988). https://www.viewer.vn/wiki

39. Zhao, T., Gasiba, T., Lechner, U., Pinto-Albuquerque, M.: Raising awareness about cloud security in industry through a board game. Information **12**(11), 482 (2021). https://doi.org/10.3390/info12110482

40. Zhao, T., Gasiba, T.E., Lechner, U., Pinto-Albuquerque, M.: Exploring a board game to improve cloud security training in industry. In: Henriques, P.R., Portela, F., Queirós, R., Simões, A. (eds.) Second International Computer Programming Education Conference (ICPEC 2021). Open Access Series in Informatics (OASIcs), vol. 91, pp. 11:1–11:8. Schloss Dagstuhl - Leibniz-Zentrum für Informatik, Dagstuhl, Germany (2021). https://doi.org/10.4230/OASIcs.ICPEC.2021.11, https://drops.dagstuhl.de/opus/volltexte/2021/14227

41. Zhao, T., Lechner, U., Pinto-Albuquerque, M., Ata, E.: Cloud of assets and threats: a playful method to raise awareness for cloud security in industry. In: Simões, A., Silva, J.A.C. (eds.) Third International Computer Programming Education Conference (ICPEC 2022). Open Access Series in Informatics (OASIcs), vol. 102, pp. 6:1–6:13. Schloss Dagstuhl - Leibniz-Zentrum für Informatik, Dagstuhl, Germany (2022). https://doi.org/10.4230/OASIcs.ICPEC.2022.6, https://drops.dagstuhl.de/opus/volltexte/2022/16610

Automated Vulnerability Detection in Source Code Using Quantum Natural Language Processing

Mst Shapna Akter[1]([⊠]), Hossain Shahriar[2], and Zakirul Alam Bhuiya[3]

[1] Department of Computer Science, Kennesaw State University, Kennesaw, USA
`makter2@students.kennesaw.edu`
[2] Department Information Technology, Kennesaw State University, Kennesaw, USA
`hshahria@kennesaw.edu`
[3] Department of Computer and Information Sciences, Fordham University,
New York, USA

Abstract. One of the most important challenges in the field of software code audit is the presence of vulnerabilities in software source code. Every year, more and more software flaws are found, either internally in proprietary code or revealed publicly. These flaws are highly likely exploited and lead to system compromise, data leakage, or denial of service. C and C++ open-source codes are now available in order to create a large-scale, classical machine-learning and quantum machine-learning system for function-level vulnerability identification. We assembled a sizable dataset of millions of open-source functions that point to potential exploits. We created an efficient and scalable vulnerability detection method based on a deep neural network model– Long Short-Term Memory (LSTM), and quantum machine learning model– Long Short-Term Memory (QLSTM), that can learn features extracted from the source codes. The source code is first converted into a minimal intermediate representation to remove the pointless components and shorten the dependency. Previous studies lack analyzing features of the source code that causes models to recognize flaws in real-life examples. Therefore, We keep the semantic and syntactic information using state-of-the-art word embedding algorithms such as Glove and fastText. The embedded vectors are subsequently fed into the classical and quantum convolutional neural networks to classify the possible vulnerabilities. To measure the performance, we used evaluation metrics such as F1 score, precision, recall, accuracy, and total execution time. We made a comparison between the results derived from the classical LSTM and quantum LSTM using basic feature representation as well as semantic and syntactic representation. We found that the QLSTM with semantic and syntactic features detects significantly accurate vulnerability and runs faster than its classical counterpart.

Keywords: Cyber security · Vulnerability detection · Classical machine learning · Feature extraction · Quantum natural language processing

G. Wang et al. (Eds.): UbiSec 2022, CCIS 1768, pp. 83–102, 2023.
https://doi.org/10.1007/978-981-99-0272-9_6

1   Introduction

Security in the digital sphere is a matter of increasing relevance. However, there is a significant invasion threat to cyberspace. Security vulnerabilities caused by buried bugs in software may make it possible for attackers to penetrate systems and apps. Each year, thousands of these vulnerabilities are found internally in proprietary code [1].

Recent well-publicized exploits have demonstrated that these security flaws can have catastrophic impacts on society and the economy in our healthcare, energy, defense, and other critical infrastructure systems [2]. For instance, the ransomware Wannacry swept the globe by using a flaw in the Windows server message block protocol [3,4]. According to the Microsoft Security Response Center, half of 2015 had an industry-wide surge in high-severity vulnerabilities of 41.7%. Furthermore, according to a Frost and Sullivan (a global growth consulting company) analysis released in 2018, there was an increase in severe and high severity vulnerabilities in Google Project, going from 693 in 2016 to 929 in 2017, with zero coming in second place in terms of disclosing such flaws. On August 14, 2019, Intel issued a warning on a high-severity vulnerability in the software it uses to identify the specifications of Intel processors in Windows PCs [5]. The paper claims that these defects, including information leaking and denial of service assaults, might substantially affect software systems. Although the company issued an update to remedy the problems, an attacker can still use these vulnerabilities to escalate their privileges on a machine that has already been compromised.

A good technique to lessen the loss is early vulnerability discovery. The proliferation of open-source software and code reuse makes these vulnerabilities susceptible to rapid propagation. Source code analysis tools are already available; however, they often only identify a small subset of potential problems based on pre-established rules.

Software vulnerabilities can be found using a technique called vulnerability detection. Static and dynamic techniques are used in conventional vulnerability detection [6]. Static approaches evaluate source code or executable code without launching any programs, such as data flow analysis, symbol execution [7], and theorem proving [8]. Static approaches can be used early in software development and have excellent coverage rates. It has a significant false positive rate. By executing the program, dynamic approaches like fuzzy testing [9], and dynamic symbol execution [10] can confirm or ascertain the nature of the software. Dynamic methods depend on the coverage of test cases, which results in a low recall despite their low false positive rate and ease of implementation.

The advancement of machine learning technology incorporates new approaches to address the limitations of conventional approaches. One key research direction is developing intelligent source code-based vulnerability detection systems. It can be divided into three categories: using software engineering metrics, anomaly detection, and weak pattern learning. To train a machine learning model, software engineering measures, including software complexity, developer activity, and code commits were initially investigated. This strategy was motivated by the idea that software becomes more susceptible as it becomes more complicated. However, in those works, accuracy, and recall need to be enhanced.

Numerous research organizations are utilizing the potential of quantum machine learning (QML) to handle massive volumes of data with the aid of quantum random access memory (QRAM) [11]. In general, the phrase "Quantum Machine Learning" refers to a field that combines quantum computing, quantum algorithms, and classical machine learning. In this field, real-world machine learning problems are addressed using algorithms that make use of the effectiveness and concepts of quantum computing [12]. Quantum computers have enormous processing capacity due to the core ideas of quantum machine learning, such as quantum coherence, superposition, and entanglement, which pave the way for the increasingly widespread use of quantum computing in technological disciplines [13]. In contrast to traditional computing, the fundamental building block of quantum computing, the Qubit, can use both 0 and 1 to pursue several computation routes concurrently [14]. A qubit state is a vector in two-dimensional space, shown by the linear combination of the two basis states ($|0>$, and $|1>$) in a quantum system: $|\psi> = \alpha|0> + \beta|1>$, where α, $\beta \in C$ are probability amplitudes required to satisfy $|\alpha|2 + |\beta|2 = 1$. Such a sequence of basis states is referred to as quantum superposition, while the correlations between two qubits through a quantum phenomenon are termed entanglement.

We have come up with a solution for detecting software vulnerabilities using a deep neural network model– Long Short-Term Memory (LSTM), and a quantum machine learning model– Long Short-Term Memory (QLSTM), that learns features extracted from the source codes. We first transformed the samples of source code into the minimum intermediate representations through dependency analysis, program slicing, tokenization, and serialization. Later, we extracted semantic features using word embedding algorithms such as GloVe and fastText. After finishing the data preprocessing stage, we fed the input representation to the LSTM and QLSTM. We found that QLSTM provides the highest result in terms of accuracy, precision, recall, and f1 score, which are 95, 97, 98, and 99%, respectively.

The contribution of this project is as follows:

1. We extracted semantic and syntactic analysis using FastText and Glove word embeddings. Sequential models have the drawback of not understanding the pattern in the text data; it is very tough to catch a similar pattern when unseen data arrives. However, it can be solved by extracting semantic features that can help the models recognize the pattern based on the context, even if unseen data comes.
2. We developed a Quantum Long-short Term Memory algorithm for dealing with sequential data. We have shown how to develop a quantum machine-learning algorithm for detecting software vulnerability.
3. We made a comparative analysis between the results derived from the classical LSTM model and the quantum LSTM model using the basic features as well as semantic and syntactic features.
4. We used both the accuracy and efficiency measurements.

We organize the rest of the paper as follows: We provided a brief background study on classical machine learning and quantum machine learning in Sect. 2. In Sect. 3, we explain the methods we followed for our experimental research. The results derived from the experiment are demonstrated in Sect. 4. Finally, Sect. 5 concludes the paper.

2   Literature Review

Researchers are interested in the recently developed quantum machine learning strategy for identifying and preventing software and cybersecurity vulnerabilities [1] to address the shortcomings of conventional machine learning techniques. For classifying software security activities like malware, ransomware, and network intrusion detection, various machine learning techniques, including Neural Networks, Naive Bayes, Logistic Regression, Recurrent Neural Networks (RNN), Decision Trees, and Support Vector Machines are successfully used. We have tried to go through the classical machine learning and Quantum machine learning-related papers that have been applied to the software security domain.

Previously, Zeng et al. [15] reviewed software vulnerability analysis and discovery using deep learning techniques. They found four game changers who contributed most to the software vulnerability using deep learning techniques. Game-changer works describe concepts like– automatic semantic feature extraction using deep learning models, end-to-end solutions for detecting buffer error vulnerabilities, applying a bidirectional Long Short Term Memory (BiLSTM) model for vulnerability detection, and deep learning-based vulnerability detector for binary code.

Yamaguchi et al. [16] showed an anomaly detection technique for taint-style vulnerabilities. It groups the variables that pass on to functions with sensitive security. Then, the violation is reported as a potential vulnerability by anomaly detection. This strategy works well with taint-style vulnerability but not with all vulnerabilities.

Wang et al. [17] proposed an automatic semantic learning process using deep learning models for defect detection in source code. They used DBN, a generative graphical model capable of learning representation that can reconstruct training data with a high probability. The input they provided are [..., if, foo, for, bar, ...] and [..., foo, for, if, bar, ...], respectively. Compared to the traditional features, their semantic features improve WPDP on average by 14.7% in precision, 11.5% in the recall, and 14.2% in F1 score.

Kim et al. [18] proposed a technique for identifying similarity-based vulnerabilities. Although, this approach is only effective against vulnerabilities brought on by code cloning.

A comparison study based on the effectiveness of quantum machine learning (QML) and classical machine learning was shown by Christopher Havenstein et al. [19]. The authors worked on reproducible code and applied ML and QML algorithms. Later, quantum variational SVMs were used instead of conventional SVMs since they exhibit greater accuracy. The future potential of quantum multi-class SVM classifiers are highlighted in their conclusion.

Quantum machine learning (QML) research was carried out by Mohammad Masum et al. [20] to identify software supply chain attacks. The researchers used a variety of cutting-edge techniques, such as the Quantum Support Vector Machine (QSVM) and Quantum Neural Network, to examine how to accelerate the performance of quantum computing (QNN). The authors discovered two open-source quantum simulators—IBM Qiskit and TensorFlow quantum for software supply chain threats detection. The study's conclusions indicate that quantum machine learning is superior to classical machine learning in terms of computing time and processing speed.

MJH Faruk et al. [21] studied quantum cybersecurity from both threats and opportunity perspectives. The authors have provided a comprehensive review of state-of-the-art quantum computing-based cybersecurity approaches. The research indicated that quantum computing can be utilized to address software security, cybersecurity, and cryptographic-related concerns. On the other hand, the malicious individual also misuses quantum computing against software infrastructure due to the immense power of quantum computers.

Payares and Martinez-Santos [22] demonstrated the importance of using generalized coherent states for the SVM model. SVM is a classical machine learning model, and coherent states are a calculational tool here. They used the RKHS concept to connect the thread in the SVM model. Such reproducing kernels are responsible for the overlapping situation of canonical and generalized coherent states. Canonical coherent states regenerate the radial kernels while the POVM calculates the overlap functions, which eventually decreases the computational times when the high dimensional feature problem arises. The Quantum version of SVM recently played an important role in solving classification and detection problems, but the quantum version of LSTM is unexplored.

Khan and Pal [23] proposed a quantum computing-based technique for developing reverse engineering gene regulatory networks using a time-series gene expression dataset. The model they used is recurrent neural networks. The method they used is comparatively new, and the results are satisfactory. They applied a 4-gene artificial genetic network model as part of experimental work and proposed a 10-gene and 20-gene genetic network. They found that quantum computing provides very good accuracy and it reduces the execution time.

Choi et al. [24] proposed a brief description of Quantum Graph Recurrent Neural Networks (QGRNN). Previously, several works have been done in the machine learning field with some optimized models. Graph Neural Networks is a subfield of machine learning which came to the focus. Researchers developed a quantum graph neural network using circuits that convert the bits into qubits. Among the other quantum machine learning models, the quantum graph recurrent neural network (QGRNN) is proven to be more effective. They proposed a Variational Quantum Eigensolver (VQE) for converting the bits into quantum states and the converting them into QGRNN.

Oh et al. [25] provided a survey on Quantum Convolutional Neural Network (QCNN). QCNN is a quantum version of classical CNN. It is sometimes very challenging when data comes with high dimensions and thus makes the model very large. But the quantum version of CNN overcomes such issues and improves performance, and makes the model efficient. The first study proposes a quantum circuit that uses Multi-scale Entanglement Renormalization Ansatz (MERA). The second work they showed used a hybrid learning model, which adds a quantum convolution layer.

Lu et al. [26] proposed a Quantum Convolutional Neural Network to find the optimal number of convolutional layers. They used CIFAR10 for training VGG-19 and 20-layer, 32-layer, 44-layer, and 56-layer CNN networks. Then they compare the difference between the optimal and non-optimal CNN models. They found that the accuracy drops from 90% to 80% as the layers increases to 56 layers. However, the CNN with optimization made it possible as the accuracy is more than 90%, and the parameters are reduced by half. Their experiment indicates that the proposed method can improve the network performance degradation very well, which causes by hidden convolutional layers, and reduce the computing resources.

3   Methodology

We adopted a Quantum Long Short-Term Memory (QLSTM), a subfield of Quantum Machine Learning (QML), for this research and applied the model to the text dataset. Figure 1 demonstrates the framework representing the implementation process. At first, we pre-processed raw data prior to providing it as input to the QML model. We used Python, keras tokenizer, sklearn LabelEncoder, Keras sequence, Keras padding, Keras embedding, Glove, and FastText embeddings for pre-processing the dataset. Keras library has been used to extract the basic input representation and the semantic and syntactic representations have been extracted using Glove and FastText Embeddings. For the experiment, we consider only the balanced portions of the dataset, which contains an almost equal number of vulnerable and non-vulnerable datasets, to avoid underfitting or overfitting. In quantum machine learning models, we need to feed numerical values, so we converted text data into numerical values, and all the numerical values were normalized to maintain a similar scale. We made a comparison with results derived from LSTM and QLSTM models with or without training the semantic and syntactic representations. Results have been shown in Sect. 4.

The sigmoid layer state's equation is:

3.1   Dataset Specification

From the standpoint of the source code, the majority of flaws originate in a crucial process that poses security risks. The function, assignment, or control statement considers the primary operation. An adversary can affect this crucial

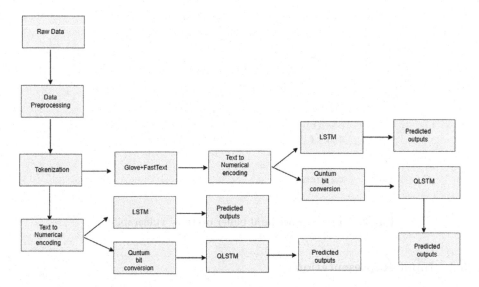

Fig. 1. Framework representation of the implementation process.

operation either directly or indirectly by manipulating certain factors or circumstances. A large number of training examples are required to train machine learning models that can effectively learn the patterns of security vulnerabilities directly from code. We chose to analyze software packages at the function-level because it is the lowest granularity level that captures a subroutine's overall flow. We compiled a vast dataset of millions of function level examples of C and C++ code from the SATE IV Juliet Test Suite, Debian Linux distribution, and public Git repositories on GitHub described in the paper of Russel [27]. In this project we have used CWE-119 vulnerability feature. CWE-119 indicates issues associated with buffer overflow vulnerability. A buffer overflow occurs when data is written to the buffer that is longer than the buffer itself, overwriting storage units outside the buffer in the process. According to a 2019 report from Common Weakness Enumeration, the buffer overflow vulnerability has evolved into the vulnerability that has been most adversely affected. Although we have used the buffer overflow issue as an example, our method can be used to find other kinds of vulnerabilities as well. Figure 2 illustrates an intra-procedural buffer overflow vulnerability.

The data we have used in this project can be found in this link: https://cwe.mitre.org/data/definitions/119.html. The dataset has a subfolder: train, validation, and test. Each of the folders contains a CSV file. The CSV file stores the text data and corresponding labeling. We analyzed the dataset and found some common words with it's corresponding counts: = (505570), if (151663), n (113301), == (92654), return (77438), * (71897), the (71595), int (53673), < (43703), + (41855), for (35849), char (33334), else (31358).

```
1   void bar(char *buf, char *src) {
2       strcpy(buf, src);
3   }
4   int main() {
5       char buf[10];
6       char src[10];
7       memset(src, 'A', 10);
8       src[10 - 1] = '\0';
9       bar(buf, src);
10      for (int i = 0; i <= 10; i++)
11      //writes buf [10] and overruns memory
12          buf[i] = 'B';
13      return 0;
14  }
```

Fig. 2. An intra-procedural buffer overflow vulnerability.

3.2   Input Representation

The basic input representation technique is representing each word with a number, eventually creating a pattern. The neural networks sometimes fail to learn in-depth patterns and thus not giving accurate results for real-life examples. The biased nature of data occurs in this case, and the model can recognize data only with the same pattern. In real life, all data are not the same. To overcome this issue, Glove and fasTest have been developed to extract the semantic and syntactic features. Even with different patterns, a model trained with semantic and syntactic features is able to recognize the vulnerability with the help of context of words.

Tokenizer. In the natural language processing project, the basic units called words are mandatory to concentrate on the computational process. In the NLP field, the word is also known as a token. Tokenization is a process that separates sentences into small units that can be used for several purposes. With this concept, Keras provides a tokenizer library called Tokenizer. Tokenizer contains two methods named tokenize() and detokenize(). The methods go through the plain text and separate the word. We used the Keras tokenizer for our initial data preprocessing step [28].

GloVe. Semantic vector space language algorithms replace each word with a vector. The vectors are useful since the machine cannot understand words but a vector. Therefore, numerous applications can make use of these vectors as features– question answering [29], parsing [30], document classification [31], information retrieval, and named entity recognition [32]. The glove is a language algorithm for prevailing vector representations of words. This is an unsupervised learning algorithm; the training process has been performed on global word-word co-occurrence statistics from a corpus [33].

Pennington et al. [33] dispute that the online scanning process followed by word2vec is inferior as it does not provides global statistical values about word co-occurrences. The model produces a vector space with a valid substructure with 75% of performance on a real-life example. GloVe was built on two concepts–local context window and global matrix factorization. CBOW and skip-Gram are Local context window methods. CBOW is better for frequent words, whereas Skip-gram works well on small datasets with rare observations. While global matrix factorization is the matrix factorization method that derives from linear algebra is responsible for reducing the long-term frequency matrices. The matrices constitute the occurrence of words.

FastText. FasText is an embedding method that uses a word's deep-down structure to improve the vector representations acquired from the skip-gram method. Modifications such as sub-word generation and skip-gram with negative sampling happen in the skip-gram method to develop the fasText model.

Sub-word generation: For a specific word, it generates character n-grams of length 3–6. The source code mostly uses words such as return, char, else, and int shown in Table 1 and Fig. 3. The first step would be to take a word and add an angular bracket. It denotes the beginning and end of the word. For instance ⟨Return⟩, ⟨char⟩, ⟨int⟩. This approach conserves the interpretation of short words that may come up as n-grams of other words. Moreover, it captures the meaning of suffixes and prefixes. The length of n-grams can be controlled by using -maxn and -minn flags for the maximum and the minimum number of characters [34]. The fastText model is somewhat considered a bag of words model aside from the n-gram window selection. No internal structure is present for the featurization of the words. However, the n-gram embeddings can be turned off by setting it as 0, which is useful for some particular words which do not bring any meaning in the entire corpus. The purpose of putting ids in words is while updating the model, fastText learns weights for each of the n-grams as well as the entire word token [35].

3.3   Classification Models

The vector representation of the software source code has been fed to the LSTM, and QLSTM models. The dataset has been divided into training and validation portions for the purpose of training the models. Finally, the test dataset is used to evaluate each trained model.

Long Short-Term Memory (LSTM). LSTM is A popular artificial Recurrent Neural Network (RNN) model, which works with datasets that preserve sequences such as text, time series, video, and speech. Using this model for sequential datasets is effectiveSince as it can handle single data points. It follows the Simple RNN model's design and an extended version of that model. However, unlike Simple RNN, it has the capability of memorizing prior value points since it developed for recognizing long-term dependencies in the text dataset. Three layers make up an RNN architecture: input layer, hidden layer, and output layer [36],[?]. Figure 3 depicts the LSTM's structural layout. The elementary state of RNN architecture is shown as the mathematical function:

$$h_t = f(h_{t-1}, x_t; \theta) \tag{1}$$

Here, θ denotes the function parameter, h_t denotes the current hidden state, x_t denotes the current input, f denotes the function of previous hidden state.

When compared to a very large dataset, the RNN architecture's weakness is the tendency to forget data items that are either necessary or unneeded. Due to the nature of time-series data, there is a long-term dependency between the current data and the preceding data. The LSTM model has been specifically developed to address this kind of difficulty. It is first proposed by Hochreiter Long [37].

This model's main contribution is its ability to retain long-term dependency data by erasing redundant data and remembering crucial data at each update step of gradient descent [38]. The LSTM architecture contains four parts: a cell, an input gate, an output gate, and a forget cell [39].

The purpose of the forget cell is to eliminate extraneous data by determining which data should be eliminated based on the state (t) − 1 and input x(t) at the state c(t) − 1.

At each cell state, the sigmoid function of the forget gate retains all 1s that are deemed necessary values and eliminates all 0s that are deemed superfluous [37]. The forget gate state's equation is stated as follows:

$$f_t = \sigma(W_f.[h_{t-1}, x_t] + b_f) \tag{2}$$

where f_t denotes sigmoid activation function, h_{t-1} denotes output from previous hidden state, W_f denotes weights of forget gate, b_f denotes bias of forgetting gate function, and finally x_t denotes current input.

After erasing the unneeded value, new values are updated in the cell state. Three steps make up the procedure: The first step is deciding which values need to update using sigmoid layer called the "input gate layer". Second, creating a vector of new candidate values using the tanh layer. Finally, steps 1 and 2 are combined together to create and update the state.

The equation for the sigmoid layer is as follows:

$$i_t = \sigma(W_i.[h_{t-1}, x_t] + b_i) \tag{3}$$

The tanh layer generates a vector of new candidates for producing a new value to the state $C(t)$, while the sigmoid layer determines which value should be updated.

The equation for tanh layer's equation is as follows:

$$\tilde{C}(t) = \tanh(W_c.[h_{t-1}, x_t] + b_C) \tag{4}$$

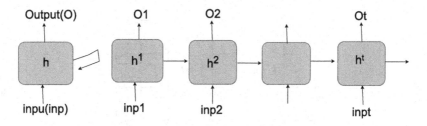

Fig. 3. LSTM neural network structure.

The addition of $\tilde{C}(t) * it$ and $Ct - 1 * ft$ updates the new cell at state $C(t)$. The updated state's equation is:

$$C_t = C_{t-1} * f_t + \tilde{C}(t) * i_t \tag{5}$$

In order to determine which output needs to be maintained, the output is ultimately filtered out using the sigmoid and the tanh functions.

$$O_t = \sigma(W_o.[h_{t-1}, x_t] + b_o) \tag{6}$$

$$h_t = O_t * \tanh(C_t) \tag{7}$$

In this state, h_t gives outputs that are used for the input of the next hidden layer.

Quantum Long Short-Term Memory (QLSTM). We propose a novel framework of a modified version of the recurrent neural network- Long short-term memory (LSTM) with Variational Quantum Circuits (VQCs), basic functions discussed briefly in the following section. The model has been implemented using a hybrid quantum-classical approach, which is fitted for NISQ devices as the approach utilizes the greater expressive power during the iterative optimization process provided by the quantum entanglement.

Variational Quantum Circuits (VQCs): A quantum circuit with tunable parameters. We choose the circuit to use in the NISQ device as it is robust against quantum noise [40]. Moreover, VQCs are more intensive than classical neural networks as it has the ability to represent certain functions with a limited number of parameters [41]. Recurrent Neural Networks approximate any computable function, even with one single hidden layer; Therefore, pairing the LSTM model with the VCQs enables the learning process very fast [42]. It has been successfully experimented on several tasks such as classification [43], function approximation [44], generative modeling [45], deep reinforcement learning [46], and transfer learning [47]. The architecture for this circuit is demonstrated in Fig. 4.

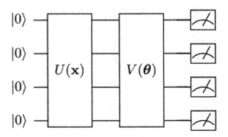

Fig. 4. Variational Quantum Circuit's architecture

The U(x) block represents the state preparation which converts the classical input x into the quantum state. In contrast, the block represents the variational part along with the learnable parameters for doing optimization during the gradient descent process. We measure a subset of the encoded qubits to retrieve a classical bit string, for example, 0100.

Quantum LSTM. We modify the traditional LSTM architecture into a quantum version by replacing the neural networks in the LSTM cells with Variational Quantum Circuits (VQCs) [42]. The VQCs play roles in both feature extraction as well as data compression. The components we used for the VCQs are shown in Fig. 5.

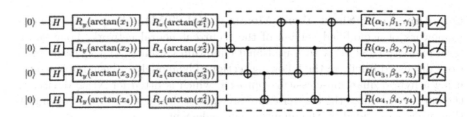

Fig. 5. Components for VQCs

The circuit consists of three parts: data encoding, variational layer, and quantum measurements. Data encoding transforms the classical data into a quantum state. The variational layer updates itself during gradient descent and plays the optimization role [42]. The quantum measurements retrieve the values for further processing. The expected values have been calculated using the simulation software, as we do not have access to the real quantum computer. We have shown the Quantum LSTM architecture in Fig. 6.

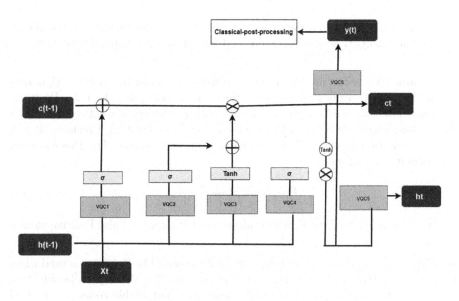

Fig. 6. QLSTM Architecture

$x(t)$ refers to the input at time t, ht refers to the hidden state, ct refers to the cell state, and yt refers to the output. The blocks σ and tanh represent the sigmoid and the hyperbolic tangent activation function, respectively. Finally, the $\otimes$ and $\oplus$ represents element-wise multiplication and addition. The mathematical functions [42] for each state of QLSTM model are stated below:

$$it = \sigma(VQC_2(v_t))$$
$$C'_t = \text{Tanh } (VQC_3(v_t))$$
$$c_t = f_t * c_t - 1 + i_t * C'_t$$
$$o_t = \sigma(VQC_4(v_t))$$
$$h_t = \sigma(VQC_5(ot * tanh(c_t))$$
$$yt = VQC_6(o_t * \tanh(c_t))$$

3.4 Evaluation Metrics

Evaluating a model's performance is necessary since it shows how close the model's predicted outputs are to the corresponding expected outputs. The evaluation metrics are used to evaluate a model's performance. However, the evaluation metrics differ with the types of models. The types of models are classification and regression. Regression refers to the problem that involves predicting a numeric value. Classification refers to the problem that involves predicting a discrete value. The regression problem uses the error metric for evaluating the models. Unlike the regression problem model, the classification problem uses the accuracy metric for evaluation. Since our motive is to detect the vulnerabilities, we used accuracy, f1 score, Precision, and Recall for our evaluation metric [?].

Precision: When the model predicts positive, it should be specified that how much the positive values are correct. Precision is used when the False Positives are high. For vulnerability classification, if the model gives low Precision, then many non-vulnerable codes will be detected as flaws; for high Precision, it will ignore the False positive values by learning with false alarms. The Precision can be calculated as follows:

$$Precision = \frac{TP}{TP + FP} \tag{8}$$

Here TP refers to True Positive values and FP refers to False Positive values.

Recall: The metric recall is the opposite of Precision. The Precision is used when the false negatives (FN) are high. In the vulnerability detection classification problem, if the model gives low recall, then many vulnerable codes will be said as non-vulnerable; for high recall, it will ignore the false negative values by learning with false alarms. The recall can be calculated as follows:

$$Recall = \frac{TP}{TP + FP} \tag{9}$$

F1 Score: F1 score combines Precision and recall and provides an overall accuracy measurement of the model. The value of the F1 score lies between 1 and 0. If the predicted value matches with the expected value, then the f1 score gives 1, and if none of the values matches with the expected value, it gives 0. The F1 score can be calculated as follows:

$$F1score = \frac{2 \cdot precision \cdot recall}{precision + recall} \tag{10}$$

Accuracy: Accuracy determines how close the predicted output is to the actual value.

$$Accuracy = \frac{TP + TN}{TP + TN + FP + FN} \tag{11}$$

here, TN refers to True Negative and FN refers to False Negative.

4   Result and Discussion

From the previous study, we found that the application of quantum models has not been applied to the software security field. Since, the majority of software companies face a surge due to software flaws, those require a system that can provide an accurate result as well as efficiency. Before training the neural networks, several criteria need to be followed. One important criterion is feature analysis. There is a huge chance that a classifier performs poorly due to the lack of feature analysis techniques. As investigators did not consider the in-depth feature analysis process in software security field, we have shown a step-by-step process for extracting the semantic and syntactic features. We developed the LSTM model with the same number of parameters for both the classical and quantum versions to get a clear observation. We implemented the classical LSTM architecture using TensorFlow with 50 hidden units.

It has a softmax layer to convert the output to a single target value y_t. The total number of parameters is 123301 in the classical LSTM. In case of QLSTM, we used 6 VQCs shown in Fig. 5. Each of the VQCs consists of 4 qubits with 2 depths in each variational layer. Additionally, there are 2 parameters for scaling in the final step. The total number of parameter is 122876. We chose pennylane as our simulation environment for the quantum circuit. Through our experimental results, we found that the QLSTM learns faster than the classical LSTM does with a similar number of parameters. Our comparative analysis between the classical Long Short-Term Memory model and the quantum long Short-Term Memory model illustrates in Tables 1 and 2.

Table 1. Vulnerable source code classification results using classical LSTM and Quantum LSTM with no word embedding algorithms

Models	Accuracy	Precision	Recall	F1 score	Execution time
LSTM	0.90	0.90	0.90	0.92	40 min 2 s
QLSTM	**0.94**	**0.99**	**0.98**	**0.99**	**13 min 52 s**

Table 2. Vulnerable source code classification results using classical LSTM and Quantum LSTM with embedding algorithms GloVe + fastText

Models	Accuracy	Precision	Recall	F1 Score	Execution time
LSTM	0.92	0.93	0.95	0.97	42 min 13 s
QLSTM	**0.95**	**0.97**	**0.98**	**0.99**	**19 min 11 s**

Table 1 shows the result derived from LSTM and QLSTM with basic input representation, whereas Table 2 shows the result derived from LSTM and QLSTM with semantic and syntactic representation. For both cases, we found that the Quantum version of the LSTM model provides better accuracy and comparatively runs faster. LSTM with basic representation provides 90% accuracy, 90% precision, 90% recall, and 92% F1-Score. In comparison, QLSTM with the same basic input representation provides 94% Accuracy, 99% precision, 98% recall, and 99% of the F1 score. Classical LSTM with semantic representation provides 92% accuracy, 93% precision, 95% Recall, and 97% F1 score. While quantum LSTM with semantic representation provides 95% accuracy, 97% precision, 98% recall, and 99% f1 score. We also found that by using the Glove +

FastText word embedding model, the accuracy improves, but the execution time becomes higher. LSTM with basic input representation, LSTM with semantic and syntactic representation, QLSTM with basic input representation, QLSTM with semantic and syntactic representation takes 40 min 2 s, 42 min 13 s, 13 min 52 s, and 19 min 11 s, respectively. Further, we explored the learning capability of the periodic function of our QML model. The sine function: $y = sin(x)$ (3) is easier to represent and more effective for comparing. The results are shown in Fig. 7 and 8. We used 30 epochs, and the models iterated through each model and learned. In each epoch, it learns and optimizes in different batches of inputs. Therefore we can make an observation by comparing the learning representation of the first and last epochs. The vertical blue line represents actual data, and the red line represents the predicted output.

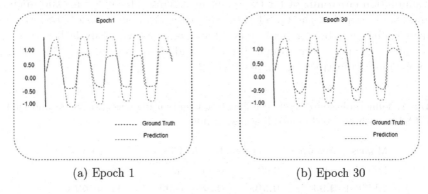

(a) Epoch 1   (b) Epoch 30

Fig. 7. Comparison between sine function learning result obtained from jupyter notebook using LSTM+ Glove + FasText model

From the sinusoidal graph, we found that QLSTM learns better than LSTM. We also point out that QLSTM learns significantly more information from the first epoch while LSTM gradually learns and improves in the last epoch, still lacking the proper learning capability.

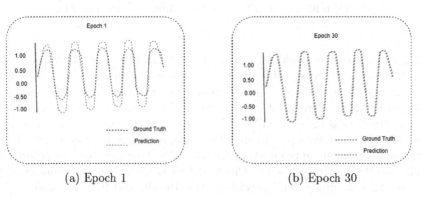

(a) Epoch 1   (b) Epoch 30

Fig. 8. Comparison between sine function learning result obtained from jupyter notebook using QLSTM+ Glove + FasText model

5   Conclusion

Quantum computing has recently gained prominence with prospects in the computation of machine learning algorithms that have addressed challenging problems. This paper conducted a comparative study on quantum Long Short-Term Memory (QLSTM) and traditional Long Short-Term Memory (LSTM) and analyzes the performance of both models using vulnerable source code. Moreover, We extracted the semantic and syntactic information using state-of-the-art word embedding algorithms such as Glove and fasText, which can make more accurate result. The QML model was used on a open sourced Penny Lane simulator due to the limited availability of the quantum computer. We have tried to implement machine learning algorithms for sequence modeling, such as natural language processing, vulnerable source code recognition on noisy intermediate-scale quantum (NISQ) device. We assessed the model's performance using accuracy and processing criteria. According to the experimental findings, the QLSTM with Glove and fastText embedding model learns noticeably more vulnerable source code features and operates more quickly than its conventional equivalent. Although advances have been made in quantum machine learning over the past few decades, more work is still needed because the current generation of quantum simulators only has a small number of qubits, making them unsuitable for sensitive source code. It is possible that a large number of convergent qubits using quantum machine learning models will have a significant impact on classification performance and computing time.

Acknowledgement. The work is partially supported by the U.S. National Science Foundation Award #2100115. Any opinions, findings, and conclusions or recommendations expressed in this material are those of the authors and do not necessarily reflect the views of the National Science Foundation.

References

1. LaToza, T.D., Venolia, G., DeLine, R.: Maintaining mental models: a study of developer work habits. In: Proceedings of the 28th International Conference on Software Engineering, pp. 492–501 (2006)
2. Yadron, D.: After heartbleed bug, a race to plug internet hole. Wall Street J. **9** (2014)
3. Manikandan, T., Balamurugan, B., Senthilkumar, C., Harinarayan, R.R.A., Subramanian, R.R.: Cyberwar is coming. In: Cyber Security in Parallel and Distributed Computing: Concepts, Techniques, Applications and Case Studies, pp. 79–89 (2019)
4. Turjo, K.R.R., et al.: Design of low-cost smart safety vest for the prevention of physical abuse and sexual harassment. In: 2021 24th International Conference on Computer and Information Technology (ICCIT), pp. 1–6. IEEE (2021)
5. Jochem, K.: It security matters
6. Brooks, T.N.: Survey of automated vulnerability detection and exploit generation techniques in cyber reasoning systems. In: Arai, K., Kapoor, S., Bhatia, R. (eds.) SAI 2018. AISC, vol. 857, pp. 1083–1102. Springer, Cham (2019). https://doi.org/10.1007/978-3-030-01177-2_79

7. Cadar, C., Dunbar, D., Engler, D.R., et al.: KLEE: unassisted and automatic generation of high-coverage tests for complex systems programs. OSDI **8**, 209–224 (2008)
8. Henzinger, T.A., Jhala, R., Majumdar, R., Sutre, G.: Software verification with BLAST. In: Ball, T., Rajamani, S.K. (eds.) SPIN 2003. LNCS, vol. 2648, pp. 235–239. Springer, Heidelberg (2003). https://doi.org/10.1007/3-540-44829-2_17
9. Böhme, M., Pham, V.-T., Roychoudhury, A.: Coverage-based greybox fuzzing as Markov chain. In: Proceedings of the 2016 ACM SIGSAC Conference on Computer and Communications Security, pp. 1032–1043 (2016)
10. Stephens, N., et al.: Driller: augmenting fuzzing through selective symbolic execution. NDSS **16**, 1–16 (2016)
11. Giovannetti, V., Lloyd, S., Maccone, L.: Architectures for a quantum random access memory. Phys. Rev. A **78**(5), 052310 (2008)
12. Alyami, H., et al.: The evaluation of software security through quantum computing techniques: a durability perspective. Appl. Sci. **11**(24), 11784 (2021)
13. Gyongyosi, L., Imre, S.: A survey on quantum computing technology. Comput. Sci. Rev. **31**, 51–71 (2019)
14. Schuld, M., Sinayskiy, I., Petruccione, F.: An introduction to quantum machine learning. Contemp. Phys. **56**(2), 172–185 (2015)
15. Zeng, P., Lin, G., Pan, L., Tai, Y., Zhang, J.: Software vulnerability analysis and discovery using deep learning techniques: a survey. IEEE Access **8**, 197158–197172 (2020)
16. Yamaguchi, F., Maier, A., Gascon, H., Rieck, K.: Automatic inference of search patterns for taint-style vulnerabilities. In: 2015 IEEE Symposium on Security and Privacy, pp. 797–812. IEEE (2015)
17. Wang, S., Liu, T., Tan, L.: Automatically learning semantic features for defect prediction. In: 2016 IEEE/ACM 38th International Conference on Software Engineering (ICSE), pp. 297–308. IEEE (2016)
18. Kim, S., Woo, S., Lee, H., Oh, H.: VUDDY: a scalable approach for vulnerable code clone discovery. In: 2017 IEEE Symposium on Security and Privacy (SP), pp. 595–614. IEEE (2017)
19. Havenstein, C., Thomas, D., Chandrasekaran, S.: Comparisons of performance between quantum and classical machine learning. SMU Data Sci. Rev. **1**(4), 11 (2018)
20. Masum, M., et al.: Quantum machine learning for software supply chain attacks: how far can we go? arXiv preprint arXiv:2204.02784 (2022)
21. Faruk, M.J.H., Tahora, S., Tasnim, M., Shahriar, H., Sakib, N.: A review of quantum cybersecurity: threats, risks and opportunities. In: 2022 1st International Conference on AI in Cybersecurity (ICAIC), pp. 1–8. IEEE (2022)
22. Payares, E., Martinez-Santos, J.: Quantum machine learning for intrusion detection of distributed denial of service attacks: a comparative overview. Quantum Comput. Commun. Simul. **11699**, 35–43 (2021)
23. Khan, A., Saha, G., Pal, R.K.: Quantum computing based inference of GRNs. In: Rojas, I., Ortuño, F. (eds.) IWBBIO 2017. LNCS, vol. 10209, pp. 221–233. Springer, Cham (2017). https://doi.org/10.1007/978-3-319-56154-7_21
24. Choi, J., Oh, S., Kim, J.: A tutorial on quantum graph recurrent neural network (QGRNN). In: 2021 International Conference on Information Networking (ICOIN), pp. 46–49. IEEE (2021)
25. Oh, S., Choi, J., Kim, J.: A tutorial on quantum convolutional neural networks (QCNN). In: 2020 International Conference on Information and Communication Technology Convergence (ICTC), pp. 236–239. IEEE (2020)

26. Lu, T.-C.: CNN convolutional layer optimisation based on quantum evolutionary algorithm. Connect. Sci. **33**(3), 482–494 (2021)
27. Russell, R., et al.: Automated vulnerability detection in source code using deep representation learning. In: 2018 17th IEEE International Conference on Machine Learning and Applications (ICMLA), pp. 757–762. IEEE (2018)
28. Kathuria, R.S., Gautam, S., Singh, A., Khatri, S., Yadav, N.: Real time sentiment analysis on twitter data using deep learning (Keras). In: 2019 International Conference on Computing, Communication, and Intelligent Systems (ICCCIS), pp. 69–73. IEEE (2019)
29. Tellex, S., Katz, B., Lin, J., Fernandes, A., Marton, G.: Quantitative evaluation of passage retrieval algorithms for question answering. In: Proceedings of the 26th Annual International ACM SIGIR Conference on Research and Development in Information Retrieval, pp. 41–47 (2003)
30. Socher, R., Bauer, J., Manning, C.D., Ng, A.Y.: Parsing with compositional vector grammars. In: Proceedings of the 51st Annual Meeting of the Association for Computational Linguistics (Volume 1: Long Papers), pp. 455–465 (2013)
31. Sebastiani, F.: Machine learning in automated text categorization. ACM Comput. Surv. (CSUR) **34**(1), 1–47 (2002)
32. Turian, J., Ratinov, L., Bengio, Y.: Word representations: a simple and general method for semi-supervised learning. In: Proceedings of the 48th Annual Meeting of the Association for Computational Linguistics, pp. 384–394 (2010)
33. Pennington, J., Socher, R., Manning, C.D.: Glove: global vectors for word representation. In: Proceedings of the 2014 Conference on Empirical Methods in Natural Language Processing (EMNLP), pp. 1532–1543 (2014)
34. Filonenko, A., Gudkov, K., Lebedev, A., Zagaynov, I., Orlov, N.: FaSText: fast and small text extractor. In: 2019 International Conference on Document Analysis and Recognition Workshops (ICDARW), vol. 4, pp. 49–54. IEEE (2019)
35. Busta, M., Neumann, L., Matas, J.: FaSText: efficient unconstrained scene text detector. In: Proceedings of the IEEE International Conference on Computer Vision, pp. 1206–1214 (2015)
36. Mandic, D., Chambers, J.: Recurrent Neural Networks for Prediction: Learning Algorithms, Architectures and Stability. Wiley, New York (2001)
37. Hochreiter, S., Schmidhuber, J.: Long short-term memory. Neural Comput. **9**(8), 1735–1780 (1997)
38. Schmidhuber, J.: A fixed size storage o (n 3) time complexity learning algorithm for fully recurrent continually running networks. Neural Comput. **4**(2), 243–248 (1992)
39. Song, H., Dai, J., Luo, L., Sheng, G., Jiang, X.: Power transformer operating state prediction method based on an LSTM network. Energies **11**(4), 914 (2018)
40. Kandala, A., et al.: Hardware-efficient variational quantum eigensolver for small molecules and quantum magnets. Nature **549**(7671), 242–246 (2017)
41. Sim, S., Johnson, P.D., Aspuru-Guzik, A.: Expressibility and entangling capability of parameterized quantum circuits for hybrid quantum-classical algorithms. Adv. Quantum Technol. **2**(12), 1900070 (2019)
42. Chen, S.Y.-C., Yoo, S., Fang, Y.-L.L.: Quantum long short-term memory. In: ICASSP 2022–2022 IEEE International Conference on Acoustics, Speech and Signal Processing (ICASSP), pp. 8622–8626. IEEE (2022)
43. Havlíček, V., et al.: Supervised learning with quantum-enhanced feature spaces. Nature **567**(7747), 209–212 (2019)
44. Mitarai, K., Negoro, M., Kitagawa, M., Fujii, K.: Quantum circuit learning. Phys. Rev. A **98**(3), 032309 (2018)

45. Dallaire-Demers, P.-L., Killoran, N.: Quantum generative adversarial networks. Phys. Rev. A **98**(1), 012324 (2018)
46. Chen, S.Y.-C., Yang, C.-H.H., Qi, J., Chen, P.-Y., Ma, X., Goan, H.-S.: Variational quantum circuits for deep reinforcement learning. IEEE Access **8**, 141007–141024 (2020)
47. Mari, A., Bromley, T.R., Izaac, J., Schuld, M., Killoran, N.: Transfer learning in hybrid classical-quantum neural networks. Quantum **4**, 340 (2020)

System Call Processing Using Lightweight NLP for IoT Behavioral Malware Detection

John Carter[✉][iD], Spiros Mancoridis[iD], Malvin Nkomo[iD], Steven Weber[iD], and Kapil R. Dandekar[iD]

Drexel University, Philadelphia, PA 19104, USA
jmc683@drexel.edu

Abstract. Although much of the work in behaviorally detecting malware lies in collecting the best explanatory data and using the most efficacious machine learning models, the processing of the data can sometimes prove to be the most important step in the data pipeline. In this work, we collect kernel-level system calls on a resource-constrained Internet of Things (IoT) device, apply lightweight Natural Language Processing (NLP) techniques to the data, and feed this processed data to two simple machine learning classification models: Logistic Regression (LR) and a Neural Network (NN). For the data processing, we group the system calls into n-grams that are sorted by the timestamp in which they are recorded. To demonstrate the effectiveness, or lack thereof, of using n-grams, we deploy two types of malware onto the IoT device: a Denial-of-Service (DoS) attack, and an Advanced Persistent Threat (APT) malware. We examine the effects of using lightweight NLP on malware like the DoS and the stealthy APT malware. For stealthier malware, such as the APT, using more advanced, but far more resource-intensive, NLP techniques will likely increase detection capability, which is saved for future work.

Keywords: Natural language processing · Machine learning · Malware detection · Internet of things

1 Introduction

IoT devices have quickly progressed from novelty technology, for early-adopting users, to ubiquitous technology that is used by many in everyday life. These devices can range from user-input speech recognition devices such as the Amazon Alexa to various micro electro-mechanical sensor systems for data acquisition. In the wake of tightly-coupled enterprise platforms, Drexel University has championed a multi-modal open-source IoT platform named `VarIoT`, comprising long and short-range wireless communication protocols. This platform can be repurposed for various use-cases due to its highly customizable and modular interfaces. The `VarIoT` gateway offers support for Bluetooth Low Energy

G. Wang et al. (Eds.): UbiSec 2022, CCIS 1768, pp. 103–115, 2023.
https://doi.org/10.1007/978-981-99-0272-9_7

(BLE), WiFi, LoRa, Zigbee and LTE/5G cellular transceivers. Other supported interfaces include mmWave radar, ultra-high frequency (UHF), radio-frequency identification (RFID), and sigfox, in order to extend the available application areas. This enables a multitude of sensors to be deployed for various scenarios. The `VarIoT` platform is built on the open-source Thingsboard platform as the gateway for server-side data collection for advanced processing, visualization and storage [22] (Fig. 1).

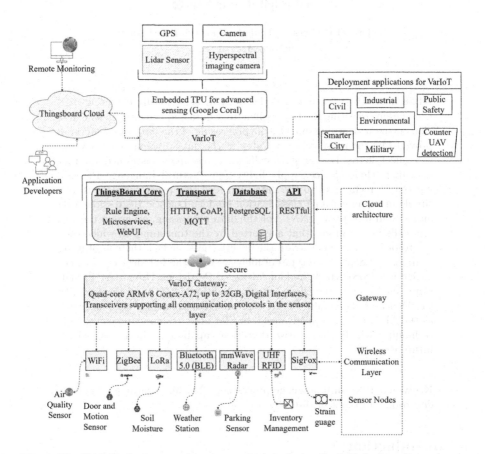

Fig. 1. The VarIoT platform architecture, which includes the IoT devices, the gateway with transceivers, capable nodes and server-side infrastructure.

In this work, we configure the VarIoT gateway to connect to a WiFi-enabled device as the sensor node to gather network data. The node used is the PurpleAir PA-II Air Quality Sensor. This framework is depicted in Fig. 2. The Air Quality Sensor communicates with the `VarIoT` server once every minute, and is dormant on the network for the remainder of the time. It uses TLS encryption for its communication, which means all data sent to or from the sensor is not easily changeable, and only the TCP header data is visible from each packet. This makes the communication less susceptible to many attacks in which the data is corrupted, such as Man-in-the-Middle attacks, but still leaves room for other attacks, such as DoS attacks, which will be explored further in Sect. 2 [18,21].

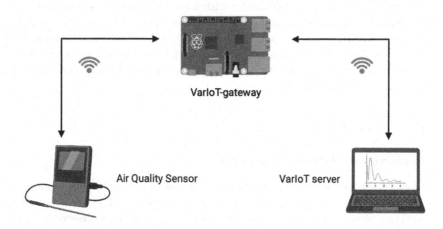

Fig. 2. The specific framework used in this work: an IoT device, the VarIoT server, and the gateway connecting them.

Our goal is to deploy malware onto the gateway and detect it using behavioral malware detection, in which kernel-level system calls issued on-device are transformed using lightweight NLP techniques and subsequently fed into two ML models.

Behavioral malware detection has been shown to be an effective method to detect malware that runs on devices, especially on resource-constrained Internet of Things (IoT) devices [2]. Machine learning (ML) models are often able to take a small amount of data, such as OS system call sequences or network traffic information, and produce an accurate classification of whether an observation is malware or not. However, this method relies heavily on what type of data is collected and how the data is processed, such that the data consists of the most explanatory features possible to use to train the models. Since the quality of the data fed to a machine learning model often dictates the model's performance, the data processing step can often be one of the most important steps in determining whether or not an effective model is produced [12].

One such data processing method is using lightweight NLP techniques to transform the data into a n-gram language model. n-gram language models make predictions using conditional word frequencies observed in the data [23]. Our work utilizes unigrams, in which the feature set comprises each observed system call issued on the VarIoT-gateway. We chose to use system calls because they provide a wider variety of observed behaviors on the device, since each process needs to issue system calls to accomplish its tasks. Although other data sources, such as network traffic, can provide useful behavioral data, system calls provide the largest breadth of device behavior. We also experimented with using system call bigrams, which means the feature set consists of each two consecutive system calls executed during the data collection period. This was not found to yield significantly better results than using the less intensive unigram method.

We show that while a model trained with a simple unigram representation of the data works well for noisier and more disruptive malware, it does not perform as well for stealthier malware. We believe classification problems for stealthier malware necessitate the use of more advanced NLP techniques, such as using a Recurrent Neural Network (RNN) or a Long Short-Term Memory (LSTM) [11], which we save for future work.

2   Previous Work

2.1   Behavioral Malware Detection

Behavioral malware detection seeks to detect malicious activity by learning the functionality and actions of malware during its execution [4,7]. Today, behavioral malware detection often uses machine learning models to observe malware behavior using system or network data – in our case, kernel-level system calls. In one study by Hasan *et al.* [10], a variety of machine learning models were used, such as Support Vector Machines, Random Forests, Decision Trees, and Neural Networks.

2.2   IoT Background

IoT is extending its impact from simple devices of convenience, such as pedometers and voice-activated home virtual assistants, to integrated home security systems, remote-controlled medical devices, and self-navigating vehicles.

IoT devices are commonly the victims of malware due to their lax security, the number of connected IoT devices, which make them useful for distributed attacks, and the fact that they are rarely monitored directly by humans. One type of malware that often infects IoT devices is DoS malware, which compromise IoT devices with the intent of using them to overload servers and other hosts that cannot handle the load of millions of requests concurrently. The most notable DoS attack is Mirai, which disabled many servers, such as Amazon, GitHub, and Netflix [3,14]. Another type of malware that can target IoT devices are APT (Advanced Persistent Threat) malware, which can passively surveil the state of the device and exfiltrate potentially sensitive information to remote command and control centers (C&C) [16].

A unique challenge for researchers who want to deploy behavioral malware detectors on IoT devices, or their corresponding ecosystems, is that such devices have computational, memory and energy limitations. Therefore, any malware detection technique that takes these constraints into account must be lightweight, such as the ones we describe in this work.

3   Malware

Two types of malware are deployed on the `VarIoT-gateway`, each of which represents malware families that are prevalent today. One is a quiet, stealthy type of malware, which we represent using an APT malware. The second type of malware is noisy and debilitating, which we represent using a denial of service attack. A DoS attack is one that is commonly carried out by IoT devices due to the scale of attack available. We explain each of these malware types in detail below.

3.1   Advanced Persistent Threat

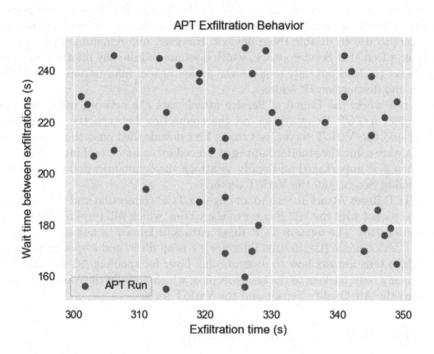

Fig. 3. The exfiltration behavior of the APT during the data collection process.

An APT is a type of malware often used for espionage and spying, sometimes by nation-states and other larger organizations [15]. In this work, the APT is designed to copy and exfiltrate the contents of files to a user-specified remote host.

It is controlled by a C&C server remotely and has the ability to be run in a *random mode*, which randomizes both the duration of each data exfiltration as well as the wait time between exfiltrations. An example of the duration and wait time parameters is depicted in Fig. 3. In Fig. 3, each data point refers to one

APT run, where the x-axis represents the duration of APT exfiltration, and the y-axis represents the amount of time the APT sleeps before the next exfiltration.

Though APTs can be found "in the wild," these often are unusable for a number of reasons, such as that they report to C&C servers that are no longer active. In addition, these APTs are not yet advanced enough to have randomized behavior, which makes their detection an easier task. In contrast, the APT we use in this work is stealthy and much more difficult to detect, which will be discussed further in the Experimental Results section of this paper.

3.2 Denial of Service

Some IoT devices are now becoming sophisticated enough to use encryption for communication with servers. In the case of the Air Quality Sensor, each packet sent to or from the sensor is encrypted using TLS. This leaves fewer options for attackers to use to disable these devices. However, one remaining option is to conduct a Denial of Service attack, which does not require any information from the packet payload but only requires the packet header information, such as the source and destination IP address.

In this work, the Denial of Service attack uses the network utility netwox to conduct a TCP Reset Attack on the connection between the Air Quality Sensor and the VarIoT server. netwox is first downloaded onto the gateway by our malware using the standard apt-get procedure common on Linux machines, and then it is unpackaged and ready to attack the communication between the Air Quality Sensor and the VarIoT server.

A TCP Reset Attack listens to an ongoing TCP connection and then sends a spoofed packet with the "R" flag set to the victim, which will terminate the TCP connection [18]. The netwox TCP Reset Attack is known as netwox 78, which takes a device name (the desired interface), a pcap filter, and a spoofip parameter, which tells netwox how to generate link layer for spoofing [9]. netwox then sends many reset packets to the host specified, which disables the communication between the Air Quality Sensor and the VarIoT server.

4 Data Collection and Processing

4.1 Initial Data Processing

The raw data consists of system calls executed on the VarIoT-gateway during periods of benign behavior as well as during periods of malware execution on the device. The malware data was collected separately for each type of malware running on the device. In addition, before the benign data was collected, the operating system was reinstalled on the device, ensuring that the environment was free of malware. The data processing step involves grouping the collected data into segments that are more useful for behavioral malware detection, and is shown in detail in Fig. 4. After the raw system calls are logged, they are grouped by timestamp using a user-specified window size.

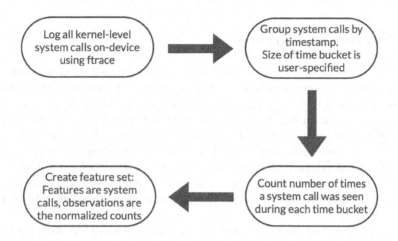

Fig. 4. The data pipeline. This describes the transformation from ROM raw kernel-level system calls to a usable feature set for a ML model.

This window size can be thought of as a parameter that breaks up the total amount of data collection time into a user-specified number of buckets. Through experimentation, we set the window size to be 10 milliseconds, though this is a tunable parameter. We chose this small window size due to the rapidity of which the system calls are executed, such that the windows could separate system calls from different processes as effectively as possible.

4.2 Data Transformation Using NLP

We then chose to use a lightweight NLP approach of grouping the data into n-grams. Often this approach is applied to written text, in which words are grouped into either unigrams (sequences of one), or bigrams (sequences of two). Longer sequences can also be used, although these are used less frequently due to larger sequences becoming intractable. We used the bag-of-n-grams approach in the groupings [13,17], where the value of n was user-specified [4]. This means that the feature set is composed of the number of observations of each n consecutive system calls in a particular time window. Through empirical analysis, we found that a value of $n = 1$ is optimal for both performance efficiency and detection efficacy in our dataset. Since we chose a value of $n = 1$, the feature set consists simply of the number of times each system call was observed during each time window. For example, using unigrams, one column of the data could be a system call such as `mutex_lock`, and each of the rows of that column will be the total number of calls to this system call for each time window. The number of observations of the system calls were then normalized using Term Frequency-Inverse Document Frequency (TF-IDF) [20], which normalizes the system call counts instead of using only the total number of times the system call was observed.

5   Experimental Results

Two typical machine learning models were used for evaluation of our data processing techniques: logistic regression and a shallow neural network. Both of these models are lightweight, which make them ideal for use on resource-constrained IoT devices. As shown in Figs. 6-7, more available training data (depicted by the x-axis of both figures) yields better models. Although the amount of training data necessary to create useful classifiers can differ between types of malware, in general, as with many ML models, more training data yields a better model. Both models are tested using a larger testing set, comprised of 120 min of benign data and 120 min of malware data. We explain each of these models in detail below.

The metric we use for evaluating the efficacy of the models is Area Under the Curve (AUC), where the curve is the Receiver Operating Characteristic curve. This metric measures the ability of a classifier to differentiate between classes in the data, and is useful as a summary of the Receiver Operating Characteristic (ROC) curve. An example ROC Curve for the neural network is shown in Fig. 5. AUC is an effective metric for evaluating classifiers, and there has been research that suggests it is actually preferable to overall accuracy for some problem domains [6].

Three types of malware are used for evaluation in this work.

1. The first is the stealthy APT malware, which was described in detail previously.
2. The second type of malware is a simple installation and uninstallation script which is responsible for repeatedly downloading netwox, unpackaging and installing it, and then removing it from the device. We chose to include this pseudo-malware because it shows how easily these simple ML models can detect the malware before any execution starts and without any execution occurring. This relies on the assumption that the device does not run automatic updates and if it were updated, the detector would not be running during that time. This rapid detection is especially important for zero-day attacks [5], since the only time a user might have to stop a malware attack from damaging their computer is to kill the download process before execution.
3. The third type of malware is the randomized netwox, which not only encompasses the installation/uninstallation process, but also executes the netwox TCP Reset Attack for a random duration of time.

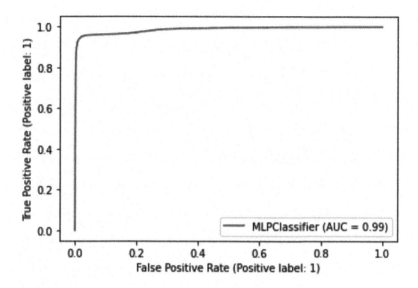

Fig. 5. An example ROC Curve using the neural network and 30 min randomized-netwox data, as shown on the right side of Fig. 7.

5.1 Logistic Regression

Perhaps the most lightweight, yet effective, machine learning model suitable for our task is logistic regression. In addition to being lightweight, it does not require much data for training, which also makes it ideal for our problem space. The results show that the LR model could easily detect the netwox-related malware, but struggled more to detect the APT.

5.2 Shallow Neural Network

Another lightweight ML model is a shallow neural network. In this work, we use a three layer NN that is provided off-the-shelf from scikit-learn called MLPClassifier [19]. This model is a three-layer neural network that optimizes the log-loss function. It uses L2 regularization ($\alpha = 1e-3$), a logistic sigmoid activation function, and the Adam optimizer with learning rate $1e-3$. Each of the parameters are user-specified and were chosen through experimentation with the data.

As with the LR model, the NN is easily able to detect the netwox-related malware, but again struggled more to detect the APT.

It is interesting to note how the AUC values for both the LR and NN models follow the same trajectory and have essentially the same values for the netwox-related malware, with the only major difference being that the NN had marginally better results for the APT malware. Similarly, both models show a slight decrease in AUC using the 15 min training data. This suggests that the slight AUC decrease has more to do with limitations from that particular training dataset rather than a model deficiency.

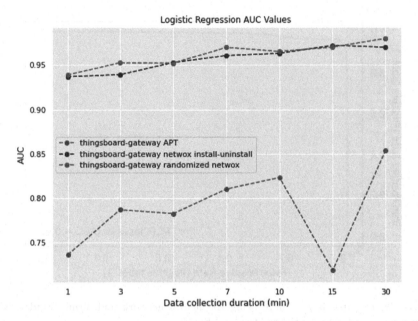

Fig. 6. Area Under the Curves for detecting the three flavors of malware on the VarIoT-gateway using a Logistic Regression model.

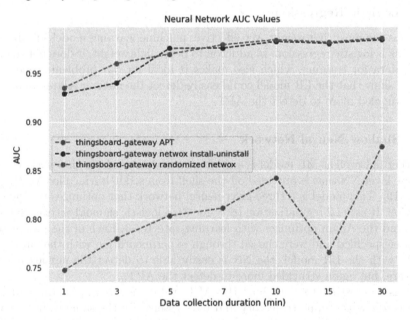

Fig. 7. Area Under the Curves for detecting the three flavors of malware on the VarIoT-gateway using a Neural Network model.

6 Conclusions

In this work, we built a simple, yet fully-functional, IoT testbed which is comprised of an Air Quality Sensor, a gateway, and an instance of a ThingsBoard server. Kernel-level system calls were logged on the gateway, which is configured specifically to connect to a VarIoT server. This gateway connects a common IoT device and a VarIoT server which relays information to users, which is shown in Fig. 2. These raw system calls were collected during periods of strictly benign behavior as well as during periods of malware execution on the gateway.

The raw system calls were then transformed into usable features using a lightweight NLP technique. Specifically, we transformed them into a feature set of unigrams, which is a lightweight representation of the data and thus ideal for resource-constrained IoT devices. Lastly, two lightweight and efficacious machine learning classifiers were built and were successful in classifying malware, especially the netwox-related malware.

The ability of the classifiers to detect the installation/uninstallation malware is quite promising and useful because with only 1 min of training data, both models were able to detect malware with greater than 90% Area Under the Curve. This finding is very useful from a user standpoint, because if the malware can be stopped early before it executes, the user has a chance to prevent malware from damaging their system. Likewise, both models were able to detect the randomized netwox just as well, which suggests that even if the data contains less obvious DoS behavior than downloading packages, the models will still perform well. However, the models were significantly less successful in classifying the stealthier APT malware. Because of the randomization of the APT's behavior as well as its much smaller system call footprint, it is harder to detect using only the lightweight NLP data representations used in this work.

6.1 Future Work

We would like to extend this work in two different directions. The first is by using more advanced NLP techniques, such as Recurrent Neural Networks, Gated Recurrent Units (GRU) [8], and Long Short-Term Memory (LSTM) [11]. We believe these techniques will work better for stealthier malware such as the APT and will result in more effective behavioral malware detection.

Secondly, we would like to explore this topic further using other IoT devices. In addition to other WiFi-enabled devices, we would like to work with devices that communicate using other protocols. These can include Bluetooth-enabled devices, which are ubiquitous, as well as devices that support protocols like LoRa, ZigBee, SigFox, UHF RFID and mmWave radar, which are both used by low-power and long-range IoT devices [1].

Since all of these devices are already natively supported by the VarIoT platform, we can replicate the work in this research and compare the effectiveness of the techniques shown here using devices that connect using a wide variety of protocols. This will not only further validate the work presented, but will also show the feasibility of using these methods for IoT devices that are less common and more often overlooked in security research.

Acknowledgments. The work was funded in part by Spiros Mancoridis' Auerbach Berger Chair in Cybersecurity.

References

1. Ali, A.I., Partal, S.Z., Kepke, S., Partal, H.P.: ZigBee and LoRa based wireless sensors for smart environment and IoT applications. In: 2019 1st Global Power, Energy and Communication Conference (GPECOM), pp. 19–23 (2019). https://doi.org/10.1109/GPECOM.2019.8778505
2. An, N., Duff, A., Noorani, M., Weber, S., Mancoridis, S.: Malware anomaly detection on virtual assistants, pp. 124–131, October 2018. https://doi.org/10.1109/MALWARE.2018.8659366
3. Antonakakis, M., et al.: Understanding the mirai botnet. In: 26th USENIX security symposium (USENIX Security 17), pp. 1093–1110 (2017)
4. Aslan, A., Samet, R.: A comprehensive review on malware detection approaches. IEEE Access **8**, 6249–6271 (2020). https://doi.org/10.1109/ACCESS.2019.2963724
5. Bilge, L., Dumitraş, T.: Before we knew it: an empirical study of zero-day attacks in the real world. In: Proceedings of the 2012 ACM Conference on Computer and Communications Security. CCS 2012, New York, NY, USA, pp. 833–844. Association for Computing Machinery (2012). https://doi.org/10.1145/2382196.2382284
6. Bradley, A.P.: The use of the area under the ROC curve in the evaluation of machine learning algorithms. Pattern Recognition 30(7), 1145–1159 (1997). https://doi.org/10.1016/S0031-3203(96)00142-2, https://www.sciencedirect.com/science/article/pii/S0031320396001422
7. Carter, J., Mancoridis, S., Galinkin, E.: Fast, lightweight IoT anomaly detection using feature pruning and PCA. In: Proceedings of the 37th ACM/SIGAPP Symposium on Applied Computing. SAC 2022, New York, NY, USA, pp. 133–138. Association for Computing Machinery (2022). https://doi.org/10.1145/3477314.3508377
8. Chung, J., Gulcehre, C., Cho, K., Bengio, Y.: Empirical evaluation of gated recurrent neural networks on sequence modeling. arXiv preprint arXiv:1412.3555 (2014)
9. Du, W.K.: Tool 78: Reset every TCP packet. https://web.ecs.syr.edu/~wedu/Teaching/cis758/netw522/netwox-doc_html/tools/78.html
10. Hasan, M., Islam, M.M., Zarif, M.I.I., Hashem, M.: Attack and anomaly detection in IoT sensors in IoT sites using machine learning approaches. Internet of Things 7, 100059 (2019). https://doi.org/10.1016/j.iot.2019.100059, https://www.sciencedirect.com/science/article/pii/S2542660519300241
11. Hochreiter, S., Schmidhuber, J.: Long short-term memory. Neural Comput. **9**(8), 1735–1780 (1997). https://doi.org/10.1162/neco.1997.9.8.1735
12. Jain, A., et al.: Overview and importance of data quality for machine learning tasks. In: Proceedings of the 26th ACM SIGKDD International Conference on Knowledge Discovery & Data Mining. KDD 2020, pp. 3561–3562, New York, NY, USA. Association for Computing Machinery (2020). https://doi.org/10.1145/3394486.3406477, https://doi.org/10.1145/3394486.3406477

13. Kang, D.K., Fuller, D., Honavar, V.: Learning classifiers for misuse and anomaly detection using a bag of system calls representation. In: Proceedings from the Sixth Annual IEEE SMC Information Assurance Workshop, pp. 118–125 (2005). https:// doi.org/10.1109/IAW.2005.1495942
14. Kolias, C., Kambourakis, G., Stavrou, A., Voas, J.: DDoS in the IoT: Mirai and other botnets. Computer **50**, 80–84 (2017). https://doi.org/10.1109/MC.2017.201
15. Lemay, A., Calvet, J., Menet, F., Fernandez, J.M.: Survey of publicly available reports on advanced persistent threat actors. Comput. Secur. **72**, 26–59 (2018). https://doi.org/10.1016/j.cose.2017.08.005, https://www.sciencedirect.com/science/article/pii/S0167404817301608
16. Li, S., Zhang, Q., Wu, X., Han, W., Tian, Z., Yu, S.: Attribution classification method of apt malware in IoT using machine learning techniques. Sec. Commun. Netw. 2021 (2021). https://doi.org/10.1155/2021/9396141 https://doi.org/10.1155/2021/9396141
17. Liu, A., Martin, C., Hetherington, T., Matzner, S.: A comparison of system call feature representations for insider threat detection. In: Proceedings from the Sixth Annual IEEE SMC Information Assurance Workshop, pp. 340–347 (2005). https:// doi.org/10.1109/IAW.2005.1495972
18. Mittal, A., Shrivastava, K., Manoria, M.: A review of DDOS attack and its countermeasures in TCP based networks. IJCSES **2**, 177–187 (2011). https://doi.org/10.5121/ijcses.2011.2413
19. Pedregosa, F., et al.: Scikit-learn: machine learning in Python. J. Mach. Learn. Res. **12**, 2825–2830 (2011)
20. Ramos, J.: Using TF-IDF to determine word relevance in document queries, January 2003
21. Surya, S.R., Magrica, G.A.: A survey on wireless networks attacks. In: 2017 2nd International Conference on Computing and Communications Technologies (ICCCT), pp. 240–247 (2017). https://doi.org/10.1109/ICCCT2.2017.7972278
22. ThingsBoard - Open source IoT Platform: Thingsboard - open source IoT platform. https://thingsboard.io
23. Wallach, H.M.: Topic modeling: Beyond bag-of-words. In: Proceedings of the 23rd International Conference on Machine Learning. ICML 2006, New York, NY, USA, pp. 977–984, Association for Computing Machinery (2006). https://doi.org/10.1145/1143844.1143967

Vulnerability Detection with Representation Learning

Zhiqiang Wang[1,2], Sulong Meng[1], and Ying Chen[1(✉)]

[1] Beijing Electronic Science and Technology Institute, Beijing 100071, China
dky_ychen@163.com
[2] State Information Center, Beijing 100045, China

Abstract. It is essential to identify potentially vulnerable code in our software systems. Deep neural network techniques have been used for vulnerability detection. However, existing methods usually ignore the feature representation of vulnerable datasets, resulting in unsatisfactory model performance. Such vulnerability detection techniques should achieve high accuracy, relatively high true-positive rate, and low false-negative rate. At the same time, it needs to be able to complete the vulnerability detection of actual projects and does not require additional expert knowledge or tedious configuration. In this article, we propose and implement VDDRL (A Vulnerability Detection Method Based On Deep Representation Learning). This deep representation learning-based vulnerability detection method combines feature extraction and ensemble learning. VDDRL uses the word2vec model to convert the source code into a vector representation. Deep representations of vulnerable code are learned from vulnerable code token sequences using LSTM models and then trained for classification using traditional machine learning algorithms. The training dataset we use is derived from actual projects and contains seven different types of vulnerabilities. Through comparative experiments on datasets, VDDRL achieves an *Accuracy* of 95.6%–98.7%, a *Precision* of 91.6%–99.0%, a *Recall* of 84.7%–99.5%, and an *F1* of 88.1%–99.2%. Both perform better than the baseline method. Our experimental results show that VDDRL is a generic, lightweight, and extensible vulnerability detection method. Compared with other methods, it has better performance and robustness.

Keywords: Static analysis · Vulnerability detection · Deep learning · Long-short-term memory network · Representation learning

1 Introduction

Vulnerability identification is a crucial and challenging problem in security. Many cyber-security incidents and data breaches are caused by exploitable vulnerabilities in software [1, 2]. The classic approaches to detecting vulnerabilities are static analysis [3, 4], dynamic analysis [5–7], and symbolic execution. However, modern software has a larger size and much more complexity. These approaches do not perform as well.

Z. Wang and S. Meng—These authors contributed to the work equally and should be regarded as co-first authors.

In order to release the time-consuming and human expert, many techniques related to machine learning (ML) have been proposed. Compared with rule-based detection, ML algorithms can learn the hidden patterns of vulnerable code and outperform the rules. Nevertheless, the performance of ML-based detection techniques still relies on the quality of features defined by human experts. This means the level of expertise and depth of domain knowledge matter significantly to the performance even when focusing on the same specific situation.

With the rapid development of computer hardware and the increasing availability of open-source software, we can easily obtain much more vulnerable source code. Meanwhile, it's possible for Deep Learning (DL) based approaches to handle a large number of code segments as training input. This means we can directly use a large amount of vulnerable source code to learn hidden vulnerability patterns without the need for feature extraction manually.

This paper proposes a vulnerability detection framework based on deep representation learning and a machine learning classifier algorithm. Previous works focused on statically-typed languages such as Java, C, and C++ [14–17]. The Python language has not attracted the corresponding attention. However, Python is one of the most popular programming languages. With the development of web frameworks such as Django and Flask, Python is related to many security problems. Hence, we choose Python as the research language codebase. Motivated by natural language processing (NLP) research using LSTMs, we assume that programming languages are similar to natural languages. To a certain extent, programming languages are more compliant than natural languages, so it is easier for neural networks to detect hidden vulnerability patterns. We use word2vec, the classic embedding model for embedding token sequences into numerical vectors. Then the LSTM model is trained using these vectors and corresponding labels to learn the representation of each code fragment, which automatically extracts hidden features besides the vulnerable codes in the form of fixed-dimensional vectors. At last, each code snippet is presented by the feature vectors obtained from the trained model. We then treat these feature vectors and labels as the input data of the ML classifier algorithm.

In summary, this paper makes the following contributions:

(1) A vulnerability detection framework based on deep representation learning and machine learning classifier algorithm which focuses on Python projects.
(2) We implemented our framework over a large natural labeled dataset gathered from GitHub.
(3) Experimental results show that VDDRL achieved a recall of 84.7%–99.5%, precision of 91.6%–99.0%, and F1 score of 88.1%–99.2%. Compared with the comparative experiments, higher Accuracy and better model robustness achieve.

2   Related Works

There are three types of research methods in source code vulnerability detection: vulnerability detection based on software metrics, vulnerability detection with Machine learning, and vulnerability detection with Deep learning. There is no absolute distinction between different research methods, and they usually mix according to different application scenarios, data types, and scales.

2.1 Vulnerability Detection Based on Software Metrics

Software metrics mean data information gathered from source code using statistical methods, such as lines of code (LOC), cyclomatic complexity, code churn, and the number of dependencies [36]. A detection model can be built through these metrics. There are some problems with relying on the organizational metrics of the source code for vulnerability detection. The first is the lack of robust-ness for the software metrics generated by one project cannot complete the task of cross-project detection. The second is that the metrics generated by statistical methods cannot retain the syntactic and semantic information in the source code, which limits its performance in vulnerability detection. Software metrics may use as part of the vulnerability features, but we cannot perform well in vulnerability prediction tasks only through the calculation and combination of metrics.

Therefore, some studies try to combine software metrics with Machine Learning (ML) to predict software vulnerabilities. Shin et al. [26] extracted nine complexity metrics from JavaScript projects combined with ML methods such as linear discriminant analysis and Bayesian networks. They achieved a low false-positive rate in the task of vulnerability prediction, but their false-positive rate is high. Chowdhury et al. [27] focus on the releases of Mozilla Firefox. For vulnerability prediction, they used decision trees, random forests, logistic regression, and simple Bayesian algorithms. Other researchers consider code commit information a form of software metrics. Zhou et al. [28] use the K-fold stacking algorithm to analyze code commit information to predict whether there is a vulnerability.

Unlike the methods above, VDDRL does not extract statistical information from the dataset as some feature but learns deep representations of vulnerabilities directly from the source code.

2.2 Machine Learning-Based Vulnerability Detection

ML techniques have been used in many programming languages to model and detect vulnerable code. There are two methods typically: supervised and unsupervised learning.

Morrison et al. [8] used a variety of ML algorithms for security testing against Windows system vulnerabilities, and the Precision and Recall of the results were very low. The final results show that this method performs well within the same project but poorly on cross-project detection tasks. Hovsepyan et al. [9] treat the source code of a Java Android project as a natural language. They use the bag-of-words technique to convert the source code into feature vectors. The features are then trained for binary classification using a support vector machine (SVM) algorithm. Research shows that treating source code as natural language appears to be able to extract deeper information.

2.3 Deep Learning-Based Vulnerability Detection

Deep learning technology does not require a manual definition of vulnerability patterns. They can extract vulnerable features by deep neural networks. The quantity and quality of the datasets have a huge impact on the final result.

Z. Li et al. [12] proposed the concept of code gadgets. Parts of code extracted from the program dependency graph are called code gadgets. Then use a bidirectional LSTM model to learn vulnerability patterns. This research work shows us the complexity and importance of collecting, cleaning, and labeling large amounts of training data.

H. K. Dam [28] was the first to apply Long Short Term Memory Networks (LSTM) to learn features automatically. The dataset they used contains open-source code from 18 Java projects. Convert all the methods in the dataset into Abstract Syntax Trees (AST) and then use the LSTM network to train syntactic and semantic features for the random forest classifier.

3 Methodology

This section presents the overview of VDDRL and expounds on each step of the proposed framework.

3.1 Overview

Figure 1 shows the workflow of VDDRL. The input is the source code of the Python project, and the output is the probability of whether the source code has vulnerabilities. There are three steps that VDDRL contains: embed the code snippets into numerical vectors and use the LSTM neural network to learn the deep representation of vulnerable features. These deep features then train an ML classifier.

Neural networks take numerical vectors as input data. Hence, we need to transform the source data with textual representations into the fixed size of numerical vectors. Previous research has demonstrated that it's unnecessary to use Intermediate Representation (IR) when mining patterns from code. Besides, many researchers [12, 14, 18, 19] have proven that we can model source code directly as text and achieve good performance. So, we choose to get the numerical vectors directly from the source code instead of transforming them into an IR.

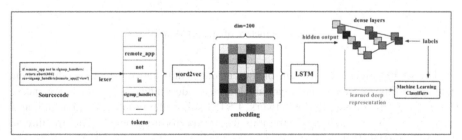

Fig. 1. The overview of the VDDRL workflow

3.2 Representation Learning

Retaining the semantic and syntactic information when transforming source code into vectors is necessary. Besides, it is also essential to keep the vectors manageable in size because neural networks are working on the fixed dimension of vectors. Word embedding is a distributed representation that distributes the meaning of a token into different parts of a numeric vector. Previous research [20] has proved that due to its strong generalization ability, word embedding has become a standard data processing method in Machine Learning (ML) and Natural Language Processing (NLP) areas. When we use word embedding to convert lexical units into vectors, the words with similar semantic information will have a closer distance in high dimensional space.

Hence, we choose the word2vec model to complete the task of dataset vectorization. We divide the code in the dataset into token sequences while removing the annotation-related content and keep all other lexical units as the corpus of the word2vec model to train the word embedding model. After this step, we can convert the input in text form into vector form suitable for neural network training input.

So far, the Python vulnerable code dataset from open-source projects has been converted into fixed-length vectors. We use it with the vulnerability labels as input to train a deep neural network to obtain a deep representation of the vulnerable code. We know that software source code data belongs to sequence data, and the role of each statement depends on its context related. Therefore, we can't just judge whether a specific token or a specific statement is vulnerable because we need to combine the statement dependencies of the context. That's why we choose LSTM as our feature extractor model.

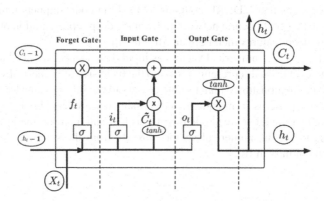

Fig. 2. Structure of an LSTM unit

The LSTM model is a variant of a recurrent neural network that introduces cell state and gating mechanisms to capture long-term dependencies of input sequences. Compared to the original RNN network, LSTM solves the problem of vanishing and exploding gradients, enabling the training of better-performing models. The structure of the LSTM model shows in Fig. 2.

In the model structure, $i_t, f_t,$ and o_t represent the Input Gate, Forget Gate, and Output Gate, respectively. W_f, W_i, W_c, and W_o correspond to the weights of the Input Unit, Input

Gate, Forget Gate, and Output Gate, respectively. There are also four loop-weights: b_c, b_i, b_f, and b_o, which come from the previous LSTM unit and the three gate structures of the current unit, respectively. The two calculation symbols, σ, and *tanh*, represent the Sigmoid activation and hyperbolic tangent functions.

3.3 Ensemble Learning with Neural Representations

Relevant studies have shown that the features learned by deep neural networks have been classified and trained in representation learning, and some methods have achieved good performance. However, combining feature extraction and classification also has its shortcomings. It is challenging to collect vulnerable codes in the real world. The datasets used in related works usually have a highly unbalanced ratio of vulnerable codes to normal codes, which leads to overfitting or non-convergence during the training process. However, we have shown through experiments that combining the output of hidden layers in deep neural networks as feature representations with ensemble classifiers such as random forests can achieve better results on the overall dataset. At the same time, separating the feature extraction and classification training process can effectively solve the problems mentioned above. In addition, when new feature sets need to be added or retrained, it is convenient and fast to use this independent classifier.

In summary, we take the hidden layer outputs of the trained LSTM model as feature representations for vulnerable codes and use these features along with the corresponding vulnerability labels to train a random forest classifier. This process can be expressed as the following equation:

$$r = LSTM\,(x) \tag{2}$$

$$p = RF\,(r)$$

x in Eq. 2 is a fixed-length vector generated from the source code data. r is the hidden layer output of the LSTM model, which we call the feature representation in this paper. The feature representation of these vulnerable codes is used to train the ensemble model and obtain the final classification result p.

4   Empirical Evaluation

In this section, we evaluate the effectiveness of VDDRL for vulnerability detection by training and classifying real-world data using VDDRL.

4.1 Data Introduction

In some previous approaches, the training and testing dataset had different problems. Some may achieve good performance because they just applied the trained model to the same project where training data comes from. Others used synthetic datasets, which are opposed to real-world code.

When testing their model on "real" projects, the performance may decrease significantly.

The Python source code dataset we used in this paper comes from VUDENC [13] which was gathered from projects publicly available on GitHub. More details on data collection can be found from that article. The data gathered from GitHub can be seen as "real" projects. This means the model trained from these data can be used for any projects in practice.

Table 1 shows the basic information of our dataset. There are seven typical and widespread vulnerability types: SQL injection, cross-site scripting, command injection, cross-site request forgery, path disclosure, remote code execution, and open redirect vulnerabilities. All those vulnerabilities are widely used in many applications and systems. The table reports the lines of code (LOC), the number of separate functions (#separate functions), and the ratio of vulnerable functions (#VF). Each vulnerability data set contains source code between around 14,000 and 83,000 lines, functions around 700 and 5000, and the ratio of vulnerable functions between 8.93% and 19.02%.

Table 1. Information of dataset

Vulnerability types	LOC	#separate functions	#VF
SQL injection [21]	83,558	5388	19.02%
XSS [22]	14,916	783	8.78%
Command injection [23]	36,031	2161	12.56%
XSRF [24]	56,198	4418	13.14%
Remote code execution [25]	30,591	2592	8.93%
Path disclosure [23]	42,303	2968	11.64%
Open redirect [26]	26,521	1762	13.67%

4.2 Evaluation Metrics

We use four metrics as the basis for this evaluation: true positives (TP), true negatives (TN), false positives (FP), and false negatives (FN). Where Positive means the predicted result is vulnerable. Negative means the expected result is not vulnerable. "true" and "false" indicate whether the prediction result is correct compared to the actual value.

By calculating the above four indicators, we can get some evaluation metrics. The Precision (cf. Eq. 3) is the proportion of true positives in all positives. It describes how precise the model is regarding how many of the predicted positives are actual positives.

The Recall (cf. Eq. 4), also called sensitivity, is a measurement of the rate of correctly identified positives compared to the total number of actual positives, which means the number of true positives in the sample that the classifier considers to be positive. F1 (cf. Eq. 5) is the harmonic mean of Precision and Recall, a measure of classification problems. Ideally, the closer the above three evaluation metrics are to 1, the better the performance of the obtained model.

$$Precision = \frac{TP}{TP + FP} \tag{3}$$

$$Recall = \frac{TP}{TP + FN} \tag{4}$$

$$F1 = 2 \cdot \frac{Precision \cdot Recall}{Precision + Recall} \tag{5}$$

In addition, another metric we also used is Accuracy (cf. Eq. 6). It represents the proportion of correct classifications among all predictions made by the classifier. It should be noted that in the field of vulnerability mining, especially when the amounts of different types of data in the vulnerability dataset used are unbalanced, this Accuracy cannot be used to judge the quality of the model. Therefore, this paper mainly uses Precision, Recall, and F1 to evaluate the model. Accuracy lists as a reference.

$$Accuracy = \frac{TP + TN}{TP + FP + TN + FN} \tag{6}$$

4.3 Experiment Settings and Environment

The LSTM networks were implemented using Keras together with a TensorFlow backend. The computational system used was a desktop running Windows10 with an NVIDIA 3080 GPU and 32G RAM.

Baseline Model. To demonstrate the performance advantage of deep representation learning, we use the methods used by previous related work on the same dataset for comparison.

LSTM [13]: This method treats the source code as a natural language. It uses the word2vec model to get the vector form of the token and feeds it into the LSTM model and the vulnerability label for classification training.

Parameter Setting. We divide the dataset into training set, validation set and test set, and their ratios are 7:2:1 respectively.

LSTM: Referring to the parameter settings mentioned in the related paper and maintaining the comparative experiments' fairness, we set the output dimension of the word2vec model to 200. The number of neurons in the LSTM model is set to 100, and the default dropout and recurrent dropout are set to 20%. The batch size is 128, and Adam optimizer is selected for optimization.

VDDRL: The parameter settings of the first part of our model are the same as the baseline. On this basis, the output of the hidden layer of the LSTM network is extracted as a 100-dimensional feature representation of each vulnerability code. The deep feature representation and corresponding labels are used as training data to train the classifier model.

Performance Evaluation. We use Accuracy, Precision, Recall, and F1 to measure the performance of different approaches. Tables 2 and 3 show the performance of the baseline model and the VDDRL model on seven different vulnerability types datasets, respectively.

Table 2. Performance of baseline model

Vulnerability	Accuracy	Precision	Recall	F1
SQL injection	93.4%	83.4%	80.6%	81.2%
XSS	97.7%	92.3%	79.9%	86.3%
Command injection	97.9%	94.2%	88.6%	91.1%
XSRF	97%	92.9%	83.8%	88.1%
Remote code execution	98.1%	95.3%	82.2%	90.2%
Path disclosure	97.4%	92.7%	84.8%	88.7%
Open redirect	96.9%	91.4%	83.9%	87.5%
SQL injection	93.4%	83.4%	80.6%	81.2%

Table 3. Performance of VDDRL

Vulnerability	Accuracy	Precision	Recall	F1
SQL injection	95.6%	91.6%	85.0%	88.1%
XSS	98.6%	99.0%	99.5%	99.2%
Command injection	98.4%	95.7%	91.2%	93.4%
XSRF	98.1%	95.2%	90.5%	92.8%
Remote code execution	98.7%	97.7%	87.7%	92.5%
Path disclosure	98.2%	95.7%	88.4%	91.9%
Open redirect	96.8%	92.1%	84.7%	88.2%
SQL injection	95.6%	91.6%	85.0%	88.1%

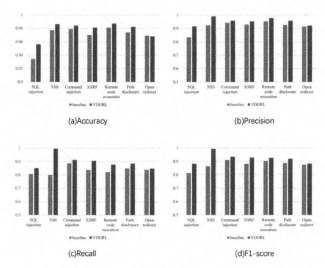

Fig. 3. Performance between VDDRL and Baseline model

From the chart, we can see that the baseline comparative model has achieved good results in vulnerability classification. The Accuracy metrics have reached more than 95% except for the SQL injection. Except for SQL injection, the Precision metrics have reached more than 90%. The Recall and F1 almost have a performance of more than 80% over the whole dataset. The vulnerability detection framework VDDRL based on deep representation learning has achieved a comprehensive improvement based on the baseline model. Figure 3 shows that our method has an average improvement of 0.86%, 3.54%, 6.2%, and 4.7% on the four metrics of Accuracy, Precision, Recall, and F1, respectively. The results mean that our VDDRL model improves the recognition accuracy and improves the model's ability to identify positive and negative samples. In other words, our model is more robust based on achieving more comprehensive vulnerability identification.

Figure 4 compares the ROC curves of the baseline model and the VDDRL model on seven vulnerabilities. It can be seen intuitively from the ROC curves that the classifier model trained by our method has a higher AUC value for each vulnerability type, which indicates that VDDRL has better classification performance than the baseline model.

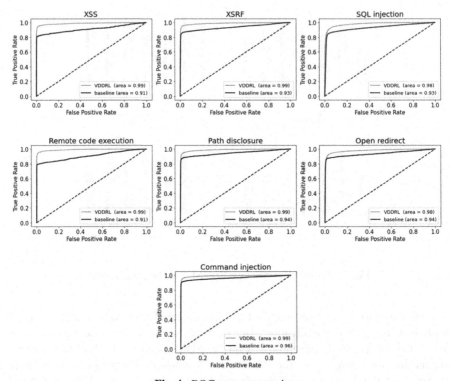

Fig. 4. ROC curve comparison

5   Conclusion

This paper proposes VDDRL, a vulnerability detection framework based on deep representation learning for python source code. We separate the vulnerability feature extraction module and the classification learning module. The former module uses LSTM for deep representation learning, and the latter uses traditional machine learning algorithms for classification training. Through comparative experiments on datasets containing seven different vulnerability types, the Accuracy of VDDRL is 95.6%–98.7%, the Precision is 91.6%–99.0%, the Recall is 84.7%–99.5%, and the F1 is 88.1%–99.2%.

Future work can consider converting the source code into the form of intermediate representation (IR), such as abstract syntax tree (AST) or data flow graph (DFG), to retain more semantic and syntactic information to improve the overall performance.

Acknowledgements. This work was supported in part by the National Key Research and Development Program of China under Grant 2018YFB0803401,in part by the China Postdoctoral Science Foundation funded project (2019M650606), and in part by the First-class Discipline Construction Project of Beijing Electronic Science and Technology Institute (3201012).

References

1. Liu, Z., Yuan, Y., Wang, S., et al.: SoK: demystifying binary lifters through the lens of downstream applications. In: 2022 IEEE Symposium on Security and Privacy (SP), Los Alamitos, CA, USA. IEEE Computer Society, pp. 453–472 (2022)
2. Hazimeh, A., Herrera, A., Payer, M.: Magma: a ground-truth fuzzing benchmark. Proc. ACM Meas. Anal. Comput. Syst. **4**(3), 1–29 (2020)
3. Ferrara, P., Mandal, A.K., Cortesi, A., et al.: Static analysis for discovering IoT vulnerabilities. Int. J. Softw. Tools Technol. Trans. **23**(1), 71–88 (2021)
4. Pecorelli, F., Lujan, S., Lenarduzzi, V., et al.: On the adequacy of static analysis warnings with respect to code smell prediction. Empir. Softw. Eng. **27**(3), 1–44 (2022)
5. Palit, T., Moon, J.F., Monrose, F., et al.: Dynpta: combining static and dynamic analysis for practical selective data protection. In: 2021 IEEE Symposium on Security and Privacy (SP). IEEE, pp. 1919–1937 (2021)
6. Wang, C.Y., You, C.Y., Hsu, F.H., et al.: SMS observer: a dynamic mechanism to analyze the behavior of SMS-based malware. J. Parallel Distrib. Comput. **156**, 25–37 (2021)
7. Li, Y., Chen, B., Chandramohan, M., Lin, S.-W., Liu, Y., Tiu, A.: Steelix: program-state based binary fuzzing. In: Proceedings of the 2017 11th Joint Meeting on Foundations of Software Engineering. ACM, pp. 627–637 (2017)
8. Morrison, P., Herzig, K., Murphy, B., Williams, L.: Challenges with applying vulnerability prediction models. In: Proceedings of the 2015 Symposium and Bootcamp on the Science of Security, pp. 4 (2015)
9. Hovsepyan, A., Scandariato, R., Joosen, W., Walden, J.: Software vulnerability prediction using text analysis techniques. In: Proceedings of 4th International Workshop Security Measurements and Metrics, MetriSec 2012, pp. 7–10 (2012)
10. Mou, L., Li, G., Jin, Z., Zhang, L., Wang, T.: TBCNN: a tree-based convolutional neural network for programming language processing. CoRR (2014)
11. Li, Z., et al.: VulDeePecker: a deep learning-based system for vulnerability detection. CoRR abs/1801.01681 (2018)
12. Wartschinski, L., et al.: VUDENC: vulnerability detection with deep learning on a natural codebase for Python. Inf. Softw. Technol. **106809** (2022)
13. Zhang, Y., Gao, X., Duck, G.J., et al.: Program vulnerability repair via inductive inference (2022)
14. Siow, J.K., Liu, S., Xie, X., et al.: Learning program semantics with code representations: an empirical study. arXiv preprint arXiv:2203.11790 (2022)
15. Schrammel, D., Weiser, S., Sadek, R., et al.: Jenny: securing syscalls for PKU-based memory isolation systems. In: USENIX Security Symposium (2022)
16. He, L., Hu, H., Su, P., et al.: FreeWill: automatically diagnosing use-after-free bugs via reference miscounting detection on binaries. In: 31st USENIX Security Symposium (USENIX Security 2022), pp. 2497–2512 (2022)
17. Liu, K., Kim, D., Bissyand'e, T.F., Yoo, S., Le Traon, Y.: Mining fix patterns for findbugs violations. IEEE Trans. Softw. Eng. **47**, 165–188 (2018)
18. J. Harer, O., et al.: Learning to repair software vulnerabilities with generative adversarial networks. In: Advances in Neural Information Processing Systems, pp. 7933–7943 (2018)
19. Gupta, R., Pal, S., Kanade, A., Shevade, S.: Deepfix: fixing common c language errors by deep learning. In: Thirty-First AAAI Conference on Artificial Intelligence (2017)
20. SQL Injection (2020). https://owasp.org/www-community/attacks/SQL_Injection. Accessed 14 May 2022
21. Cross-site Scripting (2020). https://owasp.org/www-community/attacks/xss/. Accessed 14 May 2022

22. Command Injection (2020). https://owasp.org/www-community/attacks/Command_Inje ction. Accessed 14 May 2022
23. Cross Site Request Forgery (2020). https://owasp.org/www-community/attacks/csrf. Accessed 14 May 2022
24. Code Injection (2020). https://owasp.org/www-community/attacks/Code_Injection. Accessed 14 May 2022
25. CWE-601: Open Redirect (2020). https://cwe.mitre.org/data/definitions/601. Accessed 14 May 2022
26. Shin, Y., Williams, L.: An empirical model to predict security vulnerabilities using code complexity metrics. In: Proceedings of the Second ACM-IEEE International Symposium on Empirical Software Engineering and Measurement, pp. 315–317 (2008)
27. Chowdhury, I., Zulkernine, M.: Using complexity, coupling, and cohesion metrics as early indicators of vulnerabilities. J. Syst. Arch. **57**(3), 294–313 (2011)
28. Dam, H.K., Tran, T., Pham, T., Ng, S.W., Grundy, J., Ghose, A.: Automatic feature learning for vulnerability prediction. arXiv preprint. arXiv:1708.02368 (2017)

Assessing Vulnerability from Its Description

Zijing Zhang[✉][ID], Vimal Kumar[ID], Michael Mayo[ID], and Albert Bifet[ID]

CROW, University of Waikato, Hamilton, WK 3216, New Zealand
zz199@students.waikato.ac.nz, {vimal.kumar,mmayo,abifet}@waikato.ac.nz

Abstract. This paper shows an end-to-end Artificial Intelligence (AI) system to estimate the severity level and the various Common Vulnerability Scoring System (CVSS) components from natural language descriptions without reproducing the vulnerability. This natural language processing-based approach can estimate the CVSS from only the Common Vulnerabilities and Exposures description without the need to reproduce the vulnerability environment. We present an Error Grid Analysis for the CVSS base score prediction task. Experiments on CVSS 2.0 and CVSS 3.1 show that state-of-the-art deep learning models can predict the CVSS scoring components with high accuracy. The low-cost Universal Sentence Encoder (large) model outperforms the Generative Pre-trained Transformer-3 (GPT-3) and the Support Vector Machine baseline on the majority of the classification tasks with a lower computation overhead than the GPT-3.

Keywords: Threat Intelligence · Artificial Intelligence · CVSS · Deep Learning · Natural Language Processing

1 Introduction

Large-scale cyberspace evolves as devices with new functionalities and services join and leave the network [11]. Inevitable staff turnover causes information on crucial infrastructure sometimes to go missing even with the best change management processes in place. Malicious actors constantly probe for such exploitable vulnerabilities, introduced by the gradual device changes and business fallbacks. It is therefore important to develop systems that are capable of automatically detecting vulnerabilities from configurations that may be inconceivable to an engineer. However, before we can develop such systems, we need to develop techniques that can understand the severity of vulnerabilities from their description.

Common Vulnerability Scoring System (CVSS), created by the CVSS Special Interest Group (SIG) [20], is the de facto measure for assessing the impact of a cyber vulnerability [8,17]. The CVSS scoring process requires the reproduction of the reported vulnerabilities along with a manual assessment by an evaluation panel of cyber security professionals. This process can be time-consuming and error-prone. At any given time there is always a backlog of vulnerabilities

G. Wang et al. (Eds.): UbiSec 2022, CCIS 1768, pp. 129–143, 2023.
https://doi.org/10.1007/978-981-99-0272-9_9

awaiting scoring through this manual process. An automated, intelligent system without the need to reproduce the vulnerability would greatly reduce the vulnerability assessment workloads and speed this process up.

The CVSS has two main versions CVSS 2.0 (v2) and CVSS 3.1 (v3). However, as many existing cyber security tools use the older CVSS 2.0, the adoption of the latest 3.1 metrics is slow [19]. Therefore, the National Vulnerability Dataset keeps both the CVSS version 2 and 3 metrics. The coexistence of the two forces its users to cope with both versions. A systematic conversion method for CVSS v2 and v3 would bridge this gap and unify both versions within CVSS, reinforcing the consistency of vulnerability evaluation systems.

This paper utilizes the Universal Sentence Encoder (USE) and the Generative Pre-trained Transformer 3 (GPT-3) models to estimate the severity of cyber vulnerabilities from their natural language descriptions. These models can do a quick analysis and a bidirectional conversion of the Base Scores between the CVSS 2.0 and the CVSS 3.1. We also use the Error Grid Analysis (EGA), common in medical wearable sensor evaluation methods [6], to analyze the base score predictions with more in-depth label-wise reports. Even as a lightweight sentence-level encoder, the USE model still achieves state-of-the-art performance in multiple CVSS component prediction tasks, outperforming the GPT-3 and the baseline SVM models.

Section 2 describes the background knowledge to understand the research presented in this paper. In Sect. 3 we describe the existing CVSS evaluation systems and the underlying algorithms. Section 4 describes the methods used to collect data and train the machine learning models. Section 5 shows the classification reports of the component prediction tasks and the severity level prediction task for CVSS 3.1 and 2.0. For the CVSS 2.0 severity level prediction task, we also show the Error Grid Analysis (EGA) result.

2   Background

This section describes the background of the vulnerability evaluation system and the machine learning models used in this research. There are two categories of models used: the "shallow" Support Vector Machine model and the deep learning models (the USE and the GPT).

2.1   Common Vulnerability Scoring System (CVSS)

A non-profit organization based in the United States named the Forum of Incident Response and Security Teams (FIRST) maintains the Common Vulnerability Scoring System (CVSS). FIRST selects representatives from the cyber security industry and academia from their requests to join the Special Interest Group (SIG) [8]. SIG then creates the Common Vulnerability Scoring System (CVSS) to help access vulnerabilities that are present in the cyber security domain [8].

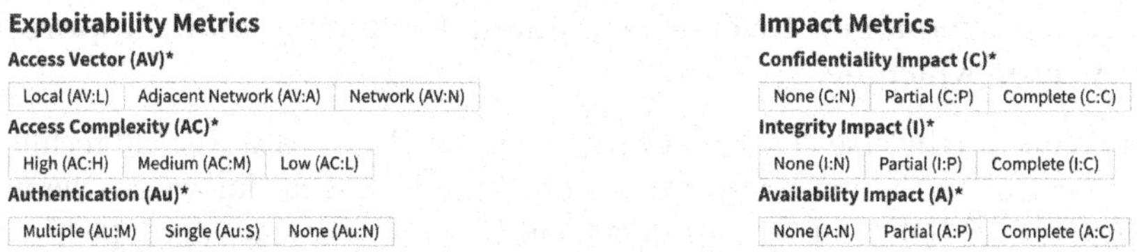

Fig. 1. The components of CVSS 2.0 base score

Fig. 2. The components of CVSS 3.1 base score

There are six components in the CVSS base score version 2 as shown in Fig. 1 [17] and eight components in the CVSS base score version 3 as shown in Fig. 2 [8]. The severity rating of a vulnerability depends on the base score components. In CVSS version 2, the "low" severity score ranges from 0.0 to 3.9, while the "medium" severity score ranges from 4.0 to 6.9, and the "high" severity score ranges from 7.0 to 10.0. Version 3 of CVSS adds two more ratings to the severity measure: "none" (0.0) and "critical" (9.0-10.0). The "low" rating starts from 0.1 instead of 0.0. The "high" rating ends at 8.9 instead of 10.0 in version 2. In version 3, the "medium" severity rating uses the same base score as in CVSS v2 [25].

The CVSS 3.1 changed from three possible values(version 2.0) to two for the Attack Complexity component, leaving only the High and the Low values [8]. Attack Vector replaces the Access Vector in version 2.0. It has four values, instead of three values, with an addition of the "Physical" value, indicating the attacker must be physically present on the victim's machine to perform attacks such as USB direct memory access [8]. Privilege Required is a new component that further categorizes the old authentication component. Along with the User Interaction component, it replaces the Authentication component in version 2.0. The User Interaction component indicates that the attacker needs misconfiguration or activity from the victim system's users(not from the attackers) to exploit the vulnerability. Scope indicates whether an attack changed the access rights of the infected system component [8].

2.2   Term Frequency Inverse Document Frequency and Support Vector Machine

Term Frequency-Inverse Document Frequency(TF-IDF) is a statistical technique used to calculate the importance of a word in a document, known as the word weight [13]. TF-IDF transforms a document into a vector space, grouped by the word's feature selection algorithms. For each task, we set the maximum feature parameter in the TF-IDF vectorization to 512, the same as the embedding size of the USE model, to speed up the computation of its Python implementation in SciKit Learn [16].

The Support Vector Machine (SVM) is a supervised machine learning algorithm [18]. It constructs a hyperplane to classify the data points. The SVM generalizes well to all types of distributions. The training data and the test/working data can have different types of label distributions such as Gaussian or Bernoulli [18]. However, the SVM model requires all the data should have the same set of attributes. Each SVM model has a hyperplane with a kernel function and a margin parameter. Express vectors(support vectors) form the decision boundaries within which the hyperplane centers itself with a certain distance, a.k.a. the margin. This margin can be "softened" to allow exceptions to avoid overfitting. The kernel function transforms low dimensional vectors into high dimensional ones so that it is easier for the model to calculate the hyperplane [18]. The choice of the kernel function is a trade-off between the ease of the hyperplane calculation and the over-fitting of the model. SVM outperforms Naive Bayes in most TF-IDF vectorized classification tasks [14] and handles nonvector data that can be a composition of multiple features of different data types. Therefore, SVM is the choice of the baseline model, representing the "shallow" learning models without neural networks.

2.3   Universal Sentence Encoder

The Universal Sentence Encoder has two components: the Deep Averaging Network (DAN) and the Transformer model [5]. The Bag-of-Words is a multiset of input strings. In a typical representation, the Bag-of-Words is a dictionary with the word as the key and the number of times the word appears in the input string as the value. The DAN adds a neural network component that collects a feature hierarchy based on the bag-of-words representation of the input [12].

$$Attention(Q, K, V) = Softmax\left(\frac{QK^T}{\sqrt{d_k}}\right) V \qquad (1)$$

The Transformer model is a linear projection of the Attention mechansim as shown in the Formula (1) [15] [26]. It replaces the recurrent neural network and other model architectures with the Self-Attentions that are capable of recognizing interdependencies in the input feature hierarchy.

Google designs the USE model for embedding textual inputs at the sentence level instead of the prior word level to transfer knowledge among different natural language processing tasks. It consists of a DAN that embeds any textual input at a linear time and a Transformer-based encoding model that prioritizes accuracy over computational cost [5]. The USE model chooses which model to use based on the input complexity. For short sentences, it uses the Transformer model; for long sentences, it uses the DAN model.

2.4 Generative Pre-trained Transformer 3

Fine-tuning is a popular learning setup for a transfer learning task. Before fine-tuning, a model has its weights initialized with the pre-trained weights from another task similar to the target task. Fine-tuned models have the best performance compared to few-shot, one-shot, or zero-shot learning. However, fine-tuning requires a large amount of data to retrain the model. The model needs to retune the weights of the pre-trained model to the fine-tuned task [4].

Few-shot learning refers to the ability of the model to learn from a limited set of examples during the model inference time, similar to the generalization capability of a human. In a few-shot learning setup, the model uses only the pre-trained weights, without any updates to its weights, to predict the target task.

The third generation Generative Pre-trained Transformer(GPT-3) model is an autoregressive model with 175 billion parameters, which is capable of few-shot learning [4]. Autoregressive means that the model can predict the next word in the sequence depending on existing words. A large number of parameters and a large amount of unsupervised training on the Common Crawl data (3.1 Billion samples [24]) enable the GPT-3 model to achieve "in-context learning", i.e. identifying the running task at inference time, instead of the conventional task-specific learning [4].

3 Related Works

This section reviews the existing works that evaluate the severity of the vulnerability with natural language descriptions. There were conventional machine learning models [27] and the more recent deep learning techniques [3,7,23].

3.1 Machine Learning for CVSS Prediction

Yamamoto et al. compared the performance of the Naive Bayes classifier, Latent Dirichlet Allocation(LDA), Latent Semantic Indexing, and supervised LDA(SLDA) model to predict the CVSS 2.0 score from January 2002 to December 2013 from the CVE descriptions. They introduced an annual weight parameter to improve the performance of the SLDA model [27].

Shahid et al. used a small BERT model with four transformer encoders to predict the CVSS 3.1 components [23]. Costa et al. compared BERT, RoBERTa, ALBERT, DeBERTa, and DistilBERT models to predict the CVSS 3.1 components with lemmatization and vocabulary addition for the tokenizer [7]. The state-of-the-art performance to predict CVSS 3.1 components is achieved by the

DistilBERT model [7]. In this paper, we choose GPT-3 as the state-of-art reference model as it is among the third generation Transformer models while the BERT model is a second-generation model similar to the GPT-2 model [4].

3.2   Conversion from CVSS V2.0 to CVSS V3.1

There is no official conversion formula for CVSS v2.0 to CVSS v3.1 [8]. Notwak et al. collected 73,179 CVSS data from the OSWASP Vulnerability Management Center [19]. The vectorization is calculated as the word frequency (if within the top 50 words) divided by 100. Through machine learning algorithms, they map the seven CVSS 2.0 components into the eight CVSS 3.1 components. They achieved a median accuracy of 62.8 % for the CVSS 3.1 score conversion task. Beck et al. proposed a method to estimate organizational risk based on the CVSS score with the help of neural network models [3]. In their work, they hypothesized that the organizational security risks depend on the terminal device implementations. Therefore, they suggest that security officers could work bottom-up to estimate the organization's security risks. The design goal of their perceptron model is then to aid the security officers with the knowledge of the environmental context and the CVSS to traverse through the device topology recursively. By recursively, Bect et al. meant to use the same perceptron model again in different cyber security contexts.

4   Methodology

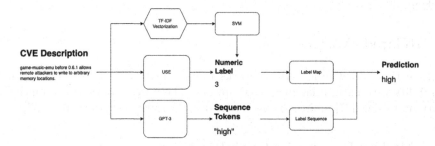

Fig. 3. The proposed methods: the three models to estimate CVSS scores from the natural language descriptions of the CVE entries in the NVD database. The SVM model takes a vector of TF-IDF values as input and outputs a numeric label. A post-processing script then converts the numeric label into the target prediction. The USE model predicts the same set of numeric labels and uses the same post-processing script. However, different from the SVM model, the USE model takes the natural language descriptions directly, without any pre-processing such as TF-IDF vectorization. The GPT-3 model takes in the natural language descriptions and outputs a string sequence, sometimes with noisy tokens. A post-processing script (the Label Map) normalizes the string sequence into target labels.

Utilizing natural language descriptions available in the NVD, we propose three types of machine learning models, shown in Fig. 3 to estimate the target labels of the cyber threats through natural language processing models. The natural language descriptions come from the requests submitted to the MITRE ATTACK framework [22]. A machine learning model maps these descriptions to the impact of cyber threats. The model aims to learn cyber security risk assessment metrics. This section details the data collected and the models used to estimate such threat intelligence.

4.1   Data

The statistical analysis of the CVSS is based on data crawled from the National Vulnerability Database(NVD), which is available at https://gitlab.com/zzj0402/nvd/, crawled up to April 2nd, 2022. The dataset has 169,000 entries, one-third is randomly split as the test set, and the rest is used as the training set. Each entry is a JSON object with a natural language description of the vulnerability and the target labels such as severity levels, CVSS score, or a CVSS component.

4.2   Tasks

Component Classification. CVSS metric consists of the Base Score, Temporal Score, and Environmental Score. This paper addresses the classification task of the CVSS base score metric components. Each CVSS component classification is a multiclass classification task. The input is the natural language description of a CVE entry. The output is a CVSS component value prediction. For example, the Access Complexity classification task for the CVSS 2.0 has the Access Complexity value(high, medium, or low) as the output. Table 1 shows the classification results for the CVSS 2.0 components. Table 3 shows the results for the CVSS 3.1 component classification tasks.

Base Score Prediction. There are two ways for the proposed machine learning models to predict the CVSS Base Score: calculate from the components using the CVSS formula or directly output a numeric value from the natural language inputs. To calculate the Base Score from each component, one would need to build six different models, each targeting a single component for the CVSS 2.0. After such modeling, one then plugs the predicted component values into the CVSS formula to calculate the Base Score, ranging from 0 to 10. This is similar to the human evaluation of the CVSS score. However, the errors would aggregate on each component value. All six models need to predict the correct component values simultaneously to have the reference Base Score value.

The alternative approach is to directly output a numeric value from the natural language inputs. It is a more challenging task than the component classification-based approach. A machine learning algorithm would need to not only estimate the component values but also its formula for the numerical Base Score prediction. However, it is an end-to-end solution, which means that it requires no intermediate stages such as plugging component values into a CVSS calculation formula to get the Base Score. Figure 5 shows the predicted Base Score values for the CVSS 2.0 with an Error Grid Analysis.

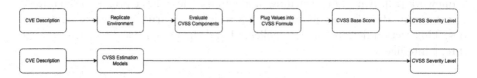

Fig. 4. End-to-end CVSS estimation workflow: the top chart shows the workflow of the CVSS severity estimation process which contains four stages. The proposed deep learning models can predict the CVSS severity level from the natural language descriptions of the CVE entries. As shown in the lower chart, it is an end-to-end solution for the severity-level estimation task.

Severity Classification. As a qualitative measure, the severity level is easier to predict than the numeric Base Score. Severity would also be a more intuitive measure to the user than the numeric Base Score. It takes the Common Vulnerabilities and Exposures(CVE) natural language description as the input and the severity level (high, medium, and low in CVSS 2.0; critical, high, medium, low, and none in CVSS 3.1) as the output. This NLP solution eliminates the need to replicate the vulnerability environment and simplifies the workflow as shown in Fig. 4 [8]. Table 2 shows the classification results for the CVSS 2.0 severity levels. Table 4 shows the results for the CVSS 3.1 severity classification tasks.

4.3   Training

Both the GPT-3 and the USE models have four training epochs. All GPT-3 models are sequence-to-sequence, taking string inputs and outputting another string. In the classification task of CVSS 2.0 components, the input is the vulnerability description, and the output is the CVSS value string, which is a vector representing the component values. This sequence-to-sequence setting sometimes causes the model to predict values from the unexpected distribution. The training/evaluation accuracy is the sequence accuracy as in GPT3 metrics since the token accuracy is irrelevant to the label, which happens to be the output sequence, typically having a single target label token.

The USE model has a trainable Keras layer available through TensorFlow's model distribution network TensorFlowHub. For each task, the upstream model is the fifth version of the "large" USE model with all the neural network parameters trained on the crawled NVD training dataset [1]. A labeled map for each sample translates the string label into a numerical one. The downstream model, a model that is appended to the upstream model, the USE, is a single-layer predictor model with a dense layer with N "neurons" where N is the number of possible labels in the dataset. Since there are three types of tasks in this paper and the component classification would have different component values, the amount of neurons in the output layer is different for each task. The whole model can then predict each label's likelihood as a real-valued probability score. Then a one-hot encoding indicates the index, which maps to a class label. ADAM is the optimizer used to train all the USE models with an empirically fine-tuned learning rate, avoiding gradient vanishing or explosion problems. These problems would cause a deep learning model to diverge. Cross-entropy loss is the training loss for both the USE and the GPT-3.

4.4 Evaluation

The evaluation test set is one-third of the whole dataset. For each task in the CVSS 3.1 classification task, a trained USE model predicts on the test set with 28,891 samples. For the CVSS 2.0 tasks, the test set has 51,000 samples. The TensorFlow framework provides a convenient KerasLayer loading function to read the trained model into the GPU memory [2]. The model then predicts the labels for each test sample description, showing the confidence for each label. An argmax function call from the NumPy library converts the predicted probabilities into the predicted labels [9]. After the label conversion, the Classification Report tool from the SciKit Learn Metrics library calculates the precision, recall, F1-score, support, and confusion matrix from the ground truth labels [16]. For each task, this paper presents a classification report produced by the Scikit-Learn toolset [21]. The GPT-3 model predicts a sequence of tokens for each task, which should match the reference tokens. However, the GPT-3 model sometimes outputs tokens partially within the target vocabulary or entirely out of distribution. A script handles this by selecting the relevant tokens from the predicted sequence. Suppose the model predicted "adjacent" in the attack vector or access vector classification task. This selection script would change "adjacent" to "adjacent_network" to match the reference value. If the model predicted "adjacentnetworkconfiguration" in the same task, this selection script would change "adjacentnetworkconfiguration" to "adjacent_network," removing the redundant tokens.

5   Empirical Evaluation Results

This section presents the results of the tasks mentioned in Sect. 4.2. Each classification report, adapted from the Scikit Learn Python toolkit [21], consists of label-specific and averaged metrics. Each cell in the label-specific metrics has three columns(the USE model, the GPT-3 model Babbage variant, and the TF-IDF SVM model). In the lower segment of each classification report, the first row only has the accuracy in the F1-Score column. The second row has the macro-averaged (sum of the label-specific score such as precision, recall, and f1-score, divided by the number of labels, which is 3 in component-specific metric classification tasks). The third row has the weighted-average precision, recall, and F1-Score. For the CVSS score versions 2.0 and 3.1, there are classification reports for each metric component prediction task, the base score prediction, and the severity classification. The best performing class is in bold. Overall, the USE model is the best-performing model. The GPT-3 performs head-to-head with the USE. Both deep learning models outclass the SVM model with TF-IDF vectorization.

5.1 Predicting Common Vulnerability Scoring System 2.0

This subsection presents the results of the CVSS 2.0-related tasks. It includes the classification reports for each of the component classification tasks(Table 1a 1b 1c 1d 1e 1f), the Error Grid Analysis for the Base Score prediction tasks (Fig. 5), and the classification reports for the severity classification task (Table 2). As shown in Table 2, the USE model performs better than the Babbage model since the USE model has a higher accuracy across the table and without out-of-distribution labels. However, the out-of-distribution prediction of the severity level labels might be due to the GPT-3 task formulation. The GPT-3 model works as a sequence-to-sequence task, while the USE model works as a multi-nomial classification task (labeling each description as low, medium, or high). The sequence-to-sequence task is more free-forming than the multi-nomial classification task as it can predict any English sentence instead of a numerical representation of the target labels.

Table 1. CVSS 2.0 Component results

Class	Precision			Recall			F1-Score			Support
	USE	GPT	SVM	USE	GPT	SVM	USE	GPT	SVM	
Adjacent	**0.83**	0.78	0.00	**0.73**	0.73	0.00	**0.78**	0.75	0.00	1779
Network	**0.97**	0.97	0.83	0.97	0.97	**1.00**	**0.97**	0.97	0.90	42176
Local	0.83	**0.85**	0.05	**0.85**	0.84	0.00	**0.84**	0.84	0.00	7132
Accuracy							**0.94**	0.94	0.82	51087
Macro	**0.87**	0.86	0.29	**0.85**	0.84	0.33	**0.86**	0.85	0.30	51087
Weighted	**0.94**	0.94	0.69	**0.94**	0.94	0.82	**0.94**	0.94	0.75	51087

(a) Access vector classification report

Class	Precision			Recall			F1-Score			Support
	USE	GPT	SVM	USE	GPT	SVM	USE	GPT	SVM	
Low	**0.87**	0.87	0.68	0.88	0.89	**0.89**	0.87	**0.88**	0.77	29858
Medium	0.80	**0.82**	0.69	**0.82**	0.80	0.42	**0.81**	0.81	0.52	20102
High	**0.54**	0.35	0.00	0.28	**0.34**	0.00	**0.37**	0.34	0.00	1400
Accuracy							**0.84**	0.84	0.68	51087
Macro	**0.74**	0.68	0.46	0.66	**0.67**	0.44	**0.69**	0.68	0.43	51087
Weighted	**0.83**	0.83	0.67	**0.84**	0.84	0.68	**0.84**	0.84	0.65	51087

(b) Access complexity classification report

Class	Precision			Recall			F1-Score			Support
	USE	GPT	SVM	USE	GPT	SVM	USE	GPT	SVM	
None	0.95	**0.96**	0.84	**0.96**	0.96	0.95	**0.96**	0.96	0.89	43265
Single	**0.78**	0.78	0.04	0.74	**0.75**	0.01	**0.76**	0.76	0.02	7802
Multiple	0.00	0.00	0.00	0.00	0.00	0.00	0.00	0.00	0.00	20
Accuracy							**0.93**	0.93	0.81	51087
Macro	**0.58**	0.58	0.29	**0.57**	0.57	0.32	**0.57**	0.57	0.30	51087
Weighted	**0.93**	0.93	0.72	**0.93**	0.93	0.81	**0.93**	0.93	0.76	51087

(l) Authentication classification report

Class	Precision			Recall			F1-Score			Support
	USE	GPT	SVM	USE	GPT	SVM	USE	GPT	SVM	
Complete	0.64	**0.65**	0.10	0.65	**0.69**	0.01	0.67	**0.68**	0.01	8591
Partial	0.82	**0.83**	0.50	0.82	0.83	**0.84**	**0.85**	0.84	0.63	25472
None	0.87	**0.88**	0.31	0.85	**0.88**	0.14	0.86	**0.88**	0.19	17024
Accuracy							0.80	**0.83**	0.47	51087
Macro	0.78	**0.80**	0.30	0.78	**0.80**	0.33	0.78	**0.80**	0.28	51087
Weighted	0.81	**0.83**	0.37	0.80	**0.83**	0.47	0.80	**0.83**	0.38	51087

(d) Confidentiality impact classification report

Class	Precision			Recall			F1-Score			Support
	USE	GPT	SVM	USE	GPT	SVM	USE	GPT	SVM	
Complete	0.65	**0.70**	0.10	**0.72**	0.68	0.01	0.68	**0.69**	0.01	8341
Partial	**0.87**	0.87	0.55	0.83	**0.87**	0.85	0.85	**0.87**	0.67	27619
None	0.87	**0.89**	0.31	**0.89**	0.89	0.16	0.88	**0.89**	0.21	15127
Accuracy							0.83	**0.85**	0.51	51087
Macro	0.80	**0.82**	0.32	0.81	**0.82**	0.34	0.81	**0.82**	0.30	51087
Weighted	0.84	**0.85**	0.40	0.83	**0.85**	0.51	0.83	**0.85**	0.42	51087

(e) Integrity impact classification report

Class	Precision			Recall			F1-Score			Support
	USE	GPT	SVM	USE	GPT	SVM	USE	GPT	SVM	
Complete	**0.72**	0.70	0.15	0.63	**0.70**	0.01	0.67	**0.70**	0.02	10100
Partial	0.77	**0.80**	0.48	**0.81**	0.80	0.48	0.79	**0.80**	0.48	22358
None	0.87	**0.88**	0.41	**0.88**	0.88	0.61	**0.88**	0.88	0.49	18629
Accuracy							0.80	**0.81**	0.43	51087
Macro	0.79	**0.80**	0.35	0.77	**0.79**	0.37	0.78	**0.79**	0.33	51087
Weighted	0.80	**0.81**	0.39	0.80	**0.81**	0.43	0.80	**0.81**	0.39	51087

(f) Availability impact classification report

Table 2. The Classification report of the severity level prediction

Class	Precision			Recall			F1-Score			Support
	USE	GPT	SVM	USE	GPT	SVM	USE	GPT	SVM	
Low	**0.64**	0.59	0.00	**0.61**	0.58	0.00	**0.62**	0.59	0.00	5271
Medium	**0.80**	0.79	0.59	0.84	0.80	**0.95**	**0.82**	0.80	0.72	30053
High	**0.76**	0.72	0.24	**0.71**	0.71	0.04	**0.73**	0.71	0.06	15763
accuracy							**0.77**	0.75	0.57	51087
macro	**0.73**	0.35	0.27	**0.72**	0.35	0.33	**0.72**	0.35	0.26	51087
weighted	**0.77**	0.75	0.42	**0.77**	0.75	0.57	**0.77**	0.75	0.45	51087

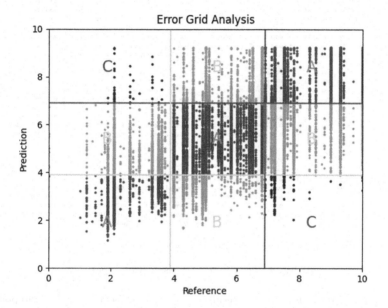

Fig. 5. Error grid analysis of the USE model for CVSS 2.0 base score prediction: the error grid consists of a "medium" threshold line (3.9, yellow) and a "high" threshold line (6.9, red). The three Zone As (colored in green, 73.7 %) in the grid indicate acceptable predictions within the same level of severity as the reference values. The four Zone Bs (colored in orange, 25.9 %) indicate predictions that are one level away from the reference severity level. The two Zone Cs (colored in red, 0.4 %) indicate predictions that are two levels away from the reference severity level. (Color figure online)

5.2 Predicting Common Vulnerability Scoring System 3.1

Table 3. CVSS 3.1 Component results

Class	Precision			Recall			F1-Score			Support
	USE	GPT	SVM	USE	GPT	SVM	USE	GPT	SVM	
Low	**0.96**	0.96	0.93	0.98	0.97	**1.00**	**0.97**	0.97	0.96	26842
High	**0.76**	0.57	0.23	**0.71**	0.53	0.00	**0.73**	0.55	0.00	2049
accuracy							0.95	0.94	0.93	28891
macro	**0.82**	0.77	0.58	**0.75**	0.75	0.50	**0.78**	0.76	0.48	28891
weighted	**0.94**	0.94	0.88	**0.95**	0.94	0.93	**0.94**	0.94	0.90	28891

(a) Attack complexity classification report

Class	Precision			Recall			F1-Score			Support
	USE	GPT	SVM	USE	GPT	SVM	USE	GPT	SVM	
Network	**0.94**	0.93	0.74	**0.94**	0.93	**0.98**	**0.94**	0.93	0.84	21051
Adjacent	**0.66**	0.54	0.63	0.63	**0.65**	0.02	**0.65**	0.59	0.03	770
Local	**0.83**	0.81	0.56	**0.84**	0.80	0.09	**0.83**	0.80	0.16	6727
Physical	**0.72**	0.62	0.00	**0.59**	0.58	0.00	**0.65**	0.60	0.00	343
accuracy							0.90	0.89	0.73	28891
macro	**0.79**	0.73	0.48	**0.75**	0.74	0.27	**0.77**	0.73	0.26	28891
weighted	**0.90**	0.89	0.69	**0.90**	0.89	0.73	**0.90**	0.89	0.65	28891

(b) Attack vector classification report

Class	Precision			Recall			F1-Score			Support
	USE	GPT	SVM	USE	GPT	SVM	USE	GPT	SVM	
None	**0.91**	0.88	0.49	0.85	**0.88**	0.54	**0.88**	0.88	0.51	11194
Low	**0.70**	0.30	0.00	0.29	**0.34**	0.00	**0.41**	0.32	0.00	697
High	0.89	**0.91**	0.66	**0.95**	0.90	0.64	**0.92**	0.90	0.65	17000
Accuracy							0.89	0.88	0.58	28891
Macro	**0.83**	0.70	0.38	0.69	**0.71**	0.39	**0.73**	0.70	0.39	28891
Weighted	**0.89**	0.88	0.57	**0.89**	0.88	0.58	**0.89**	0.88	0.58	28891

(c) Availability impact classification report

Class	Precision			Recall			F1-Score			Support
	USE	GPT	SVM	USE	GPT	SVM	USE	GPT	SVM	
None	**0.83**	0.80	0.47	**0.83**	0.82	0.19	**0.83**	0.81	0.27	6365
Low	**0.87**	0.80	0.81	0.79	**0.80**	0.22	**0.83**	0.80	0.34	5507
High	0.89	0.89	0.63	**0.92**	0.88	0.92	**0.90**	0.89	0.75	17019
Accuracy							0.87	0.85	0.63	28891
Macro	**0.86**	0.83	0.64	**0.84**	0.83	0.44	**0.85**	0.83	0.45	28891
Weighted	**0.87**	0.85	0.63	**0.87**	0.85	0.63	**0.87**	0.85	0.57	28891

(d) Confidentiality Impact Classification Report

Class	Precision			Recall			F1-Score			Support
	USE	GPT	SVM	USE	GPT	SVM	USE	GPT	SVM	
None	**0.86**	0.60	0.47	**0.89**	0.42	0.46	**0.88**	0.50	0.46	9034
Low	**0.87**	0.68	0.88	0.83	**0.75**	0.21	**0.85**	0.71	0.34	4971
High	**0.90**	0.73	0.58	**0.90**	0.84	0.73	**0.90**	0.78	0.65	14886
Accuracy							0.88	0.69	0.56	28891
Macro	**0.88**	0.67	0.64	**0.87**	0.67	0.47	**0.87**	0.66	0.48	28891
Weighted	**0.88**	0.68	0.60	**0.88**	0.69	0.56	**0.88**	0.68	0.54	28891

(e) Integrity impact classification report

Class	Precision			Recall			F1-Score			Support
	USE	GPT	SVM	USE	GPT	SVM	USE	GPT	SVM	
None	0.88	**0.89**	0.69	0.92	0.87	**0.96**	**0.90**	0.88	0.80	18707
Low	**0.76**	0.69	0.59	0.72	**0.74**	0.19	**0.74**	0.71	0.29	8033
High	**0.73**	0.60	0.33	**0.59**	0.59	0.02	**0.65**	0.59	0.04	2151
Accuracy							0.84	0.81	0.68	28891
Macro	**0.79**	0.44	0.54	**0.74**	0.44	0.39	**0.76**	0.44	0.38	28891
Weighted	**0.84**	0.81	0.64	**0.84**	0.81	0.68	**0.84**	0.81	0.60	28891

(f) Privilege required classification report

Class	Precision			Recall			F1-Score			Support
	USE	GPT	SVM	USE	GPT	SVM	USE	GPT	SVM	
Unchanged	**0.97**	0.97	0.87	0.99	0.83	**1.00**	**0.98**	0.97	0.93	24156
Changed	0.92	0.86	**0.93**	0.84	**0.97**	0.21	**0.88**	0.84	0.35	4735
Accuracy							0.96	0.95	0.87	28891
Macro	**0.95**	0.92	0.90	**0.92**	0.90	0.60	**0.93**	0.91	0.64	28891
Weighted	**0.96**	0.95	0.88	**0.96**	0.95	0.87	**0.96**	0.95	0.83	28891

(g) Scope classification report

Class	Precision			Recall			F1-Score			Support
	USE	GPT	SVM	USE	GPT	SVM	USE	GPT	SVM	
None	**0.94**	0.94	0.74	**0.96**	0.95	0.96	**0.95**	0.94	0.83	19088
Required	**0.92**	0.89	0.80	**0.89**	0.87	0.34	**0.90**	0.88	0.48	9803
Accuracy							0.93	0.92	0.75	28891
Macro	**0.93**	0.92	0.77	**0.92**	0.91	0.65	**0.93**	0.91	0.66	28891
Weighted	**0.93**	0.92	0.76	**0.93**	0.92	0.75	**0.93**	0.92	0.71	28891

(h) User interaction classification report

Table 4. Severity level classification report

Class	Precision			Recall			F1-Score			Support
	USE	GPT	SVM	USE	GPT	SVM	USE	GPT	SVM	
Low	**0.56**	0.25	0.00	0.24	**0.33**	0.00	**0.34**	0.28	0.00	517
Medium	0.76	**0.77**	0.51	**0.81**	0.77	0.53	**0.78**	0.77	0.52	11455
High	**0.73**	0.72	0.50	**0.73**	0.70	0.67	**0.73**	0.71	0.57	12474
Critical	**0.67**	0.60	0.28	0.57	**0.61**	0.01	**0.62**	0.60	0.02	4445
Accuracy							0.73	0.71	0.50	28891
Macro	**0.68**	0.59	0.32	0.59	**0.60**	0.30	**0.62**	0.59	0.28	28891
Weighted	**0.73**	0.71	0.46	**0.73**	0.71	0.50	**0.73**	0.71	0.45	28891

Table 3 presents the component classification reports. Among these models, the Universal Sentence Encoder performs best in all the classification reports. The GPT-3 Babbage performs close to the USE model. The TF-IDF SVM Model has an excellent performance in the recall metric across tasks. Table 4 shows that the Universal Sentence Encoder has the best overall performance in the Severity classification task.

6   Discussion

This work not only covers the CVSS 3.1 scoring system, but also the older CVSS 2.0 scoring system, which is the most dominant vulnerability evaluation metric in the NVD [8,10,17]. Our proposed CVSS estimation method can convert the CVSS 2.0 score to the CVSS 3.1 score, and vice versa, solely from their natural language inputs. Compared to the works from [7,19,27], we showed the reports for each label in the component-wise task and a more end-to-end approach with the state-of-the-art performance. A comparative study between the deep learning models and the human domain experts would be helpful to understand the effectiveness of predicting CVSS scores from natural language only as the CVE description by itself cannot provide a computing environment to reproduce the vulnerability.

7   Conclusion

In this paper, we present an end-to-end vulnerability evaluation system that predicts the severity level of a vulnerability based on its description. Compared to the GPT Babbage model, the Universal Sentence Encoder model consumes less computational resources to run [4] while maintaining an on-par performance as shown in Sect. 5. Since the DAN model embedded in the USE scales linearly with the input sequence [5], the USE model inferences faster than the GPT models. However, the GPT-3 models are more generalized than the USE model as they can output a token sequence, instead of an embedding vector. This ability to regressively generate such token sequences is essential to many downstream tasks such as code generation. The USE and the GPT-3 models outperform the SVM model with the TF-IDF vectorization on the tasks shown in the Sect. 4.2 and the DistilBERT, which has lemmatization and vocabulary addition, in various component classification tasks [23].

References

1. Universal-sentence-encoder.   https://tfhub.dev/google/universal-sentence-encode r-large/5
2. Abadi, M., et al.: TensorFlow: Large-scale machine learning on heterogeneous systems (2015). https://www.tensorflow.org/, software available from tensorflow.org
3. Beck, A., Rass, S.: Using neural networks to aid cvss risk aggregation-an empirically validated approach. J. Innov. Digital Ecosyst. 3(2), 148–154 (2016)
4. Brown, T., et al.: Language models are few-shot learners. Adv. Neural Inform. Process. Syst. 33, 1877–1901 (2020)
5. Cer, D., et al.: Universal sentence encoder. arXiv preprint arXiv:1803.11175 (2018)

6. Clarke, W.L.: The original clarke error grid analysis (ega). Diabetes Technol. Therap. **7**(5), 776–779 (2005)
7. Costa, J.C., Roxo, T., Sequeiros, J.B., Proença, H., Inácio, P.R.: Predicting cvss metric via description interpretation. IEEE Access (2022)
8. FIRST, E.: Common vulnerability scoring system version 3.1: Specification document (2019)
9. Harris, C.R., et al.: Array programming with NumPy. Nature **585**(7825), 357–362 (2020). https://doi.org/10.1038/s41586-020-2649-2
10. IBM: Common Vulnerability Scoring System (CVSS). https://www.ibm.com/do cs/en/qradar-on-cloud?topic=vulnerabilities-common-vulnerability-scoring-syste m-cvss
11. Iosif, A.C., Gasiba, T.E., Zhao, T., Lechner, U., Pinto-Albuquerque, M.: A large-scale study on the security vulnerabilities of cloud deployments. In: The First International Conference on Ubiquitous Security (UbiSec 2021), pp. 171–188. Springer (2021). https://doi.org/10.1007/978-981-19-0468-4_13
12. Iyyer, M., Manjunatha, V., Boyd-Graber, J., Daumé III, H.: Deep unordered composition rivals syntactic methods for text classification. In: Proceedings of the 53rd Annual Meeting of the Association for Computational Linguistics and the 7th International Joint Conference on Natural Language Processing (volume 1: Long papers), pp. 1681–1691 (2015)
13. Joachims, T.: A probabilistic analysis of the rocchio algorithm with tfidf for text categorization. Carnegie-mellon univ pittsburgh pa dept of computer science, Tech. rep. (1996)
14. Kibriya, A.M., Frank, E., Pfahringer, B., Holmes, G.: Multinomial Naive Bayes for text categorization revisited. In: Webb, G.I., Yu, X. (eds.) AI 2004. LNCS (LNAI), vol. 3339, pp. 488–499. Springer, Heidelberg (2004). https://doi.org/10.1007/978-3-540-30549-1_43
15. Kitaev, N., Kaiser, Ł., Levskaya, A.: Reformer: The efficient transformer. arXiv preprint arXiv:2001.04451 (2020)
16. Kramer, O.: Machine Learning for Evolution Strategies. SBD, vol. 20. Springer, Cham (2016). https://doi.org/10.1007/978-3-319-33383-0
17. Mell, P., Scarfone, K., Romanosky, S., et al.: A complete guide to the common vulnerability scoring system version 2.0. In: Published by FIRST-forum of incident response and security teams. vol. 1, p. 23 (2007)
18. Noble, W.S.: What is a support vector machine? Nature Biotechnol. **24**(12), 1565–1567 (2006)
19. Nowak, M., Walkowski, M., Sujecki, S.: Machine learning algorithms for conversion of CVSS base score from 2.0 to 3.x. In: Paszynski, M., Kranzlmüller, D., Krzhizhanovskaya, V.V., Dongarra, J.J., Sloot, P.M.A. (eds.) ICCS 2021. LNCS, vol. 12744, pp. 255–269. Springer, Cham (2021). https://doi.org/10.1007/978-3-030-77967-2_21
20. NVD, N.: National vulnerability database (2022)
21. Pedregosa, F., et al.: Scikit-learn: Machine learning in python. J. Mach. Learn. Res. **12**, 2825–2830 (2011)
22. Ruohonen, J.: A look at the time delays in cvss vulnerability scoring. Appl. Comput. Inform. **15**(2), 129–135 (2019)
23. Shahid, M.R., Debar, H.: Cvss-bert: Explainable natural language processing to determine the severity of a computer security vulnerability from its description. In: 2021 20th IEEE International Conference on Machine Learning and Applications (ICMLA), pp. 1600–1607. IEEE (2021)

24. Snæbjarnarson, V., Símonarson, H.B., Ragnarsson, P.O., Ingólfsdóttir, S., Jónsson, H.P., Þorsteinsson, V., Einarsson, H.: A warm start and a clean crawled corpus-a recipe for good language models. arXiv preprint arXiv:2201.05601 (2022)
25. U.S. Department of Commerce : NVD - Vulnerability Metrics, https://nvd.nist.gov/vuln-metrics/cvss
26. Vaswani, A., et al.: Attention is all you need. In: Advances in Neural Information Pprocessing Systems, vol. 30 (2017)
27. Yamamoto, Y., Miyamoto, D., Nakayama, M.: Text-mining approach for estimating vulnerability score. In: 2015 4th International Workshop on Building Analysis Datasets and Gathering Experience Returns for Security (BADGERS), pp. 67–73. IEEE (2015)

Malware Traffic Classification Based on GAN and BP Neural Networks

Yun Duan[✉], Laifu Wang, Dongxin Liu, Boren Deng, and Yunfan Tian

China Telecom Research Institute, Guangzhou 510630, China
duany4@chinatelecom.cn

Abstract. Based on the imbalance of network traffic detection samples, we propose a model based on generative adversarial network and back propagation neural networks for malware traffic classification, which is to identify malware traffic, normal traffic, and traffic types. The model is composed of generative adversarial network and back propagation neural networks. The generator of the generative adversarial network is responsible for inputting random noise and generating traffic pictures with original input characteristics. The discriminator of the generative adversarial network is responsible for identifying generated pictures and input pictures. BP neural network is used as a classifier. The pictures generated by the generator and the pictures generated by original traffic data are used as inputs of the BP neural network to identify and classify traffic. The experimental data shows that the combined model based on the generative adversarial network and BP neural network proposed in this paper performs well, and the comprehensive index F1 value has significantly improved in most situations.

Keywords: Malware traffic · Generative adversarial network · BP neural network · Sample imbalance · Flow detection

1 Introduction

According to statistics, artificial intelligence algorithms have great prospects in the field of network security and are widely used [1–5], of which supervised learning algorithms account for the vast majority. Whether it is traditional machine learning algorithms, such as logistic regression, support vector machine, or deep learning algorithms, such as convolutional neural network, recurrent neural network, etc., the actual performance of these supervised learning algorithms depends on the quality of training samples, including the balance of different types of samples, the matching of training samples with actual application scenarios, etc.

The identification and classification of malware traffic belong to the category of network traffic detection, that is to distinguish malware traffic from normal traffic, and further identify specific traffic types. However, in the actual application scenario of network traffic detection, the training samples are easy to be unbalanced. For example, before the application of the security analysis system, there are often more malicious sample data (black samples) and insufficient normal sample data (white samples); on

G. Wang et al. (Eds.): UbiSec 2022, CCIS 1768, pp. 144–160, 2023.
https://doi.org/10.1007/978-981-99-0272-9_10

the contrary, before application, the safety analysis system has more white sample data and lacks enough black sample data. This imbalance of training samples greatly restricts the practical application effect of artificial intelligence algorithms in the field of network security [6].

Imbalanced training samples raise significant challenges when building predictive models. The solutions to the sample imbalance problem [8–10] usually include: At the data level [11–13], there are usually over-sampling schemes that generate new samples for the minority class, under-sampling schemes that remove samples from the majority class, and their combination schemes. At the algorithm level [14–16], there are cost-sensitive learning, threshold method, and so on [17]. In the above schemes, over-sampling is one of the most frequently used solutions [18–20]. By balancing the class distribution through over-sampling, training on the resampled dataset can improve the classification performance of some classifiers.

The concept of the generative adversarial network (GAN) was put forward in 2014 [21], and then it made a breakthrough in the field of pictures [22–26]. GAN is an adversarial learning network, which learns the data distribution of the training set through the adversarial learning of generator (G) and discriminator (D), to learn how to generate pictures. Therefore, in the case of sample imbalance in traffic detection, we propose a combined model based on GAN and BP neural network to expand the number of small samples, identify traffic categories, improve the classification effect of malware traffic models, and improve the overall performance of model classification.

We propose a malware traffic classification model based on GAN and BP neural networks. The model is composed of GAN model and BP neural network model. BP neural network is responsible for identifying the types of normal traffic and malware traffic, and is composed of input layer, hidden layer, and output layer. The GAN model is composed of a generator and a discriminator. The generator is responsible for inputting random noise and generating a flow picture with original input characteristics. The discriminator is responsible for identifying the difference between the generated picture and the input picture. Through the training of the GAN model, the picture generated by the generator has the characteristics of the input picture. After data preprocessing, the pictures generated by the generator and the training set are used together as the data set of BP neural network, which can better identify the types of malware traffic and normal traffic.

The rest of this paper is organized as follows. The second part summarizes the network traffic detection technology and the related research work of GAN. The third part introduces the malware traffic classification model based on GAN and BP neural networks in detail. The fourth section introduces the experimental data set, data preprocessing, experimental setup, and experimental conclusion. Finally, in the fifth part, we summarize and prospect the paper.

2   Related Work

2.1 Network Traffic Detection Technology

The identification and classification of malware traffic belong to the category of network traffic detection, that is, to distinguish malware traffic and normal traffic from network traffic, and further identify specific traffic types [5]. The related technologies mainly include traffic detection based on rule matching, traffic detection based on statistical features and machine learning, and traffic detection based on deep learning. The rule design and feature design in the first two methods depend on professional knowledge, which is not easy work [27]. Traffic recognition based on deep learning directly learns the features from the original data, avoiding the manual selection of features and the design of extraction rules.

Traffic detection based on rules matches traffic categories according to manually formulated rules. The earliest rule-based traffic detection is the identification technology based on the port numbers [28]. There is a corresponding relationship between common application protocols and port numbers. The application protocol of network traffic can be identified by extracting the source port number or destination port number information of the transport layer from the network traffic. Traffic identification based on statistical features and machine learning is an analysis method based on network traffic behavior [29]. Common features include space-time features, head features, load features, statistical features, and other features that reflect network traffic behavior. In practical applications, it is necessary to design different traffic feature sets according to the network traffic classification tasks in different sub domains, and the design of features depends on the expertise of experts.

Traffic recognition based on deep learning can represent the original traffic as images or time series data, extract features from the original data through model training, and detect the category of network traffic. Wang Wei converts the original traffic data into pictures and uses a convolutional neural network to classify malware traffic [30]. Wang Maonan uses the residual network to extract features from the original traffic and uses the self-encoder to compress the statistical features of the original traffic. Through these two features, he classifies the encrypted traffic [31].

2.2 Generative Adversarial Network

The generative adversarial network (GAN) was first proposed by Goodfellow in 2014. The generative adversarial network is composed of a generator (G) and a discriminator (D). The generator generates samples by transmitting random noise through a multi-layer perceptron, and the discriminator is also a multi-layer perceptron. The optimization process of GAN is the "minimax two-player game" problem of function L (D, g) [21], and the formula is as follows:

$$\min_{G} \max_{D} L(D, G) = \mathbb{E}_{x \sim P_r(x)}\left[logD(x)\right] + \mathbb{E}_{z \sim P_z(x)}[log(1 - D(G(Z)))] \qquad (1)$$

where, p_z is the data distribution on the noise input Z, p_r is the data distribution on the real sample X.

As shown in Fig. 1, the GAN model is composed of a generator and a discriminator. The generator outputs a synthetic sample Z given the input of noise variables and is trained to capture the real data distribution. The discriminator estimates the probability that a given sample comes from a real data set. The discriminator is a two classifier and is optimized to distinguish between false samples and real samples. G and D are

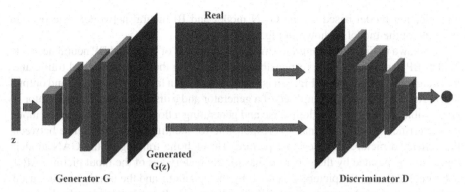

Fig. 1. The structure of the generative adversarial network

generally nonlinear mapping functions, such as multilayer perceptron, convolutional neural network, and so on.

Thomas applies the GAN model to medical images for anomaly detection and proposes an anomaly detection method based on a depth generation adversary network. That is, the GAN model is trained with normal pictures, and then the GAN model generates a normal graph corresponding to the abnormal graph to compare and find the abnormal [22]. Andrew applies the GAN model to the image modeling task, trains and synthesizes high-fidelity natural images based on the large-scale GAN model, and expands the sample images [23]. Our work is to try to introduce the GAN model to the classification task in the field of network traffic.

3 Model

3.1 Combined Model

In order to solve the problem of unbalanced traffic samples, the GAN model is introduced to generate traffic with small sample categories. We propose a malware traffic

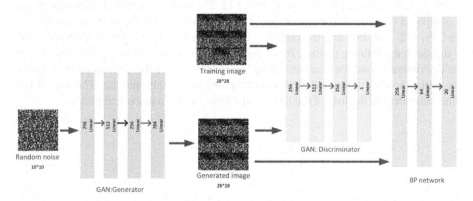

Fig. 2. The structure of the malware traffic classification model

classification model based on the GAN model and BP neural networks. The overall structure of the model is shown in Fig. 2.

As shown in Fig. 2, the combined model is composed of GAN and BP neural network model. BP neural network is responsible for identifying the types of normal traffic and malware traffic. As shown in Fig. 3, it is composed of input layer, hidden layer, and output layer. The GAN model is composed of a generator and a discriminator. The generator is responsible for inputting random noise and generating a flow picture with original input characteristics. The discriminator is responsible for identifying the difference between the generated picture and the input picture. Through the training of the GAN model, the picture generated by the generator has the characteristics of the input picture. After data preprocessing, the picture generated by the generator and the training set are used together as the input data set of the BP neural network, It can better identify the types of malware traffic and normal traffic.

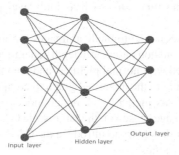

Fig. 3. The structure of the BP neural network

3.2 Design of the Generative Adversarial Network

The structure of the GAN model in this paper is shown in Fig. 4. The generator is composed of a four-layer perceptron. The input size of one-dimensional random noise is 100, and the network parameters are 256, 512, 256, and 784 in turn. The discriminator is composed of a four-layer perceptron. The input size is 784, the network parameters are 256, 512, and 256, and the output is 0 or 1, that is, whether the generated picture is similar to the training picture. BCELoss() function is selected as the loss function of the discriminator and the generator. The loss calculation of the discriminator includes two parts: the loss of the real picture and the loss of the false picture. The loss of the generator refers to the loss of the label of the false picture and the real picture.

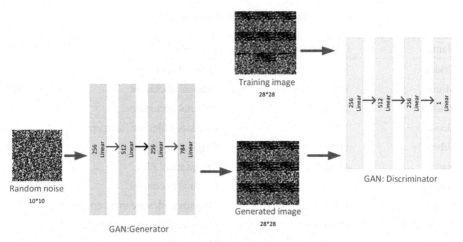

Fig. 4. The structure of the GAN model

BCELoss() is a binary cross-entropy loss function. For batch data D(x, y) containing N samples, the loss is calculated as follows:

$$loss = \frac{1}{N} \sum_{n=1}^{N} l_n \tag{2}$$

Among them, the loss corresponding to the n_{th} sample is calculated as follows:

$$l_n = -w[y_n * logx_n + (1 - y_n) * log(1 - x_n)] \tag{3}$$

In formula (3), w is a super parameter. If one input sample corresponds to one classified output, it is unnecessary to set w. The value of each element in y is 0 or 1, representing the real category.

4 Experiments

4.1 Datasets

The experimental data used in this paper are from the original traffic data set USTC-TFC 2016 [31] combined with Wang Wei. The data set includes ten types of malware traffic and ten types of normal traffic. The data format is pcap file. Among them, the ten types of malware traffic are selected from the CTU data set collected by CTU University researchers from the real environment [32], and some oversized files are intercepted. The ten types of normal traffic are collected using the professional simulation device IXIA BPS [33]. Tables 1 and 2 describe the details of malware traffic and normal traffic.

Table 1. Malware traffic types.

Name	CTU-number	Data processing
Cridex	108-1	Original document
Miuref	127-1	Original document
Zeus	116-2	Original document
Geodo	119-2	Oversized files are intercepted
Htbot	110-1	Original document
Neris	42,43	Merge small files
Nsis-ay	53	Original document
Shifu	142-1	Oversized files are intercepted
Tinba	150-1	Oversized files are intercepted
Virut	54	Original document

Table 2. Normal flow types.

Name	Type
BitTorrent	P2P
Facetime	Multimedia streaming
FTP, SMB	Data transmission
Gmail, outlook	E-mail
MySQL	Database
Skype	Instant messaging
Weibo	Social networks
WorldOfWarcraf	Computer game

4.2 Data Preprocessing

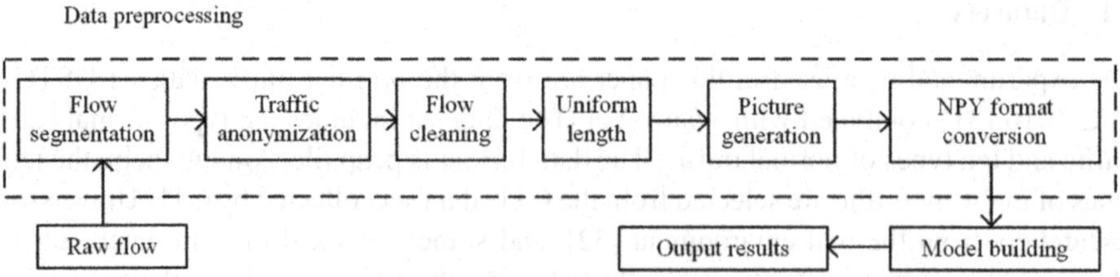

Data preprocessing

Fig. 5. Data preprocessing

Data preprocessing refers to the process flow of converting the original traffic into the input data of the model. According to the statistics of the selected dataset, the traffic between 0 bytes and 784 bytes accounts for 84% of the total [31], so we choose 784 bytes as the input size. The specific steps are shown in Fig. 5.

Step 1: traffic segmentation: divide one original traffic data into multiple traffic data according to the session layer, and the output format is still pcap file.

Step 2: anonymize. Replace the MAC address, IP address, and port number in the original packet with a zero address. The format has not changed during this process.

Step 3: traffic cleaning, sort all traffic packets by size, and intercept n pcap packets as training data. According to our statistics, the number of pcap files per traffic category after segmentation exceeds 6000, so in Experiment 1, the N size of normal traffic is set to 6000, and the N size of malicious traffic is set to 1000. In Experiment 2, the N size of normal traffic is set to 1000, and the N size of malicious traffic is set to 6000.

Step 4: unify the length, remove the pcap file header, i.e. the first 34 bytes, and then trim the filtered pcap file to 784 bytes (28 x 28). If the pcap file is shorter than 784 bytes, add 0x00.

Step 5; Image generation: files of uniform length are converted into gray image PNG in binary form.

Step 6: format conversion: convert the image to the array format in the Numpy library, and then store it in NPY format. Finally, it is used as the input of the model.

4.3 Settings

We use the USTC-TFC 2016 data set to carry out 20 classifications (type identification of normal traffic and malware traffic). In the experiment, white samples refer to normal traffic and black samples refer to malware traffic. Furthermore, in order to measure the effectiveness of the model, two sets of experimental scenarios are set up according to the imbalance of samples: more white samples, fewer black samples, and more black samples, fewer white samples. The data set is shown in Table 3:

Table 3. Experimental setting parameters.

Experiment	Number of original sample pcap packets	Number of supplementary samples generated	Model
Baseline of Experiment 1	White sample 60000 Black sample 10000	No supplement	BP neural network
Experiment 1	White sample 60000 Black sample 10000	Black sample 10000	Combined model based on GAN and BP neural network
Baseline of Experiment 2	White sample 10000 Black sample 60000	No supplement	BP neural network

(continued)

Table 3. (*continued*)

Experiment	Number of original sample pcap packets	Number of supplementary samples generated	Model
Experiment 2	White sample 10000 Black sample 60000	White sample 10000	Combined model based on GAN and BP neural network

The baseline experiment of Experiment 1: simulates the scenario of more white samples and fewer black samples. The ratio of pcap packets of white samples to black samples is 6:1, that is, 10 categories of normal traffic. Each category is sorted by pcap size. The top 6000 pcap files and 10 categories of malware traffic are selected. Each category is sorted by pcap size. The top 1000 pcap files are selected. The data set is input into BP neural network for 20 classifications.

Experiment 1: simulate the scenario of more white samples and fewer black samples. The ratio of white samples to black samples is 6:1, that is, 10 categories of normal traffic. Each category is sorted according to the size of pcap. Select the first 6000 pcap files and 10 categories of malware traffic. Each category is sorted according to the size of pcap, and select the first 1000 pcap files. Using this data set as the input of the GAN model, the GAN model generator generates 1000 pcap files for each category of output black samples and then uses the black samples generated by GAN and the original black-and-white sample data set as the training and test data set of BP neural network.

The baseline experiment of Experiment 2: simulates the scenario of more black samples and fewer white samples. The ratio of pcap packets of white samples to black samples is 1:6, that is, 10 categories of normal traffic. Each category is sorted by pcap size. The top 1000 pcap files and 10 categories of malware traffic are selected. Each category is sorted by pcap size. The top 6000 pcap files are selected. The data set is input into BP neural network for 20 classifications.

Experiment 2: simulate the scenario of more black samples and fewer white samples. The ratio of pcap packets of white samples to black samples is 1:6, that is, 10 categories of normal traffic. Each category is sorted by pcap size, and the top 1000 pcap files and 10 categories of malware traffic are selected. Each category is sorted by pcap size, and the top 6000 pcap files are selected. Using this data set as the input of GAN model, the GAN model generator generates 1000 pcap files for each category of output white samples and then uses the black samples generated by GAN and the original black-and-white sample data set as the training and test data set of BP neural network.

We select 20% of the data as the test set and 80% as the training set from the combined data set of the GAN generated data set and original data set. In this paper, the batch size of the BP neural network is 128. The initial learning rate is 0.001 and the total number of training rounds (epoch) is about 30. Precision, recall rate, and comprehensive index F1 are used as indicators to measure the effect of the model experiments. F1 is a comprehensive evaluation index that can reflect both accuracy and recall rate. The larger the F1 value, the better the model effect. The formula is as follows:

$$precision = \frac{Number\ of\ samples\ with\ correct\ classification}{Number\ of\ samples\ with\ correct\ classification\ and\ wrong\ classification} \tag{4}$$

$$Recall = \frac{Number\ of\ samples\ with\ correct\ classification}{Total\ number\ of\ samples\ in\ this\ category} \tag{5}$$

$$F1 = \frac{2*Precision*Recall}{Precision+Recall} \tag{6}$$

4.4 Results and Analysis

1) Experiment 1 (more white and fewer black): results of black sample

Table 4. Precision (%), recall (%), and F1 value of the black sample in Experiment 1.

Type	Baseline			Experiment 1			F1 comparison
	Precision	Recall	F1	Precision	Recall	F1	
Cridex	100.0	100.0	100.0	99.515	100.0	99.757	−0.243
Geodo	100.0	100.0	100.0	100.0	100.0	100.0	—
Hotbot	99.502	100.0	99.751	99.833	99.5	99.666	−0.085
Miuref	99.01	100.0	99.502	100.0	100.0	100.0	+0.498
Neris	100.0	99.667	99.833	99.668	100.0	99.834	+0.001
Nsis-ay	100.0	100.0	100.0	100.0	100.0	100.0	—
Shifu	100.0	100.0	100.0	100.0	100.0	100.0	—
Tinba	100.0	99.667	99.833	99.693	54.167	70.194	−29.639
Virut	100.0	91.0	95.288	98.529	98.049	98.289	+3.001
Zeus	90.0	81.0	85.263	97.714	83.415	90.0	+4.737

As shown in Table 4, the precision, recall, and F1 value of each flow of black samples in Experiment 1 were recorded under the condition of 20 classifications. Figures 6, 7, and 8 respectively describe the columnar comparison charts of the precision, recall, F1 value, and baseline of black samples in Experiment 1. Experiment 1 shows that in the case of insufficient black samples, GAN is used to generate black samples. Among the 10 categories of black samples, the F1 values of 4 categories are improved, and the F1 values of 3 categories are flat. The recognition effect of most categories of black samples is improved.

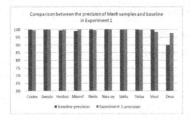

Fig. 6. Precision and baseline   **Fig. 7.** Recall and baseline

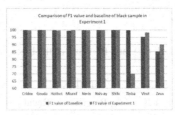

Fig. 8. F1 value and baseline

2) Experiment 1 (more white and fewer black): results of white sample

As shown in Table 5, the precision, recall, and F1 value of each flow of white samples in Experiment 1 were recorded under the condition of 20 classifications. Figures 9, 10, and 11 respectively describe the columnar comparison charts of the precision, recall, F1 value, and baseline of white samples in Experiment 1. Experiment 1 shows that in the case of insufficient black samples, GAN is used to generate black samples. Among the 10 categories of white samples, the F1 values of 5 categories are improved, the F1 values of 2 categories are flat.

Table 5. Precision (%), recall (%), and F1 value of the white sample in Experiment 1.

Type	Baseline			Experiment 1			F1 comparison
	Precision	Recall	F1	Precision	Recall	F1	
BitTorrent	99.834	100.0	99.917	93.292	99.667	96.374	−3.543
Facetime	95.098	97.0	96.04	97.073	97.073	97.073	+1.033
FTP	99.834	100.0	99.917	71.942	100.0	83.682	−16.235
Gmail	100.0	100.0	100.0	100.0	100.0	100.0	—
MYSQL	85.047	91.0	87.923	86.9	97.073	91.705	+3.782
Outlook	99.01	100.0	99.502	99.515	100.0	99.757	+0.255
Skype	100.0	99.833	99.917	99.833	99.833	99.833	−0.084
SMB	98.039	100.0	99.01	99.515	100.0	99.757	+0.747
Weibo	94.34	100.0	97.087	98.558	100.0	99.274	+2.187
WorldOfWarcraft	100.0	100.0	100.0	100.0	100.0	100.0	—

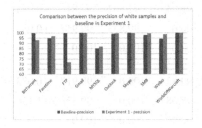

Fig. 9. Precision and baseline

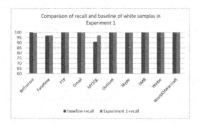

Fig. 10. Recall and baseline

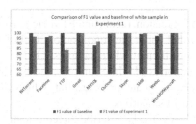

Fig. 11. F1 value and baseline

It can be seen from the figure that in the scenario of more white samples and fewer black samples, the Tinba and FTP classes have a certain index decline. Generating malware traffic is more difficult than generating normal traffic. In addition to generating byte sequences specific to traffic classes, malware traffic generation often requires sorting these byte sequences in a specific order to achieve malicious goals. We believe that for more complex malware samples, the average sample size of 1000 per class is still small. This makes the discriminator not sensitive enough to the specific order information required by some categories, which affects the generation quality of the GAN model, which is why the combined model fluctuates greatly for some categories under the scene setting of Experiment 1.

3) Experiment 2 (more black and fewer white): results of white sample

Table 6. Precision (%), recall (%), and F1 value of the white sample in Experiment 2.

Type	Baseline			Experiment 1			F1 comparison
	Precision	Recall	F1	Precision	Recall	F1	
BitTorrent	67.568	100.0	80.645	100.0	89.268	94.33	+13.685
Facetime	99.158	98.167	98.66	98.35	99.333	98.839	+0.179
FTP	93.103	54.0	68.354	90.233	94.634	92.381	+24.026
Gmail	100.0	100.0	100.0	100.0	100.0	100.0	—
MYSQL	93.399	94.333	93.864	95.043	92.667	93.84	−0.024
Outlook	100.0	99.667	99.833	100.0	99.833	99.917	+0.084
Skype	100.0	100.0	100.0	100.0	100.0	100.0	—
SMB	100.0	100.0	100.0	99.834	100.0	99.917	−0.083
Weibo	96.463	100.0	98.2	98.684	100.0	99.338	+1.138
WorldOfWarcraft	100.0	100.0	100.0	100.0	100.0	100.0	—

As shown in Table 6, the precision, recall, and F1 value of each flow of white samples in Experiment 2 were recorded under the condition of 20 classifications. Experiment 2 shows that in the case of insufficient white samples, GAN is used to generate white samples. Among the 10 categories of white samples, the F1 values of 5 categories are improved, and the F1 values of 3 categories are flat, which improves the recognition effect of white samples in most situations.

Figures 12, 13, and 14 respectively describe the columnar comparison diagrams of the precision, recall, F1 value and baseline of white samples in Experiment 2. It can be seen from the figure that in the scenario of more black samples and fewer white samples, the model improves the recognition accuracy of white samples in most situations.

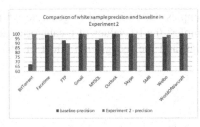

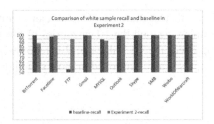

Fig. 12. Precision and baseline   **Fig. 13.** Recall and baseline

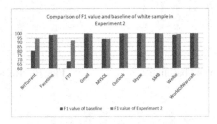

Fig. 14. F1 value and baseline

4) Experiment 2 (more black than white): results of black sample

Table 7. Precision (%), recall (%), and F1 value of the black sample in Experiment 2.

Type	Baseline			Experiment 1			F1 comparison
	Precision	Recall	F1	Precision	Recall	F1	
Cridex	99.833	99.833	99.833	100.0	99.833	99.917	+ 0.084
Geodo	99.667	99.833	99.75	99.833	99.833	99.833	+ 0.083
Hotbot	97.98	97.0	97.487	100.0	98.049	99.015	+ 1.528
Miuref	100.0	100.0	100.0	99.834	100.0	99.917	− 0.083
Neris	97.98	97.0	97.487	97.156	100.0	98.558	+ 1.071
Nsis-ay	100.0	100.0	100.0	100.0	100.0	100.0	—
Shifu	100.0	100.0	100.0	100.0	100.0	100.0	—
Tinba	98.947	94.0	96.41	94.86	99.024	96.897	+ 0.487
Virut	100.0	96.0	97.959	99.831	98.167	98.992	+ 1.033
Zeus	94.04	94.667	94.352	99.831	95.167	94.224	− 0.128

As shown in Table 7, the precision, recall, and F1 value of each flow of black samples in Experiment 2 were recorded under the condition of 20 classifications. Experiment 2 shows that in the case of insufficient white samples, GAN is used to generate white samples. Among the 10 categories of black samples, the F1 values of 6 categories are improved, the F1 values of 2 categories are flat, and the recognition effect of black samples is also improved in most situations.

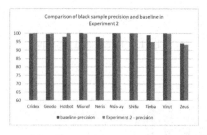

Fig. 15. Precision and baseline

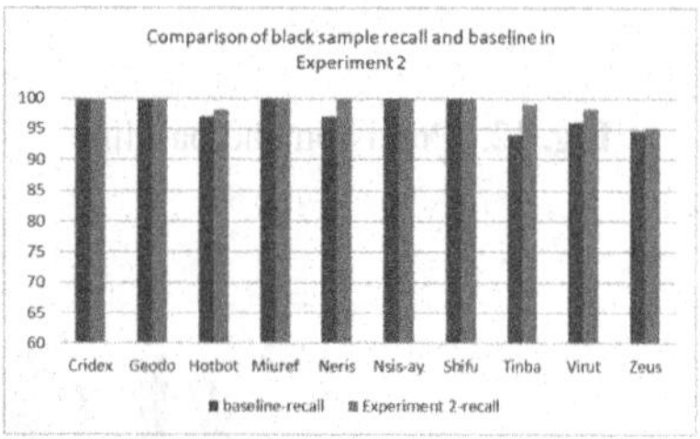

Fig. 16. Recall and baseline

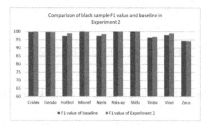

Fig. 17. F1 value and baseline

Figures 15, 16, and 17 respectively describe the columnar comparison diagrams of the precision, recall, F1 value, and baseline of black samples in Experiment 2. It can be seen from the figure that in the scenario of more black samples and fewer white samples, the model can also improve the recognition effect of black samples on the whole.

5 Summary

With the rapid development of information technology, the identification of malware traffic and normal traffic and the classification of network traffic types are of great significance to the governance of Cyberspace Security. As mentioned above, network traffic identification based on deep learning is hot research of network traffic detection. However, in practical application scenarios, there are also problems of poor application results caused by sample imbalance. Therefore, we propose a malware traffic classification model based on GAN model and BP neural networks, and the experimental results show that the combined model based on the generative adversarial network and BP neural networks proposed in this paper performs well, and the comprehensive index F1 value has significantly improved in most situations. In the long run, network traffic detection technology is closely related to application scenarios. According to actual application scenarios, more diverse structures of generative adversarial networks can also be used. There is still much room for exploration in related work.

References

1. Liu, M., Hong, Z., Liu, Q., Xing, X., Dai, Y.: A backdoor embedding method for backdoor detection in deep neural networks. In: Wang, G., Choo, K.K.R., Ko, R.K.L., Xu, Y., Crispo, B. (eds.) Ubiquitous Security. UbiSec 2021. Communications in Computer and Information Science, vol. 1557, pp. 1–12. Springer, Singapore (2022). https://doi.org/10.1007/978-981-19-0468-4_1

2. Lin, J., Wei, Y., Li, W., Long, J.: Intrusion detection system based on deep neural network and incremental learning for in-vehicle CAN networks. In: Wang, G., Choo, K.K.R., Ko, R.K.L., Xu, Y., Crispo, B. (eds.) Ubiquitous Security. UbiSec 2021. Communications in Computer and Information Science, vol. 1557, pp. 255–267. Springer, Singapore. https://doi.org/10.1007/978-981-19-0468-4_19

3. Tang, Y., Zhang, D., Liang, W., Li, KC., Sukhija, N.: Active malicious accounts detection with multimodal fusion machine learning algorithm. In: Wang, G., Choo, K.K.R., Ko, R.K.L., Xu, Y., Crispo, B. (eds.) Ubiquitous Security. UbiSec 2021. Communications in Computer and Information Science, vol. 1557, pp. 38–52. Springer, Singapore. https://doi.org/10.1007/978-981-19-0468-4_4

4. Keipour, H., Hazra, S., Finne, N., Voigt, T.: Generalizing supervised learning for intrusion detection in IoT mesh networks. In: Wang, G., Choo, K.K.R., Ko, R.K.L., Xu, Y., Crispo, B. (eds.) Ubiquitous Security. UbiSec 2021. Communications in Computer and Information Science, vol. 1557, pp. 214–228. Springer, Singapore (2022). https://doi.org/10.1007/978-981-19-0468-4_16

5. Li, W., Cai, J., Wang, Z., Cheng, S.: A robust malware detection approach for android system based on ensemble learning. In: Wang, G., Choo, K.K.R., Ko, R.K.L., Xu, Y., Crispo, B. (eds.) Ubiquitous Security. UbiSec 2021. Communications in Computer and Information Science, vol. 1557, pp. 309–321. Springer, Singapore (2022). https://doi.org/10.1007/978-981-19-0468-4_23

6. Zhang, X., Zhu, J.: Network security situation element acquisition for sample imbalance. Comput. Eng. Appl. **58**(1), 134–142 (2022)

7. Chawla, N.V., Japkowicz, N., Kotcz, A.: Session details: special issue on learning from imbalanced datasets. ACM SIGKDD Explor. Newsl. **6**(1), 1–6 (2004)

8. Barot, P.A., Jethva, H.B.: Mgini - improved decision tree using minority class sensitive splitting criterion for imbalanced data of covid-19. J. Inf. Sci. Eng. **37**(5), 1097–1108 (2021)

9. Ariannezhad, A., Karimpour, A., Qin, X., Wu, Y.J., Salmani, Y.: Handling imbalanced data for real-time crash prediction: application of boosting and sampling techniques. J. Transp. Eng. Part A. Syst. **147**(3), 1–10 (2021)

10. Ylmaz, M., Gezer, C., Aydn, Z., Güngr, V.A.: Data mining techniques in direct marketing on imbalanced data using Tomek link combined with random under-sampling. In: 5th International Conference on Information System and Data Mining, pp. 67–73. ACM, New York (2021)

11. Han, X., Jia, N., Zhu, N.: Gauss mixture undersampling algorithm for credit imbalanced data. Comput. Eng. Design **41**(1), 66–70 (2020)

12. Koziarski, M.: CSMOUTE: combined synthetic oversampling and undersampling technique for imbalanced data classification. In: International Conference on International Joint Conference on Neural Networks, pp. 1–8. IEEE, Piscataway (2021)

13. Torgo, L., Ribeiro, R.P., Pfahringer, B., Branco, P.: SMOTE for regression. In: Correia, L., Reis, L.P., Cascalho, J. (eds.) EPIA 2013. LNCS (LNAI), vol. 8154, pp. 378–389. Springer, Heidelberg (2013). https://doi.org/10.1007/978-3-642-40669-0_33

14. Folgoc, L.L., Baltatzis, V., Alansary, A., Desai, S., Devaraj, A., Ellis, S.: Bayesian analysis of the prevalence bias: learning and predicting from imbalanced data, https://doi.org/10.48550/arXiv.2108.00250. Accessed 31 June 2021

15. Hernández-Orallo, J.: Probabilistic reframing for cost-sensitive regression. ACM Trans. Knowl. Discov. Data **8**(4), 17–55 (2014)

16. Wang, D., Zhang, N., Tao, M.: Clustered federated learning with weighted model aggregation for imbalanced data. China Commun. **19**(8), 41–56 (2022)

17. Jia, S., Huang, X., Qin, S.: A bi-directional sampling based on K-means method for imbalance text classification. In: 15th International Conference on Computer and Information Science, pp. 1–5. IEEE, Piscataway (2016)

18. Chang, J.R., Chen, L.S., Lin, L.W.: A novel cluster based over-sampling approach for classifying imbalanced sentiment data. IAENG Int. J. Comput. Sci. **4**(3), 1118–1128 (2021)

19. Zhai, J., Qi, J., Shen, C.: Binary imbalanced data classification based on diversity oversampling by generative models. Inf. Sci. **585**(1), 313–343 (2022)

20. Han, H., Wang, W.Y., Mao, B.H.: Borderline-smote: a new oversampling method in imbalanced data sets learning. In: Huang, DS., Zhang, XP., Huang, GB. (eds) Advances in Intelligent Computing. ICIC 2005. Lecture Notes in Computer Science, vol. 3644, pp. 878–887. Springer, Heidelberg (2005). https://doi.org/10.1007/11538059_91

21. Goodfellow, I., Pouget-Abadie, J., Mirza, M.: Generative adversarial nets. Neural Inf. Process. Syst. **7**(8), 2672–2680 (2014)

22. Schlegl, T., Seeböck, P., Waldstein, S.M., Schmidt-Erfurth, U., Langs, G.: Unsupervised anomaly detection with generative adversarial networks to guide marker discovery. In: Niethammer, M., et al. (eds.) IPMI 2017. LNCS, vol. 10265, pp. 146–157. Springer, Cham (2017). https://doi.org/10.1007/978-3-319-59050-9_12

23. Brock, A., Donahue, J., Simonyan, K.: Large scale GAN training for high fidelity natural image synthesis. In: International Conference on Learning Representations, arXiv prints arXiv:1809. 11096 (2019)

24. Yang, G., et al.: Global and local alignment networks for unpaired image-to-image translation. arXiv preprint arXiv: 2111.10346 (2021)

25. Sun, J., Bhattarai, B., Chen, Z., Kim, T.K.: SeCGAN: parallel conditional generative adversarial networks for face editing via semantic consistency. arXiv preprint arXiv: arXiv:2111. 09298 (2022)

26. Qtmp, A., Sa, A., Js, A., Su, J.: Generating future fundus images for early age-related macular degeneration based on generative adversarial networks. Comput. Methods Programs Biomed. **216**, 106648–106662 (2022)

27. Dhote, Y., Agrawal, S., Deen, A.J.: A survey on feature selection techniques for internet traffic classification. In: 2015 International Conference on Computational Intelligence & Communication Networks, pp. 17–25. IEEE, Piscataway (2016)

28. Tian, Y., Liu, D., Wang, L.: A combined-CNN model of TLS traffic recognition and classification. In: 7th International Conference on Data Science in Cyberspace, pp. 1–10. IEEE, Piscataway (2022)

29. Hu, B., Zhou, Z., Yao, L., li, J.: Malicious traffic detection based on packet load and flow fingerprint. Comput. Eng. **46**(11), 7–17 (2020)

30. Wang, W., Zeng, X., Ye, X., Sheng, Y., Zhu, M.: Malware traffic classification using convolutional neural network for representation learning. In: 31th International Conference on Information Networking, pp. 712–717. IEEE, Piscataway (2017)

31. Wang, M., Zheng, K., Yang, Y., Wang, X.: An explainable machine learning framework for intrusion detection systems. IEEE Access **8**(1), 73127–73141 (2020)

32. CTU University: The stratosphere IPS project dataset[EB/OL]. https://stratosphere.org/category/dataset.html. Accessed June 2017

33. Ixia breakpoint overview and specifications[EB/OL]. https://www.ixiacom.com/products/breakingpoint. Accessed June 2017

Source Code Vulnerability Detection Using Deep Learning Algorithms for Industrial Applications

Akram Louati[1,2] and Tiago Gasiba[1(✉)]🆔

[1] Siemens AG, 81739 München, Germany
{akram.louati,tiago.gasiba}@siemens.com
[2] Technical University of Munich, 85748 München, Germany
akram.louati@tum.de

Abstract. Static Application Security Testing tools can be used in the industry to analyze and find potential security vulnerabilities in source code, as mandated by several industrial security standards such as the IEC 62.443. They can be easily integrated into programming environments and deployment pipelines and enable the early detection of security flaws. Our work focuses on static security vulnerability detection in C# code utilizing deep learning algorithms. We use a data set of 51 Common Weakness Enumeration identifiers widely used in the industry to train and test our models. Our results show that the method is viable for detecting and classifying source code vulnerabilities. We also compare the performance of our approach to open source tools and show that our method outperforms these. Our work contributes to understanding the effectiveness of deep learning algorithms in detecting security vulnerabilities in C# code. This work can also be used by researchers and industrial practitioners who wish to use deep learning methods to improve the security of their code.

Keywords: Machine learning security · Software and application security · Artificial intelligence security · Artificial neural networks · Deep learning · Static code analysis · Software vulnerabilities · Security in programming languages · Industry

1 Introduction

Software is an essential element of information technology systems, and its security is vital to consider, as mandated by industry standards such as IEC 62.443 [16]. However, the number of publicly known and announced software vulnerabilities in the Common Vulnerabilities and Exposures (CVE) database is steadily increasing [24]. These flaws potentially affect the security of systems and applications, e.g., by accessing sensitive data. If such software vulnerability flaws are contained in critical infrastructures, the result of a security breach through the exploitation of the corresponding vulnerability can range from financial losses [27] to a potential loss of life.

© The Author(s), under exclusive license to Springer Nature Singapore Pte Ltd. 2023
G. Wang et al. (Eds.): UbiSec 2022, CCIS 1768, pp. 161–178, 2023.
https://doi.org/10.1007/978-981-99-0272-9_11

Software vulnerabilities induced through coding errors are one of the most common origins of cyber-attacks in the industry [8]. For that reason, the industry is following industrial security coding standards such as Common Weakness Enumeration (CWE) to improve the software security of their products and services.

Ensuring that software is secure through secure coding activities is a difficult task for software developers. Several supporting activities such as secure coding reviews and pair programming can be used towards this goal. Additional support can be obtained by using source code analysis tools specifically designed to identify software vulnerabilities [17]. These tools can be categorized into two main categories: (1) Dynamic Analysis Security Testing (DAST) and (2) Static Application Security Testing (SAST). The first type of tool works through observing software behavior while running, and while its results are exact, its usage incurs a performance penalty. Furthermore, their detection capabilities are highly dependent on the process's execution path, thus requiring the development of security-specific test cases, e.g., employing fuzzing techniques that run the program with many different, potentially malicious inputs.

SAST tools, on the other hand, perform their analysis offline, i.e., without executing the program, and therefore do not incur any performance penalty, nor do they require the development of security-specific test cases. These tools work using scanning the application against a set of secure coding rules. The primary issue with this detection mechanism is that some of these rules are hard to detect, thus resulting in a marginal number of false positives and negatives. Furthermore, while DAST tools are typically more accurate than SAST tools, the latter are often fault-prone since they recognize only a fixed number of hard-coded patterns [36], Nevertheless, both these tools are not only widely deployed in practice, but their usage during the software development lifecycle is also encouraged or even mandated by several industrial security standards. Additionally, these tools can be quickly adopted in the programming environments and Continuous Integration/Continuous Delivery pipelines to automate the vulnerability detection procedure and provide immediate feedback to software developers.

Mead et al. [21] show that addressing the issue of software vulnerabilities in the early stages of software development can result in many cost savings. Therefore, by enabling the early identification and elimination of security vulnerabilities, these tools directly contribute to significant potential savings for companies and customers and reduce security incidents.

In the last decades, artificial intelligence (AI) has gained prominence as a critical research area. AI-based approaches have been shown to outperform conventional methods in various tasks, e.g. in malware detection [18]. Other fields where AI-based approaches are showing promising results include natural language processing (NLP) [34]. Deep learning-based methods have performed well in extracting meaningful patterns from textual data and understanding human languages.

Recent studies have proposed using NLP-based methods for vulnerability detection by considering the source code as text data. Deep Learning has the potential to efficiently find software vulnerabilities in source code [19,27]. However, previous work focused only on the C and C++ programming languages. Previous work also did not compare the implemented methods and existing open-source software vulnerability detection tools. Furthermore, most of the results from previous work are not provided and analyzed concerning industry-known weakness types (CWE) but instead only focus on classifying the analyzed code as simply being vulnerable or non-vulnerable.

In the present work, we extend previous work by adapting it to address the C# programming language, as this is also widely used in the industry. We investigate the performance of deep learning models in predicting C# code vulnerabilities based on the CWE industry standard. Furthermore, we compare the performance of the implemented deep learning methods to existing C# SAST tools based on individual CWEs. Additionally, we perform an initial study on the detection performance through vulnerable code samples taken from the industry. These samples differ from the original training set, taken from the NIST database [28], and correspondingly have a different structure.

We build an extensive data set of industry-relevant C# snippets to address these issues. The data set could be used in further research to train and evaluate the performance of other security detection tools. We provide our models to the research community as well as to the industry to enable further refinements of our work [20]. Our work enables and assists industry practitioners in their internal decision about selecting and adopting SAST tools.

Our work is organized as follows. Section 2 discusses previous work related to our research. Section 3 introduces our approach and details our solution. In Sect. 4 we present and discuss the results of our approach and compare them with existing tools. Finally, Sect. 5 concludes our work.

2   State-of-the-Art

In static code analysis, the proposed approaches can be mainly divided into two categories: the rule-based and the AI-based approaches. This work focuses on deep learning models and conventional open-source SAST tools.

2.1   Open Source Software Vulnerability Detection for C#

Table 1 shows a list of open-source static application security test (SAST) tools that can be used in the C# programming language.

CodeQL is a security analysis tool developed by Gitlab to automate the vulnerability detection process. The source code is first converted into a database. Second, a set of vulnerability queries are executed against the database. CodeQL supports several popular programming languages such as C/C++, Java, and C#.

Infersharp is a static analysis tool for C# developed by Microsoft. In its current version, the tool can identify only three types of security vulnerabilities: Race Condition [5], Null Pointer Dereferences [7], and Resource Leaks [6].

Table 1. Static application security testing tools for C#

	Reference
CodeQL	[4]
InferSharp	[15]
Security Code Scan	[29]

Security Code Scan (SCS) is a vulnerability patterns detector for C# and VB.NET. The tool uses a set of rules to detect software vulnerabilities from solution files.

The SAST tools mentioned previously require feature definition, which requires the expertise of security researchers and engineers [35]. Due to the feature design complexity, the task is time-consuming, and error-prone [19]. Furthermore, the SAST tools often wrongly classify vulnerable source code, which leads to a high false-negative rate [11] and consequently a possible software developer fatigue in identifying the correct issues.

2.2   Deep Learning Software Vulnerability Detection Method

Vulnerability detection using Deep Learning was first proposed in [19] through the development of the VulDeePecker tool. A data set of vulnerable and non-vulnerable C/C++ snippets related to library/API function calls is created. The obtained snippets are converted into code gadgets. These code gadgets are an intermediate representation of the source code. These are then converted into a vector representation fed to a neural network. A bidirectional long short-term memory (BLSTM) model is used. The authors show that their proposed approach outperforms open-source vulnerability detection tools. However, VulDeePecker only covers two Common Weakness Enumeration IDentifiers (CWE IDs): CWE-119 and CWE-399. Moreover, the snippets are only labeled as vulnerable or not vulnerable, and the vulnerability is not identified. Therefore, the CWE ID of the vulnerability is not detected.

Russell et al. [27] proposed the first deep learning-based vulnerability detection technique that identifies weaknesses directly in source code. Their idea was inspired by text classification tasks such as sentiment classification. In their work, C/C++ code snippets are collected and classified into vulnerable and non-vulnerable. In their work, they also build a custom C/C++ lexer to extract the context of critical tokens. The lexed features are then converted into a vector representation of the tokens by applying word embedding. Two deep learning models are used for feature extraction: Convolutional Neural Networks (CNN) and Recurrent Neural Networks (RNN). Dense layers and a random forest classifier are explored in the classification part. The implemented deep learning methods performed better than the selected SAST tools. However, the comparison provided by the authors is insufficient to understand each method's effectiveness. Moreover, the implemented approach only detects whether or not the source code is vulnerable, thus not identifying the underlying CWE ID present in the vulnerable source code.

Harer et al. [13] performed two feature extraction methods from C/C++ code: build-based and source-based feature extraction. The control flow graph (CFG) is determined for the build-based approach. Features related to basic block operations such as opcode and variable definitions such as the use-def matrix are detected. The extracted features are converted into a vector representation and fed into a random forest classifier. For the source-based method, a custom C/C++ lexer is built. The lexed tokens are represented in vectors using two different algorithms: bag-of-words and word2vec. The bag-of-words vector is used to train a random tree classifier for the training part. In addition, a TextCNN model is trained using the word2vec representation input. The classification is performed with fully connected layers and a random tree classifier. The authors' work shows that source-based models achieve better results than build-based models. The combined model outperformed the source-based model, indicating the effectiveness of build-based features. Similar to the work previously described, the work by Harer et al. only considers whether the source code is vulnerable or not. Moreover, the obtained results are not compared to conventional security detection tools.

Tang et al. [32] extended the work done in the VulDeePecker tool [19] by exploring different data preprocessing approaches and different deep learning models. Code gadgets are extracted from the C/C++ source code for the preprocessing and converted into symbolic representation using multilevel symbolization. Then, the authors apply doc2vec to derive a vector representation. Two models are trained to detect vulnerabilities: BLSTM and Random Vector Functional Link network (RVFL). The authors show that while, compared to RVFL, BLSTM results in better accuracy, RVFL outperformed BLSTM in terms of speed. Nevertheless, their work only covers two CWE IDs, namely CWE-119 (Buffer Error) and CWE-399 (Resource Management error). Furthermore, the authors do not address the difference between the performance of the implemented method compared to SAST tools.

The approach presented by Ziems et al. [36] improves earlier work by targeting the type of vulnerability rather than just predicting whether a snippet is a vulnerable one or not. Their work covers the C and C++ programming languages and employs three deep learning models: LSTM, BLSTM, and the transformer. However, their study covers only one data set, the SARD data set, and is not applied to a real-world data set from the industry. Their work compares the implemented models based on accuracy. However, the SARD data set used in their study is imbalanced since there are significantly more non-vulnerable snippets than vulnerable code, thus potentially compromising the measure of accuracy. Moreover, the results obtained by the authors' proposal were not compared with the feature-based SAST tools.

Duan et al. [9] developed the VulSniper tool, which enables the prediction of vulnerabilities in C/C++ source code. For this purpose, vulnerable and non-vulnerable code snippets are collected from the SARD dataset. Code property graphs are extracted and encoded into a feature matrix to detect correlation between nodes. An attention neural network is used to classify the code snippets. However, only buffer error and resource management error vulnerabilities are detected. Moreover, the developed tool detects whether the source code is vulnerable or not. The CWE ID is not extracted.

Chauhan [2] used the SARD dataset to train deep learning models. The work focused on vulnerability detection in Java and C# source code. A single model was trained to detect software vulnerabilities in both programming languages. However, the developed tool does not detect the CWE ID of the vulnerability. In addition, the results for C# snippets are not compared with the results of SAST tools.

3   Proposed Solution

Figure 1 represents an overview of the proposed solution. This figure shows the main components that are part of our work: (1) SARD data set (2) additional sources, (3) preprocessing step, (4) deep neural networks, (5) SAST tools, and (6) evaluation.

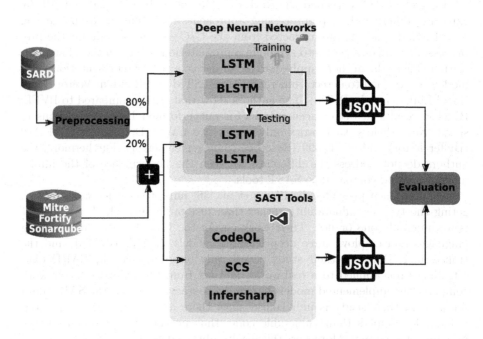

Fig. 1. Proposed solution pipeline

In order to build a deep learning-based vulnerability detection tool, an extensive data set for algorithmic training is required (1). The snippets must be labeled and classified according to the CWE ID corresponding to the vulnerability present in the source code. We opted to use the NIST Software Assurance Reference data set (SARD) [28] to train our deep learning models since these are openly available and contain many classified vulnerabilities for the C# programming language. However, these code snippets contain an inherent structure that can be picked up and affect the machine learning algorithms. Therefore, a preprocessing step is performed on the code snippets (3) to remove this structure partially. From this dataset, 80% of the snippets are used for training, while the remaining 20% are used for testing. Furthermore, vulnerable functions scraped from MITRE [25], Fortify [10], and SonarQube [31] are added to the test set (2). Afterward, the snippets are fed to the deep neural network (4) or a SAST tool (5). Snippets fed to the deep neural network are further converted into a vector representation. Finally, the results obtained from the deep learning approach and the SAST tools are evaluated and compared (6).

The models we use are built and trained using Tensorflow [30] and Keras [3]. Google colaboratory [1] is used to speed up the learning process using the available GPUs. Three C# SAST tools are selected: CodeQL, Security Code Scan (SCS), and Infersharp, as discussed in Sect. 2. Since some of these tools do not run directly on the command line, the test snippets are added and scanned in a tiny Visual Studio (VS) project. The selected tools are automatically executed and evaluated through Python [33] scripts.

Further sub-sections provide details on the data set and deep learning algorithms.

3.1 Vulnerability Detection Data Set

The data used in this work is collected from various sources. Table 2 illustrates the number of snippets used from each source - SARD data set from NIST and additional datasets from other sources.

Table 2. Number of data samples for each data source

	SARD	MITRE, Fortify, SonarQube
Vulnerable	20245	9
Non-vulnerable	26636	–
Total	46881	9

Software Assurance Reference Data Set. Automated vulnerability detection using deep learning is a recently emerging area of research. For that reason, no ready-to-use data set could be utilized, especially data sets of C# source code.

In our work, we opted for the Software Assurance Reference data set (SARD) [28], created by the National Institute of Standards and Technology (NIST). Several languages and platforms are supported in the data set. This data set includes several test cases which contain production, synthetic, and academic vulnerabilities. The security flaws are labeled with the corresponding CWE ID. Furthermore, the fixed version of the vulnerabilities is available. Hence, the trained neural network can learn to distinguish between the vulnerable and the fixed versions.

Table 3. CWE ID distribution of SARD data set

CWE ID	197	190	191	129	369	789	400	113	89	80	Others
Percentage	17.6	12.9	8.6	8.1	5.5	4.7	4.3	3.5	3.5	2.4	28.9

The C# SARD data set consists of 46881 snippets categorized into 103 different CWEs. Table 3 shows the percentage distribution of the top-10 C# code snippets for each CWE ID. As can be observed from this table, the data set is not balanced for all CWE IDs. Due to the low number of samples for some of the CWE IDs, we cut the data in half and retained only the snippets corresponding to the top 51 CWE. Therefore, the resulting dataset considers only CWEs with 35 or more vulnerable samples and captures about 98.43% of the SARD data set.

Nevertheless, inspecting the snippet percentage versus occurrence of the problem in practice, we find that the security vulnerabilities that occur more prominently in the industry are represented by a more significant amount of code snippets, in particular containing more than 3000 training samples. Therefore, due to this reason, we do not expect that this data imbalance plays a big difference in a possible training bias of the neural networks.

Pre-processing. SARD C# data set includes three types of test cases: (1) bad test cases contain only vulnerable functions, (2) good test cases include only non-vulnerable code snippets, and (3) mixed files that are composed of vulnerable functions and their corresponding patched versions.

The preprocessing pipeline is summarized in Fig. 2.

We separated the vulnerable and non-vulnerable functions from mixed test cases in our preprocessing step. Furthermore, the mixed files can include three different scenarios. The simplest test case includes functions without dependencies, i.e., no other functions are called from the vulnerable or non-vulnerable function. Functions with internal dependencies contain calls to other functions in the same file. In addition, functions can have an external dependency, occurring when a function from another file is called. The called functions are retrieved and added to the same test case file class for the test cases with internal or external dependencies. After extracting good and bad functions separately, the comments are cleaned from the source code. The comments contain information about the test case and the vulnerability, leading to a problem of overfitting when training the networks. Moreover, several duplicates were found in the data

Source code

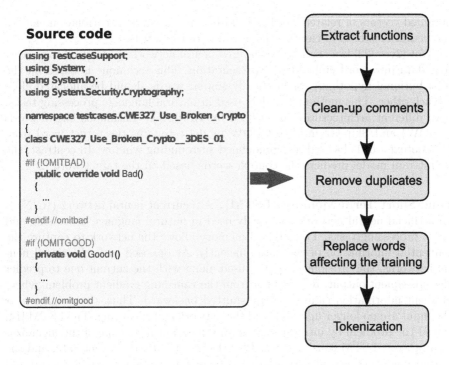

```
using TestCaseSupport;
using System;
using System.IO;
using System.Security.Cryptography;

namespace testcases.CWE327_Use_Broken_Crypto
{
class CWE327_Use_Broken_Crypto__3DES_01
{
#if (!OMITBAD)
    public override void Bad()
    {
        ...
    }
#endif //omitbad

#if (!OMITGOOD)
    private void Good1()
    {
        ...
    }
#endif //omitgood
```

Extract functions

Clean-up comments

Remove duplicates

Replace words affecting the training

Tokenization

Fig. 2. Pre-processing pipeline

set, mainly in the non-vulnerable snippets. The duplicates are removed as they could bias the models in the training phase.

Afterward, a Tokenization process is carried out, i.e., the source code is dissected into tokens. The open-source tokenizer implemented in [26] is used and adapted to the Python language.

The function name of the snippets in the SARD data set provides information about whether the function is vulnerable or not. The name of the vulnerable function contains the word "bad", and the corresponding fixed version contains the word "good". The class name of a test case specifies the type of the error based on the CWE ID. Some attributes in the code also indicate vulnerable data. These words must be removed due to their interference with the network's training; otherwise, the network learns to classify the snippets based on specific words rather than context. These attributes are replaced with random words.

3.2 Deep Learning Vulnerability Detection

Word2Vec Model. Each neural network requires data input in vector representation. For this reason, the text data should be converted to its vector representation, known as word embedding. The mapping between the text data and the corresponding vector should preserve the context. In other words, the obtained vectors of related words should be correlated. This correlation enables the neural networks to capture the meaning of the words.

Word2vec [22] is a shallow two-layered neural network model used to convert text data into word embedding representation. This technique is based on the distributional hypothesis. Semantically similar words should be allocated close to each other. This method is widely used in natural language processing tasks. Two different architectures are utilized by Word2vec: continuous bag-of-words (CBOW) and Skip-Gram. The CBOW model estimates the target word from the context words located in a predefined surrounding window. In contrast, the Skip-Gram model predicts the context words based on the target word [23].

Long Short Term Memory (LSTM). A recurrent neural network (RNN) is an artificial neural network commonly used in natural language processing and video processing tasks. The internal memory allows the network to capture the sequential information of the data efficiently. As opposed to feed-forward neural networks, the previous output is used along with the current one to predict the subsequent output. RNNs suffer from the vanishing gradient problem, where gradient information cannot be transmitted backward. Thus, the weights near the input are no longer updated, and the network stops learning. The LSTM [14] solved the problem by introducing a gating mechanism to control the memoization process. LSTM consists of 3 gates: the input gate, the forget gate, and the output gate. The neural network learns to forget existing information and add a new one depending on the current input and the previous hidden state.

Fully connected layers follow the LSTM cells to classify the code snippets. The classification model is presented in Fig. 3.

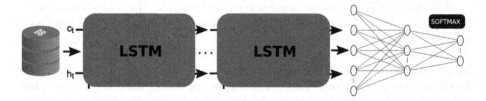

Fig. 3. Souce code classification using LSTM

Bidirectional Long Short Term Memory (BLSTM). We also use BLSTM, which was proposed as an improvement to the standard LSTM [12]. In contrast to LSTM, where inputs flow only forward, BLSTM uses information from both directions: forward and backward. The outputs of the two layers are then combined. The outcome of BLSTM is often more informative than that of LSTM since BLSTM can learn the context of the input sequence from the past and the future.

4   Experimental Results and Discussions

This section presents the clean data set obtained after performing the proposed preprocessing pipeline and the results of the implemented software vulnerability detection system.

The pipeline presented in Fig. 2 is implemented to create a C# source code data set. After running the function extractor, the extracted vulnerable and non-vulnerable files should compile successfully. This step is done automatically by running MSbuild on a C# snippets project.

SARD data set includes CWE IDs that represent only a few test cases. These snippets are eliminated given the network's inability to learn from a small number of samples. Hence, the number of CWE IDs is reduced to 51. The histogram of the collected data is presented in Fig. 4.

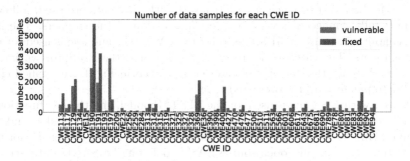

Fig. 4. Data distribution histogram

As shown in Fig. 4, the data is imbalanced. Overall, there exist many more fixed snippets than vulnerable source code.

The processed snippets are then tokenized, and a word2vec model is trained. For this step, we used the Skip-Gram model. We have chosen to set the embedding size to 30 and trained our model for 100 epochs. To evaluate the performance of the embedding model, we visualized neighboring tokens in 2 dimensions. Figure 5 illustrates the nearest tokens to the word "int."

Adjacent words are also semantically close. Thus, the trained word2vec model has captured the meaning of the words in the vector representation.

The vector representation is then fed to the neural networks, namely the LSTM and the BLSTM. The data is divided into two subsets: the more significant subset consists of 80% of the data. While this subset is used for training our model, the remaining 20% of the data are used for testing.

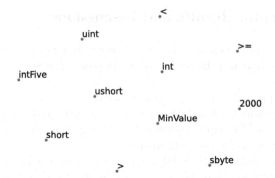

Fig. 5. Neighboring tokens to the word "int" after applying Word2vec

For the LSTM, two stacked LSTM layers with 150 units are used, followed by three fully connected layers for the classification of the snippets. The last layer contains 52 neurons: 51 are used for the CWE IDs, and one is used for the fixed snippets. The categorical cross-entropy loss and the RMSprop optimizer are utilized. Since the data is imbalanced, as shown in Fig. 4, we applied class weights to penalize over-represented classes.

A layer with 128 units is used for the BLSTM model, and the loss function is minimized with the Adam optimizer. The performance of both models and the selected SAST tools is summarized in Table 4. Deep learning models performed better than the existing open-source SAST tools on the SARD data set. As expected, our results show that the BLSTM model outperformed the LSTM model. These results show that the BLSTM can extract the context better than the LSTM.

Table 4. Performance of deep learning models and SAST tools

Model	Training accuracy	Testing accuracy	TPR	Number of detected CWE IDs
LSTM	97.64 %	97.88 %	97 %	51
BLSTM	99.54 %	99,69 %	99 %	51
CodeQL	–	57 %	3 %	11
SCS	–	57 %	3 %	7

The following part focuses on four CWE IDs from the most dangerous software errors relevant to the industry: CWE190, CWE78, CWE89, and CWE476. These are represented in the SARD data set by the following percentages: CWE190: 12.9%, CWE78: 1.31%, CWE89: 3.51%, and CWE476: 0.64%. Since the BLSTM model performed better than the LSTM, we use the BLSTM architecture to train a model that predicts the selected CWE IDs. The training outcome is then compared with the outcome of open-source SAST tools.

The comparison is performed based on the following metrics: False Positive Rate (FPR), True Positive Rate (TPR), False Negative Rate (FNR), and True Negative Rate (TNR). Moreover, we introduce the Negative Predictive Value (NPV) and the Positive Predictive Value (PPV), representing the diagnostic test's performance. In particular, PPV describes the probability that a positively detected snippet is genuinely positive. These values are calculated for each tool and each CWE ID. The selected open-source SAST tools are CodeQL, SCS, and InferSharp. Infersharp focuses on limited vulnerabilities, including CWE-476, which we use to compare the approaches.

As shown in Fig. 6, the FPR and the TNR are similar in the case of the SCS, CodeQL, and the BLSTM. However, BLSTM detected more vulnerabilities in the test set. CodeQL and SCS performed similarly with the vulnerability types CWE190 and CWE476 and did not detect vulnerabilities related to these types. In contrast, the SCS detected more vulnerabilities of types CWE78 and CWE89. For CWE476, Infersharp outperformed the other SAST tools in detecting this type of vulnerability. It identified 36% of the vulnerable snippets and returned only a few false positives.

To test the reliability of the vulnerability detection systems, we plotted the PPV and the NPV in Fig. 7. For the CWE89, the PPV obtained by SCS is higher than the value of CodeQL and similar for the other CWE IDs. Therefore, the SCS tool is more accurate when the scanned snippet is genuinely vulnerable. Furthermore, the NPV of the SCS tool is higher than the NPV of CodeQL by the CWE78 and CWE89.

This observation allows us to conclude that the SCS tool is likely correct when the scanned snippet is non-vulnerable. For the CWE476, the PPV and NPV obtained with Infersharp are higher than those obtained with the other SAST tools. Therefore, Infersharp is more reliable in detecting null pointer dereferencing errors.

Although CodeQL and SCS achieved the same accuracy, as shown in Table 4, SCS is more accurate concerning the errors CWE78 and CWE89. However, a combined model could increase the number of true positives. As shown in Fig. 8, the combined model produced a slight improvement for CWE89. While combining CodeQL and SCS tools improved the number of detected vulnerabilities from 42 to 58 snippets for CWE78. Therefore, combining both tools increases software security when dealing with CWE89 and CWE78 flaws.

Our BLSTM model was trained and fine-tuned using the SARD data set. We wanted to test our model with other vulnerable files from other data sets. For this purpose, we collected a small subset of vulnerable snippets with SQL injection vulnerabilities from SonarQube, Fortify, and MITRE. Out of 9 vulnerable snippets, our tool detected eight vulnerabilities. CodeQL and SCS did not find vulnerabilities in these snippets.

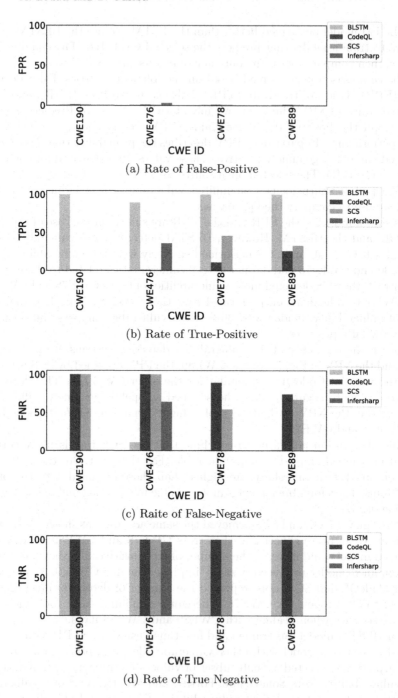

(a) Rate of False-Positive

(b) Rate of True-Positive

(c) Raite of False-Negative

(d) Rate of True Negative

Fig. 6. Comparison between deep learning methods and open source SAST tools

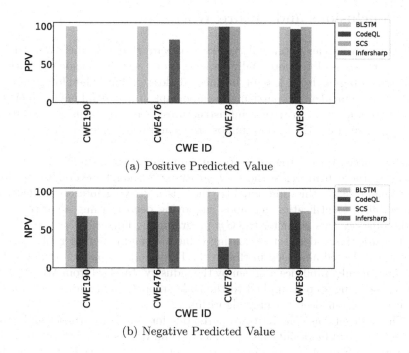

(a) Positive Predicted Value

(b) Negative Predicted Value

Fig. 7. Comparison between deep learning methods and open source SAST tools

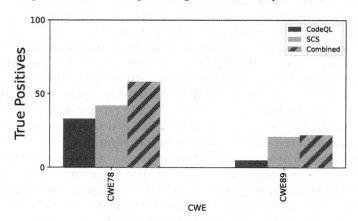

Fig. 8. Number of true positives generated by CodeQL, SCS and the combined model for the CWE78 and CWE89

The implemented deep learning method showed promising results and outperformed existing open-source SAST tools. Contrary to other tools, the chosen approach does not require the source code to be compilable. Although we trained the model using only the SARD data set, vulnerable snippets with SQL injection from other sources are also detected.

5   Conclusions and Future Work

Malicious actors can potentially exploit software that contains vulnerabilities. This fact can lead to potentially serious cyber security incidents, with consequences ranging from loss of business to loss of life. Therefore, protecting against these incidents is particularly important in industrial environments and even more important in critical infrastructures. Because of this, several security standards, such as IEC 62.443, impose rules and regulations on how to address this.

One method to mitigate software vulnerabilities includes automatically detecting these utilizing static code analysis. Although several tools already exist that provide this functionality, there is a growing interest in developing vulnerability identification methods employing deep learning algorithms. This work addresses this point for the C# programming language.

Towards this, a data set of existing vulnerable and non-vulnerable code snippets was collected and used in this work. These code snippets are mapped into well-known vulnerabilities as given by the industry standard from MITRE CWE. A preprocessing step is applied to the code snippets, and the result is used as input data to our deep learning algorithm.

The data set was split into two parts: one for training purposes and another for testing the vulnerability detection algorithm. In this work, we conducted two different experiments to test our method. In the first test, we look at the ability of the deep learning method to understand and detect software vulnerabilities in the C# source code. We compare the detection capabilities in the second test with existing open-source static code analysis tools.

Our work shows that the implemented methods can reliably and efficiently predict software vulnerabilities in C# source code based on the obtained results. We also show that, for the used test data set, our method outperforms existing open-source SAST tools on the SARD data set. Our comparison is based on the true and false-positive rates analysis. We also provide initial results on the algorithm's reliability with real-world data, in particular capturing results for software vulnerabilities that are common in the industry.

By comparing different tools and their results, our work enables industry practitioners to select appropriate tools for their environment. Our work also contributes to understanding the usage of the deep learning method to detect vulnerabilities in C# source code. We provide our algorithms and code snippets to enable researchers to study and refine our method.

In a further study, we would like to replicate our results with a more significant real-world data set of vulnerable code caught in the industry's production phase. In addition, deep neural networks' ability to predict the location of the vulnerability could be investigated.

References

1. Bisong, E.: Building Machine Learning and Deep Learning Models on Google Cloud Platform. Apress, Berkeley, CA (2019). https://doi.org/10.1007/978-1-4842-4470-8
2. Chauhan, A.: Machine Learning Based Cross-Language Vulnerability Detection: How Far Are We. The University of Texas at Dallas (2020)
3. Chollet, F., et al.: Keras. https://keras.io (2015) Accessed 21 Mar 2022
4. Codeql. https://codeql.github.com Accessed 21 March 2022
5. MITRE Corporation: Common Weakness and Exposures - CWE-366: Race Condition within a Thread. https://cwe.mitre.org/data/definitions/366.html Accessed 21 March 2022
6. MITRE Corporation: Common Weakness and Exposures - CWE-401: Missing Release of Memory after Effective Lifetime. https://cwe.mitre.org/data/definitions/401.html Accessed 21 March 2022
7. MITRE Corporation: Common Weakness and Exposures - CWE-476: NULL Pointer Dereference. https://cwe.mitre.org/data/definitions/476.html Accessed 21 March 2022
8. Department of Homeland Security, US-CERT: Software Assurance.D https://tinyurl.com/y6pr9v42 Accessed 27 Sept 2020
9. Duan, X., et al.: Vulsniper: Focus your attention to shoot fine-grained vulnerabilities. In: IJCAI, pp. 4665–4671 (2019)
10. Fortify. https://vulncat.fortify.com Accessed 21 March 2022
11. Goseva-Popstojanova, K., Perhinschi, A.: On the Capability of Static Code Analysis to Detect Security Vulnerabilities. Information and Software Technology, Butterworth-Heinemann, Newton, MA, USA vol. 68, pp. 18–33 (2015). https://doi.org/10.1016/j.infsof.2015.08.002
12. Graves, A., Schmidhuber, J.: Framewise phoneme classification with bidirectional LSTM and other neural network architectures. Neural Networks 18(5–6), 602–610 (2005). https://doi.org/10.1016/j.neunet.2005.06.042
13. Harer, J.A., et al.: Automated Software Vulnerability Detection with Machine Learning. CoRR abs/1803.04497 (2018). http://arxiv.org/abs/1803.04497
14. Hochreiter, S., Schmidhuber, J.: Long short-term memory. Neural Comput. 9(8), 1735–1780 (1997)
15. Infersharp. https://github.com/microsoft/infersharp, Accessed 21 March 2022
16. International Electrotechnical Commission: IEC 62443-4-1 - Security for industrial automation and control systems - Part 4–1: Secure product development lifecycle requirements. Tech. rep., IEC, Geneval Switzerland (2018)
17. Iosif, A.C., Gasiba, T.E., Zhao, T., Lechner, U., Pinto-Albuquerque, M.: A Large-Scale Study on the Security Vulnerabilities of Cloud Deployments. In: International Conference on Ubiquitous Security, pp. 171–188. Springer (2021). https://doi.org/10.1007/978-981-19-0468-4_13
18. Li, W., Cai, J., Wang, Z., Cheng, S.: A Robust Malware Detection Approach for Android System Based on Ensemble Learning. In: International Conference on Ubiquitous Security, pp. 309–321. Springer (2021). https://doi.org/10.1007/978-981-19-0468-4_23
19. Li, Z., et al.: VulDeePecker: A Deep Learning-Based System for Vulnerability Detection. CoRR abs/1801.01681 (2018). http://arxiv.org/abs/1801.01681
20. Louati, A., Gasiba, T.: Raw Results on Source Code Vulnerability Detection. https://github.com/XXXX,

21. Mead, N., Allen, J., Barnum, S., Ellison, R., McGraw, G.: Software Security Engineering: a Guide for Project Managers. Addison-Wesley Professional, 1 edn. (2004)
22. Mikolov, T., Chen, K., Corrado, G., Dean, J.: Efficient Estimation of Word Representations in Vector Space. In: Bengio, Y., LeCun, Y. (eds.) 1st International Conference on Learning Representations, ICLR 2013, Scottsdale, Arizona, USA, May 2–4, 2013, Workshop Track Proceedings (2013). http://arxiv.org/abs/1301.3781
23. Mikolov, T., Sutskever, I., Chen, K., Corrado, G.S., Dean, J.: Distributed Representations of Words and Phrases and their Compositionality. In: Burges, C.J.C., Bottou, L., Ghahramani, Z., Weinberger, K.Q. (eds.) Advances in Neural Information Processing Systems 26: 27th Annual Conference on Neural Information Processing Systems 2013. Proceedings of a meeting held December 5–8, 2013, Lake Tahoe, Nevada, United States. pp. 3111–3119 (2013). https://proceedings.neurips.cc/paper/2013/hash/9aa42b31882ec039965f3c4923ce901b-Abstract.html
24. MITRE Corporation: Common Vulnerabilities and Enumeration Security Vulnerability Database. https://www.cvedetails.com Accessed 4 June 2022
25. MITRE Corporation: Common Weakness and Exposures. https://cwe.mitre.org Accessed 21 March 2022
26. Multi Language Tokenizer. https://github.com/dspinellis/tokenizer Accessed 21 March 2022
27. Russell, R.L., et al.: Automated Vulnerability Detection in Source Code Using Deep Representation Learning. In: Wani, M.A., Kantardzic, M.M., Mouchaweh, M.S., Gama, J., Lughofer, E. (eds.) 17th IEEE International Conference on Machine Learning and Applications, ICMLA 2018, Orlando, FL, USA, December 17–20, 2018. pp. 757–762. IEEE (2018). https://doi.org/10.1109/ICMLA.2018.00120
28. Software Assurance Reference Data Set. https://samate.nist.gov/SRD/index.php, Accessed 21 March 2022
29. Security Code Scan. https://security-code-scan.github.io Accessed 21 March 2022
30. TensorFlow: Large-Scale Machine Learning on Heterogeneous Systems (2015). https://www.tensorflow.org/, software available from tensorflow.org
31. SonarQube. https://www.sonarqube.org Accessed 21 March 2022
32. Tang, G., Meng, L., Ren, S., Cao, W., Wang, Q., Yang, L.: A Comparative Study of Neural Network Techniques for Automatic Software Vulnerability Detection. CoRR abs/2104.14978 (2021). https://arxiv.org/abs/2104.14978
33. Van Rossum, G., Drake, F.L.: Python 3 Reference Manual. CreateSpace, Scotts Valley, CA (2009)
34. Wang, S., Jiang, J.: Learning Natural Language Inference with LSTM. In: Knight, K., Nenkova, A., Rambow, O. (eds.) NAACL HLT 2016, The 2016 Conference of the North American Chapter of the Association for Computational Linguistics: Human Language Technologies, San Diego California, USA, June 12–17, 2016. pp. 1442–1451. The Association for Computational Linguistics (2016). https://doi.org/10.18653/v1/n16-1170, https://doi.org/10.18653/v1/n16-1170
35. Wu, F., Wang, J., Liu, J., Wang, W.: Vulnerability Detection with Deep Learning. In: 2017 3rd IEEE International Conference on Computer and Communications (ICCC), pp. 1298–1302 (2017). https://doi.org/10.1109/CompComm.2017.8322752
36. Ziems, N., Wu, S.: Security Vulnerability Detection Using Deep Learning Natural Language Processing. CoRR abs/2105.02388 (2021). https://arxiv.org/abs/2105.02388

Detecting Unknown Vulnerabilities in Smart Contracts with Binary Classification Model Using Machine Learning

Xiangbin Li, Xiaofei Xing$^{(\boxtimes)}$ ⓘ, Guojun Wang ⓘ, Peiqiang Li,
and Xiangyong Liu

School of Computer Science and Cyber Engineering, Guangzhou University,
Guangzhou 510006, China
xingxf@gzhu.edu.cn

Abstract. The emergence of smart contracts has led to the wider use of blockchain, which involves a large number of virtual currency transactions. Because smart contracts are inevitably written with some vulnerabilities, which makes them vulnerable to attacks that cause property damage, and existing detection techniques and static analysis methods mainly target known vulnerability detection. We design a machine learning-based unknown vulnerability detection scheme using opcode sequences. The scheme first obtains opcode sequences of the execution path of contract transactions in the Ethereum virtual machine (EVM) by replaying them in Ethereum. Then we use a combination of N-gram model and a vector weight penalty mechanism to extract opcode features. Finally, we validate the effectiveness of our scheme by three machine learning models, namely the K-Near Neighbor Algorithm (KNN), the Support Vector Machine (SVM), and the Logistic Regression (LR). The SVM model achieves an accuracy of 91.4% and F1-score of 75.3% for the detection of unknown vulnerabilities.

Keywords: Smart contract · Unknown vulnerability · Machine learning · Opcode sequences · N-gram · Blockchain

1 Introduction

In recent years, the emergence and use of blockchain technology has raised concerns [1], especially the emergence of smart contracts, which has led to a wider application of blockchain [2,3]. On the one hand, blockchain technology with tamper-proof features and [4,5] allows people to complete transactions securely in a trustless network environment, especially the Bitcoin and Ethereum ecosystems, which have operated stably for years without systemic failures. On the other hand, as blockchain involves a large amount of wealth transactions that are not controlled by anyone, everything is controlled by the underlying code

G. Wang et al. (Eds.): UbiSec 2022, CCIS 1768, pp. 179–192, 2023.
https://doi.org/10.1007/978-981-99-0272-9_12

of the blockchain, and it is difficult to be regulated by the relevant authorities, which attracts the attention of a large number of cyber hackers.

Compared with the data layer, network layer and consensus layer of the blockchain system, the smart contract layer is relatively easy to receive attacks. This is because the former is determined by the underlying code of the blockchain system, which prevents information from being tampered with through techniques such as cryptography and the way in which everyone keeps a common ledger. It is difficult for attackers to launch attacks on the system itself, so they tend to steal information through network attacks or by controlling the hosts of the nodes, but with the continuous progress of trusted computing devices [6], the security of the nodes continues to improve, which makes the underlying blockchain system more difficult to attack. While the latter involves a large number of blockchain contract applications, which are written by users themselves and have many security vulnerabilities [1,7], such as Re-entrancy, Unexpected Function Invocation, and Incorrect Check for Authorization. A large amount of virtual currency is stored in these smart contract accounts, which quickly attracts the attention of a large number of hackers, which brings heavy losses to blockchain users.

To address the above issues, previous research mainly includes two types of approaches, namely static analysis methods and dynamic analysis methods. The former is the static analysis of smart contract source code or bytecode before contract deployment, which generally aids smart contract vulnerability detection with the help of some static analysis tools [8], or the static symbolic execution approach [9]. The latter is to perform vulnerability analysis in a real running environment after contract deployment, such as Echidna [11], which verifies the vulnerability of smart contracts by randomly generating a large number of inputs. These schemes can reduce the vulnerabilities of smart contracts to some extent, but such methods often require professional assistance to complete, and the detection efficiency is low.

Starting from the above problems, researchers have proposed some automatic detection schemes for smart contract vulnerabilities based on machine learning [13], aiming to improve the detection efficiency while increasing the detection accuracy. However, in the existing machine learning-based contract vulnerability detection research solutions mainly focus on the undeployed contract source code or bytecode, in addition to the unknown vulnerabilities of smart contracts are rarely studied. In this paper, we obtain the execution opcode sequences of smart contracts in Ethereum virtual machines (EVM) by means of contract transaction retransmission, and propose a machine learning-based detection method for unknown vulnerabilities in smart contracts based on the similarity of vulnerability characteristics. The main contributions of this paper are as follows.

(1) We propose a machine learning based unknown vulnerability detection scheme that considers the sequence of opcodes with vulnerabilities to have similar features.
(2) We propose a data feature extraction scheme that combines an N-gram model and a vector weight penalty mechanism. The N-gram model is used

to extract features such as the order and number of opcodes in opcode sequences, and the vector weight penalty mechanism is used to reduce the effect of noise such as regular opcodes in vectors.

(3) We verify our scheme by three machine learning models, and the experimental results show the effectiveness of our scheme.

The rest of this paper is structured as follows. In Sect. 2, the related works is classified and summarized. In Sect. 3 a general description of the system model for unknown vulnerability detection is given, and the details of our scheme are presented in Sect. 4. The validation and analysis of the experiments are performed in Sect. 5. We conclude this paper in Sect. 6.

2   Related Work

In smart contract vulnerability detection, static analysis tools such as Slither [8]. These tools mainly detect pattern matches in the code that may violate coding guidelines or have vulnerabilities, and the vulnerability detection checkall rate is not high. Symbolic execution [9] is another important method of static analysis, which replaces the contract program code with symbols for execution and finds the corresponding vulnerability path by the execution path of the symbols. However, such methods rely excessively on manual assistance, and although there are some intelligent pattern matching schemes, the intelligence verifies some predefined omissions. In addition symbolic execution covers paths will be too much prone to problems such as path explosion. Compared to the former, the dynamic analysis approach has better accuracy, but requires suitable inputs to generate the actual execution, and finding the correct inputs is not easy, commonly used tools are Echidna [10], ContractFuzzer [11], ReGuard [12], etc. They execute smart contracts by generating a large number of random inputs, and then detect them based on the execution logs vulnerabilities. However, both static and dynamic analysis methods require knowledge and insight into all possible execution paths, and their computational complexity increases dramatically with the depth of the path.

Compared with static or dynamic analysis statistical methods, the AI model-based automatic detection method reduces the reliance on human assistance and makes vulnerability detection more stable. It has a higher accuracy rate compared to static analysis methods. Compared with dynamic analysis methods, it has higher efficiency. Xing C et al. [14] proposed a smart contract vulnerability detection method based on neural network and slicing matrix for vulnerabilities such as short address and stream address. Xu Y et al. [15] introduced a smart contract-based analysis model to assist smart contract vulnerability detection by constructing an abstract syntax tree of smart contracts. Wang W et al. [16] extracted the dual format features from the simplified opcodes of smart contracts and used machine learning to put this contract vulnerability. Eshghie M et al. [17] proposed a machine learning-based dynamic vulnerability detection method for smart contracts, which aids data collection by building a tool to monitor transaction metadata. Zhou et al. [18] proposed a tree-based machine learning vulnerability detection method to perform vulnerability analysis of smart contracts, which captures multidimensional features by constructing abstract syntax trees. Xue et al. [19] proposed a machine learning-guided cross-contract fuzzy testing method, which focuses on vulnerability detection generated by inter-contract functions. Shakya et al. [20] proposed a machine learning-based hybrid model detection method for smart contracts, which uses both high-level syntax features and bytecode features to construct a hybrid feature space.

The above studies on smart contract vulnerability detection are for known vulnerabilities, and unknown vulnerabilities are mainly applied in traditional application vulnerability detection. Singh et al. [21] by constituting a hybrid approach for detection and prioritization of zero-day attacks, which follows a probabilistic approach to identify zero-day attack paths to detect unknown vulnerabilities that exist and have not occurred in the network. In the social network scenario, Tang et al. [22] use a neural network algorithm for secondary judgment to check unknown malicious users based on the periodic activity characteristics of active malicious accounts. Choi et al. [23] mine the target system for anomalous attacks by extracting the normal or anomalous behavior of the attacks on the target system. Periyasamy et al. [24] use vulnerability syntax trees and various predictive models together to accomplish unknown vulnerability detection in applications. Chanwoong et al. [25] propose a semi-supervised learning-based technique that uses event logs to detect unknown attacks without a priori knowledge. Al-Zewairi et al. [26] use shallow and deep ANN classifiers for unknown security attack detection. Zhang et al. [27] propose a deep learning-based scheme to detect unknown threats to information systems.

3   System Model for Unknown Vulnerability Detection

Our system consists of four main modules, which are the data collection module, data pre-processing module, the model training module, the vulnerability detection module of the model, as shown in Fig. 1.

3.1   Data Collection

In the data collection module, we use the method of Geth instrumentation collects, and later replay all transactions on Geth to collect the opcode sequences during the execution of the contract in the EVM [28]. Data collection is divided into two parts, the first part is to collect information such as opcode sequences during contract transaction execution, and the second part is to collect transaction tag information. The first part is to collect the opcode and other information during the execution of the contract transaction [29], and the second part is to collect the transaction tag information, which is based on the vulnerability detection plugin of SODA [7].

For the first part, we first modify the Ethereum client source code [29], and we deploy the modified client source code and connect it to the Ethereum public

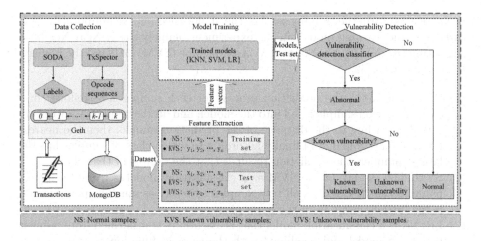

Fig. 1. System model of detecting unknown vulnerabilities

network to become a full node. Then we synchronize all the information such as transactions and accounts, because all the contract transactions will be executed during the synchronization process, so the Geth instrumentation will collect the opcode and other data during the contract execution. Finally, this data will be collected and stored in our database.

For the second part, we first deploy a plug-in to collect transaction tag information in the Ethereum client, which is based on the SODA plug-in [7], and then the plug-in will monitor information such as opcode of smart contracts in EVM in real time, where the code to collect the information has been inserted in EVM. Next, the plugin will output label data to the opcode of each contract transaction. Finally, the tag data will be associated with the data collected in the first part one by one and stored in our database.

3.2 Data Pre-processing

In the data collection module, we have stored the data into our MongoDB database, the model training module will get the training dataset from the MongoDB database, and then we need to do data preprocessing and train the model. For data preprocessing, it transforms the data into vector data that the machine learning model can learn. Our scheme uses a bigram, a bag-of-words model, and a feature vector weighting penalty scheme that we are involved in, and the data preprocessing process is described in detail in Sect. 4.

3.3 Model Training

In the model training module, our solution takes all known vulnerabilities as known vulnerability sample types as part of the training set, and all normal samples as normal sample types as another part of the training set, and the two parts together form the training set. For the model selection, we temporarily used three machine learning models in the experiment, namely the K-Near Neighbor Algorithm (KNN) [30], the Support Vector Machine (SVM) [31], and the Logistic Regression (LR) [32].

(1) KNN. For KNN, the prediction process for each sample is as follows: first each prediction sample is fed into the model, and all the training samples are sorted according to the distance of the prediction sample, then the nearest k samples are found, and finally according to which class of samples has the largest number, the prediction result is that the sample of that class.
(2) SVM. The essence of the SVM as a classification model is to find a hyperplane so that it classifies all test samples correctly as much as possible and is the furthest away from the hyperplane.
(3) LR. LR is a classification model that is essentially transformed from a linear regression model and combined with the sigmoid function to transform it into a probability between 0 and 1, thus forming a classification model.

3.4 Vulnerability Detection

In the vulnerability detection module, each pre-processed test sample (including normal samples, known vulnerability samples and unknown vulnerability samples) is first fed into the trained vulnerability detection model, which then detects each sample and determines whether it is vulnerable. As shown in Fig. 1, the vulnerability detection results have the following conditions:

(1) If the test is a normal sample, the sample is classified as a negative sample.
(2) If the test is a vulnerability sample and the sample contains a known vulnerability label (we use the SODA during the data collection phase to detect each sample for known vulnerabilities, and if present we will label the sample with known vulnerabilities), the sample is classified as a known positive sample.
(3) If the test is positive and the sample does not contain a known vulnerability label, the sample is classified as an unknown positive sample.

4   Detailed Design

In this section, we will introduce three main contents, namely the detailed scheme process of data preprocessing, the N-gram model for feature extraction, and the feature vector weight penalty scheme for eliminating common opcode sequence interference.

4.1 Scheme Process

In this subsection, we will introduce the specific scheme process of vulnerability detection, as shown in Fig. 2, which is described in detail below.

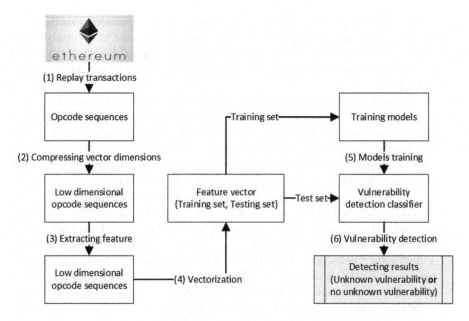

Fig. 2. The process of detecting unknow vulnerability

(1) Replay contract transaction. First, we obtain the transaction opcode sequence from the replay contract transaction in the Ethernet client Geth, which is processed as the original data of the scheme, and the specific acquisition process is described in detail in Sect. 3.1.

(2) We replace multiple opcodes with similar functions one by one to reduce the variety of opcodes and avoid dimensional disasters when opcode sequences is converted into vectors. The contents of the replacement string are shown in Table 1, the old string is the opcode that will be replaced, and the new string is the opcode that will be used to replace the old string.

Table 1. Simplified rules for smart contract opcode

Old opcode	New opcode
PUSH1-PUSH32	PUSH
SWAP1-SWAP16	SWAP
DUP1-DUP16	DUP
LOG0-LOG4	LOG

The replacement rules include: 1) replace all 32 strings of $PUSH1 - PUSH32$ with $PUSH$, 2) replace all 16 strings of $SWAP1 - SWAP16$ with $SWAP$, 3) replace all 16 strings of $DUP1 - DUP16$ with DUP, and 4) replace all 5 strings of $LOG0 - LOG4$ with LOG.

(3) Extracting feature. N-gram processes data, which is to better statistically calculate the relationship between opcodes, so that the characteristics of the are preserved to the greatest extent possible when the data is converted into vectors, and its detailed role and processing process will be described in Sect. 4.2.

(4) Vectorization. The process of converting bigram data into vectors uses a combination of a bag-of-words model and a feature vector weighted penalty scheme proposed in this paper. The bag-of-word model, which counts only the number of occurrences of each word in the opcode, regardless of the order between words. For the feature vector weight penalty scheme, the main purpose of which is to eliminate the weight influence of common opcodes in opcode sequences, the specific details of which we will discuss in Sect. 4.3

(5) Models training. The pre-processed feature vector data is divided into training and test sets, and then the training sets are put into our machine learning models of each class for training.

(6) Vulnerability detection. After the models are trained, they are turned into vulnerability detection models. We put the test set into the vulnerability detection model, and the detection results include normal samples and vulnerability samples, where the vulnerability samples can be classified into known vulnerabilities and unknown vulnerabilities according to the known vulnerability labels.

4.2   N-gram Model

In the process of data preprocessing, the N-gram model [33] was used to feature extract the data. N-gram model is an extension of the bag of words model [34], N is a number, $N = 1$ is the bag of words model. When $N = 1$, the model only takes a single opcode as a feature, completely ignoring the order between the opcodes, and the single feature cannot reflect the connection between the opcodes. When $N >= 3$, the feature dimension of the opcode sequence is too large and the classification complexity is too high. Therefore, this article uses N-gram ($N = 2$), i.e. bigram model to extract features. Let the feature number of the bigram feature be k, and the feature vector of the ith sample (i.e., the ith opcode sequence) be $[m_{i1}, m_{i2}, ..., m_{ij}, ..., m_{ik}]$, where m_{ij} represents the frequency of the jth bigram feature in the ith sample, and its equation is expressed as

$$m_{ij} = \frac{num_{ij}}{sum_i}. \tag{1}$$

where sum_i is the total number of opcodes in the ith opcode sequence, and num_{ij} is the frequency of occurrence of the jth opcode in the ith opcode sequence.

However, there are many normal opcodes in the opcode sequence that occur very frequently, so the weights of their corresponding feature vectors are so large that they interfere greatly with the prediction of the model.

4.3 Vector Weight Penalty Mechanism

To reduce the noise interference of common normal opcodes, a feature vector weight penalty mechanism is used in this paper. If a word appears in a very large number of articles, then it may be a very common word that contributes little to the special meaning of a paragraph. One processing method in natural language processing is term frequency-inverse document frequency (TF-IDF) [35], which counts the number of texts in which the word appears in all texts. In this case, the inverse document frequency is expressed as

$$IDF(t_i) = log\frac{|D|}{|\{d : t_i \in d\}|}. \tag{2}$$

where $|D| = n$ is the total sample quantity and $|\{d : t_i \in d\}|$ is the sample quantity of all samples containing feature t.

However, because in the sequence of opcodes of smart contracts, many opcodes appear in each transaction opcode sequence and many times, only the proportion of each opcode in all samples is counted, the weight penalties of many common opcodes are the same, which cannot reflect the true inverse word frequency.

Therefore, in order to adapt to this type of data for opcode sequences, this paper proposes a vector weight penalty scheme, which counts not only the number of samples containing bigram feature j, but also the number of occurrences of bigram feature j in each sample, and the detailed process is as follows.

Set w_{ij} as the penalty weight for the jth bigram feature in the ith sample, num_{ij} as the number of occurrences of the jth opcode in the ith sample, and the total number of samples is n. Then the weight penalty equation is expressed as

$$w_{ij} = log(\frac{n}{num_{1j} + num_{2j} + ... + num_{ij} + ... + num_{nj}}). \tag{3}$$

The final feature vector equation for the jth feature in the ith sample is expressed as

$$M_{ij} = w_{ij} * m_{ij}. \tag{4}$$

From the formulas (1), (3) and (4), we get

$$M_{ij} = log(\frac{n}{num_{1j} + num_{2j} + ... + num_{nj}}) * \frac{num_{ij}}{sum_i}. \tag{5}$$

where n is the total sample quantity, sum_i is the total number of opcodes in the ith opcode sequence, and num_{ij} is the number of occurrences of the jth opcode in the ith opcode sequence.

5 Experiment

5.1 Experimental Dataset

The experimental data in this article is to sequence the contract execution process by settling in the EVM and resending the contract transactions, as detailed in Sect. 3.1. These datasets contain a total of 8 types, including a normal sample denoted $S0$, and seven vulnerability samples, namely Re-entrancy, Unexpected Function Invocation, No Check after Contract Invocation, Missing the Transfer Event, Strict Check for Balance, Timestamp & Block Number Dependency. Incorrect Check for Authorization, denoted $S1, S2, S3, S4, S5, S6, S7$, respectively. For vulnerability sample, we use $S7$ as a simulated unknown vulnerability, i.e. the sample has never appeared in the training set.

Since most of these opcode sequences are not buggy, and because many contract transactions execute the same path to produce many duplicate opcode sequences, after we remove duplicate or invalid opcode sequences, we finally get that we have selected the appropriate final dataset categories and quantities as shown in Table 2. A total of 3328 samples were selected, of which 1800 were normal sample $S0$, 1342 were known vulnerability samples $S1 - S6$, and 186 were simulated unknown vulnerability sample S7. This part of the sample is not used as a training set, so as to simulate an unknown vulnerability sample that has never appeared before. 2/3 of the other samples of each class are used as training sets and 1/3 as test set, and the number of each type is shown in the following table.

Table 2. Data set of opcode sequences

Dataset	Number	Vulnerability	Quantity	Sum
Training set	S0	Normal	1200	2092
	S1	Re-entrancy	4	
	S2	Unexpected Function Invocation	333	
	S3	No Check after Contract Invocation	134	
	S4	Missing the Transfer Event	52	
	S5	Strict Check for Balance	36	
	S6	Timestamp & Block Number Dependency	333	
Testing set	S0	Normal	600	1236
	S1	Re-entrancy	2	
	S2	Unexpected Function Invocation	167	
	S3	No Check after Contract Invocation	68	
	S4	Missing the Transfer Event	27	
	S5	Strict Check for Balance	19	
	S6	Timestamp & Block Number Dependency	167	
	S7	Incorrect Check for Authorization	186	

5.2   Evaluation Metrics

The target of this article is the unknown vulnerability of the smart contract, so the simulated sample of the unknown vulnerability is a positive sample of the experiment, and the remaining normal sample and the known vulnerability sample are negative samples. For binary classification problems, statistics are a combination of results and predictions that give the Confusion matrix as shown in Table 3. Where TP means that the positive example is predicted as a positive example, FN means that the positive example is predicted as a negative example, TP means that the negative sample is predicted as a positive sample, and TN means that the negative sample is predicted as a negative sample.

Table 3. Confusion matrix

Real	Predicted	
	Positive examples	Negative examples
Positive example	True Positive(TP)	False Negative(FN)
Negative examples	False Positive(FP)	True Negative(TN)

In order to demonstrate the effectiveness of the smart contract unknown vulnerability detection scheme in this paper, we used Accuracy and F1-score rate to evaluate the model, where F1-score is calculated by recall and precision. Their calculation formula is as follows:

$$Accuracy = \frac{TP + TN}{N}. \tag{6}$$

$$Precision = \frac{TP}{TP + FP}. \tag{7}$$

$$Recall = \frac{TP}{TP + FN}. \tag{8}$$

$$F1 - score = \frac{2 * Precision * Recall}{Precision + Recall}. \tag{9}$$

5.3 Experimental Results and Analysis

For the opcode sequences samples obtained by bigram feature extraction, vector weight punishment method to reduce noise, and feature vector construction, we used three machine learning models of KNN, SVM and LR to train and detect unknown vulnerabilities in the samples respectively, and their model detection results are shown in Fig. 3. From the experimental results, it can be seen that the unknown vulnerability detection effect of the SVM model is the best, whether it is Accuracy or F1-score is higher than the other two models, and the LR model is the worst in the three models, because it adopts linear classification, which is easy to cause underfitting.

From the experimental results of Fig. 3, it can be seen that on the basis of the six known vulnerabilities of S1-S6, unknown vulnerabilities can be detected according to the similarity of the vulnerabilities. At the same time, our bigram model and vector weight penalization scheme are able to extract vulnerability features in opcode sequences.

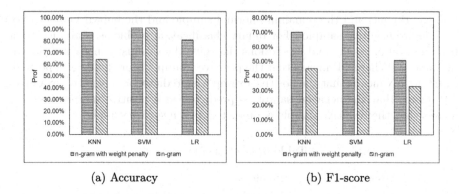

(a) Accuracy   (b) F1-score

Fig. 3. Experimental results of detecting unknown vulnerabilities

6 Conclusions

In this paper, we provide an unknown vulnerability detection method for smart contracts, which focuses on running smart contracts. The main contributions of the scheme are as follows, first, we propose a data feature extraction scheme combining N-gram model and vector weight penalty, the former extracts features such as the order and number of opcodes in opcode sequences, and the latter reduces the effect of noise such as regular opcodes in vectors. In addition, based on our existing known vulnerabilities, we propose an unknown vulnerability detection scheme based on the similarity of vulnerabilities. In the future, we will use trigram models for feature extraction of opcode sequences, and in addition we will use more machine learning models for experimental validation.

Acknowledgments. This work was supported in part by the National KeyResearch and Development Program of China (2020YFB1005804), and in part by the National Natural Science Foundation of China under Grants 61632009, 61872097, and 61802076, and Graduate Innovation Ability Training Program of Guangzhou University (No.2022GDJC-M49).

References

1. Kushwaha, S., Joshi, S., Singh, D., Kaur, M., Lee, H.: Systematic review of security vulnerabilities in ethereum blockchain smart contract. IEEE Access **10**, 6605–6621 (2022)
2. Lim, M., Li, Y., Wang, C., Tseng, M.: A literature review of blockchain technology applications in supply chains: a comprehensive analysis of themes, methodologies and industries. Comput. Indust. Eng. **154**, 107133 (2021)
3. Kirli, D., et al.: Smart contracts in energy systems. A systematic review of fundamental approaches and implementations. Renew. Sustain. Energy Rev. **158** 112013 (2022)
4. He S., Xing X., Wang G., DIV-SC.: A Data Integrity Verification Scheme for Centralized Database Using Smart Contract. In: Proceedings of IEEE TrustCom2022, pp. 1290–1295 (2022)

5. Zou, Y., Peng, T., Zhong, W., Guan, K., Wang, G.: Reliable and Controllable Data Sharing Based on Blockchain. In: Wang, G., Choo, KK.R., Ko, R.K.L., Xu, Y., Crispo, B. (eds) Ubiquitous Security (UbiSec 2021). pp. 229–240. Springer, Singapore (2022). https://doi.org/10.1007/978-981-19-0468-4_17
6. Zhou, L., et al.: A coprocessor-based introspection framework via intel management engine. IEEE Trans. Dependable Secure Comput. **18**(4), 1920–1932 (2021)
7. Chen, T., et al.: SODA: A Generic Online Detection Framework for Smart Contracts. In: Proceedings of 27th Annual Network and Distributed System Security Symposium (NDSS 2020) (2020)
8. Feist, J., Grieco, G., Groce, A.: Slither: A Static Analysis Framework for Smart Contracts. In: Proceedings of 2019 IEEE/ACM 2nd International Workshop on Emerging Trends in Software Engineering for Blockchain (WETSEB), pp. 5–8 (2019)
9. Mossberg, M., Manzano, F., Hennenfent, E., Groce, A., Grieco, G., Feist, J.: Manticore: A User-Friendly Symbolic Execution Framework for Binaries and Smart Contracts. In: Proceedings of 34th IEEE/ACM International Conference on Automated Software Engineering (ASE 2019), pp. 1186–1189 (2019)
10. Grieco G., Song W., Cygan A., Feist, J., Groce, A.: Echidna: Effective, Usable, and Fast Fuzzing for Smart Contracts. In: Proceedings of the 29th ACM SIGSOFT International Symposium on Software Testing and Analysis(ISSTA 2020), pp. 557–560 2020
11. Jiang, B., Liu, Y., Chan, W.: ContractFuzzer: Fuzzing Smart Contracts for Vulnerability Detection. In: Proceedings of the 2018 33rd IEEE/ACM International Conference on Automated Software Engineering (ASE'18), pp. 259–269 (2018)
12. Liu, C., Liu, H., Cao, Z., Chen, Z., Chen, B., Roscoe, B.: ReGuard: Finding Reentrancy Bugs in Smart Contracts. In: Proceedings of 2018 IEEE/ACM 40th International Conference on Software Engineering: Companion (ICSE-Companion), pp. 65–68 (2018)
13. Surucu O., et al.: A survey on ethereum smart contract vulnerability detection using machine learning. In: Disruptive Technologies in Information Sciences VI, 121170C (2022)
14. Xing C., Chen Z., Chen L., Guo, X., Zheng, Z., Li, J.,: A new scheme of vulnerability analysis in smart contract with machine learning. In: Wireless Networks, pp. 1572–8196 (2020)
15. Xu Y., Hu G., You L., Cao, C.: A Novel Machine Learning-Based Analysis Model for Smart Contract Vulnerability. In: Security and Communication Networks, pp. 1939–0114 (2021)
16. Wang W., Song J., Xu G., Li, Y., Wang, H., Su, C.: ContractWard: Automated Vulnerability Detection Models for Ethereum Smart Contracts. In: IEEE Transactions on Network Science and Engineering, pp. 1133–1144 (2021)
17. Eshghie, M., Artho, C., Gurov, D.: Dynamic Vulnerability Detection on Smart Contracts Using Machine Learning. In: Proceedings of Evaluation and Assessment in Software Engineering (EASE 2021), pp. 305–312 (2021)
18. Zhou Q., Zheng K., Zhang K., Hou, L., Wang, X.: Vulnerability analysis of smart contract for blockchain-based IoT applications: a machine learning approach. IEEE Int. Things J. **9**(24), 24695–24707 (2022)
19. Xue Y., Ye J., Ye J., Sun, J., Ma, L., Wang, H.: xFuzz: Machine Learning Guided Cross-Contract Fuzzing. In: IEEE Transactions on Dependable and Secure Computing (2022)

20. Shakya S., Mukherjee A., Halder R., Maiti, A., Chaturvedi, A.: SmartMixModel: Machine Learning-based Vulnerability Detection of Solidity Smart Contracts. In: Proceedings of 2022 IEEE International Conference on Blockchain (Blockchain), pp. 37–44 (2022)

21. Singh, U., Joshi, C., Kanellopoulos, D.: A framework for zero-day vulnerabilities detection and prioritization. J. Inform. Secur. Appl. **46**, 164–172 (2019)

22. Tang, Y., Zhang, D., Liang, W., Li, KC., Sukhija, N.: Active Malicious Accounts Detection with Multimodal Fusion Machine Learning Algorithm. In: Wang, G., Choo, KK.R., Ko, R.K.L., Xu, Y., Crispo, B. (eds) Ubiquitous Security (UbiSec 2021). Communications in Computer and Information Science, pp. 38–52. Springer, Singapore (2022). https://doi.org/10.1007/978-981-19-0468-4_4

23. Choi, C., Choi, J., Kim, P.: Abnormal behavior pattern mining for unknown threat detection. Comput. Syst. Sci. Eng. **32**(2), 171–177 (2017)

24. Periyasamy, K., Arirangan, S.: Prediction of future vulnerability discovery in software applications using vulnerability syntax tree (PFVD-VST). Int. Arab J. Inform. Technol. **16**(2), 288–294 (2019)

25. Chanwoong, H., Doyeon, K., Taejin, L.: Semi-supervised based unknown attack detection in EDR Environment. KSII Trans. Internet Inf. Syst. **14**(12), 909–4926 (2020)

26. Al-Zewairi, M., Almajali, S., Ayyash, M.: Unknown security attack detection using shallow and deep ANN classifiers. Electronics **9**(12), 2006 (2020)

27. Zhang, L., Liang, Y., Tang, Y., et al.: Research on unknown threat detection method of information system based on deep learning. J. Phys: Conf. Ser. **1883**(1), 012107 (2021)

28. Wang G., et al.: Generating Opcode Sequences by Replaying Ethereum Transaction Data. China Patent Application, Application Number: 202211531992.1, 2022-12-01

29. Zhang, M., Zhang, X., Zhang, Y., Lin, Z.: TXSPECTOR: Uncovering attacks in ethereum from transactions. In: Proceedings of the 29th USENIX Security Symposium (USENIX Security 20), pp. 2775–2792 (2020)

30. Hart, P.: The condensed nearest neighbor rule (corresp.). IEEE Trans. Inform. Theor. **14**(3), 515–516 (1968)

31. Hearst, M., Dumais, S., Osuna, E., Platt, J., Scholkopf, B.: Support vector machines. IEEE Intell. Syst. Appl. **13**(4), 18–28 (1998)

32. Christodoulou, E., Ma, J., Collins, G.: A systematic review shows no performance benefit of machine learning over logistic regression for clinical prediction models. J. Clin. Epidemiol. **110**, 12–22 (2019)

33. Hassan N., Gomaa W., Khoriba G., Haggag, M.: Credibility detection in twitter using word N-gram analysis and supervised machine learning techniques. Int. J. Intell. Eng. Syst. **13**(1), 291–300 (2020)

34. Liu, L., Chen, J., Fieguth, P., Zhao, G., Chellappa, R., Pietikäinen, M.: From BoW to CNN: two decades of texture representation for texture classification. Int. J. Comput. Vision **127**(1), 74–109 (2018). https://doi.org/10.1007/s11263-018-1125-z

35. Jc, A., Pkk, C., Sm, B., Sab, C., Ga, D.: An automatic software vulnerability classification framework using term frequency-inverse gravity moment and feature selection. J. Syst. Softw. **167** 110616 (2020)

Prototyping the IDS Security Components in the Context of Industry 4.0 - A Textile and Clothing Industry Case Study

Nuno Torres[1]([envelope]) [iD], Ana Chaves[2] [iD], César Toscano[2] [iD], and Pedro Pinto[1,2,3] [iD]

[1] ADiT-LAB, Instituto Politécnico de Viana do Castelo,
Viana do Castelo 4900-348, Portugal
nunotorres@ipvc.pt
[2] INESC TEC, 4200-465 Porto, Portugal
[3] Universidade da Maia, Maia 4475-690, Portugal

Abstract. With the introduction of Industry 4.0 technological concepts, suppliers and manufacturers envision new or improved products and services, cost reductions, and productivity gains. In this context, data exchanges between companies in the same or different activity sectors are necessary, while assuring data security and sovereignty. Thus, it is crucial to select and implement adequate standards which enable the interconnection requirements between companies and also feature security by design.

The International Data Spaces (IDS) is a current standard that provides data sharing through data spaces mainly composed of homogeneous rules, certified data providers/consumers, and reliability between partners. Implementing IDS in sectors such as textile and clothing is expected to open new opportunities and challenges.

This paper proposes a prototype for the IDS Security Components in the Textile and Clothing Industry context. This prototype assures data sovereignty and enables the interactions required by all participants in this supply chain industry using secure communications. The adoption of IDS as a base model in this activity sector fosters productive collaboration, lowers entry barriers for business partnerships, and enables an innovation environment.

Keywords: IDS · DAPS · Connectors · Security · Industry 4.0

1 Introduction

Data storage and exchange are essential requirements for companies operating in multiple activity sectors. Corporate services' communications include trade secrets and sensitive data; thus, protecting data integrity, authenticity and confidentiality are mandatory.

The use of Industry 4.0 technological concepts transforms how businesses produce, enhance, and distribute their products while reducing costs and enhancing

G. Wang et al. (Eds.): UbiSec 2022, CCIS 1768, pp. 193–206, 2023.
https://doi.org/10.1007/978-981-99-0272-9_13

their productivity. Thus, selecting and implementing adequate standards featuring security by design is of utmost importance. Using a standard that provides secure data sharing is a good solution for the industrial context, which still lacks implementation guides from the beginning until the end of the deployment.

International Data Spaces (IDS) is a recent standard that provides data sharing through data spaces mainly composed of homogeneous rules, certified data providers/consumers, and reliability between partners. Its primary goal is to ensure secure and standardized data exchange and linkage in a trusted business ecosystem while facilitating cross-company business processes and guaranteeing data sovereignty for data owners.

This paper proposes a prototype based on IDS for the textile and clothing sector. The communication between participants is provided by connectors and their interaction with an identity provider, as defined by the IDS. The prototype was implemented in the context of the mobilizing project Digitization of the Textile and Clothing Sector Value Chain (STVgoDigital) [1], where a set of partners in this activity sector are characterized by production orders and availability status from an industrial organization to its subcontractors. Thus, the implementation herein provided can be relevant for any set of organizations in this activity sector and other similar activity sectors, enabling all the required interactions between the companies involved in the supply chain.

The remaining document is organized as follows. Section 2 presents the related work. Section 3 presents the security-related key concepts of the IDS architecture and describes its security components Sect. 4 describes the prototype implementation. Section 5 presents a discussion regarding the prototype implementation. Section 6 presents the conclusions.

2   Related Work

The concepts of Security-by-Design and Privacy-by-Design imply that the principles of security and privacy of data and messages in a communication system are implemented and assured from the project's beginning to its end. In [2], a Security-by-Design model for Industry 4.0 is proposed, which aims to minimize system vulnerabilities and reduce the surface of attacks by ensuring security construction in every stage of the Software Development Life Cycle (SDLC). The authors divide security into three phases: the identification of security requirements, the identification of security risks and the security measures, which are divided based on software and hardware.

One of the reference modules for Industry 4.0 is the Reference Architecture Model Industry 4.0 (RAMI 4.0). It features a service-oriented model which combines all technological elements and components in a single model of layers and life cycles. RAMI 4.0 is divided into three axles: architecture, life cycle value flow and hierarchy, and finally, the inclusion of data privacy and security mechanisms [3]. In [4], a perspective towards the security of RAMI 4.0 is approached, where it is identified two sets of enablers: Smart Networking to facilitate the connection of internal logistics; and automatized systems, which utilize

Cloud-based frameworks to control the system point-to-point, report failures, and connect final users to suppliers practically and efficiently. The article [5] proposes an architecture model for Industry 4.0, based on RAMI 4.0 model, to monitor a production environment. It also presented a case study that considers good practices in the security of networks, systems and information, leading to the development of an architecture with generic use, processes, communications and data management, all based on the Cloud. In [6], the authors propose an end-to-end communication model for cyber-physical systems based on RAMI 4.0. This model is auto-adaptive to improve the trade-off between the performance of business processes and end-to-end communication safety. A recent effort is realized involving the IDS initiative that vices independent data sharing and control, guaranteeing the safety and sovereignty of data. In the article [7], the authors explored the technical architecture of GAIA-X, including the security perspective. From the security perspective, several approaches are made, from defining security-by-design and privacy-by-design as development guidelines to determining that openness, transparency, authenticity, and trust are core objectives of the architecture. In [8], the authors approach IDS from a security perspective. They identified that infrastructures must be equipped with components, such as identity managers or dynamic trust managers, to guarantee data sovereignty. Users must be certified (X.509) to participate in the data exchange, to which some restrictions on the use of data may be enforced to guarantee privacy [9] through the IDS connector, and this way, safely sharing data between parties. In [10] are presented works in progress towards implementing the IDS architecture for a heterogeneous Internet of Things (IoT) communications devices scenario. Using IDS is the leading choice for sharing data between participants. This report also presents a design for an IoT-Connector that acts as a communication interface between IoT devices and IDS connectors. In [11], the authors evaluated a real-time sovereign data exchange in IoT devices. The communication schemes were proposed and implemented following the IDS guidelines. Results showed benefits in the publish/subscribe version in longer operation times, allowing to enter low-power mode, while request/response performed better on short operations. The article [12] proposed an approach to enable the IDS for vendor-independent IoT devices, allowing data owners to benefit from providing their own data while retaining control over it. In [13] is presented an industrial scenario that simulates manufacturing as a service system for the execution of remote production orders based on the implementation of IDS connectors. The article presents a use case where IDS connectors are used in a manufacturing context and where remote production orders are securely performed. In [14], a smart factory web platform is discussed and extended by implementation with the current state of the IDS. The evaluation showed that the base connectors' communication works due to the standardized protocols and security mechanisms being re-used. In [15], the authors introduced an enterprise architecture to help companies choose which organizational and software components to implement before entering an IDS ecosystem. This paper also promotes a better understanding of the guidelines provided by the International Data Spaces - Reference Architecture Model (IDS-RAM) for companies interested in joining IDS ecosystems.

3   IDS Security Architecture and Components

The IDS architecture [16] specifies seven key concepts to achieve security: (1) secure communications, (2) identity management, (3) trust management, (4) trusted platform, (5) data access control, (6) data usage control, and (7) data provenance tracking. These key concepts are detailed as follows.

1. Secure Communications - The communication between connectors must be protected to ensure authenticity and confidentiality in data transfer. When using an IDS connector, there are two layers of security: 1) Point-to-point (between connectors) encryption, achieved through the use of a tunnel, and 2) End-to-end authorization (authorization and authenticity based on current communication endpoints). IDS connectors must communicate with each other through an encrypted tunnel (Transport Layer Security (TLS)) and must also use another appropriate protocol, such as Hyper Text Transfer Protocol Secure (HTTPS).
2. Identity Management - To control the accesses of participants, with their trusted identities and properties, a concept for Identity and Access Management (IAM) is mandatory with the following functions: Identification (claim an identity), Authentication (verify an identity), and Authorization (make access decisions based on identity). The Certification Authority (CA) issues certificates for all entities. These certificates are used for authentication and encryption between connectors. An identity could contain several attributes which are connected to the identity itself. The Dynamic Attribute Provisioning Service (DAPS) provides dynamic and updated information about the participants and their connectors.
3. Trust Management - To establish trust across the entire ecosystem, IDS uses cryptography methods. One of the methods is Public Key Infrastructures (PKI). A central concept of a PKI is that all entities are allocated with secret keys, allowing each entity to authenticate regarding other participants. Therefore, a hierarchy is created, with the Identity Provider at the top issuing certificates to other entities. Additionally, the trust regarding the creation and sharing of data in an IDS ecosystem should be strengthened through certifications assigned to the software components used to implement a data space.
4. Trusted platform - The IDS consists of multiple instances of the connector-based architecture. The trusted platform is a core element of the trusted data exchange and includes the following functions, namely, (1) to specify the minimum requirements for participants that want to exchange data and provide mutual verification of the security profiles of the participants, (2) to enable reliable execution of data applications and ensure system integrity, i.e. the Data Apps only have access to the data that is explicitly intended for them, and (3) to provide a remote integrity verification and establish a trust relationship with another Participant, with verification of the connector's properties.
5. Data access control - IDS defines access control as a resource-centred regulation of access requests from the IDS participants to resources (Data Services).

Data owners define attribute-based access control policies for their endpoints and the values of attributes a subject must satisfy to guarantee access to the resource. These attributes include (1) the identity of the connector(s) (only access requests from one or more specific connectors will be guaranteed), (2) Connector attributes (only access requests from a connector with specific attributes will be guaranteed), (3) security profile requirements (only access requests from a connector that satisfies specific security requirements will be guaranteed).

6. Data usage control - The usage control is an extension of access control and it specifies and enforces the restrictions regulating how the data is managed and what is the data consumer obligations [17]. It allows Data Providers to attach data usage policies to their data to define how a Data Consumer may use it. Usage control is a transversal concept and technology which involves the following IDS functions:
   - Broker: The IDS Broker maintains connector self-descriptions and metadata descriptions that describe the data sets provided and consumed by the Data Provider and Data Consumer entities in the context of an IDS. In this context, data usage policies can also be identified.
   - Connector: The connector is the central technical component for implementing the IDS infrastructure and is responsible for every communication inside the ecosystem. Moreover, connectors that work as Data Providers must provide technology-dependent policies for the data provided - for all types of application systems and technologies that are part of the ecosystem.
   - Clearing House: By tracking the origin of the data, it is possible to follow its use and compliance with the usage restrictions. The Clearing House can use this data later for auditing purposes.

7. Data provenance tracking - Data provenance tracking is closely related and complementary to distributed data usage control. It allows knowing when, how, and who modified the data and which data influenced the process of creating new data. This type of traceability is similar to the data protection requirements with which a data controller is faced in order to be able to fulfil the right of access to its data subjects. It is also related to the issue of proving compliance with contracts, agreements, or legal regulations. Additionally, it can facilitate the aggregation of information about data exchange transactions and data usage in a decentralized data ecosystem.

In order for IDS to assure data integrity, authenticity and confidentiality, two security components of the IDS are required: Connectors and an Identity Provider.

The connector is the central IDS component, serving as a bridge to connect existing systems and their data with the rest of the ecosystem. Its architecture and functionalities are defined by the IDS-RAM [16] and specified by the certification criteria. The connector allows data exchanges with other connectors and the data could be enriched with metadata. The Dataspace Connector [18] is an open-source implementation created by Fraunhofer ISST[1]. It uses the most recent version of the IDS Information Model[2] and the IDS Messaging Services[3] to handle messages made with other IDS components. External data sources can be connected via Representational State Transfer (REST) endpoints, allowing the Dataspace Connector to act as an intermediary between the IDS data ecosystem and the real data source. According to the requirements of a data space, communications with other IDS connectors, encrypted via TLS, and communication with an IDS Broker, are supported in the context of an IDS data ecosystem. The Dataspace Connector can simultaneously act as a data consumer and provider, providing data to an IDS ecosystem and requesting data from other IDS connectors.

The Identity Provider offers a service that allows the creation, maintenance, management, monitoring, and validation of the information identity from and for the IDS participants. Which is strictly necessary to ensure the security of IDS operations and prevent unauthorized data access. The Identity Provider is comprised by:

- Certification Authority - manages the IDS participants' digital certificates.
  - The CA is responsible for issuing, validating, and revoking digital certificates. A digital certificate is provided to a participant if both the participant and core component (i.e., connector) certificates are valid and available. The CA provides an IDS-ID for a combination of the participant and main component. The digital certificate is valid, not exceeding the validity of both certifications, i.e., the participant certification and the certification of the main component used by the participant. This component only provides the X.509 digital certificate to the participant if requested, securely sending it and notifying the DAPS. The Certification Authority is also responsible for issuing certificates to all entities, which are then used for authentication and encryption between connectors.
- Dynamic Attribute Provisioning Service - service that manages the dynamic attributes of the participants.
  - A digital identity relies on different attributes which are linked to that identity. The DAPS provides dynamic and up-to-date attribute information about participants and connectors. It was developed to enrich participants and connectors with attributes embedded into a Dynamic Attribute Token (DAT). The resulting information from the certification process is transmitted to DAPS, which includes master data and information about security profiles. The CA provides the details of the digital certificate (public key and IDS-ID). The participant is registered on the DAPS after successfully implementing the digital certificate within the component.

---

[1] https://www.isst.fraunhofer.de/en.html.

[2] https://international-data-spaces-association.github.io/InformationModel/docs/index.html.

[3] https://github.com/International-Data-Spaces-Association/IDS-Messaging-Services.

- Participant Information Service - registry for self-description documents of IDS Participant.
  - This component is responsible for making the Participants' information available, enabling business interaction between unrelated Participants. This component works as a central catalogue of information. Furthermore, as its goal is to make information available, it is mainly used by companies that have yet to work together and therefore do not trust each other. A verifiable identity management process achieves that trust through the Identity Provisioning Service and the DAPS. Both components equip each participant with the necessary attributes and cryptographic proofs for the IDS handshakes.

4   Prototype Implementation

The current research work was developed based on a scenario from a mobilising project named STVgoDigital which was intended to digitise the value chain of the Textile and Clothing Sector. The current implementation fits the project's objective and promotes the adoption and transition to the digital transition to the textile and clothing activity sector and other similar activity sectors.

The prototype implementation comprehended 4 stages: (1) definition of the requirements and architecture, (2) components configuration, and (3) communication testing. These stages are detailed as follows.

4.1   Requirements and Proposed Architecture

The scenario for an IDS ecosystem should be defined as the architecture depicted in Fig. 1. The architecture should comprehend the following items:

- Connector 1 - Facility A (Consumer)
- Connector 2 - Facility B (Provider)
- DAPS - Consortium Management Company (DAPS Server)
- Certification Chain - (via CA)
- Governance Body - Consortium Management Company (Certification Body + Evaluation Facility)

Connector 1 and Connector 2 should be installed in two different facilities. The DAPS server should be installed on the Consortium Management Company. The Certification Chain may be deployed through an external service responsible for the maintenance of the CA. The Governance Body should be deployed in the Consortium Management Company since it will be responsible for validating the participants' identities and verifying if they correspond to the facilities associated with the IDS.

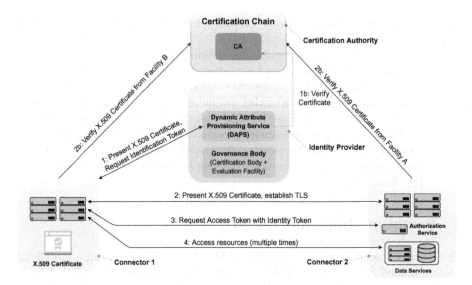

Fig. 1. Proposed architecture

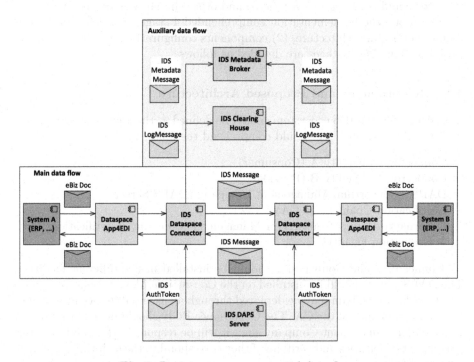

Fig. 2. Prototype components and data flow

The prototype components and the data flow are presented in Fig. 2. It is intended that this architecture and components provide the full scope for performing production orders and checking the availability status from an industrial organization to its subcontractors.

The architecture assumes that a System A (e.g., Enterprise Resource Planning (ERP)) uses the eBiz[4] document type, and pretends to share its documents with a System B, through a DataspaceApp4EDI app. This application shares the document with the IDS Connector, which shares it with the other system connector and with the DataspaceApp4EDI of System B. This process is also performed in the reverse direction, from System B to System A. The auxiliary data flow comprises three IDS Components: IDS Metadata Broker, IDS Clearing House, and IDS DAPS Server. The DAPS Server and the IDS Clearing House are called every time the connectors communicate. The first is used to validate the connector's identity, and the latter to log messages to, if necessary, serve as an auditing entity. Finally, the IDS Metadata Broker is a catalogue of available IDS participants and components. Furthermore, the DataspaceApp4EDI serves as a bridge between the ERP and the IDS Connectors, with the responsibility of sending the eBiz files to the IDS Connector or the ERP.

The implementation featured three IDS Connectors, one Producer and two subcontractors connectors (i.e., Subcontracted-A and Subcontracted-B). Furthermore, the prototype was implemented using three machines running Ubuntu 20.04 LTS to test the DAPS interaction with the connectors. One virtual machine contains the Producer, the other the Subcontracted-A and Subcontracted-B, and another the DAPS, CA, Clearing House, and Metadata Broker.

4.2   Components Configuration

To communicate with the DAPS, the connectors need valid certificates. For that, a CA was implemented to create certificates for the connectors and components (i.e., Metadata Broker and Clearing House). In order to carry out tests, the Fraunhofer AISEC[5] *Omejdn* [19], a minimal but extensible OAuth 2.0/OpenID connect server, was used. The following procedures were executed:

1. modify the file concerning the *Omejdn* configuration,
2. update the docker environment variables file to use the DAPS with HTTPS and not in localhost,
3. modify the configuration file concerning the customers, and
4. add a TLS certificate from a trusted CA to use the DAPS with HTTPS.

For the initial DAPS configuration, it was necessary to update the protocol, environment, domain, TLS key, and certificate. Then, the *Omejdn* configuration required changes to guarantee consistency with the docker environment.

The implemented prototype used a sample CA made available by the International Data Spaces Association (IDSA), used to create trusted certificates and

---

[4] https://ebiz-tcf.eu/.

[5] https://www.aisec.fraunhofer.de/en.html.

guarantee that they have a valid hierarchy, which is necessary for the architecture. The certificates were created and the connectors and components were registered on the DAPS server. For that, each X.509 certificate created by the CA was added to the "/keys" directory of the DAPS server. Once the connectors and components were registered, they were configured as clients in the DAPS. Listing 1.1 presents a client configuration with its *id*, *name*, *scope*, *attributes* and *token endpoint authentication method*. Finally, the X.509 certificates on directory "/keys" were copied onto "/keys/client", with the name being the client id encoded to serve as the verification key.

Listing 1.1. clients.yml

```
- client_id:  12:05:B7:BB:F3:EA:DE:40:AA:AE:2E:D0:94:8F:FA:94:32:7D:54:1
    C:keyid:27:A8:D6:69:E6:25:47:BA:09:8D:98:E5:DF:79:3F:09:89:F4:4D:83
  client_name:  subcontracted-A
  grant_types:
  - client_credentials
  token_endpoint_auth_method:  private_key_jwt
  scope:
  - idsc:IDS_CONNECTOR_ATTRIBUTES_ALL
  attributes:
  - key: idsc
    value:  IDS_CONNECTOR_ATTRIBUTES_ALL
  - key:  referringConnector
    value:  http://subcontracted_A.demo
  (...)
```

The keys and X.509 certificates were created and sent to the connectors. On the connector's machine, both files were used to create a *p12* file that was inserted into the connector configuration directory. Finally, its docker-composes were modified to use the instantiated DAPS instead of the default Fraunhofer one.

The Clearing House was also modified to use the new DAPS certificates and configuration, which consisted of sending the X.509 certificate and key to the component as well as the files to create a *p12* certificate inserted on the component bind mounts. As the DAPS is running HTTPS, its TLS certificate was sent to the Clearing House and moved to the directory "/docker" to be inserted into the trusted certificates folder of the operative system inside the docker container. Next, the container configuration files (i.e., *Rocket.toml*) were updated to redirect to the new DAPS instead of the Fraunhofer DAPS. Finally, the Clearing House connector was updated to also redirect to the new DAPS.

The Metadata Broker was updated to utilize the DAPS. Its docker-compose was edited to redirect to the new DAPS, and the certificates created by the CA were converted to the correct format and inserted into the proper directories. Next, the repository *application.properties* file was revised to redirect to the new DAPS and to include its URL on the trusted hosts. Finally, the DAPS TLS certificate was inserted into the docker files directory, guaranteeing that the new, untrusted certificate is inserted into the system folder when the component is built.

4.3   Communication Testing

After configuring all components to use the DAPS instance, the interactions were tested. All communications between the IDS participants use the DAPS to validate their identity and thus, any request made by or to the connectors, the Clearing House, or the Broker involves the DAPS. To test the connectors, Clearing House, and DAPS interaction, the connectors started a contract agreement process. However, to test the Broker and DAPS communication, it is necessary a request by the connectors.

The Provider and Subcontracted-A connectors and the Clearing House were used to test the Connector, Clearing House, and DAPS interaction. The process is repeated by each component, i.e. although only involving the Producer and Subcontracted-A, the Clearing House is also performing the same steps to validate the connector's identity.

The contract agreement process starts with the subcontracted-A connector communicating with a connector provider. To do that, it needs to request a DAT to the DAPS to present to the connector provider. Thus, as a first step, the subcontracted automatically creates the JSON Web Token (JWT), which contains the header, payload, and signature. The signature is created with the subcontracted's private key, and the payload contains the fields described below:

- *aud*: token audience, which can be identified as the DAPS URL in this case.
- *exp*: JWT expiration date.
- *iat*: timestamp of when the JWT has been issued.
- *nbf*: "valid not before".
- *iss*: the component which created and signed the JWT, in this case, is the subcontracted connector.
- *sub*: the combined entry of the Subject Key Identifier (SKI) and Authority Key Identifier (AKI) of the intelligent DATA solutions (iDATAs) connectors X.509 certificate.

With the JWT created, the subcontracted connector is authenticated by presenting the JWT to the DAPS. The DAPS then receives the request from the connector and, based on it, assigns the DAT or not, by identifying whether the requesting connector is valid from the configured certificate. Listing 1.2 shows the encoded and decoded DAT.

Listing 1.2. DAT Token

```
[*] Dynamic Attribute Token:
{"access_token":"eyJ0eXAiOiJhdCtqd3QiLCJraWQiOiI2MGJlZmYxYWQ2N (...)",
"expires_in":3600,"token_type":"bearer","scope":"idsc:
    IDS_CONNECTOR_ATTRIBUTES_ALL"}
[*] DAT - Decoded:
{
  "typ": "at+jwt", "alg": "RS256",
  "kid": "60
      beff1ad662e38fd8996639286e3c24e2b366e52f87d88251b854096ef78c39"
}
{
  "scope": "idsc:IDS_CONNECTOR_ATTRIBUTES_ALL",
  "aud": [ "idsc:IDS_CONNECTORS_ALL" ],
```

```
"iss": "https://vcese19.inesctec.pt/auth",
"sub": "12:05:B7:BB:F3:EA:DE:40:AA:AE:2E:D0:94:8F:FA:94:32:7D:54:1C:
    keyid:27:A8:D6:69:E6:25:47:BA:098D:98:E5:DF:79:3F:09:89:F4:4D
    :83",
"nbf": (...), "iat": (...), "jti": "b34ae7(...)", "exp": (...),
"client_id": "12:05:B7:BB:F3:EA:DE:40:AA:AE:2E:D0:94:8F:FA:94:32:7D
    :54:1C:keyid:27:A8:D6:69:E6:25:47:BA:09:8D:98:E5:DF:79:3F:09:89:
    F4:4D:83",
"securityProfile": "idsc:BASE_SECURITY_PROFILE",
"referringConnector": "http://subcontracted.demo",
"@type": "ids:DatPayload", "@context": (...),"transportCertsSha256":
    (...)
}
```

After receiving the DAT, the subcontracted-A connector shares it with the Provider connector. The provider analyzes the DAT fields, verifies if it is valid, and gives access to its services. The DAPS signs the received DAT and the client can verify this signature by retrieving the DAPS's public key(s) using a public endpoint (identified by the *iss* field in Listing 1.2). This process only shows whether the DAPS successfully authenticated the component. The exact process occurs between the Clearing House, the DAPS, and the connector that logs the message to the first component.

Regarding the Metadata Broker interaction with the DAPS, a connector is used to request the Broker. For this purpose, the description endpoint on the producer connector was used to receive the Broker's self-description.

5   Discussion

The transition of the textile and clothing industry to an Industry 4.0 environment, implies exchanging data between companies while assuring its authenticity, confidentiality, and integrity. The architecture defined had requirements of the STVgoDigital project, however, the prototype was implemented to provide the full scope for performing production orders and checking the availability status from an industrial organization to its subcontractors, as required in the textile and clothing industry sector. Thus, this architecture can be applied to other use cases within the textile and clothing industry, or other activity sectors where the requirements are similar.

The prototype is based in IDS which enables secure communications between trusted participants. The IDS Identity Provider and the IDS Connectors were implemented, which are the components responsible for guaranteeing safe data exchange. In this implementation, only trusted entities can be registered in the DAPS, which is responsible for managing the participants' dynamic attributes and a specific CA is responsible for managing the participants' digital certificates.

IDS is still a recent standard and future efforts should be dedicated to implementing this type of approach in other use cases. In order to foster these implementations, it is important to provide complete and up-to-date IDS documentation.

6   Conclusions

In order to operate their businesses, organizations from multiple activity sectors should manage their data and suppliers and manufacturers may benefit from the implementation of Industry 4.0 technical principles. Data exchange between corporations operating in the same or distinct activity sectors is required while upholding data sovereignty. Adequate standards and recommendations must be selected based on the specific requirements for these interactions, and the implementations should follow the security-by-design principles.

This paper presents the implementation of a prototype based on the IDS virtual data spaces to ensure secure communications between participants in the textile and clothing activity sector. The IDS-RAM is used as a base reference model since it meets the given requirements and aids data sharing securely while assuring data sovereignty for peers and clusters of peers. With the IDS virtual data space, the data exchange and linkage can be preserved in a reliable business ecosystem while facilitating cross-company business processes. This prototype implementation can be applied and linked with the required modifications to other textile and clothing corporations or other activity sectors, as it is valuable as a base model to encourage fruitful collaboration between all participants.

Acknowledgments. This study was developed in the context of the Master in Cybersecurity Program at the Instituto Politécnico de Viana do Castelo, Portugal.

This work was funded by European Regional Development Fund (ERDF) through the COMPETE2020 Programme, within the STVgoDigital project (POCI-01-0247-FEDER-046086).

References

1. STVgoDigital. http://www.stvgodigital.pt/. Accessed 30 Jan 2021
2. Shaabany, G., Anderl, R.: Security by design as an approach to design a secure industry 4.0-capable machine enabling online-trading of technology data. In: 2018 International Conference on System Science and Engineering (ICSSE), pp. 1–5 (2018). https://doi.org/10.1109/ICSSE.2018.8520195
3. The Internet of Things and Services Graphics Bosch Rexroth AG. https://ec.europa.eu/futurium/en/system/files/ged/a2-schweichhart-reference_architectural_model_industrie_4.0_rami_4.0.pdf. Accessed 29 Jan 2021
4. Elkhawas, A.I., Azer, M.A.: Security perspective in RAMI 4.0. In: 2018 13th International Conference on Computer Engineering and Systems (ICCES), pp. 151–156 (2018). https://doi.org/10.1109/ICCES.2018.8639235
5. Flatt, H., et al.: Analysis of the cyber-security of industry 4.0 technologies based on RAMI 4.0 and identification of requirements. In: 2016 IEEE 21st International Conference on Emerging Technologies and Factory Automation (ETFA), pp. 1–4 (2016). https://doi.org/10.1109/ETFA.2016.7733634
6. Maksuti, S., et al.: Towards flexible and secure end-to-end communication in industry 4.0. In: 2017 IEEE 15th International Conference on Industrial Informatics (INDIN), pp. 883–888 (2017). https://doi.org/10.1109/INDIN.2017.8104888

7. GAIA-X: Technical Architecture. https://www.data-infrastructure.eu/GAIAX/Re daktion/EN/Publications/gaia-x-technical-architecture.pdf?_blob=publicationFi le&v=5. Accessed 03 Mar 2021

8. International Data Spaces (IDS) makes it safe and easy to exchange data – TNO. https://www.tno.nl/en/focus-areas/information-communication-technology/road maps/data-sharing/international-data-spaces-ids/. Accessed 29 Jan 2021

9. Industrial Data Space - the secure data exchange model for industrial IoT. https:// www.i-scoop.eu/industry-4-0/industrial-data-space/. Accessed 29 Jan 2021

10. Nast, M., et al.: Work-in-progress: towards an international data spaces connector for the Internet of Things. In: 2020 16th IEEE International Conference on Factory Communication Systems (WFCS), pp. 1–4 (2020). https://doi.org/10.1109/WFCS47810.2020.9114503

11. Qarawlus, H., et al.: Sovereign data exchange in cloud-connected IoT using international data spaces. In: 2021 IEEE Cloud Summit (Cloud Summit), pp. 13–18 (2021). https://doi.org/10.1109/IEEECloudSummit52029.2021.00010

12. Nast, M., et al.: Work-in-progress: towards an international data spaces connector for the Internet of Things. In: 2020 16th IEEE International Conference on Factory Communication Systems (WFCS), pp. 1–4 (2020b). https://doi.org/10.1109/WFCS47810.2020.9114503

13. Igo, M.A., et al.: Towards standardized manufacturing as a service through asset administration shell and international data spaces connectors. In: IECON 2022–48th Annual Conference of the IEEE Industrial Electronics Society, pp. 1–6 (2022). https://doi.org/10.1109/IECON49645.2022.9968592

14. Volz, F., Stojanovic, L., Lamberti, R.: An industrial marketplace - the smart factory web approach and integration of the international data space. In: 2019 IEEE 17th International Conference on Industrial Informatics (INDIN), vol. 1, pp. 714–720 (2019). https://doi.org/10.1109/INDIN41052.2019.8972061

15. Firdausy, D.R., et al.: Towards a reference enterprise architecture to enforce digital sovereignty in international data spaces. In: 2022 IEEE 24th Conference on Business Informatics (CBI), vol. 01, pp. 117–125 (2022). https://doi.org/10.1109/CBI54897.2022.00020

16. Reference Architecture Model. https://www.internationaldataspaces.org/wp-conte nt/uploads/2019/03/IDS-Reference-Architecture-Model-3.0.pdf. Accessed 30 Jan 2021

17. Usage Control in the International Data Spaces (Position Paper), b. https://inter nationaldataspaces.org//wp-content/uploads/dlm_uploads/IDSA-Position-Paper-Usage-Control-in-the-IDS-V3..pdf. Accessed 18 Aug 2022

18. Home - dataspace connector. https://international-data-spaces-association.github. io/DataspaceConnector/. Accessed 02 Dec 2021

19. Fraunhofer-aisec/omejdn-server. https://github.com/Fraunhofer-AISEC/omejdn-server. Accessed 10 Dec 2021

An Aspect-Based Semi-supervised Generative Model for Online Review Spam Detection

Shitao Wang[1], Wenjun Jiang[1(✉)] [iD], and Shuhong Chen[2,3] [iD]

[1] College of Computer Science and Electronic Engineering, Hunan University,
Changsha 410082, China
{wangshitao,jiangwenjun}@hnu.edu.cn

[2] School of Computer Science and Cyber Engineering, Guangzhou University,
Guangzhou 510006, China
shuhongchen@gzhu.edu.cn

[3] AI Research Hub, Beijing Normal University-Hong Kong Baptist University
United International College, Zhuhai 519087, China

Abstract. With the continuous development and popularization of Internet technology and the normalization of epidemic prevention and control, people's life mode is gradually changed by the network. More and more people consume food, clothing, housing and transportation through the Internet, and the online reviews left by people have become valuable information resources. However, the authenticity of online reviews is worrying. The proliferation of review spams has become one of the most urgent security problems to be solved in the Internet economy. Review spams will lead users to make suboptimal purchase strategies and have a negative impact on the credit of the online review platform. Most of the existing studies are manual feature extraction, rule making and labeling training samples, which are usually complex and time-consuming. We propose a new semi-supervised review spam detection model for online reviews. We first compute the attention distribution over different aspects of a product in a review as the aspect coefficient. We then use the conditional variational auto-encoder (CVAE) to learn the review styles of fake and non-fake reviews for different aspects of a product, utilizing the aspect and aspect coefficients as conditions. Finally, CVAE model can distinguish fake reviews from non-fake reviews according to the review style. The model is evaluated based on restaurant reviews on yelp website, and the experimental results show the superior performance of this method.

Keywords: Spam detection · Semi-supervised learning · Onlie reviews · Aspect level · Conditional Variational Auto-Encoder (CVAE)

1 Introduction

The popularization and development of Internet technology and the normalization of epidemic prevention and control make more and more people's daily life inseparable from the Internet. The most important part is shopping and consumption through the Internet, such as restaurant reservation and ordering through the Internet. However, because they can't come to the scene to experience consumer goods in person, consumers will refer to the reviews left by other consumers to decide whether to consume or not. Michael Luca [13] analyzed 152k restaurant reviews in yelp restaurant reviews. The research shows that the restaurant's revenue will increase by 5% to 9% for each level of improvement in yelp platform restaurant's rating. The huge profit space attracts merchants or competitors to brush tickets for online reviews. In order to earn more profits, merchants will deliberately fabricate spam reviews and brush up the score of consumer goods; Competitors will maliciously brush down the score of consumer goods. This is not only unfavorable to consumers, but also not conducive to the development of the whole evaluation platform. If there are too many spam reviews on Evaluation platforms such as yelp and TripAdvisor, it will reduce the reputation of the platform, reduce user viscosity and their own profits. Therefore, it is an important task to detect spam reviews and protect the real interests of consumers and businesses.

In the past few years, academia and industry have started to detect spam reviews [5,22,24]. Liu [12] gave an initial survey and divided reviews into three types: the first is untrue reviews (malicious publicity or reviews that strongly belittle the product), and the second is reviews on the brand rather than the product itself, The third category is irrelevant content (such as advertising). Due to resource constraints, there are no manually labeled training examples. Therefore, repeated reviews are labeled as spam reviews for spam review detection, and a regression model is established on these samples. Most of the subsequent methods are supervised models. They detect spam reviews by formulating manual rules and extracting features. However, in practical application, it is very time-consuming and impractical for the review platform to label the fraudster, because the fraudster will elaborate a review like an innocent consumer to bypass the detection of the detector. In addition, the formulation of manual rules and feature extraction are more complex. Therefore, it is necessary to propose a semi-supervised spam review detection method, which makes less use of tags and alleviates the shortage of tag data.

Most of the existing work on spam review detection focuses on the text, user behavior and social network structure of reviews [19]. This paper mainly studies the spam review detection of restaurant reviews. High quality reviews and online reputation have a great impact on the restaurant's revenue. Due to the subjectivity of reviews, manually marking them is a challenging task, so the fully supervised method is no longer applicable. To illustrate our approach, refer to Fig. 1, which shows two sample comments from a restaurant. Yelp filter thinks that the first review is true and the second review is written by the fraudster. In the first review, the reviewer gave a review on the taste and presentation of the food, "Avocado toast" is short of salt or spices, "eggs" and "potatoes" are OK, but "potatoes" are a little dry, "shrimp dog" is delicious, but there is "a weird addition". A gimmicky "school tray" and "unworthy coffee" were also mentioned. In the second

Dina L.
New York, NY
93 87 3

9/11/2016

Food tries to be whimsical but fails in flavor and presentation. Went for brunch - avocado toast was totally bland, lacking any salt or spices. Eggs and potatoes were ok though potatoes were over-fried and dry. Shrimp dog was the most flavorful thing I tried, but it came with a weird addition of yogurt and fruit cereal bits. All of this served in a gimmicky school tray. Instead of trying to be original with presentation the restaurant needs to focus on their food. Also, their $1 coffee was undrinkable.

Useful   Funny 1   Cool 1

Robert M.
New York, NY
5 friends
87 reviews
2 photos

7/22/2019

The seafood pancake was strange but deliciously good. The ambience was casual, the noise level was loud, the area is small. Service is bad, the staff was busy, long time waiting.

Fig. 1. Sample reviews of a hotel.

comment, "seafood pancake", "noise", "area", "service", "the staff", "long time waiting" are mentioned. Compared with the first comment, the stars evaluated are two stars, but there are few details and the description is very concise. There are subtle differences in aspect level descriptions in true and false review, which helps to effectively find spam reviews. Inspired by this observation, it is necessary to find out the aspect level description of reviews, so as to provide more refined aspect based detection.

In order to meet the above challenges, a new spam review detection method is proposed in this paper. The method uses semi-supervised model based on aspect level and conditional variational auto encoder(CVAE). Different from the previous spam review detection methods, the model based on aspect level proposed can achieve excellent performance in the restaurant review environment. This paper probes into the characteristics of restaurant reviews, and naturally puts forward several hypotheses about spam reviews. Users pay different attention to different aspects of the restaurant (such as food, price, service, environment and others). In the process of mapping reviews to low dimensional dense vectors, the weight of feature words will increase, which can capture the aspects that users are more concerned about a restaurant. Then, the attention driven conditional variational auto encoder is used to identify specific conditional sample pairs. Using the aspect importance and the normal score of the product as the condition, the review vector is the sample. Specifically, the normal review is used to train CVAE and predict the review. If the reconstruction probability is less than the threshold α, it indicates that the review is an abnormal review, otherwise it is a normal review.

The main contributions of this paper are as follows:

1. This paper studies the characteristics of product reviews, focuses on the impact of product aspect level reviews on spam review detection, and puts forward a new spam review detection technology named ACVAE(Aspect-based Conditional Variational Auto-Encoder).
2. The model based on aspect level is introduced to find out the product aspects that reviewers are more concerned about. In word embedding, the weight of words changes adaptively according to reviewers' attention to different aspects of the product , so product aspect level reviews can be extracted and encoded into the vector representation of reviews. It could learn reconstruct the reviewer's writing and language style through CVAE, and what reviews reviewer will write under certain conditions. In addition, the semi-supervised method can effectively alleviate the problem of insufficient data labels.
3. This paper discusses and compares several other spam review detection technologies. Compared with traditional methods, proposed method can effectively detect spam reviews in restaurant review environment.

2   Related Work

Recently, the spam detection in online reviews has become a hot research topic [7, 9,18,27]. Most of the existing spam detection techniques are supervised or semi-supervised methods with predefined characteristics. Jindal et al. [12] identified three types of spam and applies logistic regression to manually labeled training examples. They selected 35 features, most of which are product features and text features. Lim et al. [14] studied several characteristic behaviors of fraudsters and modeled them. They also proposed a scoring method to measure the extent to which reviews might be fraudulent and applied it to Amazon. Rayana et al. [19] used metadata (text, timestamp, rating) and clues in relational data, and then use them to find suspicious users. Yang et al. [25] proposed a three-phase method to address the problem of spammer groups. They used approximate repetition detection, reviewer interest similarity and personal fraudster behavior. Although the previous methods have achieved good detection results, most of them are based on the text information or behavior information contained in the reviews. Yuan et al. [26] solved the potential patterns among users, products and reviews, but some useful context information is lost in the calculation process. In addition, aspect level reviews containing product attributes can be regarded as a way to identify spam reviews, because spam pays little attention to these attributes, while real users describe them more delicately and truly. Existing studies ignore the impact of aspect level information.

Word embedding is a distributed representation method, which is widely used in various natural language processing (NLP) tasks, such as viewpoint analysis [6,17], and emotion classification [11,21]. The word embedding method represents words as continuous dense vectors in low dimensional space to capture the vocabulary and semantic attributes of words. Mikolov et al. [16] proposed SkipGram, in which vectors are obtained from the internal representations from neural network. It uses negative sampling random gradient descent to optimize neighborhood preserving likelihood objectives. To be specific, given a sequence of training words $s = (w_1, w_2, ..., w_s)$, the SkipGram model seeks to maximize the average log-probability of observing the context of a word w_i conditioned on its representation $\Phi(w)$. The $\Phi(w)$ is a mapping function that maps a word to low-dimensional dense vector, and its value is the weight from the input layer to the hidden layer of the neural network. The number of neurons in the input layer corresponds to the size of the vocabulary, and that in the hidden layer is the embedding dimension.

$$\max_{\Phi} \frac{1}{|s|} \sum_{i=1}^{|s|} \sum_{-c \leq j \leq c, j \neq 0} log \ Pr(w_{i+j}|\Phi(w_i)), \tag{1}$$

where the context consists of words on both sides of a given word in window size c. A larger c may lead to more training samples, resulting in higher accuracy at the cost of training time. Introducing randomness, dynamic window size is better than fixed window size, because a central word may be related to many or only a few words in a sentence. Since the length of review is usually not too long, the window size is set to a uniform distribution of 1 to 5 in the experiment. The conditional probability $Pr(w_o|\Phi(w_i))$ is modeled as a softmax unit:

$$Pr(w_o|\Phi(w_i)) = \frac{exp(\Phi(w_o) * \Phi(w_i))}{\sum_{w \in W} exp(\Phi(w) * \Phi(w_i))}, \tag{2}$$

where w_i and w_o are the input and output words, and w are words in the vocabulary.

Anomaly detection task is a semi-supervised framework, which only uses the data of normal instances to train Conditional Variational Auto-Encoder (CVAE) [1]. Reconstruction probability is a probability measure considering the variability of variable distribution. Using the generation characteristics of variational automatic encoder, data reconstruction can be deduced and the root cause of abnormality can be analyzed. CVAE is a conditional variational self encoder. The condition we use here is the product feature.

3   Proposed Method

3.1   Problem Statement

Let X be the set of unlabeled reviews comprising M reviews, $X = \{x_1, x_2, ..., x_M\}$, and additional product information $Y = \{y_1, y_2, ..., y_M\}$. Each review $x_i = \{w_1, w_2, ..., w_{|r|}\}$ consists of a sequence of word tokens, where $w_r \in R$ represents the rth token in the sentence and R is a corpus of tokens. Review spam detection attempts to identify whether a review about a product in X is a spam or non-spam, given the auxiliary information (price, rank in sale, average rating) of this product.

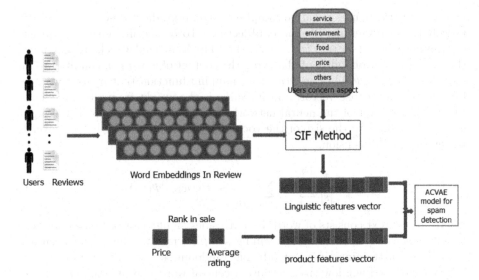

Fig. 2. A graphical illustration of the review spam detection model.

3.2   The Solution

The overall architecture of the proposed model is presented in Fig. 2. At first, the SkipGram model is leveraged to learn low-dimensional dense word embeddings from all reviews, and the SIF method calculates the weighted average of word vectors in the sentence and removing the common parts of the corpus to generate sentence embeddings. In the process, user concerns aspects are introduced and the weights of words are further adjusted according to their degree of affiliation with the concerns. The encoded product features and sentence vectors form the review pairs together, and the conditional variational auto-encoder could learn the matching relation and identify the deceptive reviews.

Table 1. Aspects and keywords

Aspect	Aspect keywords
Food	food, breakfast, lunch, delicious, tasty, yummy, tasteless, hot, salty, fresh...
Price	price, charge, deal, cost, expensive, reasonable, overpriced, unworthy, cheap, affordable...
Service	service, manager, clerk, attendant, accommodation, call, professional, friendly, helpful, staff...
Environment	environment, room, space, air condition, clean, dirty, tidy, mess, unwholesome, unsanitary...
Others	place, location, wifi, internet, connection, distance, freeway, garage, far, convenient...

3.3 Aspect Level Review and Product Information Embedding

The top 10 keywords of food, price, service, environment and others are in Table 1. Later, we will embed words according to these keywords. In simple average embedding, ordinary words (such as "the", "and") have the same weight as aspect words. In order to solve this problem, we use smooth inverse frequency (SIF) method [2]. We take the words with high frequency in the corpus as the aspect vocabulary. If the aspect word appears in the review, it is considered that the reviewer is concerned about the product aspect. SIF method text-based latent variable generation model. The model regards corpus generation as a dynamic process, that is, the tth word is generated at step. The probability of observing a word w at time t is calculated by a log-linear word production model:

$$Pr[w \ emitted \ at \ time \ t|v_t] \propto exp(< v_t, v_w >), \tag{3}$$

3.4 ACVAE: Spam Detection Based on CVAE at the Aspect Level

In this section, we describe the details of our spam model in which we explore the conditional VAE model, and we consider the aspect level review and product information. Suppose $X = \{x_1, x_2, ...x_n\}$ is a set of aspect review, that may involved several aspects, $Y = \{y_1, y_2, ...y_n\}$ (where x_k and y_k are related to the same item) is a set of product information, z is the latent variable in VAE. Connect the aspect level reviews of normal reviewers in series to obtain X and Y as the corresponding product information. Assuming that the product information y is not directly related to the latent variable z, the conditional probability (CP for short) and evidence lower bound (ELBO for short) are calculated as follows.

$$CP : p_\theta(z|y) = p_\theta(z) \tag{4}$$

$$ELBO : L(\theta, \Phi; x, y) = -KL(q_\Phi(z|x, y)||p_\theta(z)) + E_{q_\Phi}(z|x, y)logP_\theta(x|y, z) \tag{5}$$

In formula 5, the evidence lower bound L is expressed as the difference between an expectation and KL divergence. Where the expectation represents the log likelihood expectation of the output X in the case of the obtained Z variable, which can be regarded as the loss function of the decoder and can be obtained through the following Monte Carlo sampling. Because KL divergence describes the gap between two distributions, KL divergence is always greater than or equal to 0. Here we need to minimize KL divergence.

First, using the normal reviewer data X and the corresponding product information Y, train ACVAE to obtain θ, Φ, which are the probability distribution parameters of P and Q respectively.

The composition of ACVAE includes encoding and decoding stages. Using the data set X containing abnormal review and the corresponding product information data Y, the probability encoder f_Φ and decoder g_θ parameterize the isotropic normal distribution in the potential variable space and the original input variable space respectively. Monte Carlo sampling: In the test, for one sample (x_i, y_i), L samples are extracted from the trained probability encoder

f_Φ. For each sample from the encoder, the probability decoder g_θ outputs the mean and variance parameters. Using these parameters, the probability of generating raw data from the distribution is calculated. The average probability is used as the anomaly score, also known as the reconstruction probability. If the reconstruction probability (RP for short) is less than the threshold α; The data (x_i, y_i) is abnormal data.

$$RP(i) = \frac{1}{L} \sum_{l=1}^{L} P_\theta(x_i|\mu, \sigma) \tag{6}$$

The μ, σ here is obtained by decoding l samples at the probability decoder g_θ.

4   Experiment

4.1   Datasets and the Evaluation Metrics

To test and evaluate our model, our experiment uses three common datasets: YelpChi, YelpNYC, YelpZIP [19]. They include reviews of restaurants from yelp.

Table 2. Statistical information of the datasets.

	YelpChi		YelpNYC		YelpZIP	
	Non-fake	Fake	Non-fake	Fake	Non-fake	Fake
Reviews	58476	8919	322167	36885	528132	80466
Average length	170	120	141	95	140	102
Rating>=4	74.29%	70.34%	77.18%	75.24%	73.94%	70.05%
Rating<4	25.71%	29.66%	22.82%	24.76%	26.06%	29.95%
Users	30325	7738	131721	28504	198045	62232

Table 2 shows the statistics related to the dataset. The deviation between false reviews and true reviews can be observed. After analyzing the review data and the occurrence frequency of text words in the data set, we find that the average length of actual reviews is longer than that of false reviews because the probability of describing details of real reviews is very high. When examined by sentence level affective analysis, there was no significant difference in emotion between false reviews and real reviews.

Evaluation metrics: for the unbalanced datasets, we employ average precision (AP) and area under the curve (AUC) as evaluation metrics.

$$AP = \int_1^0 p(r)dr \tag{7}$$

In this integral, where p represents precision, r represents recall, and p is a function with r as the parameter, which is equivalent to finding the area under the precision-recall curve. AUC is defined as the area under the ROC (Receiver Operating Characteristic) curve, ROC curve consists of true positive rate and false positive rate.

4.2   Baselines

To illustrate the effectiveness of the proposed method, we selected several advanced anomaly detection methods for comparison, including feature engineering methods and deep learning algorithms.

Local Anomaly Factor (LOF) [3] is related to density based clustering. By calculating the outlier degree of each point, the first n points with the largest value are found and determined as outliers. The single parameter we used 10 of LOF is the number of nearest neighbors used to define the local neighborhood of the object.

One-class SVM (OCSVM) [20] It estimates the function f to learn the basic probability distribution of the data set. The functional form of f is derived by a kernel expansion. A subset of training data is obtained and controlled. The length of the weight vector in the associative feature space. The Gaussian kernel is used in the experiment.

Minimum Covariance Determinant (MCD) [8] is a distribution fitting of Mahalanobis distance, which uses robust shape and position estimation. The MCD of data points is based on the mean and covariance matrix of the sample size that minimizes the matrix determinant. The proportion of abnormal samples in the control data set is 0.

Isolated Forest (iForest) [15] builds an isolated tree set for a given data set. It detects anomalies based on the isolation concept without using any distance or density measurements. There are two variables in this method: the number of trees to build and the sub sample size, which are set to 100 and 256 respectively, depending on the size of the dataset.

Variational Auto encoder (VAE) [51] uses reconstruction probability in anomaly detection. Here it can learn the writing style and grammar habits of reviews. Because it uses the generation characteristics of variable automatic encoder to deduce the reconstruction of data, so it can analyze the potential causes of anomalies.

5   Result and Analysis

The experimental results are shown in Table 3 below, from which we can make observations as follows. Promote_1 and Promote_2 represent the improvement effect of VAE relative to iForest and ACVAE relative to VAE, respectively.

We can see the following findings by observing the results in Table 3. Since the training samples may contain some fake reviews, linear models, which map the data and learn their boundaries (e.g. OCSVM), have poor performance on review spam detection. For iForest, a random dimension is selected to build a tree, but a large amount of dimension information is not utilized, which are not mutually independent in review vectors, resulting in reduced reliability of the algorithm. We find that LOF performs well, although it is only a simple density based model. The VAE architecture detects outliers by calculating reconstruction probability. In Yelpzip dataset, VAE's AP is 11.04% higher than that of iForest, and AUC

Table 3. Results

Dataset	YelpChi		YelpNYC		YelpZIP	
Model	AP	AUC	AP	AUC	AP	AUC
LOF	35.36	77.32	36.52	79.2	48.12	80.91
OCSVM	32.31	76.12	33.69	77.46	38.2	79.33
iForest	49.26	83.24	54.5	84.94	63.13	87.63
VAE	52.72	85.33	63.82	90.88	70.1	92.11
ACVAE	**53.22**	**86.65**	**64.27**	**91.11**	**71.88**	**93.27**
Promote_1	7.02%	2.51%	17.10%	6.99%	11.04%	5.11%
Promote_2	0.94%	1.52%	0.70%	0.25%	2.48%	1.24%

is 5.11% higher. On this basis proposed ACVAE, we add users' preferences and additional information about products to judge whether the reviews are true. In same dataset, ACVAE obtained an AP value 2.48% higher and an AUC value 1.24% higher than VAE. ACVAE considers aspect level review descriptions and product information, so it achieves significantly better performance than baseline algorithms.

6   Case Study

In this section, we give two user cases to illustrate the effect of our model.

Table 4. Examples of data analysis of Yelp reviews.

Reviews	Rating	Label	User
1. The Spicy Chiken Sausage with Sesame Seaweed	5	TRUE	user1
2. The French Toast was covered in sliced pears	4	TRUE	user1
3. Classic breakfast. Cool space. Cool staff. Totally cool	4	FAKE	user2
4. Absolute dog water. Tasted terrible	1	FAKE	user2
5. Something very basic likes eggs, chicken sausage	2	TRUE	user1
6. Food was delicious and the place quiet	2	FAKE	user2

Table 5. Resolution results of examples by different models

Reviews	LOF	OCSVM	iForest	VAE	ACVAE
1	Right	Right	Right	Wrong	Right
2	Wrong	Wrong	Wrong	Right	Right
3	Wrong	Right	Right	Right	Right
4	Right	Wrong	Wrong	Wrong	Right
5	Wrong	Right	Right	Right	Right
6	Wrong	Wrong	Wrong	Right	Right

Table 4 is a restaurant review from yelp. We analyze real data derived from the yelpCHI dataset. Table 5 shows the resolution results of these examples by different models. As shown in Table 4, if a review's rating is greater than 3, this means that the review is positive. A label of "FAKE" denotes a fake review. The real user, "user1", reviews on fine grained aspects (i.e., French toast and chicken sausage) regardless of whether the review is positive or negative. The spammer, "user2", regardless of whether he or she is leaving a positive or negative review, provides a general evaluation (i.e., water, food, place). For the fourth example, Mentioned that water is hard to drink. VAE and iForest may only learn the emotional and star matching of sentences and some descriptive language, but they don't learn the fine description of each other. Our ACVAE model can find spam reviews with ambiguous descriptions of aspects. The ACVAE model can learn the data distribution of product aspect description by real users and fraudsters, and can identify real users who have a sense of authenticity in the delicate description of the product, as well as spammer. They can't make a true description of the product because the false users have not consumed the product.

7 Conclusion

In this study, we focused on the task of identifying spam reviews. Firstly, we study the impact of product aspect level reviews on spam detection, and propose a ACVAE model that pays attention to user aspect level reviews, takes users as the center and uses additional information. In word embedding, SIF method is used to determine the importance of different aspects according to the degree of users' concern. Finally, the ACVAE is trained with normal user data and product information and behavior information as conditions, so that the model can identify the writing and language styles of normal users on products. ACVAE model is user-centered, pays attention to user preferences, and can reflect users' love for products. We can improve the final effect of the model by adding product information and user behavior information as conditions. Furthermore, it is necessary for the proposed method to set the feature words manually, thus element class and feature words need to be reinvestigated for other types of reviews, which limits the generality of the model.

The following directions can be explored in the future:

(1) The paper has investigated the effectiveness of a ACVAE on spam detection. The generalization ability of the model can be further improved by mining the inherent attributes of reviews, in order to make it scalable for other types of review spam detection.

(2) ACVAE can detect reviews with rich description on aspect level, and can play a role in review recommendation. Find out high-quality reviews and recommend them to users according to the quality of reviews, the number of additional reviews and product information.

Acknowledgments. This work was supported by National Natural Science Foundation of China 62172149, 62172159, 62106240 and 61632009, the Natural Science Foundation of Hunan Province of China (2021JJ30137), and the Guangdong Provincial Natural Science Foundation under Grant 2022A1515011386.

References

1. An, J., Cho, S.: Variational autoencoder based anomaly detection using reconstruction probability. Spec. Lect. IE **2**(1), 1–18 (2015)
2. Arora, S., Liang, Y., Ma, T.: A simple but tough-to-beat baseline for sentence embeddings (2017)
3. Breunig, M.M., Kriegel, H.P., Ng, R.T., Sander, J.: LOF: identifying density-based local outliers. In: Proceedings of the 2000 ACM SIGMOD International Conference on Management of Data, pp. 93–104 (2000)
4. Crawford, M., Khoshgoftaar, T.M., Prusa, J.D., Richter, A.N., Al Najada, H.: Survey of review spam detection using machine learning techniques. J. Big Data **2**(1), 1–24 (2015). https://doi.org/10.1186/s40537-015-0029-9
5. Dewang, R.K., Singh, A.K.: State-of-art approaches for review spammer detection: a survey. J. Intell. Inf. Syst. **50**(2), 231–264 (2018)
6. Fang, Q., Xu, C., Sang, J., Hossain, M.S., Muhammad, G.: Word-of-mouth understanding: entity-centric multimodal aspect-opinion mining in social media. IEEE Trans. Multimedia **17**(12), 2281–2296 (2015)
7. Halder, S., Dutta, S., Banerjee, P., Mukherjee, U., Mehta, A., Ganguli, R.: A survey on online spam review detection. In: Emerging Technologies in Data Mining and Information Security, pp. 717–724 (2021)
8. Hardin, J., Rocke, D.M.: Outlier detection in the multiple cluster setting using the minimum covariance determinant estimator. Comput. Stat. Data Anal. **44**(4), 625–638 (2004)
9. Heydari, A., ali Tavakoli, M., Salim, N., Heydari, Z.: Detection of review spam: a survey. Expert Syst. Appl. **42**(7), 3634–3642 (2015)
10. Hussain, N., Turab Mirza, H., Rasool, G., Hussain, I., Kaleem, M.: Spam review detection techniques: a systematic literature review. Appl. Sci. **9**(5), 987 (2019)
11. Ji, R., Chen, F., Cao, L., Gao, Y.: Cross-modality microblog sentiment prediction via Bi-layer multimodal hypergraph learning. IEEE Trans. Multimedia **21**(4), 1062–1075 (2018)
12. Jindal, N., Liu, B.: Opinion spam and analysis. In: Proceedings of the 2008 International Conference on Web Search and Data Mining, pp. 219–230 (2008)
13. Kang, J.S., Kuznetsova, P., Luca, M., Choi, Y.: Where not to eat? improving public policy by predicting hygiene inspections using online reviews. In: Conference on Empirical Methods in Natural Language Processing (EMNLP), pp. 1443–1448 (2013)
14. Lim, E.P., Nguyen, V.A., Jindal, N., Liu, B., Lauw, H.W.: Detecting product review spammers using rating behaviors. In: Proceedings of the 19th ACM International Conference on Information and Knowledge Management, pp. 939–948 (2010)
15. Liu, F.T., Ting, K.M., Zhou, Z.H.: Isolation forest. In: 2008 Eighth IEEE International Conference on Data Mining, pp. 413–422. IEEE (2008)
16. Mikolov, T., Sutskever, I., Chen, K., Corrado, G.S., Dean, J.: Distributed representations of words and phrases and their compositionality. In: Advances in Neural Information Processing Systems, pp. 3111–3119 (2013)

17. Poria, S., Cambria, E., Gelbukh, A.: Aspect extraction for opinion mining with a deep convolutional neural network. Knowl.-Based Syst. **108**, 42–49 (2016)
18. Rajamohana, S.P., Umamaheswari, K., Dharani, M., Vedackshya, R.: A survey on online review spam detection techniques. In: 2017 International Conference on Innovations in Green Energy and Healthcare Technologies (IGEHT), pp. 1–5. IEEE (2017)
19. Rayana, S., Akoglu, L.: Collective opinion spam detection: Bridging review networks and metadata. In: Proceedings of the 21th ACM SIGKDD International Conference on Knowledge Discovery and Data Mining, pp. 985–994 (2015)
20. Schölkopf, B., Platt, J.C., Shawe-Taylor, J., Smola, A.J., Williamson, R.C.: Estimating the support of a high-dimensional distribution. Neural Comput. **13**(7), 1443–1471 (2001)
21. Tang, D., Wei, F., Yang, N., Zhou, M., Liu, T., Qin, B.: Learning sentiment-specific word embedding for twitter sentiment classification. In: Proceedings of the 52nd Annual Meeting of the Association for Computational Linguistics (Vol. 1: Long Papers), pp. 1555–1565 (2014)
22. Tang, Y., Zhang, D., Liang, W., Li, K.C., Sukhija, N.: Active malicious accounts detection with multimodal fusion machine learning algorithm. In: Wang, G., Choo, K.K.R., Ko, R.K.L., Xu, Y., Crispo, B. (eds.) Ubiquitous Security. UbiSec 2021. Communications in Computer and Information Science. vol. 1557, pp. 38–52. Springer Singapore, Singapore (2022). https://doi.org/10.1007/978-981-19-0468-4_4
23. Vidanagama, D.U., Silva, T.P., Karunananda, A.S.: Deceptive consumer review detection: a survey. Artif. Intell. Rev. **53**(2), 1323–1352 (2020)
24. Xue, H., Wang, Q., Luo, B., Seo, H., Li, F.: Content-aware trust propagation toward online review spam detection. J. Data Inf. Qual. (JDIQ) **11**(3), 1–31 (2019)
25. Yang, M., Lu, Z., Chen, X., Xu, F.: Detecting review spammer groups. In: Proceedings of the AAAI Conference on Artificial Intelligence. vol. 31 (2017)
26. Yuan, C., Zhou, W., Ma, Q., Lv, S., Han, J., Hu, S.: Learning review representations from user and product level information for spam detection. In: 2019 IEEE International Conference on Data Mining (ICDM), pp. 1444–1449. IEEE (2019)
27. Zhang, S., Yang, S., Zhu, G., Luo, E., Zhang, J., Xiang, D.: A fine-grained access control scheme for electronic health records based on roles and attributes. In: Wang, G., Choo, K.K.R., Ko, R.K.L., Xu, Y., Crispo, B. (eds.) Ubiquitous Security. UbiSec 2021. Communications in Computer and Information Science. vol. 1557, pp. 25–37. Springer Singapore, Singapore (2022). https://doi.org/10.1007/978-981-19-0468-4_3

Hierarchical Policies of Subgoals for Safe Deep Reinforcement Learning

Fumin Yu[1], Feng Gao[1], Yao Yuan[1], Xiaofei Xing[2],
and Yinglong Dai[3,4(✉)]

[1] College of Information Science and Engineering, Hunan Normal University,
Changsha 410081, China
[2] School of Computer Science and Cyber Engineering, Guangzhou University,
Guangzhou 510006, China
[3] College of Liberal Arts and Sciences, National University of Defense Technology,
Changsha 410073, China
[4] Hunan Provincial Key Laboratory of Intelligent Computing and Language
Information Processing, Changsha 410081, China
daiyl@hunnu.edu.cn

Abstract. Reinforcement learning is a machine learning method that relies on the agent to learn by trial and error to solve decision optimization problems. It is well known that an agent based on deep reinforcement learning in complex environments is difficult to train. Moreover, the agent will generate unsafe and strange actions due to the lack of sufficient reward feedback from the environment. To make the agent converge to a better policy and make its behavior safer and more controllable under sparse rewards, we propose a subgoal embedding method based on prior knowledge and hierarchical strategy that can make the training process converge faster. The subgoal embedding method can be combined with existing reinforcement learning methods. In this paper, we combine the subgoal embedding method with REINFORCE algorithm and PPO(Proximal Policy Optimization) algorithm to test the method in the MiniGrid-DoorKey game environment of the gym platform. The experiments demonstrate the effectiveness of the subgoal embedding method.

Keywords: Reinforcement learning · Deep reinforcement learning · Subgoal embedding · Sparse reward · Hierarchical strategies · Safe agent

1 Introduction

Deep reinforcement learning [8], as a new machine learning [17] method, provides ideas for solving perceptual decision problems for complex systems. For example, deep reinforcement learning methods were first proposed by Mnih et al. [10] and have achieved very successful game performance results in several Atari games. Alpha Go, developed by Google, and incorporating deep reinforcement learning, has defeated top human players in the field of Go several times [16]. The recommendation system based on deep reinforcement learning proposed in

G. Wang et al. (Eds.): UbiSec 2022, CCIS 1768, pp. 220–232, 2023.
https://doi.org/10.1007/978-981-99-0272-9_15

the literature [19] has been successfully applied in real business activities and has achieved good results. Deep reinforcement learning has achieved more and more research results and has been able to break through the highest human level in some fields and has also been able to be successfully used in some practical applications. In the case of complex environments, the lack of sufficient reward values from environmental feedback during the interaction of the agent with the environment, not supported by a good reward signal, can lead to very slow training of the agent and possibly failure to converge. For deep reinforcement learning solving the sparse reward [13] problem is of great significance to solve the training rate, and convergence problems of high-dimensional complex problems, which can seriously hinder the development of reinforcement learning.

The sparse reward problem of deep reinforcement learning can lead to a problem that the agent cannot converge or learn inefficiently in complex tasks. Various solutions are proposed to solve the sparse reward problem in complex environments so that the agent can converge faster in complex environments. Today's methods to face the sparse reward problem are reward design, experience replay, multi-objective learning, and auxiliary tasks. Ng et al. [11] artificially set subgoals artificially designed some rewards, as the subgoals are completed, the agent will continue to approach the final goal, and get good results in some problems. Schaul et al. [15] proposed the preferential experience replay method, which allows many samples in the experience pool to get rewards, improving the utilization of samples so that samples with rewards will play a better role in training the agent. Andrychowicz et al. [1] proposed a multi-objective learning [12] algorithm in which the agent can obtain corresponding rewards from some states that help to reach the final goal, which improves the convergence speed. Jaderberg et al. [6] proposed the UNREAL framework with three auxiliary tasks based on the A3C(Asynchronous Advantage Actor-Critic) algorithm. However, all of the above methods for solving sparse rewards have various drawbacks and shortcomings and cannot be well integrated with the current reinforcement learning algorithms.

In addition to the above methods, we embed human prior knowledge into deep reinforcement learning algorithms via concept embedding to improve the algorithm's convergence speed when targeting sparse reward problems. Moreover, by introducing prior knowledge, the behavior of the agent can be made more secure and controllable [5]. Based on this, we propose a deep reinforcement learning algorithm based on subgoal embedding in the sparse reward problem, where we decompose the problem into multiple subgoals to train separately strategies based on each subgoal, simplifying the complex problem by hierarchical strategies to solve the sparse reward problem among them.

We chose the gym-based MiniGrid-DoorKey game environment to verify the effectiveness of the method. The experimental results show that by decomposing the problem into multiple subgoals and training the strategies individually through the concept embedding method, the convergence speed of the agent can be improved by using hierarchical strategies to solve complex problems. Moreover, the subgoal embedding method can make the behavior of the agent safer, reasonable, and explainable [7], which can better enable the deep reinforcement learning algorithm to be applied in the practical field.

In the following, in Sect. 2 we briefly describe our related work. Then, in Sect. 3, we introduce the method based on subgoal embedding. In Sect. 4, we go to verify the effectiveness of our approach in the MiniGrid-DoorKey game environment. We have some discussions in Sect. 5. Finally, we conclude the paper in Sect. 6.

2   Related Work

The sparse reward problem is seen everywhere in some complex problems, and there is an urgent need to solve the sparse reward problem to make deep reinforcement learning better for real-life applications. At present, the main solution means reward design, experience playback, multi-objective learning, and auxiliary tasks. Reward design is to artificially design some rewards in a sparse reward environment to increase the probability of getting rewards in those cases where it is difficult to get rewards. The main idea of experience replay is to no longer randomly select experiences from the experience pool for training, but to prioritize those experiences that successfully obtain rewards for training, making training more efficient. Multi-goal learning increases the rewards by setting more than the final goal to make it easier for the intelligence to approach the goal and reduce the difficulty of the task. Auxiliary tasks are when we encounter a difficult task, we gradually increase the difficulty of the training task by moving from easy to difficult to finally accomplish the goal.

Ferreira et al. [3] added a rewarding design to dialogue management work and achieved some results, but inappropriate rewards can adversely affect the learning of the agent. Tavakoli et al. [18] proposed an action branching based DQN(Deep Q Network) structure based on the experience replay mechanism, which enables its good application to some continuous high-dimensional problems. Horgan et al. [4] proposed a distributed prioritized empirical replay mechanism, which can improve the diversity of samples and the usage of GPU resources, but the existence of prioritized design cannot be well migrated to some policy-based reinforcement learning algorithms. Schaul et al. [14] merged the policies of several agents in Horde into one policy and proposed an objective-based value function, which extends the value function's expressiveness, however, the problem of bias brought by the objectives in multiple objectives still exists. Mirowski et al. [9] used a similar approach to the UNREAL framework and added two auxiliary tasks to the navigation task, which helped the training process, but poor task design can lead to obtaining wrong solutions. In contrast, in our work, our approach based on subgoal embedding utilizes a hierarchical strategy to solve the problem, which will be more flexible to adjust the training process.

3   Method

In this section, we first have some conceptual knowledge of reinforcement learning and introduce the Markov process and cumulative reward in reinforcement learning, followed by the sparse reward problem in reinforcement learning. Secondly, we present our subgoal embedding-based approach, and learn different strategies according to these subgoals separately, using the hierarchical strategy approach can better solve the sparse reward problem in complex problems. Moreover the problem is still in the form of an MDP(Markov Decision Process) and we can still guarantee the theoretical convergence of the Bellman equation. Finally, we use reinforce algorithm and the ppo algorithm of reinforcement learning combined with our subgoal embedding method, respectively, to demonstrate the effectiveness of our method [2].

3.1   Reinforcement Learning

Reinforcement learning, a branch of machine learning, differs from supervised learning in that it tells the agent which action to take using the correct samples and labels, but instead uses the agent to continuously interact with the environment and learn itself through rewards fed by the environment, learning strategies to achieve maximum cumulative reward returns or to achieve specific goals.

The mathematical model for reinforcement learning is a Markovian decision process, which is a five-tuple $(\mathcal{S}, \mathcal{A}, \mathcal{P}, \mathcal{R}, \gamma)$: $\mathcal{S}$ represents the state of the agent, $\mathcal{A}$ represents the set of actions taken by the agent, $\mathcal{P}$ represents the probability that the agent will move from the current state to the next state, $\mathcal{R}$ represents the reward value obtained by taking the current action to reach the next state, and γ is the discount factor [2].

At moment t, the action a_t is taken from the learned strategy at the current state s_t. Then the current state s_t is transferred to the next state s_{t+1} according to the state transfer probability $\mathcal{P}$, and the corresponding reward value R_t is obtained. The reward is a cumulative reward starting from time step t. The discount factor $\gamma \in (0, 1]$ and the cumulative reward $R_t = \sum_{k=0}^{a} \gamma^k r_{t+k}$. The strategy of reinforcement learning is to obtain the maximum cumulative reward.

The sparse reward problem is frequent in reinforcement learning. Unlike supervised learning, reinforcement learning requires reward signals from the environment to optimize the strategy, but in real-world problems, we can see the existence of the sparse reward problem everywhere. Therefore, we propose an approach based on subgoal embedding to solve the sparse reward a problem in reinforcement learning through hierarchical strategies.

3.2   Subgoal Embedding

By decomposing a complex objective into multiple subgoals, several different strategies are trained separately based on each subgoal, and then the state and subgoals are input to the policy function at the same time and choose different substrategies based on different subgoals to make better training convergence. The action output form is as follows:

$$a_m = p_m(state_m, goal_m) \tag{1}$$

In the above formula, a_m denotes the action generated by policy p_m based on $state_m$ and $goal_m$, m represents the mth action made at the mth state and goal based on the mth policy.

The above policy is a sub policy trained based on each subgoal, and each time the current state and the subgoal are passed into the policy function at the same time, the corresponding action is obtained.

When sparse rewards are encountered in complex problems, rewards will be harvested only when the final goal is reached. We will train sub-strategies separately based on subgoals, and in one round, when a subgoal is completed, there will be a corresponding intrinsic reward obtained to train the strategy corresponding to the subgoal.

From Fig. 1, We can see that when we encounter sparse rewards, we can decompose the complex task into multiple subgoals. Based on these subgoals, we can train different strategies corresponding to these subgoals separately. Then the state the agent is in at that moment and the selected subgoals are simultaneously input to the corresponding strategy functions to output the corresponding actions to the environment. Whenever the corresponding subgoals are completed, we get the corresponding internal rewards, which can be used to train the corresponding sub-strategies.

$$R_t^{goal} = \begin{cases} \beta_i \text{ if agent finishes the goal } i \\ 0 \quad \text{otherwise} \end{cases} \tag{2}$$

R_t^{goal} is an internal reward obtained whenever a specific goal is completed and is used to train the strategy corresponding to the subgoal. β_i is a hyperparameter that can vary depending on each subgoal.

The cumulative multi-objective returns that we set and follow will be:

$$G^\pi = \sum_{k=0}^{n} \gamma^k R_{t+k+1} \tag{3}$$

G^π is the cumulative reward, γ is discount factor, R_{t+k+1} is the future reward.

In our approach, the general cumulative reward of reinforcement learning is still followed, we just use internal rewards to train the hierarchical strategy in a sparse reward environment, the goal of the agent is still to maximize the cumulative reward, the introduction of internal reward to train each sub-strategy is more conducive to reaching the final goal and the form of the problem is still MDP(Markov Decision Process), we can still guarantee the convergence of the Bellman equation.

Subgoal embedding methods can be combined with existing reinforcement learning algorithms. In this paper, we choose to embed our subgoal methods in reinforce algorithm and ppo algorithm for reinforcement learning, respectively, and in Sect. 4, we will conduct comparative experiments on our methods.

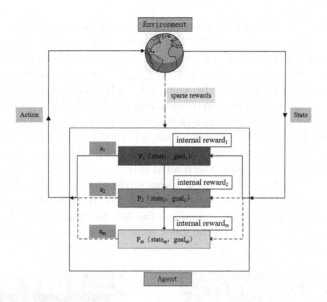

Fig. 1. The structure of the reinforcement learning method with embedded subgoals.

4   Experiments

In this section, we use the MiniGrid-DoorKey game environment in the gym platform as our experimental environment to validate our method. The game session is divided into three main steps, these three steps correspond to our three subgoals: first, get the key, then use the key to open the door, and finally reach the destination. We validate the effectiveness of our method by introducing two metrics of our method in terms of accumulated rewards and the number of steps needed in each round.

In the case of sparse rewards, our approach is based on a priori knowledge of subgoal embedding, where the agent no longer explores blindly and can make the behavior of the agent more secure and controllable, thus accelerating the learning speed, as verified by the following experiments.

4.1   Environment Set Up

MiniGrid-DoorKey is an environment of the gym framework provided by Open AI, a toolkit for developing reinforcement learning algorithms. The agent is required to complete the task of finding the key, opening the door, and reaching the destination within a fixed-size square grid. When the agent reaches the maximum number of exploration steps set in the system or reaches the end, the task will end and enters the next round, in which only the destination will be reached to get the system's reward.

The state space when the agent interacts with the environment MiniGrid-DoorKey is a three-dimensional 7*7*3. The action space mainly has five common actions: action 0 is to control the direction of the agent to the left, action 1 is to control the direction of the agent to the right, action 2 controls the agent to walk forward, action 3 is to let the agent get the key, action 5 is to let the agent opens the door with the key. The reward space will only be rewarded when the final goal is reached, where the size of the reward value obtained by reaching the end point is related to the number of steps needed to reach the end point: the smaller the number of steps to reach the end point, the larger the reward the value obtained, in other cases, the reward is 0.

Figure 2 from left to right is the game environment of MiniGrid-DoorKey-5 × 5-v0 and MiniGrid-DoorKey-8 × 8-v0. The red triangle arrow represents the agent, the yellow key-shaped represents the key to open the door, the yellow square represents the door, and the green square represents the final destination.

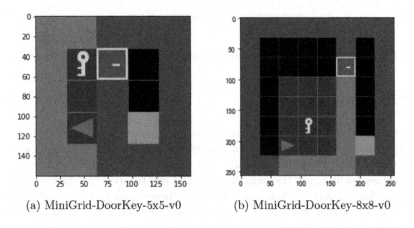

(a) MiniGrid-DoorKey-5x5-v0   (b) MiniGrid-DoorKey-8x8-v0

Fig. 2. Two different experimental environments. (Color figure online)

4.2   Subgoal Embedding in Reinforcement Learning Algorithm

The two main aspects of our experiments are to combine the subgoal embedding approach with the reinforce algorithm and the ppo algorithm of reinforcement learning in different game environments, respectively, and verifying the feasibility of our approach by examining both the metrics of the number of steps explored and the rewards obtained by the agent.

When the agent is playing the MiniGrid-DoorKey game, the only way to get a higher cumulative reward is to spend fewer steps to reach the end point to boost the reward value received. When we use subgoals embedded in existing reinforcement learning algorithms, we have done several sets of experiments for each game environment and a comprehensive comparison shows that our method is less volatile and more stable in performance.

First, we start with a reinforce algorithm based on reinforcement learning to embed our method in the game environments of MiniGrid-DoorKey-5 × 5-v0 and MiniGrid-DoorKey-8 × 8-v0, respectively, comparing the number of steps used in each round and the cumulative reward for each round.

Figure 3 below shows the experimental results. Through the experimental results, we can see from the left figure that in the same episodes, our method requires fewer steps than the original reinforcement algorithm in the same episodes, and our algorithm can reach convergence in faster rounds with a greater rate of decrease in the number of steps required as the training progresses. In the comparison experiments with the reinforcement algorithm in the right figure, we can see from the figure that our method can obtain a high cumulative reward in the same episodes compared to the original reinforce algorithm, verifying in another way that our method is feasible in the reinforce algorithm for reinforcement learning.

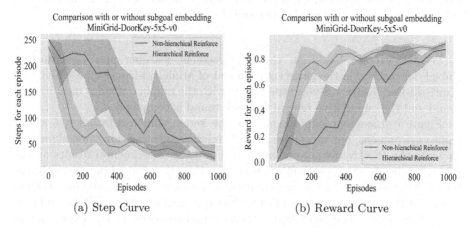

(a) Step Curve   (b) Reward Curve

Fig. 3. Comparison curve of steps and rewards. In the MiniGrid-DoorKey-5 × 5-v0 environment, the non-hierachical reinforce algorithm and the hierachical reinforce algorithm are compared in the number of training steps and rewards.

Figure 4 below shows the results of the experiment in more complex MiniGrid-DoorKey-8 × 8-v0 environments. From the experimental results, we can learn that in the left figure, our method has an advantage over the original reinforcement algorithm in terms of the number of exploration steps of the agent, with a great improvement in the convergence speed, and our method performs better in complex environments compared to the reinforcement algorithm, and in the right figure, it can be seen that our method will obtain a larger reward value in each episode, and our method will eventually obtain a higher reward value compared to the original reinforcement algorithm.

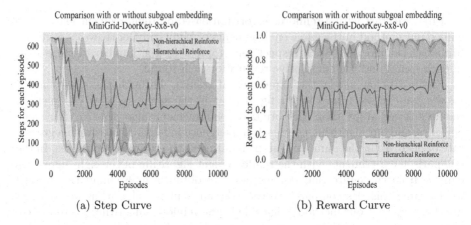

Fig. 4. Comparison curve of steps and rewards. In the MiniGrid-DoorKey-8 × 8-v0 environment, the non-hierachical reinforce algorithm and the hierachical reinforce algorithm are compared in the number of training steps and rewards.

Second, we are based on the reinforcement learning ppo algorithm to embed our method in the game environment of MiniGrid-DoorKey-5 × 5-v0 and MiniGrid-DoorKey-8 × 8-v0, respectively, with the number of steps used in each round and the cumulative reward for each round is compared.

Figure 5 shows our experiments in the same MiniGrid-DoorKey-5 × 5-v0 game environment, but we choose another reinforcement learning ppo algorithm to verify the effectiveness of our method. From the experimental results on the left, it can be seen that our method is smaller than the original ppo algorithm in terms of the number of steps used in each of the same episodes, and our method can reach the convergence state faster than the original ppo algorithm and perform even better. The right figure shows the comparison of the experimental rewards obtained in each episode, from which we can see that our method can obtain higher rewards in the same episode than the original ppo algorithm, and we can see that it can reach convergence at a faster rate, thus also verifying our method.

In the experiments in Fig. 6 below we still do comparison experiments based on the ppo algorithm, and the experimental environment chosen is the more complex MiniGrid-DoorKey-8 × 8-v0 game environment. We can see that our method still performs well in the more complex MiniGrid-DoorKey-8 × 8-v0 environment. As seen in the left figure, our method can significantly outperform the original ppo algorithm in terms of the number of exploration steps and can reach convergence in a shorter round. In the figure on the right, our approach leads to a higher reward.

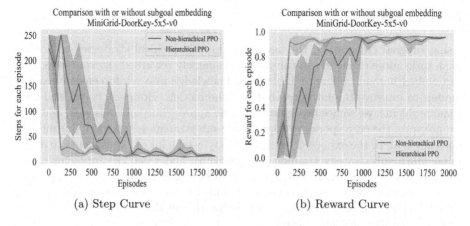

(a) Step Curve   (b) Reward Curve

Fig. 5. Comparison curve of steps and rewards. In the MiniGrid-DoorKey-5 × 5-v0 environment, the non-hierachical ppo algorithm and the hierachical ppo algorithm are compared in the number of training steps and rewards.

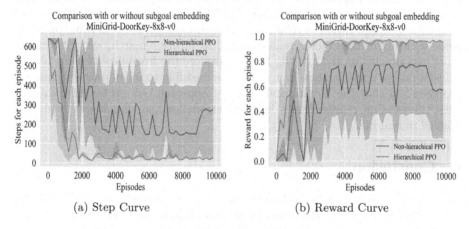

(a) Step Curve   (b) Reward Curve

Fig. 6. Comparison curve of steps and rewards. In the MiniGrid-DoorKey-8 × 8-v0 environment, the non-hierachical ppo algorithm and the hierachical ppo algorithm are compared in the number of training steps and rewards.

The experimental results from the above reinforcement learning-based REIN-FORCE and PPO algorithms show that the speed of training and the value of rewards from the environment can be improved by allowing the agent to be trained in a hierarchical strategy through the method of subgoal embedding. Based on this, we can use hierarchical strategies by embedding subgoals in more complex and sparse reward environments to improve learning efficiency and cumulative rewards of the agent, allowing us to improve the performance of the agent in a more interpretable way.

5   Discussion

Using subgoal embedding, the agent can use hierarchical strategies to accomplish tasks more efficiently in complex and sparsely rewarded environments, and can embed human understandable prior knowledge into reinforcement learning models to improve the interpretability of the models. However, it can still have some problems, we sometimes cannot set the appropriate subgoals well, and thus cannot train the corresponding appropriate sub-strategies, and when our method does not achieve the expected results, we may need a lot of experiments to determine which sub-strategy training has problems, and when the problems of the sub-strategy are determined, in the subgoal embedding approach, we also need to experiment to find out the appropriate internal reward values in subgoals and sub-strategies, which will facilitate the subgoal embedding approach to be able to solve complex problems better.

We also believe that the combination of human prior knowledge and existing deep reinforcement learning algorithms through subgoal embedding can accelerate the practical application of reinforcement learning models in real life, and also make the reinforcement learning algorithms more interpretable, which can accelerate the application of reinforcement learning algorithms in some practical fields with high safety factor requirements. In future research, we will conduct more experiments on the existing basis to explore the feasibility of using hierarchical strategy approach based on subgoal embedding to solve practical complex problems, so that the hierarchical strategy approach can be better combined with the existing reinforcement learning algorithms, so that it can be better applied in real life.

6   Conclusion

In this paper, we propose a method based on subgoal embedding using hierarchical strategies that allow the agent to learn additional strategies to accomplish the final goal in a complex, sparsely rewarded environment. The method can improve the training efficiency of the agent, and it allows the agent to receive higher reward values. The effectiveness of the method is also verified based on the MiniGrid-DoorKey game environment. Combining the method of subgoal embedding with existing reinforcement learning algorithms to train different substrategies based on respective subgoals, the training efficiency of the agent can be significantly improved, and the agent can be allowed to receive higher cumulative rewards. Through the subgoal embedding method of prior knowledge, we can embed human-understandable knowledge into the reinforcement learning algorithm, which not only improves the performance of the algorithm but also makes the behavior of the agent more interpretable and safe.

Acknowledgments. This work is supported in part by China Postdoctoral Science Foundation under Grant Number 2021M693976, Hunan Provincial Natural Science Foundation under Grant Number 2020JJ5367, Key Project of Teaching Reform in

Colleges and Universities of Hunan Province under Grant Number HNJG-2021-0251, and Scientific Research Fund of Hunan Provincial Education Department under Grant Number 21A0599.

References

1. Andrychowicz, M., et al.: Hindsight experience replay. In: Advances in Neural Information Processing Systems 30 (2017)
2. Cheng, J., Yu, F., Zhang, H., Dai, Y.: Skill reward for safe deep reinforcement learning. In: Wang, G., Choo, K.K.R., Ko, R.K.L., Xu, Y., Crispo, B. (eds.) Ubiquitous Security. UbiSec 2021. Communications in Computer and Information Science, vol. 1557, pp 203–213. Springer, Singapore (2022). https://doi.org/10.1007/978-981-19-0468-4_15
3. Ferreira, E., Avignon, F., Lefevre, F.: On the use of social signal for reward shaping in reinforcement learning for dialogue management. In: SEMDIAL 2013 DialDam, p. 44 (2013)
4. Horgan, D., et al.: Distributed prioritized experience replay. arXiv preprint arXiv:1803.00933 (2018)
5. Iosif, A.C., Gasiba, T.E., Zhao, T., Lechner, U., Pinto-Albuquerque, M.: A large-scale study on the security vulnerabilities of cloud deployments. In: Wang, G., Choo, K.K.R., Ko, R.K.L., Xu, Y., Crispo, B. (eds.) Ubiquitous Security, UbiSec 2021. CCIS, vol. 1557, pp 171–188. Springer, Singapore (2022). https://doi.org/10.1007/978-981-19-0468-4_13
6. Jaderberg, M., Mnih, V., Czarnecki, W.M., Schaul, T., Leibo, J.Z., Silver, D., Kavukcuoglu, K.: Reinforcement learning with unsupervised auxiliary tasks. arXiv preprint arXiv:1611.05397 (2016)
7. Koay, A.M.Y., Xie, M., Ko, R.K.L., Sterner, C., Choi, T., Dong, N.: Sdgen: A scalable, reproducible and flexible approach to generate real world cyber security datasets. In: Wang, G., Choo, K.K.R., Ko, R.K.L., Xu, Y., Crispo, B. (eds.) Ubiquitous Security. UbiSec 2021. Communications in Computer and Information Science, vol 1557, pp 102–115. Springer, Singapore (2022). https://doi.org/10.1007/978-981-19-0468-4_8
8. Lou, P., Xu, K., Jiang, X., Xiao, Z., Yan, J.: Path planning in an unknown environment based on deep reinforcement learning with prior knowledge. J. Intell. Fuzzy Syst. (Preprint), 1–17 (2021)
9. Mirowski, P., Pascanu, R., Viola, F., Soyer, H., Hadsell, R.: Learning to navigate in complex environments. arXiv (2016)
10. Mnih, V., et al.: Human-level control through deep reinforcement learning. Nature **518**(7540), 529–533 (2015)
11. Ng, A.Y., Russell, S., et al.: Algorithms for inverse reinforcement learning. In: Icml, vol. 1, p. 2 (2000)
12. Plappert, M., et al.: Multi-goal reinforcement learning: Challenging robotics environments and request for research. arXiv preprint arXiv:1802.09464 (2018)
13. Riedmiller, M., et al.: Learning by playing solving sparse reward tasks from scratch. In: International Conference On Machine Learning, pp. 4344–4353. PMLR (2018)
14. Schaul, T., Horgan, D., Gregor, K., Silver, D.: Universal value function approximators. In: International Conference on Machine Learning, pp. 1312–1320. PMLR (2015)
15. Schaul, T., Quan, J., Antonoglou, I., Silver, D.: Prioritized experience replay. arXiv preprint arXiv:1511.05952 (2015)

16. Silver, D., et al.: Mastering the game of go with deep neural networks and tree search. Nature **529**(7587), 484–489 (2016)

17. Tang, Y., Zhang, D., Liang, W., Li, K.C., Sukhija, N.: Active malicious accounts detection with multimodal fusion machine learning algorithm. In: Wang, G., Choo, K.K.R., Ko, R.K.L., Xu, Y., Crispo, B. (eds.) Ubiquitous Security. UbiSec 2021. CCIS, vol. 1557, pp 38–52. Springer, Singapore (2022). https://doi.org/10.1007/978-981-19-0468-4_4

18. Tavakoli, A., Pardo, F., Kormushev, P.: Action branching architectures for deep reinforcement learning. In: Proceedings of the AAAI Conference on Artificial Intelligence, vol. 32 (2018)

19. Zhao, X., Zhang, L., Xia, L., Ding, Z., Yin, D., Tang, J.: Deep reinforcement learning for list-wise recommendations. arXiv preprint arXiv:1801.00209 (2017)

Improved DeepLabV3+ based Railway Track Extraction to Enhance Railway Transportation Safety

Yanbin Weng[1(✉)], Zuochuang Li[1(✉)], Xiaobin Huang[2], and Xiahu Chen[2]

[1] Hunan University of Technology, Zhuzhou 412007, Hunan Province, China
23902@qq.com, 466904647@qq.com
[2] Zhuzhou Taichang Electronic Information Technology Co., Ltd,, Zhuzhou 412007, Hunan Province, China

Abstract. With the development of rail transit in China, rail extraction has become an important work to ensure the safety of railway transportation. The traditional railway track extraction method needs a lot of manpower and material resources, but the existing depth neural network method is inefficient. To solve the above problems, this paper proposes a railway extraction method that improves the DeepLabV3+ semantic segmentation model. The lightweight network Mobilenetv3 is used to extract railway tracks instead of the original trunk extraction network of DeepLabV3+. On the basis of not reducing the extraction accuracy, the model size and time cost are reduced; Secondly, for the problem of error in the model extraction results, this paper uses morphological algorithm to optimize the extraction results. The experimental results on the railway dataset show that the operation time of the method in this paper is 5% lower than that of the DeepLabV3+ model of the Mobilenetv2 backbone network, and the extraction accuracy is slightly improved, with the average intersection/merge ratio of 89.93% and the average pixel accuracy of 95.51%. Morphological algorithm optimization can eliminate extraction errors such as holes and spots, and this method can extract complete railway tracks.

Keywords: Semantic segmentation · Mobilenetv3 · Morphological algorithm · Railway extraction

1 Introduction

With the rapid development of China's economy, all regions in the country have put forward higher requirements for the safety and convenience of rail transit transportation. The safety of railway transportation is related to the lifeblood of the national economy and is the basic requirement of railway transportation. The acquisition of railway information is the most important step in the process of improving the safety and convenience of transportation. Remote sensing satellite images and UAV aerial images are important sources for obtaining original railway information. Remote sensing images have large observation range, high scene information comprehensiveness, simple acquisition

G. Wang et al. (Eds.): UbiSec 2022, CCIS 1768, pp. 233–247, 2023.
https://doi.org/10.1007/978-981-99-0272-9_16

method, and will not be limited by geographical region, but will be affected by weather and other factors, resulting in unstable definition; UAV aerial image observation range is small, acquisition method is difficult and restricted by geographical location, but it is not restricted by weather factors, with good timeliness and high resolution. It is more convenient to obtain railway information by using UAV aerial images.

The traditional extraction method is based on the extraction of geometric features such as texture and gray level of railway or ordinary road. This method extracts some shallow features from the image, and then manually sets corresponding rules for these shallow features to achieve the goal of extracting road information in the image [1]. M. Barzohar and Cooper. D. B proposed a geometric probability model of road image using the length, width, curvature and pixels of the road area, for a given aerial road image, it detects the road area through the maximum a posteriori probability estimation [2]. Ghaziani. M et al. proposed a method for extracting unstructured road network from satellite images based on binary image segmentation. First, obtain a threshold for statistical evaluation of satellite images, then obtain a binary image by threshold segmentation, and finally obtain the segmented road network by morphological operation on the binary image [3]. Traditional extraction methods require researchers to have rich prior knowledge. In some cases, rivers and railways have the same geometric characteristics, and buildings and railways have the same spectral characteristics. The railway information extracted by traditional methods will be affected by the above factors, and the accuracy and robustness of extraction are relatively low. Therefore, the traditional methods are not suitable for the complex environment of modern cities.

In recent years, deep learning technology has developed rapidly. Deep learning is the inherent law and representation level of learning sample data and label data [4]. Mnih. V et al. proposed a road extraction method using convolutional neural network [5]. After the road features are extracted, the road area feature map is obtained by using the thinning segmentation algorithm. However, due to the interference of environmental information, the extraction accuracy is not high. Yang Jialin et al. proposed an improved U-Net road segmentation network combining context information and attention mechanism for various interferences. First, the residual network Resnet-34 was used as the encoder to extract road image features; Then the extracted features are integrated through the context information extraction module to ensure that the geometric features of the road are extracted; Then use the attention mechanism to adjust the weight of the features transmitted by the jump connection, so that the network can get a better weight, so that the semantic segmentation network can better extract the road edge area. But because of the many parameters of the U-net network, this method has a large time cost [6]. Song Tingqiang et al. designed an AS Unet network consisting of an encoder decoder. The channel attention mechanism and spatial pyramid module were added to the encoder, and the spatial attention mechanism was added to the decoder, which significantly improved the accuracy of road segmentation. Similarly, the time efficiency of this method was low [7]. Buslaev et al. proposed a U-net semantic segmentation network, which uses ResNet-34 and U-Net network decoder pre trained on ImageNet dataset to improve the effect of road extraction [8]. The deep learning extraction method is simple in operation, wide in application and high in extraction accuracy, and has now become a common road extraction method.

At present, deep learning is mainly used to extract ordinary roads. In many cases, the acquisition of railway areas requires manual drawing by staff. This paper proposes an improved DeepLabV3+ network, which uses mobilenetv3 [9] to replace mobilenetv2 [10] and Xception [11] as the backbone structure of DeepLabV3+, further reducing the time consumption of target extraction. After using this network to extract the railway track area, morphological corrosion and expansion are used to further optimize the extraction results of the railway area. Finally, a complete railway area is obtained.

2 Methods in This Paper

2.1 Algorithm Flow

The railway track extraction method in this paper mainly consists of four modules: data preprocessing, railway track extraction, morphological optimization and calculation evaluation index. Before railway track extraction, it is necessary to use the graphic image annotation tool (labelem) to annotate the original railway aerial image semantics, generate the label image corresponding to the railway data, and then produce the railway data set. The algorithm flow of this paper is shown in Fig. 1.

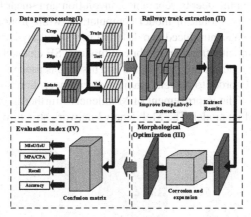

Fig. 1. Algorithm flow

In the data preprocessing phase. Name the original image and the label image to make them correspond one by one. Semantic segmentation models need sufficient sample data to learn the rules between pixels of the original image and the label image. In general, the more sample data, the better the model training effect, and the stronger the generalization ability. Data enhancement can rapidly expand the number of samples. The unsupervised learning model can directly enhance the data, but the original image of the supervised learning model and the label image need to correspond one by one, so the same operations need to be performed on the image and label at the same time. For example, the semantic segmentation model in this paper is a supervised learning model, and the same operations need to be performed on the image and label in the railway dataset, such as cutting, flipping, and rotating. After the data is expanded to a certain amount, it is also necessary to divide the data into data sets for different purposes.

In the railway track extraction phase. The data processed in the previous stage is used to improve the DeepLabv3+ network training in this paper, and the pre-training weights are used to accelerate the model convergence and get the trained weights. Then, according to the trained model, the railway track is extracted, and the initial extraction results are obtained.

In the morphological optimization stage. The errors in the initial extraction results are optimized by morphology. The combination of morphological erosion and dilation can eliminate the holes and spots in the initial extraction results.

In the stage of calculating evaluation indicators, this paper uses the intersection and merger ratio (IoU), average intersection and merger ratio (MIoU), category pixel accuracy (CPA), category average pixel accuracy (MPA), recall and accuracy to evaluate the results.

2.2 Mobilenetv3 Network

The most important thing of lightweight network is to reduce the network size and running time as much as possible on the premise of ensuring the accuracy. The Mobilenetv3 network has improved the deeply separable convolution and linear bottleneck residual structure, reducing the amount of model computation, while improving the accuracy slightly. Mobilenetv3 has introduced two different versions, Large and Small, which are applicable to different situations. In the bneck module, SE channel attention structure and inverse residual structure are introduced, and h-swish is used to replace the original activation function. In order to prevent gradient divergence, shortcut connection is also added to the module. The improvement of Mobilenetv3 further improves the accuracy and running speed of its model. The Mobilenetv3 network structure is shown in Fig. 2.

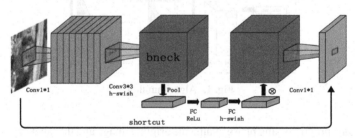

Fig. 2. Mobilenetv3 network

To further reduce the network computation, Mobilenetv3 discards the Swish activation function used in Mobilenetv2 and uses the h - swish activation function instead. The image of Swish activation function is a smooth and monotonous curve. In some deep learning models, it is approximate or slightly better than ReLU function. Therefore, Swish function is applicable to various challenging fields. Swish function includes sigmoid function, so compared with ReLU, Swish function calculation is more complex. While the h - swish activation function selects ReLU6 as the approximate function, which eliminates the complex calculation caused by sigmoid function, thus reducing the calculation cost again. The expression of h - swish activation function is:

$$h - swish(x) = x\frac{ReLU6(x + 3)}{6} \tag{1}$$

Through research, it is found that with the increase of network depth, the performance of the nonlinear activation function is also improving. Therefore, in order to better reduce the number of parameters and reduce the model time cost, in the Mobilenetv3 network, the h-swish activation function is only used in the first and later layers of the network.

2.3 Channel Attention Mechanism

In order to make the model better use of the image channel information to extract features in the local receptive field, Jie et al. proposed the SE (Squeeze and Extraction) module [12], which can explicitly model the interdependence between channels and adaptively recalibrate the channel level feature response. The structure of SE channel attention module is shown in Fig. 3. Channel attention mechanism is mainly divided into four processes. First, the feature layer is extracted. The module will extract a feature map with dimensions {W, H, C} as input, where W and H represent the width and height of the feature map respectively, and C represents the number of channels. Secondly, the compression operation, which will compress the dimension of the feature map to {1, 1, C}, that is, for each channel C1, there will be a weight corresponding to it one by one. This weight is the operation of each channel on the process when the feature map is compressed, and represents the influence of each channel on feature extraction. Then, the excitation operation sends the C dimension vector {1, 1, C} into the fully connected neural network. After two fully connected layers, the weight of each channel itself is obtained. The last is the scale operation, which multiplies the calculated weight of the channel itself with the characteristic matrix of the channel corresponding to the original characteristic map. The scale operation can be understood as that when the weight of a channel calculated by SE is significant, the corresponding channel characteristic map matrix value will increase, and the final output characteristic map result will also be greatly affected; On the contrary, when the calculated weight is small, the corresponding channel characteristic map matrix value will become smaller, and the impact on the results will also be reduced.

Because the SE module needs to calculate the channel weight additionally, that is, increase the total network calculation. In order to reduce the computation and speed up the network, h-sigmoid function is used instead of sigmoid activation function. The expression of h-sigmoid activation function is:

$$f(x) = \begin{cases} 1, (x > 3) \\ \frac{x}{6} + 0.5, (3 \geq x \geq -3) \\ 0, (x < -3) \end{cases} \tag{2}$$

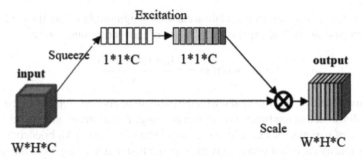

Fig. 3. Channel attention mechanism

Through the research on sigmoid activation function by researchers, it is found that the curve of the function is smooth and the function itself is easy to derive, but there is an index in the function, which greatly increases the amount of calculation. In addition, when the model operation requires back propagation to obtain the error gradient, the sigmoid derivation requires division, which is very likely to lead to the disappearance of the gradient. H-sigmoid is similar to sigmoid function, which eliminates exponential operation and greatly reduces the operation time.

2.4 Network Structure and Algorithm of This Paper

This paper uses the improved DeepLabv3+ model to extract railway tracks. In the encoder structure of DeepLabv3+, Mobilenetv3 is used to replace the original backbone extraction network, and the spatial pyramid pooling module is used behind the backbone extraction network to further process the characteristics of the backbone extraction network output; In the decoder structure, the up sampling module and concat function module are still retained to fuse and up sample the characteristics of the encoder output. The network structure of this paper is shown in Fig. 4.

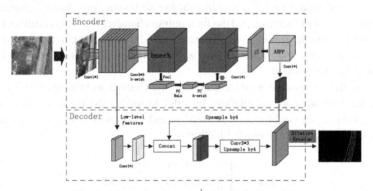

Fig. 4. Network structure diagram of this article

In the extraction phase, the new original aerial images of the railway need to be input. The original aerial images pass through the bneck structure of the Mobilenetv3 network.

With the best weight saved through model training, the railway images are first simply processed to extract low-level semantic features of the railway track. Secondly, the bneck structure sends the high-level feature map after depth extraction through the pooling layer and full connection layer to the spatial pyramid pooling structure. Finally, high-level semantic features and high-level semantic features are extracted from the encoder of this network structure. In the decoder structure, perform 1 for the low-level semantic features output by the encoder × 1 Convolution dimensionality reduction processing, upsampling and dimensionality raising processing for advanced semantic features, feature fusion of the two features through concat function, and finally upsampling to obtain the extracted railway track feature map.

The initial results extracted from the semantic segmentation model will have some errors. In this paper, the network structure reduces the running time of the model and the extraction error. In order to further improve the extraction accuracy, this paper proposes an algorithm to further optimize the initial extraction results by using morphology.

Morphological algorithm is an algorithm to change the shape of objects in binary images. In this algorithm, there is a structure that determines the specific operation, which is called the core. For an input binary image, the core determines whether to expand the area with a pixel value of 0 or 255. The size and shape of the core of the morphological algorithm are defined by the user, and there is a reference point in the core. When using the algorithm, researchers can define the core as a figure centered on the reference point. Morphological algorithms can be divided into many kinds. In this paper, expansion and erosion algorithms are mainly used. Morphological dilation algorithm is to use the set kernel to calculate the local maximum value in the binary image. In this process, it is necessary to use the core with a set shape and size to convolve the binary image read by the algorithm. The convolution operation calculates the maximum pixel value of the local area corresponding to the core, and then assigns the maximum pixel value to the area specified by the reference point. In this process, the area that needs to change shape will gradually expand. The erosion algorithm is the opposite of the expansion algorithm. It is an operation to find the local minimum value in the image, and finally makes some areas smaller. For the holes and spots in the initial extraction results, the morphological algorithm has a good optimization ability.

3 Experimental Data and Evaluation Indicators

3.1 Experimental Data Set

The data used in this paper are UAV aerial images provided by a railway information technology service company. This data set mainly uses aerial images of the railways of Lianjiang Station in Zhanjiang City, Guangdong Province, Liangjiang Station in Laibin City, Guangxi Province and Jiangcun Station in Guangzhou City, Guangdong Province, including different railway environments. The original aerial image size is 4864 pixels × 3648 pixels. This data has no ready-made label file, so you need to use Labelme software to manually draw the label file. Since the image size will be automatically reset during model training in this paper, it is unnecessary to fix the size of input image and label. In order to prevent over fitting, improve the robustness of the model, improve the generalization ability of the model, and avoid sample imbalance, this paper adopts random clipping, rotation, horizontal flipping, vertical flipping, and center flipping to enhance the data, and finally 5836 railway and its corresponding label images are obtained. This model uses the test set as a verification set, and does not separate the verification set. The training set and test set are divided by a ratio of 9:1. The background pixel value of the label dataset used in this paper is 0, and the target pixel value is 1. The original image and label image are shown in Fig. 5.

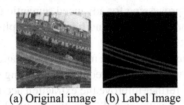

(a) Original image   (b) Label Image

Fig. 5. Original and label images

3.2   Experimental Environment and Parameter Setting

In this paper, the experimental environment is Windows 10 of 64-bit operating system, the CPU is Intel i5, and the model of the graphics card used is NVIDIA GeForce RTX 3050. The model running environment is torch 1.2.0 and python 3.7. In the training process, the initial learning rate is 7e−3; To ensure high accuracy, sgd optimizer is used; To prevent over fitting, set 1e−4 weight attenuation; A total of 100 Epochs are trained, and weight values are saved once every 5 Epochs. The loss function used in this paper is the cross entropy loss function, and the loss function expression is:

$$CE\_loss = -\frac{1}{n}\sum_x[y\ln a + (1-y)\ln(1-a)] \tag{3}$$

where, x represents a sample, y represents the actual label, a represents the output during prediction, and n represents the total number of samples. When the loss function drops to a certain value and does not continue to decline, the training weight is considered to be optimal, and the optimal weight value is stored in a separate weight file to facilitate the use of the optimal weight in prediction.

3.3   Evaluating Indicator

The model in this paper is a semantic segmentation model. In order to evaluate the advantages and disadvantages of the model in this paper, IoU and MIoU, CPA and MPA, Recall and Accuracy are selected as evaluation indicators.

The calculation of the above evaluation indicators is based on the calculation of confusion matrix. The principle of the Confusion Matrix is the classification results of the statistical model, that is to predict and classify the original images in the verification set, compare them with the label files in the verification set, and finally count the number of correct and wrong samples. The four elements of confusion matrix are TP, FP, TN and FN. TP represents the real case, that is, the model prediction result is positive, and the label result is also positive; FP represents a false positive example, that is, the model prediction result is positive, but the label result is negative; TN represents a true counterexample, that is, the model prediction result is negative, and the label result is also negative; FN means false counterexample, that is, the model prediction result is negative, but the label result is positive. In semantic segmentation, the segmentation of a category is usually represented by the intersection and union ratio (IoU), which is the intersection of the real value of the category pixel in the label and the predicted value of the model divided by its union. The average cross and merge ratio is the average of cross and merge ratios of all categories. The expressions of intersection and merger ratio and average intersection and merger ratio are:

$$IoU = \frac{TP}{TP + FN + FP} \tag{4}$$

$$MIoU = \frac{1}{N} \sum_{k=1}^{N} IoU_k \tag{5}$$

The average pixel accuracy is to first calculate the category pixel accuracy (CPA) of each class, and then accumulate the average value. The expressions of category pixel accuracy and category average pixel accuracy are:

$$CPA = \frac{TP}{TP + FP} \tag{6}$$

$$MPA = \frac{1}{N} \sum_{k=1}^{N} CPA_k \tag{7}$$

Recall rate indicates the proportion of correctly predicted target pixels in all predicted target pixels. The expression of recall rate is:

$$Recall = \frac{TP}{TP + FN} \tag{8}$$

The accuracy rate is calculated by dividing the number of correct pixels predicted by the model by the total number of pixels. The expression of the accuracy rate is:

$$Accuracy = \frac{TP + TN}{TP + TN + FP + FN} \tag{9}$$

The evaluation indicators selected in this paper are commonly used for semantic segmentation. The value range of the evaluation indicators is within [0,1]. The closer the value is to 1, the better the model is.

4 Experimental Data and Evaluation Indicators

4.1 Analysis of Ablation Experiment

To verify whether the accuracy of the improved DeepLabv3+ model in this paper is improved compared with the original model, and whether the running time consumption is reduced. This ablation experiment mainly studies the influence of Mobilenetv3 trunk extraction network, Mobilenetv2 trunk extraction network, channel attention mechanism and morphological algorithm on the accuracy and time of railway track extraction under the same other conditions. First, compare the impact of attention mechanism and morphology algorithm on the accuracy and time of DeepLabv3+ model extraction of Mobilenetv2 backbone extraction network. When attention mechanism and morphology algorithm are not used, the accuracy is low and the time consumption is less. After attention mechanism is added, the accuracy is slightly improved and the time is slightly increased. When morphology algorithm is added, the accuracy is further improved and the time is also significantly increased. Secondly, compare the impact of attention mechanism and morphological algorithm on the accuracy and time of DeepLabv3+ model extraction of the Mobilenetv3 backbone extraction network. Similar to Mobilenetv2, with the addition of attention mechanism and morphological algorithm, the accuracy and time are significantly increased. The comparison results of ablation experiments are shown in Table 1.

Table 1. Ablation experiment

Mobilenetv2(0) or Mobilenetv3(1)	SE	Morphological algorithm	Accuracy (%)	Time (s)
0	–	–	92.17%	84 s
1	–	–	93.51%	76 s
0	✓	–	93.91%	87 s
1	✓	–	96.77%	79 s
0	✓	✓	96.35%	102 s
1	✓	✓	97.69%	93 s

The ablation experiment results show that the accuracy of the improved DeepLabv3+ model is higher than that of the model using Mobilenetv2 backbone to extract the network, and the running time is significantly reduced. Secondly, attention mechanism and morphological algorithm have obvious effects on improving the extraction accuracy, but the running time also increases accordingly. To sum up, the railway track extraction accuracy of DeepLabv3+ model of the Mobilenetv3 backbone extraction network in this paper has been improved, and the morphological algorithm also has a good effect on the optimization of the extraction results.

4.2 Visual Analysis of Loss Function

In order to further verify the performance of the railway track extraction method in this paper, the convergence process of different model training loss functions is visualized on the railway dataset. The loss function is an algorithm to measure the difference between the predicted value and the true value of the model. The change of the loss value represents the improvement of the prediction accuracy of the model. When the loss function finally converges to a certain value and does not change, it represents that the model training result is optimal. Therefore, the convergence speed and minimum value of the same loss function of different semantic segmentation models represent the advantages and disadvantages of the model performance. In order to ensure no other interference conditions, different models used in the loss function visualization experiment in this paper all use the same loss function, and the number of training iterations is 100. The network used for comparison is the U-net and DeepLabv3+ model of two commonly used backbone networks. The change of loss function during training is shown in Fig. 6. The loss iteration curve of u-net network fluctuates greatly, and the training loss continues to decline. After the verification, the loss decreases slightly, and converges to the minimum loss value about the 60th iteration. The DeepLabv3+ model loss value curve of Mobilenetv2 trunk and Xception trunk fluctuates in a small range and converges to the minimum loss value in 50 to 60 iterations. The convergence curve of the loss function of the model in this paper is relatively smooth, the training loss and verification loss converge rapidly, and converge to the minimum loss value about the 40th iteration.

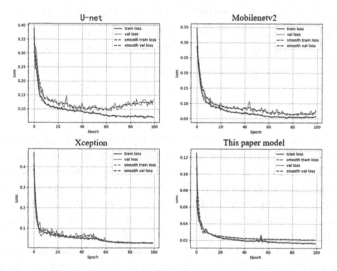

Fig. 6. Comparison of loss function convergence

The visual curve of loss function shows that the loss value of this model converges faster, the loss curve is smoother, and the loss convergence value is smaller, so the railway track extraction model proposed in this paper has better performance.

4.3 Analysis of Model Comparison Experiment

In order to compare the accuracy of this algorithm with other algorithms as a whole. Based on the railway data set, the model in this paper and the U-Net semantic segmentation network in literature [13], L-UNet network of literature [14], DeepLabv3 model of

ResNet backbone network in reference [15], and literature [16] Comparison of evaluation indicators and running time of DeepLabv3+ network using Mobilenetv2 backbone network. The comparison results are shown in Table 2. It can be seen that the prediction accuracy of U-net network and DeepLabv3+ network using Mobilenetv2 backbone network is not very different, and the accuracy of DeepLabv3+ has been slightly improved. However, the prediction duration of DeepLabv3+ is lower than that of U-net network, which indicates that the use of DeepLabv3+ model of lightweight backbone network can greatly reduce the network size and hours without reducing the accuracy. In this paper, Mobilenetv3 backbone network is used. Before morphological processing, compared with Mobilenetv2, the accuracy is improved to some extent, and the running time is reduced by about 5%. According to the above analysis, this method can improve the accuracy of a certain degree, and can also significantly reduce the running time.

Table 2. Comparison of different models

Model	IoU	MIoU	CPA	MPA	Accuracy	Time
Literature [13]	63.41%	86.16%	74.94%	93.85%	94.72%	96 s
Literature [14]	65.22%	87.60%	75.71%	94.41%	96.11%	87 s
Literature [15]	64.87%	86.68%	75.53%	94.07%	95.34%	91 s
Literature [16]	64.15%	86.35%	75.40%	93.90%	94.96%	84 s
This paper model	66.21%	88.93%	76.33%	95.51%	97.69%	79 s

The railway track area extracted by improving DeepLabv3+ model still has some holes, bulges and spots. This is because the semantic segmentation is a pixel level model. In the non railway area of the original image, there may be similar or identical pixels, which will lead to segmentation errors. The semantic segmentation results can be further optimized by using morphological corrosion and expansion. The open operation of morphological corrosion and expansion (first corrosion and then expansion) can remove spots and bulges, and the closed operation of morphological corrosion and expansion (first expansion and then corrosion) can eliminate holes in the railway area without changing the overall shape. The processing effect of morphological erosion and dilation on the results needs to adjust the size of the morphological algorithm core to achieve the optimization. After the railway area is processed, the complete railway track area is obtained. Table 3 shows the comparison between the results of morphological algorithm and those of other models.

Table 3. Visual comparison

5   Conclusion

The deep learning method can greatly reduce human resources and material consumption. Semantic segmentation is a pixel level task, which can identify and segment railway areas. However, most of the semantic segmentation models have large network scale, long training time and prediction time, and relatively low efficiency; Secondly, the railway aerial image is affected by the environment. Regional differences and weather changes will affect the resolution of the original aerial image, resulting in some errors in the image segmented by the model. This paper uses the lightweight network Mobilenetv3 as the DeepLabv3+ model of the backbone network. While ensuring the segmentation accuracy, it reduces the size of the semantic segmentation network and improves the model efficiency. Compared with the U-Net network and the DeepLabv3+ network using Mobilenetv2, the model consumption time is significantly reduced and the accuracy is slightly improved. Secondly, for the problem of error in the extraction results, this paper uses morphological algorithms to optimize the results. The combination of morphological erosion and dilation algorithm can effectively eliminate holes and spots.

This method reduces the operation time of the model to a certain extent, but it also requires morphological optimization of the extraction results separately, which increases a small part of the workload. In the future, we need to continue to optimize the model to further reduce the time cost and ensure faster and more complete railway track.

References

1. Gao, H.: Research on automatic road extraction from high-resolution remote sensing images based on deep learning. University of Chinese Academy of Sciences (Xi'an Institute of Optics and Precision Machinery, Chinese Academy of Sciences) (2020)
2. Barzohar, M., Cooper, D.B.: Automatic finding of main roads in aerial images by using geometric-stochastic models and estimation. IEEE Trans. Pattern Anal. Mach. Intell. **18**(7), 707–721 (1996)
3. Ghaziani, M., Mohamadi, Y., Koku, A.B., et al.: Extraction of unstructured roads from satellite images using binary image segmentation. In: Signal Processing and Communications Applications Conference (SIU), 2013 21st. IEEE (2013)
4. Chen, X.: Research on deep learning algorithm and application based on convolutional neural network. Zhejiang Business University (2014)
5. Mnih, V., Hinton, G.E.: Learning to Detect Roads in High-Resolution Aerial Images. Springer, Berlin, Heidelberg (2010)
6. Yang, J., Guo, X., Chen, Z.: Improved road extraction from remote sensing images based on U-Net network. Chinese J. Image Graph. **26**(12), 3005–3014 (2021)
7. Song, T., Liu, T., Zong, D., Jiang, X., Huang, T., Fan, H.: Research on road extraction from remote sensing images by improving U-Net network. Comput. Eng. Appl. **57**(14), 209–216 (2021)
8. Buslaev, A.V., Seferbekov, S.S., Iglovikov, V.I., et al.: Fully convolutional network for automatic road extraction from satellite imagery. In: 2018 IEEE/CVF Conference on Computer Vision and Pattern Recognition Workshops (CVPRW). IEEE (2018)
9. Howard, A., Sandler, M., Chu, G., et al.: Searching for MobileNetV3 (2019)
10. Sandler, M., Howard, A., Zhu, M., et al.: Mobilenetv2: inverted residuals and linear bottlenecks. In: Proceedings of the IEEE Conference on Computer Vision and Pattern Recognition, pp. 4510–4520 (2018)
11. Chollet, F.: Xception: deep learning with depthwise separable convolutions. In: Proceedings of the IEEE Conference on Computer Vision and Pattern Recognition, pp. 1251–1258 (2017)
12. Hu, J., Shen, L., Sun, G.: Squeeze-and-excitation networks. In: Proceedings of the IEEE Conference on Computer Vision and Pattern Recognition, pp. 7132–7141 (2018)
13. Ning, Y., Sheng, J.: Research and discussion on road extraction using deep learning network U-Net. J. Eng. Heilongjiang Univ. **11**(4), 1–8 (2020)
14. Miao, X., Li, Y., Zhong, J., Zuo, Z., Xiong, W.: L-UNEt: light cloud occlusion road extraction network. Chin. J. Image Graph. **26**(11), 2670–2679 (2021)
15. Han, L., Yang, C., Li, L., Liu, Z., Huang, B.: Use Deeplabv3 to extract roads from high-resolution remote sensing images. Remote Sens. Inform. **36**(01), 22–28 (2021)
16. Ren, Y., Ge, X.: An road synthesis extraction method of remote sensing image based on improved DeepLabV3+ network. Bull. Surv. Map. **6**, 55–61 (2022)
17. Stefanie, L., Tahia, D., Jerome, R.M., Valentina, R., Nicholas, C.C., Verena C.G.: Mapping trees along urban street networks with deep learning and street-level imagery. ISPRS J. Photogram. Remote Sens. **175** (2021)

18. Lin, J., Wei, Y., Li, W., Long, J.: Intrusion detection system based on deep neural network and incremental learning for in-vehicle CAN networks. In: Wang, G., Choo, KK.R., Ko, R.K.L., Xu, Y., Crispo, B. (eds.) Ubiquitous Security. UbiSec 2021. CCIS, vol. 1557. Springer, Singapore (2022). https://doi.org/10.1007/978-981-19-0468-4_19
19. Liu, M., Zheng, H., Liu, Q., Xing, X., Dai, Y.: A backdoor embedding method for backdoor detection in deep neural networks. In: Wang, G., Choo, KK.R., Ko, R.K.L., Xu, Y., Crispo, B. (eds.) Ubiquitous Security. UbiSec 2021. CCIS, vol. 1557. Springer, Singapore (2022). https://doi.org/10.1007/978-981-19-0468-4_1
20. Tang, Y., Zhang, D., Liang, W., Li, K.C., Sukhija, N.: Active malicious accounts detection with multimodal fusion machine learning algorithm. In: Wang, G., Choo, KK.R., Ko, R.K.L., Xu, Y., Crispo, B. (eds.) Ubiquitous Security. UbiSec 2021. CCIS, vol. 1557. Springer, Singapore (2022). https://doi.org/10.1007/978-981-19-0468-4_4
21. Dong, S., Wang, P., Khushnood, A.: A survey on deep learning and its applications. Comput. Sci. Rev. **40** (2021)

Analysis of Techniques for Detection
and Removal of Zero-Day Attacks (ZDA)

Khalid Hamid[1], Muhammad Waseem Iqbal[1], Muhammad Aqeel[2],
Xiangyong Liu[3]([✉]), and Muhammad Arif[2]

[1] Department of Software Engineering, The Superior University, Lahore 54000, Pakistan
[2] Department of Computer Science, The Superior University, Lahore 54000, Pakistan
[3] School of Computer Science and Cyber Engineering, Guangzhou University,
Guangzhou 510006, China
xiangyongliu@gzhu.edu.cn

Abstract. Zero-day attacks (ZDAs) are previously unknown flaws and errors in operating systems, networks, and general-purpose software. ZDAs are the cause to open security breach holes for external users or hackers for illegal operations before patches. ZDAs are different from viruses, worms and Trojans. They are very difficult to detect and remove because they are unknown to users and even programmers. Conventional defense systems are useless against such types of attacks. This paper investigates the zero-day attacks, their vulnerabilities, the intensity of these attacks and the reasons in a real-time environment. Different techniques are compared to investigate ZDAs. The hybrid technique has been used to check the behavior of data traffic coming from outside the world in the virtual environment for zero-day attacks. Static check tools (MD5 Checksum, AV-Suite, and SOPHOS) and behavioral check tools (SANDBOX) have been used for the verification and validation of results. The second comparatively best technique is Machine Learning-Based Technique which showed the best results. The results show how to choose the best solution against zero-day attacks in the real-time environment of the software.

Keywords: Behavioral tool · Flaws · Hybrid · SANDBOX · Zero-day attacks

1 Introduction

Zero-day attacks are previously unknown flaws and errors in operating systems, networks and general software that leave holes for external users or hackers for illegal operations before patches have been issued [1]. Cybercriminals have found more than eighty-five vulnerabilities in different software like Microsoft, Adobe, Oracle and Apple products but these remain unknown to the public. The software's continuously growing in size and complexity so as a result, unknown flaws allow attackers to gain illegal access and even full control over the systems.

Some software developers and distribution companies know about the errors but are bound due unavailability of solutions. Users even have big defense systems but yet they faced attacks. Patching and updating virus definitions for antivirus software will not stop them. 40% zero-day exploits occurred in 2021 as compared to the last ten years. According to the Google Report, large numbers of vulnerabilities are discovered in 2021 up to 58 more than double of the year 2020 which discloses 25 approximately. Even multiple layered defense systems are not enough to avoid zero-day attacks. In Zero-Day attacks the traditional defenses are powerless. These attacks can convert themselves into polymorphic viruses, worms, Trojans and other malware. The most dangerous attacks which are not prevented by most security systems are polymorphic worms that show different behavior every time like defense avoidance by complex mutation, multiple vulnerabilities scanners for identifying the prospective target, and targeted exploitation. Remote shells that open arbitrary ports and malware drop to download the malicious code from an outside source to continue the propagation are Zero-Day vulnerabilities [1].

1.1 Zero-Day Attacks Process

We can break the process of Zero-Day attacks into different steps. Firstly, A developer or developers develop software having unknown vulnerabilities. Secondly, A Threat Actor points out one or more vulnerabilities before the developer knows them or fixes them. Thirdly, the Attacker writes and applies the exploit code to open the vulnerability. At last, Users recognize it as information theft, or developers are aware of it and fix it by introducing patches.

When developers write patches and apply them then this exploit is not called a Zero-Day Exploit. In any case, users even have big defense systems are still open to attack. All software approximately has the chance for unknown vulnerabilities, these errors specifically frightened when known by some attackers who are used for cyber-attacks instantly are may be at some other time. According to the Security Report 2012, no defense system can avoid zero-day attacks. Till the vulnerabilities have remained and software developers cannot be developed a solution to detect them and removed these vulnerabilities by using any type of technique. In 2020, Microsoft detects vulnerabilities RCE and CVE-2020-0674 and warned attackers.

All advanced cyber-attacks are made possible due to modern malware. The modern threats are vibrant, silent, and continual leaving unknown threats for future disruption. These attacks are polymorphic and also customizable. The special characteristics of these modern exploits change for different attackers accordingly. These modern exploits are used for the following destructions:

- Cyber Crimes
- Cyber Warfare Scenarios
- Cyber Espionages

The best example of modern malware is the targeted Trojan. Modern malware in the form of a targeted Trojan is a very dangerous threat to any enterprise. These are carefully shaped attacks by skilled hackers that take advantage of a previously unknown vulnerability in the user's web or email environment and compromise the entire system. Once the attack is engaged, malware gets installed in the system, and depending on the user environment, can install other components to maximize the malware presence. The malware can be customized with additional downloads to spy on user activity, steal information, generate spam, and become part of a network of bots that perform activities directed by the attacker.

One of the most public examples of a targeted Trojan is "Operation Aurora," an attack on Google and other companies. Attackers used Zero-Day exploits for Internet Explorer which installs emails targeted malware for data-stealing on host machines. So these dangerous attacks spread dangerous links to many email accounts with just user clicks [2].

1.2 Conventional Security

Modern crime ware has insistently advanced in sophistication, technology, and scale, rendering traditional security technologies largely obsolete. While crimeware has been on an exponential growth curve, traditional security has remained architecturally stagnant. Pattern-matching signatures and rate-based heuristics are still common core features of most security methodologies. This has created a false sense of security and a significant gap in the ability of enterprises to defend against new cyber criminals. There are few current deterrents to file-based malware; AV-file scanners are available but their deployment comes with performance and stability impacts on files and shares [3, 26].

The current email security solutions focus mostly on "email hygiene" to protect the user against the storm of spam and known viruses. They use signature-based antivirus (AV) detection technologies to detect viruses, as well as reputation-based and content-based technologies to stop spam [27, 28]. However, these technologies are no match for the sophistication of attacks carried out by cyber criminals who use zero-day threats combined with sophisticated malware and the latest social engineering to stay ahead of the AV signature databases. Solutions should be far away from old and conventional security parameters and give distinct solutions to detect and remove today's complex threats. The study broadly works and classifies the defense techniques for zero-day attacks. The prime goal of every technique is to detect the exploit in a real-time environment and removed or quarantine the attack to avoid damage. The second most important challenge is to make sure that either victim's machine is not the threshold to delay for analysis or quarantine is not exceeded. There is some conventional security and protection approaches are shown in Fig. 1 below.

Fig. 1. Conventional protection techniques

2 Literature Review

Zero-Day exploits affect all organizations. Before the vulnerabilities are made public and resolve the problem, exploits circulate throughout the organizations and made them unprotected.

"ZeroWall: Detecting Zero-Day Web Attacks through Encoder-Decoder Recurrent Neural Networks" In this paper the study talks about the severe nature of zero-day attacks on web security which makes them challenging for existing signature-based firewalls because Zero-day attacks are unknown nature to users and IT experts [4]. This paper proposes an unsupervised and effective pipeline-based firewall called ZeroWall for the detection of previously unknown web attacks. This system catches the syntax and semantic patterns of benign requests through Encoder-Decoder Recurrent Neural Network for the training of a self-translation machine. Most of the benign requests proceeding by zero-day attacks are not detected by signature-based firewalls but are detected by self-translation machines well in real time. The study evaluated 8 real-world traces of 1.4 billion requests on the web and detected all zero attacks which are not detected by existing firewalls. The request processing involves four steps which are as under, firstly convert each request into the token sequence, secondly, the neural network reconstructs the token sequence, thirdly compare the score of both with a threshold value and last apply manual investigation. The results show outclass performance with best F1 scores over 0.98 which is above all baseline approaches. This paper introduces an enhanced system of existing firewalls by endorsing unsupervised and machine learning-based approaches for the detection of zero-day attacks. So, this approach with a neural network-based translation machine is highly authentic to implement in the real world immediately due to the achievement of a high F1-score over-0.98 [5].

"Efficient hybrid technique for detecting zero-day polymorphic worms" In this paper, the study told that Hybrid-based techniques are problem-solving techniques that combine various previously discussed techniques like Statistical-based techniques, Signature-based techniques, and Behavior-based techniques. This technique overcome all disadvantages of previously used techniques and adds up all the advantages of these techniques. Some of the benefits of hybrid-based techniques are as follows: This technique identifies zero-day attacks from data collected automatically on high-interaction honeypots. This technique overcome all disadvantages of previously used techniques and adds up all the advantages of these techniques. This technique does not need prior knowledge of zero-day attacks and uses Honeynet as an anomaly detector. This technique can detect zero-day attacks in their early phase and can contain the attack before major penalties occur. Hybrid-based techniques need hours against zero-day attacks and also polymorphic zero-day attacks which are very dangerous attacks due to their unknown nature and behavior-changing nature over the network or server or any other network device. Even though these types of attacks disabled your internet or cause any other potential disturbance. This technique is not only effective for zero-day attacks but also very much effective for polymorphic unknown vulnerabilities. On the other hand, this technique is also effective and valuable for known attacks and viruses over the network and servers [6, 25, 28].

"Supporting automated vulnerability analysis using formalized vulnerability signatures," The study told that Antivirus or virus software vendors having libraries of various malware signatures and virus definitions which are compiled for different malware detection are used these signature-based techniques. In this technique, all files like files of networks, files of computers, web pages, and emails are matched with these virus definitions according to predefined rules by the user. If the signature matches its means exploit and blocked otherwise continue to work. These virus definitions are updated regularly for new vulnerabilities of new attacks. There is a cost overhead in this approach to update virus definitions. Signature-based techniques are classified into Content-based Signature Techniques, Semantic-based Signature Techniques, and Vulnerabilities-based Signature Techniques. These are also effective against polymorphic worms to some extent. The first type of signature-based technique mentioned above is content-based. Content-based signature technique makes a comparison of data packets with malware signatures. Content-based signatures are categorized into Image attributes and contents which are used to input into Digital Signature Algorithm. Content signature-based techniques collect specific characteristics of different worms and used them for attack avoidance. The third type of signature mentioned above is vulnerability-based. A vulnerability-based signature has to identify the "vulnerability condition and identify the vulnerability point reachability predicate" So, the combination of all these signature-based techniques provides the best solution for known attacks but not against unknown attacks [3].

"Utilising Deep Learning Techniques for Effective Zero-Day Attack Detection" In this paper the study built a model of an Intrusion Detection System with the help of the Machine Learning Approach and Deep Learning Approach. Present Intrusion Detection Systems used signatures of historical attacks for the detection of a large number of different cyber-attacks and it's a big challenge for them. These systems are unable to detect a zero attack type like outlier-based zero-day attacks. So, these IDS are limited in the context of performance and practical uses. On the other hand, there are tremendous increases in different types of cyber-attacks which are reported by different solution provider companies. The study proposed a system for the detection of zero-day attacks called auto encoder implementer to minimize the false rate of detecting zero-day attacks. For establishing the best model, they used two well-known datasets to evaluate NSL-KDD and CICIDS2017 and also compare the results with the Support Vector Machine of Class One to check the performance of their model. Auto Encoder's abilities of encoding and decoding play a vital role to make their model very much impressive in the field of detection of complex zero-day attacks. The accuracy of detection of zero-day attacks with two datasets is given below NSL-KDD 89 to 99% and CICIDS2017 75 to 98%. These results show the best system for the detection of complex zero-day attacks. The proposed system avoided all back draws of previously used systems for the detection of zero-day attacks and provided the best solution according to results accuracy ranging from 75 to 99% as an unsupervised technique [7].

"A Hybrid Real-time Zero-day Attack Detection and Analysis System" Zero-Day exploits affect all organizations. Before the vulnerabilities are made public and resolved the problem, exploits circulate throughout the organizations and made them unprotected. In history, all the work is done based on one of the following methods. Statistical-based techniques are used previously known public vulnerabilities for finding the Zero-Day attacks. The technique uses old parameters for the detection of new attacks with help of a history profile. This technique detects zero-day exploits based on pre-set patterns and sees what is new happened and generates a signal for detecting and blocking the attack. The system should be online which is used in this approach. Present techniques in this approach carry out dynamic analysis or static analysis depending on the payloads of packets and detect only attacks having unchangeable characteristics. In the Signature-based technique, all files like files of networks, files of computers, web pages and emails are matched with these virus definitions and libraries of various malware signatures according to predefined rules by the user. Hybrid-based techniques are problem-solving techniques that combine various previously discussed techniques like Statistical-based techniques, Signature-based techniques, and Behavior-based techniques. This technique overcome all disadvantages of previously used techniques and adds up all the advantages of these techniques [8].

In "A Review on Zero-Day Attack Safety Using Different Scenarios," Harshpal R Gosavi & Anant M Bagade told that Software development companies leave some flaws in software, sometimes known to the developer but sometimes not. These flaws are used by some people to attack systems that are using the above software. When these flaws are not known to developers then no patch is available and if known to developers then no patch is available for a few months. So, Zero-Day attacks are carried out but if the administrator of the system knows about these there are possibilities to do something by changing configurations. There are more than five thousand vulnerabilities are occurred in networks per day. The proposed complete novel scenario counted these vulnerabilities efficiently. They also said that we can use the following security methods (like Encryption of different types, User ID, Firewall, Authentication & Physical Security too) to avoid such vulnerabilities. Our present systems know about known vulnerabilities but don't know about unknown flaws. They said that zero-day attacks are easily defended by using this approach of changing configurations. In this paper, they propose the method of counting thousands of vulnerabilities and then modeled a defense against these attacks. They explain future work by ranking zero-day attacks and developing various technologies for these attacks. There are also some unhandled situations and inputs which are not managed well. According to the modern scenario,s the hybrid-based system or approach should be used in the virtual environment or a hybrid system must use a machine learning environment to overcome the loopholes through which systems encounter zero-day attacks [9, 10].

"Foundations and applications of artificial Intelligence for zero-day and multi-step attack detection (2018)" In this paper researchers focus on two types of attacks which are severe. These are Zero-Day attacks and Multi-step attacks. Former are the attacks that are unknown to the user of the computer world and the second have consisted of many separate steps which are working and behave like individual codes. These multi-step attacks may create benign situations or may be malicious most of the time [1]. The solution for this scenario is possible by adopting a hybrid approach. The study used two techniques from the field of AI which are Statistical Based Analysis and Machine Learning based Analysis against complex attacks in the world of cyber-attacks. In Statistical based analysis they performed rule-based analysis and outlier detection-based analysis. On the other hand, in Machine Learning based analysis they used Behavioral anomalies detector and Event Sequence tracker. This hybrid approach from the field of Artificial

Intelligence protects unauthorized access of data on the network, integrity constraints and availability of data to only authorized and well-authenticated users [11].

3 Research Methodology

The study creates awareness about malware and unknown flaws in the wide range of software. Describe how zero-day attacks are different from viruses, worms and Trojan attacks. Comparing traditional and new techniques against zero-day attacks which are very difficult to detect and removed because these are unknown to users and even programmers of the software. Discover new and significant solutions for zero-day attacks through this review because no adequate solution has been found till now due to the incremental and unknown nature of these flaws and attacks [12].

Table 1. Techniques used for detection & removal of ZDA

Sr. no.	Techniques for detection and removal of zero-day attacks
1	Signature Based Technique
2	Anomaly Based System
3	Behavior-Based technique
4	Hybrid Based Technique
5	Machine Learning-Based Technique
6	Artificial Intelligence-Based Technique
7	Neural Networks-Based Technique
8	Intrusion Detection-Based Technique
9	Deep Learning-Based Technique
10	IoT Based Technique
11	Forensic Technique
12	Network Empirical Analysis
13	Scenario Based Technique

Table 1 shows the different techniques used for the detection of zero-day attacks previously

4 Results and Discussion

According to the cyber security report, 2020 vulnerabilities in different years are given below in Table.

Table 2. Years wise vulnerabilities

Year wise vulnerabilities			
Sr. No.	Year	%age	Remarks
1	2022	25%	Very high
2	2021	4%	Medium
3	2020	2%	Medium
4	2019	2%	Medium
5	2018	14%	High
6	2017	20%	Very high
7	2016	21%	Very high
8	2015	13%	High
9	2014	16%	High
10	2013	4%	Medium
11	2012	3%	Medium
12	2011	1%	Low

Table 2 shows percentages of vulnerabilities occurs in different years from 2011 to 2022 with their severity.

There are four major vulnerabilities of the year 2019 are shown in Fig. 2.

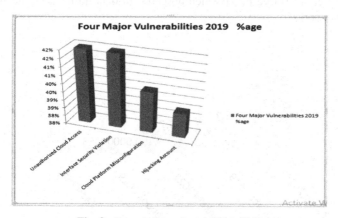

Fig. 2. Four major vulnerabilities 2019

These major vulnerabilities of the year 2020 are shown in Fig. 3 [13].

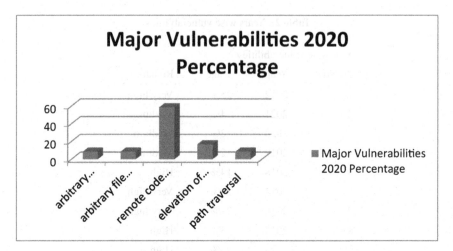

Fig. 3. Major vulnerabilities 2020

Top trends in zero-day attacks in context with the number of users affected up to 2021 [14]. MyDoom is a most dangerous virus/worm which damaged 38.5 billion dollars. It is opened the backdoor to allow the computer to access remotely and is also favorable for DDOS attacks. There are very less chances to detect it. The study reviews the literature for the purpose that how these attacks can be detected and resolved these vulnerabilities? Detection of zero-day attacks consists of two parts mean detection of Zero-Day attacks and prevention of Zero-Day attacks. They use some components of the system which first are Suspicious Traffic Filter which observes all data traffic from the edge of the internet or networks.

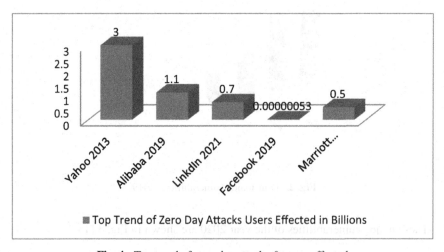

Fig. 4. Top trend of zero-day attacks & users affected

Figure 4 shows the top affected applications and their users with zero attacks in the last ten years. Then this traffic passes the same time to two components like Intrusion Detection/Prevention System and Honeynet by using Port Mirroring Switch. Another component Zero-Day Evaluation takes data traffic from STF and does the evaluation and detects Zero-Day attacks. After that Signature Generator component generates a signature that updates the STF database.

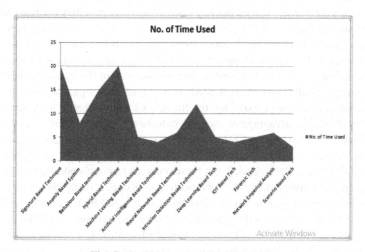

Fig. 5. Techniques used for ZDA [16].

Figure 5 shows the usage frequency of the different techniques used for the detection and removal of zero-day attacks. The study considers the following hypothesis for the defense against zero-day attacks Users and vendors need to understand the complexity and intensity of zero-day attacks in software, Comparison between different techniques against zero-day attacks gives better understanding and solution, and Analysis provides the strength to multi-layered defense security schemes to prevent a zero-day attack, Zero-Day attacks can convert itself into polymorphic viruses, worms, Trojans and other malware, and Virtualization-based solution provides solution against zero-day attacks. The virtualization technique is being used to check the behavior of data traffic coming from the outside world into computers for zero-day attacks [15]. Table and Fig. 5 show the number of time techniques used.

4.1 Analysis

From the above table and conversation we see that Signature-based frameworks are incredibly compelling against assault types that have been recognized before yet, they can't identify zero-day attacks [17]. They can be introduced rapidly and become taking effect right now. These frameworks analyze every approaching packet and look at its substance against a rundown of known assault instruments. At the point when we utilized just Whitelisting, It is successful against malware and spam. For most clients, an unadulterated whitelisting arrangement doesn't function admirably for email sifting since we frequently get mail from individuals we don't realize that is, in any case, authentic and attractive mail. It unquestionably isn't viable for sales reps who get requests from out-siders, essayists who get mail from perusers, or other finance managers who consistently get mail from likely clients. It might turn out great for the individual email records of people who just need to compare with a set gathering of loved ones. Impediments of these signature engines are that they just distinguish assaults whose signatures are recently put away in the data set; a signature should be made for each assault, and novel assaults can't be identified. This strategy can be handily hoodwinked because they are just founded on customary articulations and string coordinating. These systems just search for strings inside packets sent over the wire. More signatures function admirably against just the fixed personal conduct standard, they neglect to manage assaults made by a human or a worm with self-altering social attributes. The productivity of the signature-based frame-works is incredibly diminished, as it needs to make another signature for each variety. As the signatures continue expanding, the framework motor execution diminishes.

The significant disadvantage of anomaly detection is characterizing its standard set. The proficiency of the framework relies upon how well it is carried out and tried on all pro-tocols. The rule-characterizing measure is additionally influenced by different protocols utilized by different sellers. Aside from these, custom protocols additionally make rule characterizing a troublesome work. For detection to occur correctly, detailed knowledge about the accepted network behavior needs to be developed by the administrators.

The detriment to intrusion detection frameworks and intrusion counteraction frame-works is that they don't have a known standard of legitimate movement on which to reach inferences. They can just draw from a measurable example of what run-of-the-mill network traffic resembles. On a live endeavor network, there might be upwards of 50 million packets of HTTP traffic. These frameworks need to expect to be that if there is an expansion of traffic over some sort of edge that is normal or legitimate, at that point there is an assault in progress. Note that this framework doesn't allude to nectar pots at all and doesn't exploit distinguishing or halting zero-day assaults.

At the first level, the model used Signature-based detection, for known worm attacks, which makes the system operate in real time. Any deviation from normal behavior can be easily detected by the anomaly detector in the second level. The last level is honeypots which help in detecting zero-day attacks in a machine-learning environment [4]. This is a so-called hybrid technique of signature-based technique, anomaly-based technique and behavior-based technique in a machine learning-based environment which is the best solution for the detection and removal of zero-day attacks without compromising the security and avoidance of delay [18].

4.2 Discussion

Rules of Thumb to Avoid Zero-Day Attacks. This discussion is basically for the avoidance of zero-day attacks.

1. Divide your networks into different segments, assign limited access between these segments according to risk profiles, limited access from the Internet to Demil-itarized Zone, Demilitarized Zone to Internal networks and furthermore. Apply

preventive measures by denying access from one module to the other module without permission and need. There is no need to access the developing group system module from the accounts unit. This step can avoid attackers' access to the system due to unknown vulnerabilities.

2. Assign limited privileges on the network. All users and units should access only the required data and resources to perform their functions to limit the attack area to prevent attacks. Just because most of the attackers need high privileges to attack. Hence, reduces the risk because most of the attackers grant control from one module to another module automatically for performing destruction.

3. When administrators use a whitelisting of software in which he/she can install only permitted software, can avoid unlawful files to run on the server System. These unlawful files may include different malware payloads and exploits.

4. The administrators must have a Quick Response Plan at that place Have a Quick response (QRP) plan in place because most admins cannot guess or forecast Zero-Day attacks. In that situation, a flexible Quick Response Plan is required which is very essential at this critical time.

5. Administrators and Company members should know their environment. Security team members are not able to reduce the patch fewer flaws from the application until they have complete knowledge of the network and software to minimize or finish the problem

6. A company should patch its system with the latest patches. No doubt these latest patches are not able to completely save the system from Zero-Day attacks but some known vulnerabilities are also proved dangerous for systems. Because some systems are lack patches and available for Zero-Day attacks.

7. Every company should use the latest operating system because they have included the latest techniques to reduce the risk and sometimes avoid Zero-Day attacks but are not fully equipped to protect the system against Zero-Day vulnerabilities. An operating system should support the DEP and ASLR to minimize the risk to some extent.

8. Coordination and collaboration should be increased and faster between members of the Security Company and between security companies to overcome the latest Zero-Day attacks by communicating with them. Security companies should be intelligent enough in their field to minimize the risk.

9. Security Companies should deploy such security systems which equally successful against known threats and Zero-Day means unknown threats. Because most of the companies use signature-based techniques which are only successful against known threats only not against Zero-Day attacks. Security companies should use some behavior-based or other techniques to protect against Zero-Day attacks [19].

10. We should use advanced intelligent techniques in the system to get rid of new dangerous threats by using advanced and latest technologies [20–24].

11. Companies should use industry experts and their experiences to resolve the worst attacks. They should also enhance the capabilities of their security teams.

5 Conclusion

It is a very hot issue in today's world to secure systems from Zero-Day attacks. In this paper, we discuss and analyze different techniques like Signature-based techniques,

Statistical-based techniques, anomaly-based techniques, behavioral-based techniques, hybrid techniques and hybrid techniques in a virtual environment by using multiple tools at each level. We have also discussed and analyzed problems with existing techniques regarding Zero-Day attacks and tried to provide the best but not perfect solution to the Zero-Day, polymorphic and other known malware-related problems. In this combined approach, the different levels have been involved we used signature-based techniques at the first level, if any anomaly remains then we used anomaly-based techniques at the second level, and if any more anomaly remains then we used behavioral-based techniques at the third level and all these were done in a virtual environment which is the next level because operating system level safeguards are effective against known attacks but not against Zero-Day attacks. Our analysis of real-time malware samples shows that Web MD successfully detects malware in a virtual environment. Our results showed that a Hybrid of all techniques in a virtual environment is more appropriate in the modern world of a dynamic Zero-Day vulnerable environment. The second comparatively best technique is Machine Learning-Based Technique which showed the best results. In the future, it is recommended that research and development should be on machine learning-based malware detection tools for real-time malware detection. Research and development should be on Microvisor/sandbox-based framework for Malware Detection. Malware Detection Emulators design, and development instrumentation using open source tools for example Light Spark, and Spider Monkey for Java Script, etc.

6 Proposed Model

In light of the analysis and conclusion, we proposed a new model which adds up the advantages of the above techniques and overcomes the flaws in the techniques which are previously used. We proposed a model which used hybrid techniques in the machine learning environment (Fig. 6).

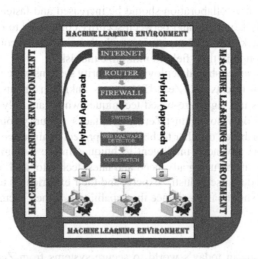

Fig. 6. Proposed model for detecting and removing ZDAs

In this proposed model known attacks are detected by signature-based techniques if an anomaly remains that will be detected by anomaly-based techniques, unknown attacks will be detected by behavioral-based techniques virtual under a machine learning environment. In future work, working of the proposed model elaborated and deployment of the model will be carried out.

References

1. Parrend, P., Navarro, J., Guigou, F., Deruyver, A., Collet, P.: Foundations and applications of artificial Intelligence for zero-day and multi-step attack detection. EURASIP J. Inf. Secur. **2018**(1), 1–21 (2018). https://doi.org/10.1186/s13635-018-0074-y
2. Venkatesan, R., Kumar, G.A., Nandhan, M.R.: A novel approach to detect ddos attack through virtual honeypot. In: 2018 IEEE International Conference on System, Computation, Automation and Networking (ICSCA), pp. 1–6 (2018)
3. Hindy, H., Atkinson, R., Tachtatzis, C., Colin, J.-N., Bayne, E., Bellekens, X.: Utilising deep learning techniques for effective zero-day attack detection. Electronics **9**, 1684 (2020)
4. Tang, R., et al.: Zerowall: detecting zero-day web attacks through encoder-decoder recurrent neural networks. In: IEEE INFOCOM 2020-IEEE Conference on Computer Communications, pp. 2479–2488. IEEE (2020)
5. Sharma, V., et al.: A consensus framework for reliability and mitigation of zero-day attacks in IoT. Secur. Commun. Netw. **2017**, 1–24 (2017)
6. Kaur, R., Singh, M.: Efficient hybrid technique for detecting zero-day polymorphic worms. In: 2014 IEEE International Advance Computing Conference (IACC), pp. 95–100 (2014)
7. Kuhn, S., Taylor, S.: Locating zero-day exploits with coarse-grained forensics. J. Inf. Warf. **14**, 43–59 (2015)
8. Zalivaka, S.S., Zhang, L., Klybik, V.P., Ivaniuk, A.A., Chang, C.-H.: Design and implementation of high-quality physical unclonable functions for hardware-oriented cryptography. In: Chang, C.-H., Potkonjak, M. (eds.) Secure System Design and Trustable Computing, pp. 39–81. Springer, Cham (2016). https://doi.org/10.1007/978-3-319-14971-4_2
9. Bherde, G.P., Pund, M.A.: Protect system using defense techniques of zero day attacks
10. Ardito, L., Coppola, R., Barbato, L., Verga, D.: A Tool-Based Perspective on Software Code Maintainability Metrics: A Systematic Literature Review (2020). https://www.hindawi.com/journals/sp/2020/8840389/
11. Ahmad, J., Baharom, S.: A systematic literature review of the test case prioritization technique for sequence of events. Int. J. Appl. Eng. Res. **12**, 1389–1395 (2017)
12. Al-Tabbaa, O., Ankrah, S., Zahoor, N.: Systematic Literature Review in Management and Business Studies: A Case Study on University–Industry Collaboration (2019)
13. Anand, P., Singh, Y., Selwal, A.: Learning-based techniques for assessing zero-day attacks and vulnerabilities in IoT. In: Singh, P.K., Singh, Y., Kolekar, M.H., Kar, A.K., Gonçalves, P.J.S. (eds.) Recent Innovations in Computing, LNEE, vol. 832, pp. 497–504. Springer, Singapore (2022). . LNEE,volume 832
14. Rajaboyevich, G.S., Rustamovna, S.H., O'g'li, G.A.M.: Characterizing honeypot-captured cyber-attacks: statistical framework and case study. Int. J. Innov. Anal. Emerg. Technol. **2**, 63–67 (2022)
15. Chatzoglou, E., Kambourakis, G., Kolias, C.: How is your Wi-Fi connection today? DoS attacks on WPA3-SAE. J. Inf. Secur. Appl. **64**, 103058 (2022). https://doi.org/10.1016/j.jisa.2021.103058
16. Aoudni, Y., et al.: Cloud security based attack detection using transductive learning integrated with Hidden Markov Model. Pattern Recognit. Lett. **157**, 16–26 (2022). https://doi.org/10.1016/j.patrec.2022.02.012

17. Aslan, Ö.: Using Machine Learning Techniques to Detect Attacks in Computer Networks (2022)

18. Sasaki, T., Fujita, A., Ganan, C., van Eeten, M., Yoshioka, K., Matsumoto, T.: Exposed Infrastructures: Discovery, Attacks and Remediation of Insecure ICS Remote Management Devices. Presented at the 2022 IEEE Symposium on Security and Privacy (SP) January 11 (2022)

19. Hasan, T., et al.: Securing industrial Internet of Things against botnet attacks using hybrid deep learning approach. IEEE Trans. Netw. Sci. Eng. 1 (2022). https://doi.org/10.1109/TNSE.2022.3168533

20. Hamid, K., Iqbal, M.W., Arif, E., Mahmood, Y., Khan, A.S., et al.: K-Banhatti invariants empowered topological investigation of bridge networks. Comput. Mater. Continua 73(3), 5423–5440 (2022)

21. Hamid, K., Iqbal, M.W., Virk, A.U.R., Ashraf, M.U., Alghamdi, A.M., et al.: K-banhatti sombor invariants of certain computer networks. Comput. Mater. Continua 73(1), 15–31 (2022)

22. Hamid, K., Iqbal, M.W., Ashraf, M.U., Gardezi, A.A., Ahmad, S., et al.: Intelligent systems and photovoltaic cells empowered topologically by sudoku networks. Comput. Mater. Continua 74(2), 4221–4238 (2023)

23. Hamid, K., Iqbal, M.W., Ashraf, M.U., Alghamdi, A.M., Bahaddad, A.A., et al.: Optimized evaluation of mobile base station by modern topological invariants. Comput. Mater. Continua 74(1), 363–378 (2023)

24. Alghamdi, A.M., Hamid, K., Iqbal, M.W., Ashraf, M.U., Alshahrani, A., et al.: Topological evaluation of certain computer networks by contraharmonic-quadratic indices. Comput. Mater. Continua 74(2), 3795–3810 (2023)

25. Shakil, M.A., et al.: Towards a two-tier architecture for privacy-enabled recommender systems (PeRS). In: Wang, G., Choo, KK.R., Ko, R.K.L., Xu, Y., Crispo, B. (eds.) Ubiquitous Security. UbiSec 2021. CCIS, vol. 1557. Springer, Singapore (2022). https://doi.org/10.1007/978-981-19-0468-4_20

26. Zou, Y., Peng, T., Zhong, W., Guan, K., Wang, G.: Reliable and controllable data sharing based on blockchain. In: Wang, G., Choo, KK.R., Ko, R.K.L., Xu, Y., Crispo, B. (eds.) Ubiquitous Security. UbiSec 2021. CCIS, vol. 1557. Springer, Singapore (2022). https://doi.org/10.1007/978-981-19-0468-4_17

27. Geman, O., Chiuchisan, I., Ungurean, I., Hagan, M., Arif, M., Ubiquitous healthcare system based on the sensors network and android internet of things gateway. In: 2018 IEEE SmartWorld, Ubiquitous Intelligence & Computing, Advanced & Trusted Computing, Scalable Computing & Communications, Cloud & Big Data Computing, Internet of People and Smart City Innovation (SmartWorld/SCALCOM/UIC/ATC/CBDCom/IOP/SCI), pp. 1390–1395. IEEE (2018)

28. Wang, T., Liang, Y., Mei, Y., Arif, M., Zhu, C.: High-accuracy localization for indoor group users based on extended Kalman filter. Int. J. Distrib. Sens. Netw. 14(11), 1550147718812722 (2018)

Android Malware Detection: A Literature Review

Ahmed Sabbah$^{(\boxtimes)}$, Adel Taweel , and Samer Zein

Department of Computer Science, Birzeit University, Birzeit, Palestine
{asabah,ataweel,szain}@birzeit.edu

Abstract. Mobile applications are increasingly being used to support critical domains such as health, logistics, and banking, to name a few. These mobile apps, hence, became a target for malware attackers. Android is an open-source operating system, which runs apps that can be downloaded from official or third-party app stores. Malware exploits these applications to penetrate mobile devices in different ways for different purposes. To address this, different approaches for malware analysis have been proposed for the detection of malware, ranging from preinstallation to post-installation. This paper presents a literature review of recent malware detection approaches and methods. 21 prominent studies, that report three most common approaches, are identified and reviewed. Challenges, limitations, and research directions are identified and discussed. Findings show most studies focus on malware classification and detection, but lack studies that investigate securing apps and detecting vulnerabilities that malware exploits to stealth into mobile apps and devices. They also show that most studies focused on enhancing machine learning models rather than the malware analysis process.

Keywords: Malware · Malware detection · Malicious software · Mobile malware · Android malware

1 Introduction

Mobile security is gaining significance due to the pervasiveness of smartphones for achieving different critical tasks, such as learning, social media, healthcare, and banking. Apple's iOS and Google's Android have been the dominant mobile device platforms. Recent statistics report that Android has 71.45% of the global mobile OS market share, while iOS has 27.83% [24].

According to Kaspersky security, in quarter one of 2022, mobile malware, adware, and riskware exceeded 6.4 million attacks. Malicious installation packages were more than 500k, among which 53,947 packages were related to mobile banking Trojans, and 1,942 packages were mobile ransomware [23]. With these huge numbers of applications and malware, there is an urgent need to develop robust malware detection approaches using analysis methods that can detect malware in a short time. Security analysis aims to understand the intent and

G. Wang et al. (Eds.): UbiSec 2022, CCIS 1768, pp. 263–278, 2023.
https://doi.org/10.1007/978-981-99-0272-9_18

behaviour of an application. Malware detection methods conduct analysis at three levels including network traffic [10,39], inner interaction-based [7], and permissions-based [4].

Malware analysis approaches can be classified as static, dynamic, and hybrid [2]. Static analysis can detect malware using the APK files without executing the application. While dynamic analysis executes and monitors apps to detect malicious behaviour during run-time. Static analysis has been shown as scalable, has a lower computational cost, and has higher code coverage compared to dynamic analysis [8]. However, static analysis that depends on signature-based methods may fail to detect new malware that has abnormal behaviour [6]. Dynamic analysis has been suggested, by [6], to mitigate the limitation of static analysis, which detects the behaviour of malicious apps during run-time.

The static analysis methods include signature-based [21,28], which focus on generating unique signatures for apps and comparing them with predefined malware signature databases; permission-based [13,17,25], which focus on different permission features, such as activity, service, and intent, that can be used by malware authors; and resource-based [22,37], which focus on apps components. The latter method uses semantic-based analysis or lexical-based, which analyses the data from different sources to extract semantic information [5,43]. Dynamic approaches analyze behaviour of apps in terms of their dynamic properties [9,32,34,39]. Dynamic analysis can be applied at the hardware level, such as monitoring memory, CPU, and battery consumption, and software level, such as analyzing network traffic, application patterns, data flow, privileges, and permissions [2]. Some studies combine both approaches, in order to avoid the weakness of static and dynamic approaches, thus are named hybrid approaches [11,12,19,35,38].

Several surveys have investigated malware detection and analysis. Razgallah et al. [31] surveyed 22 articles, from 2009 to 2020, that focused on static analysis, dynamic, and hybrid malware detection. Alzubaidi [2] surveyed studies, published between 2010 and 2021, that covered feature extraction analysis only. Qiu et al. [29], however, reported on deep learning studies on malware detection. Sk and V [33] reviewed 21 articles that covered, specifically, nine types of Android malware families. Kambar et al. [14] explored studies, from 2015 to 2021, on two malware detection methods: local analysis and network traffic analysis. Authors of [30] and [18] examined malware detection studies that, generally, employed machine learning techniques. Muzaffar et al. [27], on the other hand, reported on studies that are, specifically, based on supervised, unsupervised, deep learning, and online learning for malware detection. To be more inclusive, however, this paper conducts a literature review of the most commonly used analysis methods, as the state-of-the-art, for malware detection, identifying the most prominent studies. The differences between the contribution of this paper and previous literature review studies are shown in Table 1. The main contribution of this paper can be summarised as follows:

- Identification of most commonly used malware detection analysis methods and respective prominent studies. To achieve, we defined a set of criteria that considered the proposed analysis method, the sources of the data that were used to conduct the analysis, outcomes or results, and the limitations of the proposed analysis method.

– Identification of research directions of malware detection and analysis.

Table 1. Comparison of this paper's literature review with other related literature reviews (S: static, D: dynamic, H: hybrid, O: other).

Study	Year	Reviewed methods	Datasets	Classifiers	Result	Limitation
[29]	2021	S,D,H,O	✓	✓	✓	◗
[2]	2021	S,D,H	✓	✓	✓	◗
[31]	2021	S,D,H	✓	✓	✓	✓
[40]	2021	S	✓	✓	✓	✓
[14]	2022	S,D,H,O	◗	◗	◗	X
[33]	2022	S,D,H	◖	◖	◖	◗
[30]	2022	S,D,H	X	✓	◖	◖
[27]	2022	S,D,H	◗	✓	✓	◗
[18]	2022	S,D,H	✓	✓	◗	◗
this Study	2022	S,D,H,O	✓	✓	✓	✓

The rest of the paper is organised as follows: Sect. 2 introduces Android malware detection, Sect. 3 reviews malware detection approaches and details the most commonly used analysis methods. Section 4 discusses findings and research directions in malware detection, and finally, Sect. 5 concludes the paper.

2 Android Malware Detection

As mentioned above, there are three methods for Android malware detection: "network traffic-based" [10,39], "inner interaction-based" [7] and "permission-based" [4]. For the first, Wang et al. [39] proposed a dynamic method to analyse sensitive information in the HTTP header of data traffic transmitted by malware using HTTP GET and POST. The stream of data that passes in the HTTP packets can be used to extract features that contain semantic text unique to mobile devices, such as "IMEI", "longitude", and "latitude". But, this method cannot be efficiently used with new malware that encrypts payloads to keep their malicious code hidden. To address this, Garg, Peddoju, and Sarje [10] solved the encryption data problem by comparing the patterns of network traffic for benign and malware apps. But, it still ignores the malware whose activities do not depend on network traffic. To overcome, Somarriba and Zurutuza [34] proposed a dynamic analysis method at the network level for malware detection through monitoring the behaviour of apps in run-time. The proposed framework found malicious URLs from the app traces, which connect them with DNS service logs from the mobile operator. The limitation of this method is that it only considers URL and DNS traffic, while malware may use DNS tunneling techniques and HTTP traffic. Moreover, the experiment was conducted on an emulator, on which the malware can be detected, but may not be detected on real devices, given that the emulator does not support the anti-debugging evade method. Additionally, malware that uses certificate pinning can evade detection. The second [7] and third [4] methods focus on the Android OS and application components. Next section presents several analysis approaches based on these methods at the Android mobile level.

3   Android Malware Analysis Approaches

Malware analysis approaches are classified into three main types: static, dynamic, and hybrid. In the static approach, the application is analysed before installation on the device. The dynamic approach is concerned with monitoring the application's behaviour at run-time, while the hybrid approaches combine both to identify malicious apps.

3.1   Static Approach

Static analysis techniques extract features from the APK using various methods. Alzubaidi [2] proposed three methods of feature extraction: signature-based, permission-based, and Dalvik bytecode. The study in [15] added another method, resource-based, and renamed Dalvik bytecode as semantic-based. Muttoo and Badhani [26] used the term "misuse detection," which is synonymous with knowledge -based (or signature-based). Others used the term "anomaly detection" to mean the same as behaviour-based, in the dynamic approach, [26]. Regardless of which method is used, the main objective of static analysis is extracting features, e.g. [40], which can subsequently be used in statistical methods or machine learning for malware detection.

Signature-Based Analysis generates a unique signature pattern for known malware apps, based on the features extracted from the characteristics of Android apps, such as permissions, broadcast receivers, content strings, or bytes [21]. To detect, the signature of an app gets compared to the malware signature library, which includes a unique signature for each known Android malware. Ngamwitroj and Limthanmaphon [28] proposed a signature-based malware detection approach based on permission and broadcast-receiver data extracted from the manifest file. The malware signatures were created from 800 apps. The results of the detection of malicious signatures in the apps were 86.56% accuracy.

Permission-Based Analysis, in this approach, the unnecessary permissions requested by an app indicate that it might be a malicious activity. Ilham, Abderrahim, and Abdelhakim[13] proposed a permission-based method, that stores permissions extracted from the manifest file. Filter feature selection algorithms are then used to rank selections from 74 permission features. The critical permissions were RESTART_PACKAGES, RECEIVE, SEND _SMS, RECEIVE_SMS, READ_EXTERNAL_STORAGE and READ_PHONE_STATE. The study results were at best accuracy result of 98%, however with feature selection algorithms applied, the result reduced to 93% accuracy. Kato, Sasaki, and Sasase [17] assumed that permission-based READ_EXTERNAL_STORAGE approaches are more promising than other approaches for practical malware detection. Moreover, "permission pairs" are more practical and informative than single permission, because the "permission pairs" have the ability to provide more details about how permissions when used together. The same study proposed a scheme for Android malware detection that depends on permission pairs to satisfy efficiency, intelligibility, and stability requirements for malware detection. The composition ratio of the permission pairs was used to construct the dataset for each app, for which eight similarity scores were calculated. These scores were fed into machine learning for classification, which used a real dataset for evaluation. As an alternative technique, the study [25] suggested a risk-based fuzzy analytical hierarchy to evaluate Android applications with a multi-criteria decision. This study used static analysis to extract features including permission-based characteristics. It used risk scores to make mobile users aware of the risks involved before approving permission requests, noted as: extremely high, high, medium, and low.

Resource-Based Analysis depends on the metadata that describes app components as defined in the manifest file, such as required permissions, activity, service, intent, and other components. The authors, in [37], used reverse engineering to extract features from an Android app's source code. Seven different feature sets were used: *Permissions, API Calls, Intents, App Components, Packages, Services, Receivers*. More than 56,000 features were extracted from 100,000 applications among these feature sets. When an app attempts to access some dangerous permissions, it may indicate malware behaviour. For example, SMS, microphone, contacts, storage, and location are classified as *dangerous* permissions. The intent, related to malware, depends on the used phrase. For example, "android.net" is linked to the network manager, while "com.android.vending" is for billing transactions. API calls to resources, such as Camera, SMS, Bluetooth, GPS, network, and NFC, are controlled by the Android OS. When API calls request device resources or sensitive information, they are considered common malware. Extracted features are used to create vector mapping, which is then used in Machine learning to classify malicious applications. In this study, using a dataset, which was amalgamated from three databases (MalDroid, DefenseDroid, and GD), the malware classification result was 96.24% accuracy. Alternatively, Millar et al. [22] used Convolutional Neural Network (CNN) and static analysis on permissions, opcodes, and Android APIs as features. Evaluated for the zero-day scenario, using the Drebin and AMD datasets, their model detection weighted average, rates were 0.91 and 0.81, and F1 scores 0.9928 and 0.9963 respectively.

Semantic-Based Analysis is a branch of lexical analysis, which analyses the data from different sources to extract semantic information. Dalvik bytecode embeds semantic information, such as methods, classes, and instructions, which are used to generate data flow graphs that detect privacy leakage and misuse of telephony services. Another approach, by Bai et al.[5], proposed a scheme that uses network traffic and converts it to text, in which N-gram is used for feature representation and the CNN model for malware classification. This approach uses NLP to extract features from APK components, which are then used to form the semantic text. Alternatively, Zhang et al. [43] proposed an approach, for Android malware detection, that depends on the method-level correlation of abstracted API calls from applications. However, features are extracted from the code file. Each method code is replaced by API calls to generate a set of abstracted API call transactions. The association rules between the abstracted API calls are used to calculate a confidence level, which indicates the semantics of behaviour for an app.

3.2 Dynamic Approach

Dynamic techniques can be used for both hardware and software levels. At the hardware level, it collects data about memory, CPU, battery, sensors, camera, and screen usage. At the software level, features are extracted from network traffic, app patterns, information flows, privileges, permissions, data access, API calls, and different predefined functions [2]. Sihag et al. [32] proposed a solution, based on dynamic analysis, to explore application behaviour. The Android logs at the kernel level are used to generate app signatures by using Logcat. If the app attempts to leak information, jailbreak, gain access to dangerous permissions, or gain root privileges, that indicates the app is malware. Bhatia and Kaushal [6] used statistical analysis methods to understand the behaviour of benign and malicious apps. Their dataset was prepared from system call traces, for both benign and malicious apps. Classic machine learning algorithms were used to classify the apps based on their behaviour. Feng et al. [9] proposed EnDroid, which is a dynamic analysis framework, that used features extracted, at run-time, from system behaviour traces and application-level malicious behaviours. EnDroid used chi-square analysis to identify dangerous dynamic behaviour features.

3.3 Hybrid Approach

The hybrid approach combines both dynamic and static methods. The work in [38] suggested a hybrid method for Android malware detection that combines static and dynamic techniques. Static analysis is used to compare the differing permission patterns of malicious and benign entities using a machine-learning approach. It used a memory heap to construct a dynamic feature base by extracting the object reference relationships. The results for 21,708 apps show that the approach outperforms common detectors. The authors of [35] introduced

Android Botnet, an app to detect malicious behaviour and prevent reaching sensitive data. On the other hand, the authors of [12] proposed a solution that uses the Drebin dataset to extract static features and the CICMalDroid dataset for dynamic analysis. Extracted features were, then, fed into machine learning and deep learning models to detect malware. Alternatively, [11] built the KronoDroid dataset, which included hybrid features from the Android malware dataset. The dataset covered 12 years of Android history, from 2008-2020. The emulator and real devices were used to collect more than 70k malware and 72k benign apps. These apps belong to 449 malware families.

3.4   Other Approaches

In addition to the aforementioned approaches, for the analysis and detection of malware, there are other approaches that were not classified specifically as above. For example, the image-based approach is one that used static analysis to extract features and represent them into images, which are fed to machine learning and deep learning [41]. Another approach [36], has proposed a similar image-based technique. Features were extracted from Manifest, DEX, and Resource files for each Android app and transformed into a grayscale image. Another study [42] employed EfficientNet-B4, a CNN model, that used image-based malware representations of the Android DEX file. However, these image-based methods may be impacted by code manipulation techniques and code obfuscation, which is a weakness of most static malware analysis techniques [36]. Other malware detection methods have employed NLP and machine learning techniques, such as [20], which extracted features from raw opcode sequences of an Android app for machine learning classification. Another, [16], proposed a similar method, MalDozer framework, for detecting Android malware and their family members from raw API method calls that were extracted from DEX assembly sequences and were fed to deep learning. Similarly, CoDroid framework proposed in [44], which is a sequence-based hybrid Android malware detection method that used opcode as a static method and the system calls as a dynamic method. The generated sequence is entered into a neural network model to classify the app as malware or benign.

For the most prominent, aforementioned, studies, we summarise each reviewed study and present their main details of relevance in the following tables:

– **Table** 2 lists reviewed studies, publication year, and the type of approach of their respective malware detection analysis method.
– **Table** 3 lists reviewed studies and summarises their data sources and malware and benign apps data. The size of used data sources and the number of investigated apps provide an indication of the significance of the results of respective studies.
– **Tables** 4 and 5 show key outcomes or results of reviewed malware detection methods and their respective studies and summarize the limitations of each. For studies that develop or employ machine learning-based malware detection methods, the outcomes or results are shown as *accuracy* of their developed method.

Table 2. Studies and Malware analysis approaches/methods

Paper/study	Publication year	Malware analysis approach/method
[39]	2017	Other, Dynamic, NLP
[6,10,34]	2017	Dynamic
[28]	2018	Static, Signature-based
[13]	2018	Static, Permission, based
[9]	2018	Dynamic
[35]	2018	Hybrid
[16]	2018	Other, Static, NLP
[43]	2019	Static, Semantic, based
[32]	2020	Dynamic
[12]	2020	Hybrid
[36]	2020	Other, Static, image-based
[17,25]	2021	Static, Permission-based
[22]	2021	Static, Resource-based
[5]	2021	Static, Semantic-based
[44]	2021	Other, Hybrid, NLP
[37]	2022	Static, Resource-based
[38]	2022	Hybrid
[41]	2022	Other, Static, image-based

4   Malware Detection: Challenges and Research Directions

This section discusses limitations and challenges of the reviewed malware detection approaches and methods. It also presents identified potential research directions and research gaps. The following perspectives are identified and discussed:

– **Malware analysis and machine learning**: With the recent advances in machine learning, deep learning, and NLP, a significant number of studies investigated applying machine learning methods for malware detection. The main focus of these studies, however, is on improving machine learning models and feature selection instead of the malware analysis process. For example, studies, e.g. [10] [38], that used VirusTotal to label the apps as malware or benign, their key outcome is to improve the accuracy of the machine learning model. Similarly, experiments that adopted machine learning for malware detection are mostly conducted in virtual environments, which ignore important contextual and device features, such as sensors (i.e., malware may run only when the person is walking), thus making the output model unrealistic to deploy in real-life. Therefore, developing context-aware machine learning models for malware detection that enable auto-updatable dataset for malware

Table 3. Data sources and number of applications used for method analysis

Study	Data source
[10]	18 bot families malware selected from MalGenome and 14 apps on the devices.
[39]	8203 malware from VirusShare, and 8168 benign from Baidu.
[34]	100 Malware apps collected from MalGenome
[6]	50 benign apps from Google Play Store, and 50 malicious apps from Genome
[28]	800 apps used to create signatures from 1447 apps
[13]	673 malware apps from AMD, 58 benign from Google play
[9]	1962 benign from Google Play Store, 10000 benign from AndroZoo, 5560 malicious apps from Drebin. Datasets: dataset 1 (8806 benign and 5213 malicious), dataset 2 (5000 benign and 5000 malicious)
[35]	NA
[16]	Apps extracted from Malgenome, Drebin, MalDozer. Dataset 1: 33066 malware and 37627 benign. Dataset 2: 20089 malware and 32 families
[43]	5.9K benign and 5.6K malware from Drebin, 20.5K benign and 20.8K malware from AMD
[32]	42 malware and 260 apps from Google Play Store
[12]	For static, Malgenome and Drebin dataset (6820 malware and 12015 benign). For dynamic, CICMalDroid2020 dataset (1795 benign and 9803 malware)
[36]	4850 malware apps from Drebin, AMD and Malgenom. 4850 benign app from Google Play Store using APKPure
[17]	New mixed dataset: 7500 malware from Androzoo, 7500 malware from VirusShare, 4000 malware from Drebin, and 11500 benign from Androzoo
[25]	5000 malware from Drebin and 5000 benign from AndroZoo
[22]	1260 malware from Malgenome with 49 families, 9902 malware from Intel Security dataset, 5560 malware from Drebin with 179 families, and 24553 from AMD with 71 families. For each dataset, similar no of benign apps from Google Play
[5]	Malware and benign from CICAndMal2017. Collected network traffic reached 19.2 GB for malware, and 19 GB for benign apps
[44]	2978 malicious apps and 2707 benign from PlayDrone and Drebin
[37]	10516 malware from MalDroid, 1795 benign from MalDroid, 3062 malware from DefenseDroid, 1500 benign from DefenseDroid. 500 malware and 2421 benign from Google Play to create a new dataset
[38]	12364 malicious apps, and 9344 benign apps from VirusShare, 376 permissions and system broadcasts
[41]	VirusShare and Google Play to create three datasets. Dataset 1: 8121 malware and 2000 benign apps, dataset 2: 8121 malware and 7015 benign apps, and dataset 3: 5384 malware and 5000 benign apps

Table 4. Results and limitations of reviewed malware detection methods

Study	Result	Limitations
[10]	Overall accuracy: 0.98	Ignores malware whose activities do not depend on network traffics
[39]	Best classifier was SVM, accuracy of 0.9915 using emulator, and 54.81 with real environment	no efficient for new malware that encrypts payloads to keep their malicious code hidden. Monkey generates data randomly, can prevent detection of malware, may need semantic data to be activated
[34]	NA	It only considers URL and DNS traffic, while malware may use DNS tunnelling and HTT traffic. Only emulators used, which do not support anti-debugging evade method
[6]	The best was RF, achieved 0.88	To use system call traces, the device must be rooted, which makes applying this method dangerous on a real device.
[28]	Accuracy: 0.8656,	Only two features were used, the data source of applications not known. Introduced only 17 malicious signatures
[13]	Overall accuracy: 0.98	One type of feature only. Feature selection made the result worse than using all features
[9]	The stacking model F1-measure: 0.9735. EnDroid accuracy, on the Drebin dataset: 0.945	Labeling of benign apps is based on VirusTotal. Monkeyrunner and DroidBox may ignore triggers that indicate malicious behaviour, MonkeyRunne triggers only UI
[35]	User is the biggest reason behind the success of malware attacks	Study suggested guidelines for users to reduce malware attacks
[16]	F1-Score: 0.96-0.99	MalDozer has not supported dynamic code loading and reflection obfuscation when the app executes at runtime
[43]	Accuracy of RF and Drebin: 0.96; RF and AMD: 0.98	Used API calls to generate abstraction to reduce level of calls. The limitation: how to deal with hard coding, did not include permissions and opcode in the analysis
[32]	Results from 260 apps: 43 stole sensitive data, 2 fetched emails, 21 showed ads, 10 jailbreak device, 8 root	Limitations in experiment design: how apps run and how agents interact with it
[12]	accuracy of GB: 0.99 for static method. The hybrid model accuracy increased up to 3%	Used two existing datasets for static and dynamic. The CopperDroid framework used to obtain dynamic behaviours of apps, which limits the analysis of malware
[36]	Overall accuracy: 0.9875 with AdaBoost	Cannot detect injection attacks. The performance affected by hard coding
[17]	Overall accuracy: 97.3, feature dimensions reduced	Leak of detection app with a small number of permissions. Limitation on dangerous permission.
[25]	Accuracy: 0.9054	Only focused on permission-based features

Table 5. Results and limitations of reviewed malware detection methods

Study	Result	Limitations
[22]	Weighted average: 0.91 for Drebin, 0.81 for AMD	Only API calls. Static features and hard coding ignored
[5]	Detection rate: 0.926	Does not detect malware when network traffic uses encryption protocols
[44]	CoDroid accuracy: 0.976	Used only two features, opcode for static; system call for dynamic
[37]	Accuracy: 0.9624; 0.3 false positive	Real-time permissions; did not include API requests
[38]	Accuracy: 0.998 - static method; 0.975- dynamic	Used static to classify apps as malware or benign; it depends on static as a first step. Dynamic features not included, e.g. flow information, system load fluctuation, and dead objects [38]
[41]	Accuracy: 0.96, F-score: 0.96	labeling depends on VirusTotal; leak malware detection works in run-time; retrain complex model to detect new malware

apps and their family variations, and ranking them based on their severity and implications is a research direction that needs further exploration and investigation.

– **Zero-Day Attacks Detection**: A zero-day (or 0-day) is a type of malware that exploits a security vulnerability in the mobile ecosystem to penetrate devices. Developing preemptive abilities or approaches to discover software vulnerabilities before attackers or developers is an outstanding challenge, especially for zero-day vulnerabilities. Moreover, developing approaches that can monitor applications, at run-time, to detect zero-day attacks is, too, an outstanding challenge. Key challenges and limitations, to developing such malware detection approaches, are related to mobile resource constraints, mobile device heterogeneity, different mobile contextual uses, and speed of mobile evolution of both devices and applications to name a few. Developing approaches that overcome these challenges and limitations remain an open research direction.

– **Malware Evasion Technique**: In static analysis, for sophisticated hard-coding techniques, such as code obfuscation, malicious payload encryption, injection attacks, dynamic code loading, and so forth, apps need to run on the device to obtain the needed analysis information, which limits the abilities of these methods to detect malware. On the other hand, purely dynamic analysis methods do not cover all code execution paths, while malware authors usually select the hardest and most unusual paths for running malicious code to evade detection, thus making these methods inefficient. Hence, a potential future research area is to develop methods that make use of less hard-coding techniques combined with dynamic analysis.

– **Reverse Engineering**: Although reverse engineering is an important technique, for researchers and security companies, to understand vulnerabilities and threats in mobile apps, but equally malware authors, on the other hand, exploit reverse engineering to inject malicious code into apps. This makes it a double-edged sword that may be used to identify as well as exploit weakness of apps. This raises, however, a challenge for software engineering researchers to investigate and develop more secure techniques to protect mobile applications against exploiting reverse engineering and/or the repackaging of Android apps.

– **Preserving User Privacy**: A number of the experimental studies, e.g. [5, 6], that used machine learning were deployed on the cloud due to the large output model and constrained resources of smart devices. However, for some methods, this may cause additional privacy issues. For example, in static model malware detection, the analysis of an app is uploaded into a classifier model before installing it on the device, which, to some extent, preserves user privacy. In contrast, in dynamic malware detection, methods monitor applications and their network traffic and log their behaviour on the mobile device itself, which exposes user data to leaks, thus causing privacy issues. For such methods, privacy protection is a challenge that needs to be addressed.

– **Malware detection for iOS platform**: The paper identified prominent studies and most commonly used malware detection methods, which are summarized in Tables 3–5. It also identified outstanding challenges and directions of research, on different aspects of Android malware detection. Although, several studies focused on developing malware detection methods improving the detection and analysis processes, several other studies, particularly machine learning based, focused mainly on enhancing the employed machine learning models themselves. Many of these approaches require significant resources to process, which may render many of these methods inapplicable in reality, due to the usual resource constraints of mobile devices. Additionally, there is a clear lack of research on developing methods for securing mobile apps and detecting their vulnerabilities early to prevent malware to stealth into mobile devices. Notably, there are a limited number of studies on malware evasion techniques, cross-platform mobile malware detection, or specific types of malware, such as zero-day, and those licensed to governments, e.g., Pegasus. According to the Kaspersky report [3], over 98% of mobile banking malware targets Android mobile devices. Furthermore, the Android platform is used by more than 80% of smart devices. Additionally, Apple claimed that Android has up to 47 times more infections from malware than the iPhone due to side-loading apps [1]. But, iOS devices do not guarantee 100% security and are still vulnerable to malware attacks [3]. Although most reviewed studies focused on the Android platform, however, there is a clear lack of malware detection research on the iOS platform.

5 Conclusion

This paper presents a literature review of recent studies and approaches on Android malware detection focusing on analysis methods and techniques. Three types of malware analysis approaches are identified: static, dynamic, and hybrid. Static approaches can detect malware before running applications or before installing them on mobile devices. They extract features or characteristics of malware apps based on the analysis of the contents of APK files, using different aspects, including signature-based, permission-based, resource-based, and semantic-based. On the other hand, dynamic approaches consider static methods inefficient due to malware evasion that can happen during run-time. These methods, alternatively, extract features of applications during run-time. They monitor applications, on mobile devices or emulators, and log their behaviour. The most common dynamic methods utilise API calls and system calls. They continuously monitor and analyse network traffic data extracting information that requests sensitive data. Hybrid approaches merge the two approaches, exploiting the advantages of each. However, to achieve efficient hybrid methods, they require further investigation to reduce their complexity and applicability. Moreover, several studies combined methods from the three types of approaches with image-based and NLP techniques.

The paper identified prominent studies and most commonly used malware detection methods, which are summarized in Tables 3–5. It also identified outstanding challenges and directions of research, on different aspects of Android malware detection. Although, several studies focused on developing malware detection methods improving the detection and analysis processes, several other studies, particularly machine learning based, focused mainly on enhancing the employed machine learning models themselves. Many of these approaches require significant resources to process, which may render many of these methods inapplicable in reality, due to the usual resource constraints of mobile devices. Additionally, there is a clear lack of research on developing methods for securing mobile apps and detecting their vulnerabilities early to prevent malware from stealth into mobile devices. Notably, there are a limited number of studies on malware evasion techniques, cross-platform mobile app analysis, or specific types of malware, such as zero-day, and those licensed to governments, e.g., Pegasus.

References

1. A threat analysis of sideloading. https://www.apple.com/privacy/docs/Building_a_Trusted_Ecosystem_for_Millions_of_Apps_A_Threat_Analysis_of_Sideloading.pdf. (Accessed 28 August 2022)
2. Alzubaidi, A.: Recent advances in android mobile malware detection: A systematic literature review. IEEE Access **9** (2021). https://ieeexplore.ieee.org/document/9585476/, https://ieeexplore.ieee.org/stamp/stamp.jsp?tp=&arnumber=9585476
3. Android vs. ios security comparison (2022). https://www.kaspersky.com/resource-center/threats/android-vs-iphone-mobile-security. (Accessed 28 August 2022)

4. Arora, A., Peddoju, S.K., Conti, M.: Permpair: Android malware detection using permission pairs. IEEE Trans. Inf. Forensics Sec. **15**, 1968–1982 (2019)
5. Bai, H., Liu, G., Liu, W., Quan, Y., Huang, S.: N-gram, semantic-based neural network for mobile malware network traffic detection. Sec. Commun. Netw. **2021** (2021)
6. Bhatia,T., Kaushal, R.: Malware detection in android based on dynamic analysis. In: 2017 International Conference on Cyber Security And Protection Of Digital Services (Cyber Security), pp. 1–6. IEEE (2017)
7. Cai, H., Meng, N., Ryder, B., Yao, D.: Droidcat: Effective android malware detection and categorization via app-level profiling. IEEE Trans. Inf. Forensics Secur. **14**(6), 1455–1470 (2018)
8. Chen, Y.-C., Chen, H.-Y., Takahashi, T., Sun, B., Lin, T.-N.: Impact of code deobfuscation and feature interaction in android malware detection. IEEE Access **9**, 123208–123219 (2021)
9. Feng, P., Ma, J., Sun, C., Xinpeng, X., Ma, Y.: A novel dynamic android malware detection system with ensemble learning. IEEE Access **6**, 30996–31011 (2018)
10. Garg, S., Peddoju, S.K., Sarje, A.K.: Network-based detection of android malicious apps. Int. J. Inf. Sec. **16**(4), 385–400 (2017)
11. Guerra-Manzanares, A., Bahsi, H., Nõmm, S.: Kronodroid: Time-based hybrid-featured dataset for effective android malware detection and characterization. Comput. Sec. **110** (2021)
12. Hadiprakoso, R.B., Kabetta, H., Buana, I.K.S.: Hybrid-based malware analysis for effective and efficiency android malware detection. In: 2020 International Conference on Informatics, Multimedia, Cyber and Information System (ICIMCIS), pp. 8–12. IEEE (2020)
13. Ilham, S., Abderrahim, G., Abdelhakim, B.A.: Permission based malware detection in android devices. In: Proceedings of the 3rd International Conference on Smart City Applications, pp. 1–6(2018)
14. Kambar, M.E.Z.N., Esmaeilzadeh, A., Kim, Y., Taghva, K.: A survey on mobile malware detection methods using machine learning. IEEE (2022). https:// ieeexplore.ieee.org/document/9720753/
15. Karbab, E.B., Debbabi, M., Derhab, A., Mouheb, D.: Data-driven fingerprinting and threat intelligence. In: Springer, Android Malware Detection Using Machine Learning (2021)
16. Karbab, E.B., Debbabi, M., Derhab, A., Mouheb, D.: Maldozer: Automatic framework for android malware detection using deep learning. Digital Investigation **24**, S48–S59 (2018)
17. Kato, H., Sasaki, T., Sasase, I.: Android malware detection based on composition ratio of permission pairs. IEEE Access **9**, 130006–130019 (2021)
18. Kim, Y.-k., Lee, J.J., Go, M.-H., Kang, H.-Y., Lee, K.: A systematic overview of the machine learning methods for mobile malware detection. In: Security and Communication Networks, vol. 2022 (2022)
19. Li, W., Cai, J., Wang, Z., Cheng, S.: A robust malware detection approach for android system based on ensemble learning. In Wang, G., Choo, KK.R., Ko, R.K.L., Xu, Y., Crispo, B., (eds.) Ubiquitous Security - First International Conference, UbiSec 2021, Guangzhou, China, December 28–31, 2021, Revised Selected Papers, volume 1557. CCIS, pages 309–321. Springer (2022). https://doi.org/10. 1007/978-981-19-0468-4_23
20. McLaughlin, N., et al.: Deep android malware detection. In: Proceedings of the seventh ACM on Conference On Data And Application Security And Privacy, pp. 301–308 (2017)

21. Meijin, L., et al.: A systematic overview of android malware detection. Appl. Artif. Intell. **36**(1), 2007327 (2022)
22. Millar, S., McLaughlin, N., del Rincon, J.M., Miller, P.: Multi-view deep learning for zero-day android malware detection. J. Inf. Sec. Appli. **58** (2021)
23. Mobile malware statistics for q1 2022 — securelist. https://securelist.com/it-threat-evolution-in-q1-2022-mobile-statistics/106589/. (Accessed 28 June 2022)
24. Mobile operating system market share worldwide — statcounter global stats. https://gs.statcounter.com/os-market-share/mobile/worldwide. (Accessed 28 June 2022)
25. Arif, J.M., et al.: Android mobile malware detection using fuzzy ahp. J. Inf. Sec. Appli. **61** (2021)
26. Muttoo, S.K., Badhani, S.: Android malware detection: state of the art. Int. J. Inf. Technol. **9**(1), 111–117 (2017). https://doi.org/10.1007/s41870-017-0010-2
27. Muzaffar, A., Hassen, H.R., Lones, M.A., Zantout, H.: An in-depth review of machine learning based android malware detection. Comput. Sec. 102833 (2022)
28. Ngamwitroj, S., Limthanmaphon, B.: Adaptive android malware signature detection. In: Proceedings of the 2018 International Conference on Communication Engineering and Technology, pp. 22–25 (2018)
29. Qiu, J., Zhang, J., Luo,W., Pan, L., Nepal, S., Xiang, Y.: A survey of android malware detection with deep neural models. ACM Comput. Surv. **53**, 1–36 (2021–11). ISSN 0360–0300. https://doi.org/10.1145/3417978, https://dl.acm.org/doi/10.1145/3417978, https://sci-hub.se/10.1145/3417978
30. Rani, S.S., Eric, P.V., Sahithya, P., Priyadharshini, S., Ramyashree, S.: Pro-shield protect: Survey paper for malware detection in android application. IEEE (2022). https://ieeexplore.ieee.org/document/9743038/
31. Razgallah, A., Khoury, R., Hallé, S., Khanmohammadi, K.: A survey of malware detection in android apps: Recommendations and perspectives for future research. Comput. Sci. Rev. **39** (2021–02). ISSN 15740137. https://doi.org/10.1016/J.COSREV.2020.100358
32. Sihag, V., Swami, A., Vardhan, M., Singh, P.: Signature based malicious behavior detection in android. In: International Conference on Computing Science, Communication and Security, pp. 251–262. Springer (2020). https://doi.org/10.1007/978-981-15-6648-6_20
33. Heena Kauser, S.k., Maria Anu, V.: A literature review on android mobile malware detection using machine learning techniques. IEEE (2022). https://ieeexplore.ieee.org/document/9753746/
34. Somarriba, O., Zurutuza, U.: A collaborative framework for android malware detection using dns & dynamic analysis. In: 2017 IEEE 37th Central America and Panama Convention (CONCAPAN XXXVII), pp 1–6. IEEE (2017)
35. Tidke, S.K., Karde, P.P., Thakare, V.: Detection and prevention of android malware thru permission analysis. In: 2018 Fourth International Conference on Computing Communication Control and Automation (ICCUBEA), pp. 1–6. IEEE (2018)
36. Ünver, H.M., Bakour, K.: Android malware detection based on image-based features and machine learning techniques. SN Appli. Sci. **2**(7), 1–15 (2020). https://doi.org/10.1007/s42452-020-3132-2
37. Urooj, B., Shah, M.A., Maple, C., Abbasi, M.K., Riasat, S.: Malware detection: A framework for reverse engineered android applications through machine learning algorithms. IEEE Access (2022). https://ieeexplore.ieee.org/document/9703375/
38. Wang, H., Zhang, W., He, H.: You are what the permissions told me! android malware detection based on hybrid tactics. J. Inf. Sec. Appli. 66 (2022)

39. Wang, S., Yan, Q., Chen, Z., Yang, B., Zhao, C., Conti, M.: Detecting android malware leveraging text semantics of network flows. IEEE Trans. Inf. Forensics Secur. **13**(5), 1096–1109 (2017)
40. Wu, Q., Zhu, X., Liu, B.: A survey of android malware static detection technology based on machine learning. Mobile Inf. Syst. **2021** (2021)
41. Xing, X., et al.: A Malware Detection Approach Using Autoencoder in Deep Learning". In: IEEE Access 10 (2022). https://ieeexplore.ieee.org/document/9723074/, https://ieeexplore.ieee.org/stamp/stamp.jsp?tp=&arnumber=9723074
42. Yadav, P., Menon, N., Ravi, V., Vishvanathan, S., Pham, T.D.: Efficientnet convolutional neural networks-based android malware detection. Comput. Sec. **115** (2022)
43. Zhang, H., Luo, S., Zhang, Y., Pan, L.: An efficient android malware detection system based on method-level behavioral semantic analysis. IEEE Access **7**, 69246–69256 (2019)
44. Zhang, N., Xue, J., Ma, Y., Zhang, R., Liang, T., Tan, Y.: Hybrid sequence-based android malware detection using natural language processing. Int. J. Intell. Syst. **36**(10), 5770–5784 (2021)

Threat Modeling in Cloud Computing - A Literature Review

Mohammed Kharma$^{(\boxtimes)}$ and Adel Taweel

Department of Computer Science, Birzeit University, Birzeit, Palestine
{mkharmah,ataweel}@birzeit.edu

Abstract. Cloud computing has significantly changed the operational models of companies. This adoption has consequently caused impact on security, resulting in a wider attack surface. Due to the diverse deployment models of the cloud computing architecture, securing the environment has become a challenging task. This paper provides a narrative review of threat modeling approaches in cloud computing. It seeks to identify research challenges and gaps that new research potentially needs to address. It reviews 10 recent related studies and identifies two main types of approaches. Findings show that the next-generation threat modeling needs to introduce more formal methodologies, including a quality assessment of the threat modeling process and its output. Furthermore, automation-enabled methods are vital for advancing the threat modeling process and enabling live integration with cyber threat intelligence for developing threat identification, management, and mitigation.

Keywords: Threat modeling · Cloud computing · Threat intelligence · Security · Threat analysis

1 Introduction

Security vulnerabilities are becoming a priority than ever with the dramatic increase in the number of attacks, noting that 2021 was one of the most intense and severe periods in cyber-security records. Different levels of impact and techniques were used with a concerning increase in the number of weekly attacks by 50% compared with 2020 [1]. Recent statistics report that 37% of all businesses and organizations were affected by ransomware in 2022 with expectations that by 2031, the cost of ransomware will have increased by 13 times [1]. In 2022, there is no significant change reported in the volume of attacks. On the research side, there is an increasing focus on the security domain to reduce or fully mitigate the impact of different security threats and attacks.

Literature shows that the rapid increase in the cloud computing model adoption resulted in a wider attack surface and a rise in cyber attacks [11, 12, 25]. To address, recent focus is on applying Moving Target Defense (MTD) to mislead attackers and make their understanding of the system state incorrect and useless [25]. Modern cyber threats toward cloud computing systems are too diverse

G. Wang et al. (Eds.): UbiSec 2022, CCIS 1768, pp. 279–291, 2023.
https://doi.org/10.1007/978-981-99-0272-9_19

for traditional security measures to handle [3]. Moreover, challenges in cloud security threats identification and assessments come from the wide spectrum of services and technologies included in the operational stack, including the interactions among stakeholders and various resources [16]. Therefore, comprehensive threat modeling is one of the approaches that aim to outline potential attack scenarios along with risk rates and impact factors.

Several threat modeling methodologies exist, such as STRIDE, PASTA, LINDDUN, OCTAVE, and attack trees [20, 23]. However, these methodologies focus on predefined practices in identifying threats in systems, including the cloud domain. Consequently, existing threat modeling techniques suffer from several limitations. For example, attack trees and graphs primarily assist in discovering a complete attack-associated threat to a system [4], and both techniques are challenging to employ for large-scale systems [31]. Furthermore, there are no structured ways to establish parameter values for each node. Therefore, there is a need to introduce more formal methodologies, which incorporate the quality assessment of the threat modeling process and its output. Due to associated complexities and system diversity, methodologies that support automation are in need to automate the process of threat modeling and enable live integration with cyber threat intelligence to develop new techniques for threat identification, management and mitigation.

This paper aims to review state-of-the-art methods and approaches of threat modeling in cloud computing. To accomplish, we selected 10 recent relevant studies that have primary focus on threat modeling in cloud computing. Our findings show 1) growing interest in the adoption of threat modeling in the cloud computing domain for various architectural layers and components; 2) increasing focus towards producing a formal threat modeling for cloud computing; 3) rising research trends on employing automation to replace different manual threat modeling processes and practices; 4) increasing involvement of threat modeling to take part in predefined, adoptive and live-enabled operational environments aided with threat intelligence; 5) improving quality assessments of threat modeling to contribute to an enhanced quality of threat modeling processes and artifacts. This research presents a summary of reviewed literature seeking to identify state-of-the-art methods and their limitations, and potential research directions in threat modeling in the cloud computing domain.

The rest of this paper is organised as follows, Sect. 2 introduces related key concepts of cloud computing and threat modeling, and Sect. 3 presents thematic classification of the reviewed articles. Section 3.1 describes identified methods of modeling language-based approaches and Sect. 3.2 describes other approaches that are not. Section 4 discusses findings and identifies research challenges and directions. Finally, Sect. 5 concludes the work.

2   Background

This section introduces cloud computing and threat modeling, focusing on related key concepts that ground research in these areas.

2.1   Cloud Computing

As per Mell and Grance [17], cloud computing is defined as "... a pay-per-use model for enabling available, convenient, on-demand network access to a shared pool of configurable computing resources (e.g. networks, servers, storage, applications, services) that can be rapidly provisioned and released with minimal management effort or service provider interaction". The value of cloud computing comes from its vital characteristics, which can be summarized as follows, according to NIST [17]:

- On-demand self-service: Without the need to communicate with each service provider directly, a customer can provision computing resources as needed automatically.
- Broad network access: In order to enable usage by various tools such as mobile phones and tablets. Capabilities are made available via the network and may be accessed by conventional protocols.
- Resource pooling and enabling the multi-tenancy: This represents having more than one user who shares computing resources, storage, services, and applications with other users of the cloud provider's infrastructure.
- Rapid elasticity: This is another crucial aspect of cloud computing, it denotes the user's flexibility to scale up or down the resources assigned to services or resources depending on the demand at the time.
- Measured services: Monitoring, controlling, and reporting resource utilization allows for transparency for service providers and users.

From a service model perspective, cloud computing has three main service models based on the degree of generalization of the capability offered [9]. These degrees of generalization may also be thought of as layered architecture, where the services of one layer can be combined with those of another [32]. Figure 1 depicts how the cloud stack is organized in layers, from the physical infrastructure ending with applications. These models can be summarized as follows:

- Infrastructure as a Service (IaaS): where in this instance, the delivery of virtualized resources (computation, storage, and communication) happen on demand. One of the common examples of this model is the EC2 service from Amazon Web Services, which provides virtual machines (VMs) with configurable tools in a way similar to how a regular physical server would be configured [32].
- Platform as a Service (PaaS): offers its consumers a development environment that enables them to create and maintain their applications and cloud-specific utilities. Because PaaS provides a platform and a development environment, the cloud provider is responsible for providing all necessary infrastructure, tools, and programming environment. Red Hat OpenShift is a widely used PaaS that enables users to create and deploy applications in a seamless manner [15,32].
- Software as a Service (SaaS): is the topmost layer of the cloud computing stack where applications reside. SaaS users can access the services via Web

portals. Since online software services offer the same functionalities as locally installed computer programs, consumers are increasingly adopting SaaS provided applications [15,32].

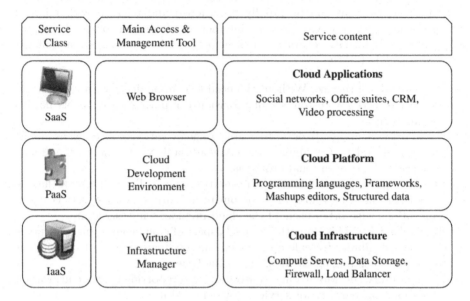

Service Class	Main Access & Management Tool	Service content
SaaS	Web Browser	**Cloud Applications** Social networks, Office suites, CRM, Video processing
PaaS	Cloud Development Environment	**Cloud Platform** Programming languages, Frameworks, Mashups editors, Structured data
IaaS	Virtual Infrastructure Manager	**Cloud Infrastructure** Compute Servers, Data Storage, Firewall, Load Balancer

Fig. 1. Cloud computing architecture- showing three main service models, depending on the generalization degree of the required capability [9].

Threats and Vulnerabilities refer to those accidental faults that can be used by attackers. Because automated methods can frequently be used to exploit vulnerabilities, it is crucial to consider their life cycles from discovery to writing, testing, and delivering a fix [6,21]. As per the Cloud Security Alliance (CSA) [22], service and account hijacking, data loss or leakage, and insecure communications are among the primary areas of security in cloud environments. Pandi et al. [18] described the most important threats in cloud computing, in reference to threat analysis mapping to STRIDE, as below:

- Data breach: unauthorized access or illegitimate viewing of access-restricted information by third parties is one of the worst circumstances that may occur to any firm. Data encryption might lessen the threat, however, compromising encryption keys allow easy decryption of encrypted data.
- Identity, credential and access management weaknesses: where each user should be uniquely recognizable by cloud service providers, through implementing federated authentication.
- Insecure interfaces: given the public availability of such cloud services, and interfaces. These services potentially would be running and in use via unauthorized access or plain text data communication.

- System vulnerabilities: where services might have an exploitable backdoor, that adversaries use to get into the system in order to steal data, to try to control or disrupt service operations.
- Account or service hijacking: when utilizing social engineering, phishing messages, or weakness exploitation to compromise infrastructure security.
- Malicious insiders: refers to an existing employee or a former employee who worked for a cloud service provider (CSP) with active access to the network and data but purposefully abused that access to harm the CSP's reputation.
- Advanced Persistent Threats (APT): is a type of parasitic cyber attack that intrudes systems to gain access to the computing infrastructure of businesses, from which they steal data and intellectual property.
- Data loss: one of the most serious and alarming threats to businesses and consumers. A consumer's data may be lost due to service data deletion or a disastrous event like a crash or operational failure.
- Insufficient due diligence: mandates creating a robust plan and specifications list when considering technologies and CSPs to get maximum benefits and safety of use for the used services.
- Abuse and wicked use of the services: spread and anonymous nature of cloud services use may appeal more to criminals.
- Denial of service: one main security risk to the availability of services when enterprises' reliance is based on public cloud services is the denial of service. This type of attack denies users access to their data or services, leaving them unable to serve their consumers. Customers must be certain about the level of availability protection offered by CSPs, who must ensure counter availability protection.
- Shared technology: distribution of resources and services among many users intensifies the need for logical seclusion and other safeguards to protect users from meddling with one another using suitable security measures.

2.2   Threat Modeling

Application threat modeling is defined by UcedaVelez and Morana [26] as "a strategic process aimed at considering possible attack scenarios and vulnerabilities within a proposed or existing application environment for the purpose of clearly identifying risk and impact levels". According to Shostack [21], "threat modeling is the use of abstractions to aid in thinking about risks. Gupta et al. [13] alternatively considered threat modeling as a way to protect the system by analyzing it from the attacker's point of view to identify the different methods that may lead to a security breach for important properties such as availability, integrity, and confidentiality. In the agile software development context, Bernsmed et al. [7] described threat modeling as the key activity to produce software that maintains functioning as planned, including under cyber attacks.

According to Xiong and Lagerström [30], the commonly used definition was given by Uzunov and Fernandez [27] as "threat modeling is a process that can be used to analyze potential attacks or threats, and can also be supported by threat libraries or attack taxonomies". It is the understanding of the attack model by formulating a detailed view of the environment, assets, processes, and actors to model the necessary mitigation measures. To accomplish, the threat modeler engineer needs to consider the different types of adversaries, including (a) external adversaries that have no legitimate access to the trusted boundaries of the environment (such as outside of the modeled data center, vehicle, smart home, or computer system); (b) insider adversaries that have legitimate access to the trusted boundaries of the environment and use their privileges to attack the environment assets; (c) insider adversaries that have legitimate access to the trusted boundaries of the environment and use their privileges to initiate an attack from inside the environment toward external environments.

3   Threat Modeling: Approaches and Methods

This section describes the reviewed studies on threat modeling. The identified approaches and methods are categorised into two types: those that are modeling language-based and those that are not. These are described in the following sub sections. The selection of this categorization is because using a modeling language is an essential part of the threat modeling framework that can address formalization and automation challenges in modeling identified threats [8]. Approaches that build on a modeling language have added characteristics, including higher scalability, applicability and adaptability, opposed to customized, system bespoke with lesser adaptability and applicability.

3.1   Threat Modeling Language-Based Approaches

Modeling language-based approaches base their threat modeling and identification on pre-defined guidelines and protocols. Several studies proposed such threat modeling solutions and methods. Saatkamp et al. [19] proposed a mitigation threat-driven security policy enforcement approach and provided a TOSCA-based technique to assist architects throughout the modeling process. Such an approach helps to identify potential threats in the solution's deployment model. It guides the user to select possible abstracted mitigation functions, mapped to a concrete implementation, and automatically injects relevant security network functions into the deployment model. Their method involves six steps with the main involvement of the architect and the security expert before the deployment model becomes ready for provisioning. Although it enables and requires more business decision involvement, such intelligence would be very helpful in terms of guiding the architect and security specialist instead of waiting for the final step. However, it lacks enough formalization and automation in threat identification. Brazhuk [8], to address, proposed a more formal ontology-driven framework, called OdTM. OdTM is developed for threat modeling for a specific domain represented by a data flow diagram. It can be used for both system design analysis and security pattern generation, using context-aware security patterns. Alternatively, Cauli et al. [10] proposed an approach that utilises description logic for threat modeling to enhance security of cloud setups. It includes a tool that converts template files into logic, using the CloudFormation declarative language developed by Amazon Web Services. The authors applied more thorough semantic reasoning to help security evaluations by augmenting the models with dataflow-specific knowledge.

On the other hand, Torkura et al. [24] focused on evaluating and identifying risks and threats in cloud brokerage systems. The authors developed a threat modeling schema, by employing attack trees and graphs along with the data flow diagrams, to show links between security threats that have been identified. They, also, proposed a method for determining acceptable scores using the Common Configuration Scoring System (CCSS), which was evaluated on two cloud-related attacks. However, it remains a challenge to evaluate the capabilities of threat modeling languages. To address, Xiong et al. [29] proposed a method to rate the effectiveness of such languages. The authors proposed the use of enterpriseLang, a language for modeling threats in enterprise applications, as an example, to test threat cases to verify its intended behavior and validate its effectiveness.

Table 1 summarizes reviewed studies that proposed modeling language-based methods, including their characteristics and limitations.

3.2   Other Threat Modeling Approaches

There are several other approaches that employ different techniques to model threats in cloud computing systems. Although the maturity level of existing threat modeling methods has been questioned Yskout et al. [33], some are frequently used in academia and industry alike. For example, STRIDE, which defines systematic threat modeling processes, has been in use more than 8 years, is considered as the state of practice. Yskout et al. [33] argues that it has mostly remained ad-hoc and dependent on "whiteboard hacking" and heavily reliant on the experience of the individuals engaged. To overcome, the authors suggested 5 maturity levels for threat modeling, influenced by other maturity models, such as COBIT and CMMI. These models include maturity level one, ad-hoc to Repeatable but intuitive, Defined process, Managed and measurable, and Optimized at level five. Similarly, Pandi (Jain) et al. [18] investigated threats, forensic problems, and their effects on distributed cloud systems and their mitigation. The authors assessed several threat modeling methods and approaches to evaluate their suitability for recognizing and handling threats in cloud computing. They found that threat modeling through pervasive computing Paradigm (TMP) was appropriate and can be used with one of the following: STRIDE, Attack Tree (AT), Practical Threat Analysis (PTA), or Attack Graph (AG).

On the other hand, Achuthan et al. [2] proposed a cloud-specific framework by implementing a threat intelligence framework to analyze and monitor the live stream of cloud logs using Splunk with mapping to MITRE ATT&CK framework matrices. Their findings show that threats can be mapped based on the attacker's behavior. The combination of threat modeling and threat intelligence improved categorizing possible cloud threats and recording real-time threats and attacks. Alternatively, Manzoor et al. [16] proposed a cloud model that spans multi-layer in the cloud stack. The authors employed Petri Nets to thoroughly

Table 1. Threat modeling language-based Studies and Approaches.

Study	Stage	Contribution type	Limitations
[19] 2019	Design	A new TOSCA-based method for STRIDE-based threat modeling with automated mitigation recommendation and injection	(1) Such a method might ignore the best practices which are normally enforced by corporate or regulator policies (2) Such mitigation might not cover the insider attack (insecure communication case for example). So, the S-NF Repository might be linked with the threat based on best practices or even with scoring for each recommended function for a particular case (3) Regarding the severity selection, it might not be a practical choice to do so as the threats are predefined in their approach, hence open-source data can be injected to contribute to risk rating calculation (4) Lastly, this method could create a good combination with threat intelligence by adding additional automation capabilities for identifying critical threats at run-time, selecting, injecting then provisioning the additional function from the S-NF Repository based on specific measures and rules
[8] 2021	All stages	Ontology-driven (OdTM) domain-specific threat model based on the base model	(1) The author relied on a security expert to create the security patterns where it might be helpful to integrate with different open sources such as ATT&CK and CVE
[24] 2018	Operation	Attack tree and Data Flow Diagram	(1) There are other threats that need to be considered as part of the threat analysis such as software and hardware Failure, and DDoS (2) There is no need to mention domain-specific tools such as Jenkins as this is a piece of environmentally specific information and the described attack tree is addressing the abstract goal which is "Get CSB Cloud Storage Buckets"
[29] 2021	Operation	Quality assessment method for threat modeling language	(1) Some of the identified improvements are to extend existing languages rather than create a new one such as the modeling language from OASIS Open or one of the well-established languages (2) Highlight the need for additional test cases in order to increase the test coverage percentage which will result in better threat modeling quality
[10] 2021	Operation	Contextual reasoning relying on descriptive logics for threats evaluation, a cloud configuration security analysis tool	(1) Authors provided a tool for threat identification on cloud configurations deployments. An additional level of context-aware analysis would be helpful in order to provide additional analysis results on the incorporated data flow. Integration with open source databases to consider vulnerabilities information such as CVE would enrich the analysis with known vulnerabilities related to the used software versions.

profile the operational behavior of services. They showed that their method can model threats in the same layer and across different layers and was able to identify vulnerabilities to reduce the attack surface of the cloud. However, it is a manually expensive domain specific approach that works at the layer level. To overcome, Välja et al. [28] proposed a semi-automated ontology-based framework for threat modeling by addressing the two issues of insufficient domain knowledge and inappropriate granularity. The authors used conceptual modeling to generalise domain knowledge to construct an ontology to support the framework. The constructed ontology enabled comparability and completeness of data from various sources as well as automating the threat modeling process.

The above approaches are briefly described in Table 2, noting their contribution and limitations.

4   Discussion and Future Directions

This literature review focused on recent studies that proposed methods that aim to enable formal processes and automatic execution of threat modeling. Such direction is a vital aspect of threat modeling, to enable automation of the complete modeling process by employing structured and systematic methodology. Such methodology requires to include defined milestones, process breakdown, and formal representation of the threat modeling output in addition to the quality assessment of the modeling process itself and its output.

Process formalisation and automation are two interdependent aspects of threat modeling. Enabling automated or semi-automated threat identification and modeling, with limited security expert intervention, is a very important element to address the gap of having a simpler, more productive, and efficient threat modeling process. Cyber threat intelligence (CTI) is the third aspect that some methods combined or integrated in the modeling process. It enables advancing threats identification, management, and mitigation. Integrating CTI into threat modeling results in a more adaptable approach that is able to learn new threats that may arise from system behavior, logs, and environmental data from the production environment.

Based on the above, identified threat modeling challenges fall into different categories as follows:

- **Lack of comprehensive threat modeling language**: Several threat modeling languages have been proposed, however, the quality of a threat modeling language is critical to its generalizability, scalability and applicability. Xiong et al. [29] created test cases to assess and verify their proposed language's intended behavior in order to validate it. Several improvements were identified, including its test coverage percentage and redesigning the modeling language to embed existing languages based on the DSL guidelines [14]. Further, it requires validating language capabilities to cover more use cases, for which more stockholders need to be involved in the language design, including enterprise system users, regulators, or ethical hackers in addition to developers.

Table 2. Other thread modeling studies and approaches

Study	Stage	Contribution type	Limitations
[16] 2018	Operation	Multi-layers cloud modeling based on Petri Nets as graph model. New model for threat analysis in the cloud	(1) The proposed approach is quite complex, where the one who will do the threat modeling needs to understand how to use Petri Nets as a graph model which is not common knowledge for developers, architects, and not-so-technical people (2) Maintaining a large design structure matrix might affect the usability of the approach
[18] 2020	Operation	Hybrid threat modeling framework	(1) Highlighted the need for creating a framework for hybrid threat modeling for cloud computing use in the healthcare domain (2) There is a need for risk assessment, risk mitigation, and technique evaluation for practical use in domain-specific standards and regulations
[2] 2022	Operation	A new threat intelligence framework with mapping to MITRE ATT&CK framework matrices	(1) A similar approach was introduced back in 2019 by Splunk Enterprise Security (2) One of the drawbacks of their work is the lack of a risk matrix (3) The complication of the categorization rules definition
[33] 2020	All stages	5 levels to enhance the threat modeling maturity	(1) The authors addressed challenges that are required in order to pass through the mentioned different maturity levels (2) Needs clear prerequisites, action items, and execution plan to achieve each level's requirements
[28] 2020	Operation	Attack path analysis based on the collected data from different scanning tools	(1) The focus of this study is primarily on command, remote file, and SQ injection in addition to cross-site scripting (XSS), their claim that the designed framework are broad enough to adopt environment-specific requirements The capability of this framework is tied to the tools as data sources such as Nessus and Nexpose that provide scanning output for vulnerability information.

- **Low maturity level for threat modeling processes and practice**: Yskout et al. [33] proposed a framework for evaluating the maturity level of threat modeling processes and practices. However, as reported, most threat modeling methods have shown low maturity in providing comprehensive, systematic and complete process. This requires a well-defined maturity model to assess process outcome and effectiveness.
- **Lack of standard cloud computing threat modeling artifacts**: [5] proposed an initial ontology-driven framework for threat modeling of cloud computing. However, having a comprehensive threat modeling of cloud computing components using a formal standardised threat modeling language

that covers the cloud modeling needs, is a challenge as well as an apparent research gap. Such language is required to address the main challenges in threat modeling, which are formalization and automation, with adaptation capability across different environments.

– **Verification and validation of the generated threat modeling artifacts**: There is a clear insufficient research on verification and validation methods of generated threat modeling outputs. The need is to develop solutions that can produce quality assured validation of threat modeling methods and tools, verifiable in practice, that may utilize generated logs of the included assets and processes in the threat modeling to ensure full capture of correct data flows.

5 Conclusion

This paper presents a narrative literature review and analysis of relevant and prominent studies that propose state-of-the-art approaches in threat modeling in cloud computing. It seeks to identify research directions and gaps that new research potentially needs to address. Cloud security vulnerabilities are becoming more of a priority than ever with the dramatic increase in the number of attacks. Threat modeling is the key precautionary step that identifies threats and implements protective models from security attacks.

Our main findings show the increasing interest in adopting threat modeling in cloud computing. They report the increased focus on research on formalization of threat modeling including its quality assessment, threat modeling automation, threat intelligence integration, and industry adoption to improve state of practice.

References

1. Cybersecurity in 2022 - a fresh look at some very alarming stats. https://www. forbes.com/sites/chuckbrooks/2022/01/21/cybersecurity-in-2022-a-fresh-look-at-some-very-alarming-stats/?sh=3b5eccd46b61, (Accessed 01 December 2022)
2. Ananthapadmanabhan, A., Achuthan, K.: Threat modeling and threat intelligence system for cloud using splunk. In: Varol, A., Karabatak, M., Varol, C. (eds.) 10th International Symposium on Digital Forensics and Security, ISDFS 2022, Istanbul, Turkey, 6–7 June 2022, pp. 1–6. IEEE (2022). https://doi.org/10.1109/ISDFS55398.2022.9800787
3. Alam, T.: Cloud computing and its role in the information technology. IAIC Trans. Sustain. Digital Innov. (ITSDI) 1(2), 108–115 (2020)
4. Alhebaishi, N., Wang, L., Singhal, A.: Threat modeling for cloud infrastructures. EAI Endorsed Trans. Security Safety 5(17), e5 (2019). https://doi.org/10.4108/eai.10-1-2019.156246
5. Andrei, B.: Threat modeling of cloud systems with ontological security pattern catalog. Int. J. Open Inf. Technol. 9(5), 36–41 (2021)

6. Andrei-Cristian, I., Gasiba, T.E., Zhao, T., Lechner, U., Pinto-Albuquerque, M.: A large-scale study on the security vulnerabilities of cloud deployments. In: Wang, G., Choo, K.R., Ko, R.K.L., Xu, Y., Crispo, B. (eds.) UbiSec 2021. CCIS, vol. 1557, pp. 171–188. Springer (2022). https://doi.org/10.1007/978-981-19-0468-4_13

7. Bernsmed, K., Cruzes, D.S., Jaatun, M.G., Iovan, M.: Adopting threat modelling in agile software development projects. J. Syst. Softw. **183**, 111090 (2022). https://doi.org/10.1016/j.jss.2021.111090

8. Brazhuk, A.: Security patterns based approach to automatically select mitigations in ontology-driven threat modelling (2020)

9. Buyya, R., Broberg, J., Goscinski, A.M.: Cloud computing: Principles and paradigms. John Wiley & Sons (2010)

10. Cauli, C., Li, M., Piterman, N., Tkachuk, O.: Pre-deployment security assessment for cloud services through semantic reasoning. In: Silva, A., Leino, K.R.M. (eds.) CAV 2021. LNCS, vol. 12759, pp. 767–780. Springer, Cham (2021). https://doi.org/10.1007/978-3-030-81685-8_36

11. Chandran, S., Hrudya, P., Poornachandran, P.: An efficient classification model for detecting advanced persistent threat. In: Mauri, J.L., et al. (eds.) 2015 International Conference on Advances in Computing, Communications and Informatics, ICACCI 2015, Kochi, India, 10–13 August 2015, pp. 2001–2009. IEEE (2015). https://doi.org/10.1109/ICACCI.2015.7275911

12. Farhat, V., McCarthy, B., Raysman, R., Canale, J.: Cyber attacks: prevention and proactive responses. In: Practical Law. pp. 1–12 (2011)

13. Gupta, R., Tanwar, S., Tyagi, S., Kumar, N.: Machine learning models for secure data analytics: A taxonomy and threat model. Comput. Commun. **153**, 406–440 (2020). https://doi.org/10.1016/j.comcom.2020.02.008

14. Hacks, S., Katsikeas, S., Ling, E.R., Xiong, W., Pfeiffer, J., Wortmann, A.: Towards a systematic method for developing meta attack language instances. In: Augusto, A., Gill, A., Bork, D., Nurcan, S., Reinhartz-Berger, I., Schmidt, R. (eds.) Enterprise, Business-Process and Information Systems Modeling - 23rd International Conference, BPMDS 2022 and 27th International Conference, EMMSAD 2022, Held at CAiSE 2022, Leuven, Belgium, 6–7 June 2022, Proceedings. LNBIP, vol. 450, pp. 139–154. Springer (2022). https://doi.org/10.1007/978-3-031-07475-2_10

15. Kumar, S., Goudar, R.: Cloud computing-research issues, challenges, architecture, platforms and applications: a survey. Int. J. Future Comput. Commun. **1**(4), 356 (2012)

16. Manzoor, S., Zhang, H., Suri, N.: Threat modeling and analysis for the cloud ecosystem. In: Chandra, A., Li, J., Cai, Y., Guo, T. (eds.) 2018 IEEE International Conference on Cloud Engineering, IC2E 2018, Orlando, FL, USA, 17–20 April 2018, pp. 278–281. IEEE Computer Society (2018). https://doi.org/10.1109/IC2E.2018.00056

17. Mell, P., Grance, T., et al.: The nist definition of cloud computing (2011)

18. Pandi, G.S., Shah, S., Wandra, K.: Exploration of vulnerabilities, threats and forensic issues and its impact on the distributed environment of cloud and its mitigation. Proc. Comput. Sci. **167**, 163–173 (2020)

19. Saatkamp, K., Krieger, C., Leymann, F., Sudendorf, J., Wurster, M.: Application threat modeling and automated vnf selection for mitigation using tosca. In: 2019 International Conference on Networked Systems (NetSys), pp. 1–6. IEEE (2019)

20. Shevchenko, N., Chick, T.A., O'Riordan, P., Scanlon, T.P., Woody, C.: Threat modeling: a summary of available methods. Tech. rep., Carnegie Mellon University Software Engineering Institute Pittsburgh United (2018)

21. Shostack, A.: Threat modeling: Designing for security. John Wiley & Sons (2014)
22. Soares, L.F.B., Fernandes, D.A.B., Freire, M.M., Inácio, P.R.M.: Secure user authentication in cloud computing management interfaces. In: IEEE 32nd International Performance Computing and Communications Conference, IPCCC 2013, San Diego, CA, USA, 6–8 December 2013. pp. 1–2. IEEE Computer Society (2013). https://doi.org/10.1109/PCCC.2013.6742763
23. Tatam, M., Shanmugam, B., Azam, S., Kannoorpatti, K.: A review of threat modelling approaches for apt-style attacks. Heliyon **7**(1), e05969 (2021)
24. Torkura, K.A., Sukmana, M.I.H., Meinig, M., Cheng, F., Meinel, C., Graupner, H.: A threat modeling approach for cloud storage brokerage and file sharing systems. In: 2018 IEEE/IFIP Network Operations and Management Symposium, NOMS 2018, Taipei, Taiwan, 23–27 April 2018. pp. 1–5. IEEE (2018). https://doi.org/10.1109/NOMS.2018.8406188
25. Torquato, M., Vieira, M.: Moving target defense in cloud computing: A systematic mapping study. Comput. Secur. **92**, 101742 (2020). https://doi.org/10.1016/j.cose.2020.101742
26. UcedaVelez, T., Morana, M.M.: Risk Centric Threat Modeling: process for attack simulation and threat analysis. John Wiley & Sons (2015)
27. Uzunov, A.V., Fernández, E.B.: An extensible pattern-based library and taxonomy of security threats for distributed systems. Comput. Stand. Interfaces **36**(4), 734–747 (2014). https://doi.org/10.1016/j.csi.2013.12.008
28. Välja, M., Heiding, F., Franke, U., Lagerström, R.: Automating threat modeling using an ontology framework. Cybersecurity **3**(1), 1–20 (2020). https://doi.org/10.1186/s42400-020-00060-8
29. Xiong, W., Hacks, S., Lagerström, R.: A method for quality assessment of threat modeling languages: The case of enterpriselang. In: Barn, B., Sandkuhl, K., Asensio, E.S., Stirna, J. (eds.) Proceedings of the Forum at Practice of Enterprise Modeling 2021 (PoEM-Forum 2021) (PoEM 2021), Riga, Latvia, 24–26 November 2021. CEUR Workshop Proceedings, vol. 3045, pp. 49–58. CEUR-WS.org (2021), http://ceur-ws.org/Vol-3045/paper06.pdf
30. Xiong, W., Lagerström, R.: Threat modeling - A systematic literature review. Comput. Secur. **84**, 53–69 (2019). https://doi.org/10.1016/j.cose.2019.03.010
31. Yeng, P.K., Wulthusen, S.D., Bian, Y.: Comparative analysis of threat modeling methods for cloud computing towards healthcare security practice. Int. J. Adv. Comput. Sci. Appli. **11**(11) (2020)
32. Youseff, L., Butrico, M., Da Silva, D.: Toward a unified ontology of cloud computing. In: 2008 Grid Computing Environments Workshop, pp. 1–10. IEEE (2008)
33. Yskout, K., Heyman, T., Landuyt, D.V., Sion, L., Wuyts, K., Joosen, W.: Threat modeling: from infancy to maturity. In: Rothermel, G., Bae, D. (eds.) ICSE-NIER 2020: 42nd International Conference on Software Engineering, New Ideas and Emerging Results, Seoul, South Korea, 27 June - 19 July, 2020. pp. 9–12. ACM (2020). https://doi.org/10.1145/3377816.3381741, https://doi.org/10.1145/3377816.3381741

A New Signal Packing Algorithm for CAN-FD with Security Consideration

Bo Zheng[1] and Yong Xie[2(✉)]

[1] Department of Computer and Information Engineering, Xiamen University of Technology,
Xiamen 361024, China
[2] School of Computer Science, Nanjing University of Posts and Telecommunications,
Xianlin 210023, China
yongxie@njupt.edu.cn

Abstract. The Controller Area Network with flexible data-rate (CAN-FD) is thought to be a good replacement for the CAN. The CAN-FD has a faster transmission rate and more data capacity than the CAN. Network security is critical for car safety, but CAN-FD has inherent network security flaws, making vehicles equipped with the protocol extremely vulnerable to malicious attacks. As a result, in order to protect against those attacks, CAN-FD requires a robust and efficient security model. In addition, as a distributed real-time network, the end-to-end timing requirement of CAN-FD should be satisfied. Otherwise, the vehicle cannot run consistently and safely. Therefore, we proposed a network security model suitable for CAN-FD. Based on the model, we further proposed an end-to-end delay optimization algorithm. Experimental results show that our proposed algorithm can effectively reduce end-to-end delay compared with the baseline algorithm.

Keywords: Security · CAN-FD · In-vehicle network · End-to-end delay

1 Introduction

With the rapid rise of the Internet of Vehicles, electronic components in vehicles are rising, and the system structure is becoming increasingly intricate. The number of Electronic Control Units (ECUs) in modern automobiles might exceed 70, and the number of interaction signals between ECUs might exceed 4700 [1]. In this context, the threat of cyber-security gradually appeared. For example, in 2015, Charlie Miller et al. invaded a Jeep Cherokee through the entertainment module and network controller [5]. In [2, 3], the authors point out that there are at least 16 possible in-vehicle interfaces that can be attacked. Those that require internet interfaces, such as the Global Positioning System (GPS), entertainment service, and so on, can be attacked more easily. Through these interfaces, the attacker can infiltrate into the vehicle's internal network, control the vehicle's brake and engine, and threaten the driver's safety. Therefore, the security of the in-vehicle network is very important for personal safety and it is gradually becoming the focus of vehicle manufacturers and researchers [10].

G. Wang et al. (Eds.): UbiSec 2022, CCIS 1768, pp. 292–303, 2023.
https://doi.org/10.1007/978-981-99-0272-9_20

The Controller Area Network (CAN) is the most widely used in-vehicle network protocol. However, with the development of automotive cyber-physical systems (ACPS), the transmission rate and the data capacity cannot satisfy control function requirements. Then Robert Bosch GmbH proposed the CAN with Flexible Data-rate (CAN-FD), which has a greater transmission rate (10 Mb/s) and larger data capacity (64 Bytes) than the CAN. Unfortunately, the CAN-FD has three security flaws: lack of message authentication, lack of encryption, and weak access control [4]. Attackers can use these flaws to take control of the vehicle's brakes, steering wheel, lighting system, wipers, and doors [6]. In [4, 9, 10], and [11], the authors used a variety of methods to ensure in-vehicle network security. Such as adding Message Authentication Code (MAC) and freshness value to the CAN-FD messages to ensure the integrity and freshness, encrypting the messages to maintain confidentiality, and so on. However, security measures can lead the end-to-end delay greater. For example, calculating the MAC several times can cause an extra 5.93 ms delay [11]. If the end-to-end delay exceeds the deadline, some functions cannot be completed in real time, it will bring serious consequences. For example, when an obstacle is detected, the collision avoidance function needs to be triggered and completed within a limited time, or else it may cause a fatal accident [9]. Therefore, the CAN-FD needs a reasonable security enhancement mechanism to compensate its inherent security flaws, as well as an efficient network design to ensure that the end-to-end delay constraint is met.

To enhance the security of the CAN-FD, we proposed a security model named Communication Security Level (CSL) suitable for CAN-FD. We also proposed a signal packing algorithm called the CSL-based Linear Programming Algorithm (CSLLP). The CSLLP is used to optimize the end-to-end delay in the CAN-FD. To demonstrate the efficiency of the CSLLP, we used the synthetic data for experimental comparison. The characteristics of the synthetic data are close to real system. The paper is organized as follows: Sect. 2 introduces the system model and the security model. Section 3 presents the CSLLP algorithm. Section 4 introduces the baseline algorithm. Section 5 shows the experimental results. Section 6 summarizes the work of this paper.

2 System Model and Security Model

2.1 System Model

As shown in Fig. 1, the system model consists of ECUs, tasks, signals, messages, and paths. The ECU set is represented by $E = \{e_1, e_2, ..., e_k, ..., e_{EN}\}$, where k is the number of ECU. The EN indicates the total number of ECUs. The task set in e_k consists of TN tasks, which are represented by $T_k = \{t_{k,1}, t_{k,2}, ..., t_{k,o}, ..., t_{k,TN}\}$. The oth task in the task set is represented by $t_{k,o} = \{\tau_{k,o}, \varepsilon_{k,o}, \theta_{k,o}, \rho_{k,o}, \xi_{k,o}\}$, which indicate the period, Worst Case Execution Time (WCET), Worst Case Response Time (WCRT), priority, and communication security level, respectively. We focus primarily on signal packing and assume that the assignment of tasks to ECUs has been designed [9]. Therefore, the period, priority, and communication security level of task are known.

The time cost of the encryption is indicated by ST. The time cost for generating the MAC and freshness value is indicated by MT. $EXE_{k,o}$ represents the basic execution time

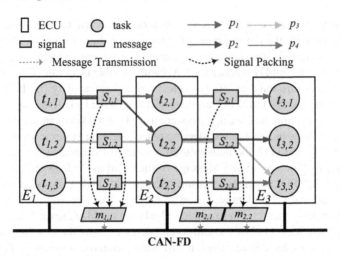

Fig. 1. System model based on CAN-FD.

of the task $t_{k,o}$. And we use the *JUD* and *JUD'* functions to discriminate what security measures the task needs. The WCET of tasks is calculated as follows [14]:

$$\varepsilon_{k,o} = EXE_{k,o} + JUD(k, o)ST + JUD'(k, o)MT \tag{1}$$

The task WCRT includes the WCET and the interfering time caused by other higher priority tasks. It can be calculated a as follows [15]:

$$\theta_{k,o} = \varepsilon_{k,o} + \sum_{o' \in HP(o)} \left\lceil \frac{\theta_{k,o}}{\tau_{k,o'}} \right\rceil \varepsilon_{k,o'} \tag{2}$$

The signal set in e_k consists of *SN* signals, which are represented by $S_k = \{s_{k,1}, s_{k,2}, ..., s_{k,i}, ..., t_{k,SN}\}$. The ith signal in the signal set is represented by $s_{k,i} = \{\tau_{k,i}, \psi_{k,i}, \theta_{k,i}, \beta_{k,i}, \xi_{k,i}\}$, which indicate the period, deadline, WCRT, size, and communication security level, respectively. Our analysis of the signal period, deadline, WCRT, and size is the same as [9]. We use the $SRC_{k,i,o}$ to indicate whether the generator of $s_{k,i}$ is $t_{k,o}$. Since the signal is generated periodically by task, the following relationship exists: $\forall SRS_{k,i,o} = 1, \tau_{k,i} = \tau_{k,o}$. And we assume $\psi_{k,i} = \tau_{k,i}$, the signal WCRT is equal to the WCRT of its carrier message. For the settings of $\beta_{k,i}$, see Sect. 5. In the part of the security model, the signal communication security level will be discussed in depth. The message set in e_k consists of *MN* messages, which are represented by $M_k = \{m_{k,1}, m_{k,2}, ..., m_{k,j}, ..., m_{k,MN}\}$. The jth message in the message set is represented by $m_{k,i} = \{\tau_{k,j}, \psi_{k,j}, \varepsilon_{k,j}, \theta_{k,j}, \rho_{k,j}, \xi_{k,j}, \beta_{k,j}, \mu_{k,j}\}$, which indicate the period, deadline, Worst Case Transmission Time (WCTT), WCRT, priority, communication security level, data size, and payload, respectively. The analysis of message period, deadline, WCTT, WCRT, data size, and data payload is the same as [9]. The period of message $m_{k,j}$ is equal to the maximum common divisor of the period of the included signals. The deadline of $m_{k,j}$ is equal to its period, i.e., $\psi_{k,j} = \tau_{k,j}$. The WCTT of $m_{k,j}$ can be calculated using the formula (3).

Constants *ARB* and *DAT* will be explained in Sect. 5.

$$\varepsilon_{k,j} = 32ARB + \left(28 + 5\left\lceil\frac{\mu_{k,j} - 16}{64}\right\rceil + 10\mu_{k,j}\right)DAT \tag{3}$$

As shown in formula (4), the WCRT of $m_{k,j}$ includes three parts: the WCTT, block time, and the interfering time caused by other higher priority messages. The block time of $m_{k,j}$ is equal to the max WCTT value in the set consisting of $m_{k,j}$ and other lower priority messages.

$$\theta_{k,j} = \varepsilon_{k,j} + \underset{j'\in LP(j)}{MAX}(\varepsilon_{k',j'}, \varepsilon_{k,j}) + \sum_{j'\in HP(j)}\left\lceil\frac{\theta_{k,j} - \varepsilon_{k,j}}{\tau_{k',j'}}\right\rceil\varepsilon_{k',j'} \tag{4}$$

In CAN-FD, the Bit-Stuffing mechanism is used to supplement the data field and impact the payload $\mu_{k,j}$ calculation of the message. To describe it, we list formulas (5) and (6) to calculate $\beta_{k,j}$ and $\mu_{k,j}$ of $m_{k,j}$ respectively. The priority of messages is assigned in a rate monotonic way, i.e., $\rho_{k,j} \propto (1/\tau_{k,j})$ [8]. The message communication security level will be described in the part of the security architecture.

$$\beta_{k,j} = \sum_{s_{k,i}\in m_{k,j}}\beta_{k,i} \tag{5}$$

$$\mu_{k,j} = \begin{cases} \beta_{k,j} & \text{if } 0 < \beta_{k,j}\leqslant 8 \\ 12 & \text{if } 8 < \beta_{k,j}\leqslant 12 \\ 16 & \text{if } 12 < \beta_{k,j}\leqslant 16 \\ 20 & \text{if } 16 < \beta_{k,j}\leqslant 20 \\ 24 & \text{if } 20 < \beta_{k,j}\leqslant 24 \\ 32 & \text{if } 24 < \beta_{k,j}\leqslant 32 \\ 48 & \text{if } 32 < \beta_{k,j}\leqslant 48 \\ 64 & \text{if } 48 < \beta_{k,j}\leqslant 64 \end{cases} \tag{6}$$

The path set is represented by $P = \{p_1, p_2, ..., p_q, ..., p_{PN}\}$. The *PN* is used to describe the total number of paths. The path is defined as an ordered sequence of tasks and signals [15]. The p_q is the *q*th path in the model, and it can be represented by $p_q = \{t_{k1,o1}, s_{k1,i1}, t_{k2,o2}, s_{k2,i2}, ..., s_{k(n-1),i(n-1)}, t_{kn,on}\}$. Taking Fig. 1 as an example, the depth-first searching can find four paths: $p_1 = \{t_{1,1}, s_{1,1}, t_{2,1}, s_{2,1}, t_{3,1}\}$, $p_2 = \{t_{1,1}, s_{1,1}, t_{2,2}, s_{2,2}, t_{3,2}\}$, $p_3 = \{t_{1,2}, s_{1,2}, t_{2,2}, s_{2,2}, t_{3,3}\}$, and $p_4 = \{t_{1,3}, s_{1,3}, t_{2,3}, s_{2,3}, t_{3,3}\}$. The end-to-end delay of p_q is expressed by $delay_q$ and can be calculated as the formula (7) [15]. The optimization goal of this paper is the sum of the end-to-end delay of all paths which is represented by the formula (8).

$$delay_q = \sum_{t_{k,o}\in p_q}(\tau_{k,o} + \theta_{k,o}) + \sum_{s_{k,i}\in p_q}(\tau_{k,i} + \theta_{k,i}) \tag{7}$$

$$\sum_{q=1}^{PN} delay_q \tag{8}$$

2.2 Security Model

In our model, there are two kinds of network attacks. The first is the passive attack. Attackers eavesdrop on the network and analyze the data. And private information, such as identification information, present or past location, navigational data, phone history, financial transaction history, etc., is often the attack target. Assuming that the attacker successfully obtains the data of the vehicle X-by-wire module, the current position can be analyzed in real-time through the data of initial position, steering angle, acceleration, and braking, so as to track the vehicle [12]. In this case, the vehicle shall give priority to ensuring the confidentiality of data. The second is the active attack. Attackers intrude on the network by masquerading, replying and tampering, etc. And the attack target is usually the vehicle control data that needs to be transmitted between different ECUs. In this case, the vehicle shall give priority to ensuring the credibility, freshness, and integrity of data.

According to the above analysis, the task can be divided into three types: general task, privacy task, and controlling task. Data loss or eavesdropping on general task will not cause any risks. Privacy task require passive attack defense capabilities to ensure the confidentiality of their data. Controlling tasks require active attack defense capabilities to ensure the credibility, freshness, and integrity of its data. As shown in Table 1, task are distinguished by communication security level, i.e., $\xi_{k,o}$.

Table 1. Task security features.

$\xi_{k,o}$	Data characteristics
1	Security protection is unnecessary
2	Data should be kept confidential
3	Data should be complete, fresh, and verifiable

The signal is generated periodically by the task, therefore the signal communication security level value is equal to that of its source task, that is, there is a relationship $\forall SRS_{k,i,o} = 1, \xi_{k,i} = \xi_{k,o}$. When the signal is packed, there are signals with different $\xi_{k,i}$ in the message, so different security mechanisms will be applied to the same message. We classify messages by different security protection measures and then determine the communication security level value $\xi_{k,j}$. See Table 2 for the description of the message communication security level.

Table 2. Message security features.

$\xi_{k,j}$	Processing of messages
1	Transmitting without any protection
2	Message is encrypted with the AES128 algorithm
3	MAC & Freshness value are added to the message
4	Message is encrypted with AES128 and with MAC & Freshness value added

3 MILP-Based Packing Algorithm

3.1 MILP Formulation

The CSLLP is based on mixed-integer linear programming (MILP). The following describes the MILP model of this paper through multiple constraints. A signal can only be packed into one message. We introduce a binary variable $packed_{k,i,j}$ to indicate whether $s_{k,i}$ is packed into $m_{k,j}$. If yes, $packed_{k,i,j} = 1$, otherwise $packed_{k,i,j} = 0$. This constraint can be expressed as follows:

$$\forall s_{k,i}, \sum_{j=1}^{MN} packed_{k,i,j} == 1 \tag{9}$$

In the system model, the period of $m_{k,j}$, i.e., $\tau_{k,j}$ is equal to the maximum common divisor of the period of the internal signal be packed into $m_{k,j}$. This constraint can be expressed as follows:

$$\forall s_{k,i}, m_{k,j}, \text{ if } \tau_{k,i} \bmod \tau_{k,j} \neq 0, \text{ then } packed_{k,i,j} == 0 \tag{10}$$

We introduce binary variables $macflag_{k,j}$ and $encflag_{k,j}$. The $macflag_{k,j}$ is used to indicate whether $m_{k,j}$ needs to add MAC and freshness value. The $encflag_{k,j}$ is used to indicate whether $m_{k,j}$ needs encryption. Function $SCSL2$ is used to indicate whether $\xi_{k,i}$ is 2. Function $SCSL3$ is used to indicate whether $\xi_{k,i}$ is 3. The following constraints are used to calculate the $macflag_{k,j}$ and the $encflag_{k,j}$.

$$\forall s_{k,i}, m_{k,j}, \begin{cases} \sum_{i=1}^{SN} (packed_{k,i,j} SCSL2(\xi_{k,i})) \geq macflag_{k,j} \\ packed_{k,i,j} SCSL2(\xi_{k,i}) \leq macflag_{k,j} \\ \sum_{i=1}^{SN} (packed_{k,i,j} SCSL3(\xi_{k,i})) \geq encflag_{k,j} \\ packed_{k,i,j} SCSL3(\xi_{k,i}) \leq encflag_{k,j} \end{cases} \tag{11}$$

The combined size of MAC, freshness value, and $\beta_{k,i}$ cannot exceed 64 bytes and there may be no MAC and freshness value in $m_{k,j}$. In the CSL model, the size of MAC and freshness value is 18 bytes [13]. Therefore, the size constraint can be expressed as follows:

$$\forall m_{k,j}, \begin{cases} \beta_{k,j} == \sum_{i=1}^{SN} packed_{k,i,j}\beta_{k,i} \\ \\ \beta_{k,j} + 18macflag_{k,j} \le 64 \end{cases} \qquad (12)$$

There is a Bit-Stuffing mechanism in CAN-FD, and we have described it with formulas (5) and (6). On this basis, the Bit-Stuffing mechanism with security constraints can be described as formulas (13) and (14).

$$\forall m_{k,j}, \ \mu'_{k,j} == \beta_{k,j} + 18macflag_{k,j} \qquad (13)$$

$$\forall m_{k,j}, \ \mu_{k,j} == \begin{cases} \mu'_{k,j} & if \quad 0 \ < \mu'_{k,j} \le 8 \\ 12 & if \quad 8 \ < \mu'_{k,j} \le 12 \\ 16 & if \quad 12 < \mu'_{k,j} \le 16 \\ 20 & if \quad 16 < \mu'_{k,j} \le 20 \\ 24 & if \quad 20 < \mu'_{k,j} \le 24 \\ 32 & if \quad 24 < \mu'_{k,j} \le 32 \\ 48 & if \quad 32 < \mu'_{k,j} \le 48 \\ 64 & if \quad 48 < \mu'_{k,j} \le 64 \end{cases} \qquad (14)$$

The calculation process of message WCTT can be described with formula (15).

$$\forall m_{k,j}, \ \varepsilon_{k,j} == 32ARB + DAT \times (28 + 5 \left\lceil \frac{\mu_{k,j} - 16}{64} \right\rceil + 10\mu_{k,j}) \qquad (15)$$

According to formula (4), the WCRT of $m_{k,j}$, i.e., $\theta_{k,j}$ includes three parts: $\varepsilon_{k,j}$, $block_{k,j}$, and the interfering time. Therefore, the calculation process of message WCRT can be described as follows:

$$\forall m_{k,j}, \ \theta_{k,j} == \varepsilon_{k,j} + block_{k,j} + grabed_{k,j} \qquad (16)$$

$$\forall m_{k,j}, m_{k',j'}, \ block_{k,j} == \underset{j' \in LP(j)}{MAX} (\varepsilon_{k',j'}, \varepsilon_{k,j}) \qquad (17)$$

$$\forall m_{k,j}, m_{k',j'}, \ grabed_{k,j} == \sum_{j' \in HP(j)} \left\lceil \frac{\theta_{k,j} - \varepsilon_{k,j}}{\tau_{k',j'}} \right\rceil \varepsilon_{k',j'} \qquad (18)$$

$$\forall s_{k,i}, \ \theta_{k,i} == \sum_{j=1}^{MN} packed_{k,i,j}\theta_{k,j} \qquad (19)$$

If $s_{k,i}$ is packed into $m_{k,j}$, then $\theta_{k,i} = \theta_{k,j}$. Therefore, the calculation process of signal WCRT can be described with formula (19).

Based on the formula (1), the calculation of task WCET can be described with formula (20).

$$\forall t_{k,o}, \ \varepsilon_{k,o} == EXE_{k,o} + ST \prod_{i=1}^{SN} \prod_{j=1}^{MN} SRC_{k,i,o} packed_{k,i,j} encflag_{k,j}$$

$$+ MT \prod_{i=1}^{SN} \prod_{j=1}^{MN} SRC_{k,i,o} packed_{k,i,j} macflag_{k,j} \tag{20}$$

The task WCRT $\theta_{k,o}$ consists of two parts: the WCET and the interfering time caused by other tasks with higher priority in the same ECU [15]. The calculation of task WCRT can be described with formula (21).

$$\forall t_{k,o}, \ \theta_{k,o} == \varepsilon_{k,o} + \sum_{o' \in HP(o)} \left\lceil \frac{\theta_{k,o}}{\tau_{k,o'}} \right\rceil \varepsilon_{k,o'} \tag{21}$$

All constraints in the system are given above and the optimization objective has been described as formula (8). We use the Yalmip tool to describe these constraints. Some of the constraints are nonlinear formulas. We leverage the linearization method proposed in [9]. After the linearization process, we use the Gurobi to solve the MILP formulation.

3.2 Execution Steps of CSLLP

If the signal packing problem of all ECUs is considered at the same time, the running time of the MILP formulation will be unacceptable. However, solving the signal packing problem of each ECU in turn will greatly reduce the running time. This is because the solution time of the MILP model will increase greatly with the expansion of the problem scale. Based on this principle, we decompose the MILP formulation of all ECUs into local MILP formulation of each ECU and solve them step by step, which can greatly reduce the running time. However, the WCRT analysis of messages in CAN-FD requires the participation of messages from other ECUs. To solve this problem, we generate a random initial solution for the signal packing of each ECU. In this way, the MILP model can only focus on one ECU at a time.

As shown in Fig. 2, the CSLLP starts by generating a random initial solution. Then select an ECU and eliminate its signal packing result from the initial solution. Next, input the incomplete initial solution into the MILP model. Since there is the signal packing of only one ECU needs to be solved, the result can be obtained quickly. And then update the initial solution. The above mentioned processes will be executed iteratively until solutions are obtained for all ECU. Finally, return the final result and end the algorithm.

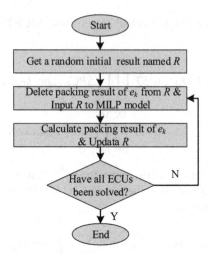

Fig. 2. The execution steps of CSLLP.

4   Simulated-Annealing-Based Algorithm

To prove the effectiveness of the CSLLP, a simulated-annealing-based heuristic algorithm named SA is proposed as the baseline algorithm. As shown in Algorithm 1, the SA also needs to obtain an initial solution. And in each experiment, the random initial solution of SA is the same as the CSLLP. We set the initial temperature TS as 1000, the termination temperature TE as 1, the cooling rate $LOSS$ as 0.99, and the disturbance times $DISTURB$ as 100. The $RAND$ function in the SA is used to generate random numbers ranging from 0 to 1. And the exponential function in the SA is represented by EXP.

Algorithm 1: SA

 1: get random initial solution OLD;
 2: TS = 1000; TE = 1; $LOSS$ = 0.99; $DISTURB$ = 100;
 3: **while** $TS > TE$
 4:      **for** $i = 1$ **to** $DISTURB$
 5:          $\forall e_k$, move a random $s_{k,i}$ to a random $m_{k,j}$;
 6:      NEW = compute the result;
 7:      **if** $NEW < OLD$
 8:          $OLD = NEW$;
 9:      **else**
10:          $\Delta = (NEW - OLD) / TS$;
11:          **if** $RAND(1) \leqslant EXP(\Delta)$
12:              $OLD = NEW$;
13:      $TS = TS * LOSS$;
14: **return** OLD;

---

5 Experimental Results

To validate the efficiency of the CSLLP, we conduct comparative experiments based on synthetic input data. The parameters of the tasks, signals, and paths are set according to [15–17]. As shown in Table 3, the test cases are divided into four groups, 100 test cases are generated for each group, and the experiment result is the average value of the 100 test cases. In all of these experiments, the general tasks account for 50%, the privacy task for 25%, and the controlling task for 25% [11, 18]. The unit time of CAN-FD arbitration field transmission is 2 μs and the data field is 0.5 μs [7, 9], i.e., $ARB = 2$ μs and $DAT = 0.5$ μs. The security overhead constants ST and MT are assumed to be 85μs and 267 μs, respectively [13]. Our experiment platform is a 2.6 GHz processor with 16 GB RAM.

As shown in formula (7), the end-to-end delay includes the period of signal and task and the WCRT of signal and task. Because the period will not change throughout the experiment, and WCRT will vary according to the signal packing result. Thus, the end-to-end delay can be divided into the constant part and the variable part, and the variable part can better evaluate the performance of the algorithms. Table 3 shows the experimental results of each group, which includes the total period and total WCRT of end-to-end path, and the run time of the algorithms. We can see that the constant part of the CSLLP and the SA are equal, but the variable part is different. The WCRT of signal and task of the CSLLP is significantly lower than that of the SA, and the maximal reduction rate is 32.2%, and the average reduction rate is 26.7%. The running time of the CSLLP is longer than that of SA, but it is within the acceptable range.

Table 3. The end-to-end delay and the runtime comparison between the SA and the CSLLP.

Group ID	Number of ECU, tasks, and signals	End-to-end delay(μs)			Reduction rate	Runtime(s)	
		Constant: period of signal and task	Variable: WCRT of signal and task			SA	CSLLP
			SA	CSLLP			
1	4, 18, 33	3814096.6	51060.8	34593.9	32.2%	285.7	809.0
2	6, 24, 55	8346400.0	94622.3	73046.1	22.8%	471.6	1181.2
3	8, 35, 70	12252333.3	158384.7	115178.0	27.2%	646.9	1797.8
4	10, 46, 92	17087833.4	242572.1	182446.0	24.7%	814.2	4540.9

6 Conclusion

Based on the security analysis of the electronic functions of the vehicles, we proposed a new security model suitable for CAN-FD. And we further proposed a signal packing algorithm named CSLLP based on MILP to optimize the end-to-end delay of vehicular functions. Experimental results show that by comparing with the baseline algorithm, the CSLLP can reduce the end-to-end delay by 26.7% on average, and 32.2% maximally.

Acknowledgments. This work was supported by Natural Science Foundation of China(61872436), and partially supported by Natural Science Foundation of Jiangsu Province(BK20211272), the Research Foundation of NJUPT for "1311 Talents Training Project" and the NUPTSF (Grant No.NY220133).

References

1. McCue, T.J.: 108 MPG with 2013 Ford Fusion Energi Plus 25 Gigabytes of Data. http://www.forbes.com/sites/tjmccue/2013/01/01/108-mpg-with-ford-fusion-energi-plus-25-gigabytes-of-data/#45211c3c46a5. Accessed 23 June 2021
2. Overview of recommended practice-SAE-J3061-16. https://www.sae.org/standards/content/j3061/. Accessed 23 June 2021
3. Xie, Y., Zhou, Y., Xu, J., Zhou, J., Chen, X., Xiao, F.: Cybersecurity protection on in-vehicle networks for distributed automotive cyber-physical systems: state of the art and future challenges. Software Pract. Exper. **51**(11), 2108–2127 (2021)
4. Woo, S., Jo, H.J., Kim, I.S., Lee, D.H.: A practical security architecture for in-vehicle CAN-FD. IEEE Trans. Intell. Transp. Syst. **17**(8), 2248–2261 (2016)
5. Miller, C., Valasek, C.: Remote exploitation of an unaltered passenger vehicle. In: Black Hat USA 2015.S 91(2015)
6. Currie, R.: Information security reading room developments in car hacking. https://www.sans.org/reading-room/whitepapers/ICS/developments-car-hacking-36607. Accessed 13 Jan 2021
7. Bordoloi, U.D., Samii, S.: The frame packing problem for CAN-FD. In: 2014 IEEE Real-Time Systems Symposium, pp. 284–293. IEEE (2014)
8. Natale, M.D., da Silva, C.L.M., Santos, M.M.D: On the applicability of an MILP solution for signal packing in CAN-FD. In: 2016 IEEE 14th International Conference on Industrial Informatics (INDIN), pp. 1202–1205. IEEE (2016)
9. Xie, Y., Zeng, G., Kurachi, R., Takada, H., Xie, G.: Security/timing-aware design space exploration of CAN FD for automotive cyber-physical systems. IEEE Trans. Industr. Inf. **15**(2), 1094–1104 (2019)
10. Lin, J., Wei, Y., Li, W., Long, J.: Intrusion detection system based on deep neural network and incremental learning for in-vehicle CAN networks. In: Wang, G., Choo, KK.R., Ko, R.K.L., Xu, Y., Crispo, B. (eds.) Ubiquitous Security. UbiSec 2021. CCIS, vol. 1557, pp. 255–267. Springer, Singapore (2022). https://doi.org/10.1007/978-981-19-0468-4_19
11. Mun, H., Han, K., Lee, D.H.: Ensuring safety and security in CAN-based automotive embedded systems: a combination of design optimization and secure communication. IEEE Trans. Veh. Technol. **69**(7), 7078–7091 (2020)
12. Munir, A., Koushanfar, F.: Design and analysis of secure and dependable automotive CPS: a steer-by-wire case study. IEEE Trans. Dependable Secure Comput. **17**(4), 813–827 (2018)
13. Wu, Z., Zhao, J., Zhu, Y., Li, Q.: Research on vehicle Cybersecurity-based on dedicated security hardware and ECDH algorithm. In: SAE 2017 Intelligent and Connected Vehicles Symposium, No. 2017-01-2005. SAE International (2017)
14. Aminifar, A., Eles, P., Peng, Z.: Optimization of message encryption for Real-time applications in embedded systems. IEEE Trans. Comput. **67**(5), 748–754 (2017)
15. Lin, C., Zhu, Q., Phung, C., Sangiovanni-Vincentelli, A.: Security-aware mapping for CAN-based real-time distributed automotive systems. In: 2013 IEEE/ACM International Conference on Computer-Aided Design (ICCAD), pp. 115–121. IEEE (2013)

16. Koay, A.M.Y., Xie, M., Ko, R.K.L., Sterner, C., Choi, T., Dong, N.: SDGen: a scalable, reproducible and flexible approach to generate real world cyber security datasets. In: Wang, G., Choo, KK.R., Ko, R.K.L., Xu, Y., Crispo, B. (eds.) Ubiquitous Security. UbiSec 2021. CCIS, vol. 1557, pp 102–115. Springer, Singapore (2022). https://doi.org/10.1007/978-981-19-0468-4_8

17. Kramer, S., Ziegenbein, D., Hamann, A.: Real world automotive benchmark for free. In: 6th International Workshop on Analysis Tools and Methodologies for Embedded and Real-time Systems (WATERS) (2015)

18. BMW X1 (E84) CAN-bus Codes. http://www.loopybunny.co.uk/CarPC/kcan.html. Accessed 24 Feb 2020

An Adversarial Sample Defense Method Based on Saliency Information

Shuqi Liu[1(✉)], Yufeng Zhuang[1,2], Xinyu Ma[1], Hongping Wang[1], and Danni Cao[1]

[1] Modern Post College (School of Automation),
Beijing University of Posts and Telecommunications, Beijing 100876, China
{liushuqi,zhuangyf,maxinyu2018,hongping.wang,
caodanni}@bupt.edu.cn
[2] Beijing Key Laboratory of Safety Production Intelligent Monitoring,
Beijing University of Posts and Telecommunications, Beijing 100876, China

Abstract. In recent years, the development of deep neural networks is in full gear in the fields of computer vision, natural language processing, and others. However, the existence of adversarial examples brings risks to these tasks, which is also a huge obstacle to implement deep learning applications in the real world. In order to solve the aforementioned problems and improve the robustness of neural networks, a novel defense network based on generative adversarial networks (GANs) and saliency information is proposed. First, the generator is utilized to eliminate disturbances of adversarial samples and clean samples, at the same time, the distance between these two distributions is minimized by loss function. Then, salient feature extraction model is used to extract salient maps of both clean examples and adversarial samples, thus improving the denoising effect of the generator by reducing the difference between salient maps. The proposed method can guide the generation networks to accurately remove the invisible disturbance and to restore the adversarial samples to clean samples, which not only improves the success rate of classification but also achieves the defense effect. Extensive experiments are conducted to compare the defense effect of our proposed method with other defense methods against various attacks. Experimental results show that our method has strong defensive capabilities against these attack methods.

Keywords: Adversarial example · Defense · Deep neural networks · Generative adversarial networks · Multi-scale discriminator

1 Introduction

In recent years, the development of deep learning is flourishing, especially in computer vision, natural language processing, unmanned driving, voice recognition and other applications [1–4]. To a large extent, deep learning provides convenience for human life. With the continuous development of the deep neural network model, the fragility of the model also appears. Hence, the robustness of deep neural networks has attracted extensive attention of many researchers.

In 2014, Szegedy [5] found that deep learning models are easily deceived by carefully designed samples. In the field of computer vision, this manifests as a neural network can be attacked by a carefully designed disturbance added to a clean image, that is,

G. Wang et al. (Eds.): UbiSec 2022, CCIS 1768, pp. 304–318, 2023.
https://doi.org/10.1007/978-981-99-0272-9_21

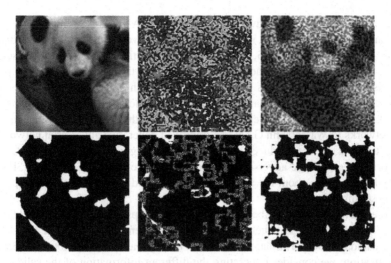

Fig. 1. Saliency information map. In the first row, from left to right are clean samples, noise, and adversarial samples. The second row from left to right is the saliency map of clean samples, the saliency map of noise, and the saliency map of adversarial samples (Best viewed in color).

the disturbance may cause misclassification of the model. Szegedy [5] calls these samples that can misclassify neural networks as adversarial samples. Essentially, because of the high dimensional nonlinear characteristics of the deep neural networks, changing a few pixels of the image would be enough to cause wrong results on different tasks. For example, in the classification task, we can even change a single pixel of the image [6] to achieve the purpose of misclassification. In the segmentation task, Metzen [7] changed the segmentation result by adding predesigned disturbance to the clean image.

Adversarial examples play an important role in real world. For example, in the scene of road traffic sign recognition, sign pollution caused by rain or snow and invisible disturbance artificially added may cause neural networks misclassification [8,9]. And this situation will undoubtedly hinder the development of driverless cars and bring potential dangers. Moreover, in the medical field, the defense against samples is still the top priority. For example, the article published on Science [10] found that the complexity and particularity of medical images make the medical image processing system more vulnerable to attack by the adversarial samples, such as misclassifying benign diseases into malignant diseases. In a word, it is the most important matter to study the defense of adversarial samples and propose appropriate defense methods in the field of deep learning.

Nowadays, people use this leak [11,12] to identify and understand potential weakness of deep neural networks, thus it can efficiently improve defense ability and robustness. Therefore, the main motivation of the proposed defense method in this paper is to denoise the adversarial samples so that the processed images can be correctly classified by the neural networks, thus achieving defensive effect.

As we know, generative adversarial networks (GANs) are the most widely used basic frameworks. For example, it not only generates adversarial samples used for attack [13,14], but also defends it [15,16]. Therefore, we initialize the GANs as baseline to propose a defense method of adversarial samples. In the traditional training process of GANs, due to the problems inherent in GAN, such as training difficulties, mode collapse, insufficient diversity, and low stability, the generation effect of the generator is affected. To address the aforementioned limitations of the prior works, we changed the basic networks to Wasserstein GAN. An improved generative adversarial network with Wasserstein distance is introduced, which can solve the gradient disappearance problem of the original generative adversarial network to some extent [17]. Moreover, Pang [3] collected some tricks about the adversarial training and GAN, like early stopping and warmup setting.

There is a huge difference between the saliency maps of adversarial and clean samples in Fig. 1. Interestingly, when displaying the difference between these two saliency maps, we find that the perturbation area added to the clean sample is obtained. Based on this motivation, we consider integrating the different information of the saliency map into our defense framework and assisting the generator to better manifest the denoising effect by reducing the difference between these two saliency maps. Our core purpose is to reduce the distribution between the clean samples and adversarial samples by denoising, so as to achieve the effect of improving the robustness of neural networks.

The main contributions of this work are as follows:

- On the one hand, a novel defense method based on the GANs against the adversarial examples is put forward. Meanwhile, we take WGAN into account and combine it into the structure to improve the stability of training.
- On the other hand, the most important point is that we utilize the salient feature extractor to generate the salient maps of the denoised image and the clean image, as well as reduce the difference between the two, so that the generator can generate better denoised image and achieve better defense effect in the salient feature level.

In terms of the experimental deployment, we not only compare the defense effects of different attack methods, but also those for different defense methods. Meanwhile, we conduct ablation experiments of the proposed model to verify the effectiveness and robustness. The experiment proved that the proposed method has a strong defense capability.

The rest of the paper is organized as follows: In Sect. 2, we introduce the background of adversarial examples and some common attack and defense methods, as well as the applications of saliency map. In Sect. 3, we discuss the details of the proposed method, including a description of the principle and settings of the objective function. Sections 4 introduces the experimental results, and the algorithm of our proposed method. Finally, we summarize the ideas and show prospects for future work in Sects. 5.

2   Related Work

In this section, we briefly review several classic attack and defense methods. At the same time, we also explain how to use WGAN to assist our method based on previous experience. Finally, we discuss the significance detection part in detail, and summarize the effectiveness of saliency map.

2.1   Existing Attack Methods

Szegedy et al. [5] first found that deep neural networks and humans may give totally different judgement on images. If perturbation is added to a clean sample, classification model may regard it as a completely different image and give a false prediction, but humans could not focus on this difference [18]. These blind spots make the neural networks model vulnerable to attacks. Generally speaking, these data with small disturbance but different prediction results are called adversarial samples. In recent years, researchers have made a lot of discussions on attack methods, among which Fast Gradient Sign Method (FGSM) was proposed by Goodfellow et al. [19] as the original method to generate adversarial samples. The principle of this method is to find the corresponding adversarial disturbance for a given input image. Equation (1) is the formula for calculating noise.

$$p_x = \varepsilon \cdot \text{sign}\left(\nabla_x J\left(w, x, y_t\right)\right) \tag{1}$$

where $J\left(\cdot, \cdot, \cdot\right)$ denotes the loss function used to train a deep neural network. $\nabla_x J\left(\cdot, \cdot, \cdot\right)$ denotes the gradient of the loss function w.r.t the input x. w is the trained network parameter. $sign$ denotes a sign function. ε denotes a constant that controls the noise intensity.

FGSM calculates the gradient of loss function, then takes sign and multiplies it by a constant, finally adds the result as adversarial noise to the original image to get the adversarial sample.

Furthermore, the PGD (Project Gradient Descent) attack proposed by Madry [20] is an iterative attack method, which can be regarded as an improved version of FGSM, and can be expressed as K-FGSM (K represents the number of iterations). The main contribution of this method is multiple iterations, one small step at a time and each iteration will clip the disturbance to the specified range. In general, PGD requires multiple iterations to find the right direction, so its overall attack performance is better than FGSM.

Moreover, the momentum iterative attack method proposed by Dong [21] can stably update the direction and avoid the local maximum value in the iterative process, thus producing a transferable adversarial sample. Moosavi-Dezfooli [22] proposed the deepfool method, which iterates to calculate the minimum norm disturbance for a given image, finds the projection of input x on the decision surface, and moves x slightly along the direction of the projection found.

CW (Carlini & Wagner) attack proposed by CarLini [11] mainly takes adversarial samples as a variable, then achieves the purpose of attack by reducing the gap between adversarial samples and clean samples and increasing the loss between the predicted label of adversarial samples and the real samples. However, JSMA (Jacobian Saliency

Map Attack) method proposed by Papernot [23] uses the Jacobian matrix to find the difference between saliency maps from input and output, so as to obtain vulnerable areas of attack.

2.2 Existing Defense Methods

Currently, several widely used defense methods have been proposed. One of the typical defense methods is MagNet [24]. MagNet proposes an attack-independent defense framework that does not rely on the adversarial sample and its generation process, but only takes advantage of the characteristics of the data itself. At the same time, this method does not modify the original network structure, and it defends against the samples from the perspective of detection. Defense-GAN [16] uses the expression ability of the generated model in WGAN [17] to defend the adversarial samples. APE-GAN [15] is a most important defense method. It is also a way to change the input image for defense, mainly by processing the image before classification. However, APE-GAN does not consider the distribution of clean samples and cannot process complex images. Defense-GAN is used to simulate the distribution of the denoised adversarial samples, and output to the classifier to achieve the purpose of defense. But this method has no reference to the distribution of clean images.

As shown in Table 1, one common feature of these defense methods is to improve the robustness of the classification model. However, our method takes into account significant information and the characteristic information of the reconstructed image. The most important feature information is the distribution information of the image. These are the three characteristics of the defense method we proposed. We have improved this limitation on this basis by using significant feature constraints, so that it can process more complex images. At the same time, we improve the generation effect by inputting clean images into the generator and obtaining the distribution of clean sample.

Table 1. Difference between existed methods and proposed method

Features	Defense		
	APE-GAN	Defense-GAN	Our method
GAN-based structure	√	–	√
Salience information	–	–	√
Reconstruction information	–	–	√
Distribution information	–	√	√

2.3 Salient Feature Extraction Methods

Generally, saliency is an important visual feature in images, which reflects the attention paid by human eyes to various regions of images. Since Laurent Itti [25] found this situation in 1998, a series of significance mapping methods have been derived. Image saliency is widely used in compression, edge enhancement, and salient object extraction. For example, if a pixel has a higher pixel value in a color image, it will be displayed in a more obvious way in saliency map. Prerana Mukherjee [26] makes use of saliency maps for denoising in 2019, and uses cyclic-consistency to denoise the adversarial samples to achieve better results. Qibin Hou [27] proposed a new method by introducing short connections to the skip-layer structures for obtaining saliency maps. Wang et al. [28] combined local estimation and global search estimation. In the local estimation phase, local block char- acteristics is used to determine the significance value of each pixel. In the global search phase, local significance mapping, global contrast and geometric information are used as prior information to describe a group of target candidate regions. Finally, they use both global and local features to get the final saliency map.

In short, there is little literature on the use of salient information for defense against adversarial samples. Therefore, in our defense method, saliency information are combined to denoise adversarial examples.

3 Our Approach

3.1 Pipeline

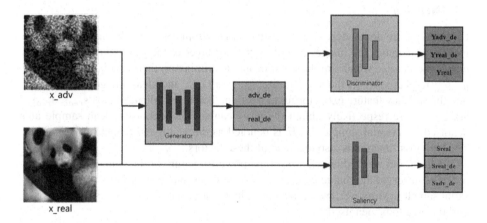

Fig. 2. *Our proposed method.* Both the adversarial sample and the clean sample are used as the input of the generator to get the denoising images, which are input into discriminators for discrimination. At the same time, the output of the generator will be used as the input of the salient feature extractor together with the clean sample to obtain the salient map.

The main defense idea of this paper is to train a better generator by using loss function and combine the saliency information to help the generator generate the denoised adversarial examples, so as to improve the classification success rate. See Eq. (2)

$$\hat{\theta}_G = \arg\min_{\theta_G} \frac{1}{N} \sum_{k=1}^{N} L_{all}\left(G_{\theta_G}\left(X_{adv}^k\right), X^k\right) \tag{2}$$

where, X is denoted as the clean images, X_{adv} is denoted as the adversarial examples. θ_G is denoted as the parameters of generator. N is denoted as the numbers of X, k is k-th images. As shown in Fig. 2, a new defense method based on GANs is proposed. The basic idea is to input clean samples and adversarial examples into the generator for joint training, so as to obtain the denoised image. Generator is used to produce denoised images and the discriminator is utilized to judge the denoised images. Due to significant informations extracted from clean samples and adversarial samples are different, salient information is considered to be a piece of useful information for improving the denoising effect of the generator. Specifically, we use saliency extractor to extract three saliency maps, including the saliency maps of denoised adversarial example, denoised clean sample and clean image. We ultimately aim to make three saliency maps above extremely similar through loss constraint. Since our method is based on GANs, which have the disadvantage of mode collapse, we apply WGAN loss to improve the stability of GAN training and denoising effect of the generator.

In a word, the motivation of our method is to capture and make use of the information of images scales. Meanwhile, we constrain the differences in saliency maps, so that our method can achieve good denoising effect and defense capability.

3.2   Notation

Clean image are denoted as x_{real} and adversarial sample as x_{adv}. We input both above into the generator. The images output by the last layer of the generator are marked as adv_{de} and $real_{de}$, which are the input of the discriminator, then we obtain $y_{adv_{de}}$ and $y_{real_{de}}$ respectively. At the same time, $x_{adv_{de}}$, $x_{real_{de}}$ and clean image x_{real} are put into the saliency feature extractor for extraction, then three saliency maps s_{real}, $s_{real_{de}}$ and $s_{adv_{de}}$ are respectively obtained from clean sample, denoised clean sample and denoised adversarial sample. W, H is denoted as the width and height of the images. The total loss function is also made up of these factors.

In short, our method benefits from the powerful nature of the generation model. It not only preserves the characteristics of clean samples, but also removes noise of adversarial samples. Moreover, we utilize the saliency information to assist the generator to find the area to be denoised.

3.3   Learning Objective

In this section, loss functions are introduced according to the role of different structures, that is, in terms of the generator, discriminator and salience feature extractor to define the loss functions. Among these functions, reconstruction loss is obtained by generator, it contains the difference of clean samples and adversarial sample; adversarial loss is produced by discriminator and it calculates the loss of GAN; saliency loss is generated by salience extractor. It mainly calculates the difference between the salience information of different images.

Reconstruction Loss l_{rec}
Since the generator's role in this paper is to denoise the adversarial samples, the loss come out by the generator is defined as the reconstruction loss l_{rec}.

In order to ensure that there is a great similarity between the denoised adversarial sample and the denoised clean sample, it is critical to minimize the distance between $x_{adv_{de}}$ and $x_{real_{de}}$. Considering the distribution of the clean samples, the distance between the clean sample x_{real} and the result of generator is also minimized. These formulas are as follows:

$$l_{rec} = l_{rec_1} + l_{rec_2} + l_{rec_3} \tag{3}$$

$$l_{rec_1} = \frac{1}{WH} \sum_{w,h=1}^{W,H} \left((x_{real})_{w,h} - (x_{adv_{de}})_{w,h} \right)^2 \tag{4}$$

$$l_{rec_2} = \frac{1}{WH} \sum_{w,h=1}^{W,H} \left((x_{real})_{w,h} - (x_{real_{de}})_{w,h} \right)^2 \tag{5}$$

$$l_{rec_3} = \frac{1}{WH} \sum_{w,h=1}^{W,H} \left((x_{adv_{de}})_{w,h} - (x_{real_{de}})_{w,h} \right)^2 \tag{6}$$

Adversarial Loss l_{adv}

It is noteworthy that the traditional GANs have some problems of mode collapse. We use WGAN to reduce the impact of the mode crash of GANs. Meanwhile, it will improve the stability of GANs.

The discriminator is introduced to discriminate the final layer output, with the main purpose of reducing the label-level loss between $x_{adv_{de}}$, $x_{real_{de}}$ and x_{real}. At the same time, WGAN loss is integrated into the discriminator structure to obtain the discriminant loss l_{adv}.

$$l_{adv_1} = \sum_{n=1}^{N} [D_{\theta_D}(x_{real}) + (1 - D_{\theta_D}(x_{adv_{de}}))] \tag{7}$$

$$l_{adv_2} = \sum_{n=1}^{N} [D_{\theta_D}(x_{real}) + (1 - D_{\theta_D}(x_{real_{de}}))] \tag{8}$$

$$l_{adv_3} = \sum_{n=1}^{N} [D_{\theta_D}(x_{adv_{de}}) + (1 - D_{\theta_D}(x_{real_{de}}))] \tag{9}$$

$$l_{adv} = l_{adv_1} + l_{adv_2} + l_{adv_3} \tag{10}$$

Saliency Loss l_{sal}

The reconstruction loss and the adversarial loss mentioned above are both basic losses based on GANs. However, we found a subtle difference in the saliency maps between adversarial sample and clean sample, thus we introduce saliency loss l_{sal} based on this observation.

Specifically, we minimize the distance between the saliency maps of the clean sample and denoised adversarial sample, as well as the distance between the clean sample and denoised sample. Moreover, since denoised clean samples and denoised adversarial samples are isomorphic, we take into account this loss. Thus, three losses are introduced to assist the generator to achieve better denoising effect in terms of saliency maps.

Significant losses are divided into three parts: l_{sal_1}, l_{sal_2}, l_{sal_3}. l_{sal_1} represents the significant loss between the clean image and the denoised adversarial sample, l_{sal_2} represents the loss between the clean image and denoised clean image, l_{sal_3} represents the significant loss between the denoised adversarial sample and the denoised clean sample.

$$l_{sal} = l_{sal_1} + l_{sal_2} + l_{sal_3} \tag{11}$$

$$l_{sal_1} = \frac{1}{WH} \sum_{w,h=1}^{W,H} \left((S_{real})_{w,h} - (S_{adv_{de}})_{w,h} \right)^2 \tag{12}$$

$$l_{sal_2} = \frac{1}{WH} \sum_{w,h=1}^{W,H} \left((S_{real})_{w,h} - (S_{real_{de}})_{w,h} \right)^2 \tag{13}$$

$$l_{sal_3} = \frac{1}{WH} \sum_{w,h=1}^{W,H} \left((S_{adv_{de}})_{w,h} - (S_{real_{de}})_{w,h} \right)^2 \tag{14}$$

In short, the total loss function L_{all} comes out by the above three parts, which is shown as the following formula:

$$L_{all} = \alpha_1 l_{rec} + \alpha_2 l_{adv} + \alpha_3 l_{sal} \tag{15}$$

The selection of weight hyperparameters has been verified under multiple combinations, and this group was finally selected, that is, α_1, α_2 and α_3 are 0.7, 0.2 and 0.1 respectively. Reconstruction loss and saliency loss focus on denoised adversarial samples' content and style, while the adversarial loss is to restore specific texture details.

4   Experimental Results and Analysis

In this section, we first outline the setup of the experiment. Secondly, in order to verify the feasibility of our method, we evaluated the proposed method qualitatively and quantitatively. Qualitative evaluation includes the defense effectiveness of the denoising method proposed in this paper at the visual level, that is, the adversarial noise samples and clean samples after denoising cannot be distinguished visually. Furthermore, we assessed the visual differences between the saliency maps of denoised adversarial samples and the saliency maps of clean samples. In theory, we expect them to be highly similar. Quantitative evaluation includes comparative experimental design, ablation experimental design. Specifically, we compared the performance of the various attack methods mentioned above with that of the various defense methods. Moreover, we also use general indicators (classification accuracy) to evaluate the effectiveness of the proposed defense approach.

4.1 Details

To verify the effect of our method, we apply the defense method to the ImageNet dataset [29]. We mainly used the ImageNet dataset, which was derived from the natural image collected by Feifei Li. It spans 1000 object classes and contains 1,281,167 training images, 50,000 validation images and 100,000 test images. This dataset was used to train the multi-scale network and saliency network. At the same time, the CIFAR10 dataset as the auxiliary dataset proves the effectiveness of the defense method. In the experiments, the learning rate is 0.0002, RMSProp is initialized by the optimizer we choose, which is used to update parameters and optimize the network. Batchsize is set as 64, device parameters are CPU: Intel I7-8700, GPU: RTX2080TI-11g, memory: DDR4-3000-32g. The code runs under the Pytorch deep learning framework, and the whole network training takes about 6 days to complete.

4.2 Algorithm Structure

The training process of this paper is as shown in the algorithm. Firstly, some basic parameters are initialized. Secondly, the salient feature extraction network was trained in advance, and the adversarial examples were generated offline. During the loop in the outer layer, when the number of iterations is less than the number of epochs, both clean samples and adversarial samples are input into the generator network for denoising, then we calculate the reconstruction losses. During the loop in the inter layer, generated denoised images are input into the discriminant for discrimination, and output corresponding label, which are compared with the ground truth to calculate the adversarial loss. Finally, the output image is input into the saliency detection network for feature extraction, then we get the saliency loss. In the process of continuous optimization, we get a good denoising image.

In the process of testing, since clean samples have been trained on the generator as the main factor in the training stage and the generator has good denoising effect, it is not necessary to input clean samples into the generator for assistance. Therefore, we only need to input the adversarial examples into the generator to complete the testing process.

4.3 Qualitative Experiments

Qualitative results are briefly described in Fig. 3. The experiments use FGSM method on the ImageNet, by setting the disturbance intensity ε as 0.10, one can see that our method has good denoising results. Before denoising, it can be seen that there is a slight disturbance on the adversarial sample. After denoising with our method, we can eliminate the disturbance, thus improving the classification success rate and achieving a good defensive effect. As shown in Fig. 4, there is a big difference between the saliency maps of clean samples and adversarial samples. However, it can be seen that the saliency maps have been significantly changed, and the edge of corn is clearer. Therefore, from the perspective of saliency, our denoising method has a good effect. In this case, the auxiliary role of saliency feature information on the network is further confirmed, and the information is conducive to improving the denoising effect of the generator.

Algorithm . Training process algorithm(taking FGSM as an example)

Initialization:
　　iterations epochs=20000; learning rate = 0.0003; loss function parameters: $\alpha_1 = 0.7, \alpha_2 = 0.2, \alpha_3 = 0.1$; batchsize=64;

Pre-training:
　　saliency detection network:Saliency; generated data:$\{x_{real}, x_{adv}\}$

1: **while** $it < epochs$ **do**
2:　　number = 5;
3:　　**for** i in $train\_loader()$ **do**
4:　　　train G:
5:　　　$G(x_{real}) \rightarrow x_{real_{de}};$
6:　　　$G(x_{adv}) \rightarrow x_{adv_{de}};$
7:　　　Calculate l_{rec};
8:　　　**if** $i\%number == 0$ **then**
9:　　　　train D:
10:　　　　$D(x_{real_{de}}, x_{adv_{de}}, x_{real}) \rightarrow y_{real_{de}}, y_{adv_{de}}, y_{real}$
11:　　　　Calculate l_{adv};
12:　　　**end if**
13:　　**end for**
14:　　$Sal(x_{adv_{de}}, x_{real_{de}}, x_{real}) \rightarrow S_{adv_{de}}, S_{real_{de}}, S_{real}$
15:　　Calculate l_{sal};
16:　　let $it \leftarrow it + 1$;
17: **end while**

4.4　Comparative Experiments

In this part, six attack methods and three defense methods mentioned in the related work will be used for a horizontal comparison on the ImageNet dataset. The main purpose is to compare the defense effectiveness of different defense methods against the same attack method. First of all, as shown in Table 2, we used various attack methods to generate corresponding adversarial samples, and conducted defense through three defense methods, so as to obtain comparative results. The results show that the classification accuracy of the FGSM attack method is 0.22 higher than that of APE-GAN [15]. Meanwhile, the classification accuracy is 0.06 higher than that of Defense-GAN [16]. Moreover, the classification accuracy of the adversarial samples after defense is 0.53 higher than that before defense, which directly proves the effectiveness of the defense method. However, under the same defense method, different attack methods have different performances. Since FGSM is a single-step disturbance generation method and PGD is an iterative disturbance generation method with better attack effect, classification accuracy of PGD is lower that of FGSM in the absence of defense. At the same time, because FGSM is relatively simple, it achieves high performance in the defense process.

4.5　Ablation Study

This section mainly introduces the effects of the different loss functions as shown in Fig. 5. Horizontal axis marked six attack methods against the generated samples, the

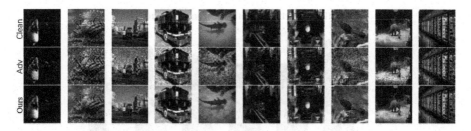

Fig. 3. The experimental results of the FGSM method on ImageNet, the first line "Normal" is a clean sample, the second line "Adv" is the generated adversarial examples, and the third line "ours" is the denoised results of our method.

Clean   Clean_sal   Adversary   Adv_sal   Denoised   De_sal

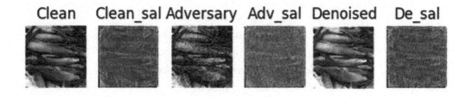

Fig. 4. From left to right are clean image, adversarial sample, denoised adversarial sample, and the corresponding saliency maps.

Table 2. Classification accuracy of six attack methods under three defense methods

Attack	Defense			
	APE-GAN	Defense-GAN	Our method	No defense
FGSM	0.72	0.88	**0.94**	0.41
PGD	0.76	0.81	**0.93**	0.35
MIM	0.68	0.85	**0.94**	0.34
DEEP-FOOL	0.65	0.82	**0.92**	0.32
JSMA	0.66	0.87	**0.91**	0.33
CW	0.60	0.84	**0.89**	0.32

ordinate is the accuracy of the classification. The first column in the chart represents classification accuracy without saliency loss ($l_{rec} + l_{adv}$), the last column is the result of taking into account the loss of all parts ($l_{rec} + l_{adv} + l_{sal}$).

The experimental results show that the performance of the significant feature extractor is better than that of the original network. This is mainly because the significant feature extractor can help the generator to find the significant region of the image, which can be used to improve the denoising effect of the generator and thus improve the classification accuracy. After the fusion, it can help the model to improve the defense capability and robustness to a great extent.

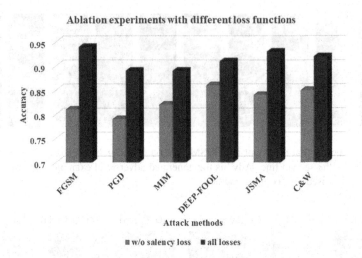

Fig. 5. Ablation experiments with different loss functions

5   Conclusion

In this paper, we propose a novel defense method based on GAN. Its main idea is to use the generator for denoising. Meanwhile, we utilize the saliency maps to further assist the generator to focus on the difference between clean samples and adversarial samples, so as to produce better denoising results. At the same time, we also use WGAN to improve the stability of generative adversarial networks and reduce the effect of the instability of generative adversarial networks. Finally, we merge the advantages of these modules to build our defense framework. We extract the corresponding saliency map by means of the saliency extraction network, to improve the denoising effect and enhance the defensive capability by constraint of loss functions. Then we deploy six common attack methods to attack the network and test the effectiveness of our proposed defense network through qualitative and quantitative experiments. Experiments show the denoising effect and the robustness of our defensive model. Although our method has some advantages, there are still disadvantages, such as the slow training due to the excessive number of parameters. In addition, the research on the disturbance of the feature space is not thorough enough.

For the future, we want to conduct in-depth research from the feature level. Finally, the application scenarios of defense methods need to be explored, which will also be presented in the future work. Moreover, we would like to discuss the application of adversarial defense methods in video classification, such as denoising and super-resolution of videos, so as to improve the classification accuracy and precision of video classification models.

References

1. Shakil, et al.: Towards a two-tier architecture for privacy-enabled recommender systems (PeRS). In: Wang, G., Choo, K.-K.R., Ko, R.K.L., Xu, Y., Crispo, B. (eds.) UbiSec 2021. CCIS, vol. 1557, pp. 268–278. Springer, Singapore (2022). https://doi.org/10.1007/978-981-19-0468-4_20

2. Zou, Y., Peng, T., Zhong, W., Guan, K., Wang, G.: Reliable and controllable data sharing based on blockchain. In: Wang, G., Choo, K.-K.R., Ko, R.K.L., Xu, Y., Crispo, B. (eds.) UbiSec 2021. CCIS, vol. 1557, pp. 229–240. Springer, Singapore (2022). https://doi.org/10.1007/978-981-19-0468-4_17

3. Pang, T., Yang, X., Dong, Y., Su, H., Zhu, J.: Bag of tricks for adversarial training. In: International Conference on Learning Representations (ICLR) (2020)

4. Ding, Z., Guo, Y., Zhang, L., Fu, Y.: One-shot face recognition via generative learning. In: 2018 13th IEEE International Conference on Automatic Face & Gesture Recognition (FG 2018), pp. 1–7. IEEE (2018)

5. Szegedy, C., et al.: Intriguing properties of neural networks. In: Bengio, Y., LeCun, Y. (eds.) International Conference on Learning Representations (ICLR) (2014)

6. Su, J., Vargas, D.V., Sakurai, K.: One pixel attack for fooling deep neural networks. IEEE Trans. Evol. Comput. **23**(5), 828–841 (2019)

7. Hendrik Metzen, J., Chaithanya Kumar, M., Brox, T., Fischer, V.: Universal adversarial perturbations against semantic image segmentation. In: International Conference on Computer Vision(ICCV), pp. 2755–2764 (2017)

8. Duan, R., Ma, X., Wang, Y., Bailey, J., Qin, A.K., Yang, Y.: Adversarial camouflage: hiding physical-world attacks with natural styles. In: IEEE Conference on Computer Vision and Pattern Recognition(CVPR), pp. 1000–1008 (2020)

9. Eykholt, K., et al.: Robust physical-world attacks on deep learning visual classification. In: IEEE Conference on Computer Vision and Pattern Recognition (CVPR), pp. 1625–1634 (2018)

10. Finlayson, S.G., Bowers, J.D., Ito, J., Zittrain, J.L., Beam, A.L., Kohane, I.S.: Adversarial attacks on medical machine learning. Science **363**(6433), 1287–1289 (2019)

11. Carlini, N., Wagner, D.: Towards evaluating the robustness of neural networks. In: IEEE Symposium on Security and Privacy (SP), pp. 39–57. IEEE (2017)

12. Co, K.T., Muñoz-González, L., de Maupeou, S., Lupu, E.C.: Procedural noise adversarial examples for black-box attacks on deep convolutional networks. In: ACM SIGSAC Conference on Computer and Communications Security, pp. 275–289. ACM (2019)

13. Bai, T., et al.: AI-GAN: attack-inspired generation of adversarial examples. In: IEEE International Conference on Image Processing (ICIP), pp. 2543–2547. IEEE (2021)

14. Jandial, S., Mangla, P., Varshney, S., Balasubramanian, V.: AdvGAN++: harnessing latent layers for adversary generation. In: ICCV Workshops, pp. 2045–2048. IEEE (2019)

15. Jin, G., Shen, S., Zhang, D., Dai, F., Zhang, Y.: APE-GAN: adversarial perturbation elimination with GAN. In: International Conference on Acoustics, Speech and Signal Processing (ICASSP), pp. 3842–3846. IEEE (2019)

16. Samangouei, P., Kabkab, M., Chellappa, R.: Defense-GAN: protecting classifiers against adversarial attacks using generative models. In: International Conference on Learning Representations (ICLR) (2018)

17. Arjovsky, M., Chintala, S., Bottou, L.: Wasserstein generative adversarial networks. In: International Conference on Machine Learning (ICML), pp. 214–223. PMLR (2017)

18. Kurakin, A., Goodfellow, I.J., Bengio, S.: Adversarial examples in the physical world. In: Artificial Intelligence Safety and Security, pp. 99–112. Chapman and Hall/CRC (2018)

19. Goodfellow, I.J., Shlens, J., Szegedy, C.: Explaining and harnessing adversarial examples. In: International Conference on Learning Representations (ICLR) (2015)
20. Madry, A., Makelov, A., Schmidt, L., Tsipras, D., Vladu, A.: Towards deep learning models resistant to adversarial attacks. In: International Conference on Learning Representations (ICLR) (2018)
21. Dong, Y., et al.: Boosting adversarial attacks with momentum. In: IEEE Conference on Computer Vision and Pattern Recognition (CVPR), pp. 9185–9193 (2018)
22. Moosavi-Dezfooli, S.-M., Fawzi, A., Frossard, P.: DeepFool: a simple and accurate method to fool deep neural networks. In: IEEE Conference on Computer Vision and Pattern Recognition (CVPR), pp. 2574–2582. IEEE Computer Society (2016)
23. Papernot, N., McDaniel, P., Jha, S., Fredrikson, M., Celik, Z.B., Swami, A.: The limitations of deep learning in adversarial settings. In: IEEE Symposium on Security and Privacy (SP), pp. 372–387. IEEE (2016)
24. Meng, D., Chen, H.: MagNet: a two-pronged defense against adversarial examples. In: ACM SIGSAC Conference on Computer and Communications Security, pp. 135–147 (2017)
25. Itti, L., Koch, C., Niebur, E.: A model of saliency-based visual attention for rapid scene analysis. IEEE Trans. Pattern Anal. Mach. Intell. 20(11), 1254–1259 (1998)
26. Mukherjee, P., et al.: DSAL-GAN: denoising based saliency prediction with generative adversarial networks. CoRR, abs/1904.01215 (2019)
27. Hou, Q., Cheng, M.-M., Hu, X., Borji, A., Tu, Z., Torr, P.H.S.: Deeply supervised salient object detection with short connections. IEEE Trans. Pattern Anal. Mach. Intell. 41(4), 815–828 (2019)
28. Mei, Y., et al.: Pyramid attention networks for image restoration. CoRR, abs/2004.13824, (2020)
29. Krizhevsky, A., Sutskever, I., Hinton, G.E.: ImageNet classification with deep convolutional neural networks. In: Advances in Neural Information Processing Systems (NIPS), vol. 25, pp. 1097–1105 (2012)

BlockLearning: A Modular Framework for Blockchain-Based Vertical Federated Learning

Henrique Dias[(✉)] [iD] and Nirvana Meratnia[(✉)]

Department of Mathematics and Computer Science, Eindhoven University of Technology, Eindhoven 5600MB, The Netherlands
mail@hacdias.com, n.meratnia@tue.nl

Abstract. Federated Learning allows multiple distributed clients to collaborate on training the same Machine Learning model. Blockchain-based Federated Learning has emerged in recent years to improve its transparency, traceability, auditability, authentication, persistency, and information safety. Various Blockchain-based Horizontal Federated Learning models are to be found in the literature. However, to the best of our knowledge, no solution for Blockchain-based Vertical Federated Learning exists. In this paper, we introduce BlockLearning, an extensible and modular framework that supports Vertical Federated Learning and different types of blockchain related algorithms. We also present performance evaluation results in terms of execution time, transaction cost, transaction latency, model accuracy and convergence, as well as communication and computation costs when BlockLearning is applied to vertically partitioned data.

Keywords: Blockchain · Blockchain-based federated learning · Horizontal federated learning · Vertical federated learning

1 Introduction

Federated Learning (FL), introduced by Google researchers in 2016 [19], allows multiple clients, in different locations, to collaborate on training a global Machine Learning (ML) model without sharing their own data with each other. Instead of sharing the raw data, clients only share their model parameters, such as weights. The first benefit of FL is that, by not sharing raw data, models can preserve clients' data privacy. In addition, since model parameters are usually much smaller than the raw data, this leads to less data being transported over the networks. Finally, since the data is distributed among different clients, a single powerful server is not required to train the model, as usually training models with smaller amounts of data is computationally less expensive.

According to [26,33], FL techniques can be broadly divided into three categories: horizontal, vertical, and transfer federated learning. In Horizontal Federated Learning (HFL), the different data sets in the different clients share the

G. Wang et al. (Eds.): UbiSec 2022, CCIS 1768, pp. 319–333, 2023.
https://doi.org/10.1007/978-981-99-0272-9_22

same feature space, but not the sample space. In Vertical Federated Learning (VFL), clients share an intersecting sample space, but different feature spaces.

Most FL solutions include a central server that coordinates the federated training process and aggregates the model weights from each of the clients into a single model. This central coordinator is a single point of failure, since it is required to always be online and behave correctly [16,30]. To address this, Blockchain-based Federated Learning (BFL) techniques have been proposed.

By combining Blockchain with the Federated Learning, not only can the central orchestrator be eliminated, but also the federated training process can be made more transparent. In the blockchain, each transaction is recorded in the distributed ledger. These transactions record information such as local updates, scores, aggregations, among others. Having this information in a public ledger allows for a transparent training process and reward distribution [16], as well as traceability, auditability, persistency, and authentication.

While the combination of blockchain and Horizontal Federated Learning has received enough attention from the research community, to the best of our knowledge, there is no work giving a practical solution on how to implement Vertical Federated Learning in the context of Blockchain-based Federated Learning. To fill this gap, we propose a modular and extensible framework for Blockchain-based Federated Learning, called BlockLearning, that supports Vertical Federated Learning. In addition to presenting the design and implementation aspects of BlockLearning, we also present its performance evaluation results in terms of execution time, transaction cost, transaction latency, model accuracy and convergence, as well as communication and computation costs when applied to vertically partitioned data.

The remainder of this paper is structured as follows. Section 2 presents a short overview of the existing work regarding BFL frameworks. Sections 3 and 4 describe the design and implementation of our framework BlockLearning, respectively, focusing on Vertical Federated Learning. Section 5 presents our performance evaluation and experiments. Section 6 presents discussion of the results. Finally, Sect. 7 gives a conclusion and future directions.

2   Related Work

As far as use of consensus algorithms in BFL is concerned, most authors have used an already existing consensus algorithm, such as Proof of Work [13,21,35], Proof of Stake [6,9,17] and Proof of Authority [14,27,34]. In addition, in the majority of existing works that used an already existing consensus algorithm, the BFL system is built on top of an already existing blockchain platform.

According to the literature, the FL model parameters may either be stored on-chain, i.e., in the blockchain itself [14,27,34], or off-chain, i.e., in a separate storage provider [2,4,18]. Even though most implementations prefer an on-chain storage, they also use custom blockchain implementations [5,13,31], which means that they can implement a platform that has different restrictions on how much data a smart contract can handle. When it comes to using already existing blockchain platforms such as Ethereum, most implementations prefer off-chain storage using a system such as the InterPlanetary File System [18,21,25].

Several works address Horizontal BFL frameworks [10,18,23,30]. However, only [22] discusses the possibility of implementing a Vertical BFS system, but provides no practical solution. In addition, very few of these frameworks provide the source code or build an extensible framework.

3   BlockLearning Framework's Design

Our modular framework, called BlockLearning, is designed in such a way that modules can be easily added, removed or changed, to accommodate both vertical and horizontal partitioned data and different blockchain-related algorithms. In this paper, we focus on its support for Vertical Federated Learning. To see how it supports Horizontal Federated Learning, one is referred to [11].

In BlockLearning, devices, identified by the address of their account in the blockchain, can be classified into three categories: *trainers*, *aggregators* and *scorers*. Additionally, the entity that deploys the contract and is responsible for starting and terminating the rounds is called *model owner*. A device, i.e., a client or a server, can be categorized as one or more categories. By allowing each device to play more than one role, the framework provides flexibility to support different architectures and algorithms.

Fig. 1. BlockLearning's execution Flow

The framework supports a modular sequential flow presented in Fig. 1 and has the following phases:

1. The model owner initializes the round, during which, depending on the participant selection algorithm, the trainers that will participate may have been selected already, or not.
2. The trainers retrieve the information such as the global weights from the last round and train the model using their local data. Then, the trainers submit their model updates.
3. The aggregators retrieve the model updates and execute the aggregation algorithm and submit the aggregation results and the backpropagation gradients to the blockchain.
4. The trainers receive the gradients and backpropagate to their local model. Then, the trainers send a message to the blockchain to confirm the backpropagation.

5. Finally, the model owner sends a transaction to the blockchain in order to terminate the round. At this point, the smart contract checks if the majority of the aggregators agreed on the aggregation. If so, the round is marked as terminated. Otherwise, the round fails, indicating that the aggregators did not reach an agreement, which may indicate that some of the aggregators are compromised.

In the last phase of the execution flow, the smart contract checks if the majority of the aggregators agree on the aggregation. The majority is defined by *at least 50%*. Therefore, the framework offers a 50% threat model. However, the threat threshold can be changed, changing the threat model.

3.1 Structure and Modules

The framework is divided into three main software components: the smart contracts, the library, and the testbed. The structure of the framework, as well as its components and their corresponding modules, are depicted in Fig. 2. Each of the components plays a different role in the overall system in order to support the logical flow shown in Fig. 1. In what follows, we explain each of the components in more detail. One should note the unexplained components are not relevant for Vertical Federated Learning and are extensions to support the Horizontal Federated Learning.

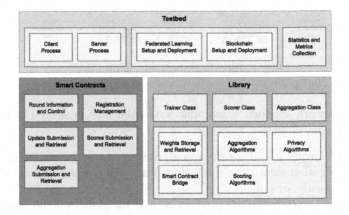

Fig. 2. BlockLearning's structure and modules

Smart Contracts live on the blockchain and are the main means of communication between FL clients and servers. In addition, they hold information regarding the current status of the round, as well as the updates, scores, aggregations, among others. The smart contracts provide the following functionality:

- *Round Information and Control*: the smart contract provides information about whether the round is ongoing and which phase, i.e., scoring, aggregation, or termination phase, it is in. It allows for flexibility such that new phases can be added in the future, such as the backpropagation confirmation phase we need for our vertical model. In addition, it allows for rounds to be started and marked as terminated. Round phase advancements are defined through pre-defined conditions that, once met, automatically move the round to the next phase.
- *Registration Management*: the smart contract allows devices to register themselves as trainers, aggregators, or scorers in the system. Finally, the smart contract provides information about which devices participate in each round.
- *Update Submission and Retrieval*: the smart contract allows trainers to submit their updates, which must include a pointer to the model weights and the amount of data points that were used to train the model. In addition, it includes the training accuracy and testing accuracy for each individual trainer. The submissions must be accessible.
- *Aggregation Submission and Retrieval*: the smart contract allows aggregators to submit the aggregations, which contain a pointer to the weights. The aggregations must be accessible.

Library encodes the algorithms, utilities, and building blocks necessary to implement the scripts that run on the clients and the servers. It includes:

- *Aggregation Algorithms*: implementation of the different aggregation algorithms with a common interface, such that adding new algorithms is easy and simple and they are interchangeable.
- *Weights Storage and Retrieval*: utilities to load and store weights on the decentralized storage provider. These provide an interface in order to make it easy to change the storage provider by providing a different implementation.
- *Smart Contract Bridge*: a contract class that provides an interface to the smart contract that lives on the blockchain. With this class, it should be possible to call the smart contract functions as if they were local functions.
- *Trainer* and *Aggregator Classes*: a class per each device category. This class must register the devices as their category upon initialization. It must also provide methods to execute the training, scoring and aggregation tasks, respectively.

Testbed provides the platform to conduct the experiments in a reproducible way, for instance by setting static seeds for randomness. The testbed includes:

- *Client, Server* and *Owner Scripts*: scripts that will be run at the clients, the servers, and at the model owner, respectively. These scripts will use the library in order to perform the right tasks according to which algorithm is being used.
- *Federated Learning Setup and Deployment*: scripts and tools to easily deploy the client and server machines in a test environment, such as containers.

– *Blockchain Setup and Deployment*: scripts and tools to easily deploy the blockchain network in a test environment using the different consensus algorithms, and to deploy the contract to such network.

In addition, the testbed includes tools to collect the required statistics and logs to retrieve the metrics necessary for the impact analysis.

4   BlockLearning Framework's Implementation

In this section, we go over the implementation details of the BlockLearning framework. The complete implementation is publicly available on GitHub[1].

Smart Contracts: We use the Ethereum [32] blockchain platform as it is the most popular and compatible with all techniques we use for our experiments and comparison with the related work. Therefore, the smart contracts must be implemented in a programming language that supports Ethereum. For this, we chose Solidity [8] as it is the most well-known with the widest support.

Our framework provides a smart contract, named `Base`, that provides the common data structures and functionality. Then, other smart contracts can derive from `Base` and provide additional functionality. In the case for Vertical Federated Learning, we have a `VerticalSplitCNN` smart contract which provides the additional functionality required to support Vertical Federated Learning through the blockchain with the Split-CNN model, which is introduced in the following section.

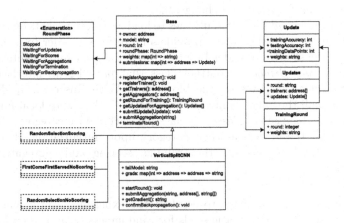

Fig. 3. Smart Contracts Class Diagram

A class diagram with the public interfaces of the contracts, as well as the data types, is depicted in Fig. 3 (adapted from [11]). It can clearly be seen that

---

[1] https://github.com/hacdias/blocklearning.

the smart contract provides round information and control, registration management, updates submission and retrieval, as well as aggregation submission and retrieval.

An interesting implementation detail to note is that score and accuracy values are stored as integers. Currently, Solidity does not support floating point numbers. To preserve fidelity, the original values are multiplied by a large integer, 10^{18}. Then, when the values are retrieved from the smart contract, they are divided by the same value in order to get the original value.

Library: is implemented in the Python [29] programming language. The main motivation for using Python is that many well-known Machine Learning libraries, such as TensorFlow [1] and PyTorch [24] are implemented in Python, as well as many data processing tools.

Aggregation Algorithms: are the first component of the library and they provide a common interface to which each algorithm must conform to. By having a common interface, we can easily implement new algorithms, or change existing ones. In the case of the aggregation algorithms, we require the following interface:

```
aggregate(trainers, updates, scorers, scores) → weights
```

The aggregators provides a function `aggregate` that receives an array with the trainer addresses, an array with the updates sorted by the same order as the trainers, an array with the scorers and an array with the scores sorted by the same order as the scorers. It is important to note that the scorers and the scores are optional arguments and related to Horizontal Federated Learning. The function returns an array with the aggregated weights.

Weights Storage and Retrieval: is the second component of the library, consisting on the utilities to store and retrieve the weights. The weights storage class also provides a common interface such that change of storage providers is possible. For our implementation, we use the InterPlanetary File System (IPFS) [3] as our decentralized storage provider since it is widely used by the community.

Smart Contract Bridge: is the third component, consisting on the smart contract bridge class. The smart contract bridge is implemented using the `Web3.py`[2] library, which provides utilities to call the functions of the smart contracts. The contract bridge class provides 1:1 functions for each functions of the smart contract.

Trainer and Aggregator Classes: implement the main flow of each of these procedures using the modules aforementioned described. For example, the trainer class is initialized with the contract bridge, the weights storage, the model, the data and an optional privacy mechanism. Then, it provides a method `train()` that executes the training procedure, and a method `backward()` that executes the backward propagation. Similarly, the aggregator class provides `aggregate()`.

---

[2] https://github.com/ethereum/web3.py.

Testbed: is the platform to conduct the experiments. It is mostly implemented using the aforementioned library and Docker [20]. Docker is a platform that allows to easily deploy applications in an isolated setting through what is called a container, allowing us to simulate multiple devices in the same network. Each container runs a piece of software called an image. In the testbed, we have the following major components:

Client, Server and Owner Scripts: are the processes that will run at the client, server and model owner, respectively. These are implemented using the BlockLearning library. In each of these scripts, we first load the required data, such as the data set in the clients, and initialize the required algorithms. Algorithm 1 presents the main loop of the client script, for Vertical Federated Learning with the Split-CNN model.

Algorithm 1. Client Script Main Loop for Split-CNN

$T \leftarrow$ Initialize Split-CNN Trainer
while True **do**
    $P \leftarrow$ Get Phase From Smart Contract
    if P is Waiting For Updates **then**
        Execute Training Procedure $T.train()$
    else if P is Waiting For Backpropagation **then**
        Execute Backpropagation Procedure $T.backward()$
    end if
end while

Blockchain Setup and Deployment: is implemented using already existing tools and our library. As previously mentioned, we use Docker containers in order to run the experiments. Moreover, we use Docker Compose in order to deploy multiple containers at once and orchestrate the deployment process.

We use different Ethereum implementations, depending on the consensus algorithm since they are not all available within the sample implementation. Ethereum's main implementation, go-ethereum[3], provides PoA and PoW. For QBFT, we use a fork called quorum [7], which is mostly identical to go-ethereum but supports QBFT. Moreover, the Blockchain setup and deployment follows the following steps:

1. *Generate Accounts.* In first place, the Ethereum accounts for the clients and servers are generated using the provided go-ethereum toolkit. Each account is pre-loaded with 100 ETH, the Ethereum currency, so that clients or servers will not run out of currency to submit their transactions.
2. *Build Images.* In second place, we build the Docker images that will be used to deploy the Blockchain network. This images are based on the images provided by each of the Ethereum's implementations that we use. In addition, they

---
[3] https://github.com/ethereum/go-ethereum.

pre-load the account information, as well as some additional configuration to ensure that all nodes are connected when the network is bootstrapped.

3. *Deploy Network*. In third place, the network is deployed using Docker Compose and the configured amount of nodes.

4. *Deploy Contract*. Finally, the contract is deployed to the network using Truffle, which is a tool designed to help developers developing and deploying smart contracts.

Federated Learning Setup and Deployment: similarly to the Blockchain setup and deployment, we also use Docker Compose for the Federated Learning system. The process is identical as in the previous section, except that we only build the images and deploy the Federated Learning network.

Statistics and Metrics Collection: the different components of the library, such as the `Trainer` and `Aggregator` classes, produce logs. These logs contain information related to timestamps and round number, and events that happen at certain points of the execution, such as: *aggregation started, aggregation ended,* among others. These logs are retrieved from the containers using command-line tools implemented into a script called `toolkit.py`. In addition, resource-related statistics, such as RAM usage, CPU usage, and network traffic, are collected directly from the Docker, through the `docker stats` command.

5   Experimental Setup and Evaluation

In this section, we provide information regarding the experimental setup and performance evaluation.

Dataset, Client Sampling, and Machine Learning Model: for our experiments, we used the MNIST [15] dataset, which includes 70,000 images of handwritten digits from 0 to 9, where each image is 28 by 28 pixels. The MINST data set is not only a well-known dataset but also widely used by the majority of the reviewed works. For the vertical data partition, we used the method of [28]. Firstly, we chose number of samples to be assigned to each client. We chose 20,000 samples in order to match the original work [28] we will be comparing with. The samples were randomly chosen from the original data set. Subsequently, each sample was assigned a unique identifier (ID) that is used as label when giving the data samples to each client. Only the servers have access to the ground truth labels. After assigning the IDs, the feature space F was divided into C parts F_c, where C is the number of clients. Finally, the features F_c, with $c \in C$ was assigned to each of the clients.

For the Vertical FL, we used a dual-headed, or four-headed, Split-CNN [12, 28], depending on whether we have two or four clients. To use this model, the model owner is expected to have the labels, while the clients are expected to have some features of each sample. For the MNIST data set, the features are vertical fragments of the image. To divide a 28 by 28 image sample between 2 clients, for example, we split the image into two 14 by 28 segments, as depicted

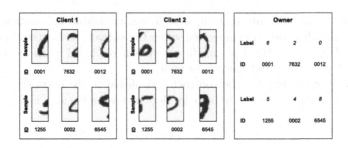

Fig. 4. Vertical Data Distribution for 2 Clients

in Fig. 4. The model at the clients is the head model, while the model at the servers is the tail model. To train this model, each client gives its input data to the models and collects the output of the last layer. Then, this intermediate output is sent to the servers, which are then given to the tail model. The servers calculate the gradients, which are then backpropagated to the clients. For more details, please consult the original works where the workings of this model are given in more detail. The architecture is depicted in Fig. 5 (adapted from [12]).

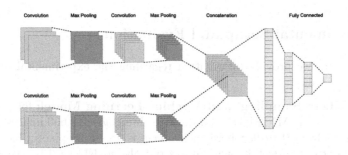

Fig. 5. Split-CNN Model Architecture

Hardware and Software Specifications: the experiments were executed on a remote machine, with a AMD Ryzen 5 3600 6-Core 4.2 GHz CPU, 64 GB of RAM, and a 500 GB NVMe disk. Use of GPUs was not needed, since if we consider that FL systems are being executed in IoT clients, it is unlikely that such resource-constrained devices would have a GPU available. In addition, the MNIST data set and the models we used are relatively simple, which means that they can be easily trained using CPUs. Nonetheless, it is worth mentioning that the training process would likely be faster on machines with GPUs.

6   Results and Discussion

We performed experiments to validate whether our implementation was successful and whether the Vertical BFL can be supported. We ran two experiments with two different number of clients: 2 and 4. The decision to use 2 clients was motivated by [12], where the Split-CNN was introduced for Vertical FL without blockchain for the first time. In addition, we also performed experiments with 4 clients.

Execution Time, Transaction Cost, and Transaction Latency: as it can be seen from Table 1, the experiments take longer with 4 clients than with 2. Regarding the transaction latency, it can be seen that it does not vary considerably with the number of clients. Similarly, the transaction costs do not present significant changes as the number of clients is relatively low. However, as expected, the transaction costs are slightly higher with 4 clients.

Table 1. Execution time, transaction cost, and transaction latency per number of clients

	2	4
E2E time (m)	18.08	24.30
Mean round time (s)	21.68	29.15
Mean transaction latency (s)	1.482	1.418
Mean transaction cost (Gas)	138659	141013

Model Accuracy and Convergence: Figure 6 illustrates the model accuracy of our experiments as well as those of Romanini et al. [28], where a Split-CNN model without blockchain was used with the MNIST data set. It can be seen that model accuracy of [28] is higher, which may be related to implementation differences like the Machine Learning library used, which is not known.

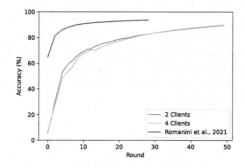

Fig. 6. Model Accuracy Per Number of Clients

Communication Costs: we can observe from Fig. 7 that at the clients there is no major difference of traffic when the number of clients increases. This can be explained by the fact that, by using a Split-CNN, each client is only required to upload its own intermediate results and downloads the gradient updates, which are similar in size. At the servers, the costs are higher as the number of clients increases. Since the higher number of clients leads to higher number of heads in the Split-CNN model, the servers are required to download more intermediate results and to upload more gradient updates. Therefore, the network traffic at the servers increases with the number of clients.

On the blockchain, the difference of number of clients is not significant to make a significant difference on traffic, since these experiments were executed with a very low number of clients.

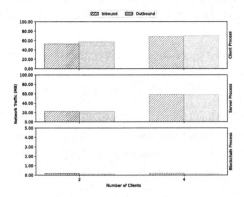

Fig. 7. Network traffic per round per number of clients

Computation Costs: Computation costs, namely RAM usage and CPU usage, are depicted in Figs. 8a and 8b, respectively. Regarding the RAM usage, we observe that with a higher number of clients, there is a higher RAM usage on the serves and the blockchain processes. This is caused by the fact that more data is being stored in-memory due to the higher amount of intermediate results that the servers store in-memory, as well as the number of blockchain transactions in the blockchain. At the clients, however, the opposite happens. This can be explained by the fact that when there are more clients, each client has less features as per the data partitioning, as explained before.

Regarding the CPU usage, we see similar results as to the RAM usage, which are explained by the same reasons.

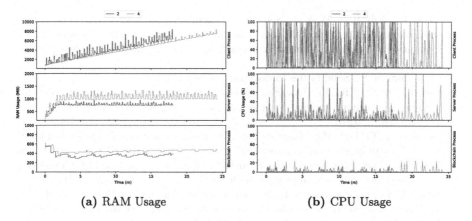

(a) RAM Usage   (b) CPU Usage

Fig. 8. Computation costs per number of clients

7 Conclusions and Future Directions

In this paper, we presented the design and implementation of a modular and extensible framework for Blockchain-based Federated Learning that supports Vertical Federated Learning. In addition, we presented its performance evaluations results in terms of execution time, transaction cost, transaction latency, model accuracy and convergence, as well as communication and computation costs.

In the future, it would be interesting to investigate how to make BlockLearning more generic in order to support other Vertical Federated Learning models. In addition, it would be valuable to incorporate the Private Set Intersection phase into our framework, allowing it to be directly applied to cases where the clients have intersecting, but not equal, sample spaces.

References

1. Abadi, M., et al.: TensorFlow: Large-scale machine learning on heterogeneous systems (2015). https://www.tensorflow.org
2. Awan, S., Li, F., Luo, B., Liu, M.: Poster: a reliable and accountable privacy-preserving federated learning framework using the blockchain. In: Proceedings of the 2019 ACM SIGSAC Conference on Computer and Communications Security, pp. 2561–2563. CCS 2019, Association for Computing Machinery, New York, NY, USA (2019)
3. Benet, J.: IPFS - content addressed, versioned, p2p file system (2014)
4. Cai, H., Rueckert, D., Passerat-Palmbach, J.: 2CP: decentralized protocols to transparently evaluate contributivity in blockchain federated learning environments (2020)
5. Cao, M., Zhang, L., Cao, B.: Toward on-device federated learning: a direct acyclic graph-based blockchain approach. IEEE Trans. Neural Netw. Learn. Syst. 1–15 (2021)

6. Chen, H., Asif, S.A., Park, J., Shen, C.C., Bennis, M.: Robust blockchained federated learning with model validation and proof-of-stake inspired consensus (2021)
7. ConsenSys: Consensys/quorum: A permissioned implementation of ethereum supporting data privacy
8. Contributors, S.: Solidity 0.8.15 documentation (2021)
9. Cui, L., et al.: CREAT: blockchain-assisted compression algorithm of federated learning for content caching in edge computing. IEEE Internet of Things J. **9**, 14151–14161 (2020)
10. Desai, H.B., Ozdayi, M.S., Kantarcioglu, M.: Blockfla: accountable federated learning via hybrid blockchain architecture. In: Proceedings of the Eleventh ACM Conference on Data and Application Security and Privacy, pp. 101–112. CODASPY 2021, Association for Computing Machinery, New York, NY, USA (2021)
11. Dias, H.: Impact Analysis of Different Consensus, Participant Selection and Scoring Algorithms in Blockchain-based Federated Learning Systems Using a Modular Framework. Master's thesis, TU Eindhoven (2022)
12. Jin, T., Hong, S.: Split-CNN: splitting window-based operations in convolutional neural networks for memory system optimization. In: Proceedings of the Twenty-Fourth International Conference on Architectural Support for Programming Languages and Operating Systems, pp. 835–847. ASPLOS 2019, Association for Computing Machinery, New York, NY, USA (2019)
13. Kim, H., Park, J., Bennis, M., Kim, S.L.: Blockchained on-device federated learning. IEEE Commun. Lett. **24**(6), 1279–1283 (2020)
14. Korkmaz, C., Kocas, H.E., Uysal, A., Masry, A., Ozkasap, O., Akgun, B.: Chain FL: decentralized federated machine learning via blockchain. In: 2020 Second International Conference on Blockchain Computing and Applications (BCCA), pp. 140–146 (2020)
15. LeCun, Y., Cortes, C., Burges, C.: MNIST handwritten digit database. ATT Labs (2010). http://yann.lecun.com/exdb/mnist
16. Li, D., et al.: Blockchain for federated learning toward secure distributed machine learning systems: a systemic survey. Soft Comput. **26**, 4423–4440 (2021)
17. Lu, Y., Huang, X., Zhang, K., Maharjan, S., Zhang, Y.: Blockchain empowered asynchronous federated learning for secure data sharing in internet of vehicles. IEEE Trans. Veh. Technol. **69**(4), 4298–4311 (2020)
18. Martinez, I., Francis, S., Hafid, A.S.: Record and reward federated learning contributions with blockchain. In: 2019 International Conference on Cyber-Enabled Distributed Computing and Knowledge Discovery (CyberC), pp. 50–57 (2019)
19. McMahan, H.B., Moore, E., Ramage, D., Hampson, S., Arcas, B.A.: Communication-efficient learning of deep networks from decentralized data. In: Proceedings of the 20th International Conference on Artificial Intelligence and Statistics, vol. 54, pp. 1273–1282 (2017)
20. Merkel, D.: Docker: lightweight Linux containers for consistent development and deployment. Linux J. **2014**(239), 2 (2014)
21. Mugunthan, V., Rahman, R., Kagal, L.: Blockflow: an accountable and privacy-preserving solution for federated learning. ArXiv (2020)
22. Nagar, A.: Privacy-preserving blockchain based federated learning with differential data sharing (2019)
23. Passerat-Palmbach, J., Farnan, T., Miller, R., Gross, M.S., Flannery, H.L., Gleim, B.: A blockchain-orchestrated federated learning architecture for healthcare consortia (2019)

24. Paszke, A., et al.: Pytorch: an imperative style, high-performance deep learning library. In: Wallach, H., Larochelle, H., Beygelzimer, A., d' Alché-Buc, F., Fox, E., Garnett, R. (eds.) Advances in Neural Information Processing Systems, vol. 32, pp. 8024–8035. Curran Associates, Inc. (2019)
25. Peyvandi, A., Majidi, B., Peyvandi, S., Patra, J.C.: Privacy-preserving federated learning for scalable and high data quality computational-intelligence-as-a-service in society 5.0. Multimed. Tools Appl. **81**, 25029–25050 (2022)
26. Pfitzner, B., Steckhan, N., Arnrich, B.: Federated learning in a medical context: a systematic literature review. ACM Trans. Internet Technol. **21**(2), 1–31 (2021)
27. Ramanan, P., Nakayama, K.: Baffle: blockchain based aggregator free federated learning. In: 2020 IEEE International Conference on Blockchain (Blockchain), pp. 72–81 (2020)
28. Romanini, D., et al.: PyVertical: a vertical federated learning framework for multi-headed SplitNN (2021)
29. Van Rossum, G., Drake, F.L.: Python 3 Reference Manual. CreateSpace, Scotts Valley, CA (2009)
30. Wang, Z., Hu, Q.: Blockchain-based federated learning: a comprehensive survey (2021)
31. Weng, J., Weng, J., Zhang, J., Li, M., Zhang, Y., Luo, W.: Deepchain: auditable and privacy-preserving deep learning with blockchain-based incentive. IEEE Trans. Dependab. Secur. Comput. **18**(5), 2438–2455 (2021)
32. Wood, G.: Ethereum: a secure decentralised generalised transaction ledger. Ethereum Proj. Yellow Paper. **151**, 1–32 (2014)
33. Yang, Q., Liu, Y., Chen, T., Tong, Y.: Federated machine learning: concept and applications. ACM Trans. Intell. Syst. Technol. **10**(2), 1–9 (2019)
34. Zhang, Q., Palacharla, P., Sekiya, M., Suga, J., Katagiri, T.: Demo: a blockchain based protocol for federated learning. In: 2020 IEEE 28th International Conference on Network Protocols (ICNP), pp. 1–2 (2020)
35. Zhang, W., et al.: Blockchain-based federated learning for device failure detection in industrial IoT. IEEE Internet Things J. **8**(7), 5926–5937 (2021)

Cyberspace Privacy

An Interactive Query Differential Privacy Protection Model Based on Big Data Analysis

Guanghui Feng[1], Wenyin Yang[2(✉)] (iD), Tao Peng[1] (iD), Xiaofei Xing[1],
Shuhong Chen[1], and Yuting Li[1]

[1] School of Computer Science and Cyber Engineering, Guangzhou University,
Guangzhou 510006, China
[2] School of Electronic Information Engineering, Foshan University,
Foshan 528000, China
cswyyang@fosu.edu.cn

Abstract. The problem of information leakage is becoming more and more serious, and how to effectively protect the security of personal privacy information has become an urgent problem at present. To this end, this paper proposes an interactive query differential privacy protection model based on big data analysis. The model is based on the irrelevance processing of differential privacy association rules to find out the hidden association information among trajectory data sets. The model uses the shared prefix method to de-compress the trajectory dataset deeply. The model constructs prefix trees to clarify useful information and remove redundant trajectory data. The model constructs a parallel gradient descent matrix decomposition algorithm based on the low-rank mechanism and alternating direction multiplier method to remove the load matrix built from the initial results and decompose the corresponding irrelevant load matrix. The model then takes reasonable values according to the user authority level to limit the privacy budget maximum. The model uses Laplace's principle to add the determined reasonable noise to the differential privacy trajectory data, reduce and delete the irrelevant attribute trajectory data, and finally feed the query results to the user. Through simulation and comparison experiments, we conclude that the proposed model can make the privacy information available to the highest degree and minimize the success probability of stealers, and thus the differential privacy track data can be protected to the best effect.

Keywords: Big data analysis · Interactive query · Differential privacy association rules · Trajectory data protection model · Parallel gradient descent algorithm

1 Introduction

Along with the continuous development of information technology, the era of big data has arrived. The application of big data is gradually expanding. The

G. Wang et al. (Eds.): UbiSec 2022, CCIS 1768, pp. 337–351, 2023.
https://doi.org/10.1007/978-981-99-0272-9_23

Internet has made people's lives easy and fast. There is also an increasing demand for data queries in daily applications. [10,26] At the same time, the problem of personal privacy leakage is becoming more and more serious. For example, the "heat map" published by the Strava application shows users' movement trajectories and leaks the location information and personnel information of U.S. military bases. There is an urgent need to address the issue of how to enhance the security of personal information when users use the Web. There are many areas of research on privacy protection, and data query privacy protection is one of them. The most basic data query in daily life is the linear query, which contains two kinds of queries: non-interactive and interactive, and the interactive query has a fast response time and can be processed online in real time [18]. However, the query will generate a lot of track data and a large amount of text to be processed, and it takes a long processing time to protect the differential privacy track data, which is extremely inefficient.

So far, most information privacy trajectory data protection algorithms are implemented through information classification and sensitive data migration. The data distortion degree, noise parameters, and other indicators are adjusted according to the regression analysis mathematical model to enhance the practicality of trajectory data. Wanjie Li [20]et al. proposed an information hierarchy privacy protection mechanism. A classification tree algorithm is used to grade users and access rights. Different levels of differential protection are employed. reasonable allocation of differential privacy budgets to achieve the protection of sensitive data. Yuxiang Fu [24]et al. proposed a privacy protection method for sensitive data migration based on the PATE-T model. The "master model," which consists of different data sets and relies on sensitive data, is established by the "black box" model. By migrating learning from the "master model," we obtain the "apprentice model," which is a set of unprotected data related to sensitive data. The attacker can only query the unimportant "apprentice model" when collecting information and cannot access the private data. The above two algorithms ignore the data availability needs of different levels of users during an interactive information query. The data availability after protection processing is low, and the information value is poor.

Combining the above-mentioned problems, this paper proposes an interactive query differential privacy protection model based on big data analysis. The model uses a redundant trajectory data removal algorithm based on differential privacy association rules. The model removes redundant trajectory data by mining the correlation between data, reduces the number of extractions of the original trajectory data, and improves the efficiency of trajectory data processing. The model uses the alternating direction multiplier method to increase the efficiency of differential privacy matrix decomposition and improve the computational speed. The model calculates a reasonable amount of noise addition based on adaptive noise, adds an appropriate amount of noise to reduce the sensitivity of query results, and uses the Laplace mechanism to achieve differential privacy trajectory data protection and maintain information security.

The rest of this paper is organized as follows. Section 2 reviews related work. Section 3 shows the redundant trajectory data removal method with our differential privacy association rules. Section 4 shows the matrix decomposition method based on the combinatorial property. Section 5 shows the trajectory data protection based on the differential privacy noise mechanism, and Sect. 6 presents the simulation experimental results. Finally, we conclude the paper in Sect. 7.

2   Related Work

Currently, the existing location data privacy protection methods are mainly classified into three categories: the heuristic privacy-measure methods; the probability-based privacy inference methods, and the privacy information retrieval methods. The heuristic privacy-measure methods are mainly to provide the privacy protection measures for some no-high-required users, such as k-anonymity [11], t-closing [2], m-invariability [17], and l-diversity [16]. Although the mechanisms such as anonymization and spatial obfuscation [1] provide location privacy through hiding identity or reporting fake locations, they ignore the adversary's knowledge about the user's access pattern and LPPM algorithm and disregard the optimal attack where an attacker may design an inference attack to reduce his calculation error. The information retrieval privacy protection methods may result in no data that can be released, and these methods have high overhead. Further, the three kinds of methods are based on a unified attack model [13], which depends on certain background knowledge to protect location data. The works [14, 21] demonstrated the shortcomings of relationship-privacy protection methods. Gedik and Liu [9] proposed the first effective location-privacy-preserving mechanism (LPPM) that enables a designer to find the optimal LPPM for a location-based service. Such an LPPM can maximize the expected distortion (error) when the adversary incurs in reconstructing the actual location of a user. Shaobo Zhang et al. [25] propose a dual privacy protection (DPP) scheme in continuous LBS to protect users' trajectory and query privacy and reduce the computation and communication overhead of a single anonymizer.

The query framework for data protection under differential privacy has two main types of queries: interactive and non-interactive. The basic architecture of the interactive differential privacy protection framework, also called the online query framework, is shown in Fig. 1. When a data analyst submits a query, the data owner designs a query algorithm to satisfy differential privacy processing according to the query requirements and returns the results to the user. The non-interactive differential privacy protection framework is shown in Fig. 2. The database owner publishes the statistical information related to the database through the differential privacy publishing algorithm. The data analyst submits a query task to get the noisy results based on the published database.

Most of the trajectory information differential privacy and trajectory data protection algorithms are implemented by information hierarchy and sensitive data migration to improve the utility of trajectory data by adjusting data distortion, noise parameters, and other indicators according to the regression analysis

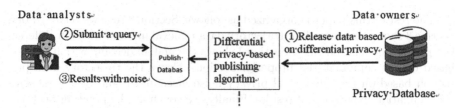

Fig. 1. Interactive framework

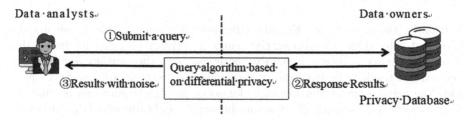

Fig. 2. Non-interactive framework

mathematical model. Li et al. [15] proposed a matrix mechanism based on the Haar wavelet mechanism and a hierarchical mechanism to study the finding strategy matrix, reduce the dimensionality of the query matrix, and reduce the amount of added noise. Thereby improving the efficiency of processing batch linear counting queries. Yuan et al. [23] proposed to use the Laplace mechanism to add noise to the number of records and the sum of attribute vectors in clustering so that the results of clustering analysis satisfy differential privacy as a way to achieve privacy protection. The amount of noise added is unreasonable because the amount of noise added is random. Yipeng Zou et al. [28] proposed the use of blockchain and attribute-based encryption techniques to provide privacy and security for data sharing.

3   Redundant Track Data Deletion Algorithm

In order to realize the construction of an interactive query differential privacy protection model, the redundant trajectory data deletion algorithm must be designed first. The algorithm proposes a data irrelevance processing technique through the correlation of information and determines whether the trajectory data is irrelevant information according to differential privacy association rules. The algorithm achieves the removal of redundant trajectory data in the interactive query process.

Differential privacy [4] is a privacy protection technique based on data distortion, which ensures the privacy of individuals in the dataset by injecting noise to make the effect of the operation of adding or deleting a data record on the output indistinguishable. A differential privacy trajectory data protection model [12] is a model that reduces the sensitivity of query results by adding noise so that an intruder cannot find out the addition or deletion of a trajectory data record from the output information, thus ensuring the security of user privacy trajectory data information in the dataset.

Assuming that differential privacy is denoted by ε and the intruder's query algorithm is denoted by $f\colon D \to R^d$, the random mechanism is supported throughout the process, from the input trajectory dataset to the output real vector d. D and D' are two adjacent trajectory datasets, respectively, and the algorithm is said to satisfy $\varepsilon - DP$ if f satisfies Eq. (1) for any of the output differentially private trajectory datasets $S \subseteq Range(f)$. It means that the algorithm satisfies $\varepsilon - DP$.

$$Pr[f(D) \in S] \le e^{\varepsilon} \times Pr[f(D') \in S] \tag{1}$$

The ε in Eq. (1) is the privacy budget [19]. It means that the smaller ε is, the smaller the frequency of attributes between trajectory datasets, which proves that the differential privacy effect is more similar, which makes it difficult for the attacker to determine the differential privacy trajectory data that needs to be stolen and specifically exists in which trajectory dataset, to increase the degree of trajectory data protection.

In order to determine the useful information of trajectory data that needs to be protected in the trajectory data set and reduce the number of times to extract the original trajectory data, this paper proposes a data irrelevance processing technique based on inter-information correlation, which determines whether the trajectory data is irrelevant information by differential privacy association rules.

Calculating the global sensitivity of the trajectory data [27]. If $f\colon D \to R^d$, $\Delta f = maxD, D' \ \|f(D)-f(D')\|$ then this function is said to be the global sensitivity of f.

The global is the maximum range of trajectory data output by applying a query algorithm on adjacent trajectory datasets D and D', and the distance L_1 between them is the metric value, determined by f, independent of the trajectory datasets. Under the ε-consistent condition, the global sensitivity is proportional to the amount of noise added in ε and also presents a positive proportion to the degree of privacy of the trajectory data. In individual scenarios, local sensitivity can replace global sensitivity.

The redundant trajectory data removal algorithm uses the global sensitivity to determine whether the current information in the current information is irrelevant. The algorithm uses a shared prefix tree approach to deeply compress the trajectory dataset to construct the FP-tree [22]. Then, based on the FP-tree, the frequent item growth method is used to highlight the high-frequency item sets, thereby reducing the mining time consumption.

There is a lot of association information hidden in the trajectory dataset, and the algorithm can find the association patterns between them using the irrelevance processing model. In this way, the algorithm removes the redundant trajectory data from the interactive query process. The whole algorithm runs as follows.

1) Obtain each attribute frequency by scanning the trajectory dataset and sorting these frequencies from highest to lowest to get a descending table.
2) Set m as the minimum supported frequency, and remove all values less than m based on the descending table in step 1.
3) Put the obtained descending table into a prefix tree and form a chain table of the nodes that appear for the first time, constructing the FP-tree by this process.
4) Using the trajectory data irrelevance processing model to integrate the FP-tree.
5) Determine whether the paths of the leaf nodes are single. If the result is no, you must return to the previous step and reconstruct the set of prefixes on each path to generate a new FP-tree. If the result is yes, you need to remove the leaf nodes and generate the set of prefixes directly to continue to the next step.
6) Finally, the interactive query association model is obtained. That is, the set of prefix paths is obtained, and the whole process of removing redundant trajectory data is completed.

4   Matrix Decomposition Method Based on Combinatorial Properties

Based on the removal of redundant trajectory data in the interactive query process, the speed of differential privacy trajectory data protection is reduced due to the large volume of trajectory data and many query rounds in the interactive query. By analyzing the sequential and parallel combinatorial nature of differential privacy, the model proposed in this paper explicitly estimates the data differential requirements. The model builds a parallel gradient descent matrix decomposition model based on the low-rank mechanism and the alternating direction multiplier method [5]. The model makes the difference privacy matrix decomposition more efficient and increases the speed of the whole algorithm.

In sequential combinatoriality [7], if there are multiple algorithms in any trajectory dataset, the differential privacy operations of each step are summed, and the resulting sum is the final result; and this process is called sequential combinatoriality. $\{A_1, A_2, \cdots, A_n\}$ are n arbitrary algorithms, D is the specified trajectory dataset, and A_i is an arbitrary algorithm. If all A_i on the trajectory dataset D satisfies $\varepsilon_i - DP$, then the sequential sequence combination of $\{A_1, A_2, \cdots, A_n\}$ on D satisfies $(\Sigma_i^n \varepsilon_i) - DP$.

In parallel combinatoriality [7], if there is information in disjoint subsets of a trajectory dataset, each information maximum privacy budget value is a parallel combinatorial type of the trajectory dataset. $\{D_1, D_2, \cdots, D_n\}$ are n disjoint subsets of the trajectory dataset D. Acting any algorithm $\{A_1, A_2, \cdots, A_n\}$ on each set, if A_i satisfies $\varepsilon_i - DP$, then it is said that $\{A_1, A_2, \cdots, A_n\}$ is a parallel sequence satisfying $(max\varepsilon_i) - DP$ combination.

The differential privacy trajectory data protection model is to reduce the sensitivity of query results by adding controlled noise. The more sub-algorithms and complex functions need to use differential privacy operations, the more noise [8] will be accumulated, and more than a certain degree will cause distortion of trajectory data and reduce the usability of trajectory data. For some queries, the value of the $\varepsilon_i - DP$ requirement seems too strict; for this reason, this paper selects the model with fewer restrictions to reduce the added noise.

Definition 1: Let $(\varepsilon, \delta) - DP$ be the differential privacy constraint. When $0 < \delta < 1$, an algorithm f on any two adjacent trajectory data sets satisfies Eq. (2) for a random output $S \subseteq Range(f)$, then f is said to satisfy $(\varepsilon, \delta) - DP$.

$$Pr[f(D) \in S] \le e^{\varepsilon} \times Pr[f(D') \in S] + \delta \tag{2}$$

Equation (2) can be interpreted as follows: if the probability of $(1 - \delta)$ of f satisfies $(\varepsilon) - DP$, then $(\varepsilon, \delta) - DP$ can be called approximate differential privacy.

The content in the trajectory dataset is not correlated before $(\varepsilon, \delta) - DP$ can be used. If this condition cannot be satisfied, even if differential privacy can be achieved, information thieves can still get differential privacy trajectory data based on data correlation. A privacy definition that can be universally applied is needed at this point. $\varepsilon - PufferFish$ privacy. $f: D \to R^d$ is the algorithm that can be randomly queried, (S, Q, Θ) is the privacy framework, $Q \in S \times S$ is the set of secret trajectory data pairs, and Θ is the set of trajectory data distributions.

Definition 2: If for any distribution $\theta \in \Theta$, any trajectory data $(S_i, S_j) \in Q(Pr(S_i|\theta) \ne 0, Pr(S_j|\theta) \ne 0)$, and any output $\omega \subseteq Range(f)$ in satisfy Eq. (3), then it is said that f satisfies $\varepsilon - PufferFish$ privacy in (S, Q, Θ).

$$e^{-\varepsilon} \le \frac{Pr[f(x) = \omega/s_i, \theta]}{Pr[f(x) = \omega/s_j, \theta]} \le e^{\epsilon} \tag{3}$$

where θ is both the data relevance description and the attacker's maximum trajectory data attack power, some trajectory data relevance description. Equation (3) shows that $\varepsilon - PufferFish$ privacy only limits the effect of any data in the set Q on S_i, S_j on the probability of the output result being not significantly different, indicating that any S_i, S_j in the secret trajectory data set Q is not significantly different from the output result after the change by $\varepsilon - PufferFish$ privacy and is not as strict as $\varepsilon - DP$ requirement. With Θ denoting the set of all trajectory data distributions, S denoting the set of all trajectory data, and Q denoting the cartesian product in S, $\varepsilon - PufferFish$ privacy is a special case of $\varepsilon - DP$.

After specifying the trajectory data differencing requirements, the load matrix built from the initial results is deleted. The irrelevant load matrix is obtained based on the above trajectory data irrelevance processing and then decomposed. Using the low-rank mechanism, the gradients $\frac{\partial G}{\partial F}$ of the decomposition matrices B and G for the decomposed matrix F are clarified.

$$B = (\beta W F^T + \pi F^T)(\beta W F^T + I)^{-1} \tag{4}$$

$$\frac{\theta G}{\theta F} = \beta B^T BF - \beta B^T W - B^T \pi)$$ (5)

In Eq. (5), W is the load matrix, β is the load matrix coefficient, and the result of B is related to F only. The parallel gradient descent matrix algorithm, which decomposes W into multiple matrices based on matrix characteristics, calculates these matrices at each node to speed up differential privacy trajectory data protection, and the whole operation steps are as follows.

1) Create the initial load matrix based on the user query specifications.
2) Remove the redundant trajectory data in the initial load matrix according to the trajectory data irrelevance processing model to obtain the irrelevant load matrix.
3) The irrelevant load matrix W_{ur} generated in step 2 is decomposed into Z components. The number of rows is represented by $\frac{u}{v}$, the number of columns is represented by r, and the number of nodes of the distributed system is represented by Z. Using the mapping process of distributed computing and the reduction process of cloud computing, the decomposition matrix process is calculated, and finally B and F are obtained, as shown in Fig. 3.

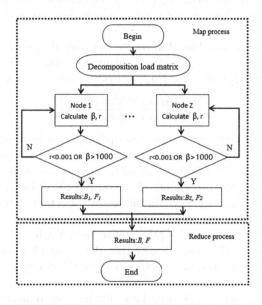

Fig. 3. Decomposition matrix flow chart

5   Adaptive Noise Tracking Data Protection

The exponential and Laplace mechanisms are often applied to many trajectory data requiring differential privacy protection. The exponential mechanism is often used for discrete trajectory data protection, limiting the output of trajectory data based on the scoring function operation principle. Numerical trajectory data protection requires the application of the Laplace mechanism, where global sensitivity can influence the amount of noise to be added to the differential privacy model, adding arbitrary noise to the query results that conforms to Laplace [6], allowing for increased trajectory data security and differential privacy trajectory data protection.

Noise mechanism 1: $f: D \rightarrow R$ is an arbitrary function, and if the randomized algorithm A conforms to Eq. (6), it shows that A conforms to $\varepsilon - DP$.

$$A(D) = f(D) + Lap(\Delta f / \varepsilon) \tag{6}$$

where $Lap(\Delta f / \varepsilon)$ is the Laplace noise to be added, and the noise variance is proportional to the global sensitivity and inversely proportional to ε. The larger the amount of noise, the smaller the ε.

The most important step in the index mechanism [3] is to construct the scoring function $u(D, r)(r \in O)$, with the output item r of the output with O as the output item.

Noise mechanism 2: $u : (D \times O) \rightarrow R$ is the scoring function of the trajectory data set D. If the randomized algorithm A conforms to Eq. (7), it shows that A conforms to $\varepsilon - DP$.

$$A(D, u) = \left\{ r : Pr[r \in o] \propto exp(\frac{\varepsilon(D, r)}{2\Delta u}) \right\} \tag{7}$$

where Δu is the maximum output value of the scoring function, which is the global sensitivity, it can be analyzed that the scoring is proportional to the probability of the selected output.

According to the noise mechanism rules for differential privacy protection of trajectory data, it is necessary to add noise that can fit the Laplace distribution to reduce the sensitivity of query results. According to the noise addition rule, it is known that adding a large amount of noise to the highly sensitive trajectory data will reduce the usability of the information, so an appropriate amount of noise addition must be chosen. The selection of ε in the differential privacy model determines the trajectory data protection effect. The smaller the selected ε value, the safer the user information, but the amount of added noise is large. The larger the selected ε value, although the amount of added noise can be reduced, the differential privacy trajectory data protection effect is not good and the information security is low. Therefore, the comprehensive Eq. (2) and Eq. (3) find a reasonable ε value that can consider the amount of added noise and the differential privacy trajectory data protection effect.

In this paper, the adaptive noise model [3] was selected to determine the reasonable value of the added noise under the premise of considering the user access rights (the higher the user access level, the closer ε is to the maximum value), combined with the condition $\varepsilon \leqslant \frac{ln2(1-p)\Delta q}{L}$. The whole algorithmic process is described as follows.

1) Limit the maximum value of ε by the condition $\varepsilon \leqslant \frac{ln2(1-p)\Delta q}{L}$, and select the appropriate ε according to the user authority level.
2) Based on Laplace's principle, the trajectory data set D, and the load matrix decomposition result F are added to the noise, respectively, and the Laplace operator is defined as.

$$\nabla^2 f = \frac{\partial^2 f}{\partial D^2} + \frac{\partial^2 f}{\partial F^2} \tag{8}$$

3) Using the trajectory data irrelevance processing model, reduce irrelevant attribute trajectory data.
4) Return the query results to the user.

6   Simulation Experiments

This experiment employs a ntel(R) Core(TM) i7-8565U CPU @1.8GHz processor, 8GB memory, the Microsoft Windows 10 operating system, the Android Studio development platform as the experimental environment, and the Java programming language to generate experimental data in order to assess the efficacy of this paper's algorithm for privacy trajectory data protection. From the perspective of information security, the differential privacy track data protection model, the information hierarchy privacy protection model, and the sensitive data migration privacy protection model proposed in this paper are compared and analyzed in the experiments.

6.1   Time Complexity

The elapsed time of model implementation is used as an evaluation index, and the shorter its elapsed time is, the lower the time complexity of the model is. The time consumption of the information hierarchy privacy protection model, the sensitive data migration privacy protection model, and this paper's model are compared, and the results of the time consumption of different methods are shown in Table 1.

Table 1. Comparison results of time consumption of different methods

Different methods	Time consuming (s)
Information hierarchy privacy model	6.48
Privacy protection model for sensitive data migration	4.77
Model of this paper	2.63

It is clear from Table 1 that the time taken by the information hierarchy privacy protection model and the sensitive data migration privacy protection model is 6.48 s and 4.77 s, respectively, while the time taken by this model is only 2.63 s. It can be seen that the time taken by this model is shorter than that of the information hierarchy privacy protection model and the sensitive data migration privacy protection model, indicating that the time complexity of this model is lower.

6.2 Information Theft Rate

Two different types of information stealers are set up. The stealer of model 1 has certain trajectory data attributes and can clarify the differential privacy and non-privacy trajectory data range of users to steal precisely; the stealer of model 2 has any information. The information theft rates of various techniques are calculated using the information hierarchical privacy protection model, sensitive data migration privacy protection model, and text model for information privacy trajectory data protection, as shown in Table 2.

Table 2. Information theft rate of different methods

Different methods	Mode 1	Mode 2
Information hierarchy privacy model	0.23515	0.06337
Privacy protection model for sensitive data migration	0.13706	0.04667
Model of this paper	0.03596	0.02246

It can be clearly seen from Table 2 that the model in this paper outperforms the other two methods in protecting differential privacy trajectory data under different types of attacks. This is because this paper uses a scoring function to limit the trajectory data attribute output traces and applies the Laplace mechanism to clarify the global sensitivity. In order to limit the likelihood of privacy information being stolen and to accomplish correct differential privacy trajectory data protection, it is possible to identify the necessary quantity of additional noise and add arbitrary noise conforming to Laplace to the query results.

6.3 Information Loss Rate

The model in this paper implements the protection function of differential privacy trajectory data. The model adds suitable noise to the user's information after achieving the preset effect. The model restores the irrelevant attributes deleted by the model based on the irrelevance of the trajectory data and then feeds the query results to the user. As a result, it causes no distortion of trajectory data and has no effect on the use of user information. The loss rate of weight information is introduced in the experiment to verify the usability of differentially private trajectory data under the protection of the model in this paper. The loss rate is the ratio of the total number of weighted items lost to the total number of items. The smaller the weight information loss rate is, the higher the trajectory data's usability is. The loss rates of information in protected trajectory data weights for different algorithms under different values of are shown in Figs. 4, 5, and 6, respectively.

The value of ε is inversely proportional to the weight information loss rate, and the smaller the ε is, the larger the loss rate is. From Fig. 4, we can see that with the increase in the number of interactive queries, the curve of weight information loss rate corresponding to different values of ε in this paper is smooth. The value of ε can be kept within a certain range, and the overall information loss rate is small. Figure 4 illustrates that the user privacy track data is protected by the algorithm in this paper, which can achieve both information security and ensure the availability.

It can be seen from Fig. 5 that the information loss rate of the information hierarchy method increases continuously with the increase in the number of queries, the utility of the trajectory data decreases, and the availability is unstable. Compared with the algorithm in this paper, under the condition that the number of queries keeps increasing, the whole curve fluctuates greatly and cannot be kept in a stable range. The overall information loss rate under the information hierarchy method is around 0.25%, while the overall information loss rate under the algorithm of this paper stably stays below 0.15%. Compared with the two, the availability of differential privacy trajectory data under the information hierarchy method is much lower than that calculated in this paper.

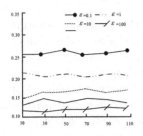

Fig. 4. Algorithm of this paper

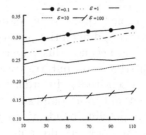

Fig. 5. Information grading method

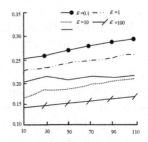

Fig. 6. Sensitive data migration method

As can be seen in Fig. 6, the weight information loss rate curve of the trajectory data under the sensitive data migration method is very similar to that of the information hierarchy privacy method. With the increase, the weighted information loss rate decreases. As the number of queries increases, the information loss rate keeps increasing, and the utility of the trajectory data decreases. The difference is that the overall information loss rate of this algorithm is lower than that of the information hierarchy privacy method, the trajectory data is better used after the information has been protected, and the overall value is around 0.2%, which is still higher than the algorithm in this paper at 0.15%. The comparison experiment can demonstrate that the algorithm presented in this paper has a good protection effect on interactive queries for differential privacy trajectory data in big data analysis, as well as a high usability of trajectory data.

7 Conclusion

In response to the current situation that the trajectory data is stolen and the user's privacy information is seriously leaked in the process of interactive information query. In this paper, we propose a differential privacy protection model for interactive query based on big data analysis. The model operates on the principle of reducing the sensitivity of query results by increasing noise. The model designs redundant trajectory data deletion algorithm to reduce the number of extractions of the original trajectory data and improve the efficiency of trajectory data processing. The model uses alternating direction multiplier method to increase the efficiency of differential privacy matrix decomposition and improve the speed of the whole algorithm. The model calculates a reasonable amount of noise addition based on the adaptive noise model, and uses adding an appropriate amount of noise to reduce the sensitivity of the query results to achieve differential privacy trajectory data protection and maintain information security. Finally, the comparison experiment proves that the algorithm of this paper can protect the differential privacy trajectory data effectively and will not affect the normal use of trajectory data.

Acknowledgements. This work was supported in part by the National Key Research and Development Program of China (2020YFB1005804), and in part by the National Natural Science Foundation of China under Grants 61632009, 61872097, and 61802076; and in part by the Natural Science Foundation of Guangdong Province (2022A1515011386). The Basic and Applied Basic Research Fund of Guangdong Province No. 2019A1515111080.

References

1. Ardagna, C.A., Cremonini, M., Damiani, E., De Capitani di Vimercati, S., Samarati, P.: Location privacy protection through obfuscation-based techniques. In: Barker, S., Ahn, G.-J. (eds.) DBSec 2007. LNCS, vol. 4602, pp. 47–60. Springer, Heidelberg (2007). https://doi.org/10.1007/978-3-540-73538-0_4
2. Bamba, B., Liu, L., Pesti, P., Wang, T.: Supporting anonymous location queries in mobile environments with privacygrid. In: Proceedings of the 17th international conference on World Wide Web, pp. 237–246 (2008)
3. Bertrand, F., Boffi, D., de Diego, G.: Convergence analysis of the scaled boundary finite element method for the Laplace equation. Adv. Comput. Math. **47**(3), 1–17 (2021)

4. Dwork, C.: Differential privacy. In: Bugliesi, M., Preneel, B., Sassone, V., Wegener, I. (eds.) ICALP 2006. LNCS, vol. 4052, pp. 1–12. Springer, Heidelberg (2006). https://doi.org/10.1007/11787006_1

5. Dolgopolik, M.V.: The alternating direction method of multipliers for finding the distance between ellipsoids. Appl. Math. Comput. **409**, 126387 (2021)

6. Dong, J., Durfee, D., Rogers, R.: Optimal differential privacy composition for exponential mechanisms. In: International Conference on Machine Learning, pp. 2597–2606. PMLR (2020)

7. Dwork, C., McSherry, F., Nissim, K., Smith, A.: Calibrating noise to sensitivity in private data analysis. In: Halevi, S., Rabin, T. (eds.) TCC 2006. LNCS, vol. 3876, pp. 265–284. Springer, Heidelberg (2006). https://doi.org/10.1007/11681878_14

8. Furtat, I.B., Nekhoroshikh, A.N., Gushchin, P.A.: Robust stabilization of linear plants in the presence of disturbances and high-frequency measurement noise. Autom. Remote. Control. **82**(7), 1248–1261 (2021)

9. Gedik, B., Liu, L.: Protecting location privacy with personalized k-anonymity: architecture and algorithms. IEEE Trans. Mob. Comput. **7**(1), 1–18 (2007)

10. Hui, H., Zhou, C., Xu, S., Lin, F.: A novel secure data transmission scheme in industrial internet of things. China Commun. **17**(1), 73–88 (2020)

11. Huo, Z., Meng, X.: A survey of trajectory privacy-preserving techniques. Chin. J. Comput. **34**(10), 1820–1830 (2011)

12. Husnoo, M.A., Anwar, A., Chakrabortty, R.K., Doss, R., Ryan, M.J.: Differential privacy for IoT-enabled critical infrastructure: a comprehensive survey. IEEE Access **9**, 153276–153304 (2021)

13. Jia, O., Jian, Y., Shaopeng, L., Yuba, L.: An effective differential privacy transaction data publication strategy. J. Comput. Res. Dev. **51**(10), 2195–2205 (2014)

14. LeFevre, K., DeWitt, D.J., Ramakrishnan, R.: Mondrian multidimensional k-anonymity. In: 22nd International Conference on Data Engineering (ICDE 2006), p. 25. IEEE (2006)

15. Li, C., Hay, M., Rastogi, V., Miklau, G., McGregor, A.: Optimizing linear counting queries under differential privacy. In: Proceedings of the Twenty-ninth ACM SIGMOD-SIGACT-SIGART Symposium on Principles of Database Systems, pp. 123–134 (2010)

16. Liu, F., Hua, K.A., Cai, Y.: Query l-diversity in location-based services. In: 2009 Tenth International Conference on Mobile Data Management: Systems, Services and Middleware, pp. 436–442. IEEE (2009)

17. Liu, L.: From data privacy to location privacy: models and algorithms. In: VLDB, vol. 7, pp. 1429–1430. Citeseer (2007)

18. Sarwar, S.M., Bonab, H., Allan, J.: A multi-task architecture on relevance-based neural query translation. arXiv preprint arXiv:1906.06849 (2019)

19. Sharma, J., Kim, D., Lee, A., Seo, D.: On differential privacy-based framework for enhancing user data privacy in mobile edge computing environment. IEEE Access **9**, 38107–38118 (2021)

20. Wangjie, L., Xing, Z., Guanghui, C., Shuai, L., Qingyun, Z.: Hierarchical data fusion publishing mechanism based on differential privacy protection. J. Chin. Comput. Syst. **10**, 2252–2256 (2019)

21. Wong, R.C.W., Li, J., Fu, A.W.C., Wang, K.: (α, k)-anonymity: an enhanced k-anonymity model for privacy preserving data publishing. In: Proceedings of the 12th ACM SIGKDD International Conference on Knowledge Discovery and Data Mining, pp. 754–759 (2006)

22. Yang, Y., Ding, J., Li, H., Jia, L., You, J., Jiang, Y.: A spark-based frequent patterns mining algorithm for uncertain datasets. Inf. Control **48**(3), 257–264 (2019)

23. Yuan, J., Tian, Y.: Practical privacy-preserving mapreduce based k-means clustering over large-scale dataset. IEEE Trans. Cloud Comput. **7**(2), 568–579 (2017)
24. Yuxiang, F., Yongbin, Q., Guowei, S.: Sensitive data privacy protection method based on transfer learning. J. Data Acquisit. Process. **34**(3), 422–431 (2019)
25. Zhang, S., Wang, G., Bhuiyan, M.Z.A., Liu, Q.: A dual privacy preserving scheme in continuous location-based services. IEEE Internet Things J. **5**(5), 4191–4200 (2018)
26. Zhang, X., Meng, X.: Differential privacy in data publication and analysis. Chin. J. Comput. **4**, 927–949 (2014)
27. Zhou, S., Lyu, Z., Ling, C., Wang, Y.: Meta-is-AK algorithm for estimating global reliability sensitivity. Acta Aeronaut. Astronaut. Sin. **41**(1), 164–173 (2020)
28. Zou, Y., Peng, T., Zhong, W., Guan, K., Wang, G.: Reliable and controllable data sharing based on blockchain. In: Wang, G., Choo, K.K.R., Ko, R.K.L., Xu, Y., Crispo, B. (eds.) Ubiquitous Security. Communications in Computer and Information Science, vol. 1557, pp. 229–240. Springer, Singapore (2022)

Decentralized Collaborative Filtering Algorithm with Privacy Preserving for Recommendation in Mobile Edge Computing

Xiangyong Liu[1], Pengfei Yin[2]([✉]), Pin Liu[3], and Shuhong Chen[1]

[1] School of Computer Science and Cyber Engineering, Guangzhou University, Guangzhou 510006, China
[2] College of Information Science and Engineering, Jishou University, Jishou 416000, China
pppypf@163.com
[3] School of Computer Science and Engineering, Central South University, Changsha 410083, China

Abstract. Mobile edge computing (MEC) deploys network services closer to the user's wireless access network side and provides IT service environment and cloud computing capabilities at the edge of the mobile network. With the advantages of low latency and high bandwidth, many context-aware services (such as recommendation) have been greatly developed. However, standard recommendation architecture in MEC focuses on individual MEC entities and the vertical interaction between end-user and a single MEC node. Its quality of service (QoS) is limited by the performance of a particular edge node, and the resources of edge servers are not fully utilized during the idle period of user activity. What's more, the user's behavioral data stored in single edge server will lead to the risk of privacy disclosure. In response to these problems, we propose a decentralized collaborative filtering algorithm in MEC, to amalgamates the heterogeneous resources at the edges and to protect user's privacy. The core of our structure is composed of user terminals, edge nodes, and cloud nodes. User terminals are the targets of recommendation services, including static and mobile devices, and can undertake a small portion of the recommendation tasks. Edge nodes are the MEC servers co-located with the base stations and are responsible for handling the low latency and computation-intensive tasks. Cloud nodes are traditional mobile cloud computing (MCC) servers located at the remote data center for latency-tolerant and computation-intensive tasks. We provide three observations on the decentralized recommendation in MEC which are from the aspects of latency, resource utilization and user privacy. In our algorithm, the rating data is divided into public and private data and processed with decentralized matrix completion.

Keywords: Mobile edge computing · Decentralized recommendation · Privacy preserving · Quality of service · Collaborative filtering

© The Author(s), under exclusive license to Springer Nature Singapore Pte Ltd. 2023
G. Wang et al. (Eds.): UbiSec 2022, CCIS 1768, pp. 352–365, 2023.
https://doi.org/10.1007/978-981-99-0272-9_24

1   Introduction

With the development of modern human society, many essential services such as water, electricity, gas, etc. are provided to people to meet the needs of daily life. These services are used so frequently that they need to be available to consumers at any time and anywhere. As a centralized computing model, cloud computing makes service-oriented architecture possible [32]. Under cloud computing, all resources, such as computing, storage, and networking, are provided to users through services, and people pay for service providers based on their usage [4]. In recent years, due to the rapid development of hardware devices and strict requirements for service quality, computing trends have begun to move from the network center to the edge of the network [5]. As an emerging computing technology, mobile edge computing (MEC) deploys network services closer to the user's radio access network, providing IT service environments and cloud computing capabilities at the edge of the mobile network [1,13,20,21]. MEC has become the core technology of the next generation Internet (e.g. Tactile Internet [8,29], Internet of Things [2]) due to its low latency and high bandwidth, and has received extensive attention from academia and industry.

The advent of mobile edge computing has driven many service-based applications into mobile devices, such as mobile retrieval, mobile payments, video applications, etc. The prosperous application generates a large amount of user interaction data that can help improve the quality of user services and puts a lot of pressure on the storage and computing of edge servers. On the one hand, Users are increasingly demanding quality of service (QoS), especially for delay-sensitive applications. On the other hand, service providers are hoping to improve the utilization of edge servers. Mobile search engine [16] and mobile recommendation system [27] are two mainstream information filtering technologies in mobile computing. The search engine solves the problem of information filtering when the user intention is clear in the mobile environment. Instead, the recommendation system considers providing recommendation services when the user is unaware. From the perspective of the service provider, the recommendation system can enhance the user experience, thereby improving service quality and promoting user loyalty.

Recommendations in MEC are different from those in mobile cloud computing (MCC), which are determined by their characteristics. The MEC server is located close to the client, co-located with the wireless gateway and the base station, and the MCC server is placed along with the data center which is away from users [13,22,31]. The control method is also different. The MEC uses hierarchical control, while the MCC is a centralized control [35]. The most important difference is that MEC features low latency and high bandwidth for latency-critical and computation-intensive applications such as autonomous driving, augmented reality (AR), online video, etc. [22], and MCC is suitable for latency-tolerant applications. One big problem in both MCC and MEC is the risk of privacy disclosure for the reason of keeping all data in centralized servers. Their architectures are shown in Fig. 1, the detailed comparison is shown in Table 1.

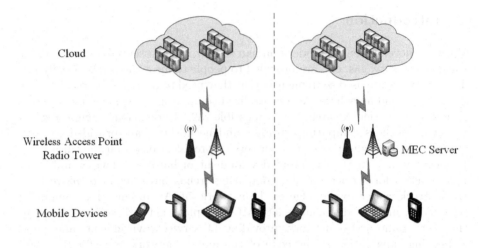

Cloud

Wireless Access Point
Radio Tower

MEC Server

Mobile Devices

Fig. 1. Illustration of mobile cloud computing (left) and mobile edge computing (right).

Therefore, when designing the recommendation algorithms in MEC, we cannot simply apply the set of methods in MCC. First of all, we must consider that the processing power of the edge server is different from the central server. In the design of the algorithm, the pressure of the edge server must be fully considered. Secondly, compared with the central server, the stability and reliability of the edge server are relatively low, so the designed algorithm also needs to take into account the issues of quality of service. In addition, the traditional recommendation algorithm must also be modified to be applied to the MEC environment, because the user's mobility is an important feature, which is not considered in the traditional recommendation system [23,26]. The recommendation in MEC has been widely studied [15,34,40].

Table 1. Comparison of MEC and MCC systems.

	MEC	MCC
Hardware	Small-scale	Large-scal
Location	Co-located with BSs or aggregation	Remote data centers
Deployment	Lightweight	Sophisticated
Scalability	High	Average
Backaul usage	Infrequent	Frequent
Management	Hierarchical control	Centralized control
Latency	Small	Larger
Applications	Latency-critical	Latency-tolerant

However, standard recommendation architecture in MEC focuses on individual MEC entities and the vertical interaction between end-user and a single MEC node. Its quality of service (QoS) is limited by the performance of a particular edge node, and the resources of edge servers are not fully utilized during the idle period of user activity. What's more, it still has great risk on disclosing user's privacy. Privacy protection and data sharing is a basic problem and has received a lot of attention [3,41]. Existing works assume that the edge servers have sufficient capacity to undertake computing and storage tasks, and do not consider energy, privacy and economic costs, only focusing on the performance of recommendation. In reality, these are very important factors. In response to these problems, we propose a decentralized recommendation algorithm. To the best of our knowledge, we are the first to propose a decentralized approach to solve the recommendation problem in MEC. The traditional approach is to consider the centralized recommendation of MCC and MEC, the former will bring the recommendation delay problem even adopt the latest streaming computing technologies, while the latter will inevitably put pressure on the edge server, thereby increasing the risk of fault, and a waste of resources due to over-deployment. Above all, they both ignores the risk of privacy disclosure.

Our contributions in this paper are threefold:

1. We propose a decentralized recommendation system architecture to address privacy, quality of service and resource utilization issues in MEC. The core of our structure is composed of user terminals, edge nodes, and cloud nodes. Service is obtained through the collaborative computing of those three components.
2. We provide three observations on the decentralized recommendation in MEC. Firstly, the low-latency services will become ultra-low latency with a small proportion of recommender tasks deployed on the client. Secondly, in a decentralized architecture, all devices work together, which makes the dynamic configuration of resources possible. Thirdly, the risk of privacy disclosure will be reduced with data distributed on all edges.
3. We propose a decentralized collaborative filtering algorithm for the consideration of user privacy. We treat the recommendation as a rating prediction problem and solve it with decentralized matrix completion. For each client, the rating data on the client is divided into public and private data. The prediction of the rating for a particular user is the integration of those data on the user client.

2 Related Work

The purpose of the recommendation system is to reduce the burden of the user while enjoying the information service. The most classic models are content-based recommendation [23] and collaborative filtering [19]. Content-based recommendation considers that people are interested in similar information services. The similarity of services is calculated by the content attributes of services. The core idea of collaborative filtering is that neighboring users will also have similar preferences, and the user's neighbors are calculated by the user's behavior data. Later, researchers found that location characteristics are particularly important in the recommendation of certain industries, such as restaurants, travel, social network, etc. Location recommendation and location-based service recommendation are of general interest to researchers [11,17,38,39].

Location awareness is a basic attribute in the mobile computing environment. The combination of the recommendation system and the mobile environment forms a mobile recommendation system [24,27]. The researchers conducted a detailed survey of the application of the mobile recommendation system in the tourism industry and classified the existing research work from three aspects [9]. How to reduce energy consumption is a problem that the transportation sectors must consider. This problem can be solved by analyzing the transportation pattern by location tracking in the mobile recommendation system and recommending a sequence of pick-up points for taxi drivers or a sequence of potential parking positions [10]. Indoor shopping still occupies an important position. Combining indoor positioning technology with a recommendation system to enhance the user's shopping experience can reduce the burden of users [7]. When people go out for a trip or leisure, the mobile recommendation system can recommend nearby popular activities by capturing the user's location information [12]. While providing mobile recommendation services, the quality of service has become more and more important [28,30,33,37].

The existing recommendation system that works in the mobile environment is based on a centralized approach, that is, in an MCC environment. With the advent of MEC, researchers began to work on the integration of edge servers and recommendation models. Starting with the caching of edge servers, the authors of [14] proposed a cache-aware recommendation method that provides cache-friendly and high-quality recommendations. Aiming at the privacy and collaboration efficiency problem brought by edge servers, a scalable mobile service recommendation method based on a two-stage local sensitive hash algorithm was proposed [25]. To ensure the quality of the recommended services, the traditional collaborative filtering algorithm was applied in the model to predict the quality of service and then make recommendations [34]. Due to the complexity of edge mobile devices, a new method that combining convolutional neural networks and matrix factorization was proposed for mining the hidden features [40]. Distance calculation is an important module in the mobile environment. To overcome the shortcomings of traditional rating-based similarity calculation, a novel service recommendation method based on the cultural distance-aware which focuses on not only the similarity but also the local characteristics and preference of users was proposed, and the experimental results prove its improvement on reliability [18].

The above methods aim at improving the metrics of recommendation systems, such as accuracy, diversity, and coverage. The quality of services and edge server performance issues have not been focused on. Because in MEC, due to the particularity of the user's location, the services they enjoy are unstable, then the quality of service (e.g. latency) becomes a very important factor. In addition, even when the edge server is well deployed, there will still be situations where some of the servers are under excessive pressure, while another part of the servers is idle, which is caused by the mobility of people. What's more, there will be higher risk on privacy disclosure with all data stored in centralized servers. Based on these considerations, we propose a decentralized recommendation architecture in MEC. In our architecture, user terminals, edge servers, and cloud servers perform collaborative computing. We propose a decentralized collaborative filtering algorithm for recommendation. Our architecture can not only improve the user experience but also greatly improve resource utilization and protect user privacy in the same time.

3   Three Observations on Decentralized Recommendation in MEC

In this section, we make three observations about decentralized recommendation architecture in MEC:

- Although mobile edge computing deploys services close to users to ensure low latency, some issues still be ignored. The first is the improvement of the user terminal hardware. The works that could only be done by the server can now be partially even fully executed on mobile terminals. If some of the recommended tasks are deployed on user terminals, then low-latency services will become ultra-low latency. The second is the instability of network conditions, which is mostly due to user mobility. The tasks performed on the user terminals are much less affected by network conditions.
- The decentralized architecture is more flexible than the centralized architecture. In a centralized architecture, resources will inevitably be wasted due to the over-configuration of edge services. On the contrary, it will bring great risks to the application services. In the decentralized architecture, the edge servers, user terminals, and cloud servers work together, which makes the dynamic configuration of resources possible.
- Both MCC and MEC exist great risk on privacy disclosure. The centralized algorithms in MCC and MEC make the data stored in centralized way, usually in one or more servers. This cannot avoid the risks of the server itself. In the decentralized architecture, all the computing nodes keep one part of the data. In extreme cases, each user can store his/her own behavior data locally, which greatly avoids the risk of data disclosure.

3.1   From Low Latency to Ultra-Low Latency

We might as well use the traditional feed recommendation as an example, as shown in Fig. 2. In the traditional centralized recommendation architecture, since all works are done on the MEC server, the user terminal simply displays the received information flow, which is shown in Fig. 2(a). The recommendation is implemented by using a paging mechanism, and each request from the user terminal will be affected by the network condition. Since the server is deployed close to the user, this delay will be relatively low. However, if the user's request is more frequent, the impact of this low latency cannot be ignored. We assume that the user's mobile terminal has a certain processing capacity and can handle some simple sorting tasks, then the terminal and the edge server can work in coordination, then the subsequent page sorting and display work can be completed on the terminal, thus avoids the limitation of network conditions and achieves the effect of ultra-low latency, which is shown in Fig. 2(b). Of course, the benefit of this is not just the delay. On the user terminal, we can also adjust the order of subsequent pages in real-time based on user feedback, thereby improving the recommended performance indicators.

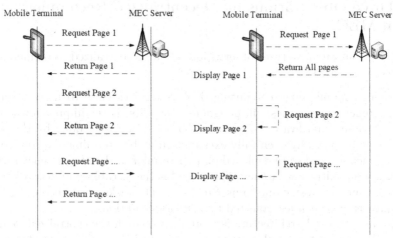

(a) All works are done on MEC server

(b) Works are done on both user terminal and MEC server

Fig. 2. Feed recommendation in MEC.

3.2   From Resource Wasting to High Utilization

In a traditional centralized architecture, the quality of services depends entirely on the performance of the central server. Due to the user's mobility and the user's dynamic use of services, the pressure on the central server changes dynamically. We assume that the user's resource requirements for the server are shown in Fig. 3. If the deployment of the central server reasonably takes into account the peak of user demand, then the server can always meet the user's demand well, as shown in Fig. 3(a). However, there will be a problem that during the nonpeak time, most of the server's resources are idle and wasted. If there is no reasonable estimation of the peak of user demand, during the peak time, some users cannot enjoy satisfactory services because they cannot obtain the resources of the server, which leads to the risk of user loss, which is shown in Fig. 3(b). If we deploy a decentralized architecture, the resources of the edge servers and user terminals will be utilized reasonably, and the resource requests will be reasonably allocated to different places so that users can enjoy satisfactory services, which is shown in Fig. 3(c). Due to the decentralized structure, the high-pressure servers can distribute their pressure to different edge servers, so that the idle servers can be fully utilized, which greatly improves the utilization of resources and the satisfaction of users.

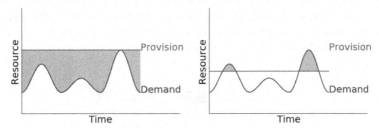

(a) The deployment satisfys the demand under centralized architecture

(b) Underestimate the spike under centralized architecture

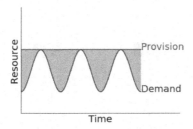

(c) The deployment satisfys the demand under decentralized architecture

Fig. 3. The estimation about the demand. (a) The estimation is correct, and there are waste resources (shaded area) during nonpeak time. (b) Underestimate the demand, some users will be provided with unsatified services during the peak time (shaded area). (c) Under decentralized architecture, the service will be satisfied most time and the utilization be greatly improved.

3.3 From High Risk to Privacy Preserving

In the traditional recommender architecture, all data is stored in the central server. We usually assume that the central server is trusted, but this is obviously inconsistent with the reality. We can often see the data leakage reports or news caused by server problems. These problems are multifaceted. Firstly, the server itself may be attacked by illegal users due to its weak security protection mechanism, which may bring danger to the data. What's more, the server administrator may be driven by interests to intentionally disclose users' personal data. What's more, the occurrence of some natural disasters will also bring hidden dangers to users' data security. In short, we cannot fully trust the security of the central server. This risk can be reduced when a decentralized architecture is adopted. We assume that user behavior data is explicit scoring data, so that all user data can form a scoring matrix, as shown in Fig. 4. From the figure, we can see that after decentralization, each edge will save a part of the scoring matrix, which greatly reduces the risk of data leakage. In the most extreme case, we can regard each user as an edge, so that the user's own data is saved locally, and the privacy risk is controlled to the maximum extent.

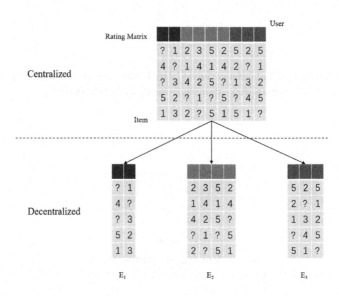

Fig. 4. Different architectures (Centralized and decentralized) related to rating matrix.

4   Decentralized Collaborative Filtering Algorithm

In this section, we provide the problem of predicting the ratings of users on unrated items in collaborative filtering. We first formulate the problem as matrix completion and then provide the decentralized solution.

Consider a system in which there are N items and M users. The user's ratings of items form a rating matrix $R^{M \times N}$. R is mostly sparse because most users only score a small part of the products in the system. Therefore, the goal of the recommender system is to predict those missing values, to make a recommendation based on the predicted scores. Without considering the characteristics of items, the traditional algorithm of prediction is collaborative filtering. The theoretical basis of it is that users with similar behaviors on rated items will also have such behaviors on unrated items. This is linked to the low-rank nature of the matrix. Therefore, our scoring prediction becomes a low-rank matrix completion problem. The problem can be formulated as follows.

$$min \ \frac{1}{2}||XY - Z||_F^2 \ \ s.t. \ \ P_\Omega(Z) = P_\Omega(R) \tag{1}$$

where $Z \in R^{M \times N}$ is an auxiliary matrix and $||\cdot||_F$ denotes the Frobenius norm.

Firstly, we review the centralized solution which based on nonlinear Gauss-Seidel iteration [36]. At iteration t, $X(t+1)$, $Y(t+1)$, and $Z(t+1)$ are calculated as follows.

$$X(t+1) = Z(t)Y^T(t)(Y(t)Y^T(t))^\dagger \tag{2}$$

$$Y(t+1) = (X^T(t+1)X(t+1))^\dagger X^T(t+1)Z(t) \tag{3}$$

$$Z(t+1) = X(t+1)Y(t+1) + P_\Omega(R - X(t+1)Y(t+1)) \tag{4}$$

where $\dagger$ is the Moore-Penrose pseudo-inverse. Since only the product XY is needed, the calculation of $X(t+1)$ can be simplified as follows.

$$X(t+1) = cZ(t)Y^T(t), c > 0 \tag{5}$$

Then, we need to calculate Eq. 5, 3, and 4 in decentralized algorithm. Assume that there are K edge servers works in a decentralized manner, then the Rating matrix R is segmented into K non-overlapped parts, that is $R = [R_1, R_2, ..., R_K]$. For each edge server, it keeps R_k. Then we can decompose Z in the same way so that each Z_k has columns corresponding to R_k and Y_k. Then at each iteration, the edge server k keeps Z_k and Y_k. Y_k becomes a private matrix. Also, we need a local copy X_k of the public matrix X. X_k will be updated at each iteration through consensus algorithm. Here, we adopt the average consensus algorithm [6], that is, set $c = \frac{1}{K}$ in Eq. 5. Then,

$$X(t+1) = \frac{1}{K} \sum_{k=1}^{K} Z_k(t)Y_k^T(t) \tag{6}$$

In decentralized manner, at iteration t, the calculation of $X(t+1)$, $Y(t+1)$, and $Z(t+1)$ for each edge server are as follows.

$$X_k(t+1) = \frac{Z_k(t)Y_k^T(t) - \alpha_k(t) + \beta|N_k|X_k(t) + \beta \sum_{j \in N_k} X_j(t)}{1 + 2\beta|N_k|} \tag{7}$$

$$Y_k(t+1) = (X_k^T(t+1)X_k(t+1))^{-1}X_k^T(t+1)Z_k(t) \tag{8}$$

$$Z_k(t+1) = X_k(t+1)Y_k(t+1) + P_\Omega(R_k - X_k(t+1)Y_k(t+1)) \qquad (9)$$

where $|N_k|$ is the cardinality of N_k, $\beta > 0$ is a constant, and $\alpha_k \in R^{M \times N}$ is the lagrange multiplier matrix with the initial value 0. The updation of α is as follows.

$$\alpha_k(t+1) = \alpha_k(t) + \beta(|N_k|X_k(t+1) - \sum_{j \in N_k} X_j(t+1)) \qquad (10)$$

The algorithm is summarized in Algorithm 1. In each iteration, the k-th edge server exchangs X_k with its neighborhood edge servers, updates X_k, and finally updates Y_k and Z_k independently.

Algorithm 1. Decentralized Collaborative Filtering Algorithm

Require: $P_\Omega(R_k), \beta, T$
Ensure: X_k, Y_k, Z_k
1: $X_k(0) = random(), Y_k(0) = random(), \alpha_k(0) = 0, Z_k(0) = P_\Omega(R_k), t = 0;$
2: **repeat**
3:     $X_k(t+1) = \frac{Z_k(t)Y_k^T(t) - \alpha_k(t) + \beta|N_k|X_k(t) + \beta \sum_{j \in N_k} X_j(t)}{1 + 2\beta|N_k|};$
4:     $\alpha_k(t+1) = \alpha_k(t) + \beta(|N_k|X_k(t+1) - \sum_{j \in N_k} X_j(t+1));$
5:     $Y_k(t+1) = (X_k^T(t+1)X_k(t+1))^{-1}X_k^T(t+1)Z_k(t);$
6:     $Z_k(t+1) = X_k(t+1)Y_k(t+1) + P_\Omega(R_k - X_k(t+1)Y_k(t+1));$
7: **until** $t = T$

---

5 Conclusion

In this paper, we studied the recommendation in mobile edge computing and proposed the decentralized architecture. The main difference between mobile edge computing and mobile cloud computing is that we can enjoy the high quality of service in MEC. In MEC, the server is deployed close to the user. But for computation-intensive and latency-tolerant tasks, the advantages of MCC are obvious. In the recommender system, we hope to get service as quickly as possible while to preserve user's privacy. In other words, we prefer real-time and secure recommendation services. In this paper, we observed that decentralized architecture has three main advantages of low-latency, high resource utilization and privacy preserve. We made a lot of comparisons between MEC and MCC and showed the recommendation architecture in both fields. In MEC, the user clients, edge servers, and cloud servers are all included and responsible for a part of recommendation tasks. Under the decentralized architecture, we proposed the decentralized collaborative filtering algorithm for the consideration of user privacy. In further, we will study more issues about the recommendation in both MEC and MCC.

Acknowledgments. This work was supported in part by the Guangdong Provincial Natural Science Foundation under Grant 2022A1515011386.

References

1. Abbas, N., Zhang, Y., Taherkordi, A., Skeie, T.: Mobile edge computing: a survey. IEEE Internet Things J. **5**(1), 450–465 (2017)
2. Al-Fuqaha, A., Guizani, M., Mohammadi, M., Aledhari, M., Ayyash, M.: Internet of things: a survey on enabling technologies, protocols, and applications. IEEE Commun. Surv. Tutorials **17**(4), 2347–2376 (2015)
3. Arif, M., et al.: Towards a two-tier architecture for privacy-enabled recommender systems (PERS). In: Proceedings of the First International Conference on Ubiquitous Security, pp. 268–278. Springer, Singapore (2021). https://doi.org/10.1007/978-981-19-0468-4_20
4. Buyya, R., Yeo, C.S., Venugopal, S.: Market-oriented cloud computing: vision, hype, and reality for delivering it services as computing utilities. In: 2008 10th IEEE International Conference on High Performance Computing and Communications, pp. 5–13. IEEE (2008)
5. Chiang, M., Zhang, T.: Fog and IoT: an overview of research opportunities. IEEE Internet Things J. **3**(6), 854–864 (2016)
6. Erseghe, T., Zennaro, D., Dall'Anese, E., Vangelista, L.: Fast consensus by the alternating direction multipliers method. IEEE Trans. Signal Process. **59**(11), 5523–5537 (2011)
7. Fang, B., Liao, S., Xu, K., Cheng, H., Zhu, C., Chen, H.: A novel mobile recommender system for indoor shopping. Expert Syst. Appl. **39**(15), 11992–12000 (2012)
8. Fettweis, G.P.: The tactile internet: applications and challenges. IEEE Veh. Technol. Mag. **9**(1), 64–70 (2014)
9. Gavalas, D., Konstantopoulos, C., Mastakas, K., Pantziou, G.: Mobile recommender systems in tourism. J. Netw. Comput. Appl. **39**, 319–333 (2014)
10. Ge, Y., Xiong, H., Tuzhilin, A., Xiao, K., Gruteser, M., Pazzani, M.: An energy-efficient mobile recommender system. In: Proceedings of the 16th ACM SIGKDD International Conference on Knowledge Discovery and Data Mining, pp. 899–908. ACM (2010)
11. Geng, B., Jiao, L., Gong, M., Li, L., Wu, Y.: A two-step personalized location recommendation based on multi-objective immune algorithm. Inf. Sci. **475**, 161–181 (2019)
12. Horowitz, D., Contreras, D., Salamó, M.: EventAware: a mobile recommender system for events. Pattern Recogn. Lett. **105**, 121–134 (2018)
13. Hu, Y.C., Patel, M., Sabella, D., Sprecher, N., Young, V.: Mobile edge computing-a key technology towards 5G. ETSI White Paper **11**(11), 1–16 (2015)
14. Kastanakis, S., Sermpezis, P., Kotronis, V., Dimitropoulos, X.: CABaRet: leveraging recommendation systems for mobile edge caching. In: Proceedings of the 2018 Workshop on Mobile Edge Communications, pp. 19–24. ACM (2018)
15. Kuang, L., Tu, S., Zhang, Y., Yang, X.: Providing privacy preserving in next poi recommendation for mobile edge computing. J. Cloud Comput. **9**(1), 1–11 (2020)
16. Leung, K.W.T., Lee, D.L., Lee, W.C.: PMSE: a personalized mobile search engine. IEEE Trans. Knowl. Data Eng. **25**(4), 820–834 (2012)
17. Levandoski, J.J., Sarwat, M., Eldawy, A., Mokbel, M.F.: LARS: a location-aware recommender system. In: 2012 IEEE 28th International Conference on Data Engineering, pp. 450–461. IEEE (2012)
18. Li, Y., Guo, Y.: Cultural distance-aware service recommendation approach in mobile edge computing. Scientific Programming 2018 (2018)

19. Linden, G., Smith, B., York, J.: Amazon.com recommendations: item-to-item collaborative filtering. IEEE Internet Comput. **7**(1), 76–80 (2003)

20. Mach, P., Becvar, Z.: Mobile edge computing: a survey on architecture and computation offloading. IEEE Commun. Surv. Tutorials **19**(3), 1628–1656 (2017)

21. Mao, Y., You, C., Zhang, J., Huang, K., Letaief, K.B.: A survey on mobile edge computing: the communication perspective. IEEE Commun. Surv. Tutorials **19**(4), 2322–2358 (2017)

22. Patel, M., et al.: Mobile-edge computing introductory technical white paper. In: White Paper, Mobile-Edge Computing (MEC) Industry Initiative, pp. 1089–7801 (2014)

23. Pazzani, M.J., Billsus, D.: Content-based recommendation systems. In: Brusilovsky, P., Kobsa, A., Nejdl, W. (eds.) The Adaptive Web. LNCS, vol. 4321, pp. 325–341. Springer, Heidelberg (2007). https://doi.org/10.1007/978-3-540-72079-9_10

24. Pimenidis, E., Polatidis, N., Mouratidis, H.: Mobile recommender systems: identifying the major concepts. J. Inf. Sci. **45**(3), 387–397 (2019)

25. Qi, L., Zhang, X., Dou, W., Hu, C., Yang, C., Chen, J.: A two-stage locality-sensitive hashing based approach for privacy-preserving mobile service recommendation in cross-platform edge environment. Futur. Gener. Comput. Syst. **88**, 636–643 (2018)

26. Resnick, P., Iacovou, N., Suchak, M., Bergstrom, P., Riedl, J.: GroupLens: an open architecture for collaborative filtering of netnews. In: Proceedings of the 1994 ACM Conference on Computer Supported Cooperative Work, pp. 175–186. ACM (1994)

27. Ricci, F.: Mobile recommender systems. Inf. Technol. Tourism **12**(3), 205–231 (2010)

28. Shah, S.H., Nahrstedt, K.: Predictive location-based QoS routing in mobile ad hoc networks. In: 2002 IEEE International Conference on Communications. Conference Proceedings, ICC 2002 (Cat. No. 02CH37333), vol. 2, pp. 1022–1027. IEEE (2002)

29. Simsek, M., Aijaz, A., Dohler, M., Sachs, J., Fettweis, G.: 5g-enabled tactile internet. IEEE J. Sel. Areas Commun. **34**(3), 460–473 (2016)

30. Soh, W.S., Kim, H.S.: QoS provisioning in cellular networks based on mobility prediction techniques. IEEE Commun. Mag. **41**(1), 86–92 (2003)

31. Tran, T.X., Hajisami, A., Pandey, P., Pompili, D.: Collaborative mobile edge computing in 5G networks: new paradigms, scenarios, and challenges. arXiv preprint arXiv:1612.03184 (2016)

32. Tsai, W.T., Sun, X., Balasooriya, J.: Service-oriented cloud computing architecture. In: 2010 Seventh International Conference on Information Technology: New Generations, pp. 684–689. IEEE (2010)

33. Wang, L., Sun, Q., Wang, S., Ma, Y., Xu, J., Li, J.: Web service QoS prediction approach in mobile internet environments. In: 2014 IEEE International Conference on Data Mining Workshop, pp. 1239–1241. IEEE (2014)

34. Wang, S., Zhao, Y., Huang, L., Xu, J., Hsu, C.H.: QoS prediction for service recommendations in mobile edge computing. J. Parallel Distrib. Comput. **127**, 134–144 (2017)

35. Wang, S., Zhang, X., Zhang, Y., Wang, L., Yang, J., Wang, W.: A survey on mobile edge networks: convergence of computing, caching and communications. IEEE Access **5**, 6757–6779 (2017)

36. Wen, Z., Yin, W., Zhang, Y.: Solving a low-rank factorization model for matrix completion by a nonlinear successive over-relaxation algorithm. Math. Program. Comput. **4**(4), 333–361 (2012)

37. Yang, K., Galis, A., Chen, H.H.: QoS-aware service selection algorithms for perva-sive service composition in mobile wireless environments. Mob. Netw. Appl. **15**(4), 488–501 (2010)
38. Yin, H., Sun, Y., Cui, B., Hu, Z., Chen, L.: LCARS: a location-content-aware recommender system. In: Proceedings of the 19th ACM SIGKDD International Conference on Knowledge Discovery and Data Mining, pp. 221–229. ACM (2013)
39. Yin, Y., Chen, L., Wan, J., et al.: Location-aware service recommendation with enhanced probabilistic matrix factorization. IEEE Access **6**, 62815–62825 (2018)
40. Yin, Y., Zhang, W., Xu, Y., Zhang, H., Mai, Z., Yu, L.: QoS prediction for mobile edge service recommendation with auto-encoder. IEEE Access **7**, 62312–62324 (2019)
41. Zou, Y., Peng, T., Zhong, W., Guan, K., Wang, G.: Reliable and controllable data sharing based on blockchain. In: Wang, G., Choo, KK.R., Ko, R.K.L., Xu, Y., Crispo, B. (eds.) Proceedings of the First International Conference on Ubiquitous Security, pp. 229–240. Springer, Singapore (2021). https://doi.org/10.1007/978-981-19-0468-4_17

Encryption Proxies in a Confidential Computing Environment

Mohamad Jamil Al Bouhairi, Mostakim Mullick[(✉)], Marvin Wolf,
Ivan Gudymenko[(✉)], and Sebastian Clauss

T-Systems Multimedia Solutions GmbH, Riesaer Street 5, 01129 Dresden, Germany
{mostakim.mullick,ivan.gudymenko}@t-systems.com

Abstract. With the increasing adoption of cloud native applications, security and privacy are among the pressing concerns hindering a wider adoption of cloud services. One of the main challenges in this context is providing reliable protection of customer data from unauthorized usage, including the cases when adversary gains root access to host systems. Using transparent data encryption, tokenizataion and pseudonymization by deploying an encryption proxy between the end user and cloud provider are some of the established approaches to protect sensitive data in the cloud. In this paper, we extend the advantages of an encryption proxy by deploying and securing it using a shielded execution framework based on Confidential Computing. Our Proof of Concept (PoC) guarantees the necessary security requirements needed to run in an untrusted computing infrastructure. The experimental evaluations show that the PoC achieves reasonable performance results while providing strong security properties with small Trusted Computing Base.

Keywords: Confidential computing · Cloud computing · Intel SGX · SCONE · Trusted execution environment

1 Introduction

Applications have moved from being a rigid monolithic package to an elastic and loosely connected set of microservices which are often hosted in a cloud infrastructure. The products have been mostly replaced by services that can be subscribed according to one's needs. Thus, a subscriber does not require any bulky infrastructure to host the application on premises but rather a terminal to access the service and a stable network is sufficient. This has certainly proven less hectic as it reduces management cost and time [11]. However, all these benefits come with a hidden cost.

Cloud computing has presented new challenges and problems that an organization must solve to fulfil its privacy and security goals. One of the key issues is data protection. The data is hosted and processed on third party machines and also being served through cloud providers. Several approaches and solutions can be used, but these approaches need to take three core aspects into

G. Wang et al. (Eds.): UbiSec 2022, CCIS 1768, pp. 366–379, 2023.
https://doi.org/10.1007/978-981-99-0272-9_25

consideration [6]: data control, usability, and data protection. Data control deals with the management oversight of cryptographic key possession and control that are necessary for encryption. Usability considers the measurement of how well cloud services and their functionalities remain usable with no restrictions to the end-user despite the data encryption. Finally, data protection involves how companies and organizations control personal data and comply with regulation. Concerns regarding data security and the need to comply with legal regulations have slowed down the process to adopt a cloud-first architecture approach. The use of encryption proxies such as the eperi Gateway [5] have used pseudonymization and encryption methods to transform personal and sensitive data into a form that could not be used in a malicious manner. This insures that *data in transit* and *data at rest* is protected at all times. Third parties with access to Personal Identifiable Information (PII) can be alarming [9]. However, anonymized and correctly pseudonymized data is not observed as PII under the GDPR [10] and therefore are not the subject of data protection. Yet, a cloud application is not able to process encrypted/tokenized data unless it has access to the cryptographic keys. A potential malicious root admin with key access is able to read the data being processed in clear text. Therefore, a practical and secure solution to protect *data in use* is needed.

One emerging technology for confidential computing, trusted execution environments (TEE) [2] (e.g Intel SGX and AMD SEV) have been widely used to deploy secure applications allowing data to be secured in all three states (at rest, in use, and in transit). However, continued adoption of TEE can be impeded by their limited support for unmodified source code implementations. Particularly, in the case of Intel Software Guard Extensions (SGX), the program's source code is expected to incorporate SGX's SDK in order to successfully execute inside of an SGX enclave. This process would entail a lot of effort and is susceptible to performance issues and attacks [7]. Addressing this usability challenge are secure container platforms like SCONE [1] which run the binary code inside SGX while also providing SGX-enabled security guarantees inside cloud environments. The security requirements regarding confidentiality and integrity are achieved by preventing unauthorized parties such as higher privileged system software (e.g OS kernel and hypervisor) and malicious users as mentioned previously to access application data. This ensures that *data in use* is also protected.

It is important that data in all three states are secured. In this paper, we take into consideration all three states and combine both existing technologies to ensure that security guarantees such as confidentiality and integrity are satisfied. Our PoC extends the data privacy techniques accompanied with the eperi Gateway and Intel SGX to design an all-rounded secure approach to data privacy. As per our knowledge, there has been no previous implementation that leveraged the features of a TEE such as Intel SGX in securing the eperi Gateway.

In this paper, we showcase the main contributions of our work as follows:

- We leverage the eperi Gateway's [5] privacy preserving features and extend the privacy preserving requirements with the Intel SGX TEE,

- Using Intel SGX and the secure container platform SCONE, we use a 'lift and shift' approach to transform the encryption proxy to a confidential application,
- We evaluate the efficacy of the proposed proof of concept using benchmarks and compare the overheads as opposed to the native version.

The rest of the paper is organized as follows. Section 2 reviews the related technologies used in this paper. Section 3 provides the implementation scenario and the procedure involved. Section 4 describes the experimental setup. Section 5–6 evaluates the proposed proof of concept with the discussion of the results, and Sect. 7 concludes the paper.

2   Background and Project Overview

In this section, we briefly review Intel SGX. We describe the existing technologies used in our implementation, SCONE and the eperi Gateway.

2.1   Intel SGX

Intel Software Guard eXtensions[1] (SGX) is a set of extensions to the Intel architecture that provide confidentiality and integrity guarantees for applications even if the underlying operating system or hypervisor is malicious [1,3]. Launched in 2015, Intel SGX uses secure hardware based TEEs known as *Enclaves*. Enclaves are isolated regions of the memory in which the code running in an enclave is isolated from other untrusted applications including higher privileged ones. Enclave code and data reside in a region of protected physical memory called the enclave page cache (EPC) [1]. Enclave code and data are guarded by CPU access controls while they are in cache. Data in EPC pages is safeguarded at the granularity of cache lines when they are relocated to DRAM. SGX provides EPC of size up to 128 MB in its first generation [12]. The EPC's cache lines written to and fetched from DRAM are encrypted and decrypted by an on-chip memory encryption engine (MEE) [1]. Enclave memory is also integrity protected, i.e., memory alterations and rollbacks are noticed in enclave memory.

In addition, Intel SGX provides *remote attestation* feature. This enables a challenger to verify the integrity of the TEE. The enclave is measured and the corresponding report is signed by the Intel's hardware keys. Combined with the sealing process (encrypting the data before storing on disk), the data confidentiality is ensured on the cloud. As a result, the use of Intel SGX provides confidentiality and integrity of application secrets at all times, despite an adversary that can compromise privileged code running on the hosts of the cloud infrastructure.

---

[1] https://www.intel.com/content/www/us/en/developer/tools/software-guard-extensions/overview.html.

2.2 SCONE

Secure CONtainer Environment (SCONE) [1] is a secure container mechanism for Docker that uses the SGX trusted execution support of Intel CPUs to protect container processes from outside attacks. SCONE takes into consideration the apparent issues with native Intel SGX SDK development such as exposed container interfaces, memory access and system call overheads and deals with them by providing alternate design suggestions while maintaining small Trusted Computing Base (TCB):

- SCONE implements File System shield to protect confidentiality and integrity of files; Network shield to enable end-to-end TLS encryption; and Console shield to protect the console streams.
- SCONE uses $M : N$ threading scheme while maintaining a thread pool where M application threads are mapped to N OS threads.
- Finally, SCONE enables asynchronous system calls by utilizing the shared memory to pass system call arguments and to collect return values.

In addition, SCONE overcomes the poor memory performance of Intel SGX SDK. Considering the original SGX design goal of protecting tailored code for security-sensitive tasks, Intel provides an SDK to facilitate the implementation of simple enclaves. It consists of an interface definition language with a code generator and a basic enclave library. Unlike SCONE, the SDK lacks the necessary support for system calls and offers only restricted functionality inside the enclave. The use of SCONE allows for better scalability than using Intel SGX SDK alone since it provides efficient thread management by using asynchronous system calls [1].

2.3 Eperi Gateway

Eperi Gateway [5] is an encryption proxy focused on data protection. It can perform a wide variety of tasks like:

- Encryption and pseudonymization of data before they are transferred to the cloud application.
- Internal cryptographic key management handling.
- Enforcing uniform data protection policies across all devices and platforms.

The Eperi Gateway consists of a transparent proxy architecture which can be integrated into any IT environment without requiring the user to apply any major modifications to the underlying infrastructure or existing workflows. The encryption and decryption process occurs transparently and in real-time. Therefore, the solution will run unnoticed in the background while preserving the core functionalities of the cloud and running applications. This process allows the user to have the sole and centralized control over the data's protection. Moreover, the eperi Gateway is flexibly tailored by allowing the client to either use eperi's standard encryption algorithm or one's own algorithm and also it allows the user to choose which fields should be encrypted, tokenized or left as plain text. Configuration data is stored encrypted in an adjacent database. Hence, unauthorized third parties are not able to gain access to the data. However, the threat model does not consider root admins as potential malicious attackers. Therefore, this scenario is specifically considered in this paper.

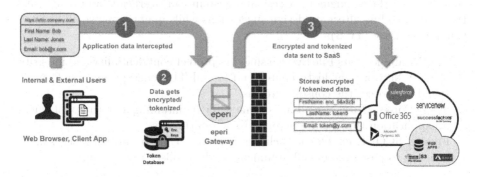

Fig. 1. Eperi Gateway workflow. Taken from [5].

The easiest way to understand the eperi Gateway is to think of it as a "broker" as show in Fig. 1. The gateway is separate from the cloud environment whose data must be protected. This decouples cloud applications from cloud data. However, this is for a particular use case. In other use cases, the eperi Gateway can be present on the cloud provider. Depending on the application and access circumstances, it can also act as a reverse, forward, or API proxy.

In essence, the eperi Gateway essentially serves as a forward and reverse proxy. According to Fig. 1, users access the eperi Gateway from their network and pass their data to the gateway which is then transparently encrypted before forwarded to the corresponding cloud application. In this way the eperi Gateway acts as a forward proxy. In the opposite direction, the eperi Gateway acts as a proxy server by accepting the data stream that is returned by a cloud service and then decrypts the encrypted data inside it with the cryptographic key already in its possession before forwarding the data to the clients in plain-text.

3   Implementation

The intent of the proof of concept is to secure the instance of a cloud encryption proxy (eperi Gateway) deployed in a cloud environment against the cloud provider and powerful adversaries possessing administration rights on the infrastructure. In this way, we wish to establish a trusted data pipeline in which the customer data is always in a protected state. This means that sensitive data can not be accessed in plain text by entities outside the TCB. Based on this motivation, we propose to leverage an encryption proxy in a confidential environment to realize this trusted pipeline. The proof of concept (PoC) was deployed on a virtual machine with Intel SGX-based CPUs. Microsoft Azure provides Intel SGX enabled confidential compute nodes, i.e, DC Series VMs which are already pre-configured with the required drivers.

3.1 Eperi with SGX

Conventional applications cannot use SGX features in the native form. To convert an application into a confidential application, it has to be modified or cross compiled and built using Intel SGX SDK. However, it is not practical to rewrite the whole application from scratch. Furthermore, Intel SGX SDK supports C/C++ whereas Eperi Gateway is built using Java. We need some other tools to convert this application into a confidential application powered by SGX. One such tool is SCONE which allows us to migrate easily to the confidential environment.

SCONE [1] introduces an efficient lift and shift transformation approach called *Sconification* which involves an automated process using a one step command, *sconify_image*, to produce the confidential version of the application. SCONE uses a native container image as input, which is created by an existing CI/CD pipeline. The image is converted or "sconified" into a confidential container image that runs inside an enclave where all data and code are protected. SCONE uses an automated single step command to achieve this:

```
sconify_image --from="$NATIVE_IMAGE" --to="$CONFIDENTIAL_IMAGE" ...
```

The *Sconification* procedure consists of the following steps:

1. The command-line tool *sconify_image* encrypts the service's code and data and copies these encrypted files into the encrypted image.
2. A security policy is created containing metadata and an additional information, e.g., the native image environment and path to working directories, to perform decryption while also checking for file integrity violations. This policy is uploaded to the attested SCONE CAS (Configuration and Attestation Service).
3. To run the confidential container from the encrypted image, SCONE CAS attests the service first to ensure its trustworthiness.
4. If successful, SCONE CAS sends the service secrets specified in the policy in order to ensure the service executes smoothly.

Confidential Application Design. In essence, our confidential application consists of three containers, i.e., *Maria DB*, *Scone LAS* (Local Attestation Service) and *Sconified Eperi*. The LAS handles the local attestation of the enclave. Furthermore, it facilitates the remote attestation by generating a verifiable quote. We aim to deploy the eperi Gateway in a confidential manner using the SCONE platform with all the necessary configuration and the required services running (see Fig. 2). In this manner, the user simply has to run the given script and use the gateway's admin portal normally without any database configurations or source code changes inside the eperi Gateway. The eperi Gateway transparently encrypts the data on its way to the cloud application. Using SGX, the encryption key is secured as opposed to the native eperi Gateway deployment.

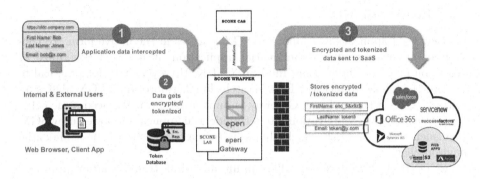

Fig. 2. Sconified eperi Gateway workflow. Adapted from [5].

During the start-up, SCONE attests the eperi container and then starts the bootstrap process for gateway services. The eperi container behaves as a transparent encryption proxy.

The container running MariaDB is not sconified. However, in our setup, MariaDB uses TLS communication while communicating with the eperi Gateway service. This is important as the lack of encryption would introduce security concerns, e.g., Man-in-the-middle attack. In addition, our setup ensures data-at-rest encryption in MariaDB as well. This is ensured through the use of eperi as a key management and encryption plugin with a negligible encryption overhead of around 3–5% [8]. The encryption key uses a 32-bit integer as a key identifier. The eperi Gateway places this key on the key server outside the MariaDB server itself while still remaining in the secure enclave allowing for an additional security guarantee. However, the encryption does not encompass the MariaDB error log, so sensitive information such as PII may be contained in the log as well. Nevertheless, our solution is generic in nature and therefore can be extended to include other confidential applications such as MariaDB. If this path is taken, it would ensure that MariaDB's encryption keys and the TLS certificate are provided only to MariaDB using SCONE's security policy. SCONE CAS enforces this policy, i.e., it ensures that only MariaDB running inside of an enclave will be able to access these keys.

Approach. Sconification simplifies the process of securing a native application to a large extent. Nevertheless, it is not completely straightforward to build a confidential encryption proxy using shielded execution as it demands supporting unaltered applications without degrading the performance. Before the deployment of the sconified image, it is required to compose the native image along with some required configurations.

Some initial configuration was needed to set up the required environment. We followed the eperi documentation [4] to set up a complete work environment and link the eperi Microsoft 365 adapter. The eperi Microsoft 365 adapter was needed to connect to a Microsoft SaaS application running on the cloud provider. In our case, our backend application was Microsoft Outlook. A custom internet domain has been set up while also the DNS within our Azure cluster has been configured to identify the new domain. The next step is to configure the eperi Gateway and specify the application used. The normal workflow starts by a client sending an email through the eperi Gateway. The eperi Gateway encrypts the sensitive content of the email according to the specified template. If the receiver accesses the Microsoft account through the normal Outlook URL, the contents would be encrypted. If accessed through the custom eperi domain, the contents would appear in plain text.

The first step of converting a native application into a confidential application is to determine the sensitive data. After initial investigation, we determined the directories that contain the application code which is compiled on image creation. The critical directories include the code directory, the data directory and the compiled binary. We cannot make any changes to the configuration inside the eperi Gateway once it is sconified. Therefore, a container with the native eperi base image has been initially created and deployed. Once the container is properly set up, it will be used as the native base image in the sconification process.

After creating a compatible base image and determining the parts to be secured, we can proceed to sconification. It is imperative that the original image supports musl libC or GLibC. In case of the latter, the application binary must be "Position Independent Code" enabled. After setting the environment variables that would be passed after attestation and the proper file system directories to encrypt, we execute the `sconify_image` command using the proper flags. After sconification, we use a normal docker compose YAML file to deploy the prepared image along with MariaDB and SCONE LAS (Local Attestation Service). It is important that we have MariaDB and LAS hosted on the same IPs which we have defined during docker compose configuration in a previous step.

4   Experimental Setup

In this section, we briefly describe the experiments performed for the proposed setup. We based our benchmarks on wrk2[2] where a web page behind the eperi Gateway proxy is fetched. The HTTP benchmarking tool produces two experimental evaluation metrics: a constant throughput load and accuracy latency details in the high percentiles. The benchmark runs for two minutes using two threads keeping 50 HTTP connections open, and a constant throughput of 100 requests per second. The setup consists of our client load generator, the eperi Gateway with the Microsoft Outlook Exchange under a custom domain as a

---

[2] https://github.com/giltene/wrk2.

back-end as shown in the Fig. 2. We implemented the services as Docker containers on the Microsoft Azure platform. The Virtual Machine (VM) has 10 vCPUs with 32 GiB of main memory. The disk configuration is irrelevant as all the services fit into memory. We tested two different setups each with different resource demand. The first setup is the plain native eperi Gateway image (v 21.17.1.0). The image has been pulled from the eperi docker repository with no modifications made. Native means execution that was performed without SGX and therefore also without SCONE. Native executions ran, like the versions using SCONE, inside a Docker container. The performance influence of Docker is therefore out of the equation. The second setup includes the eperi Gateway image converted to a secure image by using the SCONE platform running in an Intel SGX enclave.

Table 1. Average latency of both setups

Images	Average latency (ms)
Native	423
Sconified	912

5   Results

In this section, we present the results of our experiments on the different setups along with the analysis of the tests.

5.1   Latency

Latency is another key metric to assess the performance of a certain web application as the responsiveness of interactive applications directly influences the quality of user experience. This has become a critical concern for service providers. Latency can be defined as the duration it takes a request to reach its destination across the network and receive an acknowledgement. The average latency of both setups can be visualized in Table 1. The sconified version has an average latency of around twice the native Eperi deployment.

As mentioned in Sect. 2.3, the above value would outperform a setup using SGX SDK alone. When an enclave performs a system call, SCONE switches to another application thread while the system call is performed by threads running outside the enclave. This minimizes the need for the threads running inside the enclave to exit the enclave. Minimizing the enclave exits is particularly important since it is a costly operation. With this mechanism in place, we can observe a reasonable latency increase.

Figure 3 defines the percentile distribution of latency for HTTP requests from client to Microsoft Outlook via native and sconified deployments of Eperi Gateway. We can ignore the final spike in the graph as an effect of stragglers. Around *one-third* of requests are served within 450 ms and *ninety percent* within

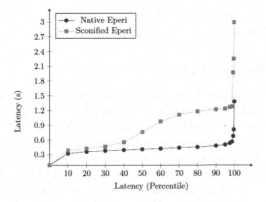

Fig. 3. Latency by percentile distribution

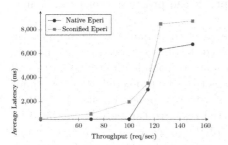

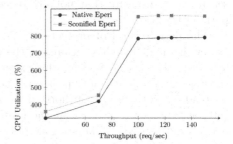

Fig. 4. Throughput versus latency for both setups

Fig. 5. CPU utilization versus latency for both setups

1.2 s in sconified version whereas *ninety percent* HTTP requests are served within 500 ms in native deployment of Eperi Gateway. We also have tested out the use of JMeter as a load testing tool. The request consisted of random strings in the payload to any increase the size of the request. The request was similar to one used in the previous experiment. The outcome showcased similar results with very minor differences in latency as shown in this section.

5.2 Throughput

The second experimental benchmark consists of issuing requests at increasing constant rates (x-axis) until the response latency spikes (y-axis). Figure 4 shows that both setups exhibit comparable performance until 100 requests per second, at which point the latency of the Sconified deployment increases dramatically. The native eperi deployment performs slightly better, reaching 110 requests per second. A closer look into the CPU utilization shown in Fig. 5 explains the aforementioned results. CPU usage was measured using Docker's built-in mechanism for viewing resource consumption, *docker stats*. Both the native and Sconified deployment reach a maximum CPU utilization at 790% and 910%, respectively under maximum throughput.

5.3 Security Requirements

In this section, we further look into the non-functional security requirements that are needed to safely run in a public cloud. The cloud provider operates the hardware, the cloud stack, and the OS. Relying on the cloud provider to do all the resource management decreases the complexity of running a cloud application. However, this also forces an application owner to give data and application sovereignty to the cloud provider. Intel SGX supported by the SCONE Platform, however, allows the application owner not to be in a position to "blindly" trust and give this power to neither the cloud provider nor malicious root users. Using SCONE, despite not having full control of neither the hardware nor the software setup, we can ensure that nobody (except for the program itself) can change parts of the program.

The desired level of protection is a design choice made by the application owner. Even if this choice changes, the program does not need to be changed. The objectives considered for this experiment are confidentiality, integrity and consistency. Confidentiality protected means that the protected resource cannot be read by entities not authorized by the security policy of the application. Integrity protected means that the protected resource can only be modified by entities authorized by the security policy of the application. All other changes are automatically detected and cause the program to terminate. Consistency protected means that changing the version of the protected resource will be detected and cause the program to terminate, unless the software update was authorized by the application owner. The assumption is that the program itself and userID are readable but not changeable. This also applies to the secrets and environment variables used by the eperi Gateway.

To verify confidentiality protection of the secrets and environment variables passed by CAS, we observe that all attempts to find values of the passed secrets and environment variables fail, since these variables are confidentiality protected as defined in the policy. However, this is not the case in the native eperi Gateway image where these variables are readable and can be configured. In fact, not even an entity with root access rights to the system of the application owner can access the secrets and environment variables, but only the application itself. To verify integrity protection, we attempt to change the environment variable path by adding another file to read the environment variables from. However, any change to the state of the application gets detected. This can be verified by looking at the hash of the environment variables is identical to the one before modification. To verify consistency protection, we simulate an attack on the consistency protection of the environment variables and check if an older version of these variables has been detected. First, we create and deploy a new version of the eperi Gateway application (version 2) which only differs from version 1 in its environment variables. However, when environment variables from version 2 are uploaded to CAS, the old variables from version 1 will no longer be present in

CAS and we therefore have nothing to which we can revert. But for the sake of argument, we can assume that the attacker in some way had indeed got hold of a copy of the version 1 eperi Gateway password. The attacker would have to upload it to CAS, in order for it to become the correct variable. As soon as the upload to CAS has taken place, however, this is considered to be a new, authorized version (version 3). Hence, we did not succeed in reverting the variables to ones present in version 1 without the change being detected and the attack on the consistency protection failed.

6 Discussion

Confidential computing provides additional security guarantees with respect to confidentiality and data integrity, which is especially relevant in a cloud setting. However, this does not solve all the security related issues. Applications are still vulnerable to threats such as side channel attacks. Nevertheless, if applied in the right way, Confidential Computing can be used to further enhance the security posture of cloud-based applications.

We have seen that Eperi Gateway behaves normally when the whole workflow is tested. This test was performed using the confidential version of the product. Despite certain performance penalties, we could still observe the results allowing for reasonable end user experience. This means that when accessing an application such as Microsoft Outlook with a load that resembles normal user behavior, the confidential eperi Gateway image results in low latencies that resembles values observed when using the native version of the eperi Gateway. Despite one-time bootrapping delays, the overall performance can be considered to be acceptable for the most use case.

7 Conclusion

Cloud Computing introduces new problems regarding data privacy and security as well as data and code sovereignty. We have to trust cloud providers with sensitive information. One solution to protect our sensitive data and code is to encrypt it before uploading it to the cloud, an approach adopted by Eperi. However, we need to secure the environment which hosts the encryption proxy. To achieve this, we use Confidential Computing.

There are different confidential computing technologies one can use. Intel SGX is one of the technologies which reduces our Trusted Computing Base significantly and provides a way to attest our platform albeit with some sacrifice in performance. AMD SEV is another technology which makes it easy to switch to a confidential virtual machine without any changes in application code. However, the TCB in this case includes the whole VM including guest OS.

8   Future Work

We plan to incorporate heavier back-end applications behind the native and confidential eperi Gateway and test their effect on the gateway's behavior. We also plan to use the confidential image of MariaDB instead of the native version we used in our experiments.

We still cannot generalize the change in performance of third party applications in confidential computing environment. From our observations, we know that there are some added overheads in SGX powered applications. Each application has its own architecture and combined with the technique one might use to convert it into a confidential application, the final architecture could vary greatly. We may try to group the performances of certain architectural and design patterns with probable overheads but that remains to be seen in future.

Confidential Computing is an evolving and dynamically developing field. In VM based trusted execution environments, until now we only had AMD's SEV in the market. However, recently, Intel announced their own VM based TEE, the Trust Domain eXtenstions (TDX) [6]. In addition, Google Cloud Platform offers Secure Encrypted Virtualization (SEV) based confidential computing solutions primarily. We could use Google Kubernetes Engine (GKE) to deploy a cluster of confidential VMs. This can be used to compare the deployment of the confidential eperi Gateway on different types of TEEs.

References

1. Arnautov, S., et al.: SCONE: secure Linux containers with intel SGX. In: 12th USENIX Symposium on Operating Systems Design and Implementation (OSDI 2016), pp. 689–703. USENIX Association, Savannah, November 2016. https://www.usenix.org/conference/osdi16/technical-sessions/presentation/arnautov
2. Confidential Computing Consortium: Confidential Computing: Hardware-Based Trusted Execution for Applications and Data (2021). https://confidentialcomputing.io/whitepaper-01-latest. Accessed 19 Dec 2021
3. Costan, V., Devadas, S.: Intel SGX explained. Cryptology ePrint Archive, Report 2016/086 (2016). https://ia.cr/2016/086
4. Eperi: Adapter for Microsoft 365. https://adminmanuals.eperi.com/administrator_manuals/en/concepts/egfca_o365_about_document.html. Accessed 06 Jan 2022
5. Eperi: Eperi gateway: the right approach to effective cloud data protection (2018). https://blog.eperi.com/en/eperi-gateway-the-right-approach-to-effective-cloud-data-protection. Accessed 19 Feb 2022
6. Intel: Intel®Trust Domain Extensions (2020). https://www.intel.com/content/dam/develop/external/us/en/documents/tdx-whitepaper-v4.pdf. Accessed 22 Feb 2022
7. Mahhouk, M., Weichbrodt, N., Kapitza, R.: SGXoMeter: open and modular benchmarking for intel SGX. In: Proceedings of the 14th European Workshop on Systems Security, EuroSec 2021, pp. 55–61. Association for Computing Machinery, New York (2021). https://doi.org/10.1145/3447852.3458722
8. MariaDB: Eperi Key Management Encryption Plugin. https://mariadb.com/kb/en/eperi-key-management-encryption-plugin/. Accessed 18 Mar 2022

9. Shakil, A.M., Sohail, S.S., Alam, M.T., Ubaid, S., Nafis, M.T., Wang, G.: Towards a two-tier architecture for privacy-enabled recommender systems (PeRS). In: Wang, G., Choo, K.K.R., Ko, R.K.L., Xu, Y., Crispo, B. (eds.) The First International Conference on Ubiquitous Security (UbiSec 2021), Guangzhou, China, 28–31 December 2021, pp. 268–278. Springer, Singapore (2022). https://doi.org/10.1007/978-981-19-0468-4_20

10. Skendžić, A., Kovačić, B., Tijan, E.: General data protection regulation - protection of personal data in an organisation. In: 2018 41st International Convention on Information and Communication Technology, Electronics and Microelectronics (MIPRO), pp. 1370–1375 (2018). https://doi.org/10.23919/MIPRO.2018.8400247

11. Srivastava, P., Khan, R.: A review paper on cloud computing. Int. J. Adv. Res. Comput. Sci. Softw. Eng. **8**, 17 (2018). https://doi.org/10.23956/ijarcsse.v8i6.711

12. Xing, B., Shanahan, M., Leslie-Hurd, R.: Intel® software guard extensions (Intel® SGX) software support for dynamic memory allocation inside an enclave, pp. 1–9 (2016). https://doi.org/10.1145/2948618.2954330

FedTA: Locally-Differential Federated Learning with Top-k Mechanism and Adam Optimization

Yuting Li, Guojun Wang$^{(\boxtimes)}$ (ID), Tao Peng, and Guanghui Feng

School of Computer Science and Cyber Engineering, Guangzhou University, Guangzhou 510006, China
csgjwang@gzhu.edu.cn

Abstract. With the explosive development of fields including big data and cloud computing, it has become a global trend for the public to place a premium on data security and privacy. A federated learning (FL) system is a useful weapon for utilizing decentralized information and files, since it enables several parties to construct a unified, robust model without disclosing their raw data, hence resolving critical issues such as data leakage and data silos. Nonetheless, an increasing number of research indicates that the federated learning algorithm cannot withstand sophisticated privacy threats. Additionally, federated learning does not guarantee privacy in a formal sense. In order to offer adequate protection for individuals' personal information, we include local differential privacy within the user uploaded settings. In addition, we proposed a framework to improve the performance of federated machine learning by employing several technologies including Top-k mechanism and Adam optimization. Detailed experimental results are provided to demonstrate the applicability and effectiveness of our approach.

Keywords: Local differential privacy · Federated learning · Top-k mechanism · Adam optimizer

1 Introduction

The rise of big data propels artificial intelligence to its new pinnacle. In recent years, however, data and computing resources are usually divided across the devices of end users, regions, and companies. As the data contain sensitive information about end users or organizations, such as facial images, location-based services, health information, or personal economic status, the distributed data and computing resources for machine learning tasks cannot be aggregated or directly shared across regions or organizations. FL is an effective way for protecting privacy in distributed environments. Multiple clients collaborate to solve an issue using machine learning with the assistance of one or more central servers. Each client's original data are stored locally and are not sent externally. The central server creates learning models by aggregating parameter updates submitted by clients; therefore, data sharing issues in untrusted situations can

G. Wang et al. (Eds.): UbiSec 2022, CCIS 1768, pp. 380–391, 2023.
https://doi.org/10.1007/978-981-99-0272-9_26

be addressed by FL. Multiple independent participants collaborate to achieve a learning objective, which not only protects the privacy of each participant's data but also considerably improves learning effectiveness.

Google's FedAvg [19] algorithm is generally regarded as the first formal investigation into federated learning. Its primary contribution consists of the weighted mean of the model parameters uploaded by each terminal in proportion to the size of the local data set. This approach Avoiding the client uploading local data directly protects user privacy to some degree. Since its introduction, federated learning has gained significant interest from academia and industry, and numerous practical applications have emerged. For instance, Google's Gboard software for Android phones initially predicted the material that users would enter in the future [14]. The mobile phone of the user gets the prediction model from the server, performs training and fine-tuning based on local user data, then uploads the fine-tuned model parameters to constantly optimize the server's global model. The asynchronous FL model can perform learning tasks efficiently, leveraging deep reinforcement learning for node selection to increase efficiency and decrease transmission burden [6]. In addition, federated learning is utilized extensively in domains like industry [33], medical care [7], the Internet of Things [5], healthcare [20], and other fields.

As federated learning is increasingly widely applied, its security and privacy protection capability have also begun to be questioned. People's continued efforts to solve this issue can be grouped into four distinct lines of attack: data poisoning attack [29,36], model poisoning attack [2,10], backdoor attack [1] and untrusted servers attack [15,16]. [29] investigates targeted data poisoning attacks against FL systems in which a malevolent subset of players intends to poison the global model by transmitting model changes generated from mislabeled data. By altering the hyperparameters of the attacker's local training, [36]adds a proportionate coefficient to the attacker's model update, so expanding the poisonous effect of the created data and boosting the influence of the attacker's update on the global model. [2] begins with targeted model poisoning by raising the updating of the harmful agent to overcome the impacts of other agents. In addition, they present two crucial principles of stealth to identify fraudulent updates and increase stealth by employing an alternating minimization technique that optimizes for stealth and the adversarial objective in a cyclical fashion. [10] formulates assaults as optimization problems and applies them to four contemporary Byzantine-resilient federated learning algorithms. In [1], the malicious party trains a malicious model with a backdoor locally before uploading a linear combination of the malicious model and the previous round of global models, such that the average aggregated global model converges to a malicious model.

Nowadays, as people have become more and more aware that privacy issues are an important issue in federated learning, more and more solutions have been proposed, such as Secure Multi-Party Computation (MPC) [22,25], Homomorphic Encryption [18,21,24] (Homomorphic Encryption), blockchain mechanism [35], data perturbation [4,26,32], etc. The trusted execution environment (TEE) represented by SGX [3] also provides a solution for privacy protection in federated learning.

The technological core and benefits and drawbacks of the following privacy protection solutions vary: Encryption technology prevents the adversary from stealing the communication messages of other nodes by concealing the transmission data between nodes. However, it is impossible to prevent the disclosure of some information, such as the aggregation results of each round or the final model, and the adversary can still infer information from these data; data perturbation technology adds noise to transmitted data so that the adversary cannot judge specific samples by analyzing intermediate results or the final model while the accuracy of the model is affected. The trusted execution environment prevents the server from tampering with data or calculating logic while aggregating data. However, its storage capacity is restricted, and it is susceptible to side channel assaults.

In reality, privacy protection technologies are not mutually exclusive; rather, one technology can be utilized to optimize other technologies. For example, [37] introduces multiple anonymizers and integrates the Shamir threshold mechanism, dynamic pseudonym mechanism, and K-anonymity technology to enhance the trajectory and content privacy in continuous LBSs; [30] Combines differential privacy with secure multiparty computation to reduce the growth of noise injection as the number of parties increases without sacrificing privacy while maintaining a pre-defined rate of trust. Hao et al. [12] introduced the privacy-enhanced federated learning framework (PEFL), which incorporates the homomorphic ciphertext of private gradients to create a secure aggregation protocol and the differential privacy technology to perturb the gradient.

In the aspect of privacy, local differential privacy (LDP) [17] is a promising privacy-protection technology to be integrated into FL due to its advantages of low computational cost and provable privacy protection. [27]provides an innovative architecture for a local differential privacy mechanism, which makes the data more distinguishable from its original value and introduces less variance. In addition, the proposed approach circumvents the curse of dimension by separating and rearranging model update data. [31] presents unique LDP techniques for collecting a numeric property, the accuracy of which is at least comparable to (and typically superior to) existing solutions in terms of the worst-case noise variance. In recent years, scholars have proposed a lot of work combining differential privacy and federated learning. For instance, Ying et al. [34] suggests an incentive FL framework with differential privacy and double insurance to secure the privacy of both the local model and bid.

Over time, machine learning itself has improved tremendously, one of which is the optimizer. Stochastic gradient-based optimization is of fundamental practical importance in numerous scientific and engineering disciplines. As a hyperparameter, the learning rate of SGD [23] is typically difficult to tune, as the magnitudes of multiple parameters change considerably, and constant adjustment is required during the training process. Several adaptive variations of SGD, including Adagrad [8], RMSprop [11], and Adam [13], were created to address this issue. The objective of these algorithms is to automatically adapt the learning rate to different parameters based on the gradient statistics.

As an illustration, Adam is a technique for first-order gradient-based optimization of stochastic objective functions that is based on adaptive estimations of lower-order moments. It is simple to implement, insensitive to diagonal rescaling of gradients, and well-suited for situations with a large number of parameters.

In light of the advantages and disadvantages of the aforementioned research approaches, our goal is to devise a system that is capable of simultaneously achieving two goals: sufficient accuracy and sufficient protection of individual privacy. The following are the contributions that we provide to the resolution of the issues described above:

- We propose a two-stage framework. This structure satisfies ϵ-LDP for any client's local vector. However, despite the fact that the Top-k mechanism performs better than LDP-FL, the accuracy diminishes with the increase of k.
- To address the accuracy obstacle, we are considering using an adaptive optimizer. To let each parameter choose its own learning depending on the current optimization state, we modified the optimizer for local parameter updating, which is based on the notion of Adam [13].
- The final experiment proves that the convergence speed is greatly improved. When compared with federated learning with the Top-k mechanism, there is little loss of precision.

The remaining parts of this work are organized as described in the following: The historical context and theoretical underpinnings necessary for our paradigm are discussed in Sect. 2. In Sect. 3, we illustrate the details of our architectures. Section 4 provides experimental results demonstrating that our proposal outperforms the state-of-art. Section 5 concludes the paper, which also covers the path that our work will take in the future.

2 Preliminary

2.1 Local Differential Privacy

Figure 1 depicts the setting for local differential privacy.

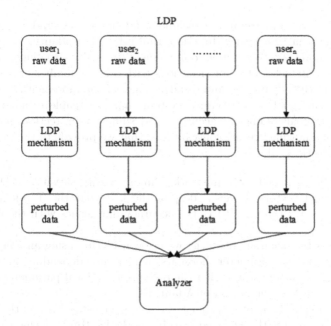

Fig. 1. Setting for local differential privacy

A person may be unwilling to share his data with the server if he lacks access to a reliable curator, which is a regular occurrence. In such circumstances, local differential privacy develops, in which each user alters vector t with a random perturbation prior to transmitting it to the analyzer.

Definition 1 (ϵ-local differential privacy). *A randomized function f satisfies ϵ -local differential privacy if and only if for any two input tuples t and t' in the domain of f, and for any output t^* of f, we have:*

$$\Pr\left[f\left(t\right) = t^*\right] \le e^{\varepsilon} \Pr\left[f\left(t'\right) = t^*\right].$$ (1)

2.2 Perturbation Mechanism

We use the classic Laplace method to add noise, that is, the added noise obeys the Laplace distribution. Since the specific value of noise added each time is random, privacy protection can be achieved. As long as certain parameters of the Laplace function are met, the final output will satisfy ϵ-LDP. The generating function of the Laplace [9] method is as follows: *Laplace mechanism.*

$$t_i^* = t_i + Lap\left(\frac{2}{\epsilon}\right)$$
$$Lap(\lambda) = \frac{1}{2\lambda} \exp\left(-\frac{|x|}{\lambda}\right)$$ (2)

t_i is the input, t_i^* is the result after perturbation with the Laplace mechanism.

2.3   Different Optimizers

Here we analyze the specific operation process of two optimizers: SGD [19], Adam [13].

SGD. At each iteration t, user i executes an SGD step based on its dataset D_i by updating its local parameter θ_t as:

$$g_t = \nabla_\theta f_t (\theta_t - 1),$$
$$\theta_t = \theta_t - 1 - \eta_t g_t,$$

where η_t denotes the constant learning rate through every training epoch. $\nabla_\theta f_t (\theta_t - 1)$ is the estimate of the gradient obtained from device i's data samples. Even though SGD can be applied to the majority of networks, it is relatively simple to become trapped at a place when the gradient is moderate, which prevents network updates for a substantial amount of time. This may be rather frustrating.

Adam. Adam can be viewed as an adaptive method that combines [28] and [11], adjusting the learning rate based on the gradients on each coordinate when running SGD. The mathematical rule for upgrading the original Adam's information may be summed up as follows:

$$m_t = \beta_1 m_{t-1} + (1 - \beta_1) g_t$$
$$v_t = \beta_2 v_{t-1} + (1 - \beta_2) g_t^2$$
$$\widehat{m_t} = \frac{m_t}{1 - \beta_1}$$
$$\widehat{v_t} = \frac{v_t}{1 - \beta_2}$$
$$\theta_t = \theta_{t-1} - \frac{\eta}{\sqrt{\widehat{v_t}} + \epsilon} \widehat{m_t}$$

m introduces first-order momentum, which reduces oscillations during stochastic gradient descent training. The second-order momentum introduced by v modifies the learning rate from η to $\frac{\eta}{\sqrt{\widehat{v_t}}+\epsilon}$. During the iterations, the adaptation of the learning rate causes the rate of learning for parameters that are seldom updated to increase, while the rate of learning for parameters that are updated frequently causes the learning rate to decrease. As a result, it is ideal for working with sparse data, despite the fact that it may exhibit some fluctuations close to the optimal point.

3   Top-k + Adam

3.1   Top-k Mechanism

In this section, we design a system that can both qualitatively and quantitatively safeguard users' privacy by combining local differential privacy with the Top-k technique. This results in an improvement in accuracy.

Assuming that a privacy budget of ϵ_l is assigned to each user in a high-dimensional network with dimension d, then the privacy budget must be evenly distributed among all d dimensions. This results in the privacy budgets allotted to each dimension rapidly decreasing, which has a significant effect on the accuracy of the network. Because the vast majority of the updated values are very near to zero, we use a sparsification method in order to ensure that each dimension is able to make use of a larger privacy budget. In each round, we rank the user-uploaded parameters by absolute value, and instead of randomly perturbing every dimension with a little budget ϵ_{ld}, we merely sample and perturb k. As a result, $\epsilon_{lk} = \frac{\epsilon_l}{k}$.

We now illustrate the proposed framework in Algorithm 1. In our framework, the server first initiates the compression rate $r = \frac{d}{k}$, the number of local iteration rounds b, clipping C for the vector, ϵ for privacy budget before allocating model to the selected users.

Algorithm 1. Top-k Framework

Server initialize r, b, C, ϵ
for each iteration t = 1,...,T **do**
    Server distributes θ^{t-1} to a batch of n users
    for i in n **do**
        $y_i \longleftarrow$ Local Update (θ^{t-1}, b)
        $\kappa_i \longleftarrow$ sparsification(y_i, r)
        $\bar{\kappa}_i \longleftarrow$ Clip$(\kappa_i, -C, C)$
        $z_i \longleftarrow$ Random Perturbation$(\bar{\kappa}_i, \epsilon_l)$
        $user_i$ sends z_i to Server
    end for
    ▷ Aggregation Process in Server
    transforms $\rho_i \longleftarrow z_i \cdot C$
    estimates $\rho \longleftarrow \frac{1}{n} \sum_{i \in [n]} \rho_i$
    updates model $\theta^t \longleftarrow \theta^{t-1} + \rho$
end for

On a local device, the method consists of three steps, which are as follows: 1. iterate b times locally according to the model that has been allocated; 2. choose the Topk indexes according to the absolute value of the update depending on the compression rate; 3. Modify the value in question by using the differential privacy technique.

The most important distinction we make from previous research is that, in addition to utilizing local differential privacy to keep our customers' data secure, we also make use of the Top-k technique in order to improve our system's overall speed. Compared to LDP-FL, experimental results in Sect. 4 demonstrate a 60% percent improvement in accuracy.

Limitation of Top-k Mechanism. As a result of the fact that gradient sparsification often requires a sparse rate of more than 90%, a sizeable portion of the parameter updates are required to be postponed. As the value of k grows, the privacy budget that is allotted to each dimension will decrease, which will lead to a decline in accuracy.

3.2   Adam Mechanism

Intuition. Although Top-k mechanism improves performance by refining the noise-adding process, the problem of lowering convergence speed has not yet been resolved. In the original version, the SGD optimizer is deployed with a set global learning rate. If the learning rate is too high, oscillation will occur, and if it is too low, the aggregation pace will be sluggish. We therefore consider that the user can vary the learning rate for different parameters when iterating locally.

In this scheme, we use Adam as the optimizer for user local updates. The specific procedure is in Algorithm 2.

Algorithm 2. Local Update Process

---

input:
x^0,b
initialize $m^0 \longleftarrow 0$, $s^0 \longleftarrow 0$
for i in b **do**
  $j \;\&\!\!\longleftarrow j+1$
  $g^i \;\& \longleftarrow \nabla_x f_j(x^{j-1})$
  $m^j \;\&\!\!\longleftarrow \beta_1 m^{j-1}+(1\text{-}\beta_1)g^j$
  $v^j \;\&\!\!\longleftarrow \beta_2 v^{j-1}+(1\text{-}\beta_2)g^j 2$
  Bias Correction
  $\widehat{m^j} \longleftarrow \frac{m^j}{1-\beta_1}, \; \widehat{v^j} \longleftarrow \frac{v^j}{1-\beta_2}$
  Update
  $x^j \longleftarrow \Pi \left(x^{j-1}\text{-}\frac{\alpha \widehat{m^j}}{\sqrt{\widehat{v^j}}+\epsilon}\right)$
end for

3.3   Top-k + Adam

The overall framework of the scheme is shown in Fig. 2. The server distributes model to a batch of users. The user first iterates b round locally using Adam optimizer, then picks the topk dimensions and uses Laplace mechanism to introduce noise to the parameters before sending them to the server. The server-side transforms the parameters and aggregates them and finally sends the updated model to a newly selected batch of users for the next iteration.

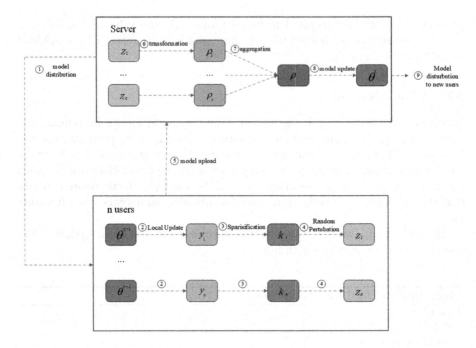

Fig. 2. The overall framework.

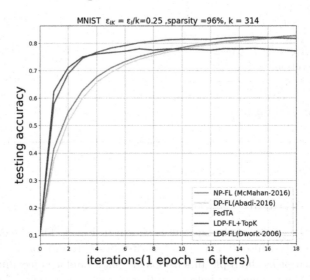

Fig. 3. Performance comparison

4   Experiment

To evaluate the accuracy of the logistic regression model on MNIST dataset under varied settings, we modified each parameter and compare our protocol with the state-of-art.

Given $\epsilon_l = 78.5$, compression rate $= 0.04$, and the selected dimension $k = 314$, the spilt privacy budget of each dimension is $\epsilon_{lk} = 0.25$. In terms of accuracy, it is evident that our protocol performs significantly better than LDP-FL as shown in Fig. 3. However, due to the use of LDP, FedTA is less accurate than NP-FL. Due to the fact that we employ Adam optimizer as the gradient descent optimizer, the precision is superior to that of LDPFL+Top-k. Compared to NP-FL, the accuracy of LDPFL+Top-k is 5% lower. The accuracy of FedTA is nearly equal to NP-FL.

5   Conclusion

We propose a framework which is combined with LDP and Top-k techniques for privacy-preserving federated learning. We then improve the accuracy by adjusting Adam optimizer and further boost the utility of our scheme via adding self-adaptation mechanisms. Ultimately, our approach can attain almost the same accuracy as federated learning. In conclusion, the studies show that using FedTA to provide privacy-preserving federated aggregation with quick convergence as in adaptive techniques and training stability is a more effective and accurate approach to do so. We plan to implement our strategy by combining it into more complex networks in order to deal with increasingly challenging circumstances.

Acknowledgments. This work was supported in part by the National Key Research and Development Program of China (2020YFB1005804), and in part by the National Natural Science Foundation of China under Grants 61632009, 61872097, and 61802076.

References

1. Bagdasaryan, E., Veit, A., Hua, Y., Estrin, D., Shmatikov, V.: How to backdoor federated learning. In: International Conference on Artificial Intelligence and Statistics, pp. 2938–2948. PMLR (2020)
2. Bhagoji, A.N., Chakraborty, S., Mittal, P., Calo, S.: Analyzing federated learning through an adversarial lens. In: International Conference on Machine Learning, pp. 634–643. PMLR (2019)
3. Brasser, F., Müller, U., Dmitrienko, A., Kostiainen, K., Capkun, S., Sadeghi, A.R.: Software grand exposure:{SGX} cache attacks are practical. In: 11th USENIX Workshop on Offensive Technologies (WOOT 2017) (2017)
4. Cangialosi, F., Agarwal, N., Arun, V., Narayana, S., Sarwate, A., Netravali, R.: Privid: practical, {Privacy-Preserving} video analytics queries. In: 19th USENIX Symposium on Networked Systems Design and Implementation (NSDI 2022), pp. 209–228 (2022)

5. Chang, X., et al.: From insight to impact: building a sustainable edge computing platform for smart homes. In: 2018 IEEE 24th International Conference on Parallel and Distributed Systems (ICPADS), pp. 928–936. IEEE (2018)
6. Chen, Z., Liao, W., Hua, K., Lu, C., Yu, W.: Towards asynchronous federated learning for heterogeneous edge-powered internet of things. Digital Commun. Netw. **7**(3), 317–326 (2021)
7. Duan, R., et al.: Learning from electronic health records across multiple sites: a communication-efficient and privacy-preserving distributed algorithm. J. Am. Med. Inform. Assoc. **27**(3), 376–385 (2020)
8. Duchi, J., Hazan, E., Singer, Y.: Adaptive subgradient methods for online learning and stochastic optimization. J. Mach. Learn. Res. **12**(7), 2121–2159 (2011)
9. Dwork, C., McSherry, F., Nissim, K., Smith, A.: Calibrating noise to sensitivity in private data analysis. In: Halevi, S., Rabin, T. (eds.) TCC 2006. LNCS, vol. 3876, pp. 265–284. Springer, Heidelberg (2006). https://doi.org/10.1007/11681878_14
10. Fang, M., Cao, X., Jia, J., Gong, N.: Local model poisoning attacks to {Byzantine-Robust} federated learning. In: 29th USENIX Security Symposium (USENIX Security 2020), pp. 1605–1622 (2020)
11. Graves, A.: Generating sequences with recurrent neural networks. arXiv preprint arXiv:1308.0850 (2013)
12. Hao, M., Li, H., Luo, X., Xu, G., Yang, H., Liu, S.: Efficient and privacy-enhanced federated learning for industrial artificial intelligence. IEEE Trans. Industr. Inf. **16**(10), 6532–6542 (2019)
13. Kingma, D.P., Ba, J.: Adam: a method for stochastic optimization. arXiv preprint arXiv:1412.6980 (2014)
14. Konečnỳ, J., McMahan, H.B., Yu, F.X., Richtárik, P., Suresh, A.T., Bacon, D.: Federated learning: strategies for improving communication efficiency. arXiv preprint arXiv:1610.05492 (2016)
15. Lam, M., Wei, G.Y., Brooks, D., Reddi, V.J., Mitzenmacher, M.: Gradient disaggregation: breaking privacy in federated learning by reconstructing the user participant matrix. In: International Conference on Machine Learning, pp. 5959–5968. PMLR (2021)
16. Zhou, L., et al.: A coprocessor-based introspection framework via intel management engine. IEEE Trans. Dependable Secure Comput. **18**(4), 1920–1932 (2021)
17. Liu, W., Cheng, J., Wang, X., Lu, X., Yin, J.: Hybrid differential privacy based federated learning for internet of things. J. Syst. Architect. **124**, 102418 (2022)
18. Madi, A., Stan, O., Mayoue, A., Grivet-Sébert, A., Gouy-Pailler, C., Sirdey, R.: A secure federated learning framework using homomorphic encryption and verifiable computing. In: 2021 Reconciling Data Analytics, Automation, Privacy, and Security: A Big Data Challenge (RDAAPS), pp. 1–8. IEEE (2021)
19. McMahan, B., Moore, E., Ramage, D., Hampson, S., y Arcas, B.A.: Communication-efficient learning of deep networks from decentralized data. In: Artificial Intelligence and Statistics, pp. 1273–1282. PMLR (2017)
20. Qayyum, A., Ahmad, K., Ahsan, M.A., Al-Fuqaha, A., Qadir, J.: Collaborative federated learning for healthcare: multi-modal Covid-19 diagnosis at the edge. IEEE Open J. Comput. Soc. **3**, 172–184 (2022)
21. Liu, Q., et al.: SlimBox: lightweight packet inspection over encrypted traffic. IEEE Trans. Dependable Secure Comput. 12 (2022). https://doi.org/10.1109/TDSC.2022.3222533
22. Liu, Q., Peng, Y., Wu, J., Wang, T., Wang, G.: Secure multi-keyword fuzzy searches with enhanced service quality in cloud computing. IEEE Trans. Netw. Serv. Manage. **18**(2), 2046–2062 (2021)

23. Robbins, H., Monro, S.: A stochastic approximation method. Ann. Math. Stat. **22**, 400–407 (1951)

24. Shakil, M.A., et al.: Towards a two-tier architecture for privacy-enabled recommender systems (pers). In: Wang, G., Choo, KK.R., Ko, R.K.L., Xu, Y., Crispo, B. (eds.) Ubiquitous Security. UbiSec 2021. Communications in Computer and Information Science, vol. 1557. Springer, Singapore (2022). https://doi.org/10.1007/978-981-19-0468-4_20

25. So, J., et al.: LightSecAgg: a lightweight and versatile design for secure aggregation in federated learning. Proc. Mach. Learn. Syst. **4**, 694–720 (2022)

26. Sun, J., Li, A., Wang, B., Yang, H., Li, H., Chen, Y.: Soteria: provable defense against privacy leakage in federated learning from representation perspective. In: Proceedings of the IEEE/CVF Conference on Computer Vision and Pattern Recognition, pp. 9311–9319 (2021)

27. Sun, L., Qian, J., Chen, X.: LDP-FL: practical private aggregation in federated learning with local differential privacy. arXiv preprint arXiv:2007.15789 (2020)

28. Sutskever, I., Martens, J., Dahl, G., Hinton, G.: On the importance of initialization and momentum in deep learning. In: International Conference on Machine Learning, pp. 1139–1147. PMLR (2013)

29. Tolpegin, V., Truex, S., Gursoy, M.E., Liu, L.: Data poisoning attacks against federated learning systems. In: Chen, L., Li, N., Liang, K., Schneider, S. (eds.) ESORICS 2020. LNCS, vol. 12308, pp. 480–501. Springer, Cham (2020). https://doi.org/10.1007/978-3-030-58951-6_24

30. Truex, S., et al.: A hybrid approach to privacy-preserving federated learning. In: Proceedings of the 12th ACM Workshop on Artificial Intelligence and Security, pp. 1–11 (2019)

31. Wang, N., et al.: Collecting and analyzing multidimensional data with local differential privacy. In: 2019 IEEE 35th International Conference on Data Engineering (ICDE), pp. 638–649. IEEE (2019)

32. Yang, P., Zhang, S., Yang, L.: Privacy-preserving cluster validity. In: Wang, G., Choo, K.K.R., Ko, R.K.L., Xu, Y., Crispo, B. (eds.) Ubiquitous Security. UbiSec 2021. Communications in Computer and Information Science, vol. 1557. Springer, Singapore (2022). https://doi.org/10.1007/978-981-19-0468-4_12

33. Yang, W., Zhang, Y., Ye, K., Li, L., Xu, C.-Z.: FFD: a federated learning based method for credit card fraud detection. In: Chen, K., Seshadri, S., Zhang, L.-J. (eds.) BIGDATA 2019. LNCS, vol. 11514, pp. 18–32. Springer, Cham (2019). https://doi.org/10.1007/978-3-030-23551-2_2

34. Ying, C., Jin, H., Wang, X., Luo, Y.: Double insurance: Incentivized federated learning with differential privacy in mobile crowdsensing. In: 2020 International Symposium on Reliable Distributed Systems (SRDS), pp. 81–90. IEEE (2020)

35. Zou, Y., Peng, W.Z.K.G., Wang, G.: Reliable and controllable data sharing based on blockchain. In: Wang, G., Choo, K.K.R., Ko, R.K.L., Xu, Y., Crispo, B. (eds.) Ubiquitous Security, UbiSec 2021. Communications in Computer and Information Science, vol. 1557. Springer, Singapore (2022). https://doi.org/10.1007/978-981-19-0468-4_17

36. Zhang, J., Chen, B., Cheng, X., Binh, H.T.T., Yu, S.: PoisonGAN: generative poisoning attacks against federated learning in edge computing systems. IEEE Internet Things J. **8**(5), 3310–3322 (2020)

37. Zhang, S., Wang, G., Bhuiyan, M.Z.A., Liu, Q.: A dual privacy preserving scheme in continuous location-based services. IEEE Internet Things J. **5**(5), 4191–4200 (2018)

Differentially Private Clustering Algorithm for Mixed Data

Kai Cheng[1], Liandong Chen[1], Huifeng Yang[1], Dan Luo[2] (ID), Shuai Yuan[3], and Zhitao Guan[2(✉)] (ID)

[1] State Grid Hebei Information and Telecommunication Branch, Shijiazhuang 050021, China
[2] School of Control and Computer Engineering, North China Electric Power University, Beijing 102206, China
guan@ncepu.edu.cn
[3] Department of Finance, Operations, and Information Systems, Brock University, Ontario, Canada

Abstract. Inspired by the current practice where mixed data is the norm instead of exceptions and the privacy concerns on data management, we propose a differentially private mixed data clustering (DPMC) algorithm considering the cluster analysis on both numerical and categorical data. First, we design an adaptive privacy budget allocation method to analyze the loss due to added noise, thus determining the number of iterations and the privacy budget given accuracy and dataset characteristics. Next, we develop an optimization method based on consistency inference for categorical attributes, in order to improve the clustering performance. Finally, comparative experiments have been carried out using four real-world datasets. The results demonstrate significant improvement in balancing between privacy protection and performance.

Keywords: Differential privacy · Clustering · Adaptive privacy budget allocation · Consistent inference · Mixed dataset

1 Introduction

The rapid adoption of artificial intelligence techniques in variety of domains has resulted in the continuous growth of data, also known as big data. However, addressing security issues with big data is still a primary concern among researchers and practitioners [1–6]. Since individual and sensitive information may be acquired by malicious users, substantial amount of research has focused on approaches for preventing data loss, exposure, and profiling [7–9].

G. Wang et al. (Eds.): UbiSec 2022, CCIS 1768, pp. 392–405, 2023.
https://doi.org/10.1007/978-981-99-0272-9_27

Cluster analysis is one of the classical techniques in the discipline of machine learning. In order to mitigate the risk of privacy leakage in the analysis, lightweight differentially private algorithms with mathematical proof are typically introduced. However, it trades off against a lower performance. Thus, balancing between the security requirement and performance of method has also been studied extensively [10–16]. In addition, most solutions do not take into account the mix of numerical and categorical data that is common in practice. Motived by these limitations, this paper presents a differentially private mixed data clustering (DPMC) algorithm for mixed datasets, where adaptive privacy budget allocation and optimization based on consistency inference are used to enhance the privacy protection, while providing better performance. Accordingly, the main contributions of this paper are as follows:

(1) We propose a DPMC algorithm for mixed datasets where adaptive privacy budget allocation and optimization based on consistency inference are incorporated.
(2) We design an adaptive privacy budget allocation method considering both numerical and categorical attributes, such that the loss caused by adding noise is analyzed. Furthermore, the number of iterations and the allocations of privacy budget are determined given accuracy and dataset characteristics.
(3) We develop an optimization method based on consistency inference. During centroid updating on a given categorical attribute, the consistency condition is applied to optimize the frequency of each attribute value after adding noise, thus improving the performance of cluster analysis.
(4) We carry out comparative experiments on four real-world datasets, i.e., Heart, Adult, CMC and DCCS. The results demonstrate significant improvement in balancing between privacy protection and performance.

2 Related Work

Because of the lack of mathematical guarantee in traditional data privacy protection methods such as k-anonymity [17] and l-diversity [18], Dwork provides the differential privacy approach by adding random noise from a specific distribution [19]. In recent years, it becomes an established paradigm for the provisioning of privacy enforcement [20, 21]. Much of the pertinent work in its extensions has focused on the balance between ensuring privacy protection and model performance. For instance, Blum et al. [22] incorporate differential privacy protection into K-means clustering method, bearing in mind the potential risks of privacy information disclosure from background knowledge and clustering outcomes.

In general, there are two schemes to allocate privacy budget in cluster analysis, fixed number and non-fixed number of iterations [23]. Su et al. [11] explore the difference on privacy budget allocation between fixed and non-fixed number of iterations and also evaluates the empirical error. Furthermore, in current practice, mixed data is the norm instead of exceptions. The differentially private technology is applied to K-modes algorithm in [24] for categorical data, while geometric mechanism [25] and exponential mechanism [26] are also used in K-modes algorithm for both interactive and non-interactive environments. K-means and K-modes algorithms are combined in [10] for the clustering on various types of data. We complement their work by introducing consistency optimization method after noise is added, and adjusting the privacy budget allocation accordingly.

3 Differentially Private Mixed Data Clustering Algorithm

In this section, we introduce the DPMC algorithm with differential privacy protection, where mixed datasets are also supported. Meanwhile, adaptive privacy budget allocation and optimization based on consistency inference are used to improve the clustering performance. We first present the overview of the approach, followed by detailed implementations on each component respectively.

3.1 Overview of the DPMC Algorithm

The DPMC algorithm proposed in this work is mainly divided into two parts. First, the number of iterations of the clustering algorithm is determined by the adaptive privacy budget allocation method, and the privacy budget for each iteration and each attribute is allocated. Second, a combined clustering approach is provided for the tasks with mixed datasets. Specifically, K-means algorithm is applied on numerical data, while K-modes algorithm is used on categorical data. During centroid updating on a given categorical attribute, the frequency of attribute values after adding noise is optimized by the optimization method based on consistency inference. The overview is presented in Algorithm 1.

The number of iterations in step (2) is determined by using the adaptive privacy budget allocation method, which is discussed in Sect. 3.3. The frequency of each attribute value in step (10) is optimized by adopting the optimization method based on consistency inference. See Sect. 3.4 for details.

Algorithm 1: DPMC

Input: D, a dataset; n, the number of data; d, the number of attributes owned by each data; p, the number of numerical attributes; q, the number of categorical attributes; K, the number of clusters; ε, privacy budget.

Output: K centroids $\left\{\hat{o}_1^{(T)}, \hat{o}_2^{(T)}, ..., \hat{o}_K^{(T)}\right\}$

---

(1) K points are randomly selected in D as initial centroids. $\left\{o_1^{(0)}, o_2^{(0)}, ..., o_K^{(0)}\right\}$.

(2) Determine the number of iterations T and privacy budget allocation scheme

(3) for $t=1 \rightarrow T$ do

(4)   for $k=1 \rightarrow K$ do

(5)   for $j=1 \rightarrow p$ do

(6) $\hat{o}_{kj}^{(t)} = \dfrac{S_{kj}^{(t)} + Lap(\varepsilon_{kj})}{C_{kj}^{(t)} + Lap(\varepsilon_{k0})}$

(7)   for $j=p+1 \rightarrow d$ do

(8)   for $r=1 \rightarrow \left|A_j\right|$ do

(9) $n_{kjr}^{(t)} = count_{kj}^{(t)}(r) + noise$

(10) $\bar{\mathbf{n}}_{kj}^{(t)} \leftarrow \mathbf{n}_{kj}^{(t)}$

(11) $\hat{o}_{kj}^{(t)} = \arg\max_r \bar{n}_{kjr}^{(t)}$

return $\left\{\hat{o}_1^{(T)}, \hat{o}_2^{(T)}, ..., \hat{o}_K^{(T)}\right\}$

3.2   Differential Privacy Protection

Let the size of the privacy budget consumed by the tth iteration be ε_t, since clusters are disjoint, the privacy budget allocated to each centroid is ε_t. Accordingly, the privacy budget of each attribute is denoted as $\varepsilon_{tj}, j \in [0, d]$.

For the jth numerical attribute, noise is added to the attribute sum S_{kj} for each attribute and the number of points C_k in the cluster before calculating the centroid. Then noise is also added to $p + 1$ number of values, including p number of attributes and the number of clusters, which are denoted as $\varepsilon_{tj}, j \in [0, p]$ where ε_{t0} is the privacy budget allocated to C_k.

For the jth categorical attribute, $j \in [p+1, d]$, the kth cluster D_k is divided into disjoint subsets D_{kjr} by different attribute values A_{jr}, and the frequency of each attribute value n_{kjr} is obtained by applying *count* on each subset. Since the calculation is performed on individual disjoint subset of D_k, the privacy budget allocated to each attribute value is equivalent, $\varepsilon_{tj}, j \in [p+1, d]$. The sensitivity of the *count* query is 1, therefore, the added noise is $Lap(1/\varepsilon_{tj})$. For simplicity, the number of points in each cluster C_k is denoted as the 0th attribute such that the privacy budget of each attribute is $\varepsilon_{tj} = \varepsilon_t/(d + 1)$.

3.3   Adaptive Privacy Budget Allocation

In this section, we present an adaptive privacy budget allocation method based on Loss analysis. It analyzes the loss caused by adding noise for both numerical and categorical attributes, calculates the sum of loss during each iteration, and determines the number of iterations and the allocation of privacy budget with regard to the accuracy level and the dataset characteristics.

Because the numerical and categorical attributes adopt different ways in calculating the centroid, the total Loss is derived as the sum of the weights of both types:

$$Loss(\widehat{o}) = \alpha \sum_{j=1}^{p} MSE_p(\widehat{o}_j) + (1 - \alpha) \sum_{j=p+1}^{d} MSE_q(\widehat{o}_j) \tag{1}$$

(1)   For a given numerical attribute $j \in [1, p]$, and $\rho = S_i/C, C \approx N/K$, we have:

$$MSE_p(\widehat{o}_j) = E\left[\left(\frac{S_j + \Delta S_j}{C + \Delta C} - \frac{S_j}{C}\right)^2\right] \approx \frac{Var(\Delta S_j)}{C^2} + \frac{S_j^2 Var(\Delta C)}{C^4} \tag{2}$$

Therefore, the loss from all numerical attributes can be derived as:

$$\sum_{j=1}^{p} MSE_p(\widehat{o}_j) \approx \frac{K^2 p(1+d)^2(1 + \rho^2)}{N^2 \varepsilon_t^2}. \tag{3}$$

(2)   For a given categorical attribute $j \in [p + 1, d]$, we have:

$$MSE_q(\widehat{o}_j) = \sum_{r=1}^{|A_j|} E\left[\left(\frac{n_{jr} + \Delta n_{jr}}{C + \Delta C} - \frac{n_{jr}}{C}\right)^2\right] \approx \sum_{r=1}^{|A_j|} \left(\frac{Var(\Delta n_{jr})}{C^2} + \frac{n_{jr}^2 Var(\Delta C)}{C^4}\right) \tag{4}$$

if $n_{jr} \approx C/|A_j|, v^2 = 1/|A_j|^2$,

$$MSE_q(\widehat{o}_j) \approx \sum_{r=1}^{|A_j|} \left(\frac{Var(\Delta n_{jr})}{C^2} + \frac{Var(\Delta C)}{C^2|A_j|^2}\right) = \sum_{r=1}^{|A_j|} \left(\frac{Var(\Delta n_{jr})}{C^2} + v^2 \frac{Var(\Delta C)}{C^2}\right) \tag{5}$$

Therefore, the loss from all categorical attributes can be derived as:

$$MSE_q(\widehat{o}) = \sum_{j=p+1}^{d} MSE_q(\widehat{o})= \sum_{j=p+1}^{d} |A_j| \left(\frac{Var(\Delta n_{jr})}{C^2} + v^2 \frac{Var(\Delta C)}{C^2} \right)$$

$$= \frac{|A|_q K^2 (1 + v^2)(1 + d)^2}{N^2 \varepsilon_t^2} \left(|A|_q = \sum_{j=p+1}^{d} |A_j| \right)$$

(6)

(3) Thus, the total loss from a centroid is:

$$Loss(\widehat{o}) = \alpha \sum_{j=1}^{p} MSE_p(\widehat{o}) + (1 - \alpha) \sum_{j=p+1}^{d} MSE_q(\widehat{o})$$

$$= \frac{\alpha K^2 p (1+d)^2 (1 + \rho^2)}{N^2 \varepsilon_t^2} + \frac{(1 - \alpha) |A|_q K^2 (1 + v^2)(1 + d)^2}{N^2 \varepsilon_t^2}$$

(7)

$$= \frac{K^2 (1+d)^2}{N^2 \varepsilon_t^2} \left(\alpha p \left(1 + \rho^2 \right) + (1 - \alpha) |A|_q \left(1 + v^2 \right) \right)$$

(4) During one iteration, the sum of loss from all centroids is:

$$Loss(\hat{O}) = \sum_{k=1}^{K} Loss(\hat{O}^k) = \frac{K^3 (1 + d)^2}{N^2 \varepsilon_t^2} \left(\alpha p (1 + \rho) + (1 - \alpha) |A|_q \left(1 + v^2 \right) \right)$$

(8)

(5) Since the sum of the loss during each iteration need to be less than the accuracy level, i.e., $Loss(\widehat{O}) \leq \delta$, the number of iterations can be determined as follows:

$$\frac{K^3 (1+d)^2}{N^2 \varepsilon_t^2} \left(\alpha p \left(1 + \rho^2 \right) + (1 - \alpha) |A|_q \left(1 + v^2 \right) \right) \leq \delta$$

$$\Rightarrow \varepsilon_t^2 \geq \frac{K^3 (1 + d)^2 \left(\alpha p (1 + \rho^2) + (1 - \alpha) |A|_q (1 + v^2) \right)}{N^2 \delta}$$

$$\Rightarrow \varepsilon_t^{min} = \left(\frac{K^3 (1 + d)^2 \left(\alpha p (1 + \rho^2) + (1 - \alpha) |A|_q (1 + v^2) \right)}{N^2 \delta} \right)^{\frac{1}{2}}$$

(9)

$$\Rightarrow T = \min \left\{ \frac{\varepsilon}{\varepsilon_t^{min}}, 7 \right\}$$

3.4 Optimization Based on Consistency Inference

In this section, we describe an optimization method based on consistency inference during centroid updating on a given categorical attribute. It uses the consistency condition to optimize the frequency of each attribute value after adding noise, leading to the improvement of the performance of cluster analysis.

For a given categorical attribute $A_j, j \in [p+1, d]$, the sum of frequencies of different attribute values should be equivalent to the number of data points in its cluster, i.e., $\forall k, j, n_k = n_{k,j,1} + \cdots + n_{k,j,|A_j|}$. However, in order to meet the requirement of differential privacy protection, noise is inevitably needed to add to the frequency of each attribute value, thus reducing the probability of incurring privacy exposure [27]. This would lead to the potential violation on the consistency conditions above. Therefore, if the consistency condition is still satisfied after adding noise, the accuracy of the analysis will be improved since some randomness is eliminated. Following this strategy, we provide the consistency inference process in Fig. 1.

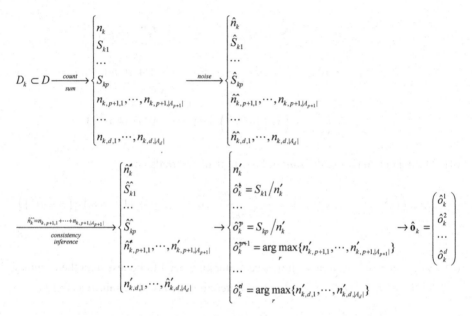

Fig. 1. Process of constraint inference

Here, we analyze the case of a given categorical attribute in a cluster during one iteration. The number of points in the cluster is denoted as μ_0, and we assume the attribute has m values with frequency $\mu_1, \mu_2, \cdots, \mu_m$, respectively. By using consistency inference, the frequency sequence after adding noise is optimized according to the constraint conditions. In other words, the sum of attribute value frequencies should be equivalent to the number of points in the cluster. Given $\hat{\mu}_0 = \hat{\mu}_1 + \hat{\mu}_2 + \cdots + \hat{\mu}_m$, the solution $\overline{\mu}$ with the smallest L_2 distance $||\overline{\mu} - \hat{\mu}||_2$ can be calculated. Specifically, for a given point $\hat{\mu} = [\hat{\mu}_0, \hat{\mu}_1, \hat{\mu}_2, \cdots, \hat{\mu}_m]$, solve the following optimization problem:

$$\min \sum_i (\overline{\mu}_i - \hat{\mu}_i)^2$$

$$s.t. \begin{cases} \overline{\mu}_0 = \overline{\mu}_1 + \overline{\mu}_2 + \cdots + \overline{\mu}_m \\ \overline{\mu}_i \geq 0, i = 0, 1, 2 \cdots, m \end{cases} (*)$$

(10)

By using the method of Lagrange multipliers, the solution $\overline{\mu} = [\overline{\mu}_0, \overline{\mu}_1, \overline{\mu}_2, \cdots, \overline{\mu}_m]$ can be derived as:

$$\begin{cases} \overline{\mu}_0 = \hat{\mu}_0 - \dfrac{\hat{\mu}_0 - \hat{\mu}_1 - \cdots - \hat{\mu}_m}{m+1} \\ \overline{\mu}_i = \hat{\mu}_i + \dfrac{\hat{\mu}_0 - \hat{\mu}_1 - \cdots - \hat{\mu}_m}{m+1}, i = 1, 2, \ldots m \end{cases} \tag{11}$$

It can also be observed that optimization result reduces the error between the processed attribute frequency and the original one.

4 Experiments

In this section, we evaluate our proposed algorithm on four selected datasets by using the Normalized Intra-Cluster Variance (NICV) and compare it with existing benchmarks. The results demonstrate that the DPMC method can significantly improve the performance and accuracy of cluster analysis.

4.1 Data Set and Parameter Setting

We conduct experiments on four mixed datasets in UCI Knowledge Discovery Archive database, including Heart, Adult, CMC and DCCS, to justify the performance of the proposed algorithm. Table 1 shows the descriptive statistics of four datasets. N is the total number of data and d is the number of attributes. In terms of data types, p represents the number of numerical attributes, q represents the number of categorical attributes, K represents the number of clusters, $|A|_q$ represents the sum of the attribute values for a given categorical attribute, $\varepsilon_t^{\min}$ represents the minimum privacy budget in each iteration. Table 2 presents the number of iterations on datasets derived from the adaptive privacy budget allocation method under various privacy budget settings.

Since $v^2 = 1/|A_j|^2 \le 0.25$ and the maximum $MSE(\widehat{o})$ occurs at time $v^2 = 0.25$, we set $\rho = 0.225$ [7] and $v = 0.5$. For the sake of brevity and without loss of generality, we set $\alpha = 0.5$ such that the weight for numerical attributes is the same as the weight for categorical attributes. Furthermore, δ is determined by the size of each dataset as follows:

$$\delta = \begin{cases} 1, N \le 1000 \\ 0.1, 1000 < N \le 10000 \\ 0.01, N > 10000 \end{cases}$$

4.2 Performance Evaluation

4.2.1 Impact of Adaptive Privacy Budget Allocation

We explore the impact of adaptive privacy budget allocation on the algorithm performance, by comparing our method with four benchmarks with given number of iterations ($T = 2,3,4,5$, respectively) over all datasets.

Table 1. Descriptive statistics of datasets

Dataset	N	d	p	q	K	$|A|_q$	ε_t^{min}
Adult	30162	12	4	8	5	80	0.348
CMC	1473	9	2	7	3	22	0.429
Heart	303	13	5	8	2	23	0.538
DCCS	30000	23	14	9	2	77	0.189

Table 2. The number of iterations on datasets under various privacy budgets

Dataset	$\varepsilon = 0.1$	$\varepsilon = 0.5$	$\varepsilon = 1$	$\varepsilon = 1.5$	$\varepsilon = 2$
Adult ($\delta = 0.01$)	2	2	3	4	5
CMC ($\delta = 0.1$)	2	2	2	3	4
Heart ($\delta = 1$)	2	2	2	2	3
DCCS ($\delta = 0.01$)	2	2	5	5	5

As shown in Table 2, the optimal number of iterations are both 2 as the privacy budget is 0.1 and 0.5 on the Adult dataset. It can be observed from Fig. 2(a) that comparing to the case where $T = 2$, the NICV of our approach is lower especially when the privacy budget is 0.1. When the privacy budget becomes 1, 1.5, and 2, the optimal number iterations are increased to 3, 4, and 5 respectively and our method yields lower NICV than the benchmarks. Similar results can be identified from Fig. 2(b, c, d) on other datasets. In general, the better performance can be achieved in error reduction as the privacy budget declines, ceteris paribus. Note that fluctuation occurs in Fig. 2 due to the random selection on the initial centroids in clustering.

Figure 2 also illustrates that given a lower privacy budget, e.g., 0.1, the NICVs are also lower when $T = 2$, in contrast to the cases with higher number of iterations. As privacy budget increases, this difference is poised to disappear. Thus, it may be advantageous to choose a lower number of iterations for ensuring the clustering performance. This is in congruence with Fig. 2(c), since the influence of adding noise on small datasets is more significant, e.g., the Heart dataset.

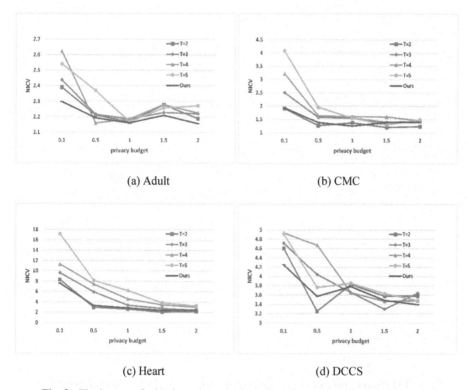

Fig. 2. The impact of adaptive privacy budget allocation on algorithm performance

4.2.2 Impact of Optimization Based on Consistency Inference

In this section, we examine the influence of the consistency inference-based optimization method on the algorithm performance. In general, the comparisons between the approaches with consistency optimization process and without (Non-OPCI) are carried out, all else being equal. Figure 3 shows the experimental results on Adult, CMC, Heart and DCCS respectively and Non-privacy denotes the method without adding noise. As expected, lower NICVs are observed on our proposed method. It is worth noting that the NICVs declines as the privacy budget increase. This empirically validates the trade-offs between privacy protection and clustering performance. Similar to the insights gained from the prior experiments, the significant improvement occurs when the privacy budget is lower, e.g., 0.1. This is because the variance of the noise is typically larger due to small privacy budget, such that a certain amount of noise is eliminated by our consistency optimization method.

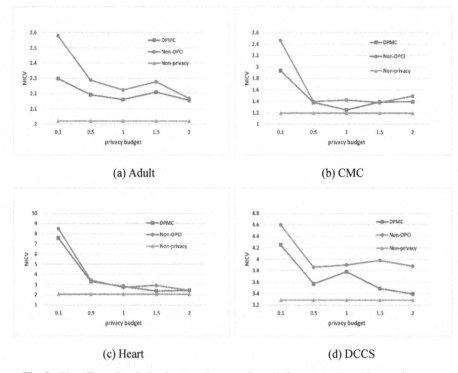

(a) Adult   (b) CMC

(c) Heart   (d) DCCS

Fig. 3. The effect of optimization based on consistent inference on algorithm performance

4.2.3 Accuracy Comparisons

Finally, we compare our DPMC approach with Non-OPCI method in [11] and the nonhybrid clustering algorithm (Non-HC) described in [24] on accuracy over Heart and DCCS datasets. Figure 4 presents the accuracy of each algorithm given privacy budget on each dataset. Consistent with our discussion earlier, higher accuracy levels are reached in the case of DPMC approach. Note that the advantage has disappeared in Fig. 4(c) due to the randomness nature of DCCS dataset, where the sensitive data may be disturbed by consistency optimization.

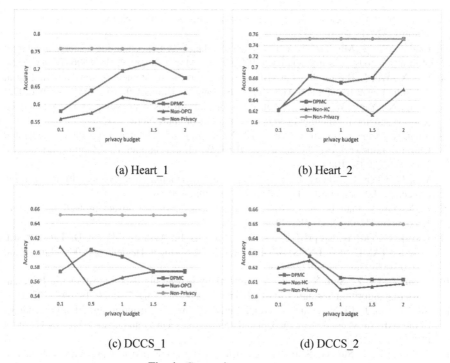

(a) Heart_1   (b) Heart_2

(c) DCCS_1   (d) DCCS_2

Fig. 4. Comparisons on accuracy

5 Conclusion

In this paper, DPMC, a mixed data clustering algorithm with differential privacy protection is proposed. Considering both numerical and categorical attributes, it determines the number of iterations and privacy budget by the adaptive privacy budget allocation method, while improving the performance by the optimization method based on consistency inference. We also conduct comparative experiments on four real-world datasets: Heart, Adult, CMC and DCCS, to evaluate the performance of DPMC with benchmarks. The results demonstrate significant improvement in balancing between privacy protection and clustering performance. How to extend the philosophy of our DPMC method to other machine learning techniques is an avenue for future investigation.

Acknowledgments. This work is supported by the science and technology project of State Grid Corporation of China entitled: "Research on Power Marketing Data Sharing and Model Fusion Technology Based on Federated Learning" (Grant No. 5700-202113262A-0-0-00).

References

1. Liu, B., Ding, M., Shaham, S., et al.: When machine learning meets privacy: a survey and outlook. ACM Comput. Surv. (CSUR) **54**(2), 1–36 (2021)

2. Ji, S., Du, T., Li, J., et al.: A review of machine learning model security and privacy research. J. Softw. **32**(01), 41–67 (2021)
3. Liao, S., Wu, J., Mumtaz, S., et al.: Cognitive balance for fog computing resource in internet of things: an edge learning approach. IEEE Trans. Mob. Comput. **21**(5), 1596–1608 (2022)
4. Lin, X., Wu, J., Bashir, A., et al.: Blockchain-based incentive energy-knowledge trading in IoT: joint power transfer and AI design. IEEE Internet Things J. **9**(16), 14685–14698 (2022)
5. Wang, N., Yang, W., Wang, X., et al.: A blockchain based privacy-preserving federated learning scheme for Internet of Vehicles. Digital Commun. Netw. (2022)
6. Yang, W., Wang, N., Guan, Z., Wu, L., Du, X., Guizani, M.: A practical cross-device federated learning framework over 5G networks. IEEE Wireless Commun. (2022).https://doi.org/10.1109/MWC.005.2100435
7. Wei, L., Chen, C., Zhang, L., et al.: The issues of machine learning security and privacy protection. J. Comput. Res. Dev. **57**(10), 2066–2085 (2020)
8. Li, Y., Yin, Y., Gao, H., et al.: Non-aggregated data sharing for privacy protection: a review. J. Commun. **42**(06), 195–212 (2021)
9. Dwork, C.: Differential privacy: a survey of results. In: Agrawal, M., Du, D., Duan, Z., Li, A. (eds.) TAMC 2008. LNCS, vol. 4978, pp. 1–19. Springer, Heidelberg (2008). https://doi.org/10.1007/978-3-540-79228-4_1
10. Guan, Z., Lv, Z., Sun, X., et al.: A differentially private big data nonparametric Bayesian clustering algorithm in smart grid. IEEE Trans. Netw. Sci. Eng. **7**(4), 2631–2641 (2020)
11. Su, D., Cao, J., Li, N., et al.: Differential private k-means clustering. In: 2016 Proceedings of the sixth ACM conference on data and application security and privacy, pp. 26–37. ACM (2016)
12. Zhu, S., Liu, S., Sun, G.: Shape-similar differential privacy trajectory protection mechanism based on relative entropy and K-means. J. Commun. **42**(02), 113–123 (2021)
13. Liu, Q., Yu, J., Han, J., et al.: Differentially private and utility-aware publication of trajectory data. Expert Syst. Appl. **180**(7), 115–120 (2021)
14. Gao, Z., Sun, Y., Cui, X., et al.: Privacy-preserving hybrid K-means. Int. J. Data Warehousing Mining (IJDWM) **14**(2), 1–17 (2018)
15. Xu, Q., et al.: Trajectory data protection based on differential privacy k-means. In: 2020 39th Chinese Control Conference (CCC), pp. 7649–7654. IEEE (2020)
16. Chen, H., Yan, Z., Zhu, X., et al.: Differential privacy high dimensional data publishing method based on cluster analysis. J. Comput. Appl. **41**(09), 2578–2585 (2021)
17. Sweeney, L.: k-anonymity: a model for protecting privacy. Internat. J. Uncertain. Fuzziness Knowledge-Based Syst. **10**(05), 557–570 (2002)
18. Machanavajjhala, A., Gehrke, J., Kifer, D., et al.: l-diversity: privacy beyond k-anonymity. In: 22nd International Conference on Data Engineering (ICDE 2006), p. 24. IEEE (2006)
19. Dwork, C., McSherry, F., Nissim, K., et al.: Calibrating noise to sensitivity in private data analysis. In: Theory of cryptography conference, pp. 265–284. Springer, Berlin Heidelberg (2006)
20. Liu, Z., Lv, H., Li, M., et al.: A novel self-adaptive grid-partitioning noise optimization algorithm based on differential privacy. Comput. Sci. Inf. Syst. **16**(3), 915–938 (2019)
21. Awan, J., Slavkovic, A.: Structure and sensitivity in differential privacy: comparing k-norm mechanisms. J. Am. Stat. Assoc. **116**(534), 935–954 (2021)
22. Blum, A., Dwork, C., Mcsherry, F., et al.: Practical privacy: the SuLQ framework. In: Proceedings of the Twenty-Fourth ACM SIGMOD-SIGACT-SIGART Symposium on Principles of Database Systems, pp. 128–138. ACM (2005)
23. Dwork, C.: A firm foundation for private data analysis. Commun. ACM **54**(1), 86–95 (2011)
24. Nguyen, H.: Privacy-preserving mechanisms for k-modes clustering. Comput. Secur. 78(sep.), 60–75 (2018)

25. Varun, R., Gangwar, R.: Geometrical link aware geocast routing for energy balancing in wireless sensor networks. J. Discrete Math. Sci. Cryptography **24**(5), 1375–1391 (2021)
26. Nguyen, H., Chaturved, A., Xu, Y.: Differentially private k-Means via exponential mechanism and max cover. In: 2021 Proceedings of the AAAI Conference on Artificial Intelligence, pp. 9101–9108. AAAI (2021)
27. Liu, M., Zheng, H., Liu, Q., et al.: A backdoor embedding method for backdoor detection in deep neural networks. In: Proceedings of the First International Conference on Ubiquitous Security (UbiSec 2021), Guangzhou, China, 28–31 December 2021, Communications in Computer and Information Science 1557, pp. 1–12, Springer (2022)

Impact of Reenactment Programs on Young Generation

Anam Fatima[1], Muhammad Waseem Iqbal[2], Muhammad Aqeel[2], Toqir A. Rana[3], Shuhong Chen[4(✉)], and Muhammad Arif[1]

[1] Department of Computer Science, Superior University Lahore, Lahore 54000, Pakistan
[2] Department of Software Engineering, Superior University Lahore, Lahore 54000, Pakistan
[3] Department of Computer Science and IT, The University of Lahore, Lahore 54000, Pakistan
[4] School of Computer Science and Cyber Engineering, Guangzhou University, Guangzhou 510006, China
shuhongchen@gzhu.edu.cn

Abstract. The influence of reenactment-based violence programs on young people is the subject of this survey-based research project. A sample of 200 respondents (100 respondents were male and 100 were female) was gathered by the distribution of a questionnaire, and their responses were examined for the study. The data was broken down into five categories: violence, instigation, language, seduction, and fear. It was intriguing to learn that a lot of teenagers believe that violence and filthy language are permissible in the reenactment program circumstances. A considerable number of young people believe that drinking and smoking are wrong and that lying in some situations is unacceptable. A significant majority of adolescent respondents considered the representation of love, relationship, flirting, seduction, physical contact, and rape attractive in various situations of reenactment crime shows. Following the violence and crimes depicted in the reenactment shows, some young viewers believed that society was unsafe for them or others. The results are shown that 53% of respondents think that the use of violence and abusive language is justified. On the other hand, only 21% of respondents believe that criminal activity and violence are justified. 53% of those polled stated that watching the shows had made them fearful. The findings demonstrate that young viewers are afraid of violence and criminality when they see it on television.

Keywords: Abusive language · Violence · Fear · Instigation · Seduction · Murder

1 Introduction

The concept of criminal re-enactment performances was somewhat novel a few years ago. However, as time has passed, viewers have grown used to crime re-enactment programs because they attract them with their narrative, production techniques, storylines, sound, and actors. Crime re-enactment performances were also categorized as programs that teach new ways to commit crimes and inspire young people to mimic them.

To promote viewership, all Pakistani television networks broadcast criminal episodes during primetime, which may create a sense of terror among teenage viewers. The

G. Wang et al. (Eds.): UbiSec 2022, CCIS 1768, pp. 406–422, 2023.
https://doi.org/10.1007/978-981-99-0272-9_28

relationship between media effect and content is based on the substance of television shows as well as the public's likes and disliking of various programs [1, 28].

Crime reenactment programs, which delight audiences by misreporting criminals and crime, have gained popularity and a high public rating. Typically, these stories are based on factual crimes for which the producers attempted to show the police method, crime plans, crime motives, actual footage, talks, and the societal issue surrounding the crimes through real film, interviews, and real footage [2].

Researchers investigated the use of alcohol in music videos. Excessive exposure to music videos, according to the research, leads to an incorrect perception of alcohol use. Musicians in these films encourage drinking in their songs, creating a false reality regarding the dangers of alcohol [3]. The number of sexual actions was more than the number of gays who appeared on television, according to Netzley [4]. According to Gerbner and Gross, people's judgment, attitudes, ideas, and views of the world are influenced by television exposure more than their social behavior.

Reiner noticed that news stations disproportionately covered crime and violence. Valier and Wardle discovered that news outlets focus on "evil others" and sex crimes, as well as strangers who commit them [5].

The whole society's youth will be considered in research work to find the results regarding the problem statement. Only dramatized programs are included in the scope; all the other programs like news and other talk shows are not included in the selected research scope.

People believe what they see, and they see what they believe. The media's exposure to content contributes to the downfall of the young. Children's violent behavior is caused by reenactment programs. According to previous studies, the violence depicted in the media causes viewers to become aggressive, desensitized, and fearful. Crime re-enactment shows were also categorized as programs that teach new ways to commit crimes and inspire young people to mimic them.

Youth nowadays are accustomed to watching television shows. As a result, watching criminal re-enactment shows has a psychological effect on young brains and can lead to the imitation of crimes depicted in these shows. To promote viewership, all Pakistani television networks broadcast criminal shows during primetime, which may create a sense of panic among teenage viewers. After watching such programs, Pakistan's young youth becomes distracted. These programs give young people fresh ideas for committing crimes, as well as dread, depression, and a variety of other voids.

Robbery, arson, abduction, child abuse, rape, domestic violence, forgery of official papers, Driving While under the influence, exposing adolescents to addictive narcotics and alcoholic goods, and other crime-related topics have received a lot of attention in Pakistani media [6]. Broadcast media agencies magnify criminal and violent acts to the point of absurdity. In today's society, the media has a vital part in the incidence of crimes [7].

Crimes that have happened in real life are reenacted on television in shows called "Crime Reenactment Programs." These programs inform viewers about the crime that is a part of their daily lives and the strategies that may be used to defend them in a criminal scenario [8, 23, 24].

Crime-based television programs cost negative impacts of different kinds given as:

Such programs are sensationalized, as they are not based on fact and rely on sensationalized actions to increase ratings and popularity. Kim et al.researched the CSI Impacts and discovered that numerous factors such as education level, race, and neighborhood difficulties were strongly linked to public perceptions of programs.

According to the researcher, people's desires had a detrimental impact on their abilities. They also claim that while CSI has little direct influence on viewers' views, it does have a significant indirect impact by increasing their cravings. The researchers discovered that persons who watched more CSI had more desire than those who watched less [9].

Various new concepts are performed in such crime-based programs that a huge number of people choose these thoughts and become involved in such activities, similar to Hollywood films, in which action and new technology are used for crime in one way or another. According to a report published by the ISRA (International Society for Research on Aggression) commission on media violence.

They employ a variety of actions that rely on fear to induce dread in these shows, and they focus on a specific target segment. Despite these flaws, there are some noteworthy findings in terms of crime fear and police performance [10, 25, 26].

Liliana et al.researched media violence and said that it is one of the most common themes of research for researchers [11]. Justified variants refer to legally relevant concerns relating to the punishment system, which analyses the type of crime committed, as well as the amount of gravity associated with the individual offense, as well as the offender's criminal background. The unjustified disparity in sentencing combines the informal classification based on one's racial background and the severity of the penalty received, according to [12].

When we watch these programs we feel we are not secured we believe we are unsecured This start permits the forecast of future Crimeevents, and therefore the most viable locations to intrude on the open doors to keep that Crime from occurring [13].

1.1 Objective of Study

The following are the study's objectives:

- To see if there is a link between crime re-enactment shows and youth violence.
- To find out why people watch re-enactment misdeed shows.
- To understand the job of reenactment misdeed shows in the development of illegal concepts.
- To get knowledge of the content of reenactment shows.
- To learn more about the impact of reenactment shows on juvenile involvement in illegal activity.
- To be aware of the societal mental implications of reenactment programs.

The reenactment program tells the entire story using real-life scenarios and settings. These crime shows are appealing and inviting due to the cast, makeover, stories, and sound effects. According to a study, media can affect viewers and their opinions. It has the potential to cause huge changes in society, both positive and negative. The reenactment shows exhibit cruelty, intolerance, retribution, lust, vulgarity, insulting language, and violence.

Cultivation theory, according to the author, is the use of television to improve people's opinions over time. They pointed out that television exposure can nurture and mold a viewer's perception. It can shape certain social behavior. The motive of this research is to provide awareness to the young generation and their parents that all the stories presented by such dramatized programs are not as reality-based as those presented. Those stories are scripted with fewer points of reality with affected audio and video graphics to raise the rating of their programs and to earn more. Users should watch the programs to be aware of happenings in their surroundings just for knowledge. By concept, these programs are reality-based but in actuality, they exaggerate the reality that proceeds toward violence. This paper aims to guide the young generations that they should watch such programs for enjoyment or for the knowledge of negative activities that are bad by seen. So such kinds of negative things and actions are not to adopt. This work's main focus is to warn users to explore their minds towards positive thinking and to avoid negative thinking as well as ignore all the actions that lead you to create violence or unethical actions.

Previous researchers did not present the work to find the impacts of reenactment programs on youth on a gender basis. Our study will evaluate either males are more affected by reenactment programs or females. There is very limited work on some factors of seduction and sexual harassment that are caused more by these reenactment programs and these factors are also leading to fear. Exaggerated information, distraction, and information complexity are all major obstacles that are not only recognized by adults as affecting youth but they express their dissatisfaction. Our study will highlight the causes and impacts of these selected factors on young males and females.

2   Related Work

Bahadur et al. did research in Pakistan that looked at violent material in the media and its effects on young people's thinking. Quantitative methodologies and easy sampling were used to survey 145 students at a university in Faisalabad. The findings revealed that through viewing crime reenactment shows, respondents acquired new techniques of committing crimes and, as a result, developed sentiments of uneasiness [8].

Sunitha and Ranjan looked at the substance of two popular crime programs on Tamil television in India, Koppiyam (Raj TV) and Thadayam (Raj TV) (News7). The crime depicted on television has a substantial influence on people's perceptions of a given crime, according to one study [14]. In this regard, Bhatti and Hassan found in their study that violent material in the media penetrates the audience and causes them to imitate it [15].

Another study surveyed 78 undergraduate students in the southeast part of the United States. These pupils were split into two groups: control and experimentation. A clear influence of violent films on the element of rage was seen [16].

Crime plays and reenactments have a long history, as crime stories were a component of mythology, folk tales, and theatres even before electricity was invented [17]. Sexual offenses are often aided by reenactment and television crime programs. There was no significant association between viewing forensic plays or reenactment programs and the crime rate in a sample of 24 convicted offenders [17].

Data were obtained from 116 responders from four institutions in Malad, Mumbai, for research done in India. The findings revealed why individuals enjoy reenactment programs and actual crime shows. This study found that viewing crime-related dramas and shows can lead to criminal imitation and studying how to commit a crime [18].

These sorts of crime re-enactment show on television have a huge influence on the types of crimes people commit. There's also a strong link between both sexual crime and television programs [19].

According to the American Academy of Pediatrics (2001), violence in movies, plays, shows, and games has a harmful influence on children and teenagers. As a result, the effects are felt throughout the human body and psyche. It was discovered that the production of children's shows is lacking and that they are not properly categorized [20].

According to research, the media depicts the truth because it makes them money. The media should be conscious that it has the potential to shape societal behavior. This duty is not unique and tough, but it is also the least profitable [21]. The author discovered that television watchers watch television as though they are consumers, and that media material is a product [22].

Hafner et al. assess how well a local mock collision reenactment affected the students' attitudes and practices regarding driving while intoxicated. Students were 1.39 times less likely to report drinking and driving in the future or getting into a car with a drunk driver after the reenactment program, nevertheless. After taking part in the program, students were 1.7 times more likely to say that they had considered the dangers of drinking and driving. After watching a simulated crash reenactment, students said they were less likely to drive while intoxicated in the future or to ride with someone who would drive while intoxicated, and they were more likely to frequently consider the risks connected with drinking and driving [24].

The association between adolescent crime reenactment programs and the perceived stress on parents was explored by Ashfaq Qazi et al. Researchers proposed a relationship between parental stress perception and exposure to youth crime reenactment programs. There were 157 parents in the sample. In Islamabad, a survey was carried out using convenient and purposeful sampling. Five components were created through factor analysis, including effects on mental health, increased stress, effects on health, situational awareness, and social isolation [25]. Additionally, a Pearson Product-Moment Correlation test was run to see whether exposure to juvenile crime reenactment programs and experienced parental stress were related. The adolescent crime prevention initiatives and perceived parental stress were found to be significantly correlated [23].

Carmody and colleagues investigate the portrayal of crime, criminals, victims, and police on reality-based crime shows. The examination is broken into two parts. First, the various types of crimes shown, as well as their normal resolution, are briefly discussed. The demographics of suspects, victims, and police officers are also summarised. The second section of the investigation contrasts how these programs depict domestic and non-domestic assaults. The study also looks at how domestic violence incidents are presented in light of misconceptions and stereotypes. It provides a preliminary examination of "Cops" and "Real Stories of the Highway Patrol," two reality-based police programs. While viewers of "Cops" are permitted to ride along with police, "Real Stories of the

Highway Patrol" includes eyewitness interviews, reenactments of dramatic instances, and some live film footage. The police programs "Cops" and "Real Stories of the Highway Patrol" are examples of a new subgenre that is a crime show modification [26] (Table 1).

Table 1. Existing work findings and limitations

Reference	Years	Parameters findings	Limitations
[18, 19]	2018,203	Such programs are influencing youngsters towards sexual crime	It is not stated in research that which gender is more influenced by these reenactment programs
[16, 22]	2016, 2018	Element of anger was seen much in the users of reenactment programs that is basic cause of violence	Domestic violence
[8, 15, 20]	2016, 2014, 2015	These programs change people's perception and penetrate them to commit crime. Also develop sentiments of uneasiness	Findings are cultural dependent
[20]	2015	These programs effect the humans mind and body by miss leading them through script addition in reality scenario	Children's shows are lacking and they are not properly categorized
[22]	2020	Media shapes the societal behavior of people. Reenactment programs are source of earn more money	Script is manipulated to increase users and their shows rating
[23]	2021	The adolescent crime prevention initiatives and perceived parental stress were found to be significantly correlated by these	Parental factor analysis based studies has been presented but not categorized by children's group

2.1 Research Gap

There was a lot of research work related to the selected area. But researchers did not describe the impact of reenactment programs ratio on gender bases that either female youth more affected by these programs or male youth; it was also not discussed what factors male and female youth is affected.

There is a lack of study found about seduction and sexual harassment that is caused more by these reenactment programs and these factors are also leading to fear. There was very limited research work to describe the suspense factor among the users created by reenactment programs that frustrate the users mentally and psychologically.

Exaggerated information, distraction, and information complexity are all major obstacles. These are issues that are not only recognized by adults as affecting youth, but also by young themselves when they express their dissatisfaction.

3 Research Design and Methodology

The UCD process model was used to examine the impact of reenactment programs on the younger generation in this study. The user-centered design model is iterative and it gives the best results against user experience evaluation. By using the UCD model researchers meet users, again and again, to find the requirements or problems according to their level of usability. Users are engaged in the whole process until the results are not evaluated.

UCD model is a very appropriate way to undertake this study because this study will evaluate the user experience related to reenactment programs and then identify the impacts of such programs on youth. Identifying the impacts of users' responses to this study are very necessary. The user's feedback gives us clear and efficient results. That's why the UCD model is used to obtain clear results. The steps in the process model are as follows in Fig. 1:

Fig. 1. Process Flow of proposed methodology

3.1 Problem Identification

Identifying the problem is the first stage in the UCD model. For this, we studied a large amount of literature and spoke with a variety of parents and teachers about the influence of reenactment programs on children.

3.2 Data Collection and Sampling

Our design of experiments included ethnography (observation), rating of such reenactment programs, and questionnaires with respondents as data-gathering approaches. Based on questionnaire replies, data was collected from users of reenactment programs. After eliminating some irrelevant users based on the pre-questionnaire, 200 users were chosen for the usability and impact evaluation of the reenactment programs and included in this research.

Sampling Technique. The survey will be conducted using a targeted sample technique. Only those young pupils and teachers who used to watch crime-based re-enactment shows would be chosen as a sample to respond to the topic.

Sample size. After eliminating some irrelevant users based on a pre-questionnaire, 200 users were chosen for the usability and impact evaluation of the reenactment programs and included in this research. This questionnaire will be distributed to 200 youth members, combining girls, boys, and teachers, ranging in age from 17 to 35, including 100 girls and 100 guys.

Variables. The following variables are analyzed using the categories below.

Violence. The intentional use of physical force to hurt injures or kills something or someone. Slaps, punches, pushbacks, fights, and verbal violence are all considered acts of violence in my study.

Language. Words that are unpleasant and offensive are used in abusive language. It will be termed abusive language if slang, offensive, or street language is utilized in some study programs.

Seduction. Arousal of emotions occurs when one's emotions are aroused by a sexual encounter.

Instigation. Inspire someone to commit an especially heinous act. For example, lying, smoking, dating, adulterous relationships, hidden marriages, public area meetings, wealth, suicide, dishonesty, and so on are all relevant to this study.

Fear. Content that deals with human feelings, such as fear or life-threatening situations.

3.3 Measurement Instruments

A questionnaire was created to capture the subjective categories of data for the evaluation. The questionnaire items for chosen characteristics such as violence, language, seduction, sexual harassment, instigation, and fear were adapted from literature. Repeated confirmation stages were included in the questionnaire design (Table 2).

Table 2. Fight scenes ratio in crime shows

Opinions	Male	Female
Strongly Agree	39	45
Agree	25	30
Neutral	20	15
Disagree	11	7
Strongly disagree	5	3
Total	100	100

3.4 Evaluation

10 questions have been put on a page and posted online to obtain feedback from a variety of people. The results are assessed based on the responses to the survey questions and results are compiled with the help of the SPSS tool (Fig. 2).

4 Experimentation

4.1 Violence

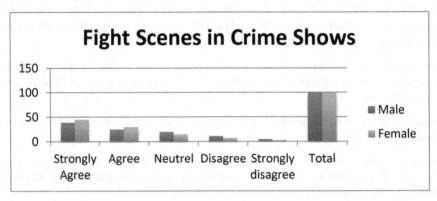

Fig. 2. Shows how violent sequences in crime re-enactment

Fighting scenes in these shows are violent, according to 39% of male and 45% of female respondents who strongly agree, and 25% of males and 30% of females who only agree. Our societal values are based on Islamic principles, and Islam is a peaceful faith in which fighting is not tolerated. These shows feature gunshots, murders, punching, encounters, poisoning, and all other innovative ways of murdering and harming people. On this, 20% of males and 15% of females are undecided. 11% of males and 7% of females disagreed that the scenes are violent, and 5% of males and 3% of females strongly disagreed that there is no violent content (Table 3).

4.2 Language

Table 3. Use of slang and foul language

Opinions	Male	Female
Strongly Agree	30	35

(continued)

Table 3. (*continued*)

Opinions	Male	Female
Agree	37	32
Neutral	5	4
Disagree	13	15
Strongly disagree	15	12
Total	100	100

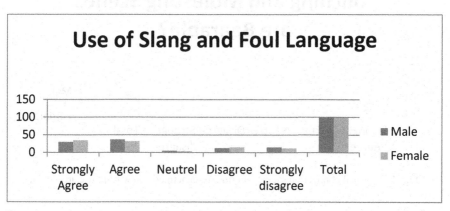

Fig. 3. Illustrates the impact of slang language in the re-enactment of crime scenes

4.3 Seduction

The language is slang, according to 30% of male and 35% of female respondents who strongly agreed and 37% of males and 32% of females who agreed. Because these are crime stories, the criminals' nasty language is shown. On this topic, 5% of male and 4% of female respondents were undecided. 13% of men and 15% of women disagree, and 15% of men and 13% of women strongly disagree, that this is not vulgar or informal language (Table 4).

Table 4. Touching and molesting scenes are bearable

Opinions	Male	Female
Strongly Agree	33	30
Agree	27	30
Neutral	13	12

(*continued*)

Table 4. (*continued*)

Opinions	Male	Female
Disagree	14	15
Strongly disagree	13	13
Total	100	100

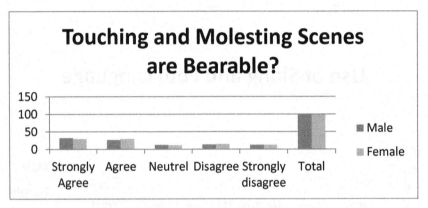

Fig. 4. Physical connection scenes of crime re-enactment show response are shown

The poignant scenes are unpleasant, according to 33% of male and 30% of female respondents who strongly agree and 27% of males and 30% of females; who agree. Because it elicits an emotional response from the viewer, the content becomes enticing. The neutral perception was held by 13% of males and 12% of females polled. The remark was disputed by 14% of males and 15% of females, with 13% of males and 13% of females strongly disagreeing (Table 5).

4.4   Instigation

Table 5. Use of Lie in re-enactment programs

Opinions	Male	Female
Strongly Agree	7	5
Agree	10	12
Neutral	13	15
Disagree	45	44
Strongly disagree	25	25
Total	100	100

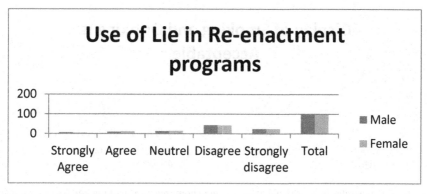

Fig. 5. Programs feedback on the use of lies in re-enactment shows

The lies in such programs do not explain the circumstances, according to 25% of male and female teenagers, who strongly disagree, and 45% of males and 44% of girls disagree. Lies are the true fault of any terrible behavior; they never justify the circumstance, but rather contaminate it. Only 13% of males and 14% of females arse undecided. This remark was supported by 10% of male and 12% of female respondents, while 7% of males and 5% of females strongly agreed (Fig. 5) and (Table 6).

Table 6. Display of Smoking and Drinking is Acceptable

Opinions	Male	Female
Strongly Agree	15	17
Agree	10	12
Neutral	15	13
Disagree	25	23
Strongly disagree	30	35
Total	100	100

When asked if smoking and drinking situations are acceptable, 30% of males and 35% of females objected, while 25% of males and 23% of females disagreed. It's wrong because these stories are widely circulated, especially among young people, and they're an easy target for incitement. The remaining 15% of males and 13% of females were undecided. This remark was supported by 10% of male and 12% of female respondents, with 15% of males and 17% of females strongly agreeing (Table 7).

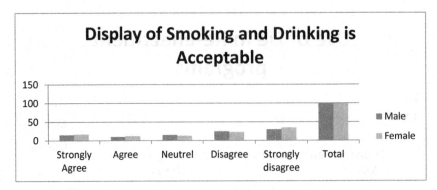

Fig. 6. Demonstrates how criminal re-enactment shows react to smoking and drinking scenes

4.5 Fear

Table 7. Crime and violence in crime shows spread insecurity

Opinions	Male	Female
Strongly Agree	34	32
Agree	19	18
Neutral	9	8
Disagree	24	25
Strongly disagree	17	17
Total	100	100

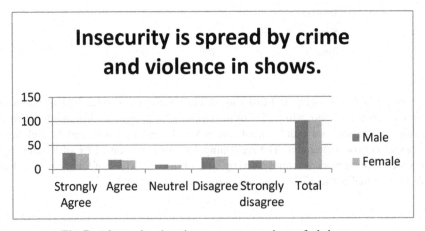

Fig. 7. After seeing the crime re-enactment shows, feels insecure

After seeing these episodes, 34% of young males and 32% of females strongly agree that they feel unsafe in their surroundings, while 19% of boys and 18% of girls only agree. 9% of boys and 8% of girls are undecided. This assertion is disputed by 24% of males and 25% of females, with 17% of males and 17% of females strongly disagreeing.

5 Results and Discussion

Viewers of re-enactment shows have been proven to be exposed to violence and foul language. The crucial phenomenon is that in many cases, they view the use of violence and abusive language to be justified. A total of 53% of respondents believe it is justified (See Fig. 1). Only 21% of respondents believe that criminal activity and violence are justified. Youths who stated that violent scenes are "OK" to view or that they are violent at all are displaying violent behavior. They have become desensitized to violence, and this exposure will cause them to act aggressively and violently.

The kids have stated that they want to experience the same predicament they see on TV by watching these criminal dramas. They want to drink, dance, do drugs, and engage in extramarital affairs. 51% of those polled say they haven't regarded smoking and alcohol consumption to be appropriate content for re-enactment shows (see Fig. 7). 60% of respondents did not approve of the usage of lying (See Fig. 4). A total of 53% of respondents said that extramarital affairs or physical relations are seductive (See Fig. 3). The scenes of these criminal shows that involve groping or molesting, according to 60% of respondents, are unpleasant (See Fig. 3).

A total of 53% of those polled stated that watching the shows had made them fearful. On the other side, 38% of those polled said that these re-enactment shows have not instilled terror in them (See Fig. 6). The findings demonstrate that young viewers are afraid of violence and criminality when they see it on television.

5.1 Discussion

The study discovered that these programs are watched by people of all ages at late hours, about 11 p.m. Youths used to watch diverse crime-related stories not only during regular hours but also during repetition hours. These shows expose viewers to violence, bad language, vulgarity, bravado, seduction, and incitement to criminality, as well as fear or emotional appeal for the attraction.

The stories involve illicit scenarios such as physical or extramarital relations, rape scenes, seduction, prostitution, sexual harassment, drunkenness, drugs, and the like. Concerning our very society, these situations are vulgar and bold. However, their "inquisitiveness" led them to view it, as a substance that has an impact on the children. These impacts might be short-term or long-term, depending on how much time they have been exposed to them. The exposure to these crime stories has enticed and encouraged them, and they are currently engaging in the same crimes. Members of the young have free time and an open mind. These types of exposure contribute to the destruction of the kids, causing them to forget about their education or their goals to be nice guys, instead of inciting them to commit crimes.

6 Conclusion

The stories depict illegal activities and performances, and they show how a crime can be carried out flawlessly. They provide warnings in the hopes of catching the person. They provide new criminal concepts for doing any crime or immoral act while exercising caution. It provides a safe passage for those planning a criminal or wrong act.

The misdeed programs feature cruelty and violent acts, which reason adolescence to become enraged and violent. Daily, their tolerance is decreasing. The programs reveal that street crime, such as aggressively snatching money, cell phones, and other valuables, is straightforward to commit. They portray criminals as "heroes" who gain everything by entering the criminal world. The shows have created an unstable and confusing social climate, with anyone at any time becoming a victim of a crime perpetrated by his family or peers. The programs' high ratings among people aged 30 and up are primarily due to their fear appeal. These presentations were attractive and exclusive because of their emotional touch. This work achieved all the objectives hence it is a result-oriented research. The results show that reenactment programs are causing the reasons to mislead young generations towards violence in different manners and these are providing different techniques to commit a crime to young users of both gender males and females.

Acknowledgments. This work was supported by the Guangdong Provincial Natural Science Foundation under Grant No. 2022A1515011386, the National Key Research and Development Program of China under Grant No. 2020YFB1005804, the Natural Science Foundation of China under Grant 61632009, and the Guangdong Provincial Natural Science Foundation under Grant 2017A030308006.

References

1. Palmgreen, P., Wenner, L.A., Rosengren, K.E.: Uses and gratifications research: the past ten years. In: Rosengren, K.E., Wenner, L.A., Palmgreen, P. (Eds.) Media Gratifications Research: Current Perspectives, pp. 11–37. Beverly Hills, CA: Sage (1985)
2. Surette, R.: Media, Crime, and Criminal Justice: Images, Realities, and Policies. Belmont, CA: Thomson Wadsworth. USA (2007)
3. Beullens, K., Roe, K., Van den Bulck, J.: Music video viewing as a marker of driving after the consumption of alcohol. Subst. Use Misuse **47**(2), 155–165 (2012)
4. Netzley, S.B.: Visibility that demystifies: gays, gender, and sex on television. J. Homosex. **57**(8), 968–986 (2010)
5. Gerbner, G., Gross, L., Morgan, M., Signorielli, N., Shanahan, J.: Growing up with television: cultivation processes. Media Effects Adv. Theory Res. **2**, 43–67 (2002)
6. Bhatti, M.A., Iftikhar, U., Mahmood, T.: Impact of reenactment-based crime shows of Pakistani private channels on youth. Rev. Econ. Dev. Stud. **6**(2), 513–530 (2020)
7. Heath, L., Gilbert, K.: Mass media and fear of crime. Am. Behav. Sci. **39**(4), 379–386 (1996)

8. Bahadur, A., Ullah, A., Zaman, L.: Analysis of various effects of television crime shows on Pakistani youth (A case study of students of Government College University Faisalabad). Pakistan J. Soc. Educ. Lang. (PJSEL), **2**(2), 65–84 (2016)

9. Kim, Y.S., Barak, G., Shelton, D.E.: Examining the "CSI-effect" in the cases of circumstantial evidence and eyewitness testimony, multivariate and path analyses. J. Crim. Just. **37**(5), 452–460 (2009)

10. Surette, R.: Media, crime, and criminal justice. Images and Realities 2nd Edition, New York: Wadsworth Publishing the Media 1(2), 15–22 (1998)

11. Liliana, S., Chaves, E., Anderson, C.A.: Media and risky behaviors. Children Electron. Media **18**(1), 147–180 (2008)

12. Bushway, S.D., Piehl, A.M.: Judging judicial discretion: legal factors and racial discrimination in sentencing. Law Soc. Rev. **35**(4), 733–764 (2001)

13. Hetsroni, A.: Violent crime on American television: a critical interpretation of empirical studies. Sociol. Mind **2**(02), 141–147 (2012)

14. Sunitha, D., Ranjani, R.: A study on construction of crime stories in tamil channels. J. Res. Soc. Sci. Humanities **6**(7), 1883–1894 (2016)

15. Bhatti, M.A., Ab ul Hassan, A.: Psychological effects of TV news violence on youth: a case study of the Students of Bahauddin Zakariya University, Multan. Pakistan J. Soc. Sci. (PJSS), **34**(1), 295–309 (2014)

16. Narvaez, P.E.N., Elsner, R.J.F.: Effects of media with violent content on college students' aggressive reaction. Psychol. Res. **6**(8), 449–454 (2016)

17. Baranowski, A.M., Burkhard, A., Czernik, E., Hecht, H.: The CSI-education effect: do potential criminals benefit from forensic TV series?. Int. J. Law Crime Justice, **52**, 86–97 (2018)

18. Mukherjee, T., Mrinal, A.: Impact of crime based indian tv reality shows on youth: a critical study. Amity J. Media Commun. Stud. (AJMCS), **8**(2) (2018)

19. Levin, J.: Representations of victims, suspects and offenders: a content analysis of four television crime shows. Undergraduate HonoursTheses. paper42. University of Colorado (2013)

20. Yasmin, M., Sohail, A., Mangrio, R.A.: Myths broken or sustained: representation of women victims in Pakistani media. Open J. Soc. Sci. **3**(07), 209 (2015)

21. Watkins, B.A., Calvert, S.L., Huston-Stein, A., Wright, J.C.: Children's recall of television material: effects of presentation mode and adult labeling. Dev. Psychol. **1980**(16), 672–674 (1980)

22. Raza, S.H., Iftikhar, M., Mohamad, B., Pembecioğlu, N., Altaf, M.: Precautionary behavior toward dengue virus through public service advertisement: mediation of the individual's attention, information surveillance, and elaboration. SAGE Open **10**(2), 1–15 (2020)

23. Shakil, M.A., Shahab, S.S., Mohammed, T.A., Syed, U., Md Tabrez, N., Guojun, W.: Towards a two-tier architecture for Privacy-Enabled Recommender Systems (PeRS). In: Wang, G., Choo, K.K.R., Ko, R.K.L., Xu, Y., Crispo, B. (eds) Ubiquitous Security. UbiSec 2021. Communications in Computer and Information Science, vol. 1557, pp. 268–278. Springer, Singapore (2022)

24. Yipeng, Z., Tao, P., Wentao, Z., Kejian, G., Guojun, W.: Reliable and controllable data sharing based on blockchain. In: Wang, G., Choo, K.K.R., Ko, R.K.L., Xu, Y., Crispo, B. (eds.) Ubiquitous Security. UbiSec 2021. Communications in Computer and Information Science, vol. 1557, pp. 229–240. Springer, Singapore (2022)

25. Geman, O., Chiuchisan, I., Ungurean, I., Hagan, M., Arif, M.: Ubiquitous healthcare system based on the sensors network and android internet of things gateway. In: 2018 IEEE Smart-World, Ubiquitous Intelligence & Computing, Advanced & Trusted Computing, Scalable Computing & Communications, Cloud & Big Data Computing, Internet of People and Smart City Innovation (SmartWorld/SCALCOM/UIC/ATC/CBDCom/IOP/SCI), pp. 1390–1395. IEEE (2018)
26. Wang, T., Liang, Y., Mei, Y., Arif, M., Zhu, C.: High-accuracy localization for indoor group users based on extended Kalman filter. Int. J. Distrib. Sens. Netw. 14(11), 1550147718812722 (2018)

Sensor Cloud Data Privacy Protection Model Based on Collaborative Deep Learning

Xiaoqian Ran[1], Yufeng Zhuang[1,2]([✉]), Hongping Wang[1], Danni Cao[1], Yulian Cao[1], and Wenjuan Gu[1]

[1] Schoolof Modern Post (School of Automation), Beijing University of Posts and Telecommunications, Beijing 100876, China
zhuangyf@bupt.edu.cn

[2] BeijingUniversity of Posts and Telecommunications, Beijing Key Laboratory of Safety Production Intelligent Monitoring, Beijing 100876, China

Abstract. The sensor cloud system includes three parts: sensor network, edge computing platform and cloud processing, which is helpful for data collection, processing, storage and sharing. But during the process of data training in the cloud, there may be malicious attacks, leading to data leakage. Traditional intrusion detection technologies are powerless against new security vulnerabilities and network attacks, and they cannot formulate effective defense strategies. The main objective of this study is to propose an improved privacy protection model for sensor cloud data based on collaborative deep learning. According to the research strategy of GAN attack model, this model sets buried points in the convolutional neural network model and combines different learning rates to eliminate the GAN attack. First of all, this paper collects sensor data and obtains the data set of the model experiment. Secondly, this paper studies the architecture of collaborative deep learning and the architecture of GAN model. Finally, by setting different learning rates, the loss values of different learning rate models are studied to verify the feasibility of the improved model.

Keywords: Sensor cloud · Privacy protection · GAN model attack · Convolutional neural network model · Collaborative deep learning

1 Introduction

The development of computing technology and sensor cloud systems is constantly removing the boundary between the physical and digital worlds. As an important application on the basis of wireless sensor network, sensor cloud not only promotes resource sharing, but also realizes large-scale application of sensor network [1]. In response to the increasing demand for sensor data storage and processing, cloud computing flexibly provides necessary computing and storage resources to achieve large-scale data collection, processing and storage [2]. But the cloud has high capacity and stores a large amount of important information, which always leads to various security problems [3]. On the one hand, irresponsible companies may leak the user's private data for their own benefit,

G. Wang et al. (Eds.): UbiSec 2022, CCIS 1768, pp. 423–435, 2023.
https://doi.org/10.1007/978-981-99-0272-9_29

thereby causing serious criminal activities such as telecom fraud, kidnapping and extortion. On the other hand, the characteristic system of sensor cloud has different types of security problems [4], which seriously threatens the security of user information [5]. Therefore, it is necessary to study the information security protection of sensor cloud and establish an appropriate model to protect the privacy of sensor cloud data.

After a lot of research, this paper found that the research on sensor cloud at home and abroad is showing an upward trend, and there are more and more researches on sensor cloud security and privacy protection. Wireless sensor networks have been deployed and applied in many aspects such as human health data in the intelligent medical field, location and business information in the vehicle network field, and power consumption information of smart grid users [6]. In these application scenarios, the privacy research of the sensor cloud cannot be ignored. However, the existing security assessment mechanisms for sensor cloud internal attacks are mostly based on the behavior level, ignoring the special attacks on the data level [7]. Aiming at the problem of hidden data attacks, Zhang, Wang et al. [8] proposes a fog computing and trust evaluation mechanism. The detection mechanism of FDS can detect hidden data attack risks in advance. In a study by Kumar, Vima et al. [9], the authors presented a method based on ABE fine-grained access control to realize secure aggregation of data in the sensor cloud. This method uses symmetric proxy re-encryption, Bloom filter and hash-based message authentication code to protect the code from eavesdropping and false code injection Attack. In another study by Thota, Chandu et al. [4], the authors propose a centralized security architecture to ensure asynchronous communication between applications and data servers deployed in the cloud environment. In another study by Saha, Sayantani et al. [10], the authors conducted a flexible security model that guarantees data confidentiality, integrity and fine-grained access control to applications. In the paper of Liang, Wang et al. [11], the author extends the classical Hungarian algorithm to use fog layer to alleviate the control mechanism. This action improves the security of cloud resources. Another study by Abdul Rahman et al. [12] use the Internet of Things technology to ensure the embedded security of each layer in the ecosystem, and apply it to the security framework of the sensor cloud to reduce the security threats faced by the sensor cloud. In another study by Zissis et al. [13], the authors propose a method based on edge computing to detect abnormal behaviors in the process of machine learning and deep learning. After actual verification, the algorithm reduces the potential risks in the use of deep learning algorithms in sensor clouds. In the paper of shojaeerad et al. [14], the threats, functions and characteristics of sensor cloud in cloud computing are discussed. Malekzadeh, Mohammad et al. [15] proposed a mechanism for converting sensor data and applications on the user's device before sharing, which eliminates the mechanism for inferring potentially sensitive activities. This mechanism ensures that external risks are reduced and gesture activity is increased. Stirapongsasuti, sopicha et al. [16] proposes a heuristic algorithm which selects a semi-optimal solution by greedily determining a better objective function value. Experiments were carried out on private data on smart home data sets, and good experimental results were obtained.

Table 1. Summarizing table

Authors	Research contents
Zhang, Wang et al.	A fog computing and trust evaluation mechanism
Kumar, Vima et al.	A method based on ABE fine-grained access control
Thota, Chandu et al.	A centralized security architecture
Saha, Sayantani et al.	A flexible security model
Liang, Wang et al.	Use fog layer to alleviate the control mechanism
Abdul Rahman et al.	Use the Internet of Things technology to ensure security
Zissis et al.	A method based on edge computing to detect abnormal behaviors in the process of machine learning and deep learning
Shojaeerad et al.	The threats, functions and characteristics of sensor cloud in cloud computing
Malekzadeh, Mohammad et al.	A mechanism for converting sensor data and applications on the user's device before sharing
Stirapongsasuti, sopicha et al.	A heuristic algorithm

From Table 1, we can learn that most of the above scholars studied from the perspective of risk detection and external risk reduction, weakening the existence of attackers to reduce the invasiveness of data. This paper takes note of this, uses the GAN model to simulate attackers copying data, and proposes a sensor cloud data privacy protection model based on cooperative deep learning. The narrative structure of this paper is: first, this paper will research the collaborative deep learning architecture; second, this paper will research the GAN attack model architecture, study the impact of learning rate on the deep learning process, and improve on the basis of the convolutional neural network model; finally, the model is evaluated experimentally, which verifies the correctness of the model.

The study main contributions are as follows:

(1) This paper studies the collaborative deep learning architecture and GAN model architecture.
(2) This paper studies the influence of different parameters on GAN deep learning process when the learning rate changes.
(3) By improving the CNN model algorithm, this paper studies the information protection capability of collaborative deep learning under the attack of GAN model.

2   Algorithm

The collaborative deep learning system is mainly divided into two parts: components and protocols. Assuming there are N training participants, and each participant has a private local data set that can be used for training. Before training, all participants reach an agreement on a common learning goal and network architecture [17–19]. We assume that the parameter server whose main role is to maintain the latest parameter values is available to all participants. In addition, the parameter server is abstract. In reality, the real server or distributed system completes the corresponding functions [20].

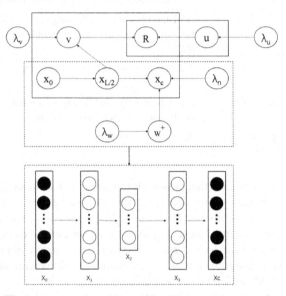

Fig. 1. Architecture diagram of collaborative deep learning

The framework of collaborative deep learning is shown in Fig. 1. In the figure, the matrix X_c represents the clean input of stacked denoised autoencoder (SDAE), the matrix X_0 represents the input with noise added, X_1 to X_l represents the middle layers of SDAE, X_l is the output layer of SDAE, and w^+ represents the weight and bias [21].

Generative adversarial networks (GAN) is mainly composed of generator model G and discriminator model D, which together form a discriminative deep learning network. Generally, the generator G and the discriminator D both are non-linear mapping functions in a multilayer perceptron or a convolutional neural network. The discriminator D is two classifiers. In the training process, generator G captures the distribution of sample data and simulates it to generate false samples similar to the original samples, which are input to discriminator D [22]. The discriminator D is used to judge whether the input sample belongs to the real sample or the false sample output by the generator, and distinguish the true and false samples as far as possible [23].

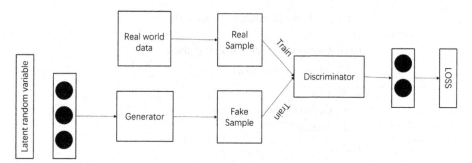

Fig. 2. GAN attack model diagram

The model consists of three parts, including the pre-training phase, the local training phase and the global parameter server training phase. First, the training process of the model in the pre-training stage is shown in Table 2. Second, the implementation process of the model in the local training phase is shown in Table 3. Finally, the process of the global parameter server training phase is shown in Table 4.

Table 2. Pseudocode description

Preliminary training
Input:
1: the V statement label $[a, b]$, the A statement label $[b, c]$; learning rate (lr);
2: percentage of parameter uploads (θ_u);
3: parameter download (θ_d);
4: buried data points (w_{ni});

Table 3. Pseudocode description

Local training stage
1: for epoch $= 1$ to nr epochs
2: do
3: user x for training
4: user x download the parameters θ_d from the parameter's server
5: the newly downloaded data replaces the respective local parameters in the user x local model

Table 4. Pseudocode description

Global parameter server training phase
1: for epoch $= 1$ to nr epochs
2: do
3: if (w_{ni}) no change:
4: $w_{ni}==0$,break;
5: else:
6: Change A's *lr*
7: return $w_j = w_j - \alpha \frac{\partial E}{\partial w_j}$
8: deny A access to the parameter server
9: end if

In the above algorithm, we first determine two participants, define the opponent or attacker as A, and define the victim as V, and then multiple users are included in the attack scope. In this paper, the detection module is added to the parameter server (*PS*) and the network protocol is modified at the same time, and then the embedded point layer is added to the local model according to the modified protocol and data embedded point. The learning rate (*lr*) determines the speed of weight update and affects the loss [24]. Here, (θ_u) and (θ_d) represent the parameters uploaded or downloaded by A or V respectively. Each participant can release any number of tags without having to cover these categories.

If we assume that the system is harmed by attacker A, the training phases of attacker A and victim V can be described as follows [25, 26]:

Training stage of victim V: victim V downloads parameters from the parameter server as local training data, updates the local model and parameters of victim V, and then uploads the rate of change to the parameter server.

The training stage of attacker A: attacker A downloads the parameters from the parameter server as the local training data, and attacker A uses GAN to train the local model to generate the same samples as victim V. In this way, attacker A achieves the purpose of stealing information from victim V.

In this paper, the buried point layer is set before the full connection layer, and the weight of the buried point layer is set to 0. When all calculated values reach the buried point layer through forward propagation, the output value will be calculated as 0. If the final result is found to be lost, the CNN model will use backpropagation to update its weights. Since the next layer of the buried point layer is the output layer, when the back propagation starts, the buried point layer is the first affected layer.

In the protocol designed for the parameter server, the training process of the local model will bypass the buried point layer, which means that the buried point layer will not affect the training process of the local model. However, the attacker does not know how the buried point layer works [27]. Therefore, once the attacker starts the training process, the backpropagation process will update the weight of the buried point layer.

When the attacker uploads the parameters to the parameter server, the detection module will immediately discover the attacker's intrusion behavior. The GAN model attack will release the parameters uploaded by the attacker, while limiting the attacker's learning speed, waiting for the attacker's next upload. If it is confirmed that the behavior is a malicious attack, the parameter server will blacklist the attacker and deny subsequent access. If this behavior is classified as a malicious parameter upload, the parameter server will directly blacklist the attacker [28, 29].

3　Experiment

In order to verify the feasibility of the method proposed in this paper, this section first introduces the experimental environment settings during the experiment, then conducts experiments under different parameters and observes the experimental results, and finally analyzes and evaluates the experimental effects of this method. The specific experimental environment settings in this paper are shown in Table 5.

Table 5. Experimental environment in the experiment

Parameters	Value
Operation system	Windows 10
Memory	8GB
CPU	Intel i5
Program language	python
Compiler	PyCharm 2020

This experiment uses the data collected by the sensor to carry out the experiment. The data set consists of 60,000 training data records and 10,000 test records. By improving the convolutional neural network system, the local parameters and global parameters in this system are encrypted and transmitted. A buried point layer is set before the fully connected layer, and its weight is set to 0. When all the calculated values pass the positive and the direction propagation reaches the buried point layer, the output value will be calculated as 0. If the final result is lost, the CNN model will use backpropagation to update its weights.

First, we change the learning rate parameters in the training process, record the response of the parameter server and the corresponding changes in the learning rate during the process of model training for the failed learning rate.

In deep learning, only an appropriate learning rate can the model get the optimal value.

Figure 3 shows the effect of learning rate on final loss. In Fig. 3, the red curve represents the low learning rate, the blue curve represents the very high learning rate, the gray curve represents the good learning rate, and the yellow curve represents the high learning rate. The figure shows the impact of 4 different learning rates on the final attack result. Among them, the very high learning rate is exponentially distributed, the model does not converge, and the attack model fails to learn. The learning rate represented by the red curve is approximately transformed in a linear manner. As the epoch increases, the loss value continues to decrease, and the model gradually converges. The good learning rate curve also shows a linear trend, but compared with the low learning rate, it has a faster convergence speed, and the final loss is smaller. Under the same epoch change, the magnitude of the loss value change is also larger. The high learning rate curve starts to converge at a certain epoch, and the loss value at this time is relatively large. The learning rate determines the step length of the weight iteration, so it is a very sensitive parameter. Its impact on the model performance is reflected in two aspects. The first is the size of the initial learning rate, and the second is the transformation scheme of the learning rate. Therefore, this paper transforms the learning rate and continuously adjusts the learning rate parameters of the model according to the feedback results of the model, so as to determine the optimal parameters to prevent GAN model attacks and protect the privacy data of the sensor cloud.

The local parameters and global parameters in this system are transmitted through encryption. Hence, even if an intruder successfully invades the system, he cannot decrypt or encrypt the parameters to be uploaded. So as to avoid the intruder from attacking the GAN model and uploading malicious parameters. The following shows the change trend of the loss value corresponding to the generator G and the discriminator D when the learning rate takes different values.

Figure 4 shows that the loss values of the generator and the discriminator change with the time slot when the learning rate is 0.001. When the learning rate is 0.001, the learning rate is low, and the loss values of the generator and the discriminator are small and relatively stable. With the increase of timeslot, the loss value does not change, the system is easy to be attacked, and the user's private information is easy to be leaked.

Figure 5 shows that the loss values of the generator and the discriminator change with the time slot when the learning rate is 0.005. When the learning rate is 0.005, the learning rate is low at this time, the loss value of the generator and the discriminator is small, and the loss value of the discriminator tends to be close to the loss value of the generator. The system is easy to be attacked, and the user's private information is easy to be leaked.

Figure 6 shows that the loss values of the generator and the discriminator change with the time slot when the learning rate is 1.0. When the learning rate is 1.0, the learning rate is large at this time, the loss value of the generator and the discriminator is large. With the increase of the timeslot, the loss value of the discriminator and the generator loss value are gradually increasing, and finally coincide. D and G cannot maintain adversarial learning, which will lead to training failure, indicating that the learning process is unsuccessful.

Figure 7 shows that the loss values of the generator and the discriminator change with the time slot when the learning rate is 10. When the learning rate is 10, the learning rate is large at this time, the loss value of the generator and the discriminator is large. With the increase of the timeslot, the loss value of the discriminator and the generator loss value are constantly fluctuating, and the loss value of the discriminator is overall greater than that of the generator Loss value. D and G cannot maintain adversarial learning, which will lead to training failure. In the end, D loss and G loss reached millions of orders of magnitude, and the generated samples did not contain any information, which indicated that the learning process was unsuccessful.

Figure 8 shows that the loss values of the generator and the discriminator change with the time slot when the learning rate is 1000. When the learning rate is 1000, the learning rate is very large at this time, the loss value of the generator and the discriminator is large, the value reaches millions, the loss value of the discriminator and the generator loss value are constantly fluctuating, and the loss of the discriminator the overall value is smaller than the loss value of the generator. D and G cannot maintain adversarial learning, which will lead to training failure. In the end, D loss and G loss reached millions of orders of magnitude, and the generated samples did not contain any information, which indicated that the learning process was unsuccessful.

It is easy to detect parameters uploaded by infected and malicious users. When an infected or malicious user uses this GAN model to attack the system, the parameter server will detect the intrusion and return high learning rate parameters. The attacker can use the GAN model to generate samples of the sensor cloud. When the learning rate is 0.001, the loss of D and G will remain stable; When the learning rate is 0.005, D and G will fluctuate. This fluctuation is caused by the imbalance in the process of finding the best value for D and G. Therefore, in the process of synchronously learning D and G, if the training effect of D is good enough, it will not return its data distribution information as feedback, which will cause G to stop learning, thereby greatly increasing the loss of G. When the learning rate increases, D and G cannot maintain adversarial learning, which will lead to training failure, and the learning process is unsuccessful. As a result, the GAN model attack can be eliminated by changing the learning rate.

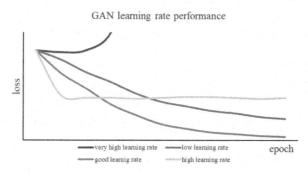

Fig. 3. The effect of learning rate on final loss

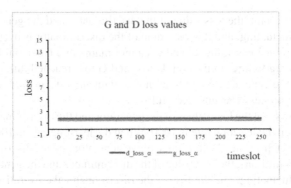

Fig. 4. G and D loss values 1

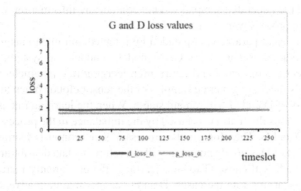

Fig. 5. G and D loss values 2

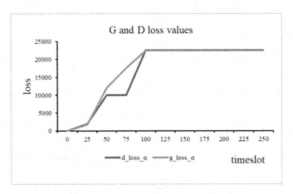

Fig. 6. G and D loss values 3

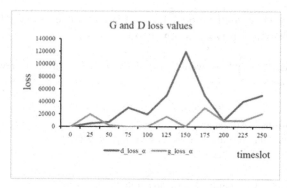

Fig. 7. G and D loss values 4

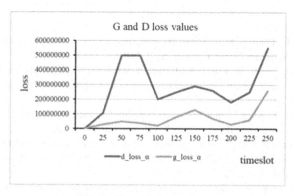

Fig. 8. G and D loss values 5

4 Conclusion and Discussion

This paper proposes a sensor cloud data privacy protection model based on collaborative deep learning, and studies a privacy protection method based on deep convolution to generate adversarial networks. First, the collaborative deep learning architecture and GAN attack model architecture are studied. Then, aiming at the leakage of privacy protection methods in the deep convolution countermeasure generation network, in the process of deep network parameter transmission, encrypted transmission is used, buried points are set, and training parameters are adjusted to make the Gan model attack training invalid and protect information security. Finally, experiments are carried out on the collected sensor data to verify the effectiveness of the model in this paper, which guarantees that the training of the GAN attack model fails to a great extent and protects privacy.

Although this paper processes and stores the cloud information of the sensor cloud system, and uses the method of setting buried points to prevent GAN attacks, the current model is not perfect, and there is still room for improvement. This paper needs to further study the characteristics of the GAN model attacks, continue to improve the protection methods for the defects related to the attacks based on the GAN model, improve the algorithms mentioned in this paper by combining artificial intelligence, big data and other algorithms, and strengthen the defense capability of sensor cloud information to improve the protection of privacy information.

Acknowledgments. The authors would like to thank the anonymous reviewers for their constructive comments.

Author Contributions. All authors contributed to the present paper with the same effort in finding available literature resources, as well as writing the paper.

Conflicts of Interest. The authors declare no conflict of interest.

References

1. Nkenyereye, L., Islam, S.M.R., Bilal, M., et al.: Secure crowd-sensing protocol for fog-based vehicular cloud. Futur. Gener. Comput. Syst. **120**, 61–75 (2021)
2. Mukherjee, P., Swain, T., Datta, A.: Issues of Some Task Scheduling Strategies on Sensor Cloud Environment. Smart Intelligent Computing and Applications, pp. 651–663. Springer, Singapore (2020)
3. Mo, Y., Liang, M., Xing, L., et al.: Network simplification and k-terminal reliability evaluation of sensor-cloud systems. IEEE Access **8**, 177206–177218 (2020)
4. Thota, C., Sundarasekar, R., Manogaran, G., et al.: Centralized fog computing security platform for IoT and cloud in healthcare system. In: Fog computing: Breakthroughs in research and practice. IGI global, pp. 365–378 (2018)
5. Madria, S.: Sensor cloud: sensing-as-a-service paradigm. In: 2018 19th IEEE International Conference on Mobile Data Management (MDM), pp. 3–6. IEEE (2018)
6. Tian, W., Yang, L.I., Weijia, J.I.A., et al.: Research progress of sensor-cloud security. J. Commun. **39**(3), 35 (2018)
7. Hitaj, B., Ateniese, G., Perez-Cruz, F.: Deep models under the GAN: information leakage from collaborative deep learning. In: Proceedings of the 2017 ACM SIGSAC Conference on Computer and Communications Security, pp. 603–618 (2017)
8. Zhang, G., Wang, T., Wang, G., et al.: Detection of hidden data attacks combined fog computing and trust evaluation method in sensor-cloud system. Concurrency Comput. Pract. Exp. **33**(7), 1 (2021)
9. Vimal, K., Sen, A., Madria, S.: Secure sensor cloud. Synthesis Lectures on Algorithms and Software in Engineering, pp. 1–140 (2019)
10. Saha, S., Das, R., Datta, S., et al.: A cloud security framework for a data centric WSN application. In: Proceedings of the 17th International Conference on Distributed Computing and Networking, pp. 1–6 (2016)
11. Liang, Y., Wang, T., Bhuiyan, M.Z.A., et al.: Research on coupling reliability problem in sensor-cloud system. In: International Conference on Security, Privacy and Anonymity in Computation, Communication and Storage. Springer, Cham, pp. 468–478 (2017)
12. Rahman, A.F.A., Daud, M., Mohamad, M.Z.: Securing sensor to cloud ecosystem using internet of things (IoT) security framework. In: Proceedings of the International Conference on Internet of things and Cloud Computing, pp. 1–5 (2016)
13. Zissis, D.: Intelligent security on the edge of the cloud. In: 2017 International Conference on Engineering, Technology and Innovation (ICE/ITMC), pp. 1066–1070. IEEE (2017)

14. Shojaeerad, Z., Taherifard, S., Jameii, S.M.: Combining wireless sensor networks and cloud computing: security perspective. In: 2015 2nd International Conference on Knowledge-Based Engineering and Innovation (KBEI), pp. 943–949. IEEE (2015)
15. Malekzadeh, M., Clegg, R.G., Cavallaro, A., et al.: Privacy and utility preserving sensor-data transformations. Pervasive Mob. Comput. **63**, 101132 (2020)
16. Stirapongsasuti, S., Nakamura, Y., Yasumoto, K.: Privacy-aware sensor data upload management for securely receiving smart home services. In: 2020 IEEE International Conference on Smart Computing (SMARTCOMP), pp. 214–219. IEEE (2020)
17. Wang, H., Liu, C., Jiang, D., et al.: Collaborative deep learning framework for fault diagnosis in distributed complex systems. Mech. Syst. Signal Process. **156**, 107650 (2021)
18. Martins, G.B., Papa, J.P., Adeli, H.: Deep learning techniques for recommender systems based on collaborative filtering. Expert. Syst. **37**(6), e12647 (2020)
19. Xiong, Y., Xu, F., Zhong, S.: Detecting GAN-based privacy attack in distributed learning. In: ICC 2020–2020 IEEE International Conference on Communications (ICC), pp. 1–6. IEEE (2020)
20. Prashar, A., Monroy, S.A.S.: A secure algorithm for deep learning training under GAN attacks. In: 2020 International Conference on Communications, Computing, Cybersecurity, and Informatics (CCCI), pp. 1–6. IEEE (2020)
21. Liao, D., Huang, S., Tan, Y., et al.: Network intrusion detection method based on GAN model. In: 2020 International Conference on Computer Communication and Network Security (CCNS), pp. 153–156. IEEE (2020)
22. Chen, X.: CNN Model Optimization Cheme and Applications. Innovative Computing, pp. 1771–1777. Springer, Singapore (2020)
23. Zeng, L., Sun, B., Zhu, D.: Underwater target detection based on Faster R-CNN and adversarial occlusion network. Eng. Appl. Artif. Intell. **100**, 104190 (2021)
24. Wen, C., Yang, L., Li, X., et al.: Directionally constrained fully convolutional neural network for airborne LiDAR point cloud classification. ISPRS J. Photogramm. Remote. Sens. **162**, 50–62 (2020)
25. Ding, H., Sun, C., Zeng, J.: Fuzzy weighted clustering method for numerical attributes of communication big data based on cloud computing. Symmetry **12**(4), 530 (2020)
26. Wang, G., Huang, H., Pan, R.: Data prediction service model based on sequential pattern mining in sensor-cloud. In: International Conference on Security, Privacy and Anonymity in Computation, Communication and Storage. Springer, Cham, pp. 281–293 (2020)
27. Dwivedi, R.K., Saran, M., Kumar, R.: A survey on security over sensor-cloud. In: 2019 9th International Conference on Cloud Computing, Data Science & Engineering (Confluence), pp. 31–37. IEEE (2019)
28. Das, K., Das, S., Mishra, A., et al.: Energy efficient data prediction model for the sensor cloud environment.In: 2017 International Conference on IoT and Application (ICIOT), pp. 1–3. IEEE (2017)
29. Zhang, T., Yan, L., Yang, Y.: Trust evaluation method for clustered wireless sensor networks based on cloud model. Wireless Netw. **24**(3), 777–797 (2018)

Cyberspace Anonymity

An Improved Cuckoo Search Algorithm and Its Application in Function Optimization

Songlv Feng, Cuina Cheng, and Liping Mo$^{(\boxtimes)}$

School of Computer Science and Engineering, Jishou University, Jishou 416000, China
zmx89@jsu.edu.cn

Abstract. An improved cuckoo search (CS) algorithm focusing on optimizing the updating of the bird's nest position is proposed to overcome the shortcomings of CS algorithm, such as low search accuracy, easy premature convergence, and weak local search ability in the late stage. The proposed algorithm employs three main strategies. First, in the early and middle stage, aiming to expand the search domain, increase the population diversity, and prevent the premature convergence of the algorithm, the global optimization strategy combining opposition-based learning and Levy flight is used to update the nest position. Second, to avoid the algorithm from falling into a local optimum, a dynamic inertia weight is employed to reduce the effect of the current nest position when the nest position is updated during the random migration. Third, in the late stage, to improve the local search ability and search accuracy, the nest position is updated using the local exploitation strategy of the Aquila optimization (AO) algorithm to replace the Levy flight mechanism. The results of comparative experiments with CS algorithm and its four variants on function optimization show that the proposed algorithm has a better global search ability, better local development ability, faster convergence speed and better search accuracy than other selected algorithms.

Keywords: Cuckoo search algorithm · Levy flight · Opposition-based learning · Inertia weight · Local exploitation

1 Introduction

Swarm intelligence optimization algorithms are a class of bionic algorithms that simulate the exchange of information and cooperation between individuals in a group of animals, it can effectively solve many complex optimization problems that cannot be solved by traditional optimization algorithms in the real world. Classical swarm intelligence optimization algorithms include the Particle Swarm Optimization (PSO) algorithm [1], the Ant Colony Optimization (ACO) algorithm [2], the Artificial Bee Colony (ABC) algorithm [3], the Whale Optimization Algorithm (WOA) [4] and the Grey Wolf Optimization (GWO) algorithm [5], and so on. These algorithms have been equipped with superior performance in finding optimal approximate solutions for complex functions and are widely employed in practical applications such as function optimization [6], engineering optimization [7] and neural network [8].

© The Author(s), under exclusive license to Springer Nature Singapore Pte Ltd. 2023
G. Wang et al. (Eds.): UbiSec 2022, CCIS 1768, pp. 439–455, 2023.
https://doi.org/10.1007/978-981-99-0272-9_30

In 2009, inspired by the parasitic brood-rearing behavior of cuckoos in nature, Yang and Deb proposed a novel swarm intelligence optimization algorithm, named the Cuckoo Search (CS) algorithm [9]. CS algorithm has the advantages of few parameters, strong robustness, easy to implement, and can find the optimum quickly in solving complex problems. However, it also has shortcomings such as low search accuracy, easy premature convergence, and poor local search ability in the late stages. Thus, some improved methods of CS algorithm in terms of parameters controlling, operators adjusting, and hybridizing with other metaheuristic algorithms have been proposed. Valian et al. [10] proposed an improved CS algorithm by adaptively varying step size and elimination probability, effectively balancing the global search and local exploitation capabilities of the algorithm. Yan et al. [11] proposed a CS algorithm for the dynamic updating parameters that makes full use of iterative information. This algorithm increases the flexibility of the local search approach by using the Cauchy distribution to generate Levy flight steps, and record the mean parameters corresponding to the optimum for each generation when generate the new Cauchy distribution required for the next generation. Walton et al. [12] improved CS algorithm by incorporating some of the optimal from the iterative process into a set to generate the next generation of solutions by randomly selecting two of the optimums in the set, enhancing the communication between populations and effectively improving the performance of the algorithm. To enhance the local search capability of the CS algorithm, Chen et al. [13] introduced the explosion operator from the fireworks algorithm into CS algorithm, and Kamoona et al. [14] proposed a hybrid algorithm of ABC algorithm and CS algorithm by using the greedy selection strategy of ABC algorithm. Huang et al. [15] introduced the teacher-student communication mechanism into CS algorithm to make up for the shortcomings of CS algorithm in local search.

The mentioned CS variants all outperform the original CS algorithm. However, some variants accelerate the convergence speed but easily fall into local optima, leading to premature convergence; some variants enhance the local search capability, but have a low search accuracy. To overcome the above shortcomings, a local search enhanced CS algorithm integrating three optimization strategies, named ECSOW, is proposed in this manuscript. First, a global optimization strategy combining opposition-based learning and Levy flight is used to complete the nest position update operation in the early and middle stage of the algorithm to expand the global search, enrich the population diversity and avoid premature convergence of the algorithm. Then, a dynamic inertia weight is employed to adjust the range of action of the current nest during the random migration, to prevent the algorithm from falling into local optimum in the late stage. Finally, the local exploitation strategy of the Aquila Optimizer (AO) algorithm [16] is utilized to replace the Levy flight mechanism for nest position updating to improve the local search capability in the late stage. In the experiments, 10 classic benchmark functions are used to compare ECSOW with other CS variants. The experimental results show that the ECSOW outperforms the selected CS variants.

The rest of this article is summarized as follows. Section 2 gives a brief introduction to CS algorithm. Section 3 presents three optimization strategies introduced in ECSOW. Section 4 illustrates the main implementation steps and explores the time complexity of the ECSOW in detail. Section 5 shows the optimization experiments and discussions. Finally, Sect. 6 presents a summary.

2 Introduction of the CS Algorithm

2.1 Algorithm Principle

CS algorithm simulates the parasitic brood-rearing behavior of cuckoos in nature based on the following three assumptions:

1) Each cuckoo lays one egg at a time and places the egg in a randomly selected nest where the host has just laid an egg.
2) The best of all randomly selected host nests is retained for the next generation.
3) The number of available host nests is fixed. The probability of a host finding a cuckoo egg is $Pa \in (0,1)$. If a host finds a cuckoo egg, it will choose to discard the egg or rebuild a new nest.

The flowchart of CS algorithm as shown on the left in Fig. 1:

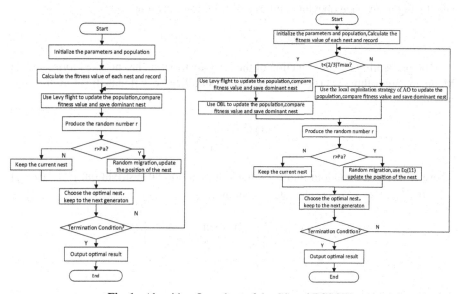

Fig. 1. Algorithm flow chart of the CS and ECSOW

As seen on the left in Fig. 1, initializing the nest position and updating the nest position are two important operations that affect the performance of CS algorithm.

In CS algorithm, the initial nest position X0 is generated by a random method shown in Eq. (1).

$$X_0 = min + (max - min) \times rand(d) \tag{1}$$

where $rand(d)$ is a random number of dimension d taking values in the range [0,1] and [min, max] denotes the search domain.

2.2 Levy Flight

To find the optimal nest quickly, CS algorithm searches all nests using the Levy flight mechanisms. Levy flight is a random migration process, consisting of frequent short-distance flights and occasional long-distance flights. Short-distance flights are beneficial for CS algorithm to search near the optimal nest, narrow the search area and increase the search accuracy. Long-distance flights are beneficial for the algorithm to jump out of the local optimum, expand the search area, and enhance the global search capability. Based on this mechanism, CS algorithm utilizes the following Eq. (2) to update nest positions.

$$X_i^{t+1} = X_i^t + \partial \otimes Levy(\lambda) \tag{2}$$

where X_i^t and X_i^{t+1} represent the positions in the t, $t + 1$ iteration of the bird's nest i, respectively; ∂ is the step size factor controlling the step size, which generally takes a positive value; $\otimes$ denotes point-to-point multiplication; $Levy(\lambda)$ denotes the random search path of the Levy flight, with the flight direction obeying a uniform distribution and the flight step size obeying the Levy distribution shown in Eq. (3).

$$Levy \sim u = t^{-\lambda}, 1 \leq \lambda \leq 3 \tag{3}$$

The probability density function of the Levy distribution has no fixed form, and the Mantegna algorithm [17] is commonly used to simulate Levy flights. It is formulated as follows:

$$Levy(\lambda) = \frac{\mu}{|v|^{1/\beta}} \tag{4}$$

where μ and v are random numbers that follow a normal distribution, $\mu \sim \left(0, \delta_\mu^2\right)$, $v \sim \left(0, \delta_v^2\right)$, $\delta^v = 1$, δ_μ is calculated as follows:

$$\delta_\mu = \left\{ \frac{\Gamma(1+\beta) \times \sin(\pi\beta/2)}{\Gamma[(1+\beta)/2] \times 2^{\beta-1/2} \times \beta} \right\}^{1/\beta} \tag{5}$$

2.3 Random Migration

CS algorithm performs a random migration after updating the nest position based on the Levy flight mechanism, and then generates a random number $r \in (0, 1)$. When $r > Pa$, a new nest position is generated by Eq. (6) to replace the current nest position, and the nest position with the better fitness of the two nests is retained.

$$X_i^{t+1} = X_i^t + rand(0, 1) \otimes H(pa - \varepsilon) \otimes \left(X_j^t - X_k^t\right) \tag{6}$$

In Eq. (6), X_j^t and X_k^t denote any two nest positions in the generation t other than the current nest position, $H(u)$ is a Heaviside function, and $rand(0, 1)$ is a random number.

2.4 Advantages and Disadvantages of the Algorithm

CS algorithm has only the elimination probability *Pa* need to be adjusted during the optimization search. Yang et al. [9] demonstrated that the convergence rate of CS algorithm is insensitive to *Pa*, which indicates CS algorithm is very robust. Moreover, CS algorithm mainly uses the Levy flight mechanism to update the nest position, and the steps are simple and easy to implement. In addition, the Levy flight has the feature of frequent small-step and occasional large-step flights, which can ensure CS algorithm has a strong global search capability.

However, CS algorithm uses the Levy flight mechanisms to update nest positions, with a single update strategy and poor population diversity, which makes CS algorithm slow to converge. Moreover, in the random migration phase, the new nest position is updated near the current nest position, which makes CS algorithm easily fall into local optimum in the late stages. In addition, in the late stage, the frequent small-step and occasional large-step of Levy's flight make individuals prone to jump around in the search domain, leading a low search accuracy.

3 Algorithm Optimization Strategies

To solve the above problems, three optimization strategies are introduced in ECSOW. Firstly, in the early and middle stage, adopting the idea of Opposition-Based Learning (OBL) combined with the Levy flight mechanism to jointly achieve global search, and enhance the global search capability of the algorithm. Secondly, introducing dynamic inertia weight parameters in the process of random migration to dynamically adjust the search range and ensure the algorithm can better transition from global exploration to local. Thirdly, two local exploitation strategies of AO algorithm are introduced in the late stage to enhance the local search capability of the algorithm.

3.1 Opposition-Based Learning Strategy

OBL is an optimization learning method proposed by Tizhoosh [18] in 2005. OBL selects the better of the current solution and its inverse solution as the new solution. Some intelligent optimization algorithms, such as differential evolutionary algorithm, combined with OBL, have now been applied in the field of intelligent computing, and show good global optimization-seeking performance [19].

The concepts related to OBL are defined as follows [18].

Definition 1. Given a real number, its inverse is defined as Eq. (7).

$$x' = a + b - x \qquad (7)$$

Definition 2. Let $X = [x_1, x_2, \cdots, x_d]$ be a point in d-dimensional space, x_i be a component of X, $x_i \in [a_i, b_i]$, then the inverse point $X' = [x'_1, x'_2, \cdots, x'_d]$ of X is defined as Eq. (8).

$$x'_i = a_i + b_i - x_i \qquad (8)$$

Definition 3. Suppose $X_i = [x_{i1}, x_{i2}, \cdots, x_{id}]$ is a feasible solution of the function $f(x)$, then its inverse solution is defined as Eq. (9).

$$\begin{cases} X_i' = [x_{i1}', x_{i2}', \cdots, x_{id}'] \\ \quad x_{ij}' = a_i + b_j - x_{ij} \end{cases} \tag{9}$$

Assuming that the optimization objective is to find the minimum value, if $f(X_i') < f(X_i)$, then X_i is replaced by X_i'. Otherwise, X_i is retained.

In the early and middle stage of CS algorithm, OBL is introduced to further optimize the nest position updated based on the Levy flight mechanism. Using this combination of OBL and Levy flight to search the solution space can expand the search range and increase the population diversity, which is conducive to enhance the global search capability of CS algorithm.

3.2 Dynamic Adjustment Strategy of Inertia Weight

During the random migration stage of CS algorithm, the random search domain for the new nest is restricted to the vicinity of the current nest position, leading to the algorithm be prone to local optimum in the late iteration. ECSOW introduces an inertia weight that is dynamically linked to the iterative process to control the influence of the current nest position on the new nest position.

In ECSOW, a non-linearly decreasing dynamic inertia weight ω as the number of iterations increases, as shown in Eq. (10), to control the range of action of the current nest position.

$$\omega = 1 - \cos\left(\frac{\pi t}{2T} + \frac{3\pi}{2}\right) \tag{10}$$

where t is the number of current iterations and T is the maximum number of iterations. The position of the new nest generated in the random migration phase is given by Eq. (11).

$$X_i^{t+1} = X_i^t * \omega + rand(0, 1) \otimes H(pa - \varepsilon) \otimes \left(X_j^t - X_k^t\right) \tag{11}$$

According to Eqs. (10 and 11), as the number of iterations increases, ω gradually decreases, which indicates that ω can dynamically control the influence of the current nest position in the iterative process. In the early and middle iterations, ω is larger, and the current nest position plays a more important role in generating a new nest position, which is conducive to finding the global optimal nest position near the current nest position. In the late iteration, close to the global optimal nest position, ω is smaller, which can effectively reduce the influence of the current nest position and prevent the algorithm from falling into a local optimum.

3.3 Local Exploitation Strategy

According to the literature [16], AO algorithm is inspired by the natural behavior of the Aquila in capturing prey in nature, simulates four behaviors of the Aquila in capturing prey. Four behaviors are searching the prey range by flying high in a vertical dive (corresponding to the selection of the search domain by expanding exploration in the early and middle stages), searching the prey range by flying contour in a short glide attack (corresponding to the searching within the search domain), flying low in a slow descent attack to approach the prey position(corresponding to the late development in the vicinity of the optimum), and capturing prey by walking or low-flying attack (corresponding to the final approach to the optimum through continuous exploitation).

The local exploitation strategy of AO algorithm reflects in the simulation of the latter two behaviors, and the corresponding formulae shown in Eqs. (12) and (13).

$$X_{t+1} = X_{best(t)} + (X_i - X_j) \times rand(0, 1) \tag{12}$$

where X_{t+1} is the new solution, $X_{best(t)}$ is the current optimum, $rand(0, 1)$ is a random number, and X_i and X_j are any two current solutions.

$$X_{t+1} = QF \times X_{best(t)} + (X_{best(t)} - X_{M(t)}) \times G_2 \tag{13}$$

where QF is the quality function of the balanced search strategy, and the calculation formula is shown in Eq. (14). G_2 is the flight slope of the Aquila algorithm, the value range is (0,2), and the calculation formula is shown in Eq. (15).

$$QF_t = t^{\frac{2 \times rand - 1}{(1-T)^2}} \tag{14}$$

$$G_2 = 2 \times \left(1 - \frac{t}{T}\right) \tag{15}$$

The features of Levy flights determine the effectiveness of CS algorithm for global searching. However, late in the iteration, it is hoped that the algorithm will only need to perform a local search in the vicinity of the global optimum, and continued use of Levy flight is not conducive to local exploitation. Therefore, the local exploitation strategy of AO algorithm can be introduced to enhance the local exploitation capability in the late iteration of the algorithm.

In ECSOW, the optimization strategy combined with OBL and Levy flight is used to carry out global searching in the early and middle stage of iteration. When the current nest position is close to the global optimal nest position, to increase the convergence accuracy, a local search is performed in the vicinity of the global optimal nest position according to Eqs. (12) and (13).

4 Description and Analysis of ECSOW Algorithm

4.1 Algorithm Description

Based on the above three optimization strategies, the steps of ECSOW are as follows:

Step 1: Initialize. Define the objective function $f(x)$, and set the population size n, dimension d, search domain [min, max], discovery probability Pa, step size factor ∂ and the maximum number of iterations $Tmax$, initialize the population using Eq. (1) and calculate the fitness of each solution.

Step 2: Check the number of iterations t. If $t < (2/3)T_{max}$, go to step 3; otherwise, go to step 4.

Step 3: Use Eq. (2) to update each solution, compare the fitness, and retain the new or old solution corresponding to the better fitness; then use Eq. (9) to calculate the reverse solution of each solution, and retain the solution with the better fitness among the current solution and its reverse solution.

Step 4: Update each solution by selecting Eq. (12) or Eq. (13) with equal probability, calculate the fitness of each new solution, and retain the new or old solution corresponding to the better fitness.

Step 5: Generate a random number r for each solution in the population. If $r > Pa$, generate a new solution using Eq. (11) to achieve a random migration of the solution, calculate the fitness corresponding to the new solution, and retain the dominant solution. Find the optimum in the population and retain the optimum until the next iteration.

Step 6: Check the termination condition. If satisfied, the algorithm ends; otherwise, go to step 2.

The flowchart for ECSOW is shown on the right in Fig. 1.

4.2 Time Complexity Analysis

Assuming that the dimension of the solution is d and the population size is n, the time complexity of the ECSOW is discussed according to the above steps as follows, where only one iteration is considered.

1) The time complexity of population initialization is $O(n \times d)$, and the time complexity of calculating the fitness of the objective function is $O(f(d))$. Therefore, the time complexity of step 1 is $O(n \times (d + f(d)))$.
2) In the early and middle iteration, Levy flight and OBL stages, the complexity of updating the solution and reverse solution according to Eq. (2) and Eq. (9) is $O(n \times (d + O(levy)))$. Since $O(levy)$ is the time complexity of computing a random number obeying the Levy distribution, its time complexity is a constant order $O(1)$. Therefore, the time complexity of Step 3 is $2 \times O(n \times (d + f(d)))$.
3) In the random migration stage, the time complexity of computing the solutions is $O(n \times d)$ using Eq. (11), and the time complexity of step 5 is also $O(n \times (d + f(d)))$.
4) In the late stage of the iteration, the time complexity of local exploitation using Eqs. (12)-(13) is also $O(n \times d)$, so the time complexity of step 4 is $O(n \times (d + f(d)))$.

Therefore, the total time complexity of ECSOW as follows:

$$O(n \times (d + f(d))) + \frac{2}{3}T_{max} \times 2 \times O(n \times (d + f(d))) + \frac{1}{3}T_{max} \times O(n \times (d + f(d)))$$
$$+T_{max} \times O(n \times (d + f(d))) \approx T_{max} \times O(n \times (d + f(d)))$$

Obviously, the time complexity of the ECSOW is essentially the same as that of CS algorithm. Theoretically, ECSOW does not increase the time complexity compared with the original CS algorithm.

5   Experiments

5.1   Experimental Environment and Test Functions

The experiment is conducted in a computer with an Intel (R) Core (TM) i5-7200 M CPU @2.50 GHz, 8 GB RAM, Win10 operating system, and Python 3.7.6 programming environment, using 10 classical benchmark functions listed in Table 1.

To verify the performance of ECSOW algorithm, it was compared with original CS algorithm, Modified Cuckoo Search Algorithm (MCSA) [20], Adaptive Step-size Cuckoo Search Algorithm (ASCSA) [21], Enhance Cuckoo Search (ECS) [14] and Snap-drift Cuckoo Search (SDCS) [22] using 10 benchmark functions run in both 50 and 100 dimensions. Each algorithm was run 30 times independently with 5000 iterations per run.

Table 1. Benchmark functions

Function	Formula	Interval	Dim	$f(x)min$
Sphere (unimodal)	$f_1(x) = \sum_{i=1}^{d} x_i^2$	$[-5.12, 5.12]$	50,100	0
Griewank (multimodal)	$f_2(x) = \sum_{i=1}^{d} \frac{x_i^2}{4000} - \prod_{i=1}^{d} \cos\left(\frac{x_i}{\sqrt{i}}\right) + 1$	$[-600, 600]$	50,100	0
Ackley (multimodal)	$f_3(x) = -20\exp\left(-0.2\sqrt{\frac{1}{d}\sum_{i=1}^{d} x_i^2}\right) - \exp\left(\frac{1}{d}\sum_{i=1}^{d}\cos(cx_i)\right) + 20 + e$	$[-32, 32]$	50,100	0
Rastrigin (multimodal)	$f_4(x) = 10d + \sum_{i=1}^{d}\left[x_i^2 - 10\cos(2\pi x_i)\right]$	$[-5.12, 5.12]$	50,100	0
Alpine (multimodal)	$f_5(x) = \sum_{i=1}^{d} |x_i \sin(x_i) + 0.1x_i|$	$[-10, 10]$	50,100	0
Schewefel2.22 (unimodal)	$f_6(x) = \sum_{i=1}^{d} |x_i| + \prod_{i=1}^{d} |x_i|$	$[-10, 10]$	50,100	0
Quartic (unimodal)	$f_7(x) = \sum_{i=1}^{d} ix_i^4 + rand[0, 1)$	$[-1.28, 1.28]$	50,100	0
Sum Squares (unimodal)	$f_8(x) = \sum_{i=1}^{d} ix_i^2$	$[-10, 10]$	50,100	0
Bohachevsky (unimodal)	$f_9(x) = \sum_{i=1}^{d-1}\left[\begin{array}{l}x_i^2 + 2x_{i+1}^2 - 0.3\cos(3\pi x_i) \\ -0.4\cos(4\pi x_{i+1}) + 0.7\end{array}\right]$	$[-15, 15]$	50,100	0
Powell (unimodal)	$f_{10}(x) = \sum_{i=1}^{d/4}\left[\begin{array}{l}(x_{4i-3} + 10x_{4i-2})^2 + 5(x_{4i-1} - x_{4i})^2 \\ +(x_{4i-2} - 2x_{4i-1})^4 + 10(x_{4i-3} - x_{4i})^4\end{array}\right]$	$[-4, 5]$	50,100	0

The parameters setting by referring to the relevant literature of the selected algorithms are shown in Table 2.

Table 2. Parameters setting

Algorithms	Parameters
ECSOW	$N = 25, \lambda = 1.5, Pa = 0.25, \alpha = 0.01$
CS	$N = 25, \lambda = 1.5, Pa = 0.25, \alpha = 0.01$
MCSA	$N = 25, \lambda = 1.5, Pa = 0.25, \alpha_{min} = 0.1, \alpha_{max} = 1.5$
ASCSA	$N = 25, \lambda = 1.5, Pa = 0.25$
ECS	$N = 25, \lambda = 1.5, Pa = 0.25, \alpha = 0.01$
SDCS	$N = 25, \lambda = 1.5, \alpha = 0.01, J = 0.3, w = 0.005$

5.2 Experimental Results and Analysis

The optimization results obtained for the six algorithms run in 50-dimension and 100-dimension on the 10 benchmark functions are shown in Tables 3 and 4, respectively. In the tables, mean and std denote the mean and variance of the optimal fitness after 30 runs of each algorithm, respectively. The smaller the value of the mean and std, the better the algorithm optimization performance.

Table 3. Optimization results on test functions (Dim = 50)

Function		CS	MCSA	ASCSA	ECS	SDCS	ECSOW
$f_1(x)$	mean	6.25e-01	5.82e + 00	6.29e−25	2.74e−81	**0.00e + 00**	**0.00e + 00**
	std	4.31e-02	4.05e + 00	4.08e−25	4.04e−81	**0.00e + 00**	**0.00e + 00**
$f_2(x)$	mean	6.29e + 01	2.77e-01	1.39e−13	3.84e−03	**0.00e + 00**	**0.00e + 00**
	std	6.92e + 01	1.73e-01	5.14e−13	8.18e−03	**0.00e + 00**	**0.00e + 00**
$f_3(x)$	mn	5.04e + 00	2.45e + 00	9.03e + 00	1.11e + 00	8.88e-16	**0.00e + 00**
	std	7.03e + 00	7.03e + 00	6.21e + 00	5.55e-01	**0.00e + 00**	**0.00e + 00**
$f_4(x)$	mean	2.04e + 02	1.44e + 02	2.19e + 02	2.62e + 01	**0.00e + 00**	**0.00e + 00**
	std	1.54e + 01	2.16e + 01	1.52e + 01	5.26e + 00	**0.00e + 00**	**0.00e + 00**
$f5(x)$	mean	9.79e + 00	7.04e + 00	3.03e + 01	2.93e−01	5.58e-155	**0.00e + 00**
	std	3.22e + 00	2.97e + 00	2.88e + 00	1.77e−01	3.11e-154	**0.00e + 00**
$f6(x)$	mean	4.46e + 00	1.76e + 01	8.87e−14	7.00e−64	**0.00e + 00**	**0.00e + 00**
	std	2.06e-01	1.14e + 01	3.45e−14	1.03e−63	**0.00e + 00**	**0.00e + 00**
$f7(x)$	mean	8.00e-01	1.53e + 00	4.45e−02	2.76e−02	3.46e-05	**1.68e-05**
	std	1.26e-01	9.94e-01	8.86e−03	6.12e−03	3.02e-05	**1.76e-05**
$f_8(x)$	mean	4.51e + 02	7.60e + 03	5.69e−22	9.47e−78	**0.00e + 00**	**0.00e + 00**

(continued)

Table 3. (*continued*)

Function		CS	MCSA	ASCSA	ECS	SDCS	ECSOW
	std	5.11e + 01	5.91e + 03	2.57e−22	3.01e−77	**0.00e + 00**	**0.00e + 00**
f9(x)	mean	2.36e + 01	6.70e + 01	**0.00e + 00**	7.50e + 00	**0.00e + 00**	**0.00e + 00**
	std	1.41e + 00	3.81e + 01	**0.00e + 00**	2.53e + 00	**0.00e + 00**	**0.00e + 00**
f10(x)	mean	8.69e + 00	1.85e + 02	2.61e−01	9.88e−03	**0.00e + 00**	**0.00e + 00**
	std	1.15e + 00	1.04e + 02	1.98e−01	4.32e−03	**0.00e + 00**	**0.00e + 00**

As shown in Tables 3 and 4, for unimodal functions $f_1(x), f_6(x), f_8(x), f_9(x), f_{10}(x)$ in 50 and 100 dimensions, and multimodal functions $f_2(x), f_4(x)$ in 50-dimension and 100-dimension, $f_5(x)$ in 100 dimensions, only ECSOW and SDCS can converge to the theoretical optimum, the other four algorithms do not; for the unimodal function $f_7(x)$ in 50-dimension and 100-dimension, none of the six algorithms can converge to the theoretical optimum, but the ECSOW outperforms the other five algorithms; for the multimodal function $f_3(x)$ in 50-dimension and 100-dimension, and $f_5(x)$ in 50-dimension, only ECSAOW can converge to a theoretically optimum, none of the other five algorithms does. Obviously, ECSOW has a stronger global search capability and better robustness than the other five algorithms.

Table 4. Optimization results on test functions (Dim = 100)

Function		CS	MCSA	ASCSA	ECS	SDCS	ECSOW
$f_1(x)$	mean	4.23e + 00	6.42e + 01	4.63e−08	3.04e−38	**0.00e + 00**	**0.00e + 00**
	std	2.29e−01	3.50e + 01	1.13e−08	7.47e−38	**0.00e + 00**	**0.00e + 00**
$f_2(x)$	mean	3.01e + 02	8.23e−01	3.78e−04	1.69e−02	**0.00e + 00**	**0.00e + 00**
	std	2.57e + 02	1.92e−01	1.83e−03	4.00e−02	**0.00e + 00**	**0.00e + 00**
$f_3(x)$	mean	4.96e + 00	5.51e + 00	1.99e + 01	4.15e + 00	8.88e−16	**0.00e + 00**
	std	5.43e + 00	1.56e + 00	1.88e−02	8.54e−01	**0.00e + 00**	**0.00e + 00**
$f_4(x)$	mean	7.36e + 02	5.90e + 02	9.80e + 02	1.20e + 02	**0.00e + 00**	**0.00e + 00**
	std	4.41e + 01	6.13e + 01	3.76e + 01	1.24e + 01	**0.00e + 00**	**0.00e + 00**
f5(x)	mean	3.95e + 01	6.06e + 01	1.17e + 02	5.10e + 00	**0.00e + 00**	**0.00e + 00**
	std	9.67e + 00	1.30e + 01	7.96e + 00	2.08e + 00	**0.00e + 00**	**0.00e + 00**
f6(x)	mean	1.69e + 01	9.72e + 01	7.64e−02	8.88e−30	**0.00e + 00**	**0.00e + 00**
	std	5.70e−01	3.57e + 01	1.80e−01	2.45e−29	**0.00e + 00**	**0.00e + 00**
f7(x)	mean	2.54e + 01	1.18e + 02	2.97e−01	1.94e−01	3.23e−05	**1.40e-05**
	std	3.01e + 00	4.51e + 01	2.96e−02	4.39e−02	2.75e−05	**1.39e-05**
f8(x)	mean	1.22e + 04	3.49e + 05	1.61e−04	9.96e−35	**0.00e + 00**	**0.00e + 00**
	std	9.70e + 02	2.09e + 05	3.41e−05	1.42e−34	**0.00e + 00**	**0.00e + 00**

(*continued*)

Table 4. (*continued*)

Function		CS	MCSA	ASCSA	ECS	SDCS	ECSOW
f9(x)	mean	7.88e + 01	5.00e + 02	1.79e−03	3.20e + 01	**0.00e + 00**	**0.00e + 00**
	std	1.54e + 00	3.45e + 02	1.27e−03	4.31e + 00	**0.00e + 00**	**0.00e + 00**
f10(x)	mean	4.82e + 01	2.70e + 02	6.98e + 03	3.16e−02	**0.00e + 00**	**0.00e + 00**
	std	3.97e + 01	1.23e + 02	3.51e + 03	1.11e−02	**0.00e + 00**	**0.00e + 00**

Figures 2, 3, 4, 5, 6, and 7 show the convergence curves of the six algorithms run on the unimodal functions in 50-dimension and 100-dimension, respectively.

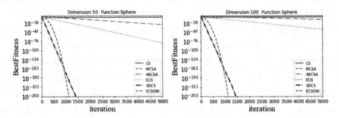

Fig. 2. Convergence curves on $f_1(x)$

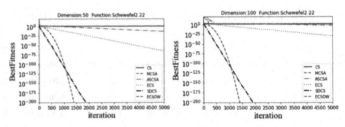

Fig. 3. Convergence curves on $f_6(x)$

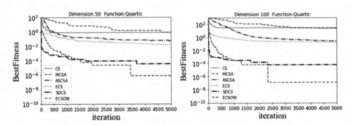

Fig. 4. Convergence curves on $f_7(x)$

As seen from Figs. 2, 3, 4, 5, 6, and 7, ECSOW converges significantly faster than the other five algorithms when run on six unimodal functions in both 50-dimension and

100-dimension; except for $f_7(x)$, ECSOW can converge to the theoretical optimum the shortest time.

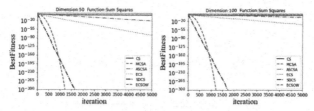

Fig. 5. Convergence curves on $f_8(x)$

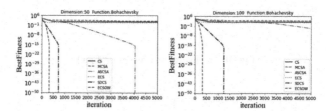

Fig. 6. Convergence curves on $f_9(x)$

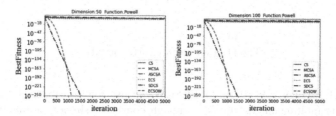

Fig. 7. Convergence curves on $f_{10}(x)$

Figures 8, 9, 10, 11 show the convergence curves of the six algorithms run on the multimodal functions in 50-dimension and 100-dimension, respectively.

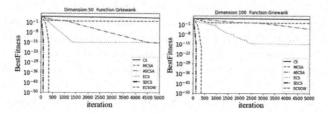

Fig. 8. Convergence curves on $f_2(x)$

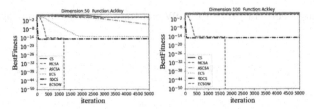

Fig. 9. Convergence curves on $f_3(x)$

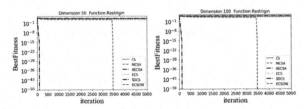

Fig. 10. Convergence curves on $f_4(x)$

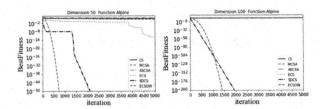

Fig. 11. Convergence curves on $f_5(x)$

As seen from Figs. 8, 9, 10 and 11, ECSOW can also converge to the global optimum when run on multimodal functions. Although converges slightly slower than SDCS algorithm on $f_2(x)$, ECSOW can converge to the theoretical optimum on $f_3(x)$, while SDCS algorithm falls into a local optimum on $f_3(x)$. It indicates ECSOW has a stronger global search capability than SDCS algorithm. When run on $f_4(x)$, ECSOW falls into a local optimum in the early and middle iteration, resulting in a slower convergence than SDCS algorithm, but can jump out of the local optimum and converge quickly in the late iteration. It reveals ECSOW has the superiority of local exploitation in the late stage.

The Wilcoxon test results shown in Table 5 further verify the above experimental results. Where the W column denotes the comparison result of ECSOW and the selected algorithms, ' +' means ECSOW is better than the selected algorithm in this case, '-' is the opposite, '≈' means the results of both algorithms are the same; the R column is the ranking of the mean of the solution accuracy; the Ave is average rank, and the Final is final rank.

As shown in Table 5, the rank of ECSAOW is 1 for all 10 functions, and the average and final rank are both first, indicating that ECSAOW outperforms all the other algorithms.

Table 5. The Wilcoxon test results

	dim	CS		MCSA		ASCSA		ECS		DCS		ECSOW
		W	R	W	R	W	R	W	R	W	R	R
$f_1(x)$	50	+	5	+	6	+	4	+	3	$\approx$	1	1
	100	+	5	+	6	+	4	+	3	$\approx$	1	1
$f_2(x)$	50	+	6	+	5	+	3	+	4	$\approx$	1	1
	100	+	6	+	5	+	3	+	4	$\approx$	1	1
$f_3(x)$	50	+	5	+	4	+	6	+	3	+	2	1
	100	+	4	+	5	+	6	+	3	+	2	1
$f_4(x)$	50	+	5	+	4	+	6	+	3	$\approx$	1	1
	100	+	5	+	4	+	6	+	3	$\approx$	1	1
$f_5(x)$	50	+	5	+	4	+	6	+	3	+	2	1
	100	+	4	+	5	+	6	+	3	$\approx$	1	1
$f_6(x)$	50	+	5	+	6	+	4	+	3	$\approx$	1	1
	100	+	5	+	6	+	4	+	3	$\approx$	1	1
$f_7(x)$	50	+	5	+	6	+	4	+	3	+	2	1
	100	+	5	+	6	+	4	+	3	+	2	1
$f_8(x)$	50	+	5	+	6	+	4	+	3	$\approx$	1	1
	100	+	5	+	6	+	4	+	3	$\approx$	1	1
$f_9(x)$	50	+	5	+	6	$\approx$	1	+	4	$\approx$	1	1
	100	+	5	+	6	+	3	+	4	$\approx$	1	1
$f_{10}(x)$	50	+	5	+	6	+	4	+	3	$\approx$	1	1
	100	+	4	+	5	+	6	+	3	$\approx$	1	1
Ave			4.95		5.35		4.40		3.20		1.25	1.00
Final			5		6		4		3		2	1

6 Conclusion

Aiming to overcome the shortcomings of CS algorithm, such as low search accuracy, easy premature convergence, and weak local search ability in the late stage, an improved CS algorithm, named ECSOW, was proposed. ECSOW is based on the global optimization strategy combining OBL and Levy flight, the dynamic adjustment strategy of inertia weight, and the local exploitation strategy of AO algorithm. In the early and middle iteration, ECSOW expands the search domain and increases population diversity by introducing OBL strategy to avoid falling into local optimum and premature convergence. In the random migration stage, ECSOW employs dynamic inertia weight to balance the effect of the current solution to avoid falling into the local optimum. In the late iteration, ECSOW introduces the local exploitation strategy of AO algorithm to improve convergence accuracy. The experimental results also show that ECSOW has a better global search ability, better local develop ability, faster convergence speed and better search accuracy than original CS algorithm and the four selected CS variants.

Acknowledgments. This work was supported by the National Natural Science Foundation of China (No. 62266019), and Jishou University Graduate Research and Innovation Project (No. JGY2022070).

References

1. Poli, R., Kennedy, J., Blackwell, T.: Particle swarm optimization. Swarm Intell. **1**(1), 33–57 (2007)
2. Dorigo, M., Maniezzo, V., Colorni, A.: Ant system: optimization by a colony of cooperating agents. IEEE Trans. System, Man, Cybernetics **26**(1), 29–41 (1996)
3. Karaboga, D., Basturk, B.: A powerful and efficient algorithm for numerical function optimization: artificial bee colony (ABC) algorithm. J. Global Optim. **39**(3), 459–471 (2007)
4. Mirjalili, S., Lewis, A.: The whale optimization algorithm. Adv. Eng. Softw. **95**(5), 51–67 (2016)
5. Mirjalili, S., Mirjalili, S., Lewis, A.: Grey wolf optimizer. Adv. Eng. Softw. **69**(3), 46–61 (2014)
6. Kang, D., Mo, L., Wang, F., et al.: Adaptive harmony search algorithm utilizing differential evolution and opposition-based learning. Math. Biosci. Eng. **18**(4), 4226–4246 (2021)
7. Wan, F., Ying, N., Huang, S., et al.: Study on efficiency improvement and capacity expansion of Nanwan reservoir based on improved cuckoo algorithm. Water Power **48**(02), 114–118 (2022)
8. Liu, M., Zheng, H., Liu Q., Xing, X., Dai, Y.: A backdoor embedding method for backdoor detection in deep neural networks. In: Wang, G., Choo, K.K.R., Ko, R.K.L., Xu, Y., Crispo, B. (eds): Ubiquitous Security. UbiSec 2021. Communications in Computer and Information Science, vol 1557, pp 1–12. Springer, Singapore (2022). https://doi.org/10.1007/978-981-19-0468-4_1
9. Yang, X., Deb, S.: Cuckoo search via Lévy flights. World Congress on Nature & Biologically Inspired Computing. IEEE (2009)
10. Valian, E., Mohanna, S., Tavakoli, S.: Improved cuckoo search algorithm for feedforward neural network training. Int. J. Artificial Intelligence & Appl. **2**(3), 36–43 (2011)
11. Yan, H., Xie, M., Zhao Q., et al.: New cuckoo search algorithm with parameter dynamic updating. J. Chinese Mini-Micro Computer Syst. 1–8 (2021)
12. Walton, S., Hassan, O., Morgan, K., et al.: Modified cuckoo search: a new gradient free optimization algorithm. Chaos, Solitons Fractals **44**(9), 710–718 (2011)
13. Chen, Y., Wang, N.: Cuckoo search algorithm with explosion operator for modeling proton exchange membrane fuel cells. Int. J. Hydrogen Energy **44**(5), 3075–3087 (2019)
14. Kamoona, A., Patra, J.: A novel enhanced cuckoo search algorithm for contrast enhancement of gray scale images. Appl. Soft Comput. **85**, 105749 (2019)
15. Huang, J., Gao, L.: A teaching–learning-based cuckoo search for constrained engineering design problems. Advances in Global Optimization. Springer, Cham, pp. 375-386 (2015)
16. Abualigah, L., Yousri, D., Abd, E., et al.: Aquila optimizer: a novel meta-heuristic optimization algorithm. Comput. Ind. Eng. **157**, 107250 (2021)
17. Yang, X.: Nature-Inspired Metaheuristic Algorithms. Luniver Press (2010)
18. Tizhoosh, H.: Opposition-Based Learning: A New Scheme for Machine Intelligence, Control & Automation. IEEE (2005)

19. Rahnamayan, S., Tizhoosh, H., Salama, M.: Opposition-based differential evolution. IEEE Trans. Evolutionary Comput. **12**(1), 64–79 (2008)
20. Ong, P., Zainuddin, Z.: Optimizing wavelet neural networks using modified cuckoo search for multi-step ahead chaotic time series prediction. Applied Soft Computing J. **80**, 374–386 (2019)
21. Li, R., Dai, R.: Adaptive step-size cuckoo search algorithm. Computer Science **44**(05), 235–240 (2017)
22. Rakhshani, H., Rahati, A.: Snap-drift cuckoo search: a novel cuckoo search optimization algorithm. Appl. Soft Comput. **52**, 771–794 (2017)

Empirical Likelihood for PLSIM with Missing Response Variables and Error-Prone Covariates

Xin Qi[1], Hongling Chen[1(✉)], and Qin Liu[2]

[1] Guangdong Polytechnic of Science and Technology, Zhuhai 519090, China
chling961@163.com
[2] College of Computer Science and Electronic Engineering, Hunan University, Changsha 410082, China
gracelq628@hnu.edu.cn

Abstract. A variety of data can be obtained through the Internet, but some data involves privacy and cannot be fully acquired. Privacy information hiding or missing problems frequently occur in many fields. In this paper, we consider some privacy missing data models and analysis problems. The empirical likelihood method is applied to study a partially linear single-index model that has the covariate X measured error and the response Y missing. The bias-corrected empirical log-likelihood ratio with asymptotic chi-square is derived, and the confidence regions are constructed. A few simulation experiments and an application to a real data set, in which some personal privacy information is hidden or missing, are conducted to illustrate our proposed method.

Keywords: Privacy missing-data · Information missing · Missing-data model · Measurement error · Partially linear single-index model

1 Introduction

We can obtain a variety of data through the Internet, but some data involves privacy and cannot be fully acquired. For example, it may be the salary data about the personal privacy information, so the response Y's can't be all acquired, and only part of Y's are available. In practice, privacy missing-data problems frequently occur in epidemiology studies, survey sampling, social science, and many other fields. So privacy missing-data model and analysis problems attract lots of attention, the research on missing-data model and analysis has become very popular. Relevant studies about privacy data problems have been done by Liu et al. (2022), Wang et al. (2022) and so on. Most of the works with missing-data problems have assumed that the covariates can be observed exactly. In fact, however, observations are often measured with errors. Therefore, it is necessary to study the models with error-prone covariates and missing response. In this paper, the missing response case is not only taken into account, but also some components of covariates with the measured error are allowed.

G. Wang et al. (Eds.): UbiSec 2022, CCIS 1768, pp. 456–470, 2023.
https://doi.org/10.1007/978-981-99-0272-9_31

The partially linear single-index model (PLSIM) can reduce the dimensionality and avoid the so-called "curse of dimensionality", therefore it has attracted much attention and been extensively studied. Relevant studies about PLSIM have been done by Xue and Zhang (2020), Zou et al. (2020), and many others. PLSIM is

$$Y = g(Z^{\mathsf{T}}\boldsymbol{\beta}) + X^{\mathsf{T}}\boldsymbol{\theta} + \varepsilon, \tag{1}$$

where Y is a response variable, $(Z, X) \in \mathbb{R}^p \times \mathbb{R}^q$ is covariate, $g(\cdot)$ is an unknown univariate link function, ε is a random error with $E(\varepsilon|Z, X) = 0$ almost surely, and $(\boldsymbol{\beta}, \boldsymbol{\theta})$ is an unknown vector in $\mathbb{R}^p \times \mathbb{R}^q$. For the identifiability of Model (1), we assume that $\|\boldsymbol{\beta}\| = 1$, where $\|\cdot\|$ denotes the Euclidean norm.

In this paper, it is assumed that the observation V is a substitute of X, $V = X + e$. The $\delta = 0$ indicates that Y is missing, otherwise $\delta = 1$. Assume that the measurement error e is independent from (Y, Z, X, δ) with $E(e) = 0$ and $Cov(e) = \Sigma_e$, and Σ_e is known at first, or else Σ_e can be estimated by the replicates of V (Liang et al. 1999). Throughout this paper, if X is observable, it can be assumed that the data missing mechanism is as follows: $p(\delta = 1|Y, Z, X) = p(\delta = 1|Z, X) = \pi(Z, X)$, for some unknown $\pi(Z, X)$. As Liang et al. (2007) pointed, Y is not missing at random without further assumptions, because X has measurement error, which is quite different from most studies of the missing data under the hypothesis of missing at random. Although this situation is more complicated, it frequently occurs in market research surveys, drug experiments, and other fields. For example, we considered a data set on manager performance in Subsect. 3.2. The role performance of the manager, which is the response variable Y, can be missing due to personal privacy. At the same time, the knowledge for the economic phases of the manager, which is the covariate variable X, is measured with error.

While Qi and Wang (2016) considered both the missing data problem and the measurement error problem in Model (1), their least-square method needs a large number of iterations to estimate parameters. Furthermore, there exists a deviation in the estimated regression coefficients caused by measurement error in semi-parametric models. To avoid these two problems, the empirical likelihood method is employed in this paper. The empirical likelihood method is introduced by Owen and has many excellent statistical properties (Owen 2001). It is universally acknowledged that the empirical likelihood method allows data to determine the shape of confidence regions, and also does not require to specify the asymptotic variance for constructing confidence regions. Therefore, the empirical likelihood method is a widely used statistical method and has been applied to many statistical models such as linear, nonparametric and semi-parametric models.

The following sections of this paper are organized as follows. Section 2 proposes the methodology for the construction of the empirical likelihood ratio, and derives the asymptotic result. In Sect. 3, some simulations are conducted to illustrate the proposed approach, and a real data set is discussed by our method, in which some personal privacy information is hidden or missing. Section 4 shows the proofs of the main result.

2 Methodology and Result

Let $\{Y_i, Z_i, V_i, \delta_i\}_{i=1}^n$ be independently and identically distributed.

2.1 Empirical Likelihood

To employ the empirical log-likelihood method to study $(\boldsymbol{\beta}, \boldsymbol{\theta})$, we need to use the link function $g(\cdot)$ and its derivative $g'(\cdot)$. Because $\|\boldsymbol{\beta}\| = 1$, the true value $\boldsymbol{\beta}$ is a boundary point on the unit sphere, and therefore $g'(Z_i^\mathsf{T}\boldsymbol{\beta})$ does not exist at the boundary point $\boldsymbol{\beta}$. For solving this problem, we adopt the "delete-one-component" method proposed by Yu and Ruppert (2002). This method is extensively used in semi-parameter models, and its details are as follows. Let $\boldsymbol{\beta} = (\beta_1, \beta_2, \ldots, \beta_p)^\mathsf{T}$ and $\boldsymbol{\beta}^{(r)} = (\beta_1, \ldots, \beta_{r-1}, \beta_{r+1}, \ldots, \beta_p)^\mathsf{T}$ be a $(p-1)$-dimensional parameter vector through deleting the rth component of $\boldsymbol{\beta}$. We assume $\beta_r > 0$; otherwise, consider $\beta_r = -(1 - \|\boldsymbol{\beta}^{(r)}\|^2)^{1/2}$. Then, $\boldsymbol{\beta} = (\beta_1, \ldots, \beta_{r-1}, (1 - \|\boldsymbol{\beta}^{(r)}\|^2)^{1/2}, \beta_{r+1}, \ldots, \beta_p)^\mathsf{T}$.

Since $\boldsymbol{\beta}$ can be derived by $\boldsymbol{\beta}^{(r)}$, only the empirical likelihood ratio of $(\boldsymbol{\beta}^{(r)}, \boldsymbol{\theta})$ needs to be taken into consideration. Moreover, $\|\boldsymbol{\beta}^{(r)}\| < 1$, which means that $\boldsymbol{\beta}$ is infinitely differentiable in a neighborhood of the parameter $\boldsymbol{\beta}^{(r)}$. Thus, the Jacobian matrix is $J_{\boldsymbol{\beta}^{(r)}} = (\gamma_1, \ldots, \gamma_p)^\mathsf{T}$, where $\gamma_s(1 \le s \le p, s \ne r)$ is a $(p-1)$-dimensional vector with the sth component being 1 and $\gamma_r = -(1 - \|\boldsymbol{\beta}^{(r)}\|^2)^{-1/2}\boldsymbol{\beta}^{(r)}$. In the following, the local linear smooth method is applied to obtain the estimators of $g(\cdot)$, $g'(\cdot)$, say $\hat{g}(\cdot)$, $\hat{g}'(\cdot)$. Let $K_{h_1}(\cdot) = K_1(\cdot/h_1)/h_1$, $K_1(\cdot)$ be a kernel function defined in $\mathbb{R}$ and $h_1 = h_1(n)$ be a bandwidth with $0 < h_1 \to 0$. For any fixed $(\boldsymbol{\beta}, \boldsymbol{\theta})$, it is easy to obtain

$$\hat{g}(t; \boldsymbol{\beta}, \boldsymbol{\theta}) = \sum_{i=1}^n W_{ni}(t; \boldsymbol{\beta})(Y_i - V_i^\mathsf{T}\boldsymbol{\theta}), \quad \hat{g}'(t; \boldsymbol{\beta}, \boldsymbol{\theta}) = \sum_{i=1}^n \widetilde{W}_{ni}(t; \boldsymbol{\beta})(Y_i - V_i^\mathsf{T}\boldsymbol{\theta}),$$

where

$$W_{ni}(t; \boldsymbol{\beta}) = \frac{n^{-1}\delta_i K_{h_1}(Z_i^\mathsf{T}\boldsymbol{\beta} - t)[S_{n,2}(t; \boldsymbol{\beta}) - (Z_i^\mathsf{T}\boldsymbol{\beta} - t)S_{n,1}(t; \boldsymbol{\beta})]}{S_{n,0}(t; \boldsymbol{\beta})S_{n,2}(t; \boldsymbol{\beta}) - S_{n,1}^2(t; \boldsymbol{\beta})}, \tag{2}$$

$$\widetilde{W}_{ni}(t; \boldsymbol{\beta}) = \frac{n^{-1}\delta_i K_{h_1}(Z_i^\mathsf{T}\boldsymbol{\beta} - t)[(Z_i^\mathsf{T}\boldsymbol{\beta} - t)S_{n,0}(t; \boldsymbol{\beta}) - S_{n,1}(t; \boldsymbol{\beta})]}{S_{n,0}(t; \boldsymbol{\beta})S_{n,2}(t; \boldsymbol{\beta}) - S_{n,1}^2(t; \boldsymbol{\beta})},$$

$$S_{n,l}(t; \boldsymbol{\beta}) = \frac{1}{n}\sum_{i=1}^n \delta_i K_{h_1}(Z_i^\mathsf{T}\boldsymbol{\beta} - t)(Z_i^\mathsf{T}\boldsymbol{\beta} - t)^l, \ l = 0, 1, 2.$$

With the enlightenment of Xue and Lian (2016), we introduce a bias-correction auxiliary random vector

$$\eta_i(\boldsymbol{\beta}^{(r)}, \boldsymbol{\theta}) = \frac{\delta_i}{s(Z_i)}\omega(Z_i^\mathsf{T}\boldsymbol{\beta})\{[Y_i - \hat{g}(Z_i^\mathsf{T}\boldsymbol{\beta}) - V_i^\mathsf{T}\boldsymbol{\theta}] \times [\hat{g}'(Z_i^\mathsf{T}\boldsymbol{\beta})(Z_i - \mu_1(Z_i^\mathsf{T}\boldsymbol{\beta}))^\mathsf{T}$$
$$\times J_{\boldsymbol{\beta}^{(r)}}, (V_i - \mu_2(Z_i^\mathsf{T}\boldsymbol{\beta}))^\mathsf{T}]^\mathsf{T} + [0, \boldsymbol{\theta}^\mathsf{T}\Sigma_e]^\mathsf{T}\}, \tag{3}$$

where $\omega(\cdot) = I\{f_\beta(\cdot) \geq c\}$ is a so-called trimming function which is expounded in the paper of Xue and Lian (2016) and c is a positive constant, $s(z) = E(\delta|Z = z)$, $\mu_1(t) = E(Z|Z^\mathsf{T}\beta = t)$, and $\mu_2(t) = E(X|Z^\mathsf{T}\beta = t) = E(V|Z^\mathsf{T}\beta = t)$.

Remark 2.1. When building the auxiliary random vector $\eta_i(\beta^{(r)}, \theta)$, we use $s(z)$ rather than $\pi(z, x)$ because X is observed with measurement errors and the exact X is not available for estimating $\pi(Z, X)$.

Remark 2.2. When building the auxiliary random vector $\eta_i(\beta^{(r)}, \theta)$, we use $\mu_1(t)$ and $\mu_2(t)$ to conditionally centralize Z and V to remove the need for under smoothing and derive the nonparametric version of the Wilk's theorem.

Remark 2.3. When building the auxiliary random vector $\eta_i(\beta^{(r)}, \theta)$, we add the term $[0, \theta^\mathsf{T}\Sigma_e]$ to avoid underestimation of parameters due to the measurement errors of X.

If (β, θ) is the true parameter, $E(\eta_i(\beta^{(r)}, \theta)) = 0$. Therefore, the empirical likelihood proposed by Owen (2001) is applied to construct the bias-corrected empirical log-likelihood ratio, which is

$$l_n(\beta^{(r)}, \theta) = -2\max\{\sum_{i=1}^{n}\log(np_i) : p_i \geq 0, \sum_{i=1}^{n}p_i = 1, \sum_{i=1}^{n}p_i\eta_i(\beta^{(r)}, \theta) = 0\}.$$

Since $s(\cdot)$, $\omega(\cdot)$, $\mu_1(\cdot)$, and $\mu_2(\cdot)$ are unknown, Formula (3) can not be applied directly. To replace them with their estimators is what researchers usually do. $\hat{s}(z)$ is the estimator of $s(z)$: $\hat{s}(z) = \sum_{i=1}^{n} W_{ni}^*(z)\delta_i$, $W_{ni}^*(z) = \frac{K^*(\frac{Z_i-z}{h_2})}{\sum_{j=1}^{n} K^*(\frac{Z_j-z}{h_2})}$, where $K^*(\cdot)$ is a kernel function defined in $\mathbb{R}^p$, and $h_2 = h_2(n)$ is a bandwidth with $0 < h_2 \to 0$. $\hat{\omega}(\cdot)$ is the estimator of $\omega(\cdot)$, $\hat{\omega}(z^\mathsf{T}\beta) = I\{\hat{f}_\beta(z^\mathsf{T}\beta) \geq c\}$, where $\hat{f}_\beta(\cdot)$ is a kernel estimator of the density function $f_\beta(\cdot)$ of $Z^\mathsf{T}\beta$, i.e., $\hat{f}_\beta(t) = \frac{1}{nh_3}\sum_{i=1}^{n} K_3(\frac{Z_i^\mathsf{T}\beta-t}{h_3})$, where $K_3(\cdot)$ is a kernel function, and $h_3 = h_3(n)$ is a bandwidth $0 < h_3 \to 0$. The trimming function $\omega(\cdot)$ can prevent small values from appearing in the denominators of $\hat{g}(\cdot)$ and $\hat{g}'(\cdot)$. In practice, quite often one may take $\omega(\cdot) = 1$, and the calculation is stable. The estimators of $\mu_1(t)$ and $\mu_2(t)$ are respectively given by $\hat{\mu}_1(t; \beta) = \sum_{i=1}^{n} W_{ni}(t; \beta)Z_i$, and $\hat{\mu}_2(t; \beta) = \sum_{i=1}^{n} W_{ni}(t; \beta)V_i$, where $W_{ni}(\cdot)$ is defined in (2).

Then an estimated auxiliary vector and an estimated bias-corrected empirical log-likelihood ratio can be respectively defined as:

$$\hat{\eta}_i(\beta^{(r)}, \theta) = \frac{\delta_i}{\hat{s}(Z_i)}\hat{\omega}(Z_i^\mathsf{T}\beta)\{[Y_i - \hat{g}(Z_i^\mathsf{T}\beta; \beta, \theta) - V_i^\mathsf{T}\theta] \times [\hat{g}'(Z_i^\mathsf{T}\beta; \beta, \theta)$$
$$\times(Z_i - \hat{\mu}_1(Z_i^\mathsf{T}\beta; \beta))^\mathsf{T} J_{\beta^{(r)}}, (V_i - \hat{\mu}_2(Z_i^\mathsf{T}\beta; \beta))^\mathsf{T}]^\mathsf{T} + [0, \theta^\mathsf{T}\Sigma_e]^\mathsf{T}\},$$

$$\hat{l}_n(\beta^{(r)}, \theta) = -2\max\{\sum_{i=1}^{n}\log(np_i) : p_i \geq 0, \sum_{i=1}^{n}p_i = 1, \sum_{i=1}^{n}p_i\hat{\eta}_i(\beta^{(r)}, \theta) = 0\}.$$

With the Lagrange Multiplier Method, $\hat{l}_n(\beta^{(r)}, \boldsymbol{\theta})$ can be represented as

$$\hat{l}_n(\beta^{(r)}, \boldsymbol{\theta}) = 2\sum_{i=1}^{n} \log\{1 + \lambda^{\mathsf{T}}\hat{\eta}_i(\beta^{(r)}, \boldsymbol{\theta})\}, \tag{4}$$

where $\lambda \in \mathbb{R}^{p+q-1}$ is determined by

$$\frac{1}{n}\sum_{i=1}^{n} \frac{\hat{\eta}_i(\beta^{(r)}, \boldsymbol{\theta})}{1 + \lambda^{\mathsf{T}}\hat{\eta}_i(\beta^{(r)}, \boldsymbol{\theta})} = 0. \tag{5}$$

2.2 Asymptotic Result

In this subsection, the main result of this paper is summarized. To state the asymptotic result, the following assumptions will be used.

($\mathbf{C_1}$) $f(z)$ is the density function of Z, which is bounded. There exist two positive constants a and b such that $\int_{u \in U(z,r_0) \cap \mathfrak{Z}} f(u)du \geq ar_0^p$, for all $r_0 \in (0, b]$ and $z \in \mathfrak{Z}$, where $\mathfrak{Z}$ is the support of Z and $U(z, r_0)$ is the closed sphere with center z and radius r_0.

($\mathbf{C_2}$) The bandwidth h_2 satisfies $nh_2^p/\log n \to \infty$ and $nh_2^{4\tau} \to 0$, where $\tau = \max\{2, p-1\}$, where p is the dimension of the parameter β.

($\mathbf{C_3}$) The function $K^*(\cdot)$ is a kernel of order τ, and there exist positive constants c_1, c_2 and ρ such that $c_1 I(\|u\| \leq \rho) \leq K^*(u) \leq c_2 I(\|u\| \leq \rho)$, where τ is defined in ($\mathbf{C_2}$).

($\mathbf{C_4}$) The function $s(z)$ has bounded partial derivatives up to order τ almost surely, and there exists a positive constant c_0 satisfying $\min_{1 \leq i \leq n} s(z) \geq c_0 > 0$, where τ is defined in ($\mathbf{C_2}$).

($\mathbf{C_5}$) The density function $f_\beta(t)$ of $Z^{\mathsf{T}}\beta$ satisfies Lebesgue measure on $\mathbb{R}$ for every $\beta \in \mathfrak{B} \subset \mathbb{R}^p$ and the Lipschitz condition of order 1 on $\mathcal{T}$, where $\mathcal{T} = \{t = z^{\mathsf{T}}\beta : z \in \mathfrak{Z}\}$. There exist a positive constant c_0 and a positive integer k_0 such that the set $\{t : f_\beta(t) = c\}$ has at most k_0 elements, for any $c_0 \geq c > 0$ and $\beta \in \mathfrak{B}$.

($\mathbf{C_6}$) $g(\cdot)$, $\mu_{1s}(\cdot)$, and $\mu_{2k}(\cdot)$ have two bounded and continuous derivatives, where $\mu_{1s}(\cdot)$ and $\mu_{2k}(\cdot)$ are the sth and kth components of $\mu_1(\cdot)$ and $\mu_2(\cdot)$, $1 \leq s \leq p$, $1 \leq k \leq q$, respectively.

($\mathbf{C_7}$) The kernels $K_1(\cdot)$ and $K_3(\cdot)$ are symmetric density functions with bounded derivatives and supported on $(-1, 1)$.

($\mathbf{C_8}$) $\sup_{z,x} E(\varepsilon^2|Z = z, X = x) < \infty$, $\sup_z E(\varepsilon^4|Z = z) < \infty$, $E(\|e\|^4) < \infty$, $E(\|Z\|^4) < \infty$, and $\sup_{t \in \mathcal{T}} E(\|X\|^2|Z^{\mathsf{T}}\beta = t) < \infty$.

($\mathbf{C_9}$) $nh_1^3 \to \infty$, $nh_1^8 \to 0$, and $\frac{nh_1^3}{\log n} \to \infty$.

($\mathbf{C_{10}}$) $V(\beta^{(r)}, \boldsymbol{\theta}) = E\{(\varepsilon - e^{\mathsf{T}}\boldsymbol{\theta})^2 \frac{1}{s(Z)}\omega(Z^{\mathsf{T}}\beta)\tilde{\Lambda}\tilde{\Lambda}^{\mathsf{T}}\} + E\{\frac{1}{s(Z)}\omega(Z^{\mathsf{T}}\beta)\Gamma\Gamma^{\mathsf{T}}\}$ is a positive definite matrix, where $\tilde{\Lambda} = [g'(Z^{\mathsf{T}}\beta)(Z - \mu_1(Z^{\mathsf{T}}\beta))^{\mathsf{T}}J_{\beta^{(r)}}, (X - \mu_2(Z^{\mathsf{T}}\beta))^{\mathsf{T}}]^{\mathsf{T}}$ and $\Gamma = [0, e^{\mathsf{T}}\varepsilon - (ee^{\mathsf{T}} - \Sigma_e)\boldsymbol{\theta}]^{\mathsf{T}}$.

Theorem 1. *Assume that* $(\mathbf{C_1})$–$(\mathbf{C_{10}})$ *are satisfied. If* $(\beta^{(r)}, \boldsymbol{\theta})$ *is the true value of the parameter, and* $\beta_r > 0$, *then*

$$\hat{l}_n(\beta^{(r)}, \boldsymbol{\theta}) \xrightarrow{L} \chi^2_{p+q-1},$$

where $\xrightarrow{L}$ *means convergence in distribution.*

Based on Theorem 1, $\hat{l}_n(\beta^{(r)}, \boldsymbol{\theta})$ can be applied to construct a confidence region for $(\beta^{(r)}, \boldsymbol{\theta})$. For any given $0 < \alpha < 1$, there exists c_α that makes $P(\chi^2_{p+q-1} > c_\alpha) = \alpha$ tenable, and then $I_\alpha(\beta^{(r)}, \boldsymbol{\theta}) = \{(\beta^{(r)}, \boldsymbol{\theta}) | \hat{l}_n(\beta^{(r)}, \boldsymbol{\theta}) < c_\alpha, \|\beta^{(r)}\| < 1\}$ is a confidence region of $(\beta^{(r)}, \boldsymbol{\theta})$ with asymptotically correct coverage probability $1 - \alpha$.

3 Numerical Examples

3.1 Simulation

This section aims to report the finite-sample performances of the proposed method. The set of data is generated from the following model:

$$Y_i = \sin\left(\pi \cdot \frac{(Z_i^{\mathsf{T}}\beta)^2 - A}{B - A}\right) + X_i\theta + \varepsilon_i, V_i = X_i + e_i, 1 \leq i \leq n, \qquad (6)$$

where $\beta = \frac{1}{\sqrt{2}}(1, 1)^{\mathsf{T}}$, $\theta = 0.5$, $X_i \sim N(0, 1)$, $\varepsilon_i \sim N(0, 0.04)$, $e_i \sim N(0, 0.01)$, the Z_i are bivariate with independent $U(0, 1)$ components, $A = \frac{\sqrt{3}}{2} - 1.645 \times \frac{1}{\sqrt{12}}$ and $B = \frac{\sqrt{3}}{2} + 1.645 \times \frac{1}{\sqrt{12}}$. The kernel function $K_i(t) = \frac{15}{16}(1 - t^2)^2$ if $|t| \leq 1$ (i = 1, 3) is used, and $K^*(z_1, z_2)$ is taken as $K_0(z_1)K_0(z_2)$, where $K_0(z) = \frac{3}{4}(1 - z^2)^2$ if $|z| \leq 1$. The above kernel functions satisfy $(\mathbf{C_3})$ and $(\mathbf{C_7})$. And take $\hat{\omega}(\cdot) = 1$. The choice of bandwidths is quite significant, which determines the quality of the adjusted curve. The least-squares cross-validation (LSCV) method is applied to choose the bandwidths in this section.

Accuracy Analysis. In this part, the coverage probabilities and average lengths of confidence intervals are calculated by the proposed empirical likelihood (EL) method and the normal approximation (NA) method. Based on Model (6), the following three data missing situations of the response are considered:

Case 1: $P(\delta = 1 | Z = z, X = x) = 0.6 + 0.1(|z^{\mathsf{T}}\beta - 0.5| + |x - 1|)$ if $|z^{\mathsf{T}}\beta - 0.5| + |x - 1| \leq 1.5$, and 0.61 elsewhere;

Case 2: $P(\delta = 1 | Z = z, X = x) = 0.8 - 0.1(|z^{\mathsf{T}}\beta - 0.5| + |x - 1|)$ if $|z^{\mathsf{T}}\beta - 0.5| + |x - 1| \leq 1$, and 0.83 elsewhere;

Case 3: $P(\delta = 1 | Z = z, X = x) = 0.8 + 0.2(|z^{\mathsf{T}}\beta - 0.5| + |x - 1|)$ if $|z^{\mathsf{T}}\beta - 0.5| + |x - 1| \leq 2$, and 0.90 elsewhere.

The average missing rates (Δ) are 0.35, 0.20, and 0.05, respectively. For each case, 1000 random samples of size n = 50, 100, 150, 200 are generated.

Our study focuses on the confidence intervals of (β_1, θ) because $\beta_1 = \beta_2$. The coverage probabilities and average lengths of confidence intervals based on confidence level 0.90 are presented in Table 1 and Table 2.

From Table 1 and Table 2, the following results can be obtained. The coverage probabilities of EL and NA are almost close to 90%. The EL method has slightly higher coverage probabilities, compared with the NA method, but the confidence intervals are widened accordingly. With a fixed missing rate, as the sample size n increases, the coverage probabilities are closer to the confidence level 0.90, and the confidence intervals are narrower. With fixed sample size n, as the missing rate increases, the coverage probabilities are away from the confidence level 0.90, and the confidence intervals become wider. It can be seen that the coverage probabilities and the confidence intervals are affected by the missing rate.

Table 1. The coverage probabilities of the confidence intervals for (β_1, θ) with the confidence level 0.90.

n	$\Delta = 0.35$		$\Delta = 0.20$		$\Delta = 0.05$	
	EL	NA	EL	NA	EL	NA
50	0.935	0.808	0.925	0.806	0.925	0.822
100	0.918	0.833	0.917	0.838	0.917	0.843
150	0.917	0.861	0.911	0.865	0.911	0.863
200	0.910	0.874	0.908	0.873	0.906	0.873

Table 2. The average lengths of the confidence intervals for (β_1, θ) with the confidence level 0.90.

Δ	n	β_1		θ	
		EL	NA	EL	NA
0.35	50	0.2403	0.2386	0.4967	0.4735
	100	0.1047	0.1028	0.2546	0.2312
	150	0.1005	0.0987	0.1656	0.1438
	200	0.0691	0.0673	0.1067	0.0601
0.20	50	0.2088	0.2061	0.4030	0.3821
	100	0.1023	0.1002	0.2318	0.2167
	150	0.0699	0.0667	0.1578	0.1402
	200	0.0596	0.0574	0.0980	0.0796
0.05	50	0.1982	0.1963	0.3021	0.2819
	100	0.0977	0.0960	0.2205	0.1998
	150	0.0600	0.0584	0.1533	0.1334
	200	0.0505	0.0487	0.0976	0.0778

Figure 1 plots the EL confidence region for (β_1, θ) based on confidence level 0.95 when the sample size is 100 and the average missing rates are 0.35 (solid curve), 0.20 (dashed curve), 0.05 (dotted-dashed curve) respectively.

Robust Analysis. To investigate the robustness of the EL method by choosing different ε_i in Model (6). We conduct simulations under three scenarios as follows:

Scenario I: Let ε_i be contaminated by some external factors and follow another normal distribution, namely: $\varepsilon_i \sim (1 - \varsigma_i)N(0, 0.04) + \varsigma_i N(0, 0.16)$, where ς_i is a 0–1 random variable with $P(\varsigma_i = 1) = 1 - P(\varsigma_i = 0) = 0.02$;

Scenario II: Let ε_i be contaminated by some external factors and follow another normal distribution, namely: $\varepsilon_i \sim (1 - \varsigma_i)N(0, 0.04) + \varsigma_i N(0, 1)$, where ς_i is a 0–1 random variable with $P(\varsigma_i = 1) = 1 - P(\varsigma_i = 0) = 0.05$;

Scenario III: Let $\varepsilon_i \sim t(2)$.

The coverage probabilities of confidence intervals for (β_1, θ) based on the EL method for Model (6) and three different contaminated samples are reported in Table 3 with the normal level 0.95. Through comparing the results presented in Table 3, we can see that the coverage probabilities have no obvious change with the change of the degree of contamination. Overall, our simulation studies indicate that the empirical likelihood method is robust.

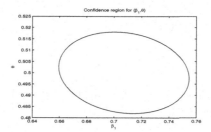

Fig. 1. Confidence regions for (β_1, θ) of Model (6) with confidence level 0.95.

Table 3. The coverage probabilities of the confidence intervals for (β_1, θ) based on Model (6) and changed samples with the confidence level 0.95.

Δ	n	Model (6)	Scenario I	Scenario II	Scenario III
0.05	50	0.967	0.967	0.974	0.967
	100	0.962	0.962	0.962	0.965
	150	0.957	0.960	0.959	0.958
	200	0.955	0.957	0.957	0.957

3.2   A Real Data Example

In this part, the empirical likelihood method will be employed in constructing the confidence regions of a real data set, in which response variables involved in personal privacy are missing. The real data arises from an experiment that has the situation of 98 managers from Iowa farmer cooperatives. Using the partially linear single-index EV model, Chen and Cui (2009) have analyzed this example without missing responses. The role performance of the manager is the response variable Y. The covariates are the knowledge for the economic phases of the manager (KEPM), the value orientation (VO), and the role satisfaction (RS). In our notation, $Z = (VO, RS)$, X is KEPM measured with error. According to Chen and Cui (2009), the error variance was estimated at 0.0203 with the replicated method. To use the proposed method, we assume that 10% of the Y value is missing. Figure 2 shows the 90% confidence regions for (β_{RS}, θ) via using the empirical likelihood method.

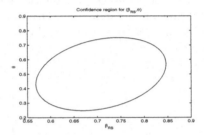

Fig. 2. Confidence regions for (β_{RS}, θ) of the real data with confidence level 0.90.

4   Proofs

Before embarking on the proof of Theorem 1, some proofs of lemmas are presented in the research. As the proofs of Lemmas 1 and 2 are similar to Xue and Lian (2016), and the proofs of Lemmas 3, 4, and 8 are similar to Zhu and Xue (2006), we omit the details here.

Lemma 1. Assume that $(\mathbf{C_1})$–$(\mathbf{C_3})$ hold. Then there exist positive constants c_3 and c_4 such that

$$c_3 \leq \min_{1 \leq i \leq n} \hat{f}(Z_i) \leq \max_{1 \leq i \leq n} \hat{f}(Z_i) \leq c_4, \ a.s.,$$

where $\hat{f}(\cdot)$ is the estimator of $f(\cdot)$, namely $\hat{f}(z) = \frac{1}{nh_2^p} \sum_{i=1}^{n} K^*(\frac{Z_i - z}{h_2})$.

Lemma 2. Assume that $(\mathbf{C_1})$–$(\mathbf{C_4})$ hold. Then

$$\max_{1 \leq i \leq n} |\hat{s}(Z_i) - s(Z_i)| = O((nh_2/\log n)^{-1/2}) + O(h_3^\tau), a.s..$$

Lemma 3. Assume that $(\mathbf{C_5})$–$(\mathbf{C_7})$ hold. If $h_1 = cn^{-\vartheta}, 0 < \vartheta < \frac{1}{2}, c > 0$, then for any integer $r \geq 2$, we have, uniformly over $1 \leq i \leq n$,

$$\begin{cases} E\{\omega(Z_i^{\mathsf{T}}\boldsymbol{\beta})|W_{ni}(Z_i^{\mathsf{T}}\boldsymbol{\beta};\boldsymbol{\beta})|^r\} = O((nh_1)^{-r}), \\ E\{\omega(Z_i^{\mathsf{T}}\boldsymbol{\beta})\sum_{j=1,j\neq i}^n |W_{nj}(Z_i^{\mathsf{T}}\boldsymbol{\beta};\boldsymbol{\beta})|^r\} = O((nh_1)^{1-r}), \end{cases}$$

$$\begin{cases} E\{\omega(Z_i^{\mathsf{T}}\boldsymbol{\beta})|\widetilde{W}_{ni}(Z_i^{\mathsf{T}}\boldsymbol{\beta};\boldsymbol{\beta})|^r\} = O((nh_1)^{-r}) + O((n^3 h_1^5)^{-r/2}), \\ E\{\omega(Z_i^{\mathsf{T}}\boldsymbol{\beta})\sum_{j=1,j\neq i}^n |\widetilde{W}_{nj}(Z_i^{\mathsf{T}}\boldsymbol{\beta};\boldsymbol{\beta})|^r\} = O(n^{1-r}h_1^{1-2r}). \end{cases}$$

Lemma 4. Assume that $(\mathbf{C_5})$–$(\mathbf{C_9})$ hold. Then for any integer $2 \leq r \leq 4$, we have, uniformly over $1 \leq i \leq n$,

$$E\{\omega(Z_i^{\mathsf{T}}\boldsymbol{\beta})|\hat{\varphi}(Z_i^{\mathsf{T}}\boldsymbol{\beta};\boldsymbol{\beta},\boldsymbol{\theta}) - \varphi(Z_i^{\mathsf{T}}\boldsymbol{\beta})|^r\} = O(h_1^{2r}) + O(n^{-\frac{r}{2}}h_1^{1-r}),$$

$$E\{\omega(Z_i^{\mathsf{T}}\boldsymbol{\beta})|\hat{g}'(Z_i^{\mathsf{T}}\boldsymbol{\beta};\boldsymbol{\beta},\boldsymbol{\theta}) - g'(Z_i^{\mathsf{T}}\boldsymbol{\beta})|^r\} = O(h_1^r) + O(n^{-\frac{r}{2}}h_1^{1-2r}),$$

where $\hat{\varphi}(\cdot) = \hat{g}(\cdot), \hat{\mu}_{1s}(\cdot), \hat{\mu}_{2k}(\cdot)$, and $\varphi(\cdot) = g(\cdot), \mu_{1s}(\cdot), \mu_{2k}(\cdot)$. $\hat{\varphi}(\cdot)$ is the estimator of $\varphi(\cdot)$.

Lemma 5. Suppose that $(\mathbf{C_5}), (\mathbf{C_7})$ *and* $(\mathbf{C_9})$ hold. Then

$$\max_{1\leq i\leq n} |\hat{f}_{\boldsymbol{\beta}}(Z_i^{\mathsf{T}}\boldsymbol{\beta}) - f(Z_i^{\mathsf{T}}\boldsymbol{\beta})| \to 0, \quad a.s..$$

The Proof of Lemma 5. Let P_t and E_t be the conditional probability and conditional expectation given $t = Z^{\mathsf{T}}\boldsymbol{\beta}$, respectively. Then,

$$\max_{1\leq i\leq n} \left|\hat{f}_{\boldsymbol{\beta}}(t_i) - f_{\boldsymbol{\beta}}(t_i)\right|$$

$$\leq \max_{1\leq i\leq n} \left|\hat{f}_{\boldsymbol{\beta}}(t_i) - E_{t_i}\{\hat{f}_{\boldsymbol{\beta}}(t_i)\}\right| + \max_{1\leq i\leq n} \left|E_{t_i}\{\hat{f}_{\boldsymbol{\beta}}(t_i)\} - E_{t_i}\{f_{\boldsymbol{\beta}}(t_i)\}\right|. \quad (7)$$

By the Bernstein Inequality in Serfling (1980), for any $\varepsilon_n > 0$, we derive that

$$P\left(\max_{1\leq i\leq n} |\hat{f}_{\boldsymbol{\beta}}(t_i) - E_{t_i}\{\hat{f}_{\boldsymbol{\beta}}(t_i)\}| > \varepsilon_n\right) \leq \sum_{i=1}^n P\left(|\hat{f}_{\boldsymbol{\beta}}(t_i) - E_{t_i}\{\hat{f}_{\boldsymbol{\beta}}(t_i)\}| > \varepsilon_n\right)$$

$$\leq \sum_{i=1}^n EP_{t_i}\left(\left|\sum_{i=1}^n \left[K_3\left(\frac{t_j - t_i}{h_3}\right) - E_{t_i}K_3\left(\frac{t_j - t_i}{h_3}\right)\right]\right| > \varepsilon_n nh_3\right) \leq 2n\exp(-cnh_3) \leq cn^{-2}.$$

Using the Borel-Cantelli Lemma, we get

$$\max_{1\leq i\leq n} |\hat{f}_{\boldsymbol{\beta}}(t_i) - E_{t_i}\{\hat{f}_{\boldsymbol{\beta}}(t_i)\}| = o(1), \quad a.s.. \quad (8)$$

On the other hand, we have $\sup_{t_i} \left|E_{t_i}\{\hat{f}_{\boldsymbol{\beta}}(t_i)\} - E_{t_i}\{f_{\boldsymbol{\beta}}(t_i)\}\right| = O_p\left(\left\{\frac{\log n}{nh_3}\right\}^{\frac{1}{2}} + h_3^2\right)$. Invoking the Borel-Cantelli Lemma, we obtain $\max_{1\leq i\leq n} |E_{t_i}\{\hat{f}_{\boldsymbol{\beta}}(t_i)\} - E_{t_i}\{f_{\boldsymbol{\beta}}(t_i)\}| = o(1)$, $a.s..$ This together with (7) and (8) proves Lemma 5.

Lemma 6. Assume that $(\mathbf{C_1})$–$(\mathbf{C_{10}})$ hold, $(\boldsymbol{\beta}^{(r)}, \boldsymbol{\theta})$ is the true value of the parameter, and $\beta_r > 0$, then

$$\frac{1}{\sqrt{n}} \sum_{i=1}^{n} \hat{\eta}_i(\boldsymbol{\beta}^{(r)}, \boldsymbol{\theta}) \xrightarrow{L} N(0, V(\boldsymbol{\beta}^{(r)}, \boldsymbol{\theta})), \tag{9}$$

$$\frac{1}{n} \sum_{i=1}^{n} \hat{\eta}_i(\boldsymbol{\beta}^{(r)}, \boldsymbol{\theta}) \hat{\eta}_i^{\mathsf{T}}(\boldsymbol{\beta}^{(r)}, \boldsymbol{\theta}) \xrightarrow{P} V(\boldsymbol{\beta}^{(r)}, \boldsymbol{\theta}), \tag{10}$$

where $V(\boldsymbol{\beta}^{(r)}, \boldsymbol{\theta})$ is defined in $(\mathbf{C_{10}})$ and $\xrightarrow{P}$ means convergence in probability.

The Proof of Lemma 6. Because the proof of (10) is similar to (9), we only prove (9) here. By Lemma 5, it follows that

$$\frac{1}{\sqrt{n}} \sum_{i=1}^{n} \hat{\eta}_i(\boldsymbol{\beta}^{(r)}, \boldsymbol{\theta}) = \frac{1}{\sqrt{n}} \sum_{i=1}^{n} \tilde{\eta}_i(\boldsymbol{\beta}^{(r)}, \boldsymbol{\theta}) + o_p\left(\frac{1}{\sqrt{n}} \sum_{i=1}^{n} \tilde{\eta}_i(\boldsymbol{\beta}^{(r)}, \boldsymbol{\theta})\right), \tag{11}$$

where $\tilde{\eta}_i(\boldsymbol{\beta}^{(r)}, \boldsymbol{\theta})$ is obtained by substituting $\hat{\omega}(Z_i^{\mathsf{T}}\boldsymbol{\beta})$ of $\hat{\eta}_i(\boldsymbol{\beta}^{(r)}, \boldsymbol{\theta})$ with $\omega(Z_i^{\mathsf{T}}\boldsymbol{\beta})$. Therefore, in order to obtain (9), we only need to prove

$$\frac{1}{\sqrt{n}} \sum_{i=1}^{n} \tilde{\eta}_i(\boldsymbol{\beta}^{(r)}, \boldsymbol{\theta}) \xrightarrow{L} N(0, V(\boldsymbol{\beta}^{(r)}, \boldsymbol{\theta})). \tag{12}$$

Thus,

$$\frac{1}{\sqrt{n}} \sum_{i=1}^{n} \tilde{\eta}_i(\boldsymbol{\beta}^{(r)}, \boldsymbol{\theta}) =: \frac{1}{\sqrt{n}} \sum_{i=1}^{n} \frac{\delta_i}{s(Z_i)} \omega(Z_i^{\mathsf{T}}\boldsymbol{\beta}) \{(\Lambda_i - E(\Lambda_i | Z_i^{\mathsf{T}}\boldsymbol{\beta})(\varepsilon_i - e_i^{\mathsf{T}}\boldsymbol{\beta}) + \Gamma_i\} + \sum_{k=1}^{5} M_k,$$

where $\Lambda_i = [g'(Z_i^{\mathsf{T}}\boldsymbol{\beta}) Z_i^{\mathsf{T}} J_{\boldsymbol{\beta}^{(r)}}, X_i^{\mathsf{T}}]^{\mathsf{T}}$, $\Gamma_i = [0, e_i^{\mathsf{T}}\varepsilon_i - (e_i e_i^{\mathsf{T}} - \Sigma_e)\boldsymbol{\theta}]^{\mathsf{T}}$, $M_1 = (M_{11}^{\mathsf{T}} J_{\boldsymbol{\beta}^{(r)}}, M_{12}^{\mathsf{T}})^{\mathsf{T}}$, $M_2 = (M_{21}^{\mathsf{T}} J_{\boldsymbol{\beta}^{(r)}}, O_{1 \times q})^{\mathsf{T}}$, $M_3 = (M_{31}^{\mathsf{T}} J_{\boldsymbol{\beta}^{(r)}}, M_{32}^{\mathsf{T}})^{\mathsf{T}}$, $M_4 = (M_{41}^{\mathsf{T}} J_{\boldsymbol{\beta}^{(r)}}, O_{1 \times q})^{\mathsf{T}}$, $M_5 = \frac{1}{\sqrt{n}} \sum_{i=1}^{n} \left\{\frac{1}{\hat{s}(Z_i)} - \frac{1}{s(Z_i)}\right\} \delta_i \omega(Z_i^{\mathsf{T}}\boldsymbol{\beta}) \{[Y_i - \hat{g}(Z_i^{\mathsf{T}}\boldsymbol{\beta}; \boldsymbol{\beta}, \boldsymbol{\theta}) - V_i^{\mathsf{T}}\boldsymbol{\theta}] \times [\hat{g}'(Z_i^{\mathsf{T}}\boldsymbol{\beta}; \boldsymbol{\beta}, \boldsymbol{\theta})(Z_i - \hat{\mu}_1(Z_i^{\mathsf{T}}\boldsymbol{\beta}; \boldsymbol{\beta}))^{\mathsf{T}} J_{\boldsymbol{\beta}^{(r)}}, (V_i - \hat{\mu}_2(Z_i^{\mathsf{T}}\boldsymbol{\beta}; \boldsymbol{\beta}))^{\mathsf{T}}]^{\mathsf{T}} + [0, \boldsymbol{\theta}^{\mathsf{T}}\Sigma_e]^{\mathsf{T}}\}.$

$$M_{11} = \frac{1}{\sqrt{n}} \sum_{i=1}^{n} [\mu_1(Z_i^{\mathsf{T}}\boldsymbol{\beta}) - \hat{\mu}_1(Z_i^{\mathsf{T}}\boldsymbol{\beta}; \boldsymbol{\beta})] g'(Z_i^{\mathsf{T}}\boldsymbol{\beta})(\varepsilon_i - e_i^{\mathsf{T}}\boldsymbol{\theta}) \frac{\delta_i}{s(Z_i)} \omega(Z_i^{\mathsf{T}}\boldsymbol{\beta}),$$

$$M_{12} = \frac{1}{\sqrt{n}} \sum_{i=1}^{n} [\mu_2(Z_i^{\mathsf{T}}\boldsymbol{\beta}) - \hat{\mu}_2(Z_i^{\mathsf{T}}\boldsymbol{\beta}; \boldsymbol{\beta})](\varepsilon_i - e_i^{\mathsf{T}}\boldsymbol{\theta}) \frac{\delta_i}{s(Z_i)} \omega(Z_i^{\mathsf{T}}\boldsymbol{\beta}),$$

$$M_{21} = \frac{1}{\sqrt{n}} \sum_{i=1}^{n} [\hat{g}'(Z_i^{\mathsf{T}}\boldsymbol{\beta}; \boldsymbol{\beta}, \boldsymbol{\theta}) - g'(Z_i^{\mathsf{T}}\boldsymbol{\beta})] \cdot [Z_i - \hat{\mu}_1(Z_i^{\mathsf{T}}\boldsymbol{\beta}; \boldsymbol{\beta})](\varepsilon_i - e_i^{\mathsf{T}}\boldsymbol{\theta}) \frac{\delta_i}{s(Z_i)} \omega(Z_i^{\mathsf{T}}\boldsymbol{\beta}),$$

$$M_{31} = \frac{1}{\sqrt{n}} \sum_{i=1}^{n} [g(Z_i^{\mathsf{T}}\boldsymbol{\beta}) - \hat{g}(Z_i^{\mathsf{T}}\boldsymbol{\beta};\boldsymbol{\beta},\boldsymbol{\theta})] \cdot [Z_i - \hat{\mu}_1(Z_i^{\mathsf{T}}\boldsymbol{\beta};\boldsymbol{\beta})] g'(Z_i^{\mathsf{T}}\boldsymbol{\beta}) \frac{\delta_i}{s(Z_i)} \omega(Z_i^{\mathsf{T}}\boldsymbol{\beta}),$$

$$M_{32} = \frac{1}{\sqrt{n}} \sum_{i=1}^{n} [g(Z_i^{\mathsf{T}}\boldsymbol{\beta}) - \hat{g}(Z_i^{\mathsf{T}}\boldsymbol{\beta};\boldsymbol{\beta},\boldsymbol{\theta})] \cdot [V_i - \hat{\mu}_2(Z_i^{\mathsf{T}}\boldsymbol{\beta};\boldsymbol{\beta})] \frac{\delta_i}{s(Z_i)} \omega(Z_i^{\mathsf{T}}\boldsymbol{\beta}),$$

$$M_{41} = \frac{1}{\sqrt{n}} \sum_{i=1}^{n} [g(Z_i^{\mathsf{T}}\boldsymbol{\beta}) - \hat{g}(Z_i^{\mathsf{T}}\boldsymbol{\beta};\boldsymbol{\beta},\boldsymbol{\theta})] \cdot [\hat{g}'(Z_i^{\mathsf{T}}\boldsymbol{\beta};\boldsymbol{\beta},\boldsymbol{\theta}) - g'(Z_i^{\mathsf{T}}\boldsymbol{\beta})] \cdot [Z_i - \hat{\mu}_1(Z_i^{\mathsf{T}}\boldsymbol{\beta};\boldsymbol{\beta})] \frac{\delta_i}{s(Z_i)} \omega(Z_i^{\mathsf{T}}\boldsymbol{\beta}).$$

Using the central limit theorem and $(\mathbf{C_{10}})$, we have

$$\frac{1}{\sqrt{n}} \sum_{i=1}^{n} \frac{\delta_i}{s(Z_i)} \omega(Z_i^{\mathsf{T}}\boldsymbol{\beta})\{(\Lambda_i - E(\Lambda_i|Z_i^{\mathsf{T}}\boldsymbol{\beta})(\varepsilon_i - e_i^{\mathsf{T}}\boldsymbol{\beta}) + \Gamma_i\} \xrightarrow{L} N(0, V(\boldsymbol{\beta}^{(r)}, \boldsymbol{\theta})). \quad (13)$$

To prove (12), we only need to infer $M_v \xrightarrow{P} 0 (v = 1, 2, 3, 4, 5)$.

Firstly, we consider M_{11}. Let $M_{11,s}$ denote the sth component of M_{11}. From Lemma 4 and the Cauchy-Schwarz inequality, we get

$$E(M_{11,s}^2) \le cn^{-1} E\{\sum_{i=1}^{n} \omega(Z_i^{\mathsf{T}}\boldsymbol{\beta})[\mu_{1s}(Z_i^{\mathsf{T}}\boldsymbol{\beta}) - \hat{\mu}_{1s}(Z_i^{\mathsf{T}}\boldsymbol{\beta};\boldsymbol{\beta})]^2 g'(Z_i^{\mathsf{T}}\boldsymbol{\beta})^2 E[(\varepsilon_i - e_i^{\mathsf{T}}\boldsymbol{\theta})^2|Z_i]\}$$

$$\le ch_1^4 + c(nh_1)^{-1} \to 0.$$

This yields $M_{11} \to 0$, and similarly $M_{12} \to 0$. Therefore, we obtain

$$M_1 \xrightarrow{P} 0. \quad (14)$$

Secondly, we consider M_{21}. Let $M_{21,s}$ denote the sth component of M_{21} and $\tilde{Z}_{is} = Z_{is} - \hat{\mu}_{1s}(Z_i^{\mathsf{T}}\boldsymbol{\beta};\boldsymbol{\beta})$. By a straightforward calculation,

$$M_{21,s} = \frac{1}{\sqrt{n}} \sum_{i=1}^{n} [\sum_{j=1}^{n} \widetilde{W}_{nj}(Z_i^{\mathsf{T}}\boldsymbol{\beta};\boldsymbol{\beta}) g(Z_j^{\mathsf{T}}\boldsymbol{\beta}) - g'(Z_i^{\mathsf{T}}\boldsymbol{\beta})] \cdot \tilde{Z}_{is}(\varepsilon_i - e_i^{\mathsf{T}}\boldsymbol{\theta}) \frac{\delta_i}{s(Z_i)} \omega(Z_i^{\mathsf{T}}\boldsymbol{\beta})$$

$$+ \frac{1}{\sqrt{n}} \sum_{i=1}^{n} \sum_{j=1}^{n} \widetilde{W}_{nj}(Z_i^{\mathsf{T}}\boldsymbol{\beta};\boldsymbol{\beta}) \cdot \tilde{Z}_{is}(\varepsilon_i - e_i^{\mathsf{T}}\boldsymbol{\theta})(\varepsilon_j - e_j^{\mathsf{T}}\boldsymbol{\theta}) \frac{\delta_i}{s(Z_i)} \omega(Z_i^{\mathsf{T}}\boldsymbol{\beta}) =: M_{21,s}^{(1)} + M_{21,s}^{(2)}.$$

From $(\mathbf{C_8})$ and Lemma 4, we know that $E\{\omega(Z_i^{\mathsf{T}}\boldsymbol{\beta})\tilde{Z}_{is} < \infty\}$. Therefore, by Lemma 3 and the Cauchy-Schwarz inequality, we have

$$E(M_{21,s}^{(1)2}) \le cn^{-1} \sum_{i=1}^{n} E^{\frac{1}{2}}\{\omega(Z_i^{\mathsf{T}}\boldsymbol{\beta}) \sum_{j=1}^{n} \widetilde{W}_{nj}(Z_i^{\mathsf{T}}\boldsymbol{\beta};\boldsymbol{\beta}) g(Z_j^{\mathsf{T}}\boldsymbol{\beta}) - g'(Z_i^{\mathsf{T}}\boldsymbol{\beta})\}^4 \le ch_1^2 \to 0.$$

For $M_{21,s}^{(2)}$, from $(\mathbf{C_8})$, Lemma 3 and the Cauchy-Schwarz inequality, we derive that

$$E(M_{21,s}^{(2)2}) \le c(nh_1^3)^{-1} + c(nh_1^2)^{-1} + c(n^2 h_1^5)^{-1} \to 0.$$

Because of the Markov inequality and the above proof, it follows that $M_{21} \xrightarrow{P} 0$, hence,

$$M_2 \xrightarrow{P} 0. \tag{15}$$

Similarly, we can prove that

$$M_3 \xrightarrow{P} 0, \quad M_4 \xrightarrow{P} 0. \tag{16}$$

At last, we consider M_5. Let

$$\xi_i = \delta_i \omega(Z_i^\mathsf{T} \beta)\{(\varepsilon_i - e_i^\mathsf{T} \theta) \times [\hat{g}'(Z_i^\mathsf{T} \beta; \beta, \theta)(Z_i - \hat{\mu}_1(Z_i^\mathsf{T} \beta; \beta))^\mathsf{T} J_{\beta^{(r)}},$$
$$(V_i - \hat{\mu}_2(Z_i^\mathsf{T} \beta; \beta))^\mathsf{T}]^\mathsf{T} + [0, \theta^\mathsf{T} \Sigma_e]^\mathsf{T}\}.$$

Similar to the proof of (11), with Lemmas 2 and 4, it follows that $M_5 = \frac{1}{\sqrt{n}} \sum_{i=1}^{n} \frac{[s(Z_i) - \hat{s}(Z_i)]\xi_i}{s^2(Z_i)} + o_p(1) =: \widetilde{M}_5 + o_p(1)$, where $\widetilde{M}_5$ is obtained by substituting $\hat{s}(Z_i)$ of the denominator about M_5 with $s(Z_i)$. Similar to the proof of Xue and Lian (2016), we get $\widetilde{M}_5 \xrightarrow{P} 0$, and hence $M_5 \xrightarrow{P} 0$. This together with (13)–(16) proves (12). And then (9) is derived.

Lemma 7. Under conditions $(\mathbf{C_1})$–$(\mathbf{C_{10}})$, it follows that

$$\max_{1 \le i \le n} \|\hat{\eta}_i(\beta^{(r)}, \theta)\| = o_p(n^{\frac{1}{2}}).$$

The Proof of Lemma 7. Invoking Lemmas 1, 2 and 4, and using similar techniques to those used to prove (9), we can complete the proof.

Lemma 8. Under conditions $(\mathbf{C_1})$–$(\mathbf{C_{10}})$, it follows that

$$\|\lambda(\beta^{(r)}, \theta)\| = O_p(n^{-\frac{1}{2}}).$$

The Proof of Theorem 1. Using a Taylor expansion in (4), we have

$$\hat{l}_n(\beta^{(r)}, \theta) = 2 \sum_{i=1}^{n} \{\lambda^\mathsf{T} \hat{\eta}_i(\beta^{(r)}, \theta) - \frac{1}{2}[\lambda^\mathsf{T} \hat{\eta}_i(\beta^{(r)}, \theta)]^2\} + o_p(1). \tag{17}$$

By calculating directly from (5), we get

$$0 = \frac{1}{n} \sum_{i=1}^{n} \hat{\eta}_i(\beta^{(r)}, \theta) - \frac{1}{n} \sum_{i=1}^{n} \hat{\eta}_i(\beta^{(r)}, \theta)\hat{\eta}_i^\mathsf{T}(\beta^{(r)}, \theta)\lambda + \frac{1}{n} \sum_{i=1}^{n} \frac{\hat{\eta}_i(\beta^{(r)}, \theta)[\lambda^\mathsf{T} \hat{\eta}_i(\beta^{(r)}, \theta)]^2}{1 + \lambda^\mathsf{T} \hat{\eta}_i(\beta^{(r)}, \theta)}. \tag{18}$$

By Lemmas 6–8, the last item on the right of Formula (18) deduces

$$\frac{1}{n} \sum_{i=1}^{n} \|\hat{\eta}_i(\beta^{(r)}, \theta)\|^3 \cdot \|\lambda\|^2 \cdot |1 + \lambda^\mathsf{T} \hat{\eta}_i(\beta^{(r)}, \theta)|^{-1} = o_p(n^{-\frac{1}{2}}). \tag{19}$$

Using (18) and (19), we obtain

$$\lambda = [\hat{\eta}_i(\boldsymbol{\beta}^{(r)}, \boldsymbol{\theta})\hat{\eta}_i^{\mathsf{T}}(\boldsymbol{\beta}^{(r)}, \boldsymbol{\theta})]^{-1} \sum_{i=1}^{n} \hat{\eta}_i(\boldsymbol{\beta}^{(r)}, \boldsymbol{\theta}) + o_p(n^{-\frac{1}{2}}), \tag{20}$$

$$\sum_{i=1}^{n} [\lambda^{\mathsf{T}} \hat{\eta}_i(\boldsymbol{\beta}^{(r)}, \boldsymbol{\theta})]^2 = \sum_{i=1}^{n} \lambda^{\mathsf{T}} \hat{\eta}_i(\boldsymbol{\beta}^{(r)}, \boldsymbol{\theta}) + o_p(1). \tag{21}$$

By (20) and (21), (17) can be rewritten as

$$\hat{l}_n(\boldsymbol{\beta}^{(r)}, \boldsymbol{\theta}) = [\frac{1}{\sqrt{n}} \sum_{i=1}^{n} \hat{\eta}_i(\boldsymbol{\beta}^{(r)}, \boldsymbol{\theta})]^{\mathsf{T}} [\frac{1}{n} \sum_{i=1}^{n} \hat{\eta}_i(\boldsymbol{\beta}^{(r)}, \boldsymbol{\theta})\hat{\eta}_i^{\mathsf{T}}(\boldsymbol{\beta}^{(r)}, \boldsymbol{\theta})]^{-1} [\frac{1}{\sqrt{n}} \sum_{i=1}^{n} \hat{\eta}_i(\boldsymbol{\beta}^{(r)}, \boldsymbol{\theta})] + o_p(1).$$

Applying Lemmas 6–7, we can complete the proof of Theorem 1.

5 Discussion

In this paper, we study some privacy missing-data model and analysis problems, that we derive the empirical likelihood inference for the partially linear single-index model when the responses are missing and linear covariates are measured with additive errors. We propose a bias-correct empirical log-likelihood ratio for the parameters and derive the nonparametric version of the Wilk's theorem. We can construct the confidence regions of the parameters with asymptotically correct coverage probabilities.

This article focuses on the inference for the parameters. When the responses are missing and linear covariates are measured with additive errors, the inference for the nonparametric component in the partially linear single-index model will be another fascinating topic, which is a future research topic.

Acknowledgements. The authors thank the editors and four referees for their constructive comments and suggestions. This work is supported by Philosophy and Social Sciences Planning Project of Guangdong Province during the "13th Five-Year" Plan Period (No. GD18CYJ08, GD20CJY50, GD20XJY05), Guangdong Province Educational Science Planning Project (No. 2021GXJK747, 2022GXJK476), National Social Science Foundation of China (No. 18CTQ032), Guangdong Provincial Department of Education Project (No. 2020WQNCX141, 2018GWQNCX039).

References

Chen, X., Cui, H.J.: Empirical likelihood for partially linear single-index errors-in-variables model. Commun. Stat. Theory Methods **38**, 2498–2514 (2009)

Liang, H., Härdle, W., Carroll, R.J.: Estimation in a semiparametric partially linear errors-in-variables model. Ann. Stat. **27**, 1519–1535 (1999)

Liang, H., Wang, S.J., Carroll, R.J.: Partially linear models with missing response variables and error-prone covariates. Biometrika **94**, 185–198 (2007)

Liu, W., Feng, W., Yu, B., Peng, T.: Security and privacy for sharing electronic medical records based on blockchain and federated learning. In: Wang, G., Choo, K.K.R., Ko, R.K.L., Xu, Y., Crispo, B. (eds.) UbiSec 2021. CCIS, vol. 1557, pp. 13–24. Springer, Singapore (2022). https://doi.org/10.1007/978-981-19-0468-4_2

Owen, A.B.: Empirical Likelihood. Chapman and Hall, New York (2001)

Qi, X., Wang, D.H.: Estimation in a partially linear single-index model with missing response variables and error-prone covariates. J. Inequal. Appl. **2016** (2016). Article number: 11. https://doi.org/10.1186/s13660-015-0941-8

Serfling, R.J.: Approximation Theorems of Mathematical Statistics. Wiley, New York (1980)

Wang, Y., Zhang, P., Zhan, H., Zhang, M.: Privacy-enhanced mean-variance scheme against malicious signature attacks in smart grids. In: Wang, G., Choo, K.K.R., Ko, R.K.L., Xu, Y., Crispo, B. (eds.) UbiSec 2021. CCIS, vol. 1557, pp. 145–158. Springer, Singapore (2022). https://doi.org/10.1007/978-981-19-0468-4_11

Xue, L.G., Lian, H.: Empirical likelihood for single-index models with responses missing at random. Sci China Math **59**(6), 1187–1207 (2016). https://doi.org/10.1007/s11425-015-5097-y

Xue, L.G., Zhang, J.H.: Empirical likelihood for partially linear single-index models with missing observations. Comput. Stat. Data Anal. **144**, 106877 (2020)

Yu, Y., Ruppert, D.: Penalized spline estimation for partially linear single-index models. J. Am. Stat. Assoc. **97**, 1042–1054 (2002)

Zhu, L.X., Xue, L.G.: Empirical likelihood confidence regions in a partially linear single-index model. J. Roy. Stat. Soc. B **68**, 549–570 (2006)

Zou, Y.Y., Fan, G.L., Zhang, R.Q.: Quantile regression and variable selection for partially linear single-index models with missing censoring indicators. J. Stat. Plann. Infer. **204**, 80–95 (2020)

High-Speed Anonymous Device Authentication Without Asymmetric Cryptography in the Internet-of-Things

Li Duan[1,2] and Yong Li[2(✉)]

[1] Paderborn University, 33098 Paderborn, Germany
liduan@mail.upb.de
[2] Huawei Technologies Düsseldorf, 64293 Darmstadt, Germany
{li.duan,yong.li1}@huawei.com

Abstract. A large portion of end-point and edge devices in the Internet-of-Things (IoT) are constrained in computational power and bandwidth, which means they cannot easily afford the resource-consuming asymmetric cryptography such as Diffie-Hellman key exchange and RSA-2048 digital signatures. On the other hand, these devices are still confronted with similar threats against conventional devices in authenticity and privacy. In this paper, we present a high-speed authentication protocol for resource-constrained devices in IoT, which provides both authenticity and anonymity without any use of asymmetric cryptography. Moreover, we show how our protocol can be extended for devices that can execute symmetric encryption for secure data transmission. The security and anonymity of the new protocols have been analyzed comprehensively, and the evaluation demonstrates their efficiency.

Keywords: Authentication · Security · Internet-of-Things · Privacy

1 Introduction

The Internet-of-Things (IoT) is expanding. According to estimates, the total number of connected devices in IoT could exceed 25 billion by the year 2030 [20]. As more devices become connected and more sensitive data go online, security of IoT has become an attractive research topic today. However, due to the heterogeneous nature of IoT architecture, conventional solutions for authentication and data security are in most cases inappropriate, especially at the edge and end-point devices. For example, Transport Layer Security (TLS) [12] depends on TCP/IP and usually needs X.509 digital certificates [5], while typical IoT edge devices may only communicate via BLE [11] or LoRaWAN [4], and cannot easily afford RSA signatures with 112-bit security or above [25]. So a natural question to ask is whether it is possible to construct reliable authentication scheme using only symmetric cryptography.

On the other hand, IoT can open more attack surfaces for privacy adversaries. The offline finding service (OF) in was released by Apple in 2019, which allows

G. Wang et al. (Eds.): UbiSec 2022, CCIS 1768, pp. 471–484, 2023.
https://doi.org/10.1007/978-981-99-0272-9_32

kindhearted finders to upload the location of lost wearable devices. However, in a detailed analysis of OF conducted in 2021 [10], Heinrich *et al.* present a server-side attack to mine a social network of finders from the data sent and the device owners' identifiers, undermining the claimed privacy guarantee of OF. Neither the service provider nor end users would like to see this attack or alike happening, so it becomes essential to consider anonymity in IoT carefully.

Besides dangers from message tampering and eavesdropping, a server database that is inadequately protected can also compromise system security. While server's private keys or other long term secrets are most likely safeguarded by designated hardware, such as Hardware Security Module (HSM), devices' authentication data are usually stored in cloud database due to their large volume. For example, in [9], the authors have assumed that the server or cloud holds the database of identifier-key pairs. Thus, by compromising the database, an adversary can simply learn all the parameters and secret inputs, breaching the security and anonymity of the entire system. As suggested by author of SRP-6 [26], having an authentication protocol resistant to server database compromise is significantly preferable to throwing perfect trust in the server.

1.1 Our Contribution and Outline of the Paper

In this paper, we develop novel authentication protocols to meet the challenges for constrained end-point and edge devices in IoT. Our core protocol is **high-speed**, with **authenticity** and excellent **anonymity** because in its execution

1. only *one* message is sent,
2. the local computation involves only cryptographic hash functions and does not rely on any designated hardware,
3. even when given the database, it is infeasible for anyone but the honest user to compute a new valid authentication message, and
4. any adversary cannot distinguish a message of device A and that of another device B.

Moreover, we implement our protocol and evaluate its performance in crucial metrics, such as speed, ROM and RAM consumption. The security analysis and the experimental results show that our design is robust and efficient.

The necessary notations and the cryptographic primitives in our protocols are introduced in Sect. 3. The concrete protocol design and security analysis are provided in Sect. 4. The evaluation of the core protocol is presented in Sect. 5. Other related works, besides those introduced in Sect. 1, are surveyed in Sect. 2. The conclusion and possible future work are presented in Sect. 6.

2   Related Work

Speed Gap Between Asymmetric and Symmetric Cryptography. Although widely deployed in the Internet, the RSA signature schemes require significantly more resources than elliptic curve cryptography (ECC) [16,23,25]. At 112-bit security

level, an ECDSA signature on secp224r1 [21] needs 64 Bytes, while an RSA-2048
signature needs 256 Bytes. Being 10 to 100 times faster than RSA [25], ECC is
still not comparable with symmetric key operation in speed [7]. For instance, on
an average personal computer[1], 1.6×10^7 blocks of 16-Byte data can be encrypted
with AES-128-CBC per second, and 3.1×10^6 64-byte data blocks can be digested
with SHA256 per second, but the fasted elliptic curve DH with X25519 [15] can
only be performed 2.5×10^4 times per second[2], leaving a speed gap of 10^2 to 10^3
times.

Symmetric Cryptography Based Authentication Schemes. Pure symmetric cryptography based authentication and identification are frequently proposed for IoT
[7,9,17,18,22] depending on hardware such as physically unclonable function
(PUF) [8] or Trusted Platform Module (TPM) [24]. As pointed in [22], existing solutions such as [17] made too strong an assumption about the security of
data on the server so that the resulting solution would be broken completely
after database compromising. Anonymity threats can be seen in [7]. Although
an alias AID_i is used, the real device identity can be recovered by XOR-ring
AID_i with the hash value of R_i, where R_i can be recovered from the message M_i
sent by the sensor and f_{2i} stored in the server database[3] without breaching the
TPM. In this paper, we provide solutions for authenticity and anonymity against
server database compromising that can run on general purposed hardware. An
overview of existing solutions can be found in Table 1.

Table 1. Comparison of existing solutions based on symmetric cryptography.

Solution	Hardware	Sec. after DB comp.	Authen.	Anonymity
Esfahani *et al.* [7]	TPM	Y	Y	N
Guin *et al.* [9]	PUF	N	Y	N
Majzoobi *et al.* [17]	PUF	N	Y	N
Nair *et al.* [18]	PUF	N	Y	N
Qureshi *et al.* [22]	PUF	Y	Y	Y
This paper	Not designated	Y	Y	Y

3   Notation and Preliminaries

3.1   Notation

The security parameter is denoted by $\kappa \in \mathbb{N}$, and 1^κ means a unary string of
length κ. Let $[n] = \{1, \ldots, n\} \subset \mathbb{N}$ be the set of integers between 1 and n. If S is

---

[1] ThinkPad, Windows 10, Intel Core i7-8565U @1.80 GHz. The speed measurement is
done with `openssl speed aes-128-cbc/sha256/ecdh`.

[2] Two EC point multiplications on each side.

[3] See "Authentication Server" column in TABLE V in [7].

a set or distribution, $e \overset{\$}{\leftarrow} S$ denotes the action of sampling a uniformly random element e from S, or taking a random sample according to S, respectively. Let $\mathcal{A}()$ be a (non-uniform) algorithm, we use $m \overset{\$}{\leftarrow} \mathcal{A}^{\mathcal{O}(\cdot)}()$ to denote that $\mathcal{A}$ outputs m with the help of another algorithm $\mathcal{O}(\cdot)$. The term $s_1 || s_2$ denotes the operation of concatenating two binary strings s_1 and s_2. We use $\Pr[E : C]$ to denote the conditioned probability that an event E happens if the condition C is met, and C can also be interactions between the attacker and the challenger in a given security experiment. We use PPT for probabilistic algorithms with their running time bounded by some polynomial $\mathsf{poly}(\kappa)$ in κ.

3.2   Cryptographic Primitives

Definition 1 (Collision-resistant Hash Function). *A hash function* $\mathsf{H} : \mathcal{M} \to \mathcal{D}$, *where* $\mathcal{M}$ *is the message space and* $\mathcal{D}$ *the digest space, is collision-resistant if there exists a negligible function* $\epsilon(\kappa)$ *such that for any PPT* $\mathcal{A}$, *it holds that*

$$\Pr\begin{bmatrix} \mathsf{H}(m_0) = \mathsf{H}(m_1), m_0 \neq m_1 : \\ (m_0, m_1) \overset{\$}{\leftarrow} \mathcal{A}(1^\kappa, \mathsf{H}) \end{bmatrix} \leq \epsilon(\kappa).$$

where κ *is the security parameter and* $m_0, m_1 \in \mathcal{M}$.

The core of our authentication protocol needs only cryptographic hash which is modeled as a random oracle. The protocol extension needs PRF and symmetric key encryption.

Definition 2 (Pseudo-random function, PRF). *A pseudo-random function* $\mathsf{PRF} = (\mathsf{KGen}, \mathsf{PRF})$ *consists of two algorithms* KGen *and* PRF *described as below.*

- $\mathsf{KGen}(1^\kappa) \overset{\$}{\to} \mathsf{k}$. *The non-deterministic key generation algorithm* $\mathsf{KGen}()$ *takes the security parameter* 1^κ *as the input and outputs the secret key* k.
- $\mathsf{PRF}(\mathsf{k}, x) = y$. *The PRF evaluation algorithm* $\mathsf{PRF}()$ *takes as the input the secret key* k *and a value* x *in the domain and outputs an image* y *in the range.*

Definition 3 (Symmetric key encryption scheme). *A symmetric key encryption scheme* $\Pi = (\mathsf{KGen}, \mathsf{ENC}, \mathsf{DEC})$ *consists of three algorithms* KGen, ENC *and* DEC *described as below.*

- $\mathsf{KGen}(1^\kappa) \overset{\$}{\to} \mathsf{k}$. *The non-deterministic key generation algorithm* $\mathsf{KGen}()$ *takes the security parameter* 1^κ *as the input and outputs one encryption-decryption key* k.
- $\mathsf{ENC}(\mathsf{k}, m) \overset{\$}{\to} \mathsf{CT}$. *The (non-deterministic) encryption algorithm* $\mathsf{ENC}()$ *takes as the input the key* k *and a message* m, *and outputs a ciphertext* CT.
- $\mathsf{DEC}(\mathsf{k}, \mathsf{CT}) \leftarrow m'$. *The deterministic decryption algorithm* $\mathsf{DEC}()$ *takes as input the key* k, *a ciphertext* CT. *It can output a plaintext* m' *or a decryption failure symbol* $\bot$.

For formal security definitions of PRF and symmetric encryption, we refer the readers to [13]. We also highlights the properties needed in our protocols in the next section.

4 High-Speed Authentication Protocols

Communication Model. We model the IoT architecture as in Fig. 1. An edge or end-point device (ED) connects with application servers via gateways. We assume that an ED has the basic resources to collect, send, and receive data, and execute symmetric cryptography such as hash and/or block cipher.

We do not consider that a gateway differs from an application server when deploying authentication protocols for ED in terms of their abundant computational resources, so henceforth we use to term server to denote both.

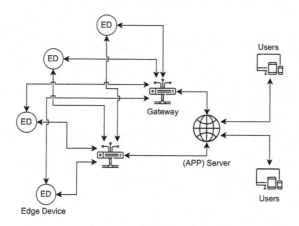

Fig. 1. IoT communication model.

Threat Model. We model an adversary $\mathcal{A}$ as a non-uniform PPT algorithm as in classical security models for authentication and key exchange [2,14]. $\mathcal{A}$ can eavesdrop and tamper with messages on the network, and $\mathcal{A}$ can also compromise some of the EDs and the server database, but cannot control the server's behavior.

More formally, the execution environment of our protocols is a group of $d \leq \mathsf{poly}(\kappa)$ parties including EDs and servers, each of which can hold up to $\ell \leq \mathsf{poly}(\kappa)$ sessions. Each session oracle is denoted by π_i^s with $i \in [d]$ and $s \in [\ell]$, and can be in the states {running, interrupted, accept}. $\mathcal{A}$ can interact with all π_i^s via the following queries.

- Send(π_i^s, m). This query sends the message m to session π_i^s. Then π_i^s processes m and $\mathcal{A}$ obtains the response messages from π_i^s as specified by the protocol. $\mathcal{A}$ can use a special message δ in this query to get the initial message from π_i^s. This query abstracts the attacks such as replay and adversarial message injection.
- Corrupt(i). If party i is an ED, this query returns to $\mathcal{A}$ the long term secret of i. If party i is a server, this query returns the complete database of i. This query models the compromising of EDs and servers.

Definition 4 (Breaking authenticity and anonymity). *An adversary* $\mathcal{A}$ *breaks the authentication if it can bring a server session* π_i^s *into* accept *without sending* Corrupt() *to its partnered ED* ***before*** *the* accept *happens.* $\mathcal{A}$ *breaks the protocol anonymity, if it can bind an identifier or a session to an ED without compromising the target ED via* Corrupt() *when there exists another uncorrupted ED.*

Definition 4 puts no restriction on whether $\mathcal{A}$ compromises the server database or not, and also allows $\mathcal{A}$ to make arbitrary **replay** and message manipulation attempts. So a protocol that cannot be broken by any adversary in Definition 4 is robust against these attacks, and thus has authenticity and anonymity.

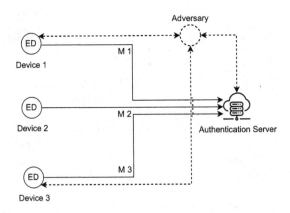

Fig. 2. Authentication pattern and the threat model.

4.1   One-Message Authentication with Anonymity

Here we present our first new high-speed authentication protocol for constrained IoT devices. All of our protocols follow the same pattern in Fig. 2. Only one message is sent to the server, which may or may not carry application data.

Keyed Hash Chain. The core mechanism of the authentication is a keyed hash chain demonstrated in Fig. 3, where $H(\cdot) : \{0,1\}^{2\cdot h} \rightarrow \{0,1\}^h$ is a collision resistant hash function with h as its output length as in Definition 1 and we set $h = 2\kappa$.

The keyed hash chain computes for $j \in [J] : T_j = H(T_{j-1}||\mathsf{CNT}_j)$. If we model $H()$ as a random oracle, then according to the conclusions on the cascaded keyed-hashing based pre-shared key schedule in [6], we can have the nice security features of this hash chain described below.

1. (Binding) Given CNT_j and T_j, there exists at most one $T_{j-1} \in \{0,1\}^h$.
2. (Pseudorandom output) Given only CNT_j but not T_{j-1}, the output T_j is pseudorandom, which is essential for security and anonymity.

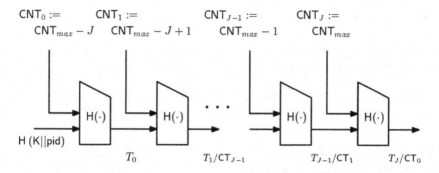

$$\text{CNT}_0 := \quad\quad \text{CNT}_1 := \quad\quad\quad\quad \text{CNT}_{J-1} := \quad\quad\quad \text{CNT}_J :=$$
$$\text{CNT}_{max} - J \quad \text{CNT}_{max} - J + 1 \quad\quad \text{CNT}_{max} - 1 \quad\quad\quad \text{CNT}_{max}$$

Fig. 3. Keyed hash chain for authentication.

3. (One-wayness) Given CNT_j and T_j, it is infeasible to recover T_{j-1}.

Therefore, we can authenticate the value of T_{j-1} with CNT_j and T_j securely, and build our protocols upon the hash chain.

Protocol Set Up. Each ED i holds its own secret key K_i, its identifier pid_i, current counter value CNT^i, a max counter value CNT^i_{max}, and an interval constrains J (lifespan of a device). Given a max counter value CNT^i_{max} and an interval constrains $J \leq \text{CNT}^i_{max}$, for an ED with K_i and pid_i, each T^i_j and a verification reference CT^i_j are defined as follows (also see Fig. 3).

$$\mathsf{K}'_i = \mathsf{H}(\mathsf{K}_i\|\mathsf{pid}_i) \tag{1}$$
$$\text{CNT}^i_j = \text{CNT}^i_{max} - J + j, \text{ for } j \in \{0\} \cup [J] \tag{2}$$
$$T^i_0 = \mathsf{H}(\mathsf{K}'_i\|\text{CNT}^0_i) \tag{3}$$
$$T^i_j = \mathsf{H}(T^i_{j-1}\|(\text{CNT}^i_j)) \text{ for } j \in [J] \tag{4}$$
$$\text{CT}^i_j = T^i_{J-j} \text{ for } j \in [J] \tag{5}$$

The server holds an anonymous data base $\text{DB} := \{\text{CT}^i_v\}$ of verification reference values for authentication. The superscript i is for notation only and the server database cannot map pid_i to CT^i_v after setup. Initially, each $\text{CT}^i_v = \text{CT}^i_0 = T^i_V$, where V is the interval constraint of the corresponding ED. Note that firstly, DB does not store any pid_i, and secondly the V can vary from ED to ED, and a different $\text{CNT}^i_{max} > V$ is chosen uniformly random for each ED i.

Protocol 1 Execution. The construction idea is that for each j, server always holds T_j, and ED provides T_{j-1} and the corresponding counter CNT_j, i.e., run the verification in a hash chain from the end to the beginning.

We use $\mathbb{F}(\mathsf{K}_i\|\mathsf{pid}_i, \text{CNT}^i_{max}, J, \text{CNT}^i_{j-1})$ as a shorthand notation for computing T_{j-1} according to Eq. (1) to (5). As shown in Fig. 4,

- ED_i computes the current authentication message $M = (T^i_{j-1}, \text{CNT}^i_j)$ from its internal states and update the counter value CNT^i_j.

- Upon receiving the message, Server reconstructs the reference value CT^* with $H()$.
- If Server can find CT_v with $CT_v = CT^*$ in its data base DB, it accepts the authentication request, updates the CT_v with T^i_{j-1}.

Note that T^i_{j-1} in the authentication message and its verification need only hash function evaluation, resulting in outstanding computational efficiency.

·········· **Edge Device ED_i** ························· Server ···········
$(\mathsf{params}, \mathsf{PID}_i, \mathsf{K}_i, \mathsf{CNT}^i_{max}, J, \mathsf{CNT}^i_{j-1})$ $\qquad\qquad\qquad$ $(\mathsf{params},\ \mathsf{DB} := \{\mathsf{CT}_v\})$

$$T^i_{j-1} \leftarrow \mathbb{F}(\mathsf{K}_i\|\mathsf{pid}_i, \mathsf{CNT}^i_{max}, J, \mathsf{CNT}^i_{j-1}) \xrightarrow{\ T^i_{j-1}, \mathsf{CNT}^i_j\ }$$

$$CT^* \leftarrow H(T^i_{j-1}\|\mathsf{CNT}^i_j)$$

Update $\mathsf{CNT}^i_j \leftarrow \mathsf{CNT}^i_{j-1} - 1$ $\qquad$ **if** $\exists \mathsf{CT}_v \in \mathsf{DB} \wedge \mathsf{CT}_v = CT^*$:

$\qquad\qquad\qquad\qquad\qquad\qquad\qquad$ Accept and update $\mathsf{CT}_v \leftarrow T^i_{j-1}$

$\qquad\qquad\qquad\qquad\qquad\qquad\qquad$ **else abort**

Fig. 4. Protocol 1: one-message anonymous authentication for ED.

The steps in dashed boxes of Protocol 1 in Fig. 4 are the core of authentication, which will be preserved in Protocol 2. We summarize the security and anonymity of Protocol 1 in the following theorem.

Theorem 1 (Authenticity and Anonymity, Protocol 1). *Let κ be the security parameter. If $H()$: $\{0,1\}^{2 \cdot h} \rightarrow \{0,1\}^h$ is modeled as a random oracle, CNT_{max} is uniformly random in $\{0,1\}^h$ with $h = f(\kappa)$ for some polynomial $f()$, and interval $J \in \mathbb{Z}^+$ a constant, then protocol 1 has authenticity and anonymity that cannot be broken by any PPT $\mathcal{A}$ as in Definition 4.*

Proof (Sketch). We give the intuition of proving Theorem 1. The threat model in Definition 4 allows an adversary $\mathcal{A}$ to obtain the server database $\mathsf{DB} := \{\mathsf{CT}^i_v\}$. To authenticate successfully, an adversary $\mathcal{A}$ has to compute a **fresh** pair (T^*, CNT^*) such that for some $\mathsf{CT}_v \in \mathsf{DB}$, $\mathsf{CT}_v = H(T^*\|\mathsf{CNT}^*)$. But a successful finding of (T^*, CNT^*) leads to attacks against the collision resistance or one-wayness of $H()$.

Given DB, breaking anonymity is to decide whether a T (or CT) is from pid_i or from pid'_i. This is also infeasible because $\mathcal{A}$ has to at least find one pre-image of some T, or invert T_0, or distinguish $H(H(\mathsf{K}_i\|\mathsf{pid}_i)\|\mathsf{CNT}^i_{max})$ from a truly random string without knowing K_i or K'_i, which all violate the pseudorandomness and one-wayness of a keyed hash chain from $H()$. $\qquad\square$

4.2   Authentication with Data Transmission

Protocol 1 achieves our design goal for authenticity and anonymity against server database compromise. As we consider that data confidentiality is orthogonal to authenticity and anonymity, we follow a more modular approach of extension. The rule of thumb is that we use separated secrets for each goal.

To extend our basic authentication protocol with secure data transmission, an additional pre-shared key K_{ss} is needed for generating one-time data key sk. K_{ss} is shared between the server and all ED and the server database is $\{(CT_v, CNT_v)\}$. This results in Protocol 2 in Fig. 5. Note that the authentication message is a single ciphertext CT' and the counter value is not sent in plaintext.

Upon receiving CT', the server searches for a counter value CNT_v in its database, such that if $sk = PRF(K_{ss}, CNT_v)$ then $DEC(K_{ss}, CT')$ also should output a plaintext that contains CNT_v. Once CT' is correctly decrypted, the authentication proceeds as in Protocol 1. The security theorem follows.

Theorem 2 (Authenticity, anonymity and confidentiality, Protocol 2). *Given the authenticity and anonymity of Protocol 1, Protocol 2 has authenticity and anonymity. If $\Pi = (KGen, ENC, DEC)$ is a semantic secure encryption scheme against chosen ciphertext attack and $PRF()$ a secure PRF, Protocol 2 also has limited data confidentiality against any PPT adversary $\mathcal{A}$, if $\mathcal{A}$ does not compromise DB and an ED simultaneously.*

Here we also give an intuition to prove Theorem 2. As the initial CNT_{max}^i value of each ED i is random, and the selected CNT_{max}^i is sparse in $\{0,1\}^h$, knowing K_{ss} alone is not enough to recover *data*. This prevents an adversary that has corrupted some ED for K_{ss} from learning the data of other ED, as long as it does not have DB. We call this *limited confidentiality* of data. On the other hand, the encryption and the random K_{ss} does not leak more information about pid_i and K_i than simple (T, CNT) pairs.

············ **Edge Device ED$_i$** ···························· **Server** ···········	
(params, K_{ss}, PID_i, K_i, CNT_{max}^i, J, CNT_{j-1}^i)	(params, K_{ss}, DB := $\{CT_v, CNT_v\}$)
$T_{j-1}^i \leftarrow \mathbb{F}(K_i \| pid_i, CNT_{max}^i, J, CNT_{j-1}^i)$	
$sk \leftarrow PRF(K_{ss}, CNT_i)$	
$CT' = ENC(sk, T_i \| CNT_i \| data)$ $\xrightarrow{CT'}$ Locate a $(CT_v, CNT_v) \in$ DB with	
$sk \leftarrow PRF(K_{ss}, CNT_v)$	
$\wedge$ $DEC(sk, CT') \neq \bot$	
Update $CNT_j^i \leftarrow CNT_{j-1}^i - 1$ **if** no such CNT_v exists : **abort**	
$T_i \| CNT_i \| data \leftarrow DEC(sk, CT')$	
$CT^* \leftarrow H(T_{j-1}^i \| CNT_j^i)$	
if $CT_v = CT^* \wedge CNT_v = CNT_i$:	
Process *data*	
Accept and update	
$CT_v \leftarrow T_i, CNT_v \leftarrow CNT_v - 1$	
else abort	

Fig. 5. Protocol 2: extended Protocol 1 with limited data confidentiality.

Due to page limitation, we put the complete proof of all the theorems in the extended version of this paper.

Further Discussion on Anonymity. We have discussed anonymity on the authentication protocol layer up to now, and ensure that no effective identifiers can be recovered from protocol messages or server's authentication database.

Although we consider the privacy threats from application data leakage or carrier protocols (e.g., BLE, IP) as out of scope in this paper, there are effective solutions proposed in other lines of research. Real application data, such as location, may leak the (pseudo-)identifier of a non-moving ED in a trivial way to other database of the server, but this threat can be mitigated by introducing privacy enhancing technologies such as local differential privacy [19]. Moreover, as suggested in [1], trusted gateways with constantly updating network address translation (NAT) or alike may provide anonymity on the carrier protocol layer.

5   Implementation and Evaluation

5.1   Experiment Configuration

We implement Protocol 1 to verify its high efficiency in the LAN setting (1 Gbps, latency 0.4 ms). The experiment configuration is illustrated in Fig. 6.

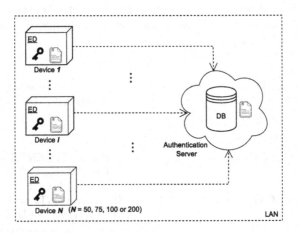

Fig. 6. Configuration in experiments.

Client Configuration. Each ED i is simulated with ROM = 250 KiB and RAM = 50 KiB as a class 2 constrained device [3], and it has its own secret key K_i and initial states.

To verify the scalability of Protocol 1, we test our implementation for of the group size $N = 50, 75, 100$ and 200, and let the EDs send their authentication requests concurrently. The hash function we choose is SHA256, with $J = 100$ and each $\mathsf{K}_i, \mathsf{pid}_i$ and $\mathsf{CNT}^i_{max} \in \{0,1\}^{128}$. A CNT^i_{max} will be sampled again if it is less than J.

For speed test, CNT^i_j will be re-initialized to CNT^i_{max} when it reaches $\mathsf{CNT}^i_{max} - J$. In real world, this should involve re-sampling a CNT^i_{max} and synchronizing the new reference value with the authentication server.

Server Configuration. Besides the protocol logic, the single server is equipped with a database DB containing all authentication references, and it has to serve all clients in parallel. Each initial CT will be reloaded again after being updated for J times. The server is a workstation (`Ubuntu Server 16.04 LTS`, with `MySQL`) with a 16-core CPU and 128 GB RAM.

Table 2. Performance of Protocol 1 with different group settings.

Total Time	Grp. Size	# Req	Avg. Resp. Time	Max. Resp. Time
480 s	50	1,436,337	16.636 ms	143 ms
480 s	75	1,160,448	30.948 ms	915 ms
480 s	100	1,089,748	43.967 ms	364 ms
480 s	200	1,103,099	86.943 ms	1008 ms

RpS	TP 50	TP 99.9	Avg. Rec. Data
2,986.147	15 ms	39 ms	304 KiB/s
2,412.573	31 ms	58 ms	304 KiB/s
2,265.588	43 ms	76 ms	304 KiB/s
2,293.345	85 ms	154 ms	304 KiB/s

Table 3. Explanation of the column names in Table 2

Column name	Meaning
Total time	Total task execution time
Grp. size	Size of ED group
# Req	Total number of authentication requests
Avg. Resp. time	Average response time for a request
Max. Resp. time	Longest response time for a request
RpS	Average number of requests per second
TP 50	The response time for the request, which takes longer than 50% of the measurements.
TP 99.9	The response time for the request, which takes longer than 99.9% of the measurements
Avg. rec. data	Average authentication data volume processed per second by the server

5.2 Result Summary

Each measurement lasts for 480 s. The results in critical metrics are listed in Table 2, with column name explanation in Table 3.

Resource Consumption. On each simulated ED i, the memory consumption is c.a. 20% on average, i.e., about 10 KiB.

The server consumes less than 10% of its total memory but 80% of its CPU. Each request generates about 110 Bytes of data in the experiments, including the 32-Byte payload (a SHA-256 digest), meta data and amortized re-sending cost.

Speed vs. Group Size. In Table 2, as can been seen in the **RpS**-column, 2200 to 3000 requests can be processed by the server per second on average.

We can see a clear impact of group size on the latency. For a group size of $N = 50$, about half the requests can be processed in 15 ms (**TP 50**) each, and 99.9% of the requests can be processed in less than 40 ms (**TP 99.9**) each. The average processing time is almost linear in the group size, but still very fast when $N = 200$, where 99.9% of the requests can be processed in less than 155 ms. The maximal request processing time (**Max. Resp. Time**) grows by a factor of 7 (from 143 to 1008 ms) when the group size is only 3 times larger (from 50 to 200), as more clients have to compete for the priority, and the database search time, probability of time-out and re-sending all increase.

To summarize, Protocol 1 performs well in terms of computational resources and speed in moderate sized ED groups in the LAN setting. We thus conjecture it can have satisfactory performance in the WAN setting if the gateway can relay messages to the remote authentication server in a reliable way.

6   Conclusion and Future Work

In this paper, we present an extremely efficient one-message protocol for anonymous authentication of edge and end-point devices in IoT that is robust against server database compromise. We also extend our core protocol for data confidentiality. Our implementation and experiments confirm the high-speed of our design for moderate and realistic sized ED groups.

Although we focus on authenticity and anonymity in this paper, we believe the forward secrecy [12] of data, which tolerates key exposure of any ED or server after a session finishes, can also be achieved with key update schemes at cost of more complicated synchronization mechanisms and more computation. Possible future works include efficient synchronization mechanisms, one-message ED-to-ED authentication, and integration with key management system appropriate for larger ED groups. We also believe it remains challenging to find optimal solution for extreme cases, such as an enormous ED group with real-time applications.

References

1. Arfaoui, G., Bultel, X., Fouque, P.A., Nedelcu, A., Onete, C.: The privacy of the TLS 1.3 protocol. Proc. Priv. Enhancing Technol. **4**, 190–210 (2019)
2. Bellare, M., Rogaway, P.: Entity authentication and key distribution. In: Stinson, D.R. (ed.) CRYPTO 1993. LNCS, vol. 773, pp. 232–249. Springer, Heidelberg (1994). https://doi.org/10.1007/3-540-48329-2_21
3. Bormann, C., Ersue, M., Keranen, A.: Terminology for constrained-node networks. RFC 7228 (informational), March 2014. http://www.ietf.org/rfc/rfc7228.txt
4. de Carvalho Silva, J., Rodrigues, J.J., Alberti, A.M., Solic, P., Aquino, A.L.: LoRaWAN-a low power WAN protocol for Internet of Things: a review and opportunities. In: 2017 2nd International Multidisciplinary Conference on Computer and Energy Science (SpliTech), pp. 1–6. IEEE (2017)
5. Cooper, D., Santesson, S., Farrell, S., Boeyen, S., Housley, R., Polk, W.: Internet X.509 public key infrastructure certificate and certificate revocation list (CRL) profile. RFC 5280 (proposed standard), May 2008. http://www.ietf.org/rfc/rfc5280.txt
6. Davis, H., Diemert, D., Günther, F., Jager, T.: On the concrete security of TLS 1.3 PSK mode. In: Dunkelman, O., Dziembowski, S. (eds.) EUROCRYPT 2022. LNCS, vol. 13276, pp. 876–906. Springer, Cham (2022). https://doi.org/10.1007/978-3-031-07085-3_30
7. Esfahani, A., et al.: A lightweight authentication mechanism for M2M communications in industrial IoT environment. IEEE Internet Things J. **6**(1), 288–296 (2017)
8. Guajardo, J., Kumar, S.S., Schrijen, G.-J., Tuyls, P.: FPGA intrinsic PUFs and their use for IP protection. In: Paillier, P., Verbauwhede, I. (eds.) CHES 2007. LNCS, vol. 4727, pp. 63–80. Springer, Heidelberg (2007). https://doi.org/10.1007/978-3-540-74735-2_5
9. Guin, U., Singh, A., Alam, M., Canedo, J., Skjellum, A.: A secure low-cost edge device authentication scheme for the Internet of Things. In: 2018 31st International Conference on VLSI Design and 2018 17th International Conference on Embedded Systems (VLSID), pp. 85–90. IEEE (2018)
10. Heinrich, A., Stute, M., Kornhuber, T., Hollick, M.: Who can find my devices? Security and privacy of apple's crowd-sourced Bluetooth location tracking system. Proc. Priv. Enhancing Technol. **3**, 227–245 (2021)
11. Heydon, R., Hunn, N.: Bluetooth low energy. CSR Presentation, Bluetooth SIG (2012). https://www.bluetooth.org/DocMan/handlers/DownloadDoc.ashx
12. Internet Engineering Task Force, Rescorla, E.: The transport layer security (TLS) protocol version 1.3. draft-ietf-tls-tls13-26 (2018). https://tools.ietf.org/html/draft-ietf-tls-tls13-26
13. Katz, J., Lindell, Y.: Introduction to Modern Cryptography. CRC Press, Boca Raton (2014)
14. Krawczyk, H.: HMQV: a high-performance secure Diffie-Hellman protocol. In: Shoup, V. (ed.) CRYPTO 2005. LNCS, vol. 3621, pp. 546–566. Springer, Heidelberg (2005). https://doi.org/10.1007/11535218_33
15. Langley, A., Hamburg, M., Turner, S.: Elliptic curves for security. RFC 7748, January 2016. https://doi.org/10.17487/RFC7748. https://www.rfc-editor.org/info/rfc7748
16. Li, X., Niu, J., Kumari, S., Wu, F., Sangaiah, A.K., Choo, K.K.R.: A three-factor anonymous authentication scheme for wireless sensor networks in Internet of Things environments. J. Netw. Comput. Appl. **103**, 194–204 (2018)

17. Majzoobi, M., Rostami, M., Koushanfar, F., Wallach, D.S., Devadas, S.: Slender PUF protocol: a lightweight, robust, and secure authentication by substring matching. In: 2012 IEEE Symposium on Security and Privacy Workshops, pp. 33–44. IEEE (2012)

18. Nair, A.S., Thampi, S.M.: PUFloc: PUF and location based hierarchical mutual authentication protocol for surveillance drone networks. In: Wang, G., Choo, K.K.R., Ko, R., Xu, Y., Crispo, B. (eds.) UbiSec 2021. CCIS, vol. 1557, pp. 66–89. Springer, Singapore (2022). https://doi.org/10.1007/978-981-19-0468-4_6

19. Nguyên, T.T., Xiao, X., Yang, Y., Hui, S.C., Shin, H., Shin, J.: Collecting and analyzing data from smart device users with local differential privacy. arXiv preprint arXiv:1606.05053 (2016)

20. Pearce, J.: Internet of Things: key stats for 2022, February 2022. https://techinformed.com/internet-of-things-key-stats-for-2022/

21. Pornin, T.: Deterministic usage of the digital signature algorithm (DSA) and elliptic curve digital signature algorithm (ECDSA). RFC 6979, August 2013. https://www.rfc-editor.org/rfc/rfc6979

22. Qureshi, M.A., Munir, A.: PUF-IPA: a PUF-based identity preserving protocol for Internet of Things authentication. In: 2020 IEEE 17th Annual Consumer Communications & Networking Conference (CCNC), pp. 1–7. IEEE (2020)

23. Srivastava, A., Kumar, A.: A review on authentication protocol and ECC in IoT. In: 2021 International Conference on Advance Computing and Innovative Technologies in Engineering (ICACITE), pp. 312–319. IEEE (2021)

24. 1889-1 International Organization for Standardization: Information technology - Trusted platform module library - Part 1: Architecture. International Organization for Standardization, Vernier, Geneva, Switzerland, ISO/IEC 11889-1:2015 (2015). https://www.iso.org/standard/66510.html

25. Suárez-Albela, M., Fernández-Caramés, T.M., Fraga-Lamas, P., Castedo, L.: A practical performance comparison of ECC and RSA for resource-constrained IoT devices. In: 2018 Global Internet of Things Summit (GIoTS), pp. 1–6. IEEE (2018)

26. Wu, T.: SRP protocol design. SRP document (2002). http://srp.stanford.edu/design.html

A-VMD: Adaptive Variational Mode Decomposition Scheme for Noise Reduction in Sensor-Cloud

Zhenru Huo[1], Guoqing Jia[1], Weidong Fang[2,3,4(✉)], Wei Chen[5,6], and Wuxiong Zhang[2,3]

[1] School of Physics and Electronic Information Engineering, Qinghai Minzu University, Xining 810007, People's Republic of China
[2] Science and Technology On Micro-System Laboratory, Shanghai Institute of Micro-System and Information Technology, Chinese Academy of Sciences, Shanghai 201899, People's Republic of China
`weidong.fang@mail.sim.ac.cn`
[3] University of Chinese Academy of Sciences, Beijing 100049, People's Republic of China
[4] Shanghai Research and Development Center for Micro-Nano Electronics, Shanghai 201210, People's Republic of China
[5] School of Mechanical Electronic and Information Engineering, China University of Mining and Technology-Beijing, Beijing 100083, People's Republic of China
[6] School of Computer Science and Technology, China University of Mining and Technology, Xuzhou 221116, People's Republic of China

Abstract. Digital signal processing is critical during the use of sensor-clouds, and the data information acquired by sensors is inevitably noisy. The Variational Mode Decomposition (VMD) algorithm can be used to reduce noise on the signal. The selection of the modal decomposition number of the VMD algorithm and the selection of the modal components of the reconstructed signal affect the effect of signal noise reduction. In this paper, an adaptive variational mode decomposition scheme is proposed. It adaptively selects the modal decomposition number through the established modal decomposition number and the input signal sample entropy model, selects the optimal modal component according to the sample entropy threshold, and reconstructs the signal after the selected modal component is processed by data smoothing. The results show that compared with traditional variational mode decomposition, empirical mode decomposition algorithms, and other algorithms, the effect of adaptive variational mode decomposition in filtering out signal noise is analyzed. The proposed adaptive VMD (A-VMD) algorithm can effectively filter out the noise of the signal obtained by the sensor.

Keywords: Signal noise reduction · Variational mode decomposition · Sample entropy

1 Introduction

With the development of the Internet of Things [1, 2] and network technology [3, 4], smart cities [5], and sensor-clouds [6] have emerged, and more and more artificial intelligence

G. Wang et al. (Eds.): UbiSec 2022, CCIS 1768, pp. 485–496, 2023.
https://doi.org/10.1007/978-981-99-0272-9_33

[7] products have also entered people's lives, refreshing people's perception of wireless sensors networks [8] vision. Sensors are used in many fields, and information about the object under test can be obtained by analyzing the data collected by the sensor. The first step in data processing is noise reduction.

The classical finite impulse response (FIR) and infinite impulse response (IIR) digital filters can only suppress the noise in a fixed frequency band, and cannot automatically modify the filter parameters according to the characteristics of the frequency domain distribution of the signal, so the noise reduction effect is not ideal. Kalman filter [9] can deal with time-varying systems, non-stationary signals, and multi-dimensional signals, but it will produce large errors when the signal changes sharply. Wavelet transform [10] has a significant impact on the processing of white Gaussian noise, but in the processing process, improper selection of wavelet base and decomposition layer will lead to the failure of adaptive denoising of noisy signals. Empirical Mode Decomposition (EMD) [11] can decompose a complex signal into a smooth data sequence set and perform adaptive processing according to the signal characteristics, but the EMD algorithm is prone to mode aliasing and has end-point effects. Konstantin Dragomire [12] proposed Variational Mode Decomposition (VMD), an adaptive signal processing algorithm. It has obvious advantages in dealing with nonlinear and non-stationary signals and has high computational efficiency. It also overcomes the modal aliasing problem in the EMD algorithm. VMD algorithm is widely used in sensor signal processing [13].

However, the quality of the VMD decomposition results is limited by the choice of the number of modal decompositions and the penalty parameters, and the choice of the modal components of the reconstructed signal is also a key factor in the noise reduction effect. Xin Wang [14] proposed to select the components needed to reconstruct the signal by calculating the correlation with the original signal and obtained good results, but in practice, the sensor signal itself contains noise, and therefore this method cannot be used to reduce noise on the sensor signal. Dibaj Ali [15] proposes a noise reduction method combining VMD with convolutional neural networks. The algorithm is highly accurate. However, it is difficult to reduce the noise of the sensor signal in real time.

In order to overcome the shortcomings of existing VMD algorithms and improve the ability to acquire vital sign information, the main contribution of this paper is to propose an adaptive VMD (A-VMD) algorithm. It adaptively selects the modal decomposition number through the established modal decomposition number and the input signal sample entropy model, selects the optimal modal component according to the sample entropy threshold, and reconstructs the signal after the selected modal component is processed by data smoothing. In the simulation data analysis, compared with EMD, wavelet threshold, and other methods, the A-VMD method proposed in this paper has a better denoising effect on sensor data and can filter noise while retaining useful signals. In the analysis of the measured data, the A-VMD algorithm has a larger signal-to-noise ratio (SNR) and smaller mean square error (MSE) than the VMD algorithm. This shows that the A-VMD algorithm keeps the time-frequency information in the signal as much as possible while filtering noise, and the instantaneous amplitude after noise reduction is closer to the instantaneous amplitude of the original signal.

2 System Model

In this section, the principle of the VMD algorithm and the calculation steps of sample entropy are described, and the basis for the proposed A-VMD algorithm is provided.

2.1 Principle of VMD Algorithm

VMD decomposition iteratively searches the optimal variational model to determine the center frequency and frequency bandwidth of each modal component and realizes the frequency domain of the signal and the adaptive division of each modal component. Assuming the original input signal is $f(t)$ decomposed into K modal components, the decomposition sequence is guaranteed to be a modal component with a limited bandwidth with a central frequency, and the sum of the estimated bandwidth of each mode is the minimum, and the constraint condition is that the sum of all modes is equal to the original signal, then the VMD constrained variational model is as follows [12]:

$$\begin{cases} \min\limits_{\{u_k\}, \{\omega_k\}} \left\{ \sum_k \left\| \partial_t \left[\left(\delta(t) + \frac{j}{\pi t} \right) * u_k(t) \right] e^{-j\omega_k t} \right\|_2^2 \right\}, \\ s.t. \sum_k u_k = f(t) \end{cases} \tag{1}$$

where $\{u_k\} := \{u_1,...,u_K\}$ is the decomposed K modal components; $\{\omega_k\} := \{\omega_1,...,\omega_K\}$ is the center frequency of the K modal components, where $k = 1,2,...,K$.

In order to calculate and solve the above constrained variational problem, the quadratic penalty factor α and the Largrange multiplication operator $\lambda(t)$ are introduced. The introduction of the quadratic penalty factor α can improve signal convergence. The role of the Lagrangian multiplication operator $\lambda(t)$ is to enforce the constraints and better solve the optimal solution of the variational constraints, where α is a large enough positive number and also can guarantee the high precision of the signal under the influence of Gaussian noise, and $\lambda(t)$ can keep the constraints stable and strict. The extended Lagrangian expression is [12]:

$$\begin{aligned} \ell(\{u_k\}, \{\omega_k\}, \lambda) := \\ \alpha \sum_k \left\| \partial_t \left[\left(\delta(t) + \frac{j}{\pi t} \right) * u_k(t) \right] e^{-j\omega_{k_1} t} \right\|_2^2 \\ + \left\| f(t) - \sum_k u_k(t) \right\|_2^2 + \left\langle \lambda(t), f(t) - \sum_k u_k(t) \right\rangle \end{aligned} \tag{2}$$

The above variational problem is solved by the alternating direction multiplication method (ADMM), and the saddle point of Eq. (1) is solved by alternately updating $u_k^{n+1}(t)$, $\omega_k^{n+1}(t)$, and $\lambda_k^{n+1}(t)$. The implementation steps are summarized as follows:

(1) Initialize u_k^1, ω_k^1, λ_k^1, and n, whose initial values are all 0, and set the decomposition modal number K to a suitable positive integer;

(2) $n = n + 1$, $k = k + 1$ executes the loop, and terminates the loop when the preset K is reached. The modal components and center frequency update formulas are respectively:

$$\hat{u}_k^{n+1}(\omega) = \frac{\hat{f}(\omega) - \sum_{i=k} \hat{u}_i(\omega) + \frac{\hat{\lambda}(\omega)}{2}}{1 + 2\alpha(\omega - \omega_k)^2}, \tag{3}$$

$$\omega_k^{n+1} = \frac{\int_0^\infty \omega |\hat{u}_k(\omega)|^2 d\omega}{\int_0^\infty |\hat{u}_k(\omega)|^2 d\omega}, \tag{4}$$

where $\hat{u}_i(\omega)$, $\hat{f}(\omega)$, and $\hat{\lambda}(\omega)$ are the Fourier transforms of $u_k(t)$, $f(t)$, and $\lambda(t)$ respectively.

(3) The formula to update $\hat{\lambda}$ is

$$\hat{\lambda}^{n+1}(\omega) \leftarrow \hat{\lambda}^n(\omega) + \tau \left(\hat{f}(\omega) - \sum_k \hat{u}_k^{n+1}(\omega) \right), \tag{5}$$

where τ is the noise tolerance, the iteration is terminated when $\sum_k \left\| \hat{u}_k^{n+1} - \hat{u}_k^n \right\|_2^2 / \left\| \hat{u}_k^n \right\|_2^2 < \varepsilon$, ε is the discrimination accuracy, and K modal components are output, otherwise, return to step (2).

2.2 Sample Entropy

The calculation of sample entropy does not depend on data length and has a good consistency, which is the advantage of sample entropy. The sample entropy calculation steps are as follows[16]:

(1) A set of vector sequences $X_m(1), X_m(2),...,X_m(N\text{-}m + 1)$ with dimension m of a time series $\{x(n)\} = x(1), x(2),...,x(n)$ composed of N data, where

$$X_m(i) = \{x(i), x(i + 1), \ldots, x(i + m - 1)\} 1 \leq i \leq N - m + 1 \tag{6}$$

(2) The distance $d[X_m(i), X_m(j)]$ between the definition vectors $X_m(i)$ and $X_m(j)$ is the absolute value of the largest difference between the corresponding elements of the two:

$$d[X_m(i), X_m(j)] = max_{k=0,1,...,m-1}(|x(i + k) - x(j + k)|). \tag{7}$$

(3) For a given $X_m(i)$, count the number of $j(1 \leq j \leq N\text{-}m, j \neq i)$ of $d[X_m(i), X_m(j)] \leq r$, and denote it as B_i. For $1 \leq j \leq N\text{-}m$, $B_i^m(r)$ is defined as

$$B_i^m(r) = \frac{B_i}{N - m - 1}. \tag{8}$$

(4) Define $B^m(r) = \frac{1}{N-m} \sum_{i=1}^{N-m} B_i^m(r)$.

(5) Increase the dimension to $m + 1$, and calculate the number of distances between $X_{m+1}(i)$ and $X_{m+1}(j)$ $(1 \leq j \leq N\text{-}m, j \neq i)$ that are less than or equal to r, denoted as A_i. $A_i^m(r)$ is defined as

$$A_i^m(r) = \frac{A_i}{N - m - 1}. \tag{9}$$

(6) Define $A^m(r) = \frac{1}{N-m} \sum_{i=1}^{N-m} A_i^m(r)$ such that $B^m(r)$ is the probability that two sequences match m points under a similarity tolerance r, and $A^m(r)$ is the probability that two sequences match $m+1$ points. The sample entropy is defined as

$$S(m, r) = \lim_{N \to \infty} \left\{ -\ln\left[\frac{A^m(r)}{B^m(r)}\right] \right\}. \tag{10}$$

3 A-VMD Algorithm

In this section, the proposed A-VMD algorithm model and calculation steps are presented, and the algorithm flow chart is designed.

3.1 Number of Decomposition Modes

In the VMD algorithm, the selection of the decomposition modal number K value is more important. If the value is too small, it will lead to under-decomposition, and if the value is too large, it is easy to cause over-decomposition. The above two situations will have adverse effects on the reconstruction of the signal. Obtaining the correct K value is a critical step in VMD decomposition.

After research, it is found that the number of VMD decomposition layers K is related to the sample entropy of the input signal. The higher the signal complexity, the larger the sample entropy value and the larger the number of VMD decomposition modes. Therefore, through data analysis, the relationship model between K and input signal sample entropy S is established as:

$$\left\{ \begin{array}{l} K = 2 \ S \le 0.5, \\ K = 3 \ 0.5 < S \le 1, \\ K = 4 \ 1 < S \le 1.2, \\ K = 5 \ 1.2 < S \le 1.5, \\ K = 6 \ 1.5 < S \le 2.5, \\ K = 7 \ 2.5 < S. \end{array} \right. \tag{11}$$

By calculating the sample entropy of the signal, this relational model can be used to adaptively select the number of decomposition modes of the signal.

3.2 Quadratic Penalty Factor

Through multiple simulation analyses, it is concluded that VMD decomposition is performed on the signal. Among the obtained modal components, the sample entropy value of the first modal component is the smallest. The signal is decomposed by VMD by presetting the value range of α as 100 ~ 2,000, with a step size of 100, and taking different α values. Calculate the sample entropy of the first modal component obtained by each decomposition, and select the α value with the smallest sample entropy as the VMD decomposition penalty parameter.

3.3 Component Selection and Processing of Reconstructed Signals

Using the size of the sample entropy to measure the noise level of each modal component after VMD decomposition. Select the optimal modal component signal by setting the sample entropy threshold. Use the Gaussian smoothing filter function to smooth the selected modal components and reconstruct the signal [17]. The purpose of data smoothing is to reduce the influence of noise on the signal and improve the signal-to-noise ratio.

3.4 A-VMD Algorithm Flow

(1) Calculate the sample entropy of the input signal and adaptively select the number of decomposition modes K according to (11).

(2) The value range of α is preset, and different α values are used to decompose the signal by VMD. Calculate the sample entropy of the modal components obtained by each decomposition, and select the α value with the smallest sample entropy as the VMD decomposition penalty parameter. Initialize other parameters in the VMD algorithm, noise tolerance, direct-current component, center frequency, and convergence criterion tolerance.

(3) According to the set sample entropy threshold, select the appropriate modal component, perform data smoothing on the selected modal component, and then reconstruct the signal to obtain the denoised signal (Fig. 1).

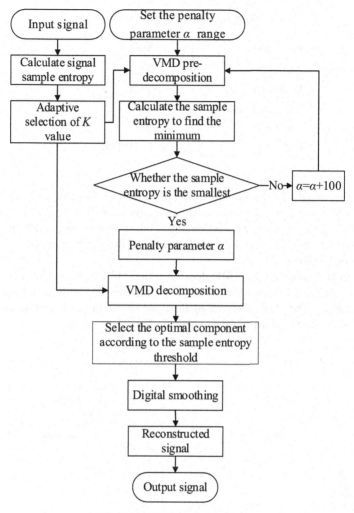

Fig. 1. A-VMD algorithm flow.

4   Noise Reduction Comparison

In this chapter, to verify the proposed theory and the A-VMD algorithm, simulation analysis is carried out by Matlab software.

4.1   Simulation Data Analysis

The parameter settings of the signal are as follows in Table 1.

Table 1. Analog signal parameters.

Parameter	Value
Amplitude	2
Frequency	10 Hz
Sampling frequency	200 Hz
Initial phase	$\pi/3$
SNR	$[-155]$ dB

To compare and analyze the noise reduction effect of different methods, SNR and MSE are selected as noise reduction evaluation indicators. It is generally believed that the higher the SNR, the greater the information content of the signal, the better the noise reduction effect; and the smaller the MSE, the closer the signal after noise reduction is to the original input signal.

The signal is denoised by VMD decomposition [12], Kalman filter [9], empirical mode decomposition [11], wavelet threshold processing [10], data smoothing [17], and A-VMD method. The MSE of several methods are shown in Fig. 2, and the comparison results of SNR of several methods are shown in Fig. 3.

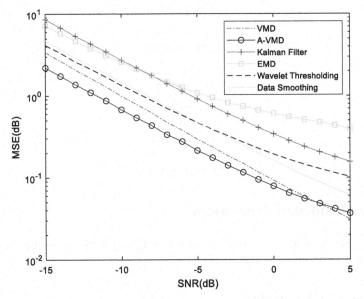

Fig. 2. MSE comparison results

It can be seen from Fig. 2 and Fig. 3 that when the same noise content is added to the signal, the SNR of the signal is the highest after the noise-containing signal is denoised by the A-VMD method. However, using EMD, wavelet threshold, and other methods to

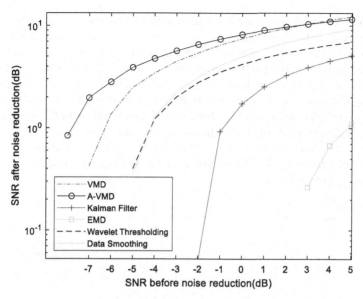

Fig. 3. SNR comparison results

reduce noise, although the SNR of the signal has been improved, it is significantly lower than that of the A-VMD method. Under different noise contents, the MSE value of the denoised signal by the A-VMD method is the smallest. When the SNR before denoising of the signal increases, the SNR after denoising by the A-VMD method is significantly improved. It shows that under different noise contents, the proposed A-VMD method has a better denoising effect, and can retain useful signals while filtering out noise. Compared with EMD, wavelet threshold denoising, and other methods, it has obvious advantages.

4.2 Measured Data Analysis

In the experiment, the actual measured data of the JXZK-MRL radar sensor was processed, and the relevant parameter information was shown in Table 2.

Table 2. Data parameter information.

Parameter	Value
Sampling frequency	128 Hz
FMCW radar Operating frequency	24 GHz
Frequency modulation period	7.8125 ms
Number of sampling points	128

The VMD algorithm and the A-VMD algorithm were used to reduce the noise of the signal collected by the FMCW radar, and the noise reduction comparison results were shown in Fig. 4 below. The MSE value of the VMD algorithm is 0.0034 and the SNR value is 10.93. The AMD algorithm has an MSE value of 0.0015 and an SNR value of 14.98. It can be seen that the noise reduction effect of A-VMD is significantly better than that of the VMD algorithm. In the comparison results, A-VMD has a large signal-to-noise ratio and a large number of interrelationships with the original signal, indicating that the scheme retains the time-frequency information in the signal as much as possible while filtering out the noise. The MSE of A-VMD is minimal, which means that when noise reduction is used, the instantaneous amplitude information of the signal is closer to that of the signal.

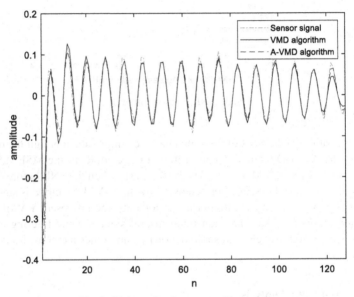

Fig.4. Noise reduction comparison results

5   Conclusion

In order to improve the accuracy of sensor cloud information processing, an A-VMD algorithm is proposed to overcome the shortcomings of existing VMD algorithms from the aspect of sensor signal noise reduction. The scheme adaptively selects the modal decomposition number through the established relationship model between the modal decomposition number and the sample entropy of the input signal, adaptively selects the optimal modal component according to the sample entropy of the calculated modal component, and reconstructs the signal after the selected modal component is processed by data smoothing. The following conclusions can be drawn from the simulation data analysis and the measured data analysis:

(1) The A-VMD method can adaptively select the number of decomposition modes according to the sample entropy of the signal, which avoids the influence of over-or under-decomposition of VMD.

(2) The A-VMD method selects the optimal modal component for reconstruction according to the sample entropy threshold, so it retains the features of the signal more completely, which is beneficial to improving the accuracy of the subsequent calculation of the target's vital feature information.

(3) The A-VMD method performs data smoothing on the selected modal components before reconstructing the signal, so the noise reduction effect of the signal is better than that of algorithms such as VMD.

Acknowledgment. This work was funded by the Applied Basic Research Program of Qinghai Province (Grant Number 2020-ZJ-724) and the Shanghai Natural Science Foundation (Grant Number 21ZR1461700).

References

1. Keipour, H., Hazra, S., Finne, N., Voigt, T.: Generalizing supervised learning for intrusion detection in IoT mesh networks. In: Wang, G., Choo, K.K.R., Ko, R.K.L., Xu, Y., Crispo, B. (eds): Ubiquitous Security. UbiSec 2021. Communications in Computer and Information Science, **1557** (2022). Springer, Singapore. https://doi.org/10.1007/978-981-19-0468-4_16

2. Carter, J., Mancoridis, S.: Evaluation of an anomaly detector for routers using parameterizable malware in an IoT ecosystem. In: Wang, G., Choo, K.K.R., Ko, R.K.L., Xu, Y., Crispo, B. (eds): Ubiquitous Security. UbiSec 2021. Communications in Computer and Information Science, **1557** (2022). Springer, Singapore. https://doi.org/10.1007/978-981-19-0468-4_5

3. Song, X., Li, J., Lei, Q., Zhao, W., Chen, Y., Mian, A.: Bi-CLKT: Bi-graph contrastive learning based knowledge tracing. Knowledge-Based Syst. **241**, 108274 (2022)

4. Song, X., Li, J., Tang, Y., Zhao, T., Chen, Y., Guan, Z.: JKT: a joint graph convolutional network based deep knowledge tracing. Information Sci. **580**, 510523 (2021)

5. Weidong, F., Ningning, C., Wei, C., Wuxiong, Z., Yunliang, C.: A trust-based security system for data collection in smart city. IEEE Trans. Industr. Inf. **17**(6), 4131–4140 (2021)

6. Liu, J., Yu, J., Shen, S.: Energy-efficient two-layer cooperative defense scheme to secure sensor-clouds. IEEE Trans. Information Forensics and Security **13**(2), 408420 (2018)

7. Fang, W., Zhu, C., Yu, F.R., Wang, K., Zhang, W.: Towards energy-efficient and secure data transmission in ai-enabled software defined industrial networks. IEEE Trans. Industrial Informatics **18**(6), 4265–4274 (2022)

8. Fang, W., Zhang, W., Yang, W., Li, Z., Gao, W., Yang, Y.: Trust management-based and energy efficient hierarchical routing protocol in wireless sensor networks. Digital Communications and Networks **7**(4), 470478 (2021)

9. Gilda, S., Slepian, Z.: Automatic Kalman-filter-based wavelet shrinkage denoising of 1D stellar spectra. Monthly Notices of the Royal Astronomical Society **490**(4), 52495269 (2019)

10. Bae, C., Lee, S., Jung, Y.: High-speed continuous wavelet transform processor for vital signal measurement using frequency-modulated continuous wave radar. Sensors **22**(8), 3073 (2022)

11. He, K., Xia, Z., Si, Y., Peng, Y.: Noise reduction of welding crack AE signal based on EMD and wavelet packet. Sensors **20**(3), 761 (2020)

12. Dragomiretskiy, K., Zosso, D.: Variational mode decomposition. IEEE Trans. Signal Process. **62**(3), 531544 (2014)

13. Li, R., Luo, J., Hu, B.: Lamb wave-based damage localization feature enhancement and extraction method for stator insulation of large generators using VMD and wavelet transform. Sensors **20**(15), 4205 (2020)
14. Wang, X., Pang, X., Wang, Y.: Optimized VMD-wavelet packet threshold denoising based on cross-correlation analysis. International J. Performability Eng. **14**(9), 2239 (2018)
15. Dibaj, A., Ettefagh, M.M., Hassannejad, R., Ehghaghi, M.B.: A hybrid fine-tuned VMD and CNN scheme for untrained compound fault diagnosis of rotating machinery with unequal-severity faults. Expert Systems with Appl. prepublish (2020)
16. Huachun, W., Jian, Z., Chunhu, X., Yiming, H.: Two-dimensional time series sample entropy algorithm: applications to rotor axis orbit feature identification. Mechanical Systems and Signal Process. **147**, 107123 (2021)
17. Velleman, P.F.: Definition and comparison of robust nonlinear data smoothing algorithms. J. American Statistical Association **75**(371), 609615 (2012)

A Thermal-Aware Scheduling Algorithm for Reducing Thermal Risks in DAG-Based Applications in Cyber-Physical Systems

Irfan Ali[1], Muhammad Naeem Shehzad[2]([⊠]) [iD], Qaisar Bashir[3],
Haroon Elahi[4][iD], Muhammad Naeem Awais[2], Oana Geman[5], and Pin Liu[6][iD]

[1] Department of Computer System Engineering, Institute of Business Administration
Sukkar, Sukkur 65200, Pakistan
[2] Department of Electrical and Computer Engineering, COMSATS University
Islamabad, Lahore Campus, Lahore 54000, Pakistan
`Naeem.shehzad@cuilahore.edu.pk`
[3] Intel Corporation, Austin, TX 78746, USA
[4] Department of Computing Science, Umeå University, 9036 Umeå, Sweden
[5] Department of Computers, Electronics and Automation, Stefan Cel Mare
University of Suceava, 720229 Suceava, Romania
[6] School of Computer Science and Engineering,
Central South University, Changsha 410083, China

Abstract. Directed Acyclic Graph (DAG)-based scheduling applications are critical to resource allocation in the Cloud, Edge, and Fog layers of cyber-physical systems (CPS). However, thermal anomalies in DVFS-enabled homogeneous multiprocessor systems (HMSS) may be exploited by malicious applications posing risks to the availability of the underlying CPS. This can negatively affect the trustworthiness of CPS. This paper proposes an algorithm to address the thermal risks in DVFS-enabled HMSS for periodic DAG-based applications. It also improves the current list scheduling-based Depth-First and Breadth-First techniques without violating the timing constraints of the system. We test the algorithm using standard benchmarks and synthetic applications in a simulation setup. The results show a reduction in the temperature peaks by up to 30%, average temperature by up to 22%, temperature variations up to 3 times, and temperature spatial gradients by up to 4 times as compared to the conventional Depth-First Scheduling algorithms.

Keywords: Cyber-physical systems · Cloud computing · Edge computing · Thermal-risks · Trust

1 Introduction

Directed Acyclic Graph (DAG) and scheduling applications can help in robustly exploiting resources in the cyber-physical systems (CPS), [24]. However, while

G. Wang et al. (Eds.): UbiSec 2022, CCIS 1768, pp. 497–508, 2023.
https://doi.org/10.1007/978-981-99-0272-9_34

running these applications, Dynamic Frequency and Scaling (DVFS) enabled homogeneous multiprocessor systems can face thermal issues that affect their efficiency and lifespan [18]. For example, research shows that a ten-degree centigrade increase in operating temperature approximately halves the lifespan of a System-on-Chip (SoC) [23]. Such a scenario is even more critical for the battery-operated devices common in CPS's Cloud, Edge, and Fog layers [26]. Further, compared to the single processor, these issues are more common in multiprocessor systems required to serve CPS needs due to the neighboring effects of the operating cores and relatively limited cooling area [13]. Hence managing the thermal issues along and energy and power optimization is a significant security problem that may affect the lifespan and performance of DAG-based scheduling applications and the trustworthiness of their underlying CPS.

A significant amount of research work focuses on thermal management of independent task sets application model [12,13,21]. However, the dependent task set application model closer to real-world CPS scenarios like DAG-based applications, where a job's execution depends on executing one or more tasks in the system, is under-researched. Further, the existing algorithms for solving DAG-based tasks ignore temperature issues due to unbalanced workload allocation [9,17]. This leaves the Cloud, Edge, and Fog layers of CPS where DAG-based applications are extensively used [24,25] vulnerable to potential attacks involving thermal exploitations by malicious parties [5]. This research aims to enable the trustworthy execution of DAG-based applications in CPS while obeying the precedence constraints and minimizing thermal emergencies. The main contributions of this research are as follows.

1. In this paper, we propose an algorithm to address the thermal issues in DVFS-enabled homogeneous multiprocessor systems for periodic DAG-based applications.
2. The proposed algorithm lowers the temperature peaks, average temperature, temperature temporal gradients, and temperature spatial gradients on a DVFS-enabled homogeneous multi-core system. Instead of just using the execution time of running tasks, the load balancing is performed based on the power consumed by each processing core by incorporating the nature of each task.
3. The algorithm is evaluated in a simulation environment using benchmark and synthetic applications for 4-core and 8-core systems. We compare the results with the conventional algorithms.

The rest of the article is organized as follows. Section 2 highlights the important work in literature. Section 3 describes the system model. The proposed algorithm is discussed in Sect. 4. Section 5 details the experimental setup and results and discussion given in Sects. 6. The conclusion is given in Sect. 7.

2 Related Work

Conventionally, techniques such as Dynamic Power Management (DPM) [19], Dynamic Voltage and Frequency Scaling (DVFS) [4], Load balancing, task migration, or modification of these techniques has been the focus of processor optimization research. However, the use of DAG and scheduling applications in robustly exploiting resources in the cyber-physical systems (CPS) [24] has changed the focus. For example, Alsubaihi et al. [1] propose PETRAS (Performance, Energy, and Thermal aware Resource Allocator and Scheduler), which uplifts the system performance using task mapping, core scaling, and thread migration to lower energy, power, and peak temperatures. King et al. [11] propose multiple static schemes that identify the nodes of DAG applications that can be executed at lower clock speeds under DVFS-enabled cores to optimize the energy.

Baskiyar and Abdel-Kader [2] propose EADAGS (Energy-Aware DAG Scheduling) which reduces energy consumption by reducing the operating frequency when necessary using the principle of dynamic voltage scaling (DVS) in heterogeneous processors. It also reduces the scheduling length. Geng et al. [6] propose a scheduling algorithm based on the task duplication technique that minimizes the scheduling length while balancing the workload among the cores of a multi-core cluster system. In another work [18], the authors propose two algorithms to optimize performance, energy, and temperature while scheduling DAG-based applications on a multi-core system.

Bhatti et al. [3] propose a list scheduling heuristic called Noodle heuristic that reduces the average scheduling length. Contrary to conventional solutions, priorities are assigned to the ready tasks using proportionate fairness. Guo et al. [7] present an energy and power-aware scheduling algorithm for sporadic DAG-based tasks with implicit deadlines on multi-core systems. They use federated scheduling for intelligent task allocation with the decomposition of a task.

Finally, it has long been known that DAG-based applications are vulnerable to thermal security risks [5]. However, to the best of our knowledge, prior work does not address temperature peaks, average temperature, temperature spatial, and temporal gradients simultaneously for the DAG-based task sets model to improve the security of these applications. Our proposed algorithm is novel because it addresses all these parameters for the DAG-based task model.

3   System Model

3.1   Application Model

Our workload comprises an application represented by the DAG graph $G = (\tau, E, WCET, CC)$, wherein each node T_i belongs to the set τ and represents a task. The edge $E(i, j)$, belonging to a set of edges, represents the dependency between node T_i and T_j. Dependencies can be data and/or control-flow dependencies. The $WCET(T_i)$ represents the worst-case execution time of the node and is non-negative. The $WCET$ is the sum of $WCET$ of each node. A positive weight $CC(E(i, j))$ on edge $E(i, j)$ shows the communication cost between tasks if they run on different processors. If the tasks run on the same processor, there is no communication cost. Communication cost is the cost of transferring the data required for task execution from one processor to another. It is measured by the consumed time. P is the time after which the application restarts itself.

In our case, the application deadline D is equal to its time period, i.e., implicit deadlines. The utilization requirement of the application is obtained by dividing the $WCET$ of the application by the product of the time period and the number of cores M in the system.

Further, in this application, a source node is the starting point of DAG. And it does not have any predecessor task. A sink node is the end point of DAG, and it does not have any successor task. The critical path is the path with the largest path length. The critical path doesn't need to have the largest number of nodes/tasks in it. It depends upon the $WCET$ of the nodes. The schedule length L is the total time taken to completely finish the execution of all tasks in a DAG by the scheduler. It cannot be less than the critical path. Finally, parallelism is the ratio between total execution time over Critical Path length. A DAG with parallelism value 1 indicates that it is a sequential execution.

For feasible schedule of DAG-based application with worst case execution time $WCET$, time period P equals to its deadline D, and schedule length L on M core processing system, the following two necessary conditions must be met.

$$\frac{WCET}{P} \leq M \tag{1}$$

$$L \leq D \tag{2}$$

3.2   Power Model

We use the power model as proposed by Jejurikar et al. [8]. In this model, the total power comprises dynamic and static power as given in Eq. 3.

$$P_{Total} = P_{Dynamic} + P_{Static} \tag{3}$$

The dynamic part of the power $P_{Dynamic}$ is given by Eq. 3.

$$P_{Dynamic} = C * F * V^2 \tag{4}$$

In the Eq. 4, C represents the value of switching capacitance. The V and F represents the supplied voltage and switching frequency respectively.

The value of the static power is dependent on the leakage current as given by Eq. 5.

$$P_{Static} = I_L * V \tag{5}$$

Where I_L represents the leakage current and has a direct relation with the temperature. The relation between temperature and leakage current is given in Eq. 6.

$$I_L = I_O * T^2/(T_O^2) * e^{(a*V*(T-T_O))/(T*T_O)} \tag{6}$$

where I_O represents the value of leakage current at a reference temperature T_O. The increase in the leakage current increases the static power which in turns raises the total power consumption.

The consumed energy in a time interval $[a, b]$ can be computed using Eq. 7.

$$E = \int_a^b P(t)dt \tag{7}$$

3.3 Thermal Model

The employed thermal model is proposed in ATMI (Analytical Model of Temperature in Microprocessors) [16]. ATMI is a linear thermal model. It models a processor core as two layers: a silicon layer over a metal layer of given dimensions. The user provides the physical dimension and parameters like thermal conductance and diffusivity. The model does not consider the impact of edges. ATMI computes the transient temperature using core functions employing the power states of the core. The steady-state response is computed using the superposition principle. The steady state and transient temperatures are modeled using the following heat equation.

$$dT/dt = b * (T_S - T) \tag{8}$$

In Eq. 8, b is a hardware-dependent thermal parameter while steady state temperature is represented by T_S. The core temperature is estimated using the superposition principle. ATMI assumes uniform ambient temperature. The value of ambient temperature is provided by the user.

3.4 Threat Model

In the Edge and Fog layers, due to resource constraints, it is hard to implement sophisticated security systems. Therefore, it is possible that the threat actor bypasses the limited security controls, identifies dependent task set DAG-based applications, and triggers such applications repeatedly. Such repeated executions will cause thermal emergencies and reduce the lifespan of the underlying devices. Furthermore, if multiple such applications are running on different devices in the system, CPS will face failures at random points. Finally, since the attacker achieves it through normal application execution, it is challenging to identify such attacks.

4 Proposed Algorithm

We propose an algorithm that lowers the temperature peaks and temperature temporal and spatial gradients in the DAG-based application. The algorithm works in two steps. In the first step (lines 6–9) of the algorithm, the temperature peaks are reduced by lowering the operating frequency using the principle of DVFS. The frequency is computed such that timing constraints are not violated. In the second step (lines 10–17), M new scheduling points are introduced to perform the load balancing mechanism. Instead of using just the running time of each core, the proposed algorithm performs the load balancing based on power consumed by each core by incorporating the power deviation factor of each task

Algorithm 1. Pseudo code of Proposed Algorithm

1: **Input:**
2: *A DAG based taskset containing N nodes with period P. A multiprocessor system with M cores (Cr), All the processing cores can run at discrete values of frequencies $F_1, F_2, ...,$ and F_H. F_H is the highest frequency. F is newly computed frequency*
3: **Output:**
4: *Thermal aware schedule for DAG based taskset*
5: **procedure**
6:     **Step1.** Offline computation of lowest operating frequency
7:       *WCET ← Sum of execution time of all the nodes*
8:       *Util = WCET/(P * M)*
9:       *F ← ⌈Util * F_H⌉ //Ceil the computed value to the higher available discrete frequency value*
10:     **Step2.** Online Load Balancing of workload
11:       *L = P/M // Length to add new scheduling event*
12:       *@ (each tick of time t)*
13:       *If (t/L == 0)*
14:       *For (i : 1toM)*
15:         $Cr(i)_{Pow.Con} = \sum (Execution\ time\ of\ task\ T_n * T_n.Power.Deviation)$ // Data is recorded only for the last interval
16:       *End For*
17:       *End If*
18: **end procedure**

---

executed over it. It is mentioned in line 12 of the pseudo code. The value of power deviation of task Tn denoted by Tn. Power-Deviation varies from 1 to 100. A task with power deviation 100 will consume double power as compared to the task with power deviation 50. However, the product cannot be less than a specified minimum power value provided in the data sheet for each operating frequency. Balancing is performed only on the record of the most recent interval of length P/M. The pseudo-code of the proposed algorithm is given in the listing 1.

5 Experimental Setup

The proposed algorithm is evaluated in a simulation environment comprising a scheduling simulation tool STORM (Simulation Tool for Real-time Multiprocessors) [22] and thermal modeling software. STORM can execute a given task set over a defined processing platform according to the user's defined scheduling policy and has been used by many recent studies [14,20]. The user defines the details of the task set and provides information about the processing platform. Further, we use a thermal modeling tool ATMI (Analytical Model of Temperature in Microprocessors) [16]. By employing the processor details like physical dimensions, material properties, and packaging information, ATMI models the system. Using the power profile values recorded by STORM, ATMI estimates the temperature of the individual core by solving the heat equations of the system.

The power profile carries each core's power consumption as a time function. We have used the PXA270 processor [15], which is an XScale® technology and is a popular choice for embedded system applications. It is a DVFS-enabled processor capable of operating at different couple voltage and frequency levels shown in Table 1. The proposed algorithm is evaluated using the benchmarks Standard

Table 1. PXA270 processor power consumption at different operating frequencies

Operating frequency (MHz)	Active power (Watt)	Idle power(Watt)
624	0.925	0.26
520	0.747	0.222
416	0.570	0.186
312	0.390	0.154
208	0.279	0.129
104	0.116	0.064

Task Graph (STG) [10] as well as the synthetic applications. The application comprised of 10, 26, 52 and 100 nodes task sets. The 52 node task set STG is used as the bench mark application. The worst-case execution time of the this application is 288.

6   Result and Discussion

This section provides detailed results and necessary discussion. The results were generated using the simulation setup discussed in the previous section. We compare our results with the conventional DAG-solving DFS algorithm. We use temperature peaks, average temperature, spatial and temporal gradients, and power consumption for comparisons. Detailed information about the two datasets is provided in Table 2.

Table 2. PXA270 processor power consumption at different operating frequencies

Details	Case1	Case2
Origin	Synthetic	Bench Mark
Nodes	26	52
WCET	99	291
Critical Path	45	74
Time period	69	175
% Utilization	36	21

Case 1. The execution of a 26-nodes synthetic application over a 4-core system.

Figure 1 shows the execution of a synthetic application over the 4-core system using conventional DFS at 624 MHz. The horizontal axis represents the time in seconds while the vertical axis represents the temperature in degree centigrade. In the conventional DFS algorithm, the maximum temperature of the hottest core rises up to 65 °C. This is because core-1 always gets the highest priority during workload allocation. The workload is allocated to the next core, i.e., core-2, only if core-1 is busy. This phenomenon is valid for all the cores, resulting in the maximum temperature of core-1 and the minimum temperature of core 4. It causes a spatial gradient of 13 °C in this case. Further, the application is executed at 624 MHz which allows the application completion in 60% of the allocated time. Therefore the core remains idle for the rest of the time. This results in periodic peaks of the temperature after a specific time period. The average temperature of the four cores in the conventional DFS algorithm is 55 °C.

The results of the temperature curves using the proposed algorithm at 416 MHz frequency are given in Fig. 2. The value of the frequency is computed using the principle of DVFS technique in the first part of the algorithm. This is the minimum frequency at which the workload may be executed without missing the timing constraints. Operation at this relatively lower frequency lowers the energy which results in reducing of temperature peaks. The peak temperature is around 53 °C. In the second part, the algorithm creates some extra scheduling points that balance the workload among the cores while considering the recent thermal history of the individual core. This cause approximate equal temperature among all the cores. It lowers the spatial gradient among the cores. The maximum value of the spatial gradient, in this case, is 7 °C. The average temperature of the four cores in the proposed algorithm also lowers to 47.2 °C. This is because lowering the frequency lowers the energy of each core.

Case 2. The execution of 52 nodes STG benchmark application over an 8-core homogeneous system.

Figure 3 shows the execution of the STG benchmark application over the 8-core system using conventional DFS at 624 MHz. In the conventional DFS algorithm, the maximum temperature of the hottest core, i.e., core-1, rises to 76 °C. This is because the workload is always allocated to core 1 in the first choice. The workload is assigned to core-2 only if core 1 is busy, and so on. As a result of this behavior, the core-8 is rarely utilized. This causes a considerable temperature difference between the temperature of the cores of the system. The maximum value of the spatial gradient is 26 °C. Moreover, significant peaks of the system are observed because the execution of the workload is completed far earlier than the completion of the time period of the application. The average temperature of the eight cores in the conventional DFS algorithm is 53.2 °C.

The results of the proposed algorithm for the benchmark application are given in Fig. 4. The peak temperature is reduced because of the scaling down of the frequency to 316 MHz. The maximum value of the peak temperature is 52 °C. Due to the balancing of workload among the cores, the spatial gradient is

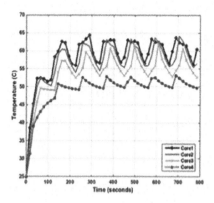

Fig. 1. Temperature profile of 4 cores system using conventional DFS at 624 MHz.

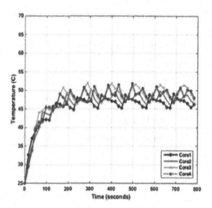

Fig. 2. Temperature profile of 4 cores system using proposed technique at 416 MHz.

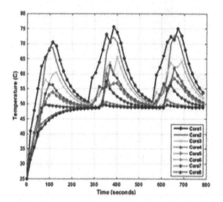

Fig. 3. Temperature profile of 8 cores system using conventional DFS algorithm at 624 MHz.

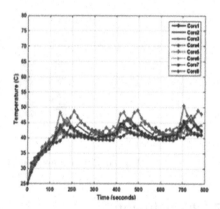

Fig. 4. Temperature profile of 8 cores system using proposed algorithm at 316 MHz.

also reduced to 8 °C. The average temperature of the eight cores in the proposed algorithm also lowers to 41.4 °C.

Table 3 provides the summary of peak and average temperature as well as temperature spatial and temporal gradients. It shows that proposed algorithm significantly lowers the spatial gradients, temporal gradients and temperature peaks.

Figure 5 shows the total and individual power utilized by the two algorithms in the 4-core system. The graph shows that the total power used by the systems remains the same. However, there is significant difference in power utilized by individual cores in conventional algorithm. The proposed algorithm incurs almost equal power utilization among all the cores using the load balancing algorithm.

Table 3. Summary of various parameters in 4 and 8 core system

Parameters	4 - Core System		8 - Core System	
	DFS	Proposed	DFS	Proposed
Temperature peaks (°C)	64	52	76	49
Average temperature (°C)	55	47.2	53.2	41.4
Spatial gradients (°C)	13	7	26	8
Temporal gradient (°C /100 s)	8	4	20	7

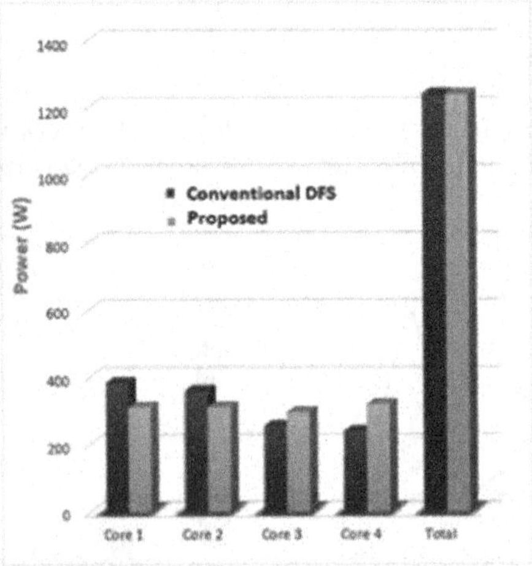

Fig. 5. Power consumed by individual cores for 800 s.

7   Conclusion

DAG-based applications manage critical resource allocation in the Cloud, Edge, and Fog layers of CPS. Thermal issues encountered in DVFS-enabled homogeneous multiprocessor systems can be exploited by malicious parties, which may affect the availability of DAG-based applications and the security of underlying systems. This paper proposed a thermal-aware scheduling algorithm for executing DAG-based applications over a homogeneous multi-core processing platform. The proposed algorithm reduces thermal risks by operating the processor at the minimum operating frequency while meeting timing constraints and balancing the workload among the cores. We evaluated the algorithm in a simulation setup and compared the results with conventional DFS for 4-core and 8-core processing platforms. The results show a significant reduction in temperature peaks and average temperature compared to the traditional method. The proposed algorithm also decreases the spatial gradients by up to 4 times and temporal gradients by up to 3 times. The power used by the system in each case remains the same; however, it is efficiently balanced among the cores in the proposed algorithm. The proposed technique can improve the security and trustworthiness of the Edge and Fog layers of CPS by removing the risk of thermal exploitation.

References

1. Alsubaihi, S., Gaudiot, J.L.: PETRAS: performance, energy and thermal aware resource allocation and scheduling for heterogeneous systems. In: Proceedings of the 8th International Workshop on Programming Models and Applications for Multicores and Manycores, PMAM 2017,. pp. 29–38. ACM, New York, NY, USA (2017)
2. Baskiyar, S., Abdel-Kader, R.: Energy aware DAG scheduling on heterogeneous systems. Clust. Comput. **13**(4), 373–383 (2010)
3. Bhatti, M.K., Oz, I., Popov, K., Brorsson, M., Farooq, U.: Scheduling of parallel tasks with proportionate priorities. Arab. J. Sci. Eng. **41**(8), 3279–3295 (2016)
4. Burd, T., Pering, T., Stratakos, A., Brodersen, R.: A dynamic voltage scaled microprocessor system. IEEE J. Solid-State Circuits **35**(11), 1571–1580 (2000)
5. Dadvar, P., Skadron, K.: Potential thermal security risks. In: Semiconductor Thermal Measurement and Management IEEE Twenty First Annual IEEE Symposium, 2005, pp. 229–234. IEEE (2005)
6. Geng, X., Xu, G., Fu, X., Zhang, Y.: A task scheduling algorithm for multi-core-cluster systems. J. Comput. **7**(11), 2797–2804 (2012)
7. Guo, Z., Bhuiyan, A., Saifullah, A., Guan, N., Xiong, H.: Energy-efficient multi-core scheduling for real-time DAG tasks. In: Bertogna, M. (ed.) 29th Euromicro Conference on Real-Time Systems (ECRTS 2017). Leibniz International Proceedings in Informatics (LIPIcs), vol. 76, pp. 22:1–22:21. Schloss Dagstuhl-Leibniz-Zentrum fuer Informatik, Dagstuhl, Germany (2017)
8. Jejurikar, R., Pereira, C., Gupta, R.: Leakage aware dynamic voltage scaling for real-time embedded systems. In: Proceedings of the 41st Annual Design Automation Conference, DAC 2004, pp. 275–280. ACM, New York, NY, USA (2004)
9. Juarez, F., Ejarque, J., Badia, R.M.: Dynamic energy-aware scheduling for parallel task-based application in cloud computing. Futur. Gener. Comput. Syst. **78**, 257–271 (2018)
10. Kasahara Lab., Waseda Univ: Standard task graph set. https://www.kasahara.cs.waseda.ac.jp/schedule/
11. King, D., Sheikh, H., Ahmad, I.: Stretch and compress based re-scheduling techniques for minimizing the execution times of DAGs on multi-core processors under energy constraints. In: International Conference on Green Computing, pp. 49–60. IEEE Computer Society, Los Alamitos, CA, USA (August 2010)
12. Lee, J.S., Skadron, K., Chung, S.W.: Predictive temperature-aware DVFS. IEEE Trans. Comput. **59**(1), 127–133 (2010)
13. Liu, W., Yi, J., Li, M., Chen, P., Yang, L.: Energy-efficient application mapping and scheduling for lifetime guaranteed MPSoCs. IEEE Trans. Comput. Aided Des. Integr. Circuits Syst. **38**(1), 1–14 (2019)
14. Magdich, A., Kacem, Y.H., Kerboeuf, M., Mahfoudhi, A., Abid, M.: A design pattern-based approach for automatic choice of semi-partitioned and global scheduling algorithms. Inf. Softw. Technol. **97**, 83–98 (2018)
15. Marvell Technology Group: Marvell pxa270 processor electrical, mechanical and thermal specification data sheet. https://tinyurl.com/wqrk3q8

16. Michaud, P., Sazeides, Y.: Atmi: analytical model of temperature in micropro-
    cessors. In: Third Annual Workshop on Modeling, Benchmarking and Simulation
    (MoBS), vol. 2, pp. 12–21 (2007)
17. Shakil, Arif, M., Sohail, S.S., Alam, M.T., Ubaid, S., Nafis, M.T., Wang, G.:
    Towards a two-tier architecture for privacy-enabled recommender systems (PeRS).
    In: Communications in Computer and Information Science, pp. 268–278. Springer
    Singapore (2022). https://doi.org/10.1007/978-981-19-0468-4_20
18. Sheikh, H.F., Ahmad, I.: Fast algorithms for simultaneous optimization of perfor-
    mance, energy and temperature in DAG scheduling on multi-core processors. In:
    Proceedings of the International Conference on Parallel and Distributed Process-
    ing Techniques and Applications (PDPTA), Athens, pp. 1–7. Athens: The Steering
    Committee of The World Congress in Computer Science, Computer Engineering
    and Applied Computing (WorldComp) (2012)
19. Srinivasan, J., Adve, S.V.: Predictive dynamic thermal management for multime-
    dia applications. In: Proceedings of the 17th annual international conference on
    Supercomputing - ICS 2003. ACM (2003)
20. Sun, J., Cho, H., Easwaran, A., Park, J.D., Choi, B.C.: Flow network-based real-
    time scheduling for reducing static energy consumption on multiprocessors. IEEE
    Access 7, 1330–1344 (2019)
21. Tyagi, S.K.S., Jain, D.K., Fernandes, S.L., Muhuri, P.K.: Thermal-aware power-
    efficient deadline based task allocation in multi-core processor. J. Comput. Sci. 19,
    112–120 (2017)
22. Urunuela, R., Deplanche, A.M., Trinquet, Y.: STORM a simulation tool for real-
    time multiprocessor scheduling evaluation. In: 2010 IEEE 15th Conference on
    Emerging Technologies and Factory Automation (ETFA 2010). IEEE (September
    2010)
23. Wilcoxon, R.: Does a 10 c increase in temperature really reduce the life of elec-
    tronics by half? Electronic Cooling, pp. 1–1 (August 2017)
24. Wu, H., Hua, X., Li, Z., Ren, S.: Resource and instance hour minimization for
    deadline constrained DAG applications using computer clouds. IEEE Trans. Par-
    allel Distrib. Syst. 27(3), 885–899 (2016)
25. Xu, L., Yang, D.: An edge-cloud collaborative object detection system. In: Wang,
    G., Choo, K.K.R., Ko, R.K.L., Xu, Y., Crispo, B. (eds.) Ubiquitous Secur., pp.
    371–378. Springer Singapore, Singapore (2022). https://doi.org/10.1007/978-981-
    19-0468-4_28
26. Zou, Y., Peng, T., Zhong, W., Guan, K., Wang, G.: Reliable and controllable
    data sharing based on blockchain. In: Communications in Computer and Informa-
    tion Science, pp. 229–240. Springer, Singapore (2022). https://doi.org/10.1007/
    978-981-19-0468-4_17

Short Papers

Garbage Recognition Algorithm Based on Self-attention Mechanism and Deep Sorting

Haiyang Huang[1], Falong Xiao[2], Xiaofang Zhang[2], Wanting Yan[2], Fumin Liu[1], and Yuezhong Wu[2][✉]

[1] College of Artificial Intelligence, Hunan University of Technology, Zhuzhou 412007, Hunan, China
[2] College of Railway Transportation, Hunan University of Technology, Zhuzhou 412007, Hunan, China
wuyuezhong@hut.edu.cn

Abstract. Garbage sorting plays a very important role in ensuring a life safety. Aiming at the problems of poor real-time detection and low recognition accuracy of current garbage classification, an improved multi-objective real-time garbage classification recognition algorithm based on YOLOv5s is proposed. By combining the Coordinate Attention (CA) self-attention module and the neck part of YOLOv5s, the defect of insufficient receptive field is reduced to improve the detection accuracy, and the DeepSort algorithm is introduced to optimize the multi-target garbage feature recognition and strengthen the real-time detection ability. The experimental results show that the improved YOLOv5s garbage classification detection model can effectively identify 44 different types of garbage. Compared with the original YOLOv5s algorithm, the detection mAP value is 76.56%, an increase of 11.3%, and the precision is 85.63%, an increase of 12.38%. While ensuring the multi-target real-time detection efficiency, the improved algorithm can have better detection accuracy Rate.

Keywords: Machine learning and AI security · Computer vision · Self-attention mechanism · DeepSort

1 Introduction

Since 2019, the total amount of garbage in China has exceeded 1 billion tons per year, and the annual growth rate is 5–8%. At least two-thirds of cities in China are facing the dilemma of "garbage siege", so the establishment of a systematic garbage classification system has become imminent [1]. Modern waste contains chemicals, some of which raise safety concerns. If the garbage is disposed of in landfill or stacked, even if the landfill is far away from the living place and the corresponding isolation technology is adopted, it will endanger human safety. These harmful substances will enter the entire ecosystem with the circulation of the earth, pollute water sources and land, and ultimately affect people's life's safety through plants or animals [2]. Garbage classification plays a very important role in life safety. Therefore, it is of great research significance to use computer vision technology [3] for automatic garbage identification to replace human.

Vision-based target detection algorithms are roughly divided into target detection algorithms based on traditional methods and target detection algorithms based on deep learning. Until 2012, the rise of convolutional neural networks [4, 5] pushed the field of object detection to a new level. With the rapid development of deep learning, many researchers have proposed a variety of methods beyond traditional image recognition. The mainstream image recognition algorithms of deep learning can be divided into two categories according to the completed steps: Two-stage target detection algorithms (eg: RCNN series) [6, 7] and One-stage target detection algorithms (eg: YOLO series) [8]. YOLO [9] is the originator of one-stage detectors, and it has also achieved real-time in the true sense. Ye A et al. [10] introduced the Variational Autoencoder (VAE) into the YOLO model to reduce the model size, improve the accuracy of automatic garbage identification and classification, and enhance the model calculation speed. Bohong L et al. [11] proposed an efficient channel attention YOLO (ECA-YOLO) detection algorithm. By improving a lightweight cross-channel interactive attention mechanism in the YOLOv3 residual unit, the model can be more complete and effective. Yang G et al. [12] adopted a garbage identification and detection algorithm based on YOLOV5, and used data augmentation to improve the robustness of the model and achieve fast and accurate identification of different types of garbage. He Y et al. [13] replaced the standard convolution in YOLOv3 with depthwise separable convolution, and introduced triple attention in the backbone network, reducing the parameters and arithmetic operations of YOLOv3, improving the detection speed of the model, and enhancing the effective features The channel weights enhance the feature extraction capability.

This paper aims to improve the real-time performance and accuracy of real-time garbage classification identification and detection in different environments. In the field of garbage classification, real-time detection has not been well used. The main reason is that the speed of real-time detection is not enough, the real environment is complex, and the algorithm recognition ability is low. Although the above algorithms have improved the accuracy of the YOLO algorithm, there are still problems such as low real-time detection efficiency, misjudgment for overlapping or deformed objects in the detection of a large amount of domestic waste. In view of such problems, our improvements are as follows:

1) Using CA combined with the neck of YOLOv5s improves the sensitivity and detection accuracy of the network for small objects and occluded objects.
2) Combined with the DeepSort algorithm to improve the accuracy of real-time monitoring. In the following, this paper will solve the above problems from related work, improvement of the YOLOv5s network and ablation experiments.

2   Related Work

2.1   YOLOv5s

The YOLOv5s [14] architecture consists of four different models, which differ only in the parameters controlling the depth of the network and the width of the network. As shown in Fig. 1, its network structure mainly includes four parts: input, backbone, neck, and head [15]. The main work of the input side is the preprocessing of image data. The main function of the backbone network is to extract a series of feature maps of different scales in the image.

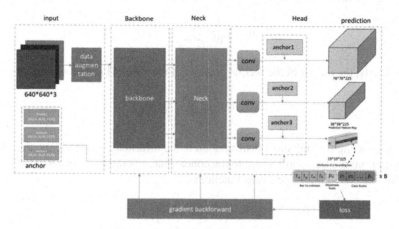

Fig. 1. YOLOv5s network structure

2.2 CA Self-attention Mechanism

Attention mechanism [16] is a method for processing data in machine learning. It is to increase the weight of the attention mechanism in the hidden layer of the neural network, so that the content that does not conform to the attention model is weakened or forgotten. The structure diagram of CA mechanism is shown in Fig. 2

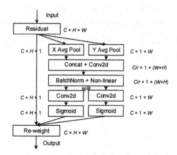

Fig. 2. The CA self-attention mechanism

Specifically, given the input, each channel is first encoded separately along the horizontal and vertical coordinates using the pooling kernel with the dimensions of (H, 1) or (1, W). Therefore, the output of the first channel of height h can be expressed as:

$$z_c^h(h) = \frac{1}{W} \sum_{0 \leq i < W} x_c(h, i).$$

(1)

Similarly, the output of the second channel of the width H can be written as:

$$z_c^w(w) = \frac{1}{H} \sum_{0 \leq j < H} x_c(j, w)$$

(2)

After passing through the transformation in the information embedding, the section proceeds from the transform above to the concatenate operation, and then transforms it by using the convolution transform function:

$$f = \delta\left(F_1\left(\left[z^h, z^w\right]\right)\right)$$

(3)

where is the concatenate operation along the spatial dimension, is the nonlinear activation function, and is the intermediate feature map that encodes the spatial information in the horizontal and vertical directions. Here, it is used to control the reduction rate of the SE block size. It will then be decomposed into 2 separate sums of tensors along the spatial dimension. Using another 2 convolutional transforms and transforming the sum into a tensor with the same number of channels to the input respectively, we get:

$$\begin{cases} g^h = \sigma\left(F_h\left(f^h\right)\right) \\ g^w = \sigma\left(F_w\left(f^w\right)\right) \end{cases}$$

(4)

In order to reduce the complexity and computational overhead of the model, an appropriate reduction ratio is usually used to reduce the number of channels. Then the output sum is expanded, respectively, as attention weights. Finally, the output of the Coordinate Attention Block can be written as:

$$y_c(i, j) = x_c(i, j) \times g_c^h(i) \times g_c^w(j)$$

(5)

2.3 DeepSort Algorithm

To track each garbage detected by the YOLOv5s model, define an 8-dimensional state vector that defines the state of the object to be detected:

$$x = (u, v, \gamma, q, \dot{u}, \dot{v}, \dot{\gamma}, \dot{q})$$

(6)

In the formula: (u, v) are the center coordinates of the object to be detected; γ, q are the aspect ratio and height of the bounding box of the object to be detected; $(\dot{u}, \dot{v}, \dot{\gamma}, \dot{q})$ are the objects to be detected (u, v, γ, q) corresponding velocity information in the image coordinate system[17].

The algorithm flowchart is shown in Fig. 3.

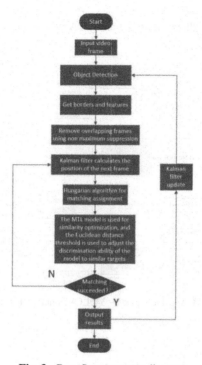

Fig. 3. DeepSort structure diagram

3 Improvement of YOLOv5s Network Structure

3.1 DeepSort and CA Algorithm Combined with YOLOv5s

DeepSort algorithm is an improved SORT multi-target tracking algorithm. On this basis, convolutional neural network is used to extract appearance information features to reduce the number of ID switches generated. Cascaded matching is used to give priority to frequent objects to solve the discontinuity problem in target tracking. It is mainly divided into four steps: ①Based on the original video frame, using the target detector to obtain the target candidate box, and the Non-Maximum Suppression screen is used to remove the multiple frames, and the detection results are obtained. ②Using Kalman filtering algorithm to predict the location and state of the target in the next frame, and IOUs are matched between the prediction frame and the detection frame to calculate the cost matrix. ③Using the Hungarian algorithm to optimally match the detection frame according to the input cost matrix, and using the re-identification model to extract the appearance characteristics of the object, giving priority to the matching weight of the tracking frame of the confirmed state. ④Outputting tracking results, and updating the parameters of the tracker through Kalman filter, looping the algorithm process again until the end of the video frame.

The YOLOv5s block diagram after fusing CA with neck and adding the DeepSort algorithm is shown in Fig. 4.

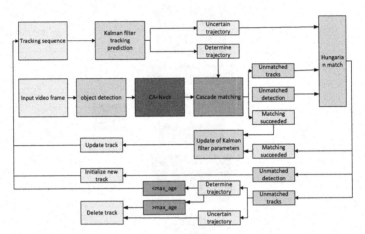

Fig. 4. CA + DeepSort + YOLOv5s network structure

4   Experimental Setup and Results Analysis

4.1   Dataset Settings

In this experiment, 1.4 w spider images were crawled and classified into 44 different types. Each type is classified as a folder, including common garbage types such as cigarette butts, pillows, shoes and fish bones. The number of images in each category is more than 300, considering different shapes, angles, light, and stains. Labelimg is used to annotate each type of image, and the number of manually annotated images is more than 150. The annotation process is shown in Fig. 5:

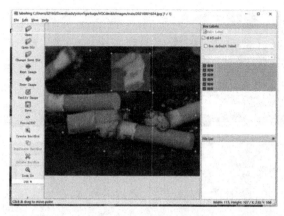

Fig. 5. Labelimg annotation example diagram

4.2 YOLOv5s Network Training

The experimental environment is shown in Table 1:

Table 1. Experiment environment

Environment	Cpu	Gpu	System	Frame	Development language
Model	amd	Tesla	Ubuntu	pytorch	python
Version	7-5800h	v100 (32G)	16.02	1.5	3.8

Parameter training using SGD optimization algorithm, parameter settings are as follows: Batchsize is 32; epoch is 300; the momentum factor is 0.9; the weight attenuation coefficient is 0.0005. The learning rate is dynamically adjusted by annealing strategy, and the initial learning rate is 0.01. Use GIOU Loss as the loss function.

4.3 YOLOv5s Ablation and Comparative Test

The trained model is tested under same background, same scale and occlusion. The experimental results are shown in Fig. 6–7, and the values on the figure are confidence. It can be seen from the test results that YOLOv5s (CA + DeepSort) can better detect occluded and small garbage under the same conditions. However, in the case of occlusion, the confidence of detecting the target is reduced.

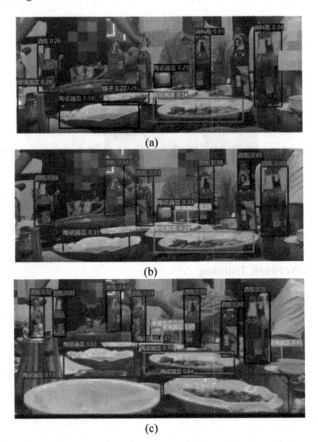

(a)

(b)

(c)

Fig. 6. Comparison of YOLOv5s(a),YOLOv5s + CAeffects(b) and YOLOv5s + CA + DeepSort effects(c) under complex background

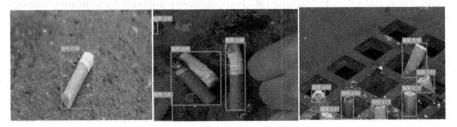

Fig. 7. Identification of different environments, light and shapes of the same object

As can be seen from the above figure, for the original YOLOv5s model, under the conditions of using the same data set and equipment, the recognition effect of occluded objects and small objects is not as good as the improved YOLOv5s model, and the best effect is (CA + Deepsort) YOLOv5s model, the detection of small objects and occluded objects has been significantly improved, and the confidence of objects has also been improved.

4.4 Algorithm Test Results Analysis

This paper uses the commonly used average accuracy rate, average precision, and detection frames per second to measure the effect of the algorithm. The IOU is set to 0.5, and three algorithms, YOLOv5s, YOLOv5s (CA), and YOLOv5s (CA + DeepSort) are tested based on the 3144 test set. The results are shown in Table 2:

Table 2. Network comparison experiment results

Model	Precision/%	mAP@0.5/%	Training time/h	Frame rate/fps
YOLOv5s	73.25%	65.4%	216	30.00
YOLOv5s (CA)	81.32%	70.3%	120	30.00
YOLOv5s (DeepSort + CA)	**85.63%**	**76.3%**	**120**	30.00

The comprehensive analysis shows that the CA + DeepSort has certain advantages in accuracy and mAP compared with original YOLOv5s algorithm. But the frame rate compared with the original algorithm, the advantage is not prominent. This paper focuses on the problem of poor recognition accuracy under occlusion. At the same time, considering the complex background and different garbage forms in the data set, the detection ability of small target objects is enhanced. The improved algorithm has improved in accuracy, mAP and other indicators. The accuracy of the improved CA + DeepSort YOLOv5s algorithm is 12.38% higher than that of the YOLOv5s algorithm, 4.31% higher than that of the YOLOv5s algorithm with only CA, 10.9% higher than that of the mAP algorithm, and 6.0% higher than that of the YOLOv5s algorithm with only CA. In summary, the good performance of the proposed algorithm can be verified, and it has certain advantages in the actual tracking scene. The final results are shown in Fig. 8–9. Figure a represents the native YOLOv5s network; Figure b represents the YOLOv5s network after adding only the ca mechanism; Figure c represents the YOLOv5s network after adding the YOLOv5s and CA mechanisms.

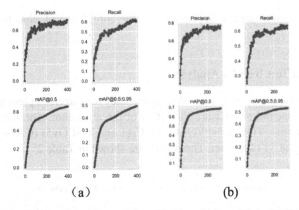

Fig. 8. Results without adding CA (a) and after adding CA (b)

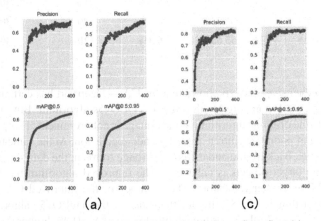

Fig. 9. Results without CA (a) and with CA + DeepSort (c)

5   Conclusion

In this paper, we use the modified YOLOv5s-based model to train on the homemade garbage classification dataset, and obtain the final garbage identification model. The experimental results show that the overall performance of the garbage classification detection model based on YOLOv5s constructed in this experiment is significantly better than that of the YOLOv5s model without CA and DeepSort algorithms. It has the advantages of high real-time detection accuracy, good robustness, small size and high accuracy. In the next step, we will study how to further improve the accuracy of garbage identification, and combine this algorithm with unmanned vehicles to create drones that can automatically identify and clean up garbage, and integrate it into urban waste treatment systems to promote people's life safety.

Acknowledgments. This work was supported in part by the National Key R&D Program of China under Grant nos. 2022YFE010300 and 2019YFE0122600, in part by the Major Project for New Generation of AI under Grant no. 2018AAA0100400, in part by the Natural Science Foundation of Hunan Province under Grant no. 2021JJ50050 and 2022JJ50051, in part by the Scientific Research Fund of Hunan Provincial Education Department under Grant nos. 21A0350 and 21C0439 and in part by the Hunan Provincial Innovation Foundation For Postgraduate under Grant nos.CX20220835.

References

1. Xie, Q.S., Yang, X.: Why does the garbage classification policy have very little effect? this is based on a content analysis of the 1986–2019 central policy text. China Public Policy Rev. **19**(02), 53–75 (2021)
2. Duan, J.H.: Research on Problems and Countermeasures of Grid Management of Urban Public Environmental Sanitation in Kunming. Yunnan Normal University (2022)
3. Lu, W., Chen, J.: Computer vision for solid waste sorting: a critical review of academic research. Waste Manage. **142**, 29–43 (2022)
4. Yang, L., Zhang, R.Y., Li, L., et al.: Simam: A simple, parameter-free attention module for convolutional neural networks. In: International Conference on Machine Learning. PMLR, pp. 11863–11874 (2021)
5. Sarvamangala, D.R., Kulkarni, R.V.: Convolutional neural networks in medical image understanding: a survey. Evolutionary Intelligence **15**(1), 1–22 (2021)
6. Pramanik, A., Pal, S.K., Maiti, J., et al.: Granulated RCNN and multi-class deep sort for multi-object detection and tracking. IEEE Trans. Emerging Topics in Computational Intelligence **6**(1), 171–181 (2021)
7. Mansour, R.F., Escorcia-Gutierrez, J., Gamarra, M., et al.: Intelligent video anomaly detection and classification using faster RCNN with deep reinforcement learning model. Image Vis. Comput. **112**, 104229 (2021)
8. Jiang, P., Ergu, D., Liu, F., et al.: A review of Yolo algorithm developments. Procedia Computer Sci. **199**, 1066–1073 (2022)
9. Redmon, J., Divvala, S., Girshick, R., et al.: You only look once: unified, real-time object detection. In: Proceedings of the IEEE Conference on Computer Vision and Pattern Recognition, pp. 779–788 (2016)
10. Ye, A., Pang, B., Jin, Y., et al.: A YOLO-based neural network with VAE for intelligent garbage detection and classification. In: 2020 3rd International Conference on Algorithms, Computing and Artificial Intelligence, pp. 1–7 (2020)
11. Bohong, L., Xinpeng, W.: Garbage detection algorithm based on YOLOv3. In: 2022 IEEE International Conference on Electrical Engineering, Big Data and Algorithms (EEBDA). IEEE, pp. 784–788 (2022)
12. Yang, G., Jin, J., Lei, Q., et al.: Garbage classification system with YOLOV5 based on image recognition. In: [C]//2021 IEEE 6th International Conference on Signal and Image Processing (ICSIP). IEEE, pp. 11–18 (2021)
13. He, Y., Li, J., Chen, S., et al.: Waste collection and transportation supervision based on improved YOLOv3 model. IEEE Access, pp. 81836–81845 (2022)
14. Wang, D., He, D.: Channel pruned YOLO V5s-based deep learning approach for rapid and accurate apple fruitlet detection before fruit thinning. Biosys. Eng. **210**, 271–281 (2021)
15. He, T., Zhang, Z., Zhang, H., et al.: Bag of tricks for image classification with convolutional neural networks. In: Proceedings of the IEEE/CVF Conference on Computer Vision and Pattern Recognition, pp. 558–567 (2019)

16. Bello, I., Zoph, B., Le, Q., et al.: Attention augmented convolutional networks. In: /2019 IEEE/CVF International Conference on Computer Vision (ICCV), IEEE, pp. 3285–3294 (2020)
17. Veeramani, B., Raymond, J.W., Chanda, P.: DeepSort: deep convolutional networks for sorting haploid maize seeds. BMC Bioinformatics **19**(9), 1–9 (2018)

Approaches for Zero Trust Adoption Based upon Organization Security Level

Muntaha Alawneh[1(✉)] and Imad M. Abbadi[2]

[1] Computer Engineering, Al Ain University, Abu Dhabi, UAE
muntaha.alawneh@aau.ac.ae
[2] Security, Risk, and Compliance Practice, Hewlett Packard Enterprise, Dubai, UAE
imad.abbadi@hpe.com

Abstract. The "Trust but Verify" principle, which majority of enterprises follow, would need to be revamped. It is agreed that the problems resulting from the "Trust but Verify" principle can be addressed using the Zero Trust principles alongside a risk-driven enterprise security approach. Despite the importance and increasing popularity of Zero Trust, it is still not widely adopted by many organizations. This is because adopting and enforcing the principles and mechanisms behind Zero Trust are unclear. The majority of the work done in this space is industrial and usually customized and scoped to address specific enterprise business requirements. We believe Zero Trust adoption must not be homogeneous across all types of organization, neither it should be scoped to component level. The adoption should rather get processed within an enterprise security architecture framework and should consider the security maturity of an organization. In this paper, we do not cover the mechanisms for implementing Zero Trust; but rather propose, based on our practical experience, the different possible classifications of organization security maturity and the various approaches for Zero Trust Adoption. We then map the proposed approach of Adopting Zero Trust to the classified organizations.

Keywords: Zero trust adoption · Organization security maturity · Insiders · Lateral movement · Enterprise security architecture

1 Introduction

The advanced level of cyberattacks have changed the game. This is especially the case when attackers get insider privileges, for example, by attacking trusted resources and emanating the attack from there. The threats behind insiders and creeping insiders have expanded exponentially over the past couple of years [3]. This is because many painful attacks came from entities that were assumed to be trusted. Zero Trust and insiders are associated concepts. Zero Trust principles were mainly introduced to treat the threats emanating from "Trust but Verify" which typically gets exploited by insiders or once an attacker privilege

© The Author(s), under exclusive license to Springer Nature Singapore Pte Ltd. 2023
G. Wang et al. (Eds.): UbiSec 2022, CCIS 1768, pp. 523–533, 2023.
https://doi.org/10.1007/978-981-99-0272-9_36

gets escalated to act on behalf of an insider. As explained by John [6], Zero Trust main objective is to change gears and move from "Trust but Verify" to "Never Trust/Always Verify".

Although the principles of Zero Trust are important to improve an organization security posture; however, most organizations still do not know how to adopt Zero Trust and where to start. Most work done on this space focuses on individual mechanisms for enforcing Zero Trust [4], but not much work focuses on the approaches of adopting Zero Trust. We believe the complexity of Zero Trust adoption resulted from inconsistencies around the security position across organizations; for example, majority of organizations, despite following best practices, still do not adopt a structured method for securing their infrastructure. This leads us to believe the complexity of adopting Zero Trust is not only related to technical issues or mechanisms but also to the lack of understanding about the relationship between organizational security maturity and the processes/mechanisms of Zero Trust adoption. As a result we found the initial steps for adopting Zero Trust require understanding the classification of organizations by considering their security maturity and then integrate Zero Trust accordingly.

This paper starts by briefing an example of enterprise security architecture views that are required to understand some principles in follow up sections. We then proposed a classification of organizations by considering their security maturities. Next, we proposed two approaches for adopting Zero Trust that can address the needs of different organizational requirements. Subsequently, we map the approaches and design principles based upon the suggested classification of organizations. During our work we found most organizations are in the process of adopting cloud, which has several mechanisms for improving Zero Trust adoption. We highlighted the cloud subject; but it is not covered in any details - the integration with clouds require extensive research that needs dedicated paper, which is a planned future work. Our work, to the best of our knowledge, is the first to discuss Zero Trust adoption based on organization security maturity (see related work section for more details).

This paper is structured as follows: Sect. 2 covers related work; Sect. 3 provides the background; Sect. 4 covers our proposal for Zero Trust Adoption; we briefed the importance of cloud for Zero Trust Adoption in Sect. 5; and finally Sect. 6 summarizes the paper.

2 Related Work

Most of the previous work on Zero Trust focused on analyzing specific angle about Zero Trust. To the best our knowledge Zero Trust adoption processes and mechanisms are subjects that have not been touched beforehand. Our main contribution in this paper is in providing, based on our practical experience, foundation processes that enables organizations to understand their maturity in Zero Trust adoption and the initial steps they need to follow to prepare for Zero Trust.

The idea of building Zero Trust architecture using Kubernetes is discussed in [7]. Kubernetes by itself is a component view which completely differs from our work which focuses on the adoption cycle. Kubernetes or any other mechanisms could fit within our future directions and get integrated with several other technologies.

The work done in [14] covers several aspects that is related to implementing Zero Trust principles. The work deep dives in the domains of identity and access management, network security, and infrastructure orchestration. Our work completely differs from this in the direction that we provides a fundamental steps that should be prepared prior adopting Zero Trust, while their provides few aspects related to the design and building up views.

The work in [5] discusses literature gaps in Zero Trust (academic and industrial) and claims that previous work mainly misses economic studies as well as limitations and impact on user technologies. We disagree with the author's finding as there are several other directions that still need to be studied as in the case of ours.

The same discussion, as above, equally applies to other work. For example, the work in [17] presents few technologies in Zero Trust and their applications; the work in [16] presents challenges when adopting Zero Trust; and the work in [8] discusses the importance of Zero Trust.

3   Background

Business View	Contextual Architecture
Architect's View	Conceptual Architecture
Designer's View	Logical Architecture
Builder's View	Physical Architecture
Tradesman's View	Component Architecture
Manager's View	Management Architecture

Fig. 1. SABSA architecture views [11]

Adopting enterprise security architecture framework is a core factor for differentiating organizations based on their security maturity. This paper is not meant to deep-dive into this complex domain and not even to cover any part of an enterprise security architecture in detail. We rather aim to clarify the terms, which are required to understand some of the core concepts in this paper. This section briefs the architecture view of one of the most-popular enterprise security architecture frameworks, SABSA (Sherwood Applied Business Security Architecture) [11]. SABSA is originally authored by John Sherwood in 1995. Its methodology is used for developing business-driven risk and opportunities focusing on enterprise security and information assurance architecture. SABSA is also used for delivering security infrastructure solutions that traceably supports critical business initiatives.

Figure 1 illustrates the architecture views of SABSA which is composed of the following set of integrated layers (also called views).

- Contextual Architecture (also called Business View) – this view analyzes the business goals and values aiming to derive the business risks of opportunities and threats. The outcome of the Business View is fed into the follow-up layer which is the Conceptual Architecture.
- Conceptual Architecture (also called Architect View) – this view builds up the business value and knowledge strategy in the form of business attribute taxonomy and profile aiming to understand the risk management strategy and objectives. The risk management strategy focuses on Enablement and Control Objectives, Policy Architecture, Risk Categories, Risk Management Strategies, Risk Architecture, Risk Modelling Framework, and Assurance Framework. The outcome of the Architect View is fed into the Logical Architecture.
- Logical Architecture (also called Design View) – this view develops the information assets which is composed of inventory of information assets and information model of the business, and aims to understand the risk management policies. The outcome of the Design View is fed into the follow up layer which is the Physical Architecture.
- Physical Architecture (also called Builder View) – this view examines the data assets aiming to prepare for the risk management practice. The outcome of this view is fed into the Component Architecture.
- Component Architecture (also called Tradesman View) – this view focuses on the component assets (i.e. products and tools including data repositories and processes) aiming to do the risk management using risk analysis tools, risk registration, and risk monitoring and reporting tools.
- Management Architecture (also called Manager View) – this view focuses on the delivery and continuity management (assurance of operational excellence and continuity) aiming to control the operational risk management. The outcome of this view is assessed and analyzed and any deviation is returned back to the top view (Business view) for re-assessment.

In most use cases, the architecture processes and data flow run in a loop from the Business View to the Tradesman View that are managed using the Manager View. This is called Top-Down Architecture Principle. By following this principle, any security control should be bound to business goals and objectives. Although this approach sounds solid; however, we experienced certain use cases under which the Top-Down principle was not the most efficient to start with; i.e. in certain use cases we prefer to start from the Tradesman View and go backward; once the environment is ready we switch back to the Top-Down principle. Adopting Zero Trust requires following both principles. Subsequent parts of this paper discuss the use cases for both principles and where they could be applied.

4 Zero Trust Adoption and Deployment

In this section, we discuss our proposal about the approaches for adopting Zero Trust by considering the maturity of security within organizations. This section starts by categorizing organizations based on their security level. It then proposes two approaches for Zero Trust adoption. Finally, it maps the approaches into the categories.

4.1 Organizational Categories

In this subsection, we provide the different possible categories of organizations by considering their security maturity. Organizations would typically follow a framework and/or a set of standards for securing their valuable assets. The security position, for the majority of organizations, is measured by being compliant with well-known standards such as ISO27k, CSA, PCI DSS, and HIPAA. However, being compliant does not necessarily reflect the security maturity of the infrastructure. Compliance rather states that certain practices are followed [12,13,15]. This is because compliance with security standards is eventually mapped into a checklist that does not relate to business use cases, needs and requirements. That is to say, an organization could be compliant with a set of standards but have the following issues:

- being compliant but the followed mechanisms are not enough to address the security requirements of the organizational use cases;
- being compliant but using excessive security control that results in unjustified costs and complexities; and/or
- being compliant but the mechanisms in place conflict with each other which could result in unforeseen threats.

Thus, we believe security should be rather thought about as an integral part of an enterprise security architecture by following a standard security framework such as SABSA (see Sect. 3 for a quick introduction). By considering what we have just discussed, we suggest categorizing organizations into four categories based on their security maturity.

- *Newly Established Organizations* – This refers to startup organizations that is yet to develop their IT and security strategies. Such organizations are welling to explore new "opportunities, adopt new frameworks and start with major changes. This is because such changes within startup organizations do not result on major business impacts. All newly established businesses would fall under this category.
- *Immature Organizations* – This refers to organizations that have established their IT infrastructure but with limited security capabilities. Such organizations would typically follow certain standards when building up their security maturity but does not adopt any security framework. That is, the security within organizations under this category is adopted on an ad hoc approach and/or by being compliant with certain practices. Majority of organizations would fall under this category [13,15].

- *Hybrid Organizations* – This refers to organizations which have established their IT infrastructure and have the following two approaches to secure their environment.
  - *Approach (a)* – well-structured enterprise security architecture framework that applies to the majority of the their infrastructure, and
  - *Approach (b)* – ad hoc security approach which applies to other parts of the infrastructure on selected use cases.

  We call such organizations as hybrid as they follow two approaches based on predefined criteria. Organizations that fall under the hybrid category are those that are flexible in adopting new models and business lines for the part of the infrastructure that falls under Approach (b); but, on the other hand, for the parts of the infrastructure that falls under Approach (a) they are not willing to accept major changes and rather prefers to adopt changes in slow pace by following a complex management process.

- *Mature Organizations* – This refers to organizations that have well established IT infrastructure and follow a formal enterprise architecture approach including a security framework. Organizations of this category would be found very security-sensitive and stricter to changes. Such organizations are almost static in nature; very hard to change; and very hard to add new lines of business. In most cases, Mature Organizations would not be up to date in security as they are always looking for steady and very well verified changes. Examples of such organization are the Operational Technology (OT) industry and defense sector.

4.2   Zero Trust Approaches

In this section, we propose, based on our practical experience, the following two approaches for adopting Zero Trust within organizations as illustrated in Fig. 2 (the mechanisms for implementing Zero Trust is outside the scope of this paper and planned future work which we started in [4]).

- *Greenfield Approach for Adopting Zero Trust* – This approach uses either of the following design principles for integrating Zero Trust mechanisms within organizations (the principle that should be followed would eventually depend on several factors including the maturity of the organization and their risk tolerance level as discussed next).
  - *Greenfield Bottom-Up Architectural Principle* starts from the Component Architecture (i.e. the Tradesman View), going all the way to the Contextual Architecture (i.e. the Business View). We mean by this, organizations can freely start to plan and integrate Zero Trust mechanisms in the best possible shape without expecting any major restrictions from the business. This principle assumes the following:
    * the implementer have full flexibility to adopt a proper security architecture framework;
    * the implementer can reshape the infrastructure, build security controls, and securely operate the environment using the adopted security

framework by applying clear sets of trust assumptions (as required to establish Zero Trust) which are capable to achieve the required levels of trust.

Once this is established across the overall environment, i.e. getting into a satisfactory security maturity status, the organization should stop using the Bottom-Up approach; and rather switch to a different approach for adopting Zero Trust. In this approach, the organization are required to keep following the agreed security architecture framework when adding or adjusting use cases (e.g. adding a software platform, re-platforming a software application, phasing out a software platform, etc.).

The Greenfield Bottom-Up Architectural Principle is the best fit for a fresh startup environment that is willing to do major changes but quick wins with moderate risk impact.

- *Greenfield Top-Down Architectural Principle* starts from the Business View going all the way to the Tradesman View. We mean by this, organizations start integrating Zero Trust within their existing ecosystem gradually either at a slow or fast pace. The Greenfield Top-Down Architectural principle assumes organizations have full flexibility for adopting a proper security architecture framework for reshaping of their infrastructure. It requires the security control design to start from business use cases that are mapped into risks, goals, and opportunities.

  The Greenfield Top-Down Architectural Principle is the best fit for well-established IT infrastructures but does not yet follow any security frameworks and aims to do so as part of Zero Trust adoption. Such organizations do not accept major changes with high or even moderate risk impacts.

- *Adaptable Approach for Adopting Zero Trust* – This approach designs Zero Trust from the Top-Down starting at the Business View and going all the way through to the Tradesman View. Organizations adopting this principle have a well-practice security architecture framework. Zero Trust adoption, under this approach, must follow a slow pace when it gets introduced into the existing ecosystem. The Adaptable Approach does not have the flexibility to introduce changes that have a high impact on business. In several cases, under this approach high-impact changes take considerable time to get optimal results; i.e. it is developed as part of a long-term roadmap that gets executed for 2–5 years. In different wordings, Zero Trust adoption under the Adaptable Approach should be integrated as part of the organization's long-term strategic planning.

4.3   Mapping Zero Trust to Organization Categories

Based on our practical experience we found organizations adopt Zero Trust by considering three factors: a) do they have and follow a well-established security framework; b) the risk tolerance they are willing to take, and c) the status (new or well-established) of the part of the infrastructure they plan apply Zero Trust. Our discussion next clarifies this in more detail.

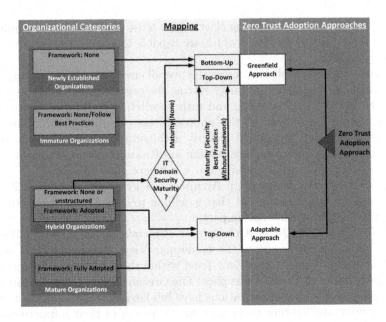

Fig. 2. Our proposal of adopting zero trust by considering organization security maturity

As illustrated in Fig. 2, Zero Trust Greenfield Approach is a good candidate for the following:

- newly established businesses;
- organizations that are yet to build their security strategy and mechanisms (i.e. immature in security and/or those that do not follow a structured security framework); or
- new business units but within well-established organizations.

In different wording, the Greenfield Approach applies to the following types of organizations (based on our categorizations): Newly Established Organizations, Immature Organizations, and the parts of Hybrid Organizations that do not have a security framework. The architectural principle that should be followed (i.e. Bottom-UP or Top-Down), as we discussed earlier, would depend on several factors importantly the risk impact the organization is willing to take. The majority of Newly Established Organizations would start with the Bottom-Up approach, and once Zero Trust is enabled the Top-Down approach is always preferred. On the other hand, the majority of Immature Organizations, and the part of the Hybrid Organizations that do not follow a security framework would use the Top-Down design principles but under the Greenfield approach.

Well-established security-aware enterprises are unlikely to follow the Greenfield Approach. This is because, following the Greenfield Approach for the overall environment, shall replace the existing principles and security controls that would result in high-impact risk, additional expenditures, operational problems, and complexities. As a result, we propose Zero Trust Adaptable approach to be applied to the following organization types: Mature Organizations, and the part of Hybrid Organization that follows a structured security framework. The architectural principle, as we discussed earlier, that would be applied is mainly the Top-Down design principle, as otherwise the risk impact is likely to be very high and would not be economically visible.

5   Zero Trust and the Cloud

Cloud computing is a critical domain that is gaining worldwide popularity. Major public cloud providers have been expanding over the past few years, racing amongst each other to have physical data centers covering most geographical locations. Organizations adopt the cloud for several reasons including scalability, adaptability, availability, new business models, and changing from Capital Expenditure (CapEx) to Operational Expenditure (OpEx) [2]. In this paper, we claim that the cloud is a Zero Trust enabler as it comes with great attributes that can by far enable stronger forms of Zero Trust. We believe cloud attributes are the best for supporting Zero Trust principles. At first instance, this might not seem so, especially for those organizations that resist the cloud. Such originations believe the cloud is insecure and would result in loss of control over data, and/or they believe the cloud does not address specific regulatory requirements [10]. The majority of decision-makers, in such cases, do not trust the cloud because it is a quickly evolving domain and they lack clarities around the new directions in the cloud and especially around the keep-evolving mechanisms for establishing trust within it. Over the past decade, several mechanisms have been developed to establish trust in the cloud and assure its trustworthiness. As a result, enterprises can better adapt Zero Trust principles under the cloud properties over anything else.

Adopting Zero Trust under cloud principles, by no means replaces the two approaches which we covered earlier. The mechanisms and security architecture principles for the two discussed approaches, i.e. the Greenfield and the Adaptable Approach, would require expansion to integrate with security architecture principles in the cloud. As discussed by Abbadi [1], the cloud is associated with eighteen different deployment models, and each is associated with different trust attributes. Enterprises can build their intra-cloud trust models around the variations of trust attributes across the Zero Trust deployment approaches. This concept is referred to as cybersecurity mesh architecture in the cloud [9] which provides a rich environment for organizations to adopt Zero Trust principles - enabled by the dynamics of the cloud, and simultaneously support data security and control in the cloud, as in the case of treating insider threat and move to data-centric security approach. The detailed discussion of cloud and Zero Trust requires deep diving around each of the eighteen methods to deploy and consume cloud. We plan to extend this paper to cover this important angle in a future work.

6   Conclusion

We believe, based on our practical work in this field, the adoption process of Zero Trust is not static but would be applied by considering several factors, most importantly, the organization's security maturity. Thus, we started our work by categorizing organizations based on their security maturity and the risks they are willing to take when adopting Zero Trust. We then proposed two approaches with design principles for adopting Zero Trust. We next mapped the proposed adoption approaches and the design principles to the suggested organization categories. We believe this work would help organizations to understand the different means for adopting Zero Trust. It also helps them to realize from where to start and to build their strategies accordingly. As we stated earlier, Zero Trust adoption is not a trivial task; this paper established the core for much wider research work in this domain. Our plans are to extend this work in several directions: propose the mechanisms to achieve Zero Trust Principles, integrate the principles within an enterprise security architecture framework; and discuss the techniques for adopting Zero Trust building on cloud attributes.

References

1. Abbadi, I.M.: Cloud Management and Security. Wiley, Hoboken (2014)
2. Abbadi, I.M., Martin, A.P.: Trust in the cloud. Inf. Secur. Tech. Rep. 16(3–4), 108–114 (2011). https://doi.org/10.1016/j.istr.2011.08.006, https://doi.org/10.1016/j.istr.2011.08.006
3. Alawneh, M., Abbadi, I.M.: Sharing but protecting content against internal leakage for Organisations. In: Atluri, V. (ed.) DBSec 2008. LNCS, vol. 5094, pp. 238–253. Springer, Heidelberg (2008). https://doi.org/10.1007/978-3-540-70567-3_19
4. Alawneh, M., Abbadi, I.M.: Integrating trusted computing mechanisms with trust models to achieve zero trust principles. In: The 9th International Conference on Internet of Things: Systems, Management and Security (IOTSMS) (2022)
5. Buck, C., Olenberger, C., Schweizer, A., Völter, F., Eymann, T.: Never trust, always verify: a multivocal literature review on current knowledge and research gaps of zero-trust. Comput. Secur. **110**, 102436 (2021). https://doi.org/10.1016/j.cose.2021.102436, https://www.sciencedirect.com/science/article/pii/S0167404821002601
6. Cunningham, C.: A look back at zero trust: Never trust, always verify (2020). https://www.forrester.com/blogs/a-look-back-at-zero-trust-never-trust-always-verify/
7. D'Silva, D., Ambawade, D.D.: Building a zero trust architecture using kubernetes. In: 2021 6th International Conference for Convergence in Technology (I2CT), pp. 1–8 (2021). https://doi.org/10.1109/I2CT51068.2021.9418203
8. Embrey, B.: The top three factors driving zero trust adoption. Comput. Fraud Secur. **2020**(9), 13–15 (2020). https://doi.org/10.1016/S1361-3723(20)30097-X, https://www.sciencedirect.com/science/article/pii/S136137232030097X
9. Gartner: What is cybersecurity mesh? (2022). https://www.gartner.com/en/conferences/na/security-risk-management-us/conference-resources/cybersecurity-mesh

10. Iosif, A.C., Gasiba, T.E., Zhao, T., Lechner, U., Pinto-Albuquerque, M.: A large-scale study on the security vulnerabilities of cloud deployments. In: Wang, G., Choo, K.K.R., Ko, R.K.L., Xu, Y., Crispo, B. (eds.) Ubiquitous Secur., pp. 171–188. Springer Singapore, Singapore (2022). https://doi.org/10.1007/978-981-19-0468-4_13

11. SABSA: SABSA enterprise security architecture (2022). https://sabsa.org

12. SecurityWeek: Best practice: Can you really define 'best' security? (2012). https://www.securityweek.com/best-practice-can-you-really-define-best-security

13. Stack, T.: When is good enough good enough? meeting compliance without losing your mind (2022). https://www.threatstack.com/blog/is-good-enough-good-enough-meet-compliance-without-losing-your-mind

14. Syed, N.F., Shah, S.W., Shaghaghi, A., Anwar, A., Baig, Z., Doss, R.: Zero trust architecture (ZTA): A comprehensive survey. IEEE Access 10, 57143–57179 (2022). https://doi.org/10.1109/ACCESS.2022.3174679

15. ca technologies: Regulatory compliance is irrelevant... or is it?(2018). https://docs.broadcom.com/doc/regulatory-compliance-is-irrelevant-or-is-it

16. Teerakanok, S., Uehara, T., Inomata, A.: Migrating to zero trust architecture: reviews and challenges. Secur. Commun. Netw. 2021, 1–10 (2021). https://doi.org/10.1155/2021/9947347

17. Yan, X., Wang, H.: Survey on zero-trust network security. In: Sun, X., Wang, J., Bertino, E. (eds.) Artif. Intell. Secur., pp. 50–60. Springer Singapore, Singapore (2020)

Multi-Mobile Agent Security by Design Itinerary Planning Approach in Wireless Sensor Network

Saad Khan$^{(\boxtimes)}$, Tariq Alsboui, Richard Hill, and Hussain Al-Aqrabi

School of Computing and Engineering, University of Huddersfield,
Huddersfield HD1 3DH, UK
{saad.khan,t.alsboui,r.hill,h.al-Aqrabi}@hud.ac.uk

Abstract. Due to the distinctive advantages of mobile agents (MAs) in wireless sensor networks (WSNs), such as network bandwidth and energy savings as well as flexibility in their use for various applications, MAs have drawn substantial research interest in recent years. The majority of the suggested agent-based dynamic itinerary planning algorithms are effective at addressing node failure due to energy shortage. However, they do not account for the (1) MAs' expanding size when visiting a series of nodes (2) producing inefficient groups of MAs itineraries, causing a delay in reporting data back to a sink node, and (3) most importantly, they lack support for securing the overall itinerary planning from an attacker who could spoil the execution of the MA when visiting a sequence of nodes and the data itself. In this paper, we propose a dynamic and secure multi-mobile agent itinerary planning approach based on a Directed Acyclic Graph modelling and AES algorithm to secure the itinerary planning mechanism from an attacker. The network will apply DAG technique to generate efficient groups based on leader nodes where encryption/decryption will also occur.

Keywords: Wireless sensor network · Itinerary planning · Dynamic itinerary · Encryption · Data security

1 Introduction

A wireless sensor network's (WSN) primary objective is to give users access to the pertinent data gathered by spatially dispersed sensors. To ensure a complete exposure of the monitored physical environment, sensors are frequently placed in large numbers in real-world applications. As a result, huge amounts of data are anticipated to be produced by such networks [1]. The methodologies utilised for mobile agent itinerary planning are primarily responsible for the success of WSNs applications due to the need to identify and route mobile agents in an energy-efficient manner. The selection, determination, and migration cost of the mobile agent itinerary planning, as well as the techniques utilised to define such a plan, are the main issues when dispatching a mobile agent.

© The Author(s), under exclusive license to Springer Nature Singapore Pte Ltd. 2023
G. Wang et al. (Eds.): UbiSec 2022, CCIS 1768, pp. 534–544, 2023.
https://doi.org/10.1007/978-981-99-0272-9_37

Itinerary planning are the main issues to be taken into consideration while dispatching a mobile agent. Planning an MA itinerary is a difficult distributed task due to practical constraints on sensor node implementation, such as power consumption (battery limits), computing capability, and maximum memory storage, which makes planning an MA itinerary a difficult decentralized task. Collaborative information processing, or using the patterns in the data of geographically correlated nodes to reduce the amount of data broadcast to the sink, is one of the most crucial aspects of WSN [2].

Over the past few years, there has been ongoing research into mobile agent technology (MA) for WSNs [3–6]. We direct interested readers to the recent survey [7] and the references therein for a thorough literature assessment. These studies focused on data dissemination, data collecting, and data fusion, as well as itinerary planning based on certain architectures. To optimise the effectiveness of agent planning and the quality of the information given, security aspect in protecting the overall itinerary planning and the data itself from an outside attack has not received much attention.

Contributions: Our main contributions are summarised as follows:

- An energy efficient and fault-tolerant multi-mobile agent framework to improve the scalability and security of WSNs;
- A new node grouping technique to avoid delays when dispatching mobile agents to collect data from WSNs; and
- Finding a suitable lightweight cryptography systems by reviewing state-of-the-art.

The rest of this paper is organized as follows: Sect. 2 presents an overview of the dynamic itinerary planning algorithms and lightweight cryptography systems. Next, Sect. 3 presents the proposed secure, dynamic multi-mobile agent framework, along with the grouping mechanism. In Sect. 4, we conclude the paper and discuss future work.

2   Multi-mobile Agent Itinerary Planning in WSN

2.1   Dynamic Itinerary Planning

In dynamic itinerary planning for MA in WSN, most of the published work in the literature consider that a MA has no prior knowledge of their path. Additionally, they use multi-agent to collect data. For example, a dynamic Energy and Trust Aware Mobile Agent Migration (ETMAM) is proposed in [8]. ETMAM main idea to identify and bypass the faulty or malicious nodes during mobile agent migration process. ETMAM combines energy and trust as selection criteria to build routes on the fly for the traveling agent to complete the data aggregation tasks. The proposed approach is energy efficient, and responds efficiently to nodes failure in the network, and secure. In addition, ETMAM uses cloning mechanism to optimize agent migration path and reduces agents payload. However, ETMAM does not take into consideration the growing size of the MA when visiting sensor nodes. In addition, it introduces a delay in reporting data back as the cloned MAs are still required to visit a large number of nodes. Furthermore, due to the need of detecting malicious nodes, the whole approach is considered complicated and requires heavy computation.

The work in [9] proposed a dynamic building method of mobile agent path with minimum payment based on referral. Referral is a collaborative model for finding the answer with help, assuming that the inquirer does not know who the answer would be, but who can help him. Therefore, the next workplace (host) of a mobile agent can be recommended by the current workplace provider based on his acquaintance knowledge. The proposed approach is energy efficient and does not require a pre-fixed system; thus, it can adapt to open environment. However, the approach lacks scalability, and security. Also, it introduces a delay since it uses a single MA.

A dynamic itinerary planning approach that is based on Mobile Agent Electronic Triage Tag (MAETT) system is proposed in [10]. The idea is to separate the itinerary data structure from the agent itself in order to provide a simple mechanism to flexibly define and track how an agent travel. The proposed approach is energy efficient and scalable. Also, it reacts to nodes failure efficiently. However, the approach lacks security, and the need to leave the injecting node, which is the one attached to the handheld device, in connection range of the created WSN. This forces the medical personnel to use that node as part of the WSN, having to replace the injecting node every time a new WSN is created.

Similar approaches have been suggested in [11,12]. In [11] the authors build upon their previous work by introducing a dynamic planning method for mobile agent path based on the Markov decision process (MDP) and social acquaintance recommendation variable decision space. The path planning model is described with MDP, and social acquaintance recommendation, assuming that every social member can provide workplace and service recommendation for a mobile agent in a cooperative work manner. The approach is energy efficient, and responds efficiently to nodes failure. However, their technique is time-consuming and complicated to apply in practice. Also, it lacks security, scalability, and introduces a delay.

2.2   Data Security

Data confidentiality, integrity and availability are considered as the main challenges in all IoT deployments as they collect personal/sensitive data from the environment and transfer it over the network [13]. Despite being a critical problem, it has not been not fully addressed in existing research as in resolving particular challenges of IoT according to a recent survey [14]. At present, the information leakage and data breach in IoT networks are usually prevented by implementing robust access control management and encryption. There are several types of encryption schemes designed for varying processing power and memory capabilities. The conventional encryption methods, such for AES, 3DES, and RSA, are no longer suited to every IoT environment, as most of the IoT devices

(RFID tags, sensors, smart cards, etc.) have easy physical access and are limited in energy, memory, and processing power resources [15]. A report [16] published by NIST presents and standardises other performance metrics as well, such as ciphertext expansion that can increase storage and transmission costs, key-related attacks, ciphertext security, latency, throughput, etc. Latency is defined as the time between the initial request for an encryption or decryption operation and the response that returns the corresponding result. Throughput is the rate at which results are generated. As a result, researchers have been proposing various lightweight cryptography algorithms and protocols to overcome the problems of conventional cryptography in IoT networks, having different strengths and disadvantages [17], by using smaller block and key sizes, simpler iterations, and key schedules. This can help in establishing (1) which encryption algorithm is the most suitable one for our proposed architecture and (2) how to ensure proper key management, as this will directly impact the strength of data secrecy, trust, and availability in the resource-constrained IoT environment.

According to a recent extensive review [18] of 50+ lightweight encryption algorithms, it is claimed that block cipher algorithms perform better in resource-constrained IoT devices than stream cipher, due to using both confusion and diffusion properties. The confusion uses substitution (S-box) to obscure connection between the ciphertext and the key, whereas diffusion reduces the statistical relationship between the structure of ciphertext and the plaintext using permutation. Furthermore, the number of iterations, number of S-boxes and key size have critical impact on resource consumption and security of a cipher as increasing them makes the cipher more secure but it will require more energy, time, memory, CPU and consequently more cost for execution [19]. Another article [20] compared 54 lightweight block ciphers, stream ciphers, hash functions, and Elliptic curve cryptography (ECC) against several performance metrics. Based on the results, GFN based algorithms (TWINE, SPECK and DESL) and SPN based algorithms (PRESENT, RECTANGLE, LED, and KLEIN) performed best in terms of power and energy requirements.

Contrary to symmetric cryptography, the relatively larger key size and high memory requirements make asymmetric cryptography unsuitable for IoT devices; however, lightweight ECC [21] can provide similar level of security with smaller key size as compared to other similar algorithms, such as RSA that is not suitable due its high requirements [22]. There are many challenges, ranging from architecture design to actual implementation, that need to be resolved in order to make an ECC viable for IoT devices. But still, AES can be 10–1000 times faster than ECC, depending on the micro-controller. Another research [23] concluded that lightweight implementation of AES is the most suitable solution for resource-constrained IoT network in terms of performance and security, mainly due to its architecture, Mix-Column/S-box modify strategy and resilience to several hardware and software attacks.

2.3   Limitations of Prior Work

From the above we can see that most of the existing approaches to dynamic itinerary planning in IoT suffer from inherent problems. (1) they are limited to a specific set of applications where consistent changes occur across the network, e.g. agricultural applications [8] (2) they are more difficult to design and complex to execute, as they first need to group sensor nodes into subsets in a way that will create itineraries of approximately equal cost [9, 10] (3) they require more time due to the fact that the decision about the next node to be visited is taken at each sensor node [24] (4) they require a careful selection of the number of MAs and the number of nodes in a different group to achieve an optimized task duration [25]. Finally, they lack support for security, which is a fundamental challenge and should be support in dynamic multi-mobile agent itinerary planning approaches [8–10, 12, 24, 26].

3   A Dynamic Multi-mobile Agent Itinerary Planning Approach in WSNs

The problems and limitations presented above lead to future research opportunities. Possible solutions that we are currently investigating is to develop a secure and dynamic multi-mobile agent itinerary planning through the use of a Directed Acyclic Graph [27] to model the network with an efficient grouping mechanism and utilising a lightweight encryption algorithm for securing stationary and in-transit data. Considering the existing literature, we believe a lightweight AES algorithm is the most suitable encryption scheme for our proposed solution, due to several reasons. First, AES is a symmetric key cryptography algorithm, which means it is relatively faster and more resource efficient, unlike asymmetric algorithms. Most block ciphers are suitable for lightweight cryptography as they are tailored for implementation in constrained environments (according to ISO/IEC 29192–2:2012). It is the one of the most commonly used, well-tested algorithms with applications ranging from encrypted data storage to wireless communication. It is also found to be a suitable choice for mobile devices [28]. Second, due to utilising SPN and longer key, it will provide an excellent level of security than other algorithms. Third, AES is sufficiently flexible to be integrated with a variety of platforms, even with other security protocols, and does not require making significant changes in the underlying infrastructure. Last but not least, it is publicly and freely available in both hardware and software implementations, thus making it a robust, and ubiquitous security protocol.

3.1   Lightweight AES Implementation

An integral part of our proposed solution is to achieve the best possible data security, but without significantly increasing power and energy consumption of the nodes. Therefore, a lightweight implementation of AES algorithm that is resource efficient would serve the purpose. There are several implementations available having different approaches and designs to reduce time delays and increase effective utilisation of energy and computing resources. The remaining section presents some of the lightweight AES algorithms, along with their strengths and weaknesses, that we believe are suitable for our sensor network. A research article [29] proposes to simply exclude mix column operation from each round and directly use the output from shift row operation, whilst keeping all operations exactly the same as of traditional AES 128-bit. There results show 10.67% reduction in setup delay time and 17.34% in hold delay time for one voice communication device, and 58.51% in setup delay and 64.20% in hold delay time for another type of similar device. However, this work does not discuss how it impacts the security after eliminating mix column operation, which might lead to several security flaws.

Another article [30] proposes Lightweight AES (LAES) algorithm for securing IoT sensor data. LAES utilises a multi chaotic systems and replaces several components in the traditional AES. The Shift row operation is performed by Initial Permutation technique and mix columns by dynamic shift rows. Also, the S-Box is created using a chaotic logistic map system. The author claim using chaotic system brings higher level of security as a small change in the input results in significant change in the output. The results shows that LAES is faster than the original AES and other lightweight AES algorithm, and passes all NIST statistical tests [31]. It is evident from existing literature that the most suitable (lightweight) AES version for IoT devices is achieved by optimising the S-Box and the number of rounds it takes for byte substitution, which we will consider and implement accordingly in our future work.

3.2   Proposed Grouping Mechanism

Directed Acyclic Graph (DAG) is an information or data structure, which can be used to demonstrate diverse problems. It is an acyclic graph in topological ordering. It can be used to model WSN where a set of nodes are connected with each other via edges. Within the DAG graph, we will generate a set of routes (route 1, route 2 and route 3 that cover all nodes, including private nodes and leader nodes, in the network. Private nodes are nodes that belong to a particular route only. Shared nodes are source nodes that are on multiple routes. In addition, a group is a collection of private nodes and allocated leader nodes in a particular route. The groups are generated based on allocating leader nodes to the group of a route with the least number of nodes.

Figure 1 is an illustration of how one of the algorithms' underlying ideas works. It displays a series of routes (in this example, routes 1, 2, and 3) that cover all nodes in the network, including leader and private nodes. Private nodes are those that are exclusive to a given route. Source nodes on several routes are referred to as leader nodes. In this example, there is just one leader node, and it is present on both routes 1 and 2. A group is also a collection of assigned leader nodes and private nodes in a specific route. The groups are created by assigning shared nodes to the group of a route that contains the fewest nodes overall. As an illustration, see Fig. 1. We assign the leader node to the group for

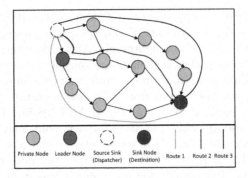

Fig. 1. An example of the grouping technique and working principles of the proposed solution

route 2 since there are only two private nodes in the group for route 2, compared to three private nodes in the group for route 1. It should be noted here that, in practise, the source sink (such as the dispatcher) and the sink node (such as the destination) must be the same (sink) node. Here, since the entire network is modelled as a DAG, it is virtually split into two nodes that each exploit a portion of the network's links to source nodes.

3.3   A Secure Dynamic Itinerary Planning Approach

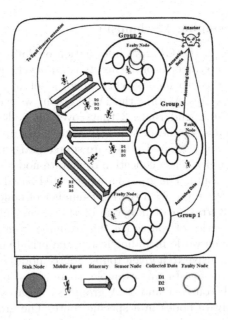

Fig. 2. A secure and dynamic Multi-mobile agent itinerary planning approach

Fig 2 presents an abstract view of the proposed Secure Dynamic multi-mobile agent itinerary planning approach. It describes all relevant components including mobile agents, itinerary, sensor nodes,, faulty node, network attack and collected data each of which is responsible for a specific task. It shows a set of sensor nodes in each route and how nodes are grouped together. The grouping is based on the identified leader nodes. A leader node is considered as a node with multiple routes. The routes are generated to cover all nodes in the network. It also shows that when a node is faulty as a result of energy depletion, the MAs will dynamically move to the next node in each group. The sink node is responsible for dispatching MAs to a particular group in order to collect data from. The MAs collect data from the groups that they are assigned to. For example, the itinerary (e.g., gray lines) represents the routes to the assigned group.

Considering Fig. 2, there are several ways an attacker can compromise the confidentially, integrity, and availability of the sensor network. For example, apart from sensor nodes susceptible to physical capture, attacker can breach the nodes at any layer of of the communication protocols, thereby making it difficult to protect the network at all times. Similar to attacks originating from outside of the network, insider attacks can also occur when legitimate but malicious nodes act in unintended or unauthorised manner. As any real-time network is dense population of nodes, it can be hard to detect and remove such malicious nodes. The attacker can also easily spoil the itinerary execution by injecting malicious messages into the network. This might include active interference, such as interception, modification, fabrication, and replay attacks, as well as passive eavesdropping. Furthermore, a malicious node present in the routing path can send the packets in incorrect direction, causing destination unreachable error. Due to the nature of the network, attacker can target the network in different ways, leading to leaking of secret information, interfering message, etc.

A lightweight implementation of AES algorithm is proposed to be integrated into our approach for the purpose of securing data. To achieve overall security, following two aspects should be considered. First, the data residing in both sink node and group nodes should be encrypted to prevent loss of confidentiality and availability in case any node is breached or compromised by the attacker. Second, the communication between sink node and group nodes (itinerary) should also protected to ensure confidentiality and integrity in MAs. The sink node has sufficiently large number of computing resources than group nodes and is also connected to a power; therefore, sink node will responsible for generating the key for the lightweight AES algorithm, one for each group. Note that all nodes in each group will share the same key, rather than each node having a different key. This is done to have an energy efficient, cost effective approach. Considering two-way communication, the encryption and decryption of plaintext and ciphertext, respectively, will be performed in both the sink node and group nodes, which involves all the steps discussed in Sect. 3.1.

As discussed earlier, it is well-established in the existing research that the lightweight AES algorithm provides a right balance between security and performance, which is sufficient for our proposed solution. However, a major challenge remains on how the key will be shared across sink node and group nodes, and how and where it will be stored, in a safe manner. A key leakage of any sort will result in the loss of security of the entire system. It will render the cryptography system completely useless, and in fact will become a massive strain on the resources. Note that secure key management issue is not unique to any specific type of network, but again, resource and energy constraints magnify this issue. Therefore, it is critical to employ a safe management mechanism for the full lifecycle of cryptography keys and one of the best ways to do this is by utilising an online service, such as AWS or any other Cloud based service.

4   Conclusion and Future Work

This paper has addressed the issue of efficient and secure dynamic multi-mobile agent itinerary planning. A secure and energy-efficient itinerary planning approach has been proposed in order to achieve scalability and reduce energy consumption. A lightweight version of an AES algorithm has been identified along with a grouping strategy, which plays an important role when nodes in the network are assigned into smaller sets, making energy depletion less of a problem. In future, we are planning to implement our proposed solution and evaluate it against some of the existing dynamic multi-mobile agent itinerary planning algorithms.

References

1. Hammoudeh, M., Newman, R., Mount, S.: An approach to data extraction and visualisation for wireless sensor networks. In: 2009 Eighth International Conference on Networks, pp. 156–161 (2009)
2. Alsboui, T., Hammoudeh, M., Abuarqoub, A.: A Service-Centric Stack for Collaborative Data Sharing and Processing. In: Cho, H., Kim, T., Mohammed, S., Adeli, H., Oh, M., Lee, K.-W. (eds.) GST/SIA -2012. CCIS, vol. 338, pp. 320–327. Springer, Heidelberg (2012). https://doi.org/10.1007/978-3-642-35251-5_45
3. Aloui, I., Kazar, O., Kahloul, L., Servigne, S.: A new itinerary planning approach among multiple mobile agents in wireless sensor networks (WSN) to reduce energy consumption. Int. J. Commun. Networks Inf. Secur. (IJCNIS) 7(2) 116–122, (2015)
4. Alsboui, T., Qin, Y., Hill, R., Al-Aqrabi, H.: An energy efficient multi-mobile agent itinerary planning approach in wireless sensor networks. Computing 103(9), 2093–2113 (2021)
5. Karthik, S., Karthick, M., Karthikeyan, N., Kannan, S.: A multi-mobile agent and optimal itinerary planning-based data aggregation in wireless sensor networks. Comput. Commun. 184, 24–35 (2022)
6. Nidhi, S.U.: Fuzzy c-means clustering of network for multi mobile agent itinerary planning. In Yu-Dong Zhang, Tomonobu Senjyu, Chakchai So-In, and Amit Joshi, editors, Smart Trends in Computing and Communications, pp. 589–598, (2023) Springer Nature https://doi.org/10.1007/978-981-16-9967-2_55
7. El Fissaoui, M., Beni-hssane, A., Ouhmad, S., El Makkaoui, K.: A survey on mobile agent itinerary planning for information fusion in wireless sensor networks. Arch. Comput. Methods Eng. 28(3), 1323–1334 (2021)

8. Gupta, G., Misra, M., Garg, K.: Energy and trust aware mobile agent migration protocol for data aggregation in wireless sensor networks. J. Netw. Comput. Appl. **41**, 05 (2014)

9. X. Xu. X. Wang, G. Zeng. A dynamic building method of mobile agent path based on referral networks. Int. J. Innovative Comput. Inf. Control, 19(1–5), 2014

10. Mercadal, E., Vidueira, C., Sreenan, C.J., Borrell, J.: Improving the dynamism of mobile agent applications in wireless sensor networks through separate itineraries. Comput. Commun. **36**(9), 1011–1023 (2013)

11. Zeng, G., Wang, X.: A dynamic building method of mobile agent path based on referral networks. Appl. Math. Inf. Sci, 19 (1–5), (2014)

12. Camponogara, E., Shima, R.B.: Mobile agent routing with time constraints: a resource constrained longest-path approach. J. JUCS, **16**(3), 372–401, Feb 2010

13. Ahanger, T.A., Aljumah, A., Atiquzzaman, M.: State-of-the-art survey of artificial intelligent techniques for IoT security. Comput. Networks, p. 108771 (2022)

14. Shah, A., Engineer, M.: A Survey of Lightweight Cryptographic Algorithms for IoT-Based Applications. In: Tiwari, S., Trivedi, M.C., Mishra, K.K., Misra, A.K., Kumar, K.K. (eds.) Smart Innovations in Communication and Computational Sciences. AISC, vol. 851, pp. 283–293. Springer, Singapore (2019). https://doi.org/10.1007/978-981-13-2414-7_27

15. Wang, X., Zhang, J., Schooler, E.M., Ion, M.: Performance evaluation of attribute-based encryption: toward data privacy in the IoT. In: 2014 IEEE International Conference on Communications (ICC), pp. 725–730. IEEE (2014)

16. McKay, K., Bassham, L.: Meltem Sönmez Turan, and Nicky Mouha. Report on lightweight cryptography. Technical report, National Institute of Standards and Technology (2016)

17. Buchanan, W.J, Li, S., Asif, R.: Lightweight cryptography methods. J. Cyber Secur. Technol, **1**(3–4), 187–201 (2017)

18. Thakor, V.A, Razzaque, M.A, Khandaker, M.R.A.: Lightweight cryptography algorithms for resource-constrained IoT devices: a review, comparison and research opportunities. IEEE Access, **9**, pp. 28177–28193 (2021)

19. Rana, M., Mamun, Q., Islam, R.: Lightweight cryptography in IoT networks: a survey. Futur. Gener. Comput. Syst. **129**, 77–89 (2022)

20. Dhanda, S.S., Singh, B., Jindal, P.: Lightweight cryptography: a solution to secure IoT. Wirel. Pers. Commun. **112**(3), 1947–1980 (2020)

21. Nino, -L., Andres, C., Perez, -D., Sandoval, A.-M.: Elliptic curve lightweight cryptography: a survey. IEEE Access, **6**, 72514–72550 (2018)

22. Sadkhan, S.B., Salman, A.O: A survey on lightweight-cryptography status and future challenges. In: 2018 International Conference on Advance of Sustainable Engineering and its Application (ICASEA), pp. 105–108. IEEE (2018)

23. Dutta, I.K., Ghosh, B., Bayoumi, M.: Lightweight cryptography for internet of insecure things: a survey. In: 2019 IEEE 9th Annual Computing and Communication Workshop and Conference (CCWC), pp. 0475–0481. IEEE (2019)

24. Rech, L., De Oliveira, R. S. Montez, C.: Dynamic determination of the itinerary of mobile agents with timing constraints. In: IEEE/WIC/ACM International Conference on Intelligent Agent Technology, pp. 45–50, (2005)

25. Aloui, I., Kazar, O., Kahloul, L., Servigne, S.: A new itinerary planning approach among multiple mobile agents in wireless sensor networks (WSN) to reduce energy consumption. Int. J. Commun. Netw. Inf. Secur. (IJCNIS), **7**116–122, (2015)

26. Ota, K., Dong, M., Wang, J., Guo, S., Cheng, Z., Guo, M.: Dynamic itinerary planning for mobile agents with a content-specific approach in wireless sensor networks. In: 2010 IEEE 72nd Vehicular Technology Conference - Fall, pp.1–5 (2010)

27. Thost, V., Chen, J.: Directed acyclic graph neural networks (2021)
28. Andres, C., Nino, L-., Sandoval, M.-M., Perez, A.-D: An evaluation of AES and present ciphers for lightweight cryptography on smartphones. In: 2016 International Conference on Electronics, Communications and Computers (CONIELECOMP), pp. 87–93. IEEE (2016)
29. Kumar, K., Ramkumar, K.R., Kaur, A.: A lightweight AES algorithm implementation for encrypting voice messages using field programmable gate arrays. J. King Saud Univ. Comput. Inf. Sci. (2020)
30. Fadhil, M.S., Farhan, A.K., Fadhil, M.N.: A lightweight AES algorithm implementation for secure IoT environment. Iraqi J. Sci. 62(8), 2759–2770 (2021)
31. Jenny, W. Y., Aagaard, M.d.: Benchmarking and optimizing AES for lightweight cryptography on ASICs

On the Variability in the Application and Measurement of Supervised Machine Learning in Cyber Security

Omar Alshaikh$^{(\boxtimes)}$ [ID], Simon Parkinson [ID], and Saad Khan [ID]

Department of Computer Science, University of Huddersfield, Huddersfield HD1 3DH, UK
Omar.alshaikh@hud.ac.uk

Abstract. Supervised learning (SL) is being increasingly adopted to enhance capability and mitigate cyberattacks. Published literature containing empirical studies often demonstrates an optimistic viewpoint, with promising results achieving greater than 90% in terms of accuracy when detecting and mitigating cyberattacks. These results are often generated on well-refined test scenarios. Cyberattack statistics show a continued increase in occurrence and continue to result in significant damage. This is resulting in organisations becoming increasingly worried about suffering a cyberattack, increasing their desire to identify and adopt suitable solutions. The optimistic result presented in research studies might misrepresent the application's true capabilities and set unreachable expectations. The purpose of this paper is to investigate how SL technique is applied to cybersecurity challenges and how it is evaluated. To pursue this aim, a literature review is undertaken, classifying the most common SL performance measurements in cybersecurity research. The key finding of this paper revealed that SL is mostly used because of its capabilities in detecting known patterns on a restrictive application challenge. This could therefore be misleading for those wanting to utilise such systems.

Keywords: Machine learning · Cybersecurity · Cyberattacks · Performance measurements · Supervised learning

1 Introduction

The need to consider cyber security has become increasingly crucial for individuals and organisations alike. The severity of a successful attack is high, with the potential to lose valuable data and suffer reputation and financial damage. The threats surrounding people and organisations by cybercriminals have been classified as the fourth-highest security risk (Cabinet Office, 2010). As stated in the UKs HM Government National Cyber Security Strategy 2016–2021 (2016), the nation's prosperity and growth are depending on the capability of obtaining the highest standards of security for technology, data, and networks. The techniques utilised to commit cybercrime are continuously progressing as cybercriminals are inventing and utilising new means to unexpectedly affect computing systems.

© The Author(s), under exclusive license to Springer Nature Singapore Pte Ltd. 2023
G. Wang et al. (Eds.): UbiSec 2022, CCIS 1768, pp. 545–555, 2023.
https://doi.org/10.1007/978-981-99-0272-9_38

Numerous organisations aiming to enhance security readiness have embedded AI applications in the production processes and operations. The result achieved in research and development could entice end-users to invest or use an AI application. At the same time as the uptake of AI application is increasing, so is the rate of cybercrime is still increasing. This presents a significant challenge for AI systems, where new attacks require the system to evolve to detect and mitigate, but this may require extensive modification to the AI in terms of utilising additional data sources and performing more training. However, end-users of AI systems may not be aware of this as the quoted accuracy might lead them to believe that it will remain at this level of accuracy throughout its use, which in cybersecurity is not feasible as new attacks have cautiously been detected. AI can be loosely categorised into the two forms of model-based reasoning and data-driven approaches. Model-based reasoning approaches are often deliberating to solve a problem using domain knowledge, whereas a data-driven approach is often trying to identify meaning from data. Most AI applications in cybersecurity utilise ML techniques as the application challenge is often data driven, such as performing anomaly detection (Khan et al. 2018).

This paper aims to review and group existing research studies that are utilising supervised ML in cybersecurity and investigate their capabilities in the cybersecurity domain. The main contribution of this paper is discovering themes in using accuracy metrics for measuring and quantifying capability. Given that supervised learning is the most often used ML technique in cybersecurity application, the study was inspired to further investigate. The paper is structured in three sections as follows: In Sect. 2, the method of this study is provided. In Sect. 3, a comprehensive review of published literature is performed to examine existing knowledge on supervised ML applications implemented to mitigate cyberattacks, as well as highlighting the metrics used to evaluate the model's performance. Section 4 provides a discussion, including a critical analysis of observations. Finally, a conclusion is presented.

2 Method

To achieve the aim of this paper, an investigation of the existing literature is conducted in the field of supervised ML application and their use in cybersecurity applications. As there are many cyber threats that could be considered as a security challenge, this study is focussed on those that are most common. These have been established by two independent surveys conducted by two private sector organisations targeting businesses from various sectors. The first report is published by the INTERPOL and the second survey published by a UK entity (Department for Digital, Culture, Media & Sport). The top threats are phishing, ransomware, denial of service, electronic fraud, social engineering, intrusion, and malware.

Only literature published in leading journals within the last five years are considered. In addition, impact metrics such as the journal's metrics as well as influence measure such as citations are used to identify works that are of sufficient scientific rigor. Suitable papers were identified through using the Google Scholar search engine with the keywords "cybersecurity AND machine learning". The literature review has been divided into two subsections. The first section will briefly demonstrate different types of machine learning in terms of concepts, utilisation and drawbacks, as well as reviewing the measurement implemented for the supervised learning to evaluate performance. The second section will present the implementation of supervised ML applications in the field of cybersecurity, highlighting and discussing how the measurements could be interpreted by the research end-users. To keep the paper concise, only a selected extract of the surveyed papers is included. Those included were chosen based on the breadth of their content and importance in the field.

3 Literature Review

3.1 Supervised Machine Learning and Measurements

Machine Learning (ML) has been embedded in a large range of research studies, and it can be considered as the most common type of AI implementation (Rashid et al. 2020). ML uses a set of data points to build models, which are then trained using mathematical methods to anticipate previously unseen data without being specifically programmed. As described by Li (2018).

In terms of a supervised approach, the learning function that maps an input to an output based on example input-output pairs is known as supervised learning. It derives a function from labelled training data, which consists of a collection of training samples (Goodfellow et al. 2020). One example of supervised implementations in the cybersecurity field is distinguishing between spam and non-spam email in a scenario of binary classification (Goodfellow et al. 2014). ML is often criticised due to result are based on pre-defined data and it cannot handle new, previously unseen patterns.

The performance of the ML model is measured via several metrics that are assigned to a model depending on the learning criteria (Rashidi et al. 2019). As the research focus is on the supervised learning technique, the performance measurements of supervised machine learning are examined. Classification and regression are considered as two main categories of supervised learning (Kumar et al. 2017). Classification has been implemented for categorisation between different elements, where regression utilises trained data to find the relationship between different variables in a continuous manner (Makridakis et al. 2018). Based on the performed literature study, Fig. 1 has been produced and illustrates the common metrics that are used to measure two types of supervised learning approaches, which are classification and regression. Generally, classification examples in literature are categorised in three types depending on their input type (numeric, text, and images).

Regression approaches are commonly presented in applications with high dimensionality, typically including datatypes such as hypertext, text, and images. The prediction in regression is measured based on proximity between expected and real value. I.e., a lower error rate could indicate high prediction accuracy.

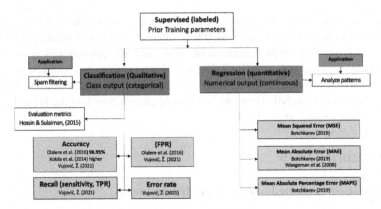

Fig. 1. Supervised leaning categorisation & common metrics

Generally, the literature review examination indicates that classification accuracy is the most used measure as part of the confusion metrics. True positive (TP), True Negative (TN), False Positive (FP), and False negative (FN) are used to establish Accuracy and Error rates (Caelen, 2017). TP is referring to a correct prediction identified by the model, such as a spam email being correctly identified as spam. TN is an indication to a negative prediction being correct where an email is correctly predicted as not been spam. FP occurs when the prediction is not accurate as it predicts that an email is spam when in fact it is normal. Finally, FN is referred to a false prediction but this time when predicting that an email is normal, but it is a spam email (Hong et al. 2021). In some instances, individual measures of the confusion matrix are used in isolation to better communicate specific measurements, such as the False Positive or False Negative rates, which are often used in generating the Equal Error Rate (Parkinson et al. 2021). These measures can be particularly useful for demonstrating specific characteristics of the system, which can be lost in an accuracy measure. For instance, if false positive values are particularly important from the application's perspective, such as in security, reporting the accuracy has the chance to mislead as false positive values could be lost in an aggregate measure containing high numbers of true positives. As highlighted in Fig. 1, other measurements have been utilised in addition to accuracy, as in all cases accuracy alone has been identified as not being valid in dealing with imbalanced datasets (Saputra and Suharjito, 2019).

Evaluation measures are however slightly different for regression, where we see Mean Squared Error (MSE), Mean Absolute Error (MAE), and Mean Absolute Percentage Error (MAPE) being utilised. The average of the squared discrepancies between predicted and actual values in a dataset is used to determine the MSE. The MAE does not assign distinct errors weight to model result as it is in MSE, instead, the score increases linearly as the number of errors increases. It is considered as a mathematical function that turns a negative value into a positive number. As a result, the difference between an expected and anticipated value is presented in a positive manner (Sammut and Webb, 2011). Lastly, the MAPE is to measure the average of absolute errors in a model in terms of percentage (De Myttenaere et al. 2016). The common metrics for the regression model were extracted based on a survey conducted by Botchkarev (2019), which highlighted top regression metrics utilised in research over the last 25 years. Supervised learning classification can be implemented in four different approaches in which the input and the output could be binary, multi-class, multi-labelled and hierarchical (Grira et al. 2004). It has been argued by several researchers that generating model accuracy could be misleading while dealing with imbalanced data in the supervised learning causing overfitting model result (Liu, 2021). On the other hand, several techniques were discussed and implemented in place to overcome the imbalanced data. Liu (2021) proposed a novel imbalance data classification method, this could be implemented by processing data through several layers utilizing a Support Vector Machine (SVM).

In this section, it has been established that accuracy metrics and the confusion matrix are widely used for supervised classification technique. In addition, it been noted that several researchers implemented accuracy with other performance measurements to overcome accuracy limitations and to generate a higher accuracy percentage. The next section will concentrate on the supervised ML application in the field of cybersecurity, aiming to explore the research orientation in supervised machine learning types, understand the implementation and presentation of the measurement technique of the research outcome.

3.2 ML Applications in the Field of Cyber Security

Considerable research has been conducted to test and validate algorithms to obtain optimum results. This literature review surveyed fifteen research studies that concentrate on supervised machine learning implementation and is shown in Table 1. Notably, the majority of examined research studies attempt to improve on model performance, either by fusing several algorithms in a hybrid methodology or by implementing several performance metrics to evaluate the model performance. There is variation in each application, and interestingly, it is argued by Shahrivari et al. (2020) that there is no consensus on the hybrid approach generating optimum results in comparison with individual classifiers.

Variants of supervised learning implementation in the field of cybersecurity were examined in Table 1, out of 15 examined applications in cybersecurity, 14 utilised supervised learning, and 1 paper utilised both supervised and unsupervised as a hybrid learning technique, where supervised learning was implemented to provide the basic knowledge to the model and unsupervised learning to aid the system to identify the new patterns. This demonstrates that supervised learning applications are being used widely to tackle different cybersecurity challenges. The reason behind mentioning the hybrid technique is to present further aspects for future study.

Information on the splitting methodology between training, testing, and validation. And the performance measure used by the researcher to evaluate the model performance were examined. Notably, research tends to implement various metrics to evaluate the performance of the model with differentiating in using the performance measurement depending on the learning style and algorithm used. Confusion Matrix, Precision, Recall, Accuracy and Error rate have been widely used among other performance measurements. It can be observed from Table 1 that the splitting of datasets varies in different applications and there is no standardised method to implement. For example, 7 out of 15 have not mentioned the splitting of the database in the methodology section. Further, the works have implemented different splitting percentages between training and testing to identify the highest accuracy rate. It is assumed that the researchers have based their methodology on performing early stage empirical testing, otherwise there is the risk that the technique could have been trained to be more accurate with a different split. There are consequences beyond the accuracy measures. For example, training the data on a large portion of the data could result in the model being better at handling future 'unseen' data, whereas training on a small portion of data might result in a trained model that is insufficiently flexible. These issues may not become apparent if the training and testing data are lacking variation.

A survey ran by Singh and Singh (2021) attempts to establish an ML model for malware detection, analysed a significant amount of previous research, consisting of forty research papers utilising detection techniques such as signature-based, behaviour-based, and hybrid-based. Most previous analysed papers used accuracy to evaluate the performance model. This is also stated by Sokolova and Lapalme (2009), where they identify accuracy as the top metric being used in the research, due to its ease of use for model validation. The results demonstrate that there are significant differences in metric use, which could make comparison challenging, especially for those working in the application area.

Even though accuracy is a widely used metric for classification performance, its implementation with an imbalanced class will mislead the model outcome as the result will tend towards most of the class (Saputra and Suharjito, 2019). Furthermore, Fan et al. (2019) conducted research in the field of energy management illustrated that accuracy is misleading and could not be implemented separately and other metrics should be utilised in parallel. Finally, as described by Vujović (2021) accuracy could not be isolated and other metrics shall embed for better justification of the model performance. According to Table 1, all the examined papers present accuracy as the performance measure, which indicates that this metric is utilised by vast research studies, despite the knowledge that it might present the results in an overly optimistic way if the datasets are imbalanced.

Supervised ML inevitability is a technique that can enhance human ability in achieving tasks (Bikeev et al. 2019). However, as it is stated by Segars (2018) there are concerns associated with supervised ML implementation in terms of security assurance. As businesses are increasingly embracing supervised ML as an indispensable process in the production, the outcome of supervised ML is difficult to establish and evaluate due to differences in training and evaluation processes and metrics (Keipour et al. 2021). Thus, further study is suggested to understand how supervised ML metrics are interpreted and to better understand how they influence adoption.

4   Discussion

Supervised ML is a powerful and generalised tool, resulting in it being implemented in various cybersecurity application areas. Funds are invested in supervised ML cybersecurity with high expectations to improve the detection system of malicious activities and mitigate the intrusion to systems (Ransbotham et al. 2017). For example, organisations are keen to preserve beneficiaries' personal data, and supervised ML technology has been implemented to increase cybersecurity defence (Vinayakumar et al. 2019). For instance, Dada et al. (2019) has implemented a spam detection for email utilising AI technique that extracts a frequent feature of the spam to block the sender achieving a decrease in spam rate by 46.6%; however, the rate of spam and phishing are still increasing as stated by Wood et al. (2016) with total loses reach up to 27 billion in 2021. This raises uncertainty over how effective the 46.6% reduction can be in the future. This concern is shared across all supervised implementations, where training has been performed on historical data. This could result in the system having limited efficacy in the future, resulting in a poor return on investment.

The research paper highlighted the different ML techniques in the first section of the literature review to capture the different ML technique concepts, usages, and limitations; that aid the authors in providing some understanding on the existing ML types as well as clearly emphasise the research study motivation. In the second section the most common performance measurement utilised for supervised machine learning has been presented as illustrated in Fig. 1. This aids in providing an overview of the existing utilised metrices and presents potential misleading in the usage of accuracy as a performance measurement.

This study demonstrates the suitability and capability of supervised ML at solving specific security challenge. There is however a pessimistic side, where research claiming that supervised ML is merely built on pre-defined data and the lack of consciousness in of new patterns will not be capable of handling new, previously unseen data (Sharma et al. 2021). As seen in Fig. 1, and Table 1, there are a wealth of applications trained using well-known and understood datasets. These applications demonstrate good accuracy values, more than 95%, yet it is not understandable the readiness of supervised ML to handle new attack instances. This has the potential to mislead as it might be assumed that the unsupervised technique is very capable at detecting new attack patterns, when in fact its ability to deal with new, previously unclassified attack instances, has not been tested.

The steady increase of cybercrime over the years has created the necessity for a sophisticated solution that can make new ground in cybersecurity defense (Dawson et al. 2019). Ransomware, phishing, and social engineering are considered as top threats as some of the top threats facing businesses (Verizon, 2021). Many ML techniques have been developed and implemented to create generic, intelligent solution. This is proving to generate good utility, where supervised ML techniques can be applied to multiple cybersecurity challenges.

As provided in Table 1, Kesavamoorthy and Soundar (2019) proposed a new method for model optimisation readiness in detecting denial of services (DOS) attacks that generates almost 99% accuracy. However, a survey conducted by Mahjabin et al. (2017) examine all eminent supervised ML technique to mitigate the DOS presenting the possible challenges of the technique. The survey conducted by Kesavamoorthy and Soundar (2019) proposed that the model has a limitation in which it is not able to suitably identify a DOS attack. Hence, it can be established that significant research is concerned to present the research outcome without presenting the research limitation. This can mislead the non-specialist. The paper is built on a systematic approach as the concentration was on cited papers that are not older than five years, this approach aid to gain an insight on current research trends. However, it could be considered as a limitation as older relevant research studies have been omitted. The finding of this paper reveals that numerous existing research studies concentrate on the use of supervised ML techniques, which are based on labelled, pre-defined and historical knowledge used to train the module to learn the relationship between the input data and the labelling. Accuracy could be considered as a key performance indicator (KPI) in which it is one of the common performance measurements utilised by the researcher as noticeably provided an optimistic result that the system could identify malicious movement with a percentage that exceeds 90%.

The accuracy of supervised ML could be interpreted by the beneficiaries that supervised learning is an optimum solution, and it could lure the end-users to set unreachable expectations, motivate investors to fund futile investment. Furthermore, it could be analysed from the literature that testing methodology of the model is varied in terms of how the dataset is divided into a training and testing dataset. Nevertheless, several researchers either have not presented the testing methodology in detail or have initiated a new database utilising synthetic or real data, raising concerns over how well it represents the real application. The percentage of splitting the data between training validation testing notably there are no consensus standard (Liu et al. 2020). In reference to Table 1, it is argued that increasing the percentage of data used to train the model will lead to increasing the percentage of the model accuracy as more patterns will be recognised previously by the system where more data dedicated for testing will decrease the model accuracy (Olalere et al. 2016). According to Shahrivari et al. (2020), most of the spam features are similar and follow the same theme that can be identified by the model, whereas the model longevity to prevent or mitigate new patterns, techniques, viruses, and unrecognised features is doubtable as they could remain undetected by supervised ML model. Thus, continuous updating of the detection tool is required to keep the system in line with the latest features and behaviour (Singh and Singh, 2021). A framework or a system shall be in place to organise the role, duties of parties, avoid illegal entice, and to ensure better communication of supervised learning capability.

5   Conclusion

This paper investigated existing literatures in the field of supervised ML application for mitigating cyberattacks and investigates the potential influence on cybersecurity defense. This paper discovered consistency in using accuracy as a metric for measuring the model performance. As supervised learning is the most common mechanism used by researchers to train a model, it has been discovered that there is a variation in how supervised ML techniques are trained and evaluated as well as that there is no consensus in the splitting the dataset into training, testing and validation. This paper was built on secondary data based on surveying papers in the field of supervised machine learning attempting to enhance the cybersecurity against most common cyber challenges. In future work, primary data can be collected from those implementing, testing, and adopting supervised ML solutions to validate and test the obtained result. A framework for ideal implementation based on the analytics of the primary data for the ideal implementation of the performance measurements could also be developed in which a better communication of ML capability could be presented. The scope of this paper concentrates on supervised ML implementation in the field of security, yet other ML types could be investigated as well as other sectors of ML implementation such as ML in business operations; where there are different application impacts of how the ML is evaluated.

Appendix

Table 1. Research summary of ML performance measurement

Security challenge	ML type	Testing methodology	Key metrics
Phishing (Smadi et al. 2018)	Supervised and Unsupervised ML	70/30	Accuracy, Confusion Matrix
Malware (Olalere et al. 2016)	Supervised ML	90/10, 80/20, 50/50	Accuracy, Confusion Matrix
Malware (Liu et al. 2020)	Supervised ML	N/A	Accuracy
Phishing (Rashid et al. 2020)	Supervised ML	90/10	Accuracy, Confusion Matrix, F1
Phishing (Jain and Gupta, 2017)	Supervised ML	N/A	Accuracy, TPR
Phishing (Selvakumari et al. 2021)	Supervised ML/DL	70/30	Accuracy, Precision
Phishing (Shahrivari et al. 2020)	Supervised ML	70/30	Accuracy
Intrusion Detection (Dada, 2017)	Supervised ML	N/A	Accuracy
Intrusion Detection (Dada, 2017)	Supervised ML	75/25	Accuracy
Fraud Detection (Hindy et al. 2020	Supervised ML	N/A	Accuracy, Confusion Matrix, G-mean, F1-Score
Fraud Detection (Saputra and Suharjito, 2019)	Supervised ML	80/20	Accuracy, Confusion Matrix, F1
Ransomware (Vinayakumar et al. 2019)	Supervised DL	67/33	Accuracy, Confusion Matrix, F1
Ransomware (Poudyal et al. 2018)	Supervised ML	N/A	Accuracy
Denial of Service (Vidal et al. 2018)	Supervised ML	N/A	Accuracy, Confusion Matrix
Denial of Service (Kesavamoorthy and Soundar, 2018)	Supervised ML	N/A	Accuracy

References

Bikeev, I., Kabanov, P., Begishev, I., Khisamova, Z.: Criminological risks and legal aspects of artificial intelligence implementation. In: Proceedings of the International Conference on Artificial Intelligence, Information Processing and Cloud Computing, pp. 1–7 (2019)

Botchkarev, A.: A new typology design of performance metrics to measure errors in machine learning regression algorithms. Interdisciplinary J. Information, Knowledge Manage. **14**, 45-76 (2019)

Cabinet Office: A strong Britain in an age of uncertainty: the national security strategy (Vol. 7953). The Stationery Office (2010)

Caelen, O.: A Bayesian interpretation of the confusion matrix. Ann. Math. Artif. Intell. **81**(3–4), 429–450 (2017)

Dada, E.G., Bassi, J.S., Chiroma, H., Adetunmbi, A.O., Ajibuwa, O.E.: Machine learning for email spam filtering: review, approaches and open research problems. Heliyon **5**(6), e01802 (2019)

Dada, E.G.: A hybridized svm-knn-pdapso approach to intrusion detection system. In: Proc. Fac. Seminar Ser, pp. 14–21 (2017)

Dawson, M., et al.: Applying software assurance and cybersecurity NICE job tasks through secure software engineering labs. Procedia Computer Sci. **164**, 301–312 (2019)

De Myttenaere, A., et al.: Mean absolute percentage error for regression models. Neurocomputing **192**, 38-48 (2016)

Fan, C., et al.: A novel methodology to explain and evaluate data-driven building energy performance models based on interpretable machine learning. Applied Energy **235**, 15511560 (2019)

Goodfellow, I., et al.: Generative adversarial networks. Commun. ACM **63**(11), 139–144 (2020)

Goodfellow, I., et al.: Generative adversarial nets. Advances in Neural Information Processing Syst. **27** (2014)

Grira, N., et al.: Unsupervised and semi-supervised clustering: a brief survey. A review of Machine Learning Techniques for Processing Multimedia Content **1**, 9–16 (2004)

HM government: National Cyber Security Strategy 2016–2021 (2016)

Hong, C.S., et al.: TPR-TNR plot for confusion matrix. Communications for Statistical Appl. Methods **28**(2), 161–169 (2021)

Jain, A.K., Gupta, B.B.: Towards detection of phishing websites on client-side using machine learning based approach. Telecommun. Syst. **68**(4), 687–700 (2017)

Keipour, H., Hazra, S., Finne, N., Voigt, T.: Generalizing supervised learning for intrusion detection in IoT mesh networks. In: Inernational Conference on Ubiquitous Security, pp. 214–228. Springer, Singapore (2021). https://doi.org/10.1007/978-981-19-0468-4_16

Kesavamoorthy, R., Ruba Soundar, K.: Swarm intelligence based autonomous DDoS attack detection and defense using multi agent system. Clust. Comput. **22**(4), 9469–9476 (2018)

Khan, S., Parkinson, S.: Review into state of the art of vulnerability assessment using artificial intelligence. In: Guide to Vulnerability Analysis for Computer Networks and Systems, pp. 3–32. Springer, Cham (2018). https://doi.org/10.1007/978-3-319-92624-7_1

Kumar, S.S., et al.: Assessment of various supervised learning algorithms using different performance metrics. In: IOP Conference Series: Materials Science and Engineering, **263**(4), p. 042087). IOP Publishing (2017)

Li, J.-H.: Cyber security meets artificial intelligence: a survey. Frontiers of Information Technol. Electronic Eng. **19**(12), 1462–1474 (2018)

Liu, H., et al.: A novel imbalanced data classification method based on weakly supervised learning for fault diagnosis. IEEE Trans. Industrial Informatics **18**(3), 15831593 (2021)

Liu, X., et al.: A novel method for malware detection on ML-based visualization technique. Comput. Secur. **89**, 101682 (2020)

Mahjabin, T., et al.: A survey of distributed denial-of-service attack, prevention, and mitigation techniques. Int. J. Distributed Sensor Networks **13**(12), 15501477 (2017)

Makridakis, S., Spiliotis, E., Assimakopoulos, V.: Statistical and Machine Learning forecasting methods: concerns and ways forward. PLoS ONE **13**(3), e0194889 (2018)

Olalere, M., et al.: Identification and evaluation of discriminative lexical features of malware URL for real-time classification. In: 2016 International Conference on Computer and Communication Engineering (ICCCE), pp. 90–95 (2016). IEEE

Parkinson, S., et al.: Password policy characteristics and keystroke biometric authentication. IET Biometrics **10**(2), 163–178 (2021)

Poudyal, S., Subedi, K.P., Dasgupta, D.: A framework for analyzing ransomware using machine learning. In: 2018 IEEE Symposium Series on Computational Intelligence (SSCI), pp. 1692–1699 (2018). IEEE

Ransbotham, S., et al.: Reshaping business with artificial intelligence: closing the gap between ambition and action. MIT Sloan Management Rev. **59**(1) (2017)

Rashid, J., et al.: Phishing detection using machine learning technique. In: 2020 First International Conference of Smart Systems and Emerging Technologies (SMARTTECH), pp. 43–46 (2020). IEEE

Rashidi, H.H., et al.: Artificial intelligence and machine learning in pathology: the present landscape of supervised methods. Academic Pathology **6**, 2374289519873088 (2019)

Sammut, C., Webb, G.I.: Encyclopedia of Machine Learning. Springer Science & Business Media (2011). https://doi.org/10.1007/978-0-387-30164-8

Saputra, A., Suharjito, S.: Fraud detection using machine learning in e-Commerce. Int. J. Adv. Comput. Sci. Appl **10**(9), 332–339 (2019)

Segars, S.: AI today, AI tomorrow. Awareness, Acceptance and Anticipation of AI: A Global Consumer Perspective (2018)

Selvakumari, M., et al.: Phishing website detection using machine learning and deep learning techniques. In: Journal of Physics: Conference Series **1916**(1), p. 012169 (2021). IOP Publishing

Shahrivari, V., et al.: Phishing Detection Using Machine Learning Techniques. arXiv preprint arXiv:2009.11116 (2020)

Sharma, S., et al.: A survey on analysis and detection of android ransomware. Concurrency and Computation: Practice and Experience **33**(16), e6272 (2021)

Singh, J., Singh, J.: A survey on machine learning-based malware detection in executable files. J. Syst. Architect. **112**, 101861 (2021)

Smadi, S., Aslam, N., Zhang, L.: Detection of online phishing email using dynamic evolving neural network based on reinforcement learning. Decis. Support Syst. **107**, 88–102 (2018)

Sokolova, M., Lapalme, G.: A systematic analysis of performance measures for classification tasks. Inf. Process. Manage. **45**(4), 427–437 (2009)

Verizon 2021 Data Breach Investigations Report (2021)

Vidal, J.M., et al.: Adaptive artificial immune networks for mitigating DoS flooding attacks. Swarm Evol. Comput. **38**, 94–108 (2018)

Vinayakumar, R., et al.: Ransomware triage using deep learning: twitter as a case study. In: 2019 Cybersecurity and Cyberforensics Conference (CCC), pp. 67–73 (2019)

Vujović, Ž: Classification model evaluation metrics. Int. J. Advance Computer Science and Appl. **12**(6), 599–606 (2021)

Wood, P., et al.: Internet Security Threat Report 2011, 17 (2016)

Author Index

Printed in the United States
by Baker & Taylor Publisher Services